VIVA
TRAVEL GUIDES

Guatemala

1st Edition
March 2011

Guatemala City - Antigua - Central Highlands - Western Highlands - Verapaces - Pacific Coast - Oriente and Atlantic Coast - The Petén

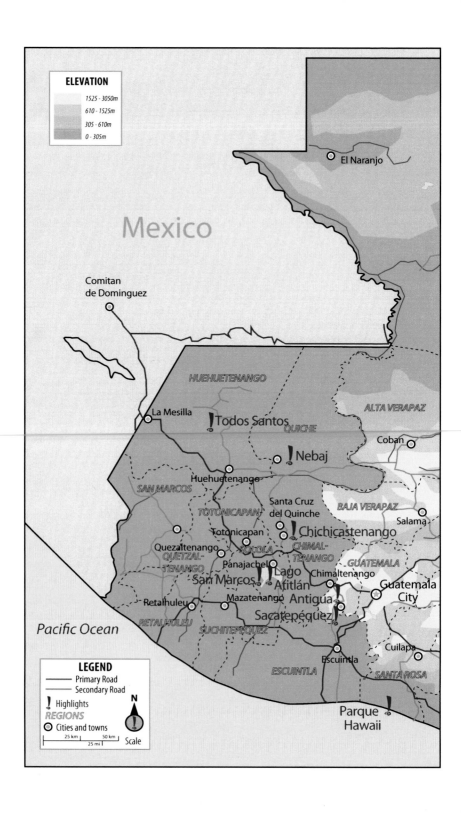

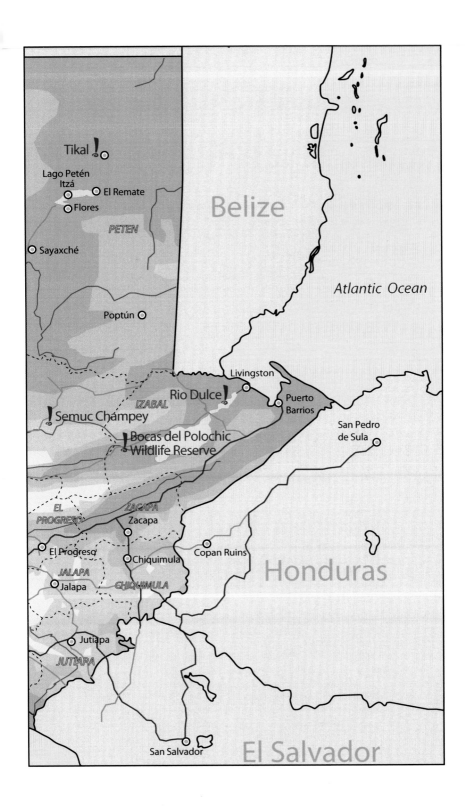

▲ Tikal

This ancient Mayan city, made famous by the movie *Star Wars*, are some of the most impressive ruins in the world. Engulfed by dense rainforest and abundant wildlife, one gets an eerie sense of what life must have been like in the day of the Maya. Climb to the top of Temple IV to watch the sunset or sunrise while perched high above the jungle canopy.

▲ Sea Turtles in Parque Hawaii

Two types of turtle species nest on the beaches of Parque Hawaii, the smaller, more common (but still threatened) Olive Ripely and the larger endangered Leather Back. At Parque Hawaii, there are several volunteer opportunities to help rescue these turtles from extinction. They also have hatcheries where turtle eggs are collected and hatched to help ensure their survival. Lucky visitors might get a change to see hatching babies or mamas laying their eggs.

▲ Sailing Down Río Dulce

If you are looking for a mellow adventure in the Caribbean head to Río Dulce. For only a few dollars, you can sail down the river to the port town of Lívingston. If you get too hot sunbathing on the deck, hop in the calm water for a refreshing swim.

▲ Hiking around Nebaj

Located in the Cuchamatan Mountains, the region draws hikers in from all over the country. It is covered in trails that run deep into the mountains, pass by incredible waterfalls and will lead you to ancient Maya ruins and charming out-of-the-way villages. Hikers of all levels will find something to suit their needs.

GUATEMALA

Formed by the Río Cahabón, Semuc Champey is a series of turquoise pools that offer a nice reprieve from the heat of Alta Verapaz. Spend all day relaxing in the electric blue and green pools or hike up to the top of the ridge for an outstanding view of the whole area.

▲ Birdwatching in the Cloud Forests

Although the cloud forests of Guatemala are filled with diverse wildlife and lovely scenery, the chance to catch a glimpse of the Resplendent Quetzal, a bird known to be as elusive as it is beautiful, is the major draw for most birders. In addition to the Quetzal, Guatemala's national bird, there are hundreds of rare avian species waiting to be spotted and plenty of guides to show you where to look.

▲ Studying Spanish

Because of an abundance of schools and the low prices for classes, Guatemala has become a popular destination for those wanting to learn Spanish. Whether you're looking to brush up on your language skills for a week while taking in the sites or you're serious about learning to speak Spanish fluently in a place with few distractions, there is a school that will fit your needs.

▼ Antigua

Finding something to fill a day in Antigua isn't hard. Finding a way to spend a week isn't either. A lazy day can be spent browsing colonial art and artifacts at the Museo de Santiago or the Museo Casa del Tejido, then shopping for traditional Maya crafts at Nim Po't Market before lounging at one of the many coffee shops. On more adventurous days, climb to the top of Cerro de la Cruz and get a view of the entire city, or plan a day trip up one of the four surrounding volcanoes.

▲ Yoga at San Marcos

If you're ready to relax, take a boat across Lake Atitlán to the small village of San Marcos. Known as the spiritual healing and yoga center of Central America, this village offers several types of yoga retreats including five-week courses. Travelers looking for something a little less intense will have no problems finding a massage or practicing their sun salutation on the beach.

▲ Todos Santos Cuchumatán Horse Racing

On November 1, Todos Santos offers up festivals unlike any other in the country. In celebration of All Saints Day, traditional dances are performed in the street and horse riders, most of whom have been drinking for several days prior to the event, race down from point to point taking a drink of strong alcohol at each stop. The winner is the last person to fall from his horse.

▼ Lake Atitlán

Surrounded by volcanoes and small villages, Lake Atitlán is a nice place to relax, play and get a taste of Guatemalan culture you won't find anywhere else. Take in the nightlife or meet other travelers in Panajachel, kayak from village to village on the serene waters, or ride a horse through the remote hills of Santiago Atitlán to explore abandoned coffee fincas. When you go, make sure to brush up on your Tzutuhil, a Mayan language still spoken in many of the villages.

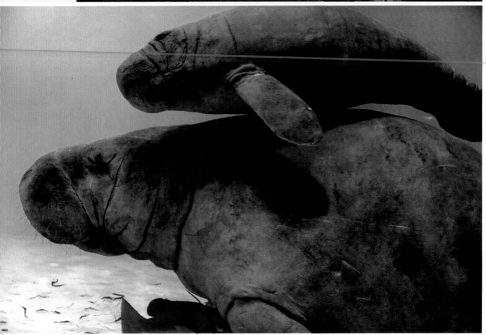

▲ Manatee Viewing at Bocas del Polochic Wildlife Reserve

As its name suggests, Bocas del Polochic Wildlife Reserve sits at the mouth of the Río Polochic delta and is home to wetlands, dense forests, savannahs and, most importantly, the last of the remaining manatees of Lake Izabal.

▲ Chichicastenango Market

The town of Chichicastenango is most well-known for its Thursday and Sunday markets. The K'iche' Maya cultural market sells handcrafts, textiles, tools, food and even live animals. The city itself is well-known for its woodcarvings, especially those made for masks used in traditional dances.

▲ Santiago Sacatepéquez for Day of the Dead

Santiago Sacatepéquez is known for its impressive Day of the Dead festival, during which elaborate kites fill the sky in honor of those who have passed on. Made from cloth, colorful paper, bamboo and wire, these kites range from the size of a man to the size of a small building. They are flown from graveyards and are said to be a way to communicate with the dead who speak through the movement of the wind.

RECOMMENDED ITINERARIES

The Gringo Trail in one week

Day 1: Arrive at the international airport in Flores. From here you can spend the rest of the day discovering the Maya ruins of Tikal and marvel at the surrounding jungle, either on your own or through a Flores tour operator. Stay at the park overnight to see the sunrise from the top of Temple IV.

Day 2: Check out more ruins at Yaxhá, which is where one season of *Survivor* was filmed.

Day 3: Fly back to Guatemala City, and take a bus to Antigua, the country's old colonial capital. Take a city tour, or explore on your own, starting out from the Plaza Mayor.

Day 4: Check out nearby coffee farms and/or bike through Antigua's neighboring villages. Head to nearby Jocotenango, just 3.5 km/2.2 m away, and visit the La Azotea Cultural Center, which houses a coffee, costume and music museum.

Day 5: Take a bus to Panajachel, the main tourist locale on Lake Atitlán. Buy some authentic Maya handicrafts along Calle Santander, and then enjoy the lively nightlife Panajachel has to offer (try to spend a Friday or Saturday night here).

Day 6: Take a shuttle boat to San Pedro La Laguna, a village nestled in between Lake Atitlán and the San Pedro Volcano. Here you can find a birdwatching tour through the Atlitán Natural Reserve, or rent a kayak/canoe to explore the lake. After a day of outdoor activities, relax and recuperate in the thermal pools.

Day 7: Try the 4-hour trek up the San Pedro Volcano—you won't regret it (no climbing experience necessary). Then head to the thermal pools again—you deserve it.

Lake Atitlán

Ruin Exploration

In one week:

Day 1: Arrive in Guatemala City. Hop on a bus and head north to the riverside town of Sayaxché.

Day 2: Take a short boat trip across the river to the ruins of Ceibal, Aquateca and Dos Pilas. Take a full day to explore the area.

Day 3: Board a bus to Flores. Check into your hotel then walk across the bridge that crosses Lago de Petén Itzá to Santa Elena. Check out the caves on the edge of town. Walk back to Flores and spend the rest of the day exploring this peaceful island town.

Day 4: Wake up early the next morning and take a short bus ride to Tikal. Walk through the dense jungle and climb up impressive Maya ruins. Book a room in the park and take in the sunset from the top of Temple IV.

Day 5: Spend the day exploring the less-visited ruins of the area, including El Chal, Ixlú and Machaquilá. Spend the night in the village of El Remate.

Day 6: Take a taxi to the ruins of Uxaxtan located just north of Tikal. Spend half a day there and then take a taxi to the Yaxhá.

Camp for free along the lakeshore or spend the night in the nearby eco-lodge.

Day 7: Finish your archeological journey by watching the sunrise over the lake then take a bus to Guatamala City, stopping for lunch in Cobán.

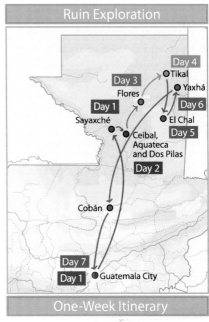

Ruins neat Antigua

Guatemala for the Adventurer

Two Weeks:

Days 1-5: Arrive in Guatemala City. Take a bus to Antigua and set up a base camp there. Take a day trip to Volcán Agua and take your time hiking to the peak. This is a relatively moderate climb and a good place to start. Get up early the next morning and head out on a two-day trip to Volcán Acatenango. Reach the summit and camp under the lava cones. The next day, cross over to the peak of Volcán Fuego and then make your descent. Spend a day resting in Antigua and preparing for your final hike up the active Volcán Pacaya. Wake up early. Check the safety conditions and if they are good, head up Volcán Pacaya to see flowing lava.

Days 6-9: From Antigua, hop on a bus to Panajachel. Take a boat across Lake Atitlán to the village of Santiago Atitlán. Rent a kayak and watch the sunset while paddling through the calm waters of the lake. Spend the evening in one of the many shoreline restaurants. The next morning, rent a mountain bike and follow the trails around the lake to the nearby coffee fincas. Safety can be an issue, so it's a good idea to hire a guide. Then take a boat to San Marcos for a day of yoga and day hikes. The next day, head back to Panajachel and catch a bus to Nebaj. Spend the rest of the day gearing up for a few days of hiking in the cloud forest.

Days 10-11: Stop in town and hire a guide to take you across the mountains to some

Rock Climbing

Volcán Pacaya

of the remote villages only accessible by trail. Come back to rest your feet and get a good night's rest. Wake up and do some early morning birdwatching in the cloud forest before heading to Cobán.

Days 12-13: From Cobán, take a short bus ride to Semuc Champey. Spend the day swimming in the turquoise pools and hiking up to the ridge for amazing views. Camp out or grab a room at the lodge. The next morning, get up and enjoy a refreshing swim before heading back to Cobán for zip-lining through the jungle canopy.

Day 14: Spend the morning whitewater rafting down the rapids of Río Cahabon. After your adventure, rest up and have a late lunch in Cobán before catching a bus back to Guatemala City.

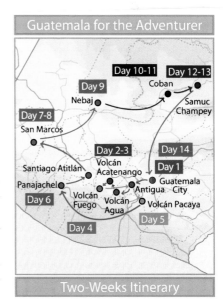

Guatemala for the Adventurer

Day 10-11 · Day 12-13 · Coban · Day 9 · Nebaj · Samuc Champey · Day 7-8 · San Marcos · Day 2-3 · Day 14 · Volcán Acatenango · Day 1 · Santiago Atitlán · Panajachel · Antigua · Guatemala City · Day 6 · Volcán Fuego · Volcán Agua · Volcán Pacaya · Day 4 · Day 5

Two-Weeks Itinerary

Experience the Culture of Guatemala City, Antigua and Chichicastenango

One Week:

Day 1: Start you trip in Guatemala City. Visit the museum of Museo Ixchel and browse through impressive examples of Maya textiles and weavings, then head next door to the Museo Popol Vuh, full of Maya art and archeological pieces. Next, tour Museo Miraflores, which houses many relics from the nearby Kaminaljuyú ruins. If you aren't exhausted by the evening, take in a play at the Centro Cultural Metropolitano.

Day 2: In the morning, take a short bus ride from Guatamala City to Antigua. Begin your day by walking up to the Cerro de la Cruz to get your bearings by looking down on the city from the top of the hill. On your way back into town, stop off at the Museo de Santiago and experience the colonial history of Guatemala. Stop at Plaza Mayor and rest by the fountain while eating food from one of the many delicious street carts. Spend the after-noon browsing the Museo del Libro Antiguo, also known as the Historical Book Museum, and then head to the Iglesia de San Francisco to visit the tomb of Santo Hermano Pedro de San José de Betancurt.

Day 3: Start the next day off by watching local women do their laundry in the public sinks at Iglesia y Convento de Santa Clara, then head over to Iglesia y Convento de Nuestra Señora de la Merced to tour the sanctuary of one of Antigua's most impressive churches. Spend the afternoon shopping for handmade crafts at Nim Po't Market. If you don't find what you're looking for, head for the outdoor Antigua Market.

Day 4: Visit Las Capuchinas, the maze-like convent with incredible towers and arches. After lunch, take a trip out of town to the ruins of Iglesia y Convento de La Recolección.

Day 5: Take the seven-kilometer (4.3 mi) walk to the village of Ciudad Vieja, where you can see the site of the first capital of Guatemala and then tour the nearby coffee plantation, Finca de los Nietos.

Flower carpet in Iglesia y Convento de Nuestra Señora de la Merced

Day 6: Take a tour of the Museo de Arte Colonial to see paintings by some of Mexico's most predominate artists of the era. Then take a stroll to Monumento a Landívar and catch up on some reading or rest up for your journey to Chichicastenago in the peaceful park.

Day 7: On the final day, take a bus to the village of Chichicastenango. Make sure you plan your trip so that you arrive on a Thursday or Sunday for the famous market. Spend the morning shopping and the afternoon touring the Iglesia de Santo Tomás and Museo Regional, where you can find a collection of ceremonial masks and other artifacts from the pre-colonial era. Leave enough time to visit Pascual Abaj, the ancient Maya sacrifice stone and a shrine to the god Huyup Tak'ah.

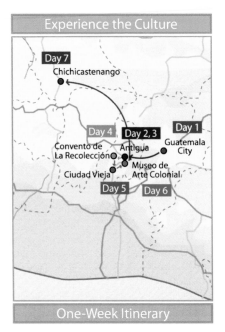

Experience the Culture

One-Week Itinerary

Semana Santa in Antigua

Guatemala

About this Book

At V!VA, we believe that you shouldn't have to settle
for an outdated guidebook. You can rest assured that in your hands
is the most up-to-date guidebook available on Guatemala because:

-- The final research for this book was completed on October 24, 2010.
-- Each entry is "time stamped" with the date it was last updated
-- V!VA's hyper-efficient web-to-book publishing process brings books to press
  in days or weeks, not months or years like our competitors
-- V!VA's country guides are updated at least once per year.

When you buy a V!VA Guide, here's what you're getting:

-- The expertise of professional travel writers, local experts and real travelers
  in-country bringing you first-hand, unbiased recommendations to make the
  most out of your trip
-- The wisdom of editors who actually live in Latin America, not New York,
  Melbourne or London like other guidebook companies
-- Advice on how to escape the overly-trodden gringo trail, meet locals and
  understand the culture
-- The knowledge you'll need to travel responsibly while getting more for your money

Contribute to V!VA

V!VA is an online community of travelers, and we rely on the advice and opinions of
vagabonders like yourself to continuously keep our books accurate and useful. YOU
are our best resource.

Take a part in this ongoing effort by writing about the places you have been on our
website, www.vivatravelguides.com. We want to know about that rarely visited town
you stumbled upon, about that bus company you will never take again, about that
meal you just can't stop thinking about. Together, we can help enhace each other's
travel experiences and share in our love and passion for exploring Latin America.

Go ahead! Log on and create a free user account and profile on our site, click
around, and create original reviews for hotels you have stayed at, restaurants
you have eaten at, activities you have tried and nightlife you have experienced, or take a moment to comment on already existing reviews. We look
forward to hearing from you soon!

VIVA
TRAVEL GUIDES

Guatemala

Guatemala City - Antigua - Central Highlands - Western Highlands

The Verapaces- Pacific Coast - Oriente and Atlantic Coast - The Petén

1st Edition

April 2011

V!VA Travel Guides Guatemala.

ISBN-10: 0-9825585-4-6

ISBN-13: 978-0-9825585-4-6

Copyright © 2011, Viva Publishing Network.

Voice: (831) 824-4395

Website: www.vivatravelguides.com

Information: info@vivatravelguides.com

◇ Cover Design: Jason Halberstadt, 2011 ◇
◇ Front Cover Photo: 11-26-07 © lubilub ◇
◇ Back Cover Photo: "Lake Atitlan, Guatemala" by Szeke, http://www.flickr.com/photos/pedrosz/4154059153, 2005 ◇
◇ Title Page Photo: "Guatemala-0744" by Archer10 (Dennis) ©, http://www.flickr.com/photos/archer10/2214416010/, 2007 ◇

The following photos are licensed under the Creative Commons license (see http://creativecommons.org/licenses/by/2.0/ and http://creativecommons.org/licenses/by/3.0/ for details):

"Back from School" (Antigua), by Alexis Lê-Quôc ©, http://www.flickr.com/photos/alq666/2339417596/in/set-72157604132912630/, 2008; "Central Acropolis at Tikal," by Jo Ann Deasy ©, http://www.flickr.com/photos/7682623@N02/2267613630/, 2006; "Juvenile Green Sea Turtle" (Parque Hawaii), by Silke Baron ©, http://www.flickr.com/photos/silkebaron/2796414636/, 2008; "crabbing" (Sailing Down Río Dulce), by Jake Brown ©, http://www.flickr.com/photos/manbeastextraordinaire/3926260472/, 2009; "acul-nebaj express" (Hiking around Nebaj), by Seth Pipkin ©, http://www.flickr.com/photos/thepinksip/2765690706/, 2008; "one can" (the Cloud Forests), by cito ©, http://www.flickr.com/photos/cito/156964061/, 2006; "DSCN1146" (Semuc Champay), by Micah & Erin ©, http://www.flickr.com/photos/micahmacallen/30422532/, 2005; "Day 194" (Studying Spanish), by Oisin Prendiville ©, http://www.flickr.com/photos/prendio2/3772755945/, 2009; "Volcán de Agua, Antigua, Guatemala," by James Wu ©, http://www.flickr.com/photos/beautiful-taiwan/3630898681/, 2009; "Yoga at San Marcos, Lake Atitlán, Guatemala," by Bomba Rosa ©, http://www.flickr.com/photos/bombarosa/2110995672/; "Horse Races in Todos Santos Cuchumatán" by Yves Picq http//veton.picq.fr ©, http://en.wikipedia.org/wiki/Todos_Santos_Cuchumat%C3%A1n, 2008; "Atitlán," by Guillermo Ramírez ©, http://www.flickr.com/photos/gramz/2139354893/, 2007; "manatee" (Bocas del Polochic Wildlife Reserve), by psyberartist ©, http://www.flickr.com/photos/psyberartist/4292444316/, 2010; "Día de Los Muertos Figure

CONTENTS

INTRO & INFO

INTRO & INFO

INTRO & INFO

8

At the age of 18, **Joanne Sykes** left her native Yorkshire, England to work a ski season in Switzerland and has since traveled to more than 30 countries, living in Mexico, Japan, Spain, France, Ecuador and Guatemala. With an MA in International Politics and Human Rights, as well as BA degrees in Spanish and French, she considers herself a student of the world. After three months supporting V!VA from the office in Quito, Joanne traveled to Guatemala and is a major freelance writer contributing to this first edition.

Javier España was born in Guatemala in 1970. He is a systems engineer, writer, musician, poet, photographer, sportsman and avid traveler. Javier served as a volunteer firefighter, as director of the 78th Fire Company. Married to Katherine, who is his great support, and father of three beautiful daughters, Stephanie, Alessandra and Alida, he currently works as webmaster for an entity of the justice sector in Guatemala.

Born in France, **Claire Bourgin** has traveled around the world since she was a child. She has lived in Quetzaltenango, Guatemala for three years and has enjoyed every bit of it. Claire has been working as a travel writer for a year, and she contributed heavily to the Western Highlands and The Petén sections of this Guatemala guide.

Born in Hong Kong and raised in SE Asia and Europe, it was no real surprise that exploring the world held such a strong call and became the lifestyle of choice for **Kathryn Witts** in May of 2000. Over 10 years and 80 countries later, Kathryn is still going strong and has only two continents left–South America and Antartica. What happens after that is anyone's guess!

OUR CONTRIBUTORS:

Nellie Huang contributed to Tikal and Cobán and **Lucy Brown** hit the cobblestones of Antigua. Also thanks to Juan Manuel Marroquin, Will Gray, Kaylie Jensen, Peter Aras, Eugenia Herrera, Michelle Forbes, Francisco Vasquez Jacquet, Martin Crossland and dozens more who shared their knowledge. Additionally, Andrea Davoust, Dr. Crit Minster, Mark Samcoe, Margaret Rode, Chris Hughes and Lorraine Caputo contributed reviews.

MANY THANKS TO:

Clémence Duron, Thomas Griffin, Eli Mangold, Jen O'Riordan, Jon Moore and **Emily Ellis**—V!VA's intern superheroes; and to **Jesua Silva** (map-maker extraordinaire). Thanks to **Lisa W. Blackwell-Sayles, Stephanie Witkin** and **Emily Thiersch** for helping out with last-minute touches. Also, thanks to **Rigoberto Pinto** and **Cristián Ávila**, the programming masterminds who keep www.vivatravelguides.com running smoothly and are always willing to lend a hand to the not-so-computer-savvy staff; and to the whole **Metamorf** team for their support.

Last but not least, thanks to the hundreds of Guatemalans who taught us about the culture, history & beauty of their country.

ABOUT THE EDITORS

Paula Newton was the Managing Editor for this book and for many other V!VA guidebooks. With an MBA and a background in New Media, Paula was the organizing force behind the editorial team. With an insatiable thirst for off-the-beaten-track travel, Paula has traveled extensively, especially in Europe, Asia and Latin America, and has explored more than 30 countries. She currently lives in Quito.

Nick Rosen is a staff writer and editor for VIVA. He holds a BA in International Development from Montreal's McGill University and has worked on public health projects in Kenya and Ghana. He maintains that nothing compares to the sublime beauty of his native New Jersey.

Libby Zay is a staff writer and editor at V!VA Travel Guides. She grew up in Cleveland, Ohio and earned degrees in Popular Culture Studies and Women's Studies from The Ohio State University, where she also minored in Film. Her wanderlust has led her to circle the U.S. in a smelly conversion van, as well as journey to the far reaches of Moldova. Before moving to Quito, Ecuador, Libby worked as an editorial assistant at AOL Travel in Washington DC.

Desiree Andrews has worked as a writer and editor since 2006. She received a BA in Creative Writing at Prescott College. She has worked as a journalist in Reykjavik, Iceland, rescued sea turtles in Hawaii, and served as an editorial assistant and marketing assistant at Tin House Books in Portland, OR. She currently lives in Quito, Ecuador and works full time as a staff writer for V!VA Travel Guides.

Jena Davison is a staff writer and editor at V!VA. Shortly after graduating from University of Wisconsin-Madison with a BA in Journalism and Mass Communication, Jena packed her backpack and headed across the equator to travel solo through South America. Born and raised in New Jersey, Jena's itch for travel has previously brought her to 20 countries, mostly in Europe and Latin America. She currently lives in Quito, Ecuador.

Rachel Tavel is a half-Argentine NYC girl. She graduated from Bowdoin College in 2005, where she earned her BA in Spanish and archaeology. Since graduating, her adventures have included: working for Travel + Leisure and Food & Wine magazines, co-authoring the Frommer's guidebook MTV Best of Mexico and serving as a staff writer for VIVA Travel Guides in Ecuador. Rachel has traveled everywhere from Argentina, Turkey and Japan to Portugal, Austria, the Netherlands and Jamaica.

"In Chichicastenango," by David Dennis ©, http://www.flickr.com/photos/davidden/4390948561/, 2010; "Los Barriletes" (Santiago Sacatepéquez), by Johnatan Moran ©, http://www.flickr.com/photos/visionfutura/3062378878/, 2008; "Atitlán" (The Gringo Trail), by Alexis Lê-Quôc ©, http://www.flickr.com/photos/alq666/2339444058/, 2008; "View of Volcano Thru Ruins" (Antigua), by Jo Ann Deasy ©, http://www.flickr.com/photos/7682623@No2/2274753272/, 2006; "Rock Climbing" (by Neto Gonzalez ©, http://www.flickr.com/photos/netogonzalez/4239551834/, 2009; "Walking to the Volcano" (Pacaya Volcano), by Bruno Girin ©, http://www.flickr.com/photos/brunogirin/28481526/, 2005; "Flower Carpet - La Merced" (Convento de Nuestra Señora de la Merced), by Roger Price ©, http://www.flickr.com/photos/rwp-roger/3414541592/in/set-72157615986231425/. 2009; "Maria Nuestra Auxiliadora" (Antigua), by Roger Price ©, http://www.flickr.com/photos/rwp-roger/3423780081/in/set-72157615986231425/, 2009.

About VIVA Travel Guides

VIVA Travel Guides pioneers a new approach to travel guides. We have taken the travel guide and re-designed it from the ground up using the Internet, geographic databases, community participation, and the latest in printing technology, which allows us to print our guidebooks one at a time when they are ordered. Reversing the general progression, we have started with a website, gathered user ratings and reviews, and then compiled the community's favorites into a book. Every time you see the V!VA insignia you know that the location is a favorite of the V!VA Travel Community. For you, the reader, this means more accurate and up-to-date travel information and more ratings by travelers like yourself.

Community and Free Membership:
The accuracy and quality of the information in this book is largely thanks to our online community of travelers. If you would like to join them, go to www.vivatravelguides.com/members/ to get more information and to sign up for free.

Your Opinions, Experiences and Travels:
Did you love a place? Will you never return to another? Every destination in this guidebook is listed on our website with space for user ratings and reviews. Share your experiences, help out other travelers and let the world know what you think.

Corrections & Suggestions:
We are committed to bringing you the most accurate and up-to-date information. However, places convert, prices rise, businesses close down, and information, no matter how accurate it once was, inevitably changes. Thus, we ask for your help: If you find an error in this book or something that has changed, go to www.vivatravelguides.com/corrections and report them (oh, and unlike the other guidebooks, we'll incorporate them into our information within a few days).

If you think we have missed something, or you want to see something in our next book, go to www.vivatravelguides.com/suggestions and let us know. As a small token of our thanks for correcting an error or submitting a suggestion, we'll send you a coupon for 50 percent off any of our E-books or 20 percent off any of our printed books.

Coming soon on www.vivatravelguides.com
This is just the beginning. We're busy adding new features that our users have requested to our books and website. A few coming attractions to improve community functions include the ability to: join specialized groups, find travel partners, participate in forum discussions, write travel blogs, add maps and much more!

How to Use This Book:
This book is a best-of Guatemala taken straight from our website. You can check out www.vivatravelguides.com to read user reviews, rate your favorite hotels and restaurants, and add information you think we are missing. The book also features highlighted sections on national parks, volunteering opportunities and Spanish study . While you are out and about in Guatemala, use our helpful tear-out sheet in the back of the book, complete with emergency contact details and helpful numbers.

Join V!VA on Facebook. Like "V!VA Travel Guides Guatemala."

REGIONAL SUMMARIES

Guatemala City

Guatemala City is the administrative, geographical and political center of the country. Centrally located, this capital city provides a good starting point for those planning to visit such popular sites as Tikal, Antigua and Lake Atitlán. While many travelers quickly zoom off to those spots, Guatemala's most vibrant city rewards those who take the time to explore it. At 1,600 meters (5,000 ft) above sea level, Guatemala City, known as Guate to the locals, is a sprawling capital divided into zones that start at the center and radiate outward.

The center area, Zona 1, is the colonial part of the city, home to governmental buildings, cathedrals and several examples of impressive architecture. During the day, this part of town is packed with locals selling affordable goods and produce. Some of the more inexpensive hotels, popular with backpackers and budget travelers, can be found around here. Another zone of interest to travelers is Zona 4, a commercial area that also houses the national theater: the Centro Cultural Miguel Ángel Asturias, named after one of Guatemala's greatest writers. Along Avenida de la Reforma are zones 9 and 10, a pleasant area with tree-lined streets, small parks, and the best hotels and restaurants in the city. The area has the nickname "Zona Viva," or "lively zone" due to its numerous clubs and bars.

The city is packed with cultural, archeological, historical and architectural sites. Archaeology buffs will appreciate the Museo Nacional de Arqueología and Etnología in Zona 13, which displays pre-Colombian artifacts found at Maya sites throughout Guatemala. The Kaminaljuyú ruins boast some 100 small structures and are also located close to the center of town. There are a few exciting excursions just outside of Guatemala City as well, including the Pacaya Volcano National Park and the Mixco Viejo Ruins. The former is Guatemala's most active volcano, and the latter was the capital city of the Chojoma Maya.

Antigua

The charming colonial city of Antigua, founded in 1543, lies in a highland valley surrounded by three volcanoes: Volcán de Auga to the south, and Volcán Acatenango and Volcán Fuego to the southwest. Once the Spanish capital of Central America, Antigua oversaw a vast area stretching from southern Mexico to the impenetrable Darién Gap, the undeveloped swampland that separates Panama from Colombia.

Declared a UNESCO World Heritage Site in 1979, Antigua has managed to preserve and restore its colonial architecture and old-world appeal. The cobblestone streets are splashed with colorful houses, shops and old churches, and crumbling ruins are dotted throughout. Due to its location, beauty, history, variety of cultural activities and outdoor excursions both inside Antigua and close by, it has become a thriving landing place for globetrotters. Around 47,000 people call Antigua home, and the mixture of locals, travelers and expats gives it a certain worldly air.

There are ruins and museums to visit, handicraft markets to comb through, a wide variety of cuisine to try, and just outside the city, there are coffee plantations to explore. Many visitors are lured by the well-earned reputation of the city as one of the choice spots to study Spanish, and there are hordes of language schools of all calibers vying for the bucks. Volunteering opportunities are endless both in Antigua and in outlying areas with NGO organizations and various projects focusing on different social, educational, health and environmental issues. Forever a popular place to learn salsa, there are qualified instructors running classes for all levels in dance studios around town.

Central Highlands

Guatemala's Central Highlands has something for everyone, from history buffs to nature lovers. It is home to several Maya ruins; El Biotop del Quetzal, a protected ecosystem where Central America's most famous bird resides; Chicicastenango, Pacaya Volcano National Park; and Chichicastenango, Guatemala's most important market. Visitors come from all over the world to wander in the maze of smoky streets, shopping for masks, textiles and other locally made treasures. The market is easily done in a day from Antigua or from many of the towns in the Lake Atitlán region.

The Central Highlands, which includes the provinces of El Quiché, Alta Verapaz and Baja Verapaz, are also the site of some important Guatemalan history: The Verapaz region–"true peace" in English–was where the legendary Defender of the Indies, Fray Bartolomé de Las Casas, proved to the Spanish crown in the 16th century that warlike natives could be brought peacefully to Christianity by patient missionaries. In the 1970s and 1980s, Guatemala's brutal insurgency was fought all over the country, but the province of El Quiché was particularly affected.

Western Highlands

Guatemala's Western Highlands, which include the provinces of Huehuetenango, Totonicapán, Quetzaltenango and San Marcos, are mostly for die-hard travelers who are looking for some adventure off the beaten path of the typical gringo trail. Here you can study Spanish and shop in authentic artisan markets in a less touristy atmosphere, and experience a region of Guatemala where the population is largely indigenous. Away from the main cities, local women still wear *huipiles* (native blouses), and more people speak traditional languages such as Mam, Jacalteco and Quiché.

Crossed by the picturesque Cuchumatanes mountain chain, Guatemala's Western Highlands are rugged and beautiful, and there are several towns, cities and sites of interest for visitors in the region. The city of Quetzaltenango, also referred to as Xelajú or Xela ("SHAY-la"), is the country's second largest city and a popular spot studying Spanish. Todos Santos Cuchumatán is a traditional Maya village, located in the remote mountains above bustling Huehuetenango. It is known for its traditional lifestyle, men who still wear native clothing, and its annual festival of Todos Santos, which takes place from October 31 to November 2. The province of Huehuetenango is also home to the ruins of Zaculeu, a Maya stronghold that fell to the Spanish early in the conquest. The province of Totonicapán is noteworthy for having genuine native markets in both the city of Totonicapán and Momostenango.

The Verapaces

The geographical heart of Guatemala, the Verapaces is a beautiful land of hidden waterfalls, gently rushing rivers and mysterious caves. From the drier valleys around Salamá, the land rises into low mountains covered with misty cloud forest, then north of Cobán, its only real city, evens out into cardamom-planted hills, from which curious limestone bumps bulge.

In this region you'll find a number of outdoor adventures, from spelunking to underground river tubing and quetzal-spotting hikes. You can also visit one of the many coffee plantations, or even a tea plantation. Indeed the region is a very agricultural one; Alta Verapaz concentrates 80 percent of Guatemala's cardamom production, Guatemala being the number one exporter of the aromatic seeds, and Baja Verapaz exports vegetable seeds and ornamental ferns around the world. The area is also an indigenous stronghold, where many people in the rural areas speak Q'eqchi' before Spanish and still practice ancient Maya rites.

Although the region is home to one of Guatemala's major attractions, the spectacular pools of Semuc Champey, it is not overly touristy. Enough visitors come that the infrastructure is there, from shuttles to hotels, but you are not swamped by tourists as in Flores or Antigua.

Pacific Coast

Located toward the southwestern part of the country, the Pacific Coast consists of the provinces of San Marcos, Retalhuleu, Suchitepequez, Escuintla and Santa Rosa, which lie just beyond the volcanic mountain ranges that divide the rest of the country from these western flatlands.

These provinces have thriving agricultural and livestock industries, as well as a booming fishing business. Home mostly to working-class Guatemalans with little or no indigenous blood, these provinces tend to be somewhat rough-and-tumble, and more than a little dangerous. The main towns, such as Escuintla and Puerto San José, have little to offer visitors.

This region has a little bit of everything ancient archeological ruins, surfing, farm-stays, adventure parks, volcanoes, mangrove tours, turtle watching, volunteering projects, deep sea fly fishing and more. The most notable ruins are found at Takalik Abaj, near the city of Retalhuleu. A relatively small site with only about 80 structures, Takalik Abaj is most interesting for its several impressive stone carvings and possible links to the ancient Olmec culture.

Accommodation varies from the divine to the squalid but invariably comes with a swimming pool. Fresh fish and seafood can be found in abundance, but apart from a handful of exceptions, there are few alternative options. Transport is local-style, but in a part of Guatemala that is predominantly visited by locals, what better way to understand the heart of its people.

Oriente and Atlantic Coast

The hot provinces of El Progreso, Jalapa, Jutiapa, Zacapa, Chiquimula and Izabal make up Guatemala's Oriente, or eastern region, where the population is mostly ladino, or mestizos with little or no indigenous ancestry. There a few small pockets of indigenous communities, as well as some West African descendents (Garifuna) on the Caribbean coast, most notably in the village of Livingston. There is a local festival of dancing and partying there in late November, but the town is lively any time of year.

There are several ruins and natural wonders to admire in this region, including the Parque Nacional Río Dulce, a large protected natural area home to many species of birds and animals; Lake Izabal; and the Maya site of Quiriguá, Guatemala's most important ruins outside of Petén. On the northern shore of Lake Izabal sits the Castillo San Felipe, a more-or-less preserved Spanish fortress built in 1595. It protected Izabal from Caribbean pirates and served as a military prison.

One of the biggest draws of this area is a dark-skinned wooden carving of Jesus known as the Cristo Negro, or the Black Christ, located in the Basilica of the city of Esquipulas. The festival of the Cristo Negro is on January 15.

The Petén

This rugged and densely forested northeastern appendage of Guatemala makes up roughly one-third of the country's total landmass. Although once home to hundreds of thousands of Maya inhabitants, today it is a sparsley populated area that thrives on basic agriculture, logging and tourism. The Petén has several important Maya sites, including Uaxactún, Yaxhá, Seibal and Piedras Negras. The region's greatest attraction is the ruins of the mighty Maya city of Tikal, a sprawling complex that contains hundreds of structures, including some of the most spectacular temples in the Americas.

The Petén is also a popular destination for nature lovers; thousands of species of mammals, reptiles, birds, insects and plants live in the rainforests. Some of the more interesting ecosystems are protected, but unfortunately the Petén is in danger of losing much of its biodiversity to logging and development.

Guatemala

Guatemala may only be the size of Iceland, but the country's landscape and history are amazingly diverse and complex. Travelers are drawn to the country's breathtaking mountain landscapes, colorful markets, centuries-old Maya culture, modern cities, colonial-era gardens and magnificent ruins. These are just some of the reasons more and more travelers come to this small Central American country every year.

Guatemala is probably best known to the western world as the site of a horrific civil war that lasted from the late 1950s until the mid 1990s. The worst years were during the late 1970s and early 1980s, when thousands of Guatemalans were murdered or displaced, and entire villages were razed. Fortunately, the civil war is over, and Guatemala is once again safe to visit. Updated: Sep 30, 2009.

Geography

Guatemala shares borders with El Salvador, Honduras, Belize and Mexico. The country is situated on the intersections of the Cocos, the Caribbean and the North American tectonic plates. Tectonic shifts are the reasons behind the country's interesting and varied scenery, which ranges from the black sand beaches of the Pacific Coast to the highest mountain in Central America: Tajumulco, at 4,220 meters (13,845 ft). Due to the country's location, frequent earthquakes have historically caused turbulent conditions, including seismic activity such as volcanic eruptions. There is also a hurricane season between June and November.

Guatemala is located in the tropics, but contrary to popular belief, the climate is not always hot and humid. Temperatures are cooler in the highland region that cuts through the center of the country, especially at night. There are a large number of volcanoes in this area, a few of which are currently active. Running to the south of Guatemala's mountainous region is the Pacific Coast, an area that features beaches, mangroves and wetlands. This heavily farmed area produces coffee and sugar, two of the county's staple crops. The hot and humid Petén area, comprising most of the north, has an extensive limestone foundation that supports large forested regions. The small section of Caribbean Coast in Guatemala is characterized by white sand beaches, rainforests and swamplands. Banana plantations are common in this area. Updated: May 13, 2010.

Flora and Fauna

Guatemala means "land of the trees," and as such, it is no surprise that 35 percent of the country is forested. In the Petén region, you can find what are known as tropical moist and tropical wet forests. In these forests, you may come across the ceiba, a tree variety with branchless trucks that the Mayas thought was sacred. Cloud forest ecosystems exist around the Alta Verapaz region, whereas the Pacific and Caribbean Coasts are home to mangrove forests. Guatemala is thought to have more than 8,000 species of plants, including 600 orchid species, 200 of which are endemic to Guatemala. In the cloud forests, you may see Guatemala's national flower, known as "white nun" (*monja blanca*). Unfortunately, deforestation for both illegal and legal purposes is having an impact on the country's diversity.

Birdlife in Guatemala is varied, particularly in the rainforest areas of Petén and around Tikal. In these jungle areas, there are a variety of colorful parrots and toucans. Harpy eagles are also common in the Tikal area, as are ocellated turkeys, a bird that is similar to a peacock. There are approximately 700 bird species in Guatemala, the most famous of which is is the quetzal. The iridescent bird, known for a bright red chest and long tail feathers, is most commonly found around Lake Atitlán. The Guatemalan national currency is named after the quetzal, and in some areas there are projects dedicated to preserving the species.

Guatemala has a variety of interesting mammal life, with monkeys being the most predominant species. In the Petén area, howler and spider monkeys are so abundant they are easy to spot. Elusive jaguars live around Petén, Verapaces and Izabal, but sightings of these creatures are very rare. Other cat species include ocelot, puma and margay. Bats are particularly common in Guatemala, with more than 100 species recorded. Other mammals to be found are the Tamandua anteater and the White-lipped and Collared Peccaries.

The coastal areas are home to a number of different sea turtles. At Monterrico, on the Pacific Coast, you can visit the Monterrico-Hawaii Biotope to see olive ridley, hawksbill and loggerhead turtles. While you are at the beach, try your hand at deep sea fishing. Or head to the

National Parks in Guatemala

With 19 ecosystems spanning the country, Guatemala has a lot to preserve. The government has dedicated nearly 30 percent of the country's total land as protected areas. More than 1,000 species of birds, mammals, reptiles and amphibians call these protected places home. As if that wasn't impressive enough, more than 8,000 species of plants are known to exist in the country, plus a multitude of butterflies and other insects. Visitors are pretty much guaranteed to find something spectacular in the national parks of Guatemala.

Cuevas del Silvino in Izabal: A limestone cave system that can be found on the road connecting Guatemala City to Puerto Barrios.

El Reformador in El Progreso: A well-known lookout point.

El Rosario in El Petén: Formerly a state-owned coffee finca, this tropical jungle park is named for the small lake within its boundaries.

Grutas de Languín in Alta Verapaz: Remember to bring a flashlight into this limestone cave system, because the electric-lighted path has been known to go out.

Laguna Lachuá in Alta Verapaz: This area of tropical jungle is home to half the species of mammals found in Guatemala, 30-40 species of reptiles and nearly 180 bird species.

Laguna El Pino in Santo Rosa: Around this lake you can find many species of waterfowl and floating flora, such as the water hyacinth.

Laguna del Tigre: This national park is within the Maya Biosphere Reserve.

Las Victorias in Alta Verapaz: Formerly a plantation owned by Belgian coffee grower Julio Rossingnon, this site was declared a national park in 1980.

Los Aposentos in Chimaltenango: In this national park, you will find two small lakes and several natural springs.

Mirador Río Azul in El Petén: Although the biodiversity in this park has not been studied sufficiently, many species found within this tropical jungle are considered vulnerable or were not previously recorded in Guatemala. Part of the Maya Biosphere Reserve.

Naciones Unidas in Guatemala: Just 145 kilometers (90 mi) away from Guatemala City, this park has popular hiking and mountain biking trails.

Tikal in El Petén: Set in the jungle, this national park is dotted with thousands of structures leftover from the pre-Columbian Maya civilization and is home to an abundance of wildlife. Tikal is the first national park to be declared in Guatemala, as well as a UNESCO World Heritage Site.

Quiriguá in Izabal: An ancient Maya archeological site well known for its abnormally large, elaborately carved monuments. A UNESCO World Heritage Site.

Río Dulce in Izabal: This jungle area along the banks of the "Sweet River" is a popular sailing destination.

Riscos de Momostenango in Totonicapán: This national park is famous for its strange sandstone cliffs and nearby market.

San José la Colonia in Alta Verapaz: This park sits in the jungle on the northern outskirts of the city of Cobán.

Sipacate Naranjo in Escuintla: In this tropical savannah, endangered turtles lay their eggs on beaches and more than 90 bird species make for great birdwatching.

Sierra del Lacandón in El Petén: This tropical park connects protected areas in northern Guatemala to those in southern Mexico. The park has a few ancient Maya archeological sites within its bounds, and is part of the Maya Biosphere Reserve.

Volcán Pacaya in Escuintla: This active volcano is a popular tourist attraction because it has been erupting continuously since 1965. Updated: Jun 10, 2010.

Guatemala has a variety of reptiles, including snakes and crocodiles, such as the Morelet's crocodile and the American crocodile. You can find snakes around Lake Yaxhá, and crocodiles around Petén and Izabal. Poisonous snakes that are native to Guatemala include the pit viper and rattlesnakes; there are also non-poisonous Boa constrictors. Among the interesting amphibian life you may encounter are the Morelet's tree frog, the red-eyed tree frog and the Fleischmann's glass frog. Updated: Jul 20, 2010.

Climate

The mountainous regions of Guatemala tend to have pleasantly warm days and cool nights year round. For this reason, Guatemala has been dubbed the "Land of Eternal Spring." The daytime temperature makes the mountain region a delightful place to visit at any time, but do not forget a sweater for the chilly evenings. There are two basic seasons: wet and dry. The wet season is from approximately the middle of May to the middle of October. Wet weather can last for longer in the Petén region, where rains can continue into December. During the rainy season, the downpours do not last all day, but instead, there are daily showers that normally fall in the afternoons. Humidity can also be high during these times. Roads can become more difficult to travel during the rainy season, particularly when you are heading farther off the beaten track. The dry season runs roughly November-April. During these months, temperatures can be very high along the coast and in the Petén area. Updated: May 13, 2010.

History

THE MAYA

The first settlers of present-day Guatemala arrived thousands of years ago, and a number of early civilizations developed in the area. Most notable was the Maya, whose empire peaked between 700-1100 AD. The Maya were great astronomers, builders, warriors and traders. They built great palaces and cities and left behind several fascinating ruin complexes such as Tikal in Guatemala and Palenque in Mexico.

Today, opinions vary as to the reason for their decline. Some believe that a series of natural disasters such as earthquakes and famines are responsible, while others say the Maya warred among themselves

too heavily. In any event, by the time the Spanish arrived in Maya lands in 1523, most Maya civilizations had disintegrated into small, weak ethnic groups that continued to war among themselves even as the Spanish picked them off one by one.

THE SPANISH CONQUEST

There was little in the Maya region of interest to the Spanish. They found very little gold and silver, and the natives were difficult to govern. Nevertheless, the Spanish established a colony in the area, and put an *encomienda* system in place. Under this type of labor system, vast tracts of land—and the natives who lived there—were given to Spanish conquistadors and bureaucrats. In turn, the landowners made the land productive and gave the crown a percentage of the profits. Needless to say, this system led to a number of abuses and horrors.

One man who denounced the horrors of the conquest and the encomienda system was the Dominican friar Bartolomé de Las Casas. He eventually became Bishop of Chiapas, and worked tirelessly his entire life to stop the abuses of the colonial system. He is known in Guatemala for the "Verapaz Experiment," in which he sent missionaries into a troubled area of northern Guatemala to see if the natives there could be peacefully brought into the Spanish fold. The experiment worked, and the region is still known as Verapaz.

Spanish rule in Guatemala came to an end in 1821, when Mexico declared independence and took Guatemala with it. In 1823, Guatemala and other Central American nations seceded from Mexico and established the Central American Federation. The new republic was unwieldy, as communication between Central American countries was very difficult. By 1839 the republic had disintegrated, and Guatemala was an independent nation.

INDEPENDENCE AND THE UNITED FRUIT COMPANY

For the next few decades, Guatemala went through a succession of leaders but always remained a poor nation of wealthy landowners and repressed peasants. Around the turn of the century, Guatemala attracted the attention of the United Fruit Company, a powerful American firm dedicated to raising and importing fruit—primarily bananas—from Central America and the Caribbean.

The legacy of the United Fruit Company in Guatemala is mixed. The company provided jobs, infrastructure, schools and electricity to many regions that never would have had those things. But it also supported corrupt, repressive governments and shared little of its profits. In 1944, the repressive tyrant José Ubico was overthrown and in the elections that followed, the people elected the socialist Dr. Juan José Arévalo Bermej.

Another free election followed, and the people selected Jacobo Arbenz. The new president continued his predecessor's social programs, but went too far. He wanted to implement a land redistribution program that would allow the poorest Guatemalans to own land. When he announced his plans to nationalize and redistribute some of the United Fruit Company's vast land holdings, the company went to the United States government to ask for help. As early as 1952, the CIA was working on plans to overthrow Arbenz and replace him with someone more agreeable to big business.

U.S. INTERVENTION
In 1954, the CIA was ready. They found a dissident colonel living in Honduras, Carlos Castillo Armas, and enlisted him to lead an uprising. Castillo Armas entered Guatemala with only 150 men and marched on Guatemala City. Meanwhile, the CIA arranged for American pilots to bomb strategic targets in the capital and began a misinformation campaign that made the people believe a much larger force was coming. Arbenz and his government fled, and the coup was complete. The CIA considered it a rousing success, a textbook example of how to defeat communism in the post-war world.

In the long run, however, the plan backfired. The people of Guatemala, fed up with imperialism and the United Fruit Company, soon took up arms in rebellion. By the early 1960s, there was a full-scale guerrilla war taking place. In the 1970s, the war escalated and tens of thousands were massacred, mostly rural peasants. By 1977, the Guatemalan government had become so repressive and violent that the United States ceased military support.

CIVIL WAR AND MORE CORRUPTION
In 1982, General Efraín Ríos Montt took power in a coup. Although Ríos Montt was only in power for about a year before he was also deposed by a military coup, his administration is considered to have presided over the most violent and repressive period in the whole civil war. Under his rule, entire towns and villages were burned to the ground, hundreds of thousands were

displaced, and thousands were murdered and buried in unmarked mass graves.

In 1983, Maya peasant Rigoberta Menchú wrote a testimonial account of the war, "I, Rigoberta Menchú." Although some of the details were found to have been fabricated, the story brought global attention to the plight of Guatemala's poor during the war. As global pressure mounted on Guatemala, Ríos Montt's successor, Oscar Humberto Mejía Victores, decided to restore democracy and drafted a new constitution. Vinicio Cerezo, a civilian, won the presidency in 1986 and ruled until 1991, when another civilian government took power through the ballot box. Under presidents Ramiro De León and Álvaro Arzú, the peace process accelerated, and a final agreement was signed with the leftists in December of 1996.

Gaspar Ilóm

Rodrigo Asturias is a Guatemalan guerrilla leader and politician who fought under the name Gaspar Ilóm, which he adopted from the book *Men of Maize* by Nobel Prize winner Miguel Angel Asturias (Rodrigo's father).

Ilóm became involved in the revolution in 1971 when he founded the ORPA, or Armed People's Association.

ORPA was one of four rebel groups that united to establish the Guatemalan National Revolutionary Unity (URNG), and Ilóm was named its head. He generally directed his forces from exile in Mexico. Ilóm was the head of the URNG from the early 1980s until 1996, when a peace treaty was finally signed.

The URNG was converted into a legitimate political party and Ilóm ran for president, but was defeated. He died of a heart attack in 2005. Upon learning of his death, his former adversary Otto Pérez Molina described him as "a brave man, with grand ideas, who did a great deal to bring about the end of the war." Updated: Nov 23, 2009.

GUATEMALA TODAY
Guatemala's transition from dictatorship and war to democracy and peace has not been an easy one. Although a Truth Commission set out to document the atrocities of the war, the

Political Timeline

800 BC-200 AD: Takalik Abaj serves as one of the most important economic and cultural centers of the pre-Columbian Maya civilization.
700-1000: Peak of the Maya civilization.
1519: The Spanish began expeditions to Guatemala, resulting in devastating epidemics.
1522: Spanish armies conquer Guatemala.
1524: The first Guatemalan capital, Santiago de los Caballeros de Guatemala, is founded.
1527: Capital is moved to Ciudad Vieja.
1541: A mudslide engulfs Ciudad Vieja after a volcano crater fills with water. The capital is moved six kilometers (4 mi) to Antigua, now a UNESCO World Heritage Site.
1773-1774: Antigua is destroyed by several earthquakes. The capital is moved about 50 kilometers (30 mi) to modern day Guatemala City.
1821: Mexico declares independence and takes Guatemala with it, ending Spanish rule.
1823: Guatemala and other Central American nations secede from Mexico and establish the Central American Federation. The union dissolves by 1840.
1901: The government hires the United Fruit Company to manage the postal service. By 1930, the company becomes the largest employer in Central America.
1954: The U.S. Central Intelligence Agency organizes a coup to overthrow President Jacobo Árbenz Guzmán, who instituted a controversial land reform program that redistributed land—including a vast portion of the United Fruit Company's holding—to Guatemalan peasants.
1959: Belize and Guatemala sign a border treaty.
1960-1996: The longest civil war in Latin America is fought between the government of Guatemala and insurgents.
1985: Guatemala adopts the country's current constitution.
1996: A peace accord between the guerrillas and the government, negotiated by the United Nations, ends the Guatemalan Civil War. More than 200,000 people were killed and more than 1 million had been displaced within Guatemala or fled the country.
2005: Guatemala ratifies the U.S.-Central American Free Trade Agreement (CAFTA-DR). Updated: Jun 10, 2010.

enactment of amnesty laws and the harassment of human rights investigators prevented a full airing of the truth. Politically, the democratically elected governments have been mired in corruption charges. Ríos Montt emerged as a major political force, but has been barred from serving as president. In 2007, a center-left government under Álvaro Colom came to power. Although the violence of the war subsided, gang violence has become a major problem in Guatemala City. The drug smuggling routes between Colombia and Mexico run through Guatemala, leading to significant amounts of crime, as well as corruption in the judicial and political systems. Updated: Aug 17, 2010.

Politics

Guatemala's politics have been troubled at best, though the political system is a democratic, multi-party system. Álvaro Colom, the current president of Guatemala, was elected in 2007 and came to office in January 2008. Colom is the first left-wing president elected in more than half a century, reflecting a sweeping tide toward leftism across much of Latin America. As president, Colom is also head of state and government. Presidents are legally able to hold power for four years. Guatemala is divided up into 22 departments that are headed up by governors who are elected by the president.

In the 2007 elections, the parties securing the highest numbers of votes were the current president's party, National Unity of Hope (UNE), and also the party who ran the country for the preceding term, Grand National Alliance (GANA). The Patriotic Party (PP) also secured a significant number of votes. There is a general level of despondency with politics in Guatemala. Most people believe that politicians are inefficient and corrupt. The current president has not been exempt from these perceptions, so no one yet knows how successful he will be. One of Colom's objectives has been to reduce criminal activity, which he believes can be accomplished by reducing poverty. Updated: Jul 20, 2010.

Banana Republic: The United Fruit Company and Guatemala

Before 1870, bananas were essentially unheard of in the United States. By the turn of the century, more than 16 million bunches were imported every year. The U.S.'s insatiable taste for the little yellow fruit came at a huge cost to Guatemalans, a legacy that starts with the exploitation of cheap labor, climaxes with a CIA-organized government coup, and ends with a 36-year-long civil war.

The U.S.-owned United Fruit Company began to acquire land in Latin America for banana plantations at the end of the 19th century, ultimately snatching up around 42 percent of Guatemala's total farmland. The company was given the exclusive right to transport mail in 1901, and eventually clinched a stranglehold on all of Guatemala's transportation and communication systems. Through bribes and concessions, the company essentially controlled the conservative government. The UFCO was "top banana" in Guatemala, and the country became what is now known as a "banana republic."

The people of Guatemala called the UFCO *el pulpo*, or "the octopus." Workers labored grueling hours but were paid low wages and provided minimal benefits. By 1944, the Guatemalans had had enough. The conservative dictator was overthrown, a democratic constitution drawn up, and a socialist president was freely elected. Over the next few years, progress was made in education and health care. The next freely elected president, Jacobo Arbenz Guzmán, proposed an even larger reform: the redistribution of unused land to Guatemalan peasants.

To say the least, the UFCO was unhappy with Guzmán's proposal. At the time, only 10 percent of land in Guatemala was available to 90 percent of the population—and the UFCO owned nearly half of the unused land. With the aid of the Central Intelligence Agency, the UFCO organized a successful coup that placed a right-winged dictator in power.

Guatemala, a country with a long history of domination, had barely enjoyed 10 years of progress before being thrown back into suppression. A 36-year-long civil war soon broke out between insurgents and the conservative government. The UFCO made efforts to change their reputation, and was eventually bought by Chiquita Brands International. Updated: Jul 20, 2010.

Economy

Guatemala lays claim to the largest economy of any Central American country, but it is stuck on the short list of poorest countries in Latin America. More than half the population lives below the poverty line, while the richest 10 percent of Guatemalans eat up half the country's income. The gap between rich and poor is evident throughout the country, especially in Guatemala City, where the poor beg for change from expensive cars that pass by. The agricultural sector employs around half of the labor force, with coffee, bananas and sugar making up the bulk of Guatemala's exports. Tourism is also an ever increasing source of revenue for the country, now employing around 35 percent of the nation's total workforce.

Since the time of the Spanish conquest, Guatemala's economy has been dependent on the export of a handful of agricultural products. Indigo and cochineal dominated the market during colonial times, until synthetic dyes made the materials obsolete. Cocoa and essential oils filled the void, until coffee and bananas eventually became principal exports. Since 1960, a civil war in Guatemala stifled foreign investment in the country. In 1996, peace accords ended the war, allowing the country to focus on major economic reforms after decades of unrest. Guatemala further improved the investment climate by recently ratifying free trade agreements with the United States, Taiwan, Colombia and several Central American nations.

Today, the United States is Guatemala's largest trading partner, receiving over a third of the country's exports and providing Guatemala with around 41 percent of its imports. Nontraditional agricultural products such as cut flowers have been a blooming source of revenue for Guatemala in recent years, but sugar, bananas, and coffee dominate the export

Colom and Rosenberg—Videotape and Murder

Rodrigo Rosenberg, an attorney in Guatemala City, was murdered while riding a bicycle near his home on May 10, 2009. In a country with 20 murders per day, such a crime would usually be met with shrugged shoulders, except that Rosenberg left something truly disturbing behind.

Earlier, Rosenberg had submitted a video to El Periódico and La Prensa, two leading dailies, and asked that it be released in the event of his death. The day after Rosenberg's murder, the video surfaced on El Periódico's website.

In the short clip, Rosenberg chillingly prophesied his death. The truly troubling part, however, is to whom he assigned blame: President Álvaro Colom, his wife and his personal secretary. He then went on to build a convincing case against the three.

Rosenberg's most high-profile client was Khalil Musa, a textile tycoon. Colom had asked Musa to serve on the board of an influential bank, but Musa quickly resigned over the corruption he found among Colom's cronies on the board; a short time later, in mid-April, Musa and his daughter were shot and killed while waiting at a red light. The crime is unsolved, and the police report that two assassins escaped on motorbikes.

Rosenberg did not hesitate to connect the dots. He told everyone he could that Colom and his inner circle were responsible for the death of his client. This, Rosenberg claimed, was tantamount to signing his own death warrant.

For several weeks, Guatemala shook with the news. Protesters took to the streets and other outlets such as Twitter to express their outrage. For a little while, it looked like Colom might be forced to resign over what he had done.

Except that Colom had not done anything. After months of investigation, an international team of detectives pointed the finger at an unlikely suspect: Rosenberg himself. The investigators found that Rosenberg, distraught over the deaths of the Musas, had decided to frame Colom by organizing his own death, and hired hit men to have himself killed. It was an appropriately surreal conclusion to a shocking and strange case. Updated: Aug 20, 2010.

market. Guatemala is the top receiver of remittances in Central America, mostly due to the large number of Guatemalan expatriates who fled to the U.S. during the Guatemalan Civil War. The amount of money sent to Guatemala in remittances is equivalent to nearly two-thirds of the total made from exporting goods. Updated: Jul 20, 2010.

Population

The population of Guatemala was estimated in January 2010 to be at approximately 13 million. Nearly half of the population is made up of Maya Amerindians, including groups such as Mam, Kaqchikel and Quiché. The largest percentage of the Maya population lives in the highlands. There are smaller pockets of Mayas in other rural areas of the country, such as the Petén. Mestizos, of mixed indigenous and European descent, form the next largest population group, and are found mostly in cities in towns. On the coast, there

is a small population of people of mixed African and indigenous descent, known as Garifuna. The white population, forming the traditional upper crust of Guatemalan society, is relatively small and concentrated in a few major cities. Updated: Jul 20, 2010.

Language

Spanish is the most widely spoken language in Guatemala. The country is a great place to learn Spanish because Guatemalans speak a relatively clear form of the language. Antigua has a particularly large number of Spanish schools; Quetzaltenango is another good option if you are looking for a different place to learn. Due to Guatemala's Maya ancestry, indigenous languages are still predominant in more rural sections of the country. There are estimated to be around two million Quiché speakers, primarily located in the highland regions. Mam is another commonly used language, mainly in western Guatemala. If you are interested in learning indigenous languages, the larger language centers usually offer classes. Updated: Jul 20, 2010.

INDIGENOUS LANGUAGES

Spanish is the official language in Guatemala, but 23 languages are recognized by the government. Twenty-one distinct Mayan languages are spoken in Guatemala, and two other Amerindian languages—Garifuna and Xinca—round out the list. Garifuna is spoken by roughly 17,000 descendants of the original Carib Indians of the island of St. Vincent, who trace their ancestry to escaped West African slaves. In the southern portion of Guatemala, near El Salvador, around 13 percent of the 16,214 indigenous Xinca people speak their own isolated language, not believed to be part of the family of Mayan languages. Updated: Jun 10, 2010.

Religion

As is the case in most Latin American countries, the predominant religion in Guatemala is Roman Catholicism, practiced by approximately 55 percent of the population. There is a surprisingly large Protestant following as well; around 40 percent consider themselves to be Protestants and a large number of these are Evangelical, a denomination that has been on the rise. The indigenous Maya faith is reported to be practiced by around just one percent of the population, though Maya traditions are often mixed with Christian customs during holidays and ceremonies. There are a small number of Guatemalan followers of Judaism, Buddhism and Islam. Updated: Jul 20, 2010.

Culture

The Guatemalan way of life is heavily influenced by two very different cultures: the Maya and the Spanish. This curious mixture of culture can be seen, tasted, heard, and even celebrated throughout Guatemala. Take, for example, the assortment of architecture in the country: One day you can be exploring the ancient Maya ruins of Tikal and the next you may find yourself in Guatemala City's neo-Gothic cathedral, Iglesia Yurrita. The same mishmash of culture can be tasted in Guatemalan food. Although most plates are still based on the Maya diet of corn and beans, the Spanish added rice, European vegetables and generous portions of meat. The marimba, Guatemala's national instrument, is another tradition expanded on by the Spaniards. Although the marimba is

believed to have been around since 1550, two Spanish musicians developed a chromatic scale for the instrument in 1894. Finally, holidays are an assortment of religious customs and indigenous traditions, usually taking a Catholic holiday and throwing in plenty of traditional music, dancing, and food. Updated: Jul 20, 2010.

ART

Art can be found around every corner in Guatemala, from traditional weaving to spray-paint stained walls. Guatemala City hosts several art festivals throughout the year, while browsing handicraft boutiques and cozy art galleries in Antigua is a great way to spend the night.

Guatemala's rich art legacy dates back to murals and carvings made by the Mayas. If interested in these types of relics, check out the Museo Popol Vuh in Guatemala City, considered to house one of the world's best Maya art collections. Guatemala City also has an entire museum dedicated to the traditional textiles of the Mayas, Museo Ixchel del Traje Indígena, where the textiles from around 140 communities are on display.

Many artists produced great works during the colonial period as well, though most pieces were done anonymously. The Museo de Arte Colonial in Antigua houses a great deal of sculptures and paintings from this era, including many religious-themed works. Two famous painters from this period, Cristóbal de Villalpando (1649-1714) and Tómas de Merlo (1694-1739), are also represented here. Although Villaplando is Mexican, he did a substantial amount of work in Guatemala.

Another Guatemalan artist, Andrés Curruchich (1891-1969), is credited with pioneering the "primitivist" style of painting. Born in San Juan Comalapa, Curruchich was a Kaqchikel Maya who depicted the daily lives of those around him in a very simple, easy-to-understand form. His colorful paintings are still romanticized, replicated and sold in markets today. Carmen Petterson (1900-1991) used watercolors to paint the clothing styles of rural highland villagers. Although born in Guatemala, her parents were of mixed European and Latin descent, and she painted in a style that was obviously European influenced. Her work can be seen at the Museo Ixchel del Traje Indígena in Guatemala City. Carlos Mérida (1891-1984), a contemporary of Pablo Picasso born to Maya and Zapotec parents, may be the most famous Guatemalan

Architecture in Guatemala

Tikal: Deep in the jungle of northern Guatemala is Tikal, one of the largest archaeological sites of the pre-Columbian Maya civilization. The dense rainforest is dotted with thousands of limestone structures, only a fraction of which have been excavated after decades of archaeological work. Six steeply stepped pyramids are the most iconic structures at Tikal, but the site also contains plenty of palaces, tombs and temples to explore. Declared a UNESCO World Heritage Site in 1979, daily flights from Guatemala City reach Flores, about 64 kilometers (40 mi) southwest of Tikal.

Antigua: Three volcanoes tower in the distance of Antigua, once the colonial capital of Guatemala. Despite a number of earthquakes, the Spanish Mudéjar-influenced Baroque architecture is spectacularly well preserved in Antigua's colonial churches, monuments, fountains and other ruins. Antigua, the Old City of Guatemala, has been designated a UNESCO World Heritage Site. The city makes a great home base for exploring the rest of the country.

Guatemala City: In Guatemala City, colonial buildings exist alongside modern skyscrapers. At the heart of the city is the Centro Histórico, home to the National Palace and Cathedral of Guatemala City, the main church of the city that began construction in 1782. Another must-see is the neo-Gothic Iglesia Yurrita, rumored to be the work of famous Spanish architect Antoni Gaudí. Admission to the building is free, and it only takes 15 to 20 minutes to tour the whole thing—so your best bet is to have a cab wait for you outside.

Flores: Flores town proper is an island on Lago Petén Itzá, instantly recognizable for its patchwork of colonial, red-roofed buildings. The city's narrow, cobblestone streets are easily walkable, and a circle around the village takes only 15 minutes. Spend some time taking it all in at the Parque Central, where you can easily spot the two white domes that top off the Flores Church, the most striking architectural attraction on the island.

Quetzaltenango: Quetzaltenango, Guatemala's second largest city, has a mix of neo-Classical and colonial buildings. The city's central plaza, Parque Centro América, is surrounded by buildings with Neoclassical flourishes, most of which date from the early 20th century. The Catedral del Espíritu Santo on the southeastern corner dates from 1535, but only the walls of the original building remain. Near the Parque Benito Juárez is Iglesia de San Nicolás, a building known for Baroque finishes of gold moldings and arches. Updated: Jul 20, 2010.

of all. Mérida's indigenista style of art can be found in several public buildings in Guatemala City, as well as at the Museo Nacional de Arte Moderno, which was named after him.

Today, weaving still reins king as Guatemala's primary craft. Traditional dress can be seen throughout the country, particularly in highland villages. Other popular crafts include jewelry making and wooden mask production. It is also not uncommon for each village to have a specialty, whether it be the woolen blankets of Momostenango, lacquered boxes of Totonicapán, or canvas replicas of Curruchich's paintings from his hometown, San Juan Comalapa. Updated: Jul 28, 2010.

ARCHITECTURE

When it comes to Guatemalan architecture, visitors are delighted to discover Maya temples, colonial buildings and modern skyscrapers all within a country slightly smaller than the state of Tennessee.

Ruins from the pre-Columbian Maya civilization can be found in countless sites throughout the country, most notably in Tikal National Park, once one of the most powerful kingdoms of the ancient Maya. Starting in the 16th century, the Spanish brought Baroque touches to many Guatemalan cities, including the magnificently preserved colonial capital of Antigua. Guatemala City is an urban area of stark contrasts, where spectacular skyscrapers cast shadows on colonial buildings and tin-roofed shantytowns. Architecture lovers will find so much to see and do in Guatemala; the hardest part is deciding where to begin. Updated: Jul 20, 2010.

MUSIC

The styles of popular music in Guatemala are extremely varied. From the highlands to the cities, you can find just about any type of music style, including but not limited to traditional folk music, tropical salsa, mariachi bands, hip hop, reggaeton, classical orchestras, meringue bands, opera vocalists and even heavy metal. Wind and percussion bands are popular in many towns, but the younger people tend to prefer rock and pop music.

Cumbia, a style of music from Colombia, is also very popular. The cumbia bands in Guatemala are unique because they are influenced by other traditional styles of music found in Guatemala. On the northern coast, the Garifuna people have their own Caribbean-influenced folk music. You can also find traditional indigenous music played on instruments such as the pan flute and fiddle.

Of course, you cannot talk about music in Guatemala without mentioning the county's national instrument, the marimba. This xylophone-like instrument made with wood bars and played with mallets is the principal instrument in most Guatemalan folk music. The first documentary evidence of a marimba is from 1680, but it is very probable the instrument is much older. In fact, the marimba may have been introduced by West African slaves as early as 1550. Today, the famous waltz played on the marimba, "Luna de Xelajú," is regarded as an unofficial national anthem by many Guatemalans.

As far as the history of music in Guatemala goes, archaeological evidence suggests the Mayas were making music as early as 600-900 AD. Drums, shakers, whistles and rattles have been found throughout the Maya region, as well as figurines and other relics depicting Maya people playing instruments. Documents and murals have also been found that detail musical instruments and dance in writing and drawings.

When the Spaniards came to Guatemala, they corresponded back home about the styles of music found at the time. Guatemalan music became known as *villancico*, which the Spanish regarded as akin to Christmas carols. Indigenous, European and African influences continued to act upon one another, morphing traditional Guatemalan music into what it is today. Traditional music is still popular in highland Maya settlements today, usually featuring a lot of percussion and woodwind accompaniments.

Recently, Guatemala has had a surge of rock bands and pop vocalists. The most popular is probably Alux Nahual, a pop-rock group that has recorded a dozen albums and promotes peace in Central America. In 2006, the last rock station playing music on FM radio went off air, creating a surge in the underground music community. The lack of support from the media caused hundreds of musicians to begin self-producing records and promoting themselves through Internet venues such as www.MySpace.com and www. RockRepublik.net. Today, underground musical projects are extremely diverse, including reggae dub, folk, electronic, instrumental and metal. Updated: Jul 29, 2010.

MUSEUMS

A day at the museum in Guatemala is great if you are into ancient relics, trade route maps and textile displays. Those interested in Guatemalan history, art and culture will find lots to explore, but do not expect to be wowed by enormously expansive—or expensive—art collections found in other major cities. You should not assume museums come with English translations; it is a wise decision to keep your Spanish-to-English dictionary as a backup if necessary.

In Guatemala City, museums range from quirky to contemporary, and most are centered around Zona 1, 10 and 13. In Zona 1 (Centro Histórico), you will find the unusual but intriguing Railway Museum, where you can explore passenger carriages parked on the tracks of the city's old main terminal. The Museo Ixchel in Zona 10 is a favorite for those interested in Maya culture, particularly indigenous clothing and other textiles. The Museo Nacional de Historia Natural in Zona 13 is not as extensive as natural history collections in other major cities, but is worth a visit if you are interested in flora and fauna native to Guatemala. Nearby is the Museo Nacional de Arte Moderno as well as the Museo Nacional de Arqueología y Etnolgia, home to Guatemala's largest collection of Maya artifacts.

A simple stroll around the colonial city of Antigua will have you popping your head in several one-of-a-kind museums. The Handicraft and Kitchen Museum and the Pharmacy Museum are windows into the way Guatemalans have lived in years past. Art lovers will enjoy exploring the dozens of art galleries throughout the city, plus the Central American Art Gallery,

Marimba

The origin of the marimba, Guatemala's national instrument, is unknown. Some maintain it came from Indonesia, others from the Amazon, yet it's more widely believed that slaves brought it over from Africa in the 16th century. This theory is most widely accepted because a Zulu myth tells of a goddess named Marimba creating a musical instrument of wooden palings and hanging gourds.

The marimba is an integral part of Guatemalan culture beloved by all. The soundtrack of many festivals, both in rural areas and in the city, a fiesta without marimba would be considered no fiesta at all. The sound of the marimba's lively melodies echoing through the streets is a sure sign that something is being celebrated. A poem about the marimba is recited during the commemoration of independence and gigantes, the giant figures that are such an important part of pueblo pageants, and is accompanied only by the sound of its music. There are also a number of traditional dances that go along with various marimba rhythms.

Similar to a wooden xylophone, this beautiful percussion instrument is played by differing numbers of musicians depending on its size. The keys, usually made of rosewood, are arranged like a piano and are tapped with mallets, creating distinctive musical tones. There is a Guatemalan saying about large families having *una marimba de hijos*, likening the horde of children to the abundance of keys on the instrument.

It's said that the marimba evolved from simple wooden bars placed over a hole in the ground, which the indigenous people of Guatemala copied and refined to create their own style. The first documented account of the existence of marimba is from a performance in front of the cathedral in Antigua in 1680, and it can still be heard every year on July 25, Antigua's Patron Saint Day. Modern marimba bands dress formally and consist of a smaller marimba for three players or a larger one for four, accompanied by a string bass and drum kit or other percussion.

Jades, S.A., a jade factory and archaeological museum in Antigua, recently made the first marimbas with jade keys. They were inspired by the Chinese, who have used the semi-precious stone for thousands of years to make musical instruments, due to its special acoustic properties. Now three various-sized marimbas of jade, each producing a different sound, are on display in their museum in Antigua.

To get a taste of the marimba while in Antigua, head for the 5a Avenida Norte on a Sunday. A father and his family, including young children, all dressed in indigenous attire, perform together in the street. Marimba is also played in La Fonda de la Calle Real and sometimes in Parque Central at weekends and festivals. Updated: Nov 23, 2009.

Contemporary Art Museum, and the VIGUA Museum of Pre-Columbian Art and Modern Glass, which displays ancient objects juxtaposed next to contemporary glass pieces.

Those curious about Guatemalan culture should visit La Azotea Cultural Center in nearby Jocotenango. The complex includes a coffee plantation, botanical gardens, and trio of exhibits dedicated to coffee, costumes and music. To get there, hop on a Chimaltenango-bound bus from Antigua's terminal. Updated: Jun 10, 2010.

DANCE

In this modern era where technology reigns supreme, it is a wonder to behold something as rich in history and tradition as a Guatemalan folkloric dance. Well-orchestrated through centuries of practice, folkloric dancing is the highlight of any party or festival. Dating back to pre-conquest times, Guatemalan folkloric dances reflect ancient Maya, Spanish and even African cultures. Each dance weaves an elaborate story as dancers prance about in vibrant Maya costumes and ceremonial masks or traditional Guatemalan fashion to the rhythms of the marimba, flute or drums.

The quintessential Guatemalan dances convey spectacular historical accounts and captivate audiences of all ages. The horrific conquest of indigenous populations by the Spaniards is poignantly evident in the traditional dance of La Conquista. La Punta, on the other hand, is a symbolic reenactment of the cock-and-hen mating dance, a feat of strength as participants remain poised on the balls of their feet for hours at a time. Moros y Cristianos captures a single historical event in which the Moors were expelled from Spain in 1462. Gender barriers blur as men don feminine masks to participate in El Yancunú. Perhaps the most incredible of these folkloric dances is the Palo Volador, in which men climb up a 10-story wooden pole and attempt a primitive form of bungee jumping as nail-biters gasp and hold their breath below.

Arguably the best troupe featuring traditional dances is the Guatemalan National Modern and Folkloric Ballet that has delighted audiences for more than 40 years. Not only a treasure to Guatemalans, this dance group has also entranced international crowds with its performances in Europe, the Caribbean and throughout the Americas. Keep an eye peeled for performances by this dynamic crew.

Numerous opportunities to witness these gorgeous dances arise throughout the year. The Guatemalan National Folk Festival, hosted every August since 1972, is an excellent way to view Guatemalan heritage through dance and other indigenous art forms as well, such as pottery, crafts and painting. In Cobán, the National Folklore Festival Rabin Ajau held in July features several impressive renditions of folkloric dance. Near the finale of this festival, local indigenous women compete for the title of Rabin Ajaw in a pageant where the emphasis lies not in the beauty of the women, but in their cultural pride and preservation. Updated: May 13, 2010.

CINEMA

Guatemala's film industry has yet to really take off and remains fledgling and fragile. There is very little institutional support for cinema, and films are made on scant budgets. The current generation of filmmakers is keen to expose the country's many social issues, focusing on the struggles of its most marginalized people.

Filmmakers also wish to showcase Guatemala's attractiveness and viability as a filmmaking location. The diverse geography and improvement of film production levels have yet to draw many shoots to the Land of the Eternal Spring. Tikal makes an appearance in *Star Wars* (1977); a season of U.S. reality series *Survivor* (2005) was set in Yaxhá-Nakúm-Naranjo National Park; and, recently, *Looking for Palladin* (2008) was filmed in Antigua and Guatemala City.

The country's 36-year civil war is popular film fodder: Political upheaval and violence are often foreground or background of films. Maya culture, past and present, is also mined heavily for content. Documentaries make up a large portion of Guatemalan film, exploring the effects of the war as well as giving attention to social problems, which are rarely covered by the mainstream media. *Estrellas de la Línea* (2006) documents a football team formed by sex workers and the conflict surrounding their expulsion from a local five-a-side league.

One of Guatemala's most successful films is *El Silencio de Neto* (1994), the country's first independent film entirely produced by nationals. Luis Argueta's first feature-length film is an acclaimed, coming-of-age drama set against the events of the 1954 CIA-backed coup. *El Norte* (1983), though filmed outside of Guatemala, deals with the plight of a teenage Guatemalan brother and sister fleeing from their war-torn home to the United States.

In spite of the dependence on government support and a TV monopoly that has limited the attention given to cinema, the quality of Guatemalan productions has been on the rise, and more and more films are getting play and winning accolades in international festivals. *Gasolina* (2007), a story of the precarious friendships of a group of gasoline-stealing, joy-riding teens, won three prizes, including one for the best Latin American entry at the San Sebastian Film Festival in Spain. The film's post-production would not have been possible without the financial benefits that came with the awards.

Back in Guatemala, support for the development of the industry comes from film studies courses and one of Central America's biggest film and TV festivals. Every November for over a decade, the Icaro Festival has been celebrating Latin American and international works in Guatemala City. Updated: Nov 23, 2009.

LITERATURE

Guatemala's literary history dates back to the ancient stories of pre-Columbian Mayas. The creation myths in "El Popol Vuh" and historical myths of the Kek'chi people in the theatrical play "El Rabinal Achí" have influenced the writing of many contemporary Guatemalan writers. *El Popol Vuh*, or the Book of the Community, is one of the few major remaining works of Mesoamerican mythologies. It contains accounts of the creation of the world, the cosmos and all living things.

The Spanish conquest of Mesoamerica had conflicting impacts on Mayan writing. On one hand, Spanish missionaries were the primary translators of these texts, making them accessible to future generations of Guatemalans as well as the rest of the world's audience. However, many Maya stories were destroyed by the Spanish in their attempt to make the church ideologically dominant.

The Spanish colonization of Guatemala produced writers and poets who strongly opposed the worst abuses of colonial rule, notably Bartolomé de las Casas (1474-1566), poet Rafael Landívar (1731-1793) and Antonio José de Irisarri (1786-1868). Like many other writers of this time living under colonial oppression, Guatemalan authors and poets fused both indigenous and nationalist influences into beautiful, complex and often politically slanted literature. Many Guatemalan writers were forced into exile due to these criticisms, which stunted the growth of a cohesive literary movement. However, when independence was granted in 1821, Guatemalan literature began to develop its own distinct style, separate from the powerful Spanish influence.

Guatemalans began to appear on the international stage with mostly political works influenced by the European techniques of the day. Miguel Ángel Asturias (1899-1974), arguably Guatemala's best-known and most respected author, won the Nobel Prize in 1967 for his novel *El Señor Presidente*, an outspoken criticism of the Estrada Cabrera dictatorship (and all Latin American dictators, by extension). In Asturias' other best-known work, *Men of Maize*, he adapts the ancient Mayan text "El Popol Vuh" into a contemporary context using the literary style of magical realism.

Magical realism, made popular by authors such as Gabriel García Márquez and Toni Morrison, is a technique that combines realistic objectivity with fantastical events to add depth and meaning. The effect in *Men of Maize* is a stunning, surrealist account of the European conquest of the Maya, woven into the contemporary role of maize in both the capitalist system and the indigenous Guatemalan culture.

Another famous writer and activist from Guatemala is Rigoberta Menchú, whose autobiographical account of her life during the Guatemalan Civil War, "I, Rigoberta Menchú" (1983), has been widely disseminated. Her writings shed light on the atrocities committed by the Guatemalan government, and she has been one of the leading voices for indigenous peoples in Latin America. However, American anthropologist David Stoll discovered that part of her story was fabricated when he traveled to Guatemala to research her story, including the descriptions of her family's role in the war. However, her work is still considered to be an important indictment of genocide and violence toward indigenous peoples. Menchú won the Nobel Peace Prize in 1992. Updated: Jun 22, 2010.

Holidays and Fiestas

The Guatemalan calendar is packed with special dates. Thanks to influence from the Maya and the Spanish, holidays and fiestas are a mixture of indigenous traditions and religious customs. With every celebration comes the liberal consumption of *boj*, an alcohol made from sugar cane that is also known as "white lightning." Pretty much every celebration, procession or fiesta is also accompanied with fireworks—but be careful, as injuries are not uncommon.

Small, local fiestas called *cofradias* are prevalent throughout the country, usually dedicated to the town's patron saint. During these celebrations, it is normal to see a group of people carry a religious icon through the street while fireworks light up the sky to scare away evil spirits. There is always plenty of dancing, usually accompanied by musicians joyfully playing the marimba, Guatemala's national instrument. The traditional meal of choice is *kak'ik*, a turkey dish with white sauce, which is always served with an abundance of boj.

The most rejoiced holiday celebrated universally in Guatemala is Semana Santa, or Holy Week. Antigua, famous for its vibrant traditions, draws thousands of visitors during the holiday. The main event is on Good Friday, when the people of Antigua place elaborate handmade carpets outside of their homes. At first glance the colonial- and Maya-influenced carpets appear to be real, but a closer look shows they are actually made of flowers, pines and leaves. In the morning, men and boys dressed in purple robes line the carpeted streets, while around 70 people carrying

Holidays and Fiestas in Guatemala

Below is a list of the major holidays, fiestas and celebrations in Guatemala. As in other places, banks and government offices close on holidays. These include New Years', Holy Thursday, Holy Friday, Holy Saturday, Labor Day, Army Day, Assumption Day, Independence Day, Revolution Day, All Saint's Day and Christmas.

January 1: New Years' Day
It is Guatemalan tradition to bring in the new year in a new outfit, which is supposed to bring good luck.

March/April: Semana Santa (Holy Week)
This is the most celebrated of all holidays in Guatemala. During the week leading up to Easter, expect to see religious processions as well as mock crucifixions and resurrections. Thousands of visitors come to Antigua for Holy Week, where the most famous celebrations take place.

May 1: Labor Day
Parties and parades commemorate this day all over Guatemala.

June 30: Army Day
Known locally as Día del Ejército, this day pays tribute to Guatemala's armed forces. The holiday is set in place in remembrance of the day conservative president Vicente Cerna was overthrown in 1871.

August 15: Assumption Day
This day is observed in Guatemala City and the town of Santa María Nebaj, both of which claim the Virgin Mary as patron saint.

September 15: Independence Day
Guatemala celebrates independence from Spain by setting off fireworks and dancing. After weeks of practice, school children parade throughout the streets during the day. The largest holiday fair is in Quetzaltenango.

October 20: Revolution Day
On this day, Guatemala celebrates "October Revolution," when dictator Jorge Ubico was overthrown in 1944. In Guatemala City, thousands of people celebrate in the streets near Plaza Mayor. Expect lots of music, dance, and as always, fireworks.

November 1/2: All Saints' Day/ Day of the Dead
In the town of Santiago Sacatepepéquez near Antigua, giant kites are flown in the cemeteries in an effort to communicate with the deceased. Throughout Guatemala, *fiambre*—a homemade salad made of deceased relatives' favorite ingredients— is traditionally served.

December 7: Burning of the Devil
Guatemalans gather everything worth burning—such as waste paper and old household items—and set it ablaze to cleanse their homes for the holy weeks to come.

December 13-21: Tribute to Santo Tomás
In Chichicastenango, there is a big festival that mixes Christian and Maya traditions with lots of fireworks and dancing. On the last day, men swing from a 10-story-high pole, known as Palo Volador.

December 25: Christmas Day
Guatemalans celebrate Christmas throughout the entire month of December, placing large emphasis on the nativity scene.

December 31: New Years' Eve
An abundance of fireworks make this the noisiest of all Guatemalan holidays. Tamales are traditionally eaten at midnight.

There is also a Maya New Year celebration that emphasizes life and renewal. Since the Maya calendar has 260 days, the date varies. In addition, each town in Guatemala also has its own holiday, usually dedicated to exalting the town's patron saint.

a giant sculpture of Christ bearing the crucifix on their shoulders pass by. The processions last into the night as onlookers watch from the streets and balconies. The town of Santiago Sacatepepequez has a unique tradition on All Saints' Day, also known as "Day of the Dead." Locals dress in bright-colored clothing and walk through the streets carrying giant, circular kites—some as tall as two-stories high. Messages to the dead are tied to the kite tails in hopes that locals can fly the kites high enough to communicate with the departed. A rainbow of kites dots the sky in this celebration of the dead, each hue meaning something different. Across the country, Guatemalans eat *fiambre*, a salad topped with a mixture of the favorite ingredients of deceased relatives. This traditional salad is only eaten during the holiday.

Much like other Latin American countries, Guatemala celebrates Carnaval. Although the celebrations are not as outrageous as in Brazil, Guatemalans do bring their own special touches to the holiday. One tradition is to have children clean out eggs, fill the shells with confetti and then cover the opening with tissue paper. On the day of Carnaval, children dress in colorful costumes and have confetti fights in the schoolyards. In the end, the ground—and the children—are covered in a blanket of sparkling confetti. Mazatenango is a city famous for an eight-day feast during Carnaval. The cheerful celebration brings the city to life through colorful parades, an abundance of food and traditional music.

Many national holidays in Guatemala may seem familiar, but Guatemalans celebrate them with a different twist. Take New Years', for example: Guatemalans typically ring in the new year by wearing new clothes, a tradition that is supposed to bring good luck. Men wearing masks make their way through crowds and set off fireworks from cages that are fitted around their body. New Years' is a lively holiday, with lots of music and plenty of boj. September 15 is Independence Day, Guatemala's most widely celebrated national holiday. The holiday brings fireworks, parades and lots of dancing. In the city of Quetzaltenango, locals deck out buses with vibrant, patriotic symbols and students march around the central square singing the national anthem and playing in bands. Updated: Jul 20, 2010.

Social and Environmental Issues

INCOME INEQUALITY AND POVERTY

Guatemala is one of the poorest countries in Latin America, a sad reality for the most populous Central American country. According to the CIA World Fact Book, more than half the population lives below the poverty line, and the country's unemployment rate is at 3.2 percent. It is estimated that 40 percent of Guatemalans survive on less than $1 per day, while 10 percent of the population accounts for half of the country's income.

The gap between rich and poor is evident throughout the country. In rural areas, more than 70 percent of the population is classified as living in "extreme poverty." The middle class is growing in urban areas, but income disparities are still clear-cut in Guatemala City, where those who have almost nothing beg for change from expensive cars stopped at intersections.

DIASPORA

A 36-year-long civil war in Guatemala forced many people to restart their lives elsewhere. The majority of Guatemalan refugees fled to the United States, but many others moved to Mexico, Belize and Canada. Remittances sent home from these refugees now constitute the largest single source of foreign income for Guatemala, around $3.5 billion per year. The influx of money is quickly hurtling traditional villages into the modern world. It is hard to know for sure, but some believe more people in Guatemala own cell phones and TVs than toilets.

THE 2009 FOOD CRISIS

Drought, global warming and the global financial crisis have each been huge hindrances to Guatemala's ability to grow and import food. The food shortage situation became so grim that Guatemalan President Álvaro Colum declared a national emergency in September of 2009, asking the international community to contribute emergency food supplies. The most recent update from the United Nations, released April 2010, said Guatemala has received less than 10 percent of the $34 million the country requested.

The UN also estimated the number of children under the age of five suffering from chronic malnutrition is as high as 43 percent—the highest rate in the world. The "dry corridor" in the east and center of the country has been hit particularly hard, and children in indigenous families have a 70 percent chance of suffering from malnutrition.

POLLUTION

A curtain of smog hangs over Guatemala City, where air pollution is severe. Pollution is mainly due to industrial causes such as vehicle exhaust, factory emissions and garbage burning, but sporadic eruptions from nearby Volcán Pacaya also contribute to the city's pollution.

Other areas of the country may not exceed the World Health Organization safety standards for air pollution (as is the case in Guatemala City), but even the countryside has its own set of pollution problems. Around half of Guatemalans living in the countryside lack access to safe drinking water, and nearly two million Guatemalans live within direct contact with pesticides. Lake Atitlán, "the most beautiful lake in the world," is also being threatened by pollution. The lake developed a film of green scum in October of 2009 that was so dense it could be seen from space. The culprit was cyanobacteria, single-celled organisms that multiply rapidly when elements such as phosphorus and nitrogen are abundant in still water. Volcanoes and Maya settlements encircle Lake Atitlán, which act like a bowl that collects runoff from sewage, agriculture and deforestation. Although the amount of cyanobacteria has receded because of cooler weather, experts expect more outbreaks in years to come.

DEFORESTATION
Although nearly 30 percent of Guatemala is set aside as protected land, it is not all sunshine and roses. The UN reported deforestation in Guatemala averaged 1.7 percent each year between 1990 and 2000. The situation is particularly grim in the Petén region, where logging companies and slash-and-burn farming techniques threaten the tropical forest. Conservationists are working hard to preserve the Petén, which is also threatened by oil companies interested in the resources of the area.

OIL EXPLOITATION
Although the largest oil deposits of Central America are found in Guatemala, in the early 1990s, the country was only producing around one-third the amount of oil it consumed every day. During the Persian Gulf War, Guatemala's import bill for oil nearly doubled, so the country opened up the Petén rainforest for oil exploitation. Oil production spiked from 4,000 barrels per day in 1990 to 20,140 barrels per day in 2006. In January 2010, President Álvaro Colom said the country expects oil production to reach as high as 60,000 barrels per day in the coming months.

INDIGENOUS MOVEMENT
As in many other Latin American countries, the indigenous population faces discrimination in schools, at restaurants, in the workplace and in the political arena. Guatemala, however, has faced many obstacles unique to the country's indigenous population. First of all, the community is fragmented by the diversity of Guatemala's Maya population. There are 22 distinct linguistic groups throughout the country, and Mayas have a history of differentiation between these groups. Furthermore,

Guatemala Facts

Official Name: Republic of Guatemala

Capital: Guatemala City

People: White and mestizo, 59.4%; Amerindian, 40.5%; other, 0.1%

Religion: Roman Catholic, Protestant, indigenous Maya beliefs

Population: 13.6 million (as of July 2010)

Language: Spanish 60%, Amerindian languages 40%

Government: Democratic Republic

President: Álvaro Colom, elected January 14, 2008

Economic Facts: Unemployment is 3.2%; 56.2% of the population is below the poverty line

Agriculture: Sugarcane, corn, bananas, coffee, beans, cardamom, farm animals

Main Industries: Sugar, textiles and clothing, furniture, chemicals, petroleum, metals, rubber, tourism

Main Exports: Coffee, sugar, petroleum, apparel, bananas, fruits and vegetables, cardamom

Departments: Alta Verapaz, Baja Verapaz, Chimaltenango, Chiquimula, Petén, El Progreso, El Quiché, Escuintla, Guatemala, Huehuetenango, Izabal, Jalapa, Jutiapa, Quetzaltenango, Retalhuleu, Sacatepéquez, San Marcos, Santa Rosa, Sololá, Suchitepéquez, Totonicapán, Zacapa

Time: UTC-6 (1 hr behind Washington, DC during Standard Time)

Electricity: 120 Volts at 60 Hertz. Outlets generally accept two-prong plugs the Guatemalan government also has a history of brutal violence directed at the indigenous population. Throughout the Guatemalan Civil War, the government led a brutal insurgency campaign directed at a guerrilla movement. Entire Maya villages had been massacred and nearly 200,000 people killed. Today, many indigenous people are coming together to actively participate in the peace process. The goal of these groups is to increase awareness on indigenous issues such as poverty, land claims and discrimination. Updated: Jun 10, 2010.

Before You Go

Guatemala's tourism infrastructure may not be as developed as other Latin American countries, but visitors are pleased to find the country is accessible and very affordable. Most travelers head straight for the colonial city of Antigua, the Maya ruins of Tikal or the waters of Lake Atitlán—but if you are willing to step off the beaten path, you will find there is natural beauty everywhere you look.

When packing, take Guatemala's diverse landscape and climate into consideration: Much of the country is tropical, but there are other regions in the mountains where the temperature can drop below freezing at night. Antigua and Lake Atitlán both lie in the temperate zone, where daily temperatures rarely rise above 30°C (85°F).

Bring a small first aid kit with any medicine you take on a regular basis, along with some anti-diarrhea pills, aspirin, insect repellent and sunscreen. Although you can find most of these items throughout Guatemala, it is best to pick them up at home than to risk going without. Updated: Jul 20, 2010.

Insurance

If you are planning a trip to Guatemala, travel insurance may be a worthwhile investment. Travel insurance is an important tool for protecting yourself from financial losses due to medical expenses, theft, lost valuables or luggage, trip cancellations and legal fees. Indeed, for most travelers, using travel insurance in Guatemala is an excellent idea.

There are many Guatemala travel insurance products on the market, so you should thoroughly research which policy best suits you. Before you commit to anything, you should make sure that you do not already have travel insurance coverage through your homeowner's policy, medical insurance or credit card.

MEDICAL INSURANCE

Medical fees are the most costly unexpected expenses for travelers. A good medical insurance policy should have a high ceiling for costs, as well as provisions for emergency evacuation in case you need specialized treatment back home. Whether or not you have travel insurance, Guatemalan hospitals will require payment up-front. Most hospitals in Guatemala will want cash, though some smarter places will take credit cards. Make sure to get receipts, as you will need these for your insurance claim to be processed. Note that many travel insurance policies exclude medical expenses incurred during adventure and extreme sports. If you are going to participate in anything outdoorsy, you should check that the activities are covered before you buy.

LOST OR STOLEN ITEMS

Crime is, sadly, a fact of life in Guatemala. Most travel insurance claims in Guatemala relate to lost or stolen items. If you plan to bring expensive goods with you, it is important to get insurance that covers the value of those goods. If your goods are stolen, you will need a copy of a police report to submit with your insurance claim. This means heading to a police station within 24 hours of the crime and filling out a good deal of paper work. Generally, the level of coverage for stolen or lost good is directly proportional to the price of the insurance policy. Cheaper policies have low limits and high deductibles, or they may not cover goods at all.

STUDENT TRAVEL INSURANCE

Students traveling to Guatemala for study abroad programs are advised to get travel insurance for their stay; in fact, many universities and programs will require proof of insurance. A few specialty student insurance policies will cover things such as course refunds if you are ill or have to leave the country. Such policies also usually cover goods—such as pricey laptops and cameras—and medical expenses incurred during outdoor activities.

TIPS ON INSURANCE

While traveling in Guatemala, travel insurance companies recommend that you carry your prescriptions, a list of allergies and the 24-hour international hotline for your insurer. It is also a good idea to have this information saved in an E-mail account and photocopied back home. Updated: Jul 20, 2010.

Getting To and Away

Most travelers arrive to Guatemala by plane at La Aurora International Airport in Guatemala City. An increased demand in tourism as well as a large number of Guatemalans living in the United States has pushed carriers to step up their presence in the country, and the government has also made improvements to both of Guatemala's international airports. Traveling between Guatemala and other Central American countries can be done by air, land or water. Air is faster and more reliable, but sometimes if you depart by bus or boat, you will not have to pay a departure tax. Bus travel is extremely common in Guatemala, with options ranging from air-conditioned coaches to rickety old school buses and everything in between.

BY AIR

La Aurora International Airport in Guatemala City is the county's largest point of entry and exit. The government recently invested millions of dollars in a massive modernization project for the airport, which is still underway. Guatemala City is about 6.5 kilometers (4 mi) north of the airport, easily reachable by bus, taxi or private shuttle. Travelers can reach La Aurora from many points in North America, including from Dallas/Fort Worth and Miami on American Airlines; from Houston-Intercontinental and Newark on Continental Airlines; from Cancún and Fort Lauderdale on Spirit Airlines; and from Chicago O'Hare, Los Angeles, Mexico City and Orlando on TACA.

Those skipping around Central America can fly in from Belize City and San Pedro Sula on Maya Island Air or from San José de Costa Rica, San Pedro Sula, San Salvador and Tegucigalpa on TACA. The only other international airport in Guatemala is in Flores, the Mundo Maya International Airport. Mundo Maya serves traffic for the surrounding areas, including the Maya site Tikal. Mundo Maya can be reached from Cancún and Guatemala City on TACA, or from Belize City on Tropic Air.

BY LAND

There are a number of ways for travelers to cross into Guatemala by land. The Pan-American Highway cuts through the country, allowing access to Mexico in the north and El Salvador in the south. Accessing Guatemala from Belize and Honduras is also possible, but be careful to only cross at officially recognized border crossings no matter where you are coming from. If traveling by car or bus, it is also a good idea to leave as early in the day as possible, as border towns in Guatemala are notoriously seedy places to get stuck in overnight.

Bus service is available from various points in Mexico, Belize, Honduras and El Salvador. Buses crossing borders are sometimes subject to considerable delays, so plan accordingly. Ticabus (URL: www.ticabus.com) is a popular bus company for budget travelers, which offers direct daily service from El Salvador and Mexico to Guatemala City, as well as several connecting routes. More expensive buses are air conditioned and comfortable, however, when traveling through Guatemala, a fleet of retired U.S. school buses rules the road. These buses, which have been recycled and fragrantly repainted, have been dubbed "chicken buses" by English-speaking travelers because it is very likely you may share a seat next to a local bringing livestock to or from a market.

No passenger trains currently run in Guatemala. Two steam trains were previously chartered by tour companies on the Ferrovias Guatemala, a historic 800-kilometer (500 mi) railway running through Guatemala from Mexico to El Salvador. However, the service was forced to end in October 2007 pending the outcome of a claim filed against the U.S.-Dominican Republic-Central American Free Trade Agreement (CAFTA).

BY BOAT

Cruise ships call on Puerto Quetzal on the Pacific Coast and Puerto Santo Tomás de Castilla on the Caribbean side. There is not much to see near either dock, but cruise lines offer a whole host of land excursions for those who want to visit local resorts and beaches or travel to Antigua, Tikal or Lake Atitlán. Water taxi services connect Punta Gorda, Belize, to the Guatemalan towns of Puerto Barrios and Lívingston. From Lívingston, you can also catch a ride to Omoa, Honduras. Transportes El Chato leaves daily at 9 a.m from Punta Gorda to Puerto Barrios, a trip that takes only a little more than an hour in length and costs $15-18 each way. The taxi returns around 2 p.m., so plan accordingly. On Tuesdays and Fridays, Exotic Travel traverses the waters between Punta Gorda or Omoa and Lívingston. Tickets can be purchased at the waterfronts of each town. If the weather is bad, you may want to consider postponing your trip, because life jackets are not always readily available. Also, be prepared to fork over a $10 departure tax when leaving Guatemala by sea.

Boats also travel the Usumacinta River, which divides Mexico and Guatemala. The route, from Frontera Corozal in Mexico to La Técnica and Bethel in Guatemala, is popular for travelers interested in various Maya ruins. Yaxchilán is on the banks of the Usumacinta, but buses take travelers to Palenque on the Mexican side and from La Técnica and Bethel in Guatemala to Flores. Package deals combining water and land transport are available from several transport agencies in Palenque and Flores for around $35. Updated: Jul 20, 2010.

TAXES AND FEES

A departure tax may or may not be included in the price of your airplane ticket. Check with your airline representative before leaving for your trip. If the fee was not included in your ticket, expect to pay somewhere around $30 to leave Guatemala. Cash is the only accepted form of payment. Updated: Jun 10, 2010.

Border Crossings

Guatemala shares one border crossing with Belize, and several with Mexico, Honduras and El Salvador. To enter Guatemala, you will need a passport valid for six months after the date of arrival, and you will have to fill out immigration and customs forms.

Although there are no fees to enter the country, depending on which border you cross and who stamps your passport, you may be asked to pay unofficial fees anywhere up to $20. Always ask for a receipt, in which case your fee may be magically dropped. A proper receipt will always have the Guatemalan emblem on it. When in doubt, observe what other travelers are paying in front of you.

Border crossing should only be done during daylight hours, so try to allow plenty of time for border formalities as well as transport to a major town on the other side before dark. Many border posts are closed for lunch and some cease operations as early as 6 p.m.

From Belize, the only major border crossing to Guatemala is at Melchor de Mencos. Many buses service the popular route between Belize City and Flores, a four to five hour drive.

The main crossing point from Mexico to Guatemala is in Ciudad Hidalgo, near Tapachula. There is also a crossing on the Pan-American Highway at Ciudad Cuauhtémoc, which sits between Comitán, Mexico, and Huehuetenango, Guatemala. Both

these routes are well traversed by buses, which have a frequent service to nearby cities in both countries.

There are three main border crossings between Honduras and Guatemala, all of which are well-paved. The first is at El Florido, between Chiquimula, Guatemala, and Copán Ruinas, Honduras. Another is Agua Caliente, between Esquipulas, Guatemala, and Nueva Ocotepeque, Honduras. Finally, there is also a crossing at the Caribbean town of Corinto, between Puerto Barrios Guatemala, and Omoa, Honduras. Buses run frequently between the main Honduras cities to Guatemala City and Antigua.

El Salvador and Guatemala share many borders at all the main highways. On the Pan-American Highway (CA-1), there is a crossing at San Cristóbal. From Highway CA-8, there is a crossing between La Chinamas, El Salvador, and Valle Nuevo, Guatemala. A third crossing point is between La Hachadura, El Salvador, and Ciudad Pedro de Alvarado on the Pacific Coast Highway (CA-2). Finally, on Highway CA-10, there is a crossing at Anguiatu.

If crossing into Guatemala by car, be prepared for the mountain of paperwork that goes along with bringing an automobile into the country. You will need a current registration and a valid driver's license or an International Driving Permit (IDP), which can be issued by automobile associations such as AAA. You will also need to have proof of vehicle ownership on hand. If the car is not yours, you will need to get a notarized letter allowing possession of the vehicle from its owner.

At the border, you will receive a temporary import permit that is valid for a maximum of 30 days. The permit is free, so do not be fooled by crooked border officials who may try to tell you otherwise. You may have to pay a fumigation fee to have your car sprayed at the border. Additionally, you will have to purchase insurance locally, because Guatemala does not recognize foreign insurance. This can be done at the border post, but remember to ask for a receipt. Finally, Guatemalan law says travelers must exit the country in the same vehicle used to enter. Updated: Jul 20, 2010.

Visa Information

All travelers to Guatemala will need to present a passport valid for at least six months beyond the date of entry. North Americans, Central Americans,

Europeans, Australians and most South Americans do not need advanced visas or proof of return tickets for stays lasting less than 90 days. In 2006, Guatemala joined the Central American Border Control Agreement (CA-4), which permits the free passage of people and goods throughout El Salvador, Guatemala, Honduras and Nicaragua. Travelers are allowed to tour these four countries for a period of up to 90 days without completing any entry and exit formalities at border checkpoints. If you plan on being in the CA-4 region for a period longer than 90 days, you can request an extension or simply leave for a period of 72 hours (possibly to Mexico or Belize) and then reenter to renew your length of stay for another 90 days.

Some nationalities need either a visa or a tourist card to enter Guatemala. These include Czechs, Filipinos, citizens of the Gulf States, Poles, Slovaks and South Africans. Those who are required to obtain an advanced visa are citizens of most Caribbean and African countries, Bolivians, Colombians, Egyptians, Hungarians, Romanians, Russians and South Koreans.

WORK VISAS

Work visas are issued for six months and can be extended once for the same amount of time. Applicants will need to present a Consulate of Guatemala or the Ministry of Foreign Affairs with several documents, usually including an original and notarized copy of your passport, a recent photo and a letter from the company for which the applicant works explaining the purpose of the trip. Check with your local consulate to find out the official requirements, as they vary from place to place.

The price to apply for a work visa is $50. When renewing the work visa, applicants will need to again supply an original and notarized copy of their passport, as well as a certificate of economic solvency. Be sure to extend before the expiration of the first work visa, not after, or else you will be fined. If it is necessary to extend your stay past the expiration of the second visa term, temporary residence should be requested.

STUDENT VISAS

Student visas require more paperwork that work visas. Along with your original passport and a recent photo, you will be asked to supply an education license or acceptance letter from the institution you will be studying at, a certificate of economic solvency, a criminal background check and a letter of authorization from your parents if you are under age. Again, check with your local consulate to find out the official requirements.

TOURIST VISAS

Tourist visas are issued for single entry ($25) and multiple entries ($50), but both types are only valid for a period up to 90 days. To obtain a tourist visa, you will need to submit the following to the Ministry of Foreign Affairs: an application form, proof of economic solvency, an affidavit of your contact in Guatemala, a letter of recommendation, a copy of your round-trip ticket or itinerary and two passport-sized pictures.

Note: Please be aware, visa and passport requirements are subject to change at any time. It is recommended to check with your embassy or consulate for verification. Updated: Jul 20, 2010.

Getting Around

Most travelers get around Guatemala by bus. Distances between destinations are generally short, which is good, because you are likely to be crammed in. For those who want to travel in a bit more comfort and are willing to pay more, shuttle buses operate between most of Guatemala's main traveler destinations. Long trips, such as the bus ride from Guatemala City to Flores and Tikal, can be time-consuming and uncomfortable, so you may want to shell out for a flight instead. If you wish to see the country a bit more closely and you have time to spare, mountain biking across Guatemala can be enjoyable. Train travel is not currently an option in Guatemala. Updated: Jul 20, 2010.

BY AIR

In February of 2009, the only regularly scheduled domestic flights in Guatemala were from Guatemala City's La Aurora airport (GUA) to Flores. The airport in Flores is commonly known as Aeropuerto Internacional Santa Elena (FRS), but is also sometimes Called Aeropuerto del Mundo Maya. The airport is located on the outskirts of Flores.

Two airlines operate the Guatemala City to Flores route: TAG (URL: www.tag.com.gt) and TACA (URL: www.taca.com). The flight takes around an hour. The cheapest round-trip flights with TACA cost around $210 including taxes, while those with TAG cost a few dollars more. One-way trips cost about half of that price. TAG does not have an online booking option, but it can be contacted by E-mail (reservaciones@tag.com.gt) or by telephone (502-2360-3038/61-1180). The TAG flight from Guatemala City to Flores leaves at 6:30 a.m., with the return journey departing at 4:30 p.m. Chartered flights can also be organized with TAG to Copán. TACA has a number of flights leaving daily, either early in the mornings (6:50 a.m., 7:15 a.m., 9:15 a.m.) or late afternoons (5:25 p.m. and 5:45 p.m.). The return journeys depart slightly later in the morning (8:25 a.m. and 8:50 a.m.) and in the early evening (7 p.m. and 7:20 p.m.). Updated: Jul 20, 2010.

BY BUS

By far the most common method of getting around Guatemala is by bus, whether it be by the so-called "chicken buses," first-class bus or by shuttle bus. Traveling by bus is a great way to get to know the real Guatemala up close. Passengers are often packed in like sardines, but the journeys usually do not last much more than four hours. There are some inherent dangers with bus travel in Guatemala. Buses may be robbed, with everyone forced to hand over their valuables. Accidents are also relatively frequent. As with public transport in most of Latin America, petty theft is rife. You should not use buses after dark.

Chicken buses are school buses that were decommissioned in the United States and are now widely used in Guatemala. The chicken buses are considered "second class" buses, and as a rough guide, you can expect to pay a fare of around a dollar an hour. They are usually very brightly colored and do not normally leave from bus terminals, but more often depart from the outskirts of towns.

One option that is generally safer is the "Pullman," or first-class bus. These buses often leave from the bus company offices, and they tend to only cover the main routes, such as those along the Pan-American Highway. In some cases, Pullmans have toilets and TVs, and in rare cases, they have air conditioning. Often none of these services will be working. Tickets can be purchased in advance, but unless you are traveling during a public holiday, you usually do not have to buy your ticket ahead of time.

Travelers have also started to use shuttle buses, mainly because they are safer than other options. The shuttles operate along the routes that tourists most frequently use, for example, between Guatemala City and Antigua, Antigua and Panajachel, Panajachel and Chichicastenango, and Tikal and Flores. The cost of a shuttle ticket is significantly more than for a public bus. Shuttle buses companies include Atitrans, Turansa and Grayline Tours. You can also organize private transportation through these types of companies.

Approximate travel times from Guatemala City by bus:

To Antigua: 1-1.5 hr
To Panajachel: 3-3.5 hr
To Quetzaltenango: 4-5 hr
To Flores: 7-10 hr
To Lago Izabal: 4 hr
To Puerto Barrios: 5-6 hr
To Monterrico: 3-3.5 hr
To Cobán: 4-5 hr
Updated: Jul 20, 2010.

BY TRAIN

There are currently no passenger trains operating in Guatemala. The last such train traveled between Guatemala City to Puerto Barrio. The route was discontinued in 2007 as the national rail company began to be privatized. There are currently plans to create a train route that will cross all of Central America. The project is Called FERISTSA, and the current proposal has the line linking Guatemala to Mexico's rail system in the north, with the railroad continuing south as far as the Panama Canal. Provided that the project goes ahead as planned, the FERISTSA will be an extremely important transportation system in the region. Updated: Jul 20, 2010.

BY TAXI

Taxis are available all over Guatemala. In Guatemala City, taxis have meters; in the rest of the country, they do not. You should always agree on a fare with the driver before you start the journey or you may have a nasty shock at the end of your ride. Especially in Guatemala City, calling a cab is a safe and convenient option. How quickly you are able to find a taxi depends on the district you are in and the time of day. Taxi drivers are not usually able to change big bills, so be sure to have as close to the correct change as possible before you get in.

Taxis may be hired for longer trips, such as visiting attractions that are out of the city. You should agree to a fee upfront, and expect to pay the driver for the time spent waiting for you. Taxis can also be arranged to travel the distance between two cities, for example, between Guatemala City and Antigua. For a ride of this length, expect to pay somewhere between $35-40.

Tuk-tuks have become more common of late around some of the popular tourist destinations, such as Panajachel and Antigua. These open-sided rickshaws (or mototaxis) can be a fun way to get around the city. Expect to pay similar fees as for a cab, and always agree to the fee in advance. Updated: Jul 20, 2010.

BY HITCHHIKING

Although hitchhiking is possible in Guatemala, it is not generally recommended or safe in most parts of the country. That said, in some areas of Guatemala, hitchhiking is the only means of transport available. If you stand on the side of the road and put your arm out, sooner or later somebody will stop to collect you. The rides are not free—as a general rule, you can expect to pay about the same prices as the bus (approximately one dollar per hour). In the Alta Verapaz and Ixil Triangle regions, pickup trucks are practically the only mode of transportation. You will likely ride in the back, often crammed in with many other people. Again, fees are similar to those on buses. Updated: Jul 20, 2010.

BY CAR

Driving in a rental car is an easy way to get around Guatemala. If you plan to drive, you need to make sure you have an International Driving Permit (IDP). Driving in Guatemala can be an interesting experience, as the rules of the road are likely to be different than in your country. Most notably, Guatemalans have a tendency to overtake on blind bends and continually honk their horns for no apparent reason. Gas stations are easy to come by, and most of the major roads, such as the Pan-American Highway, are in fairly good condition.

In terms of your personal safety, you should consider the following: Rent a 4x4 if you are planning to travel off the main roads. Be careful where you leave the car, especially if parking in parts of cities where security can be an issue. Never drive at night. If you do, you are at risk of armed robbery, especially in rural areas. Drunk driving is a problem that persists throughout the country.

All the larger urban centers, including Guatemala City, Antigua, Quetzaltenango, Flores and Huehuetenango, have car rental agencies. It is possible to rent a car for as little as $25 a day. To hire a car, you will need to present your license, passport and a credit card. For insurance purchases, you must be at least 25 years old. Furthermore, you will need to buy insurance from the rental agency unless you can show that you already have insurance that covers collision or a loss-damage waiver.

Major rental agencies in Guatemala include:

Avis: www.avis.com
Dollar: www.dollar.com
Budget: www.budget.com
Hertz: www.hertz.com
National: www.nationalcar.com
Updated: Jul 20, 2010.

BY BIKE

Bike travel in Guatemala is becoming much more common and is a pleasant way to see and experience what the country has to offer. You can bring your own bike, but there are also companies that offer bicycle rentals in Antigua, Panajachel and Quetzaltenango. If you decide to go solo, keep in mind that the roads can be bad in condition and may pass through seedy places.

Your best option is to go for a mountain bike. The good news is that, when your bike breaks down, there are shops throughout the country that can repair it. Guatemalans are usually fairly willing to help, so if you want a break for a while, it is not too hard to find a bus that will hoist your bike up onto the roof, or a boat that will take your bike.

Another good option is to take a biking tour, which will get you a bit more off-the-beaten track. Guatemala Adventures (URL: www.guatemalaventures.com) offers a variety of tours, including half- and full-day trips of Antigua, and multi-day trips exploring the Lake Atitlán region, the northern highlands or the Atlantic coastline.

If you plan to take a motorcycle across country, be forewarned: If something goes wrong, parts may be either expensive or impossible to come by. Since motorcycles are a less common means of transportation in Guatemala, the mechanical assistance available to you may also be limited. Updated: Jul 20, 2010.

BY BOAT

There are a number of places to travel by boat in Guatemala, two of which are of great

INTRO & INFO

importance to tourists: The use of boat to navigate Lake Atitlán and traveling by boat to Lívingston on the eastern coast. One of the best—and quickest—ways to get around Lake Atitlán is by boat. The boats run for most of the day up until late afternoon. The best place to depart for any of the smaller villages around the lake is Panajachel. From here, boats go to Santiago Atitlán, San Pedro La Laguna, San Marcos La Laguna, Santa Cruz La Laguna, Jaibalito and Tzununá. None of the journeys take very long. You can hire a private boat, known locally as a *lancha*, if you so wish, but expect to pay more. On the Caribbean coast, the town of Lívingston can only be accessed by boat. There are two options: The first is to take a boat from Puerto Barrios. The journey lasts approximately one and a half hours, and boats leave a few times per day in each direction. For those looking for a more scenic option, the trip along the Río Dulce, from the town of Río Dulce to Lívingston is long, but spectacular—don't miss this experience if you have the time. Updated: Jul 20, 2010.

Tours

Guatemala runs the gamut of travel activities, allowing numerous opportunities to get close to nature or explore ancient civilizations. From the lava-spitting volcanoes in the Western Highlands to the dense forests shadowing ancient ruins, it is easy to see why Guatemala is fast becoming one of the most popular stops on the Central American travel circuit.

This vibrant country is marked by so many colorful natural and cultural landscapes it may be hard to choose where to start. Architecture lovers should check out the colonial city of Antigua, while it would be a shame for those interested in archeology to miss the ruins of Tikal. Nature lovers have plenty of options, from volcano-climbing tours to birdwatching and wildlife excursions in Guatemala's multitude of biosphere reserves.

Those looking for some adventure can hike or trek in various regions, and can easily find places to bike, climb, canoe or kayak. Finally, those who want to take in Guatemala's natural and cultural beauty should head to Lake Atitlán, a captivating body of water ringed by volcanoes and quaint Maya villages.

VOLCANO CLIMBING TOURS

Guatemala is part of the Central America Volcanic Arc, a chain of volcanoes formed by an active zone along the Caribbean Plate. The country is home to more than 30 volcanoes, which vary in size, type and activity level. At 4,223 meters (13,935 ft), Tajumulco is the highest volcano in Central America, but it is not the most difficult to climb. Tours can be arranged in nearby Quetzaltenango, and it is possible to complete the climb in one day; however, many hikers choose to camp overnight about 150 meters (500 ft) below the summit to get acclimatized to the altitude.

Three peaks near Antigua are also popular climbs: Agua, Fuego and Acatenango. Agua and Acatenango are blanketed with forest, while the more-active Fuego has a bare peak and often a small ash cloud that rises from the summit. Volcán Pacaya is also easily accessible from Antigua and lies just 29 kilometers (18 mi) from Guatemala City. Pacaya last erupted in May of 2010, spewing ash on Guatemala City and disrupting airport traffic at La Aurora airport. Updated: Jul 20, 2010.

ARCHAEOLOGICAL TOURS

Remains from the Maya civilization that flourished from 700 BC to 900 AD can be found throughout Guatemala. Tikal is the most famous site, and for good reason: Thousands of Maya temples, pyramids and other structures are tucked away in the dense, tropical forest. In addition to exploring the ruins, the native flora and fauna still flourish relatively undisturbed; chances are you will catch glimpse of a howler monkey or a toucan. The abundance of history and wildlife in Tikal also means it is well worth the price of hiring a tour guide.

Another idea for a unique archaeological tour is a boat tour of the sites along the Usumacinta River, which divides Mexico and Guatemala. Explore Yaxchilán or Palenque in Mexico, and then from La Técnica or Bethel in Guatemala, you can take a bus to Flores where you can make your way to Tikal. Package deals combining water and land transport are available from several transport agencies in Palenque and Flores for around $35. Updated: Jul 20, 2010.

ANTIGUA CITY TOURS

The colonial city of Antigua makes for a perfectly charming sightseeing tour. You can easily explore its cobblestone streets, churches and art galleries on your own, but you may also want to hire a guide so you do not miss any important historical tidbits. The best place to start a tour is at the heart of the city in Parque Central. Here you will find the fountain of Las Sirenas, as well as several other masterpieces of colonial architecture, such as the fantastic Catedral de San José, built in 1541.

Before you take in the rest of the city, make sure you are wearing proper footwear: If the soles of your shoes are flimsy, you will feel every cobblestone under your feet. Antigua's narrow streets do not allow for double-decker sightseeing buses, but you can hire one of the many horse-drawn carriages that congregate in Parque Central to take you around the city. The tour should cost $25 per hour, and drivers are usually happy to give commentary on the surroundings—an English-speaking driver, however, may be tough to come by. Updated: Jul 20, 2010.

Photo by: Douglas J. Klostermann

LAKE ATITLÁN TOURS

Lake Atitlán is Guatemala's pride and joy, a clear-blue lake ringed by towering volcanoes and tiny Maya villages. The best thing to do at Lake Atitlán is simply to take in the view, whether you are being led by a local on a private boat tour, day hiking or biking along the shores, hovering above the forest canopy on a zip line, riding on horseback, or simply swinging to the rhythm of the lake breeze on a hammock. Three volcanoes sit on the edge of the lake's southern shore: San Pedro (3,020 m/9,908 ft), Toliman (3,158 m/10,361 ft) and Atítlan (3,535 m/11,598 ft). San Pedro offers breathtaking views on clear days and can be climbed in a day, but be sure to go with a guide. Guides also lead boat tours that crisscross the lake to local villages or land excursions to nearby villages, such as the lively Chichicastenango market, about a one hour drive away. On Thursdays and Sundays, the town becoming a bustling center of activity where handicrafts and produce are sold. Updated: Jun 15, 2010.

Ecotourism in Guatemala

Guatemala is a nature lover's dream location, with virgin jungles, shimmering lakes, more than three dozen towering volcanoes, and a myriad of flora and fauna. There are more than 18 ecosystems throughout the country waiting to be explored. However, in order to keep things in balance, it is important to make your best effort to have a minimal impact on your environment.

Conventional tourism can have ecological and social downsides, as many hotels and tour companies do not respect the cultural and natural heritage of their surroundings. From recycling and conserving water to using local labor and building materials, it is important to research the places you stay and decide whether or not those businesses and organizations are having a negative impact on the local environment.

The principles of ecotourism are simple: minimize impact, built cultural awareness and empower local people. From the ruins of Tikal to the flora and fauna of the rainforest, there is a lot worth protecting in Guatemala. Always be aware of the influences you have on your surroundings, including both the natural and cultural richness of Guatemala.

Currently, Guatemala is poised to become one of the leading ecotourism destinations in the world, alongside places like Costa Rica, Galapagos, Kenya and Australia. To help preserve the country's natural treasures for future generations, travelers should try to support businesses that have minimal impact on the environment. Updated: Aug 12, 2010.

BIRDWATCHING TOURS

Guatemala is a paradise for birders. More than 720 different bird species live in varying ecosystems scattered throughout the country, about a dozen of which are so rare they are listed as "globally threatened." In the Central American Highlands, around 10 percent of the bird species population is not found anywhere else in the world. The Atlantic slope is particularly diverse—more than 500 species have been found in the area. Hiring a professional guide on a birdwatching or wildlife tour will enhance your experience. Guides know exactly where to look for nests, and are attune to the species of the area.

April is supposed to be the best month to go birding in Guatemala, as this is the extremely active breeding season when birds sing much more frequently. If you are lucky, you may even be able to catch a glimpse of the quetzal, Guatemala's national bird. In Maya times, the bird's iridescent feathers were used as currency, which is why Guatemala's currency is called a quetzal today. Tours that specifically seek the quetzal are offered in Guatemala, particularly in the Chelemhá Cloud Forest Reserve and at Biotopo del Quetzal, a biosphere reserve established to preserve populations of the bird. Updated: Aug 09, 2010.

PRE-ARRANGED TOURS

Many travelers choose to pre-arrange tours with companies that offer organized packages before setting off for Guatemala. This is a fairly easy task, as several tour companies provide online services that can be booked from home or elsewhere on the road. Your best bet is to go online and research what it is you want to do, when you want to do it and how you want it done; it's all out there. Check out Tucan Travel or GAP Adventures Worldwide, two of the leading organized tour companies that service Central America. Updated: Aug 09, 2010.

Sport and Recreation

Like many of its Central American neighbors, soccer is Guatemala's most popular sport. Although the national team has never qualified for the final tournament of the World Cup, the team has been to the Olympics three times. In 1950, the country hosted the Central American and Caribbean games, which are held every four years and include all countries in Central America, Mexico, Bermuda, and several countries in the Caribbean and South America. The national team has also participated in the Pan-American games—also held every four years—and has won seven times. The major clubs are Comunicaciones and Municipal, both based in Guatemala City. In addition to these, there are several other clubs that play around the country. If you would like to become a spectator, you can generally get tickets to see a game for about $4.

Baseball, American football and basketball are also popular sports but have a much smaller fan base than soccer. Guatemala's national basketball team competes regularly with other Latin American teams but is often ranked near the bottom of the table. Guatemala also has an organized American Football League that is a member of the Pan-American Federation of American Football. Updated: Aug 11, 2010.

Adventure Travel

From rock climbing to bungee jumping, travelers in Guatemala will have no problems finding activities that will keep their hearts pumping and their blood flowing. Rock climbing doesn't have an especially long tradition in the area, but the popularity of the sport is growing and the climbing community is getting stronger. It's now possible to find several good routes, mostly near Antigua. If you are interested in water sports, you have plenty of options. Certified divers can explore Lake Atitlán while kayakers can run Río Dulce. With Guatemala's 35 volcanoes, hikers will find no shortages of places to wander. Updated: Aug 11, 2010.

HIKING

Travelers who come to Guatemala for the culture stay for the hiking. With a choice of trekking active volcanoes, descending into valleys filled with waterfalls and tropical cloud forests, and exploring caves and ancient ruins, who can blame them? The country is brimming with exciting places to discover and a wealth of resources to help you along the way. Whether you are planning an extensive, 10-day trip or a casual day-hike, Guatemala has you covered. Not only does Antigua have an abundance of colonial charm, it also happens to be a fantastic playground for hikers. The town has four volcanoes within 25 kilometers (15.5 mi), which makes for happy adventure seekers and volcanologists alike.

Stunning views from Quetzaltenango's volcanoes, leisurely day-hikes around Lake Atítlan and winding trails through Maya ruins are just some of the things that await you in the Guatemalan highlands. Take a multi-day expedition that retraces the paths of the ancient Mayas along the Mayan Highland Trail or spend a day hiking the lush paths that wind through Santiago Atitlán. There are tours that offer jaunts up volcanoes and into cloud forests, where wildlife is abundant and where the views stretch all the way to the coast.

Nebaj is generally considered to be a hiker's paradise. Located in the Cuchumatán Mountains, the region is rich with pristine trails that meander through mountains, and past waterfalls and sacred Maya sites. There are options for all levels of hiking, including multi-day trips.

If you want to feel like a real explorer, head to Tikal. No matter the number of tourists, the dense jungle trails have an isolated and adventurous feel. Although the trails are clearly marked, coming across the dramatic ruins that rise about the jungle's canopy feels like a true discovery.

Meanwhile, hikers and wildlife enthusiasts could not ask for more than what they will find in central and eastern Guatemala. The Sierra de Las Minas watershed and the Bocas del Polochic Wildlife Refuge comprise 80 percent of the country's biodiversity. Hikers can spot more than 300 species of birds, as well as howler monkeys, butterflies and even the occasional jaguar. Farther west, the area around Cobán is ripe for exploration. The underworld of Alta Verapaz, made up of deep and winding cave systems, is another great place to look for adventure. Above ground, trails will take you to turquoise pools, tranquil waterfalls and into some of the country's most unique landscapes. Updated: Aug 06, 2010.

CLIMBING
Guatemala is not known for rock climbing, but the sport's popularity is growing with locals and travelers alike. Because of Guatemala's volcanic geology, there are a number of areas around the country that offer good climbing. More sites and routes are being discovered all the time, and a few tour companies offer organized tours for beginners and intermediate climbers.

The country's most developed climbing lies just outside of Quetzaltenango, in a place called Cerro Quemado. On this active volcano, the crag starts at about 2,745 meters (9,000 ft), and routes are rated from 5.9 to 5.12. If you are looking to meet new climbing partners or just want to get reliable information from locals, head to Cerro Quemado during the weekends.

Many climbers say that Sunday is the most popular day for climbing here. There are also hot springs nearby to sooth sore muscles after a long day of climbing.

Located just 45 minutes away from Guatemala City on the banks of Lake Amatitlán, Filón de Amatitlán is another popular hiking spot. This area is reported to have 20-30 routes and most of them are easy to find. Grades here range from 5.9 to 5.12. This is another great place to meet other climbers and get insider advice on climbing in Guatemala.

If you are into bouldering, Huehuetenango is the place for you. Located in the Cuchumatanes Mountains, this unofficial park offers a range of limestone boulders to climb. Although there are a few bouldering problems that have been established (v0-v3), many more await discovery. Climbers recommend that you bring your own brushes and crash pad. Several of the climbing areas are located on private property. It is highly recommended that you ask the land owners before you enter.

On the border of the highlands and Pacific slope region, Escuintla is a sleepy little town that attracts travelers who are looking to relax by the river or maybe take in a little birdwatching. This town has a handful of little-known climbing spots just off the road, offering climbers the opportunity to ascend established routes or discover their own. Updated: Jul 06, 2010.

RAFTING & KAYAKING
There is adventure at every turn on Guatemala's vast waterways. Tour companies offer single and multi-day outings in the highlands, along the Pacific Coast, and in the Verapaz and El Petén regions. Everyone from the first-timer to the seasoned veteran can challenge themselves with rapids running from Class II to VI. Come face-to-face with magnificent natural wonders such as caves, hot springs, waterfalls and lush jungle vegetation as you navigate volcanic lakes, mangroves and raging rivers. You may even have the chance to see some wildlife or Maya ruins on your trip.

Many rafting trips are limited to the rainy season, which runs June-October. However, excursions are possible year round in the Petén region and near Maya sites such as Tikal, Ceibal and Aguateca.

Río Cahabón (Class III-IV), located in the Alta Verapaz region near Lanquín, is thought to have the best whitewater rafting in the country. It is famed for its rigorous rapids (Class IV), grottoes, waterfalls, hot springs and a variety of birds. Mellow Río Coyolate (Class II-III rapids) in the lowland tropics is home to herons, hawks and falcons. Within easy reach of Antigua and Guatemala City, you can traverse the family-friendly Río Nahualate (Class III-IV), the challenging Ríos Naranjo or the demanding Los Esclavos (Class III-IV).

Kayaking highlights include paddling through a gorge along the Río Dulce to Lívingston on the Caribbean coast, birdwatching in the maze of mangroves in Monterrico on the Pacific coast, visiting tiny villages and coves on Lake Atitlán, and floating through the caves along Río Candelaria. Check out the thriving wildlife during a relaxed outing on Lake Petén Itzá, and explore the canals near Punta de Manabique. Updated: Jul 20, 2010.

HORSEBACK RIDING

Horseback riding in Guatemala is as much of a pleasure as it is an adventure. Picture a day-trip through dense, tropical forests and green coffee fincas, or saddling up for a seven-day journey across terrain that is as diverse as the country itself. Horses can take you almost anywhere in Guatemala. No matter your skill level—from novice to expert—seeing the countryside from the back of a horse is easily done. Whether winding though the cobblestone streets of Antigua in a carriage or galloping around the base of one of the country's many volcanoes, Guatemala has several opportunities for horseback riding enthusiasts.

Riding though the lush hills of Santiago Atitlán is generally a relaxing experience, but the narrow, steep trails can make for a bit of an adventure, too. The horses are often small and gentle, but they are not afraid to gallop if you want them too. Do not be surprised if your guide shows up riding a mountain bike instead of a horse; it's a fairly common practice. If that's the case, do not worry; the horses follow their leaders faithfully, and it is unlikely they will lead you astray. The guides are usually very knowledgeable about the area and are a good resource if you want to learn about the politics and the history of the region.

In Nebaj, horseback riders will find breathtaking views, rich culture and trails that have been relatively untouched by tourism. Tours offered include day-trips through the nearby mountains, which promise the rider a unique and fun way of viewing a region where many residents continue to practice ancient Maya rituals. Multi-day rides are also an option, including trips that lead riders though open plains, up mountain peaks, into wooded forests and across coffee plantations. More adventurous riders can choose to be out on the trail for up to nine days, taking in Guatemala's beautiful landscapes during the day and reflecting on the experience around a campfire at night.

In the villages surrounding Tikal, visitors have several options for horseback riding tours. Travelers often recommend El Remate, a small village near the border of Belize. The town sits at the edge of a picturesque lake and offers horseback riders the chance to trot through abundant tropical forests and Maya ruins that seldom see tourists. Updated: Jul 06, 2010.

Birdwatching

In a country that is home to more than 720 species of birds, it would be a sin to leave your binoculars at home. Guatemala's diverse habitats enable birdwatchers to view endangered Cherry-throated Tanager on the coast of Lake Atitlan or spot Golden-cheeked Warblers in the wetlands of the Atlantic coast. Some of the region's rare endemic species can not be seen outside of the region.

THE PACIFIC SLOPE

Biotopo Monterrico-Hawaii nature reserve is well known for its nesting leatherback and ridley turtles, but it is also full of avian activity and a good place to catch a glimpse of birds that are on your must-see list, as well as many of the birds that characterize the mangrove swamps of the Pacific.

THE HIGHLANDS

The Guatemalan highlands offer an astonishing array of colorful birds, such as the Hooded Grosbeak and Pink-headed Warbler. The cloud forests of the region are perfect for finding rare species of hummingbirds and parakeets. If you are lucky, you may spot the elusive resplendent quetzal that nests in the cloud forests. Located at the base of Atitlan volcano, Los Tarrales Reserve is a hotspot for bird activity. With reliable access on 4X4 roads, tour guides will get you to the teeming cloud forest. The reserve has several local bird guides on hand to answer questions and to point you in the direction of the best spots to see birds, such as Green-throated Mountain-gems and Black-throated Jays.

EL PETÉN

In addition to the stunning sight of ancient ruins that rise up above the jungle canopy, travelers are drawn to Tikal for the opportunity to see birds they will not find elsewhere. It's known to be one of the best places in the country to see birds of prey. You may find an Orange-breasted Falcon or a Black Hawk-eagle while you are hiking though the jungle. Tops of temples make for excellent bird-watching perches. The nearby Yaxhá offers a similar type of birding experience. In addition to the birds near Tikal, birders are likely to see aquatic and migratory birds that are drawn to the permanent water supply here.

Photo by: Jonathan Nolasco

CENTRAL AND EASTERN GUATEMALA

Birders will find a rich diversity of species along the Atlantic coast. Many types of birds have been recorded in the region, including the Black-crested Coquette, a variety of parakeets, and the Northern Potoo. The Patrocinio Reserve is a highly recommended place for birdwatching. Visitors can rest comfortably in a recently constructed observation tower while watching flocks of parakeets fly by. Those who used the tower reported spotting as many as 60 different types of birds within only a few days. Parque Nacional Laguna Lachuá, located northwest of Cobán, is another great place for birding. There, winding trails allow you to go deep into the rainforest to view several of the 177 species living in the park. If you are a fan of waterbirds, Laguna Lachuá will most likely have something to offer. The lake attracts Blue-winged Teal, Black-bellied Whistling-duck, Snowy Egret and many other varieties of waterbirds. Updated: Jul 06, 2010.

Wildlife Watching

Guatemala is rich with wildlife. Within a few-days journey, travelers can visit butterfly pavilions, sea turtle rescue centers, and reserves that are home to jaguars, spider monkeys and elusive manatees. If you are a nature lover who is looking for a unique experience, just keep your eyes peeled.

Biotopo Monterrico-Hawaii nature reserve is celebrated for its nesting leatherback and olive ridley turtles. Just down the beach in Parque Hawaii, a turtle research center and hatchery run by a non-profit NGO called ARCAS specializes in the conservation of these endangered turtles. They also breed iguana and spectacled caiman, releasing the offspring into the wild. ARCAS runs tours to help support its project, including bird-watching excursions, and whale, dolphin and sea turtle sailing voyages.

When combined with the neighboring Calakmul reserve in Mexico, the Mayan Biosphere Reserve is the second largest tropical forest in the Americas. It is most often associated with its most famous attraction, the ruins of Tikal, but should also be noted for its incredible amount or biological diversity. The reserve is home to several endangered species, including Scarlet Macaws, jaguars and howler monkeys, to name a few. Visitors are almost guaranteed to glimpse some sort of spectacular wildlife just by hiking around. But, sadly, because of poaching and illegal pet trading, the majestic jaguar is even harder to find. Wildlife tours can be set up through many different companies, but it is highly recommend you go with a non-profit so your money will go to help support the conservation of the area.

Initially set aside to protect the resplendent quetzel, Biotopo del Quetzal is a 1,500-hectare (2,841 ac) reserve ripe for wildlife watching. The reserve is one of the few remaining cloud forests in the country and is prime habitat for nesting quetzals, as well as spider and howler monkeys. Updated: Jul 06, 2010.

Studying Spanish

From the cobblestone streets of Antigua to the Maya village of Nabja in the highlands, Guatemala is famous for its many Spanish language schools. Students can find almost any type of experience they desire, whether volunteering on a farm, living with a host family or studying in a garden under the remains of ancient buildings. There are even classes that cater to medical professionals.

Guatemalan Spanish is often fairly clear and relatively easy to understand. Many classes provide one-on-one instruction and teachers are sometimes willing to teach as you tour the town. The full-immersion style of these classes helps immensely with your conversational skills and prepares you to continue your travels with confidence.

Schools in Guatemala are known to be cheaper than those in Mexico, and students are usually extremely satisfied with the quality of instruction, interdependent of whether they are a beginner or a well-practiced speaker. Many schools across the country run non-profit programs and offer volunteers opportunities for their students. It is common for schools to organize field trips and social events that strengthen the learning community. Some schools, however, do not employ qualified instructors. These schools can charge more for classes that may not be of the same caliber as less-expensive schools. Make sure to do a little background research before you choose a place to study.

Some schools hire recruiters to fish for newly arriving travelers at bus stops. Beware if someone offers you a free lunch if you come and see a school. If someone seems too eager to get you in the door, it is likely they are not offering the best deal. It pays to shop around, and if you don't, you could end up paying twice as much as the going rate. Updated: Jul 06, 2010.

Studying Mayan Languages

Guatemala may be well-known as a destination to study Spanish, but it is also the best country in which to learn one of the Mayan languages. Many people—particularly linguists and anthropologists—come to Guatemala to study one of the 21 distinct Mayan dialects spoken throughout the country.

Around 40 percent of the population speaks one of these languages, but unfortunately they are quickly becoming marginalized. Today, strong efforts are being made to learn and preserve Mayan languages, including those who wish to understand their cultural heritage. One of the most popular Mayan languages to learn is Quiché, spoken by around one million Guatemalans. There are schools offering Quiché language study in various parts of the country, including Quetzaltenango, where a large percentage of indigenous Mayas live.

One of the best ways to learn is to take up residency in a community with a large indigenous population and immerse yourself in the language. Finding a school that offers Mayan language studies is much more difficult than enrolling in a Spanish school. It is recommended you seek out a school that gives you the opportunity to visit villages where the language of your choosing is widely spoken so that you can practice with native speakers. One good option is the Celas Maya School in Quetzaltenango (URL: www.celasmaya.edu.gt). The school offers one-on-one classes for four hours per day and can set you up with a Quiché-speaking host family to live with while you are enrolled. Updated: Aug 11, 2010.

Volunteering

In Guatemala, opportunities exist for a wide variety of volunteering options. You can help construct houses in poor communities, teach English, assist with the care of sea turtles or look after orphaned children. In particular, those in the medical profession, teachers, and people with Internet development or design skills are highly sought after.

In order to volunteer in the country, most posts require basic Spanish skills. Depending on the job you are undertaking, more advanced Spanish may be required. You are normally required to pay for your accommodation and food during your stay. Language schools are a good place to pick up information about volunteering opportunities, a number of which are detailed below.

ARCAS

ARCAS is a non-profit NGO that was formed in 1989 by Guatemalans. The focus is on wildlife, in particular caring for wildlife being sold on the black market. This organization has a research center that houses anywhere between 300 and 600 animals. It also works with the ecological center in Monterrico to help with the preservation of turtles and the wetlands. Areas of focus are: Guatemala City, Petén and Parque Hawaii on the coast. URL: www.arcasguatemala.com.

Asociación COED (Cooperative for Education)

This Cincinnati-based non-profit is dedicated to breaking the cycle of poverty in Guatemala by providing textbooks and educational opportunities to underprivileged schoolchildren. The cooperative's projects are aimed at improving traditional and technological literacy in impoverished schools. Placement can be anywhere from Guatemala City, where the organization is headquartered, to the department of Quetzaltenango. URL: www.coeduc.org.

EntreMundos

This NGO was founded in 2001 and is based in Quetzaltenango. The organization focuses on providing assistance to the rural poor in the Western Highlands region. EntreMundos has a database of opportunities to explore. URL: www.entremundos.org.

Escuela de la Calle

Based in Quetzaltenango, Escuela de la Calle is an organization dedicated to serving at-risk youth. The school is hoping to stop kids from turning to the street by giving academic, health and nutritional education. URL: www.escueladelacalle.org.

Project Mosaic

Project Mosaic is a German non-profit organization that helps to place volunteers in both Guatemala and Nicaragua. It has a large database of opportunities and requests a donation of $55-270 to take part. URL: www.promosaico.org.

Proyecto Ecológico Quetzal

In 1988, a group of German students working in the cloud forest region took inventory of the number of quetzals in the department of Alta Verapaz. Following their effort, this organization was created, with goals of providing assistance in the fields of agriculture, ecotourism, environmental education and biology to local communities. URL: www.ecoquetzal.org/volunteer.php.

Other websites to check out for volunteer opportunities are:

www.casa-alianza.org.uk
www.casa-guatemala.org
www.casaxelaju.com
www.aktenamit.org
www.animalaware.org
www.upavim.org
www.care.org
Updated: Jul 20, 2010.

Working in Guatemala

Opportunities for paid work in Guatemala are harder to come by than volunteering ones. As a general rule, wages are extremely low. One of the easiest options for paid work is to teach English, but foreigners can often find work in hotels, restaurants and bars. This type of work is not well paid, but can help if you need a little extra cash.

English teachers are in high demand in Guatemala, a country where English proficiency is often required for Guatemalan jobs and universities. It is easier to pick up this work if you have a TEFL or ELT qualification. Opportunities for those without such qualifications are harder to find and tend to not pay as well. Quetzaltenango is a good place to find English-teaching jobs. In addition to teaching, the schools themselves sometimes have a need for people who can coordinate between the students and the teachers, and who can keep things running smoothly. This is true for both English schools and Spanish schools.

Teaching positions can be organized before you leave home or while on the ground in the country. The Internet is a great resource for the first option, while the telephone directory is a good place to start in the latter instance. Updated: Jul 20, 2010.

Living in Guatemala

More and more people who visit Guatemala are deciding to extend their stays, and some are even making the big move. It's easy to see why: Guatemala entices travelers with natural beauty, tons of colonial charm and a low cost of living. Who wouldn't want to stay for awhile?

Antigua is the most popular place for expatriots to move. There is a budding expat community here, as well as plenty of Spanish schools and cheap housing. You can live rather luxuriously here for relatively cheap: A room with private bath can be rented for around $120 a month; or a private, one-bedroom apartment with all the best amenities will cost around $200 a month. Food is cheap, too. Meals average $2-5, and you could live on much less if you shop in markets and cook at home.

If you do plan on relocating to Guatemala, whether for a short or long period of time, you should be aware of the visa requirements. Tourist visas are only valid for a period of up to 90 days, but there is a loophole: You can leave to Mexico or Belize for a period of 72 hours and then renew your visa for another three months. Work, student and volunteer visas can also be issued, usually for a period of six months. Check the requirements put in place by your local consulate for more information. Updated: Aug 11, 2010.

Lodging

Accommodation options in Guatemala are as varied as the country's landscapes. Travelers on a shoestring budget can stay in dirt-cheap hostels or even set up camp, whereas those looking to live it up in Central America can book their stay at a luxury high-end hotel in Guatemala City's Zona Viva. You will also find everything else in between: colonial hotels in Antigua, beach cabañas along the Pacific Coast, eco-lodges in the Petén region and more. Other, lesser-known options include *posadas* (inns) and *casas de huéspedes* (guesthouses). In many ways, these small, family-run affairs are the most intimate way to get to know Guatemala. If you are planning on staying for a few weeks or more, the best way to immerse yourself in Guatemalan culture is to arrange a homestay with a Guatemalan family. This will not only help you improve your Spanish, but you are pretty much guaranteed to learn a whole lot about Guatemalan culture. Updated: Aug 11, 2010.

CAMPING

In comparison to other countries, there are not very many designated campsites in Guatemala. With hostel, guesthouse and hotels costing so much cheaper than the norm, camping is not really necessary for those traveling on a budget.

However, if you are traveling through Guatemala in a RV, there are some options. Truck stops, gas stations and sometimes hotels will allow you to park your car in their lot overnight. Always be sure to ask permission before staying the night. Usually such places do not charge, but buying a meal at the restaurant or filling up on gas while you are there is a nice way of saying "thank you."

If you really want to go off-the-beaten path and camp with a tent, it is doable, but for safety reasons, it is not preferable in some places. Many national parks, reserves, lakes, ruins or cultural monuments will allow you to set up camp for a night. In most instances, camping is free if you have your own gear, but it is usually a good idea to tip the warden or ranger. If you do plenty of research before you go, it makes camping in Guatemala a whole lot easier.

Corazón del Bosque is a private ecotourism reserve situated near Panajachel that charges a small fee for camping but has hot showers on-site. Rangers at the various ruins near Sayaxché, such as Ceibal or Aguateca, will usually let you camp for the night if you ask nicely. Laguna Yaxja is another well-equipped site with toilets and fire pits. Places such as Poptún, Finca Ixobel and Fuentes Georginas also allow camping. Whether you plan on camping in a tent or in your RV, always give yourself plenty of time before dark to scout out a suitable area. Always try to ask a local if it is all right to camp at a place you have picked, or if they know of anywhere that is better. A good place to ask about the best places to set up camp is in towns or cities where there is a tourist information office. The staff will generally do its best to help you out. Updated: Aug 11, 2010.

ECO-LODGES

If you are looking to appreciate Guatemala's natural beauty with as little environmental impact as possible, book a stay at one of the country's many eco-lodges. The majority of eco-lodges in Guatemala are located in the Petén region, but they are also found in other areas of the country, such as along Guatemala's Pacific Coast.

The good news is that the number of eco-lodges are growing. However, some hotels claim to be "eco-lodges" but are not actually making any strides in ecological protection. To make sure your hotel is not cheating the system by just slapping "eco" in their title, do not be afraid to ask what guidelines they follow to promote eco-responsibility. Every guest should leave an eco-lodge having learned something about eco-responsibility. Updated: Aug 11, 2010.

HACIENDAS

One of the most unique places to stay in Guatemala is in a *hacienda*, a restored country home formerly owned by wealthy citizens. As in the rest of Latin America,

Guatemalan haciendas were once elegant, single-family estates that ruled the surrounding areas. As such, haciendas are linked to oppression and exploitation of indigenous society; basically, they were plantations of the colonial era.

Today, many haciendas have been turned into first-rate guest homes akin to B&Bs in the U.S. Haciendas not only come with a storied history, they also often feature stately gardens, horse stables and elegant accommodations. Although more expensive than other places to stay in Guatemala, most haciendas are tranquil, even romantic, retreats that offer excellent meals and can easily arrange horseback riding trips or other excursions. Updated: Aug 11, 2010.

Food and Drink

Corn and beans are the backbone of all three meals in Guatemala. Much of the cuisine resembles Mexican short orders such as tacos and enchiladas, but soups and spicy stews are also popular dishes. Fresh fruit and vegetables flourish here, and are always ripe for the picking. Travelers on a budget will be happy to know Guatemalan food is reasonably priced, and even though some consider the cuisine to be bland, hot sauce is almost always within arm's reach.

Since the time of the ancient Maya civilization, food in Guatemala has centered around corn. Tortillas are at the heart of most meals; Guatemalan families can eat dozens of the thin, corn pancakes each day. Smaller and a bit thicker than their Mexican counterpart, Guatemalan tortillas are always served fresh and piping hot. Many restaurants make tortillas right before your eyes, a "hot-off-the-presses" testament to their freshness. Other foods used by the Mayas—black beans, squash, potatoes and chilies—have long been staples of the Guatemalan kitchen.

The Spanish expanded on these local flavors, introducing rice, bread, European vegetables and greater portions of meat to the Guatemalan diet. Today, other cultures have infiltrated Guatemala, so much so that Chinese restaurants can be found in even small towns.

Chicken, turkey and beef are the most common meats, and it is not unheard of for a chicken to be served with its feet still attached. Seafood is easy to find on the coasts and in tourist centers but is uncommon elsewhere. Extremely poor Guatemalans consider meat a luxury, and sometimes eat little more than corn, beans and fruit.

Vegetarian food in Guatemala is easy to come by, especially since a basic meal of beans, rice and tortillas can be found on just about any menu. When in doubt, be sure to ask if the beans were cooked in lard or soups were made with meat stock. Restaurants catering solely to vegetarians have also started popping up in tourist areas.

To stay healthy—and keep from falling into a carbohydrate coma—Guatemalans eat plenty of fruits and vegetables. Both temperate and tropical fruits are plentiful in Guatemala, where you can find apples, peaches and oranges sold alongside bananas, papayas and mangoes. Some less familiar fruits such as *tuna*, the fruit of a prickly pear cactus, are worth a try. Many varieties of vegetables sneak onto menus and into markets, just be sure all your produce is washed with purified water to avoid sickness.

BREAKFAST, LUNCH AND DINNER
Meals are eaten around similar hours as in North America and much of Europe, and there is frequently a mid-afternoon snack of a light sandwich or pastry and coffee. Guatemalans keep breakfast simple: usually some combination of eggs, beans, tortillas and plantains. Tropical fruits, such as bananas and mangoes, are a sweet addition, as is a cup of world-famous Guatemalan coffee. However, much of the good stuff is exported, and locals tend to like their coffee weak with plenty of sugar. Lunch is the most important meal of the day, and as a result, the largest. A generous bowl of soup or stew is usually served, followed by a plate of meat, rice, vegetables and a simple salad. Fresh fruit or pudding may also be presented as a light dessert. Dinnertime is typically between 7 and 9 p.m. in the cities but earlier in rural areas. Few restaurants are open past 10 p.m., even in major cities, and you will be hard pressed to find a restaurant open after 8 p.m. outside of the city. Dinner foods resemble lunch but can be more elaborate.

WHERE TO EAT
Comedor: If you are looking for a cheap meal, try stopping in a *comedor*, a no-fuss eatery serving set breakfasts, lunches and dinners. So long as the place looks clean and busy, you will probably get a good meal for around $2-4.
Restaurante: At least one step above the comedor is a *restaurante*, where you can order a sit-down meal off a menu of soups, salads,

sandwiches, pastas and meat dishes for some-where between $3-6. More expensive establish-ments are found in cities, but even the classiest should never cost more than $30. Be sure to tip around 10 percent when eating at a restaurante, a practice unnecessary at simpler eateries, un-less you have received exceptional service.

Pepián: An Authentic Guatemalan Dish

Vegetarians aside, nobody should visit Guatemala without trying *pepián*, a traditional dish that has been served in the country for centuries. At first glance, the dish may look like Mexican mole, but a closer look reveals a dis-tinctly Guatemalan blend of European and Maya influences.

Pepián typically starts with chicken or turkey, but on some menus, you will also find pork or beef. Rice and *güis-quil*, a green potato-like fleshy vegeta-ble, are also on the plate, and the entire dish is smothered in *recardo*, a rich gravy-like sauce made from roasted to-matoes, chilies, cinnamon, and sesame and squash seeds. There is always a basket of warm, freshly made corn tor-tillas to soak up the extra sauce, which should never go to waste. Generally, it is not very spicy but on a rare chilly evening in Antigua, you can always ask for the heat to be turned up.

Food can vary across Guatemala's 22 departments, but pepián knows no boundaries; from the coasts to the highlands, you will find this dish all across Guatemala. You can sample this delicious meal from streetside stalls to high-end restaurants. Some may reserve this dish for special occasions, such as birthdays and holidays, whereas others will lap it up any day of the week. And even though fast food may be grow-ing in popularity, Guatemalans still love fresh, home-cooked meals—so make the most of it. Updated: Nov 23, 2009.

Café or Cafetería: In addition to coffee, you can pick up a light snack at a café or caféteria.
Fast Food: International fast food is widely available, as is the country's resident fried chicken fast food joint, Pollo Campero.
Bars: As a general rule, bars stay open 11

a.m.-11 p.m. By law, no alcohol may be served in Guatemala after 1 a.m.

GUATEMALAN SPECIALTIES
Plato típico: Found on most menus, this plate of meat is served with black beans, tortillas, rice and a simple salad. Usually, the dish is topped off with salty cheese and a dollop of sour cream.
Chiles rellenos: Peppers stuffed with rice, cheese, meat and vegetables.
Tamales: There are hundreds of varieties of tamales throughout Guatemala, a dish made of starchy dough and other fillings wrapped in a leaf and boiled. Traditionally, tamales are eaten on Christmas Eve around midnight.
Chilaquilas: A mix of eggs, beef, onions, cheese and tortillas.
Ceviche: Raw seafood marinated in lime juice, chopped onion and garlic. Served chilled.
Jocón: A spicy stew made with either chick-en or pork that varies regionally, but can in-clude green tomatoes, peas, squash, onions, chile peppers and cilantro.
Caldo de gallina: The Guatemalan version of chicken soup, served with chunks of chicken, carrot, squash, tomatoes and other vegetables.
Pepián: Meat in a spicy tomato, pumpkin and sesame seed sauce.
Kak'ik: A regional specialty of Cobán, this spicy turkey stew is made with an ancient recipe calling for 24 ingredients.
Tapado: Served along the Caribbean Coast of Izabal, this seafood stew is made with co-conut milk and plantains.
Mosh: This sloppy oatmeal porridge is the perfect breakfast dish on chilly mornings.

NON-ALCOHOLIC GUATEMALAN DRINKS
Limonada: A simple, refreshing drink made with limes, water and sugar. Try it *con soda* for a fizzy burst of flavor.
Licuado: Sweetened juices made from any combination of fruits available. You may want to ask to have yours prepared without sugar (*sin azúcar, por favor*).
Sodas: Sweetened, bottled soft drinks (in-cluding international brands) are available just about everywhere, but are often poured in a sandwich bag with a straw so the seller can bank in on the glass deposit.
Water: For health reasons, avoid drink-ing tap water. Ask for *agua pura* or *agua mineral*, and add *con gas* if you would like the water carbonated.

ALCOHOLIC GUATEMALAN DRINKS
Cocos locos: Found on the Guatemalan

coast, this drink is simply a green coconut with the top sliced off, plus a shot of rum.
Rompopo: A spiked eggnog found in the town of Salcajá, near Quetzaltenango.
Aguardiente: Moonshine made in Maya highland towns, also known as "guaro."
Beer: The most well-known brand of beer is Gallo, a lager recognizable by the stylized rooster on its label. Moza is a dark beer that is also widely available. Updated: Jul 30, 2010.

Shopping

Guatemalan marketplaces are well worth a visit for their beautiful textiles, delicious aromas and general hustle and bustle, which stimulate the senses. Stores often have established prices, but shopping in Guatemalan markets revolves around bargaining. Oftentimes, the seller will name a price significantly higher than what he or she expects to receive, so it's up to you to find a happy medium. However, try to avoid offering too low of a price, which is considered to be rude.

The primary wares available in these markets include handicrafts, textiles, leather products, silver jewelry, jade and coffee. The handicrafts are generally very high quality, and many of the textiles are hand woven and come in brilliant colors. The coffee, depending on its quality—going directly to the grower or roaster is advised—can be some of the finest in the world.

There are many notable markets in Guatemala. The most famous is Chichicastenango, which is about two hours northwest of Guatemala City by bus. The journey makes a nice day trip; however, if you want to escape the city for longer, there are a few hotels in town. The nicest is the Hotel Santo Tomás, livened up with gardens and artwork. On Thursdays and Saturdays, the marketplace reaches its fullest vibrancy, with plenty to buy and see. Vendors from all over Guatemala come to the town, and you are sure to find good deals on textiles and other crafts.

Another popular market (Tuesdays and Thursdays) is Sololá, west of the capital near Lake Atitlán. This market has a much less touristy and more relaxed atmosphere than Chichicastenango. There are beautiful views of the lake and surrounding volcanoes.

In addition to these two markets, there are plenty of other indigenous markets all over Guatemala. In many substantial towns and villages, there is a good likelihood that they have a central marketplace where indigenous Guatemalans sell their goods, including textiles and produce.

If you would rather not make your shopping trip a lengthy excursion, there are also lively, centrally located marketplaces in the major cities, especially Guatemala City and Antigua. Bargaining is not as common in the city markets as in the countryside, but the goods can be just as special. These areas are also prone to pickpocketing thieves, so be careful!

Marketplaces offer more than just high quality and low prices; they provide visitors with an immersion experience of indigenous Guatemalan culture. Whether you just want a cheap souvenir or a one-of-a-kind textile, these marketplaces have a galaxy of products.

Aside from the buzz of the marketplace, more upscale and trendy options exist in the major cities. If you are looking for the costlier goods, Zona Viva in Guatemala City has a good deal of swanky stores. However, these stores lack the vibrant, colorful atmosphere that the marketplaces have.

For the convenience of the modern shopping experience, Gran Centro Los Próceres is perhaps the largest and most modern shopping mall, offering a movie theater, restaurants and a variety of stores. It is located in the capital's Zona Viva on 16 Calle 2-00, and has some American stores and restaurants in addition to domestica businesses. Other American chains, such as Starbucks, Dunkin' Donuts and Burger King, can also be found in the major cities. There are also more than 125 supermarkets in Guatemala, where you are sure to find some familiar products. Updated: Jun 23, 2010.

MAPS

It's a good idea to pick up a comprehensive map of Guatemala before you depart on your trip, as a good map is not always easy to come by once you touch down. If you forgot or lost a map, you can find some sold in souvenir shops, bookstores or travel agencies in Guatemala City, Antigua, Panajachel and Quetzaltenango. The most comprehensive map on the market is probably the one made by International Travel Maps, which goes for about $10 in Guatemala. Intelimapas' Mapa Turístico Guatemala is cheaper and updated more often, as it is produced locally. In order to walk around Guatemala without being bothered, be discreet about where you pull out your map. Updated: Aug 12, 2010.

Health

Health and safety concerns are numerous in Guatemala, but avoiding them is not difficult if the proper precautions are taken. Due to poor sanitation, questionable drinking water and tropical climate, Guatemala is a hotbed for bacteria and viruses. Many of these are transmitted through contaminated water, food and insects. Avoid drinking non-purified water and eating fruits, vegetables and meats that have been thoroughly cooked or cleansed. Take care to use insect repellent in many areas where viruses like malaria, dengue and yellow fever are endemic. Vaccinations are not required to enter Guatemala, but shots for yellow fever, hepatitis A and B, typhoid and a tetanus booster come heavily recommended. If you plan on traveling in malaria-prone areas, taking some sort of preventative pill will dramatically reduce your risk, but DEET repellent is important as well. Updated: Aug 11, 2010.

Minor Health Problems

While traveling, especially in developing countries, there is always the possibility of catching a minor illness, especially in rural or remote areas. Although relatively uncommon, the list below is of possible illnesses that can be contracted while traveling throughout Guatemala. Above all, heed your doctor's advice and come prepared!

CHAGAS DISEASE

Chagas is most common where thatched roofs are commonly used, mostly in rural areas of the country. It is an illness carried by parasitic insects that pass infection through bites and defecation on exposed skin. The severity of the disease varies, as most symptoms show local swelling and possible fever or tiredness. If Chagas goes untreated, there is the possibility of swelling in the lymph glands, spleen and liver. If you suspect you have been infected, see a doctor immediately.

SUNBURN/HEAT EXHAUSTION

The sun is hottest and most harmful from 10 a.m. to 4 p.m. in Guatemala. If you are looking for a tan, it is safest to sit outside early mornings or late afternoons. However, travelers should take proper precautions to protect themselves from ultraviolet radiation. Note that you will burn faster here than in Europe or the U.S.

For prevention, apply sunscreen with at least an SPF of 30 every few hours you are outside. If you get severe sunburn, treat it with a cream and stay out of the sun for awhile. To avoid overheating, wear a hat and sunglasses, and drink lots of water. Overweight people are more susceptible to sun stroke. The symptoms of heat exhaustion are profuse sweating, weakness, exhaustion, muscle cramps, rapid pulse and vomiting. If you experience heat stroke, go to a cool, shaded area until your body temperature normalizes and drink lots of water. If the symptoms continue, consult a doctor.

MOTION SICKNESS

Even the hardiest of travelers can be hit by motion sickness on the bumpy buses in Guatemala. Sit near the front of the bus or stay above deck on any boats you may take, and focus on the horizon. If you are prone to motion sickness, eat light, non-greasy food before traveling and avoid drinking too much, particularly alcohol. Over-the-counter medications such as Dramamine can prevent it: Go to a pharmacy and ask for Mareol, a liquid medicine similar to Dramamine. If you know that you commonly suffer from severe motion sickness, you may want to get a prescription for something stronger for your travels, such as a medicinal patch.

TRAVELER'S DIARRHEA

This is probably the most common disease for travelers. There is no vaccine to protect you from traveler's diarrhea; it is avoided by eating sensibly. Contrary to popular belief, it is usually transmitted by food, not contaminated water. To best prevent traveler's diarrhea, eat only steaming hot foods that have been cooked all the way through in clean establishments. Avoid raw lettuce and fruit that cannot be peeled, such as strawberries. Vegetables are usually safer than meat. If you are cooking your own meals, an inexpensive vegetable wash can be purchased at large supermarkets. Make sure any milk you drink has been boiled. In some areas, milk is unpasteurized and therefore powdered or tinned is advised. Bottled water is always recommended, and remember to avoid ice cubes.

If you do get diarrhea, the best way to remedy it is to let it run its course while staying hydrated with clear soups, lemon tea, Gatorade and soda that has gone flat. Bananas are also a good source of potassium and help stop diarrhea. If you need to travel and cannot afford to let the illness run its course, any pharmacy will give you something that will make you comfortable enough for a bus trip. If the diarrhea persists for more than five days, see a doctor. Updated: Aug 12, 2010.

Major Health Problems

While traveling, especially in developing countries, there is always the possibility of being affected by a major health problem, especially in rural or remote areas. Travelers should not fixate on these relatively uncommon maladies, but should consult with their doctors before coming.

DENGUE FEVER

In recent years, there have been growing reports of dengue fever in Guatemala. While it is not a great threat, this mosquito-borne disease is present, and it is recommended to wear long sleeves and pants, as well as proper repellent, in order to dramatically reduce the risk.

DYSENTERY

This digestive illness is the far more serious version of traveler's diarrhea. It involves mucus and blood in feces, and is contracted most often from eating or drinking foods that are untreated or washed with unsanitary water. This water carries micro-organisms, or parasites, that destroy the intestinal lining and cause bacterial infections in the system. The best way to remedy dysentery is by oral rehydration therapy given in proper medical facilities.

HEPATITIS A

Hepatitis A is a severe and infectious disease of the liver that is caused by the ingestion of microscopic amounts of fecal matter. Hepatitis A causes jaundice and liver inflammation, and while the disease usually lasts for a few weeks, it does not lead to chronic infection. If you are planning to visit Guatemala, it is strongly advised you get a vaccination against hepatitis A.

MALARIA

Most of Guatemala is not at risk for malaria, but the disease cannot be ruled out and proper precautions should be taken when traveling here. Rural areas, especially by the coasts, show reports of the mosquito-borne disease. Symptoms are flu-like, followed by exhaustion, fever, and at severe stages, a coma. Chloroquine is recommended as an antimalarial drug, however, consult your doctor before traveling to any at-risk areas.

RABIES

There are stray dogs throughout Guatemala that are, for the most part, harmless. However, many homeowners train guard dogs to attack trespassers, and other feral dogs can be dangerous. On long hikes in rural areas, always carry a walking stick to defend yourself if a dog starts to attack, and in the city,

do not feed or antagonize strays. It is recommended to be pre-vaccinated for rabies, however treatment against rabies should be available in major cities if you happen to get bit. Be sure to see a doctor immediately if you believe you were infected, whether or not you have had the vaccine.

TYPHOID

This disease is caused by ingesting contaminated food and water, and symptoms include dangerously high fever, profuse sweating and severe diarrhea. Wash your hands as frequently as possible, and try your best to eat food from restaurants with good reputations. Oral or intraveneous vaccinations are recommended by the World Health Organization and should be taken before travel if you are planning to be in Central America for an extended period of time (six months or more). The injection needs boosting every three years. Updated: Aug 12, 2010.

Hospitals

If you need to go to the hospital, private hospitals such as Hospital Herrera Llerandi (6a. Av. 8-71, Zona 10, Guatemala City. Tel: 502-2384-5959) are preferable to public hospitals, which suffer from a severe lack of resources. Private hospitals generally have an English speaker on staff, which can be a critical factor in receiving proper treatment. However, private hospitals are more expensive, so make sure you are covered by insurance. Many hospitals expect to be paid in cash, so it is good to bring extra money if you plan on going to the hospital. A list of hospitals in Guatemala, courtesy of the U.S. State Department, is available at: http://guatemala.usembassy.gov/uploads/Hn/Et/HnEtZZzHbEKHReSCkh4nRA/acsehospitals.pdf. Updated: Jun 23, 2010.

Doctors

Doctors in Guatemala diminish in quality and frequency the farther you get outside of the large cities. There are many public clinics that will treat you in an emergency, but private clinics offer better service at a higher price. Many doctors expect to be paid in cash. Updated: Jun 23, 2010.

Pharmacies

Pharmacies in Guatemala are both privately and state owned, and will stay open all night in major cities on a rotating basis. However, due to language barriers and poor training, some pharmacists will prescribe inaccurate doses and/or medicines. Some medications that must be prescribed by a doctor in the U.S. or Europe are available over the counter in Guatemala, but playing doctor is not necessarily advised. Consider consulting a prescription pill guidebook or asking your doctor prior to taking the medicine. Updated: Jun 23, 2010.

Safety

Safety is a genuine concern for all travelers and tourists, but in developing countries like Guatemala, you should be a little more vigilant. Violent attacks are generally rare, but some have been reported in the past, mainly in the larger cities such as Guatemala City and Antigua. Pickpocketing and petty theft are a lot more common, so make sure to keep a close eye on your personal belongings at all times, especially cameras, laptops, iPods, handbags and cell phones.

Try not to walk around alone at night, even in small groups. In the more populated areas, there are usually plenty of taxis that do not cost very much. Often your hotel or the restaurant where you are eating will call one for you. For women, walking around alone is not a good idea, and everyone is advised to avoid wearing flashy jewelry or expensive-looking clothing, as these can attract unwanted attention.

When you are hiking or climbing around Guatemala, make sure you are wearing suitable footwear for the terrain and that you let someone nearby know where you are hiking. Even better, hire a guide if possible. They tend to have a better knowledge of an area and can make a hike or a climb much easier and more enjoyable. Also, be careful when swimming in the ocean or in lakes. Do not swim at night and try to stick to areas where there are other people swimming. Sea currents can be hard to predict and getting caught in one is not worth the risk. When traveling around some of the more rural parts of Guatemala, try to keep in mind that taking photographs of the local indigenous can be found offensive. Some tourists have experienced hostile reactions to photos taken without permission or in an intrusive manner. Be especially careful if children are involved. Guatemalans can be very wary of westerners taking too much of an interest in indigenous children. Reported cases of small children being kidnapped have made many communities very protective. Updated: Aug 18, 2010.

Communications

Postal services in Guatemala are run by a fairly reliable and inexpensive Canadian company, known as El Correo, but international mail can take weeks to reach its destination. A quicker, cheaper form of correspondence is through E-mail, a method that is easily accessible in most substantial towns and cities in the form of Internet cafés. Some hostels provide web-equipped computers as well. Cell phones are the way to go in Guatemala, and there are a few carriers to choose from, the most visible being Tigo. Updated: Aug 12, 2010.

Phones

GUATEMALA CALLING CODE

The international calling code for Guatemala is 502, which is dialed after the international access code and before the eight-digit number.

CALLING GUATEMALA

Calling Guatemala from the United States and Canada: 011 + 502 + Eight-digit number.

Calling Guatemala from Europe: 00 + 502 + Eight-digit number.

Calling Guatemala from Latin America: 00 + 502 + Eight-digit number.

Calling Guatemala from elsewhere: 00 + 502 + Eight-digit number.

CELL PHONES

In Guatemala, most people use cell phones as the primary means of communication. You have multiple options when it comes to choosing a cell phone. First, you can use your own cell phone if it has unlocked triband capability (ask your provider). If it does, you can purchase a SIM card to replace your existing card once you are in Guatemala. These are sold by the following providers, who offer cheaper prices on local calls than what you would pay with an American or European provider:

Movistar (URL: www.movistar.com.gt)

Claro (URL: www.claro.com.gt)

Tigo (URL: www.comcel.com.gt)

These prepaid cards will cost you about $20-25 per month, and most rates run about $0.15 per minute within the country or to the U.S., but vary among other international calls. The cards are widely available at most grocery stores, malls and convenience shops, and whenever you run out of credit, you can purchase another one.

Your other option is to buy a cheap phone in Guatemala with a pre-paid plan. Phones should cost about $30 and come with some credit to make calls and text messages. This may be a better option if your phone does not have international capability or if your phone is an expensive model that may be a primary target for pickpocketing.

CALLING CARDS

If you plan on buying a pre-paid calling card, you can purchase them at grocery stores and convenience stores in denominations of $1-6. Depending on the provider, these cards can be inserted directly into certain pay phones or have a code that you enter into the keypad. Telgua and Telefónica are the most common, and have phones all over the country. Telgua is cheaper if you plan to make more local calls or calls to Europe, and Telefónica is cheaper for calls to the U.S. ($0.20 compared to $0.50). It is recommended to buy the calling card once you arrive in Guatemala, because it is most likely cheaper than buying one in your home country.

CALLING WITHIN GUATEMALA

When calling a local number in Guatemala, only the eight-digit number is used; there are no area or city codes.

CALLING HOME FROM GUATEMALA

To dial home from Guatemala, you dial 00 + the country code (1 for the U.S.) + the area code + the number.

There are multiple options for making international calls in Guatemala. International calling cards are a cheap alternative to making collect calls to North America. The cheapest options are Internet-based phones, found in calling centers and some hotels. Some calling centers may have less reliable connections than others, but it is still a good option compared to costly cell phone calls. Computer communication programs such as Skype and Apple iChat are free if both you and the person you want to talk to have computers with fast Internet connections. Skype calls from your computer to any phone run about $0.02 per minute and up. Updated: Jun 23, 2010.

Mail

For parcel post, both international and regional couriers are available in addition to El Correo, which has very expensive international rates. International couriers such as DHL, Fed Ex and UPS operate in Guatemala and make

up for high prices with more reliability. If you have valuable items you want to ship, this is the way to go. Do not expect packages mailed from Guatemala to reach the U.S. quickly, unless you want to pay around $63 for delivery within three days with a private courier.

For receiving mail, use a private address because general deliveries are no longer available in the Guatemalan post. If you are staying at a hotel, you can ask them to receive it for you. El Correo's website, www.elcorreo.com.gt, has useful information. Updated: Jun 21, 2010.

Internet

Internet is commonly available throughout Guatemala. Medium-sized towns usually have Internet cafés with a decent connection. While Internet cafés may exist in the smaller towns, connection speeds tend to be slower. In the cities and bigger towns, connectivity is good, with fast speeds available.

In some cases, you can use Internet in the hostel where you are staying, or if you are studying Spanish, at your school. This benefit will often be included in the price of your stay or classes, though there may be a limit placed on usage, such as 30 minutes per day. Sometimes these places will charge you a little extra for the use of their Internet facilities. WiFi access is becoming more commonplace. Many of the Spanish schools have WiFi, as do the higher-end hotels and a few hostels. If you are looking for a room, you may be charged a little more at hostels that have WiFi connectivity. Updated: Jul 20, 2010.

Media

The Guatemalan press enjoys almost unrestricted free speech, though some journalists have been punished for making caustic remarks. Defamation is taken very seriously by the Guatemalan judicial system and can result in long jail sentences. However, the Guatemalan press has been a very robust source for criticism of corrupt or unfair governmental practices, and in the past, the media has shed light on some major human rights and environmental violations committed by the government and multinational corporations.

There are six national newspapers, varying in quality and content. The most-reputable newspapers include *Prensa Libre* and *La Hora*. Every paper has a sort of tabloid format, but are still well-written, and reading one is a great way to practice

Spanish. Consult the monthly magazine *Revue* for practical information as well as what is going on around the country.

There are only five Guatemalan TV channels and two news programs, so many channels are syndicated from other parts of Latin America or the United States. *Telenovelas* (soap operas) and junky American action flicks abound on cable. The only Guatemalan cable channel is Guatevisión. Radio is very popular in Guatemala, and there are many local stations. Some of the most popular include Patrullaje Informativo, Radio Sonora, and broadcasts from "El Independiente," part of www.NuevoMundoRadio.com, a popular electronic newspaper. Updated: Aug 12, 2010.

Money and Banks

The currency of Guatemala is the quetzal. In February 2011, the exchange rate was 7.849 quetzales to the U.S. dollar. Since exchange rates vary frequently, check on up-to-minute conversion rates at the time of your trip.

Opening hours for banks vary from place to place. Most banks are open 9 a.m.-4 p.m. Monday-Friday, with many open until 6 p.m. and a few open as late as 7 p.m. Often, if a bank is open later, it may not exchange currencies up until closing time—in many cases, the exchange service ends at 4 p.m. Most banks are open 9 a.m.-1 p.m. on Saturdays, and are closed on Sundays and public holidays.

Some of the bigger banks in Guatemala are Banco Occidente, BAC and Banco Indus-trial. Most banks have ATMs. You will find ATMs (known as *cajeros automáticos*) in most larger urban centers, but not in small towns. You should not rely on being able to draw money out from an ATM in villages and smaller centers. Additionally, over pub-lic holidays, be prepared for the possibility of ATMs running out of money. Common ATMs are Bancared, Banco Industrial and Credomatic, which accept most card types.

Be cautious when you are using ATMs. Always draw out money during daytime hours. Try to use ATMs inside banks rather than outside. Usually the banks are heavily guarded, a safe bet you will have no hassles when using the ATM. Always get receipts and keep records of money withdrawn, in case of any discrepancies later, which have been known to happen. Note: If you have a five-digit pin, it will not be possible to use this in Guatemala; the banks are set up for four-digit pins.

Credit cards are starting to become more widely accepted, but they still cannot be used everywhere. Visa and MasterCard (and less commonly, American Express) can be used in the more upscale hotels, restaurants and shops, and with some tour companies. Do not expect to be able to use your credit card at a beach shack or mom-and-pop store. In many cases, using your credit card will cost you— often charges of 8 percent or so will be added to the cost of your transaction.

Traveler's checks can be exchanged at major bank branches in large urban areas, or areas that are important for tourists. You can occa-sionally change them in shops or travel agen-cies, but this is much less common. Always bring checks that are in U.S. dollars—other currencies such as the euro and the pound are notoriously difficult to exchange. Ameri-can Express traveler's checks are the most commonly known brand, so it is better to stick with those. To change checks, you will always need your passport (original, not a copy) and in many cases, you will also need your proof of purchase. Do not forget to keep the check numbers separate from the checks for your own security in case of theft.

There are a variety of ways to wire money to Guatemala. It is common for banks to have Western Union as an affiliate because many Guatemalans working abroad send money home to their families. However, you do not need to go through Western Union, as many banks in the U.S. or Europe will wire money to a Guatemalan bank. Before doing so, inquire about exchange rates. Expect the transfer to take at least a few days. In emergency situations, U.S. citizens can have money transferred through the U.S. Embas-sy, for a fee of $30. Updated: Sep 03, 2010.

Etiquette and Dress

When traveling, the importance of being polite, observant and respectful goes without saying. However, every destina-tion has a few local idiosyncrasies. Pick-ing these up sooner rather than later will help you avoid embarrassing situations or causing offense.

In Guatemala, it is customary to say "bue-nos dias" or "buenas tardes" to strangers as you pass them in the street and to shake hands with friends or cheek-kiss in more urban areas. Say "mucho gusto" when you are introduced so someone for the first time. Titles are important, especially to the older generation. Use Señor, Señora or Señorita, or address a person using his or her professional title, such as Profesor(a) for teachers, Abogado/a for lawyers or Doctor for physicians. Speaking softly is proper, and good topics for general conversation are Guatemalan food, geography and culture; do not initiate conversations about the civil war and its associated violence.

If you are staying with a host family, you could take a small gift from your home country as an offering. Do not give white flowers, as these are only for funerals. Likewise, graciously accept food, drinks or gifts offered, and do not overuse alcohol. For business or visiting government offices, men should always wear a suit, while women should wear a knee-length skirt and shirt. The main meal of the day is usually eaten at lunchtime so this is preferable for a business meal also.

Trying to blend in a bit to avoid unwanted attention can be useful in some situations. Chauvinistic attitudes prevail in some communities. Women are fine to travel and eat out unaccompanied, but should avoid going to bars alone or walking home alone at night. Same-sex relationships are not illegal in Guatemala, but it is still frowned upon in some areas, so gay and lesbian couples are advised to refrain from public displays of affection.

Tipping 10 percent of the bill is expected in mid-range and high-end restaurants and bars, but not at street stalls or basic comedores. You can also tip taxi or tuk-tuk drivers and tour guides. There is usually a charge for using public toilets, but this is only a few quetzales. Updated: May 13, 2010.

Officialdom and Business

When dealing with Guatemalans on official or business terms, it is important to maintain professional composure. Unlike many other Latin American countries, it is considered rude to be late, so make sure you arrive on time for a meeting.

Also, try to address anyone in a business setting by their professional title. It is important that at least one person on your staff is fluent in Spanish to ensure proper communication. If you need to hire an interpreter, make sure to ask your client first. Attire is formal, generally a lightweight suit for men, and business casual clothing for women, such as blouses and dresses. It is appropriate to make small talk before starting the meeting as an icebreaker. Corruption can be a problem in Guatemala, so take this into consideration in your initial impression of the client; try to determine if you can trust them. Updated: Jul 22, 2010.

Responsible Tourism

Responsible tourism involves a little more than making sure you do not throw your garbage out of the bus windows, as the local norm goes. True, you must take responsibility for your day-to-day actions when visiting a foreign place, but you should also think about the wider implications of your travel choices. You can use your buying power as a customer to influence business practices, as well as fellow travelers and locals alike. Deciding to go with a tour agency that has built into its working practices environmental sustainability is important, as is choosing to spend your tourist dollars in locally owned artisan shops rather than foreign-owned chains.

Responsible tourism should, in short, be about minimizing negative economic, environmental and social effects. It is also important to contribute positively to the conservation of the natural and cultural heritage, provide more meaningful connections for locals and tourists, and encourage a greater understanding of other cultures while building opportunities for locals to make decisions about their own working conditions, environment and society in general.

Responsible and sustainable tourism is a growing trend, and there are many tools out there to direct your travel behavior in the right direction. The website www.wtmwrtd.com organizes a world responsible tourism day every year sponsored by BBC World News and supported by the World Tourism Organization. The site www.responsibletravel.com can help you pick out feel-good vacations. Idealist.org lists many volunteer opportunities with social and environmental projects. Updated: May 13, 2010.

Photography

With its smoking volcanoes, imposing Maya ruins and colorful cities, Guatemala is a photographer's goldmine. If using a film camera, supplies are easily found in most cities and towns, including both color and black and white film. For those who do use roll film, there are also processing centers in most substantial cities.

Due to import fees, digital cameras sold in Guatemala are a bit more expensive than you would think. You can upload your digital images at some film processing centers and Internet cafés. As in many other Latin American countries, try to keep your camera and equipment out of sight as much as possible, because expensive electronics attract thieves.

Photographic etiquette is a salient topic in Guatemala due to the protective stance many Maya take over their children in areas not frequented by tourists. This attitude has to do with widespread rumors in rural Guatemala that foreigners steal indigenous children and sell their organs. A Japanese tourist was beaten to death a few years ago after attempting to pick up a Maya child. If you want to take up-close pictures of Guatemalans, asking for permission is necessary. Some may charge you a few quetzals, especially children. If it's a landscape photograph and there happen to be people in it, there is no need to worry. Updated: Aug 11, 2010.

Tips for Women Travelers

As in many Latin American countries, a certain level of the machista culture still exists in Guatemala. The best way to deal with catcalls, car horns and lingering stares is to ignore them. While sometimes it may be difficult, the spontaneous suitors usually do not mean any harm and do not tend to bother continuing with their comments once they are ignored.

If someone gets too close or gropes you, scare them off by shouting and causing a bit of a scene; perverts generally do not like being exposed as such in public. Dress demurely, particularly in the less touristy parts of the country. Shorts are best kept for the beach, skirts should fall to the knee and necklines should not be too low.

Women traveling alone should avoid traveling between destinations at night. Attacks or assaults on women are not necessarily commonplace, but they have been known to happen. Try to sit beside women or children on the bus if it makes you feel more comfortable. Travel by taxi after dark and, if possible, try to share a taxi back to where you are staying.

Along the coast, you may notice some locals wearing T-shirts over their bathing suits when they are swimming. If this is the case, you may choose to follow suit. Also, be aware of how going to a bar alone

may appear if you are not particularly interested in getting to know some locals. Do not hitchhike and if you feel a bit vulnerable traveling alone around some of the more remote areas, inquire with the nearest tourist office about hiring a guide. Updated: Jul 29, 2010.

Tips for Gays and Lesbians

Machista culture can also prove troublesome for gay couples traveling in Guatemala. Some parts of the country may be slightly more tolerant of homosexuality than others, but rather than risk harassment, it is best to be discreet with your partner. Open displays of mutual affection in public should be avoided.

In the more urban areas, such as Guatemala City and Antigua, there are a number of openly gay venues. Zona 1 and the "Old City" in Guatemala City are where most of the gay bars and clubs can be found. Antigua can even appear a bit more laidback than the capital; however, in general, homosexuality is still kept behind closed doors. Some hostels, hotels or lodges may not be comfortable with providing gay couples with a double room. The website www.gayguatemala.com is a good one and provides lots of information on places to stay and visit that are gay and lesbian friendly. Updated: Jul 29, 2010.

Tips for Seniors

There is no reason whatsoever why seniors should not feel comfortable about traveling in Guatemala. Visitors with medical conditions should consult with their doctors before traveling to Guatemala, and should carry medicine and their prescriptions with them. It could also be worth your while inquiring with hotels and tour operators about a reduced rate for seniors.

Museums, theaters and attractions usually offer a senior discount, and there is no harm in asking if you do not see anything displayed. The same situation can also apply to car rental. Public transport in Guatemala is often rickety, but there are plenty of travel companies around that offer specific tours tailored to suit seniors or those with specific interests. Updated: Jul 29, 2010.

Tips for Disabled Travelers

Guatemala is not very well equipped to cater to the needs of the disabled. The rugged rural terrain and awkward streets and pavements make moving around for those in a wheelchair quite difficult. This is particularly true in Antigua, where the charming cobblestone streets deter a lot of wheelchair users. While there are curb ramps onto the pavement at most street corners, sometimes the pavements themselves are not navigable.

For those with hearing or visual impairment, facilities are almost non-existent. Even at some of the bigger attractions, there is rarely any assistance provided for the blind or deaf.

In terms of transport around Guatemala, the shuttle buses that travel between tourist centers are your best bet if you want to use public transport. "Chicken buses" are a no-no. You can also always look into renting a car or a driver who will take you from one destination to another. The airports have improved greatly, particularly Guatemala City, where elevators and ramps were a key feature of its recent upgrade.

In terms of accommodation, many of the smaller hotels and hostels tend to be wheelchair accessible because rooms are often located on the ground floor. The newer, more expensive hotels have elevators, ramps and often wheelchair-accessible bathrooms. There are also plenty of travel operators willing to organize trips suited to an individual's disability, so if you want to avoid the hassle of researching everything yourself, that is also an option. Updated: Jul 29, 2010.

Tips for Traveling with Children
Children are highly regarded in Latin America and can often help to break the ice with indigenous families. Local children are not as shy as their parents when it comes to approaching foreigners of their own age. Families with children are also viewed with less suspicion than westerners traveling alone. On most modes of public transport, there is a reduced rate for children; buses and planes generally charge less for kids under 12 years old and even less again for those under 2 years old.

Internal flights are something to think about if traveling long distances in Guatemala, as buses can often be uncomfortable and exhausting for adults, let alone children. However, check the baggage allowances for children, as they differ depending on the airline. Some budget hotels in Guatemala do not charge for children at all, while with others you can negotiate a family rate. You can also try to negotiate family tickets to attractions and museums, if they do not already exist.

Guatemala has a very dense and rich history that some kids may get bored with. It's worth looking into some theme parks, zoos or children's museums to help break up the more historical-based activities. Most restaurants are accommodating when it comes to the picky eating habits of some children, and many will assemble some form of a high chair for smaller children. Make sure you carry a copy of your child's birth certificate and a few passport-sized photographs.

Diapers and certain other baby supplies are easier to come by in the cities and tourist areas. Also, take note that fresh milk is rare and not always pasteurized, so you may have to make do with UHT milk or powdered milk. Ensure children are vaccinated sufficiently before you go, and make sure they keep away from tap water and street food stalls, as they are more susceptible than adults to bugs that can be carried in these. Updated: Jul 29, 2010.

Tips for Budget Travelers
Guatemala is perhaps the cheapest country to visit in all of Latin America. If you shop around, you can find decent transportation, meals and lodging for less than you would imagine.

Transportation by "chicken bus" generally costs about a dollar an hour, just do not expect rigid schedules and routes. These buses run all over the country and are a great option to get to places where few taxis or coach buses run. The towns surrounding Antigua are difficult to get to by another means than a *camioneta*, or pickup truck. Hitchhiking is another low-cost option, and sometimes the only option if you are out in the sticks.

Meals are also a bargain. If you have the ability to cook for yourself long term or do not mind a steady diet of rice and beans, you can eat for under $5 a day. Fixed-price menus for breakfast and lunch should run anywhere from $2-4. If you are OK with hole-in-the-wall comedores or street food, dinners can cost about the same. However, street food is more likely to get you sick, which could end up costing you quite a bit to take care of.

Lodging offers another pleasant surprise; beds in shared rooms can cost as low as $2, while a comfortable private room is easily available for under $10. Family-run *hospedajes*, essentially a house with a few extra rooms, are usually the cheapest option, along with the more modest of the hostels. Camping is also available, and is generally cheaper than any proper lodging in the area. Updated: Jul 22, 2010.

Tips for Mid-Range Travelers

Traveling in Guatemala on a mid-range budget will afford you a much more comfortable stay, because a little goes a long way in this country. For about $30 a day, you can avoid crowded buses, dingy hostel rooms and the mundane comedores that make budget traveling a bit tiresome. Private, secure buses run throughout the country. Taxis are fairly expensive, but are cheaper in the cities where there is a lot of competition. However, avoid taking taxis to remote areas, because the driver may charge you an arm and a leg. Make sure to bargain, as travelers are an easy target for rip-offs.

Food substantially improves in portion-size and quality as you move into the $5-10 price range. You will also have a much better variety of food to choose from if you opt for a restaurante instead of a comedor. Expect better service and a more pleasant dining experience, including chairs with backs and waiters with uniforms.

Having your own private room with bath and hot water makes for a much more comfortable experience. Fortunately, these amenities will only cost you about $10 a night, with cheaper rates outside of the cities. Updated: Jul 22, 2010.

Tips for Luxury Travelers

Expect to be continuously, unabashedly pampered if you have a lot of money to spend while traveling in Guatemala. For the price of a Holiday Inn in the United States, you can stay in a five-star hotel on the beach in Guatemala. However, you do not need to go blow all of your cash on imitation jewelry and exorbitant cab fares.

If you have the money, consider renting a car to get around. It should cost about $50 a day, but will afford you flexible travel free of crowded buses. Another benefit is your ability to stop anywhere you like, whereas on a bus you just have to watch the once-in-a-lifetime scenery pass you by.

Guatemala has some world-class restaurants in the major cities, allowing you to dine in a luxury environment similar to that of the U.S. or Europe. However, once you are out in the country, you will have to settle for lower-quality establishments. For a price, many gringo-run places serve up meals of higher quality than the local fare.

Since most high-quality liquor is imported, alcohol can be fairly expensive for the nicer drinks. If you have the ability to shell it out, there is nothing more relaxing than reclining on a hammock with an well-made daiquiri.

Lodging affords perhaps the most noticeable improvement for the price, and luxury options are available even in the middle of nowhere. Jungle lodges, boutique spas and waterfront bungalows are all available for about $50 a night—often less, depending on the season. Beware that some places lose their charm as the price goes up, so a higher price tag does not necessarily mean a better experience. Some of the best options are the cheap, quaint places that cannot offer hydro-massages or complimentary wine, but will afford you the authentic experience. Updated: Jul 22, 2010.

Suggested Reading List

NON-FICTION
I, Rigoberta Menchú–Rigoberta Menchú
Popul Vuh–Dennis Tedlock (trans.)
Beyond the Mexique Bay–Aldous Huxley
Breaking the Maya Code–Michael Coe
What Prize Awaits Us–Bernice Kita

FICTION
Men of Maize–Miguel Angel Asturias
El Señor Presidente–Miguel Angel Asturias
Dust on Her Tongue–Rodrigo Rey Rosa

!)))

INTRO & INFO

Travelers' discussions. User reviews. Feedback.
Photo contests. Book updates.
Travel news. Apps.
Writing contests.
Give-aways.

V!VA
TRAVEL GUIDES

Follow us online
www.facebook.com/vivatravelguides
www.twitter.com/vivatravelguide
www.vivatravelguides.com

Don't leave home without travel insurance. Get it at vivatravelguides.com/insurance/

GUATEMALA CITY

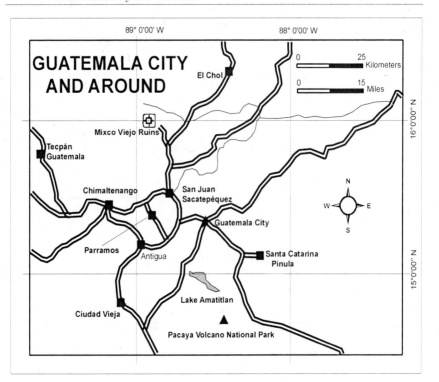

Guatemala City and Around

Guatemala province, dominated by Guatemala City, is the administrative, geographical and political center of the country. The province is centrally located, providing travelers a good starting point for their travels to such visitor hotspots as Tikal, Antigua and Lake Atitlán. While many travelers quickly zoom off to those spots, Guatemala's most vibrant city rewards those who take the time to explore it.

GUATEMALA CITY

 1600 m   502

Guatemala's sprawling capital city, Guatemala City ("Guate" to the locals) is considered by most as simply a place to catch a plane or pass through on the way to a more pleasant part of the country. This is somewhat unfair, as the city—the largest in Central America—has plenty to offer.

The city is divided into zones, which start at the center and radiate outward. The center area, Zona 1, is the colonial part of the city and is home to governmental buildings, cathedrals and several examples of impressive architecture. This part of town is packed with locals during the day, selling affordable goods and produce. Some of the more inexpensive hotels, popular with backpackers and budget travelers, can be found around here. Another zone of interest to travelers is Zona 4, a commercial zone that also houses the national theater: the Centro Cultural Miguel Ángel Asturias, named after one of Guatemala's greatest writers. Along Avenida de la Reforma are zones 9 and 10, a pleasant area with tree-lined streets, small parks, and the best hotels and restaurants in the city. The area has the nickname "Zona Viva," or "lively zone," due to its numerous clubs and bars.

Archaeology buffs will appreciate the Museo Nacional de Arqueología and Etnología in Zona 13, which displays pre-Columbian artifacts found at Maya sites throughout Guatemala. The Kaminaljuyú ruins boasts some 100 small structures and is also located close to the center of town. Updated: Aug 18, 2010.

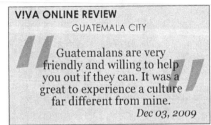

When to Go

Guatemala has two tourist high seasons: the first is July-August, and the second is between November and April. For years, the country has been known as "The Land of Eternal Spring" due to its pleasant climate and almost constant average temperature of 21°C (70°F) during the day and around 15°C (59°F) at night. The rainy season lasts May-October, while March and April are generally considered summer, as temperatures around this time can reach up to 40°C (104°F) in parts of the country.

If you want to experience Guatemalan culture at its best, then festival time is definitely the time to go. Easter week, Christmas, the day of the Virgin of the Assumption on August 15 and New Year's are all great times to visit. There are also more modern festivals and holidays such as the annual film festival, Icaro Central, held in November. Check out what is happening before you go: Communities and towns hold various celebrations throughout the year. Updated: Aug 18, 2010.

Getting To and Away

Bus is probably the easiest way to travel to and from Guatemala City from other parts of the country. Buses leave and arrive frequently along a series of routes in all directions. For buses traveling south, it is best to head to the Central Wholesale or CENMA, Zona 12. West-bound buses leave from El Trebol, Zona 7. To go east, make a beeline to the 19th Street station in Zona 1, and buses usually leave from 8th Avenue in Zona 1 for northern destinations such as Tikal and Flores. International buses arrive into, and leave from, company offices.

La Aurora is Guatemala City's main airport and the largest in Central America. It has recently been refurbished and a wide range of airline carriers fly through La Aurora. There

are a number of international routes, but the only domestic destination reached from La Aurora is Flores. Updated: Aug 18, 2010.

Getting Around

There is plenty of public transportation to take you around Guatemala City. However, it is important to remember that petty thieves and pickpockets target commuters and visitors using the busy public transport networks. Be careful of your belongings and stay vigilant. Getting around by bus will cost you roughly $0.12 between 5 a.m. and 6 p.m., but then increases to $0.24 a trip at nighttime. Transmetro and Transurbano are convenient ways of getting around the city, costing $0.12 a trip; they usually also have police officers stationed onboard. Plenty of white taxis can also take you around for somewhere between $3.75 and $12.50, depending on how far you are going.

If you are not happy to take the white taxis, then Corporación Amarillo is a recommended yellow cab company (Tel: 1766). Driving in Guatemala City is not recommended due to the serious traffic problems and risk of crime, but if you want to get out of the city, Hertz (URL: www.rentautos.com.gt) has five offices around the city, plus an office at La Aurora Airport. Updated: Aug 18, 2010.

Safety

As in other large cities, you should be vigilant of yourself and your belongings. Guatemala City doesn't have the best reputation when it comes to safety, and as a tourist, you need to be careful. Don't have valuables such as your camera, cell phone, laptop, jewelry or wallet out in plain sight. Don't walk alone. The easiest thing to do is to just travel by taxi whenever possible. Transmetro and Transurbano are the best public transport options, and the Zona Viva is usually a much more relaxed and safer area. For assistance from the National Civil Police, dial 110, or to get in touch with the fire brigade or paramedics, call 122 and 123, respectively.

Services

For medical services, www.hospitalesdeguatemala.com and www.medicosdeguatemala.com give plenty of information on the various hospitals and medical services available in the city and country.

There is also the Red Cross (URL: www.guatemala.cruzroja.org) and the city is full of pharmacies; Carolina y H is one of the bigger pharmacies and has branches throughout the city with home delivery (URL: www.

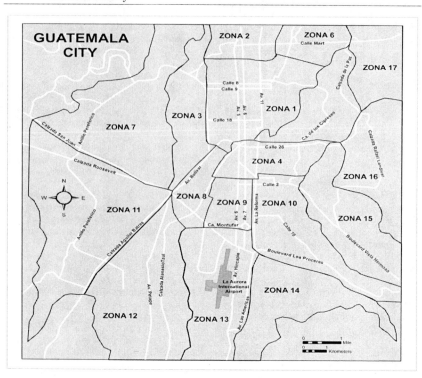

carolinayh.com). In the historic center, there is a gym called Smartraining (5a Av. 8-40. Tel: 502-223-82499; $3 per day), and Worldgym (Boulevard Los Proceres 25-74, Zona 10. Tel: 502-2423-6000, URL: www.worldgym.com. gt) is another popular gym in the Zona Viva.

You can print photos from your digital camera at Quickphoto agencies throughout the city and country. There are also lot of laundromats in Guatemala City. La Sercha (URL: www.lasercha.com) is a popular choice with locations all around the city.

For some relaxation, Rebeccana Spa (Centro Comercial Los Proceres 3rd floor. Tel: 502-2361-8514) offers massage services, a sauna, haircuts, beauty treatments and more. The spa is usually quite busy, so it is advisable to make an appointment to ensure availability. Donald's (Tiffany Plaza, 13a Ca. "A" 7-19, Zona 10.) is a good barbershop that offers cuts for both adults and children.

TOURISM

INGUAT
INGUAT is the national office of tourism. You can visit its headquarters at 7a Av. 1-17, Zona 4. Tel: 1500/502-2421-2810, E-mail: asistur@inguat.gob.gt/info@inguat.gob.gt., URL: www.visitguatemala.com. Updated: Aug 18, 2010.

CAMTUR
There is also a Chamber of Tourism, comprised of the non-profit organization Cámara de Turismo (CAMTUR), which is especially helpful when it comes to facilitating special requests and needs, and it offers comprehensive information on tour operators, transport companies, hotels, rural tourism, birdwatching and extreme sports, among other things. It is located at 12a Ca. 6-61, Zona 1. Tel: 502-2220-9916. URL: www.camtur.org. Updated: Aug 18, 2010.

MONEY
There are plenty of banks throughout the city, including Bank Gytcontinental (6a Av. 9-08, Zona 9. URL: www.gytcontinental.com.gt), Industrial Bank (7a Av. 5-10 Zona 4, in the Financial Center. URL: www.bi.com.gt) and the Banrural (Av. La Reforma 2-56 Zona 9. URL: www.banrural.com.gt).

Guatemala has a unified ATM network, so you shouldn't have any trouble withdrawing money from your home account, but take note that a small fee usually applies.

KEEPING IN TOUCH

Letters and postcards can be sent via the El Correo postal service. The prices are generally quite reasonable and there are plenty of offices situated in Guatemala City. In Zona 1, the office is located at 7a Avenida and 12a Calle. Almost all of the hotels and some restaurants offer Wi-Fi. If they don't, there are Internet cafés everywhere. An hour of Internet usually costs $1.

SHOPPING

Shopping in Guatemala is a great experience. Prices are low and there is a huge variety of quality artisan crafts, clothing, pottery and jewelry for you to take home with you. Central Market, located in the Historic Center, the Craft Market in Zona 13, and Proceres Mall in the Zona Viva are the most popular districts to shop in.

If you are looking for handicrafts from all corners of the country, make the Central Market your first stop. Located on 9th Avenue and 6a Street in the heart of the historic center, this large market is divided into several sections. One section deals almost entirely with leather goods including boots, holsters, hats and wallets. Then there is a craft section where you'll find authentic woven huipils, clothes, table centerpieces, clay items and handmade sandals.

Situated close to the airport, in Zona 13, the craft market is where you can also buy an assortment of souvenirs, ceramics, wooden objects, leather goods and jewelry. The market is generally open Monday-Saturday 8 a.m.-6 p.m.

For those after a more western shopping experience in Guatemala, there is Los Proceres Mall. Located close to some of the best hotels on 16a Calle in Zona 10, prices are mid-range to high, and there is an extensive choice of clothing stores and restaurants, along with several movie theaters. Updated: Aug 27, 2010.

Things to See and Do

A few days to explore all of Guatemala City is simply not enough. There are so many cultural, archaeological, historical and architectural sites to visit that if you are interested in seeing them all, you will need more than a weekend.

If you are low on time, then identify what you are really interested in experiencing while in Guatemala City and perhaps talk to a tour operator about the best way to maximize your time there. A visit to the National Palaceof Culture, La Plaza de la Constitución, Central Market,

the Museum of Archaeology and Ethnology, and the Kaminaljuyú Archaeological Park are some of the more popular choices among visitors. Updated: Aug 19, 2010.

CHURCHES

Catedral Metropolitana

Guatemala City's cathedral is not particularly attractive, but it was built to survive earthquakes—and it has. Indeed, it is one of the only buildings around the square that survived the city's major earthquake in 1917. Inside the cathedral are many colonial paintings, some brought here from Antigua when the capital was moved. However, the most interesting detail is on the outside: Etched into the stone pillars are the names of the vanished victims of the country's internal conflicts, a poignant affirmation of the permanent fight for justice. Daily 8 a.m.-noon and 3 p.m.-7 p.m. 7a Av. and 8a Ca., Zona 1. Updated: Sep 03, 2009.

Iglesia de San Francisco

This Catholic church was built between 1800 and 1851 and is home to numerous artistic and religious treasures. Iglesia de San Francisco also houses several famous images of the Crucified Jesus and the Virgin of the Immaculate Conception. It has 18 altars decorated in a Baroque style and draws large crowds for its famous Easter processions. Religious services are held there every day, but the most popular one is Sunday at 11 a.m. 6a Av. and 13a Ca., Zona 1. Tel: 502-2421-2800. Updated: Aug 19, 2010.

Iglesia de Santo Domingo

One of the largest churches in the capital's historic center, the Iglesia de Santo Domingo is a well-preserved example of 18th-century architecture and also has its own quiet park-like courtyard. The church was built in a Neoclassical style and features several images of the Virgin of the Rosary. Its main festival is held in October and is accompanied by a popular fair, with gambling, street food and fun rides for the kids. 12a Av. and 10a Ca.

Cerrito Del Carmen

This simple, 16th-century hermitage stands atop a wooded hill. The building enjoys a magnificent view of the city, and many say the hill was once the site of an ancient Mayan pyramid. The site hosts painting classes and musicians on Sunday, and many artists like to paint there, saying they feel that the temple holds a special energy. 1a Ca. and 12a Av. Zona 1.

GUATEMALA CITY

Iglesia San Miguel de Capuchinas

This beautiful church features Neoclassic and Baroque influences as well as altars with wooden carvings and stunning gold detail. The church has been around since 1789 and has been restored in various parts over the years. Something that sets San Miguel apart from other churches is the presence of several oil paintings by the famous religious painter Tomás de Merlo. One of the more famous examples of his work is the image of Jesús de las Palmas riding a donkey. Religious services are held daily. 10a Av. and 11a Ca., Zona 1. Updated: Aug 19, 2010.

Iglesia Yurrita

This church was built by Felipe Yurrita in honor of Our Lady of Sorrows and combines neo-Gothic elements with other more modern styles that inspired the architect at the time. The structure is dominated by a 30-meter-high (100 ft) tower that houses valuable treasures, such as splendid stained glass representations of the Stations of the Cross from Europe. Due to its elegant interior, this church has become hugely popular for weddings. Ruta 6 and Mariscal Cruz, Zona 4. Updated: Aug 20, 2010.

MUSEUMS

Museo Nacional de Arqueología y Etnología

This museum is widely regarded as the best museum on Maya culture in the world. Different rooms show various aspects of the country's history; some are filled with Mayan relics and others are filled with stone-carved monuments that depict some of the ancient civilization's defining moments. 6a Ca. and 7a Av., Finca La Aurora, Zona 13. Tel: 502-2475-4399, URL: www.munae.gob.gt. Updated: Aug 25, 2010.

Palacio Nacional de la Cultura

Every day, except Sunday, 30-minute guided tours of the former presidential palace are available. This National Palace, built by prisoners during the despotic reign of dictator Jorge Ubico, is a fascinating blend of colonial, Neoclassical and indigenous elements, including stained glass windows and murals depicting scenes of Guatemalan history. Highlights include the Patio de la Paz, Salas de Recepción, and the beautiful green courtyards, each side with five arches representing the number of syllables in the former president's name. Tours available in English and Spanish leave from inside

the main entrance every 30 minutes 9:30 a.m.-noon, and 1-4:30 p.m. 6a Ca. and 6a Av., Zona 1. Updated: Sep 02, 2009.

Museo Nacional de Historia

The personal belongings of former presidents and some of Guatemala's leading figures are some of the more unusual items at this fascinating museum. Visitors here will also find numerous objects and furniture from around 1821, when the country finally achieved independence from Spain. Opened in 1896, the Museo Nacional de Historia is also home to one of Guatemala's largest photo libraries. The building itself features stunning Renaissance-style architecture and has been used as the headquarters of numerous institutions and organizations over the years. Guided tours are available. Ca. 9a 9-70, Zona 1. URL: www.mcd.gob.gt. Updated: Aug 19, 2010.

Museo del Ferrocarril

Guatemala City's main train station was constructed in 1884 and symbolized significant technological and economic advancements in Guatemala at the time. However, over the years, the building suffered greatly from damage by natural disasters and fire. In 2003, the entire building was remodeled and today stands as a fine railway museum full of memorabilia, locomotives, clothing, photographs and interactive exhibitions relating to the country's railway history. Daily 10 a.m.-4 p.m. 9a Av. and 18a Ca., Zona 1. Tel: 502-2232-9270. Updated: Aug 19, 2010.

Museo Ixchel

This private museum focuses on one particular aspect of Maya culture: traditional dress. The museum charters Guatemala's infamous textile history as reflected in the various traditional costumes that both men and women have proudly worn since colonial times. Garments worn for special occasions and ceremonies are displayed alongside typical everyday dress, highlighting the important part textiles play in Maya culture. Museo Ixchel also serves as an attractive space for painting exhibitions, cultural events and conferences. Guided tours are available. 6a Av., Zona 10, Universidad Francisco Marroquin's Cultural Center. Tel: 502-2331-3634, URL: www.museoixchel.org. Updated: Aug 25, 2010.

Museo Popol Vuh

A part of the Francisco Marroquin University, the Popol Vuh Museum aims to preserve the rich cultural and archaeological heritage of Guatemala. It houses an extensive collection of both Mayan and colonial art from around the country and has a library specializing in art history and Guatemalan culture. The space is divided into a number of themed rooms and hosts guided tours and workshops, making it a great place to explore Guatemalan art. Monday-Saturday 9 a.m.-3 p.m. 6a Ca., Zona 10. URL: www.popolvuh.ufm.edu.gt. Updated: Aug 25, 2010.

Museo Miraflores

Miraflores Museum is situated right where the ancient Mayan city of Kaminaljuyú once stood. There, visitors can explore the permanent exhibition of Maya objects and three mounds that form part of a pre-Hispanic archaeological zone. In the lobby, there is a model of the old city showing how Guatemala City was built directly over it. The museum displays the work of many well-known contemporary artists. 7a Ca., 21-55, Zona 11, to the side of Tikal Futura Hotel. Tel: 502-2470-3415, URL: www.museomiraflores.org. Updated: Aug 25, 2010.

Museo de los Niños

The Children's Museum is one of the city's newer museums and was established as an education base for children. It promotes interaction with nature and science, and encourages young people to take an interest in natural phenomena such as electricity and earthquakes. Children are also invited to engage with literature, books, poems and tongue-twisters in a relaxed, fun environment. There are always a few temporary art exhibitions at the museum, which are designed to awaken a sense of appreciation for the arts in Guatemala's younger population. 5a Ca., 10-00, Zona 13. Tel: 502-2475-5076, URL: www.museodelosninos.com.gt. Updated: Aug 25, 2010.

Museo Nacional de Historia Natural Jorge Ibarra

Created in 1950 by naturalist Jorge Ibarra, this museum seeks to collect and preserve examples of Guatemala's flora and fauna. The focus is clearly one of learning and conservation. Displays include "The Origin of the Universe" and "The Origin of Life on Earth," featuring mineral paleontology, birds, reptiles, mammals and butterflies. There is also a small botanical garden where you can walk around and sample some of Guatemala's natural history. 6a Ca. and 7a Av., Finca La Aurora, Zona 13. Tel: 502-2472-0468. Updated: Aug 25, 2010.

Tipografía Nacional

The Tipografía Nacional was founded in 1894 for the purpose of producing and printing official texts and educational materials. Several earthquakes destroyed the original site and the organization was eventually moved to its current location. The new building, featuring Neocolonial architecture was completed in 1943. The in-house museum displays the evolution of typography machinery from the 19th century to today's more modern technology. 18a Ca. and 6a Av., Zona 1. Tel: 502-2421-5600, URL: www.tipnac.gob.gt. Updated: Aug 20, 2010.

Casa Mima

Casa Mima was opened in 1999 and offers visitors the opportunity to explore an 1870s house that still has its original furniture, kitchenware, personal effects and even toys from the early 20th century. Displays include a living room, bedroom, kitchen, bathroom and an exhibition of period costumes. There are guided visits, cultural activities and photographic exhibitions. 8s Av. and 14a Ca., Zona 1. Tel: 502-2253-6657, URL: www.portalmuseosguatemala.net. Updated: Aug 20, 2010.

Museo Nacional de Arte Moderno

The Museum of Modern Art was named after the Maestro Carlos Merida, one of Guatemala's most infamous contemporary artists. Merida's work can be found at the heart of the museum and is surrounded by temporary exhibitions by other well-known artists. A while back, visitors were treated to a display of Picasso's imaginary portraits, so big names are frequently shown at the museum. Besides various exhibitions throughout the year, the Museo de Arte Moderno also hosts a number of cultural events. 6a Ca. and 7a Av., Finca La Aurora, Zona 13. Updated: Aug 25, 2010.

PARKS AND PLAZAS

Parque Central

Also known as the Plaza de la Constitución, this large (and now quite bland) square was originally laid out as the city's central focus of power, with the cathedral and important government buildings lining its edges. A redesign in the 1980s robbed the square of much of its architectural legacy, but a bit of grandeur remains.

A brass plaque in front of the Palacio Nacional marks the country's ground zero, the point from which all distances in Guatemala are measured, and a huge national flag flies above an underground parking garage. The park is pretty quiet during the week, but on weekends, Guatemalans come here to promenade, eat ice cream and shop at the huipil market.

Of particular interest is the monument to the 1996 peace accord, but the eternal flame for peace has now been moved inside the palace. The square is also known for being the site of occasional protests. Between Ca. 6 and 8 and Av. 6 and 7. Updated: Nov 23, 2009.

Photo by: Tracy T.

Parque Arqueológico Kaminaljuyú

Before Guatemala City was ever built in the Valley of the Hermitage, there existed the ancient Maya city of Kaminaljuyú. Kaminaljuyú, which means "Hill of the Dead" in Quiché, was originally built in the vicinity of Lake Miraflores. However, a combination of the lake drying up, among other factors, attributed to its abandonment. Unfortunately, those building the new capital did not take into account the historical value of relics and ruins at the site of the former city and only a few structures and building remain.

Today, you can visit the Kaminaljuyú Archaeological Park and see tombs, ceremonial sites, ceramics and other Mayan artifacts. Many of the objects found at Kaminaljuyú can also be seen at the Museo Miraflores and the city's Museum of Archaeology and Ethnology. Open daily. 23a Av., Zona 7. Updated: Aug 20, 2010.

Mapa en Relieve

This is basically a giant map of Guatemala that shows its geography and political organization by department. Spanning some 2,000 square meters (12,500 sq ft) on a scale of 1 to 10,000, visitors can view various parts of the map from a series of platforms. The map was built by engineer Francisco Vela way back in 1905, after years of extensive study. End of Av. Simeon Canas, Zona 2. URL: www.mapaenrelieve.org. Updated: Aug 20, 2010.

Parque Centenario

Parque Centenario is where the old National Palace once stood and where Guatemala's government used to convene. It is here that Central America's independence from Spain was signed in 1821. The park has now been renovated, but retains an old theater-like structure with great acoustics where free art exhibitions and music concerts frequently take place. It is wise to leave the area before nightfall. 6a Av. and 6a Ca., next to the Plaza de la Constitución. Updated: Aug 19, 2010.

Plaza Estado de Israel

This small plaza is instantly recognizable thanks to the giant Star of David that adorns it. The square is used for Israeli celebrations and symbolizes the sturdy bond that exists between Guatemala and Israel. It was recently renovated by the local council and features several monuments and memorials to the countries Guatemala considers itself close to. Av. Reforma and 5a Ca., Zona 9. Updated: Aug 20, 2010.

Jardín Botánico

El Jardín Botánico de Guatemala was opened in 1922 and is home to multiple collections of both local and foreign plant species. Nearly extinct varieties are carefully preserved here, and there is an extensive collection of dried plants, used for research and study. The garden has also managed to recreate a number of habitats, including the wetlands where orchids and the national flower "The Monja Blanca" are cultivated. Av. La Reforma 0-63, Zona 10. URL: www.natureserve.org. Updated: Aug 20, 2010.

Plazuela España

This square is a tribute to the historical, social and cultural bonds that exist between Spain and Guatemala. The main attraction is the central fountain dedicated to King Charles III, who established Guatemala and its boundaries when the country was part of the Spanish colony. Despite surrounding traffic, the plaza is a pleasant place to rest and visitors can relax amid beautiful flowers and tiles depicting the conquest of Guatemala. 7a Av. and 12a Ca., Zona 1. Updated: Aug 20, 2010.

Plaza Berlín

This small plaza offers beautiful views of the city and acknowledges the presence of a small German community in the city. Its main attraction is a genuine piece of the infamous Berlin Wall that was brought to Guatemala City by a small group of Germans that lived in the capital. There is a small food market held here and the calm atmosphere allows visitors to sit and relax and perhaps reflect on memorable part of European history. Unfortunately, it is not recommended that you visit the plaza after dark. End of Av. de las Americas, Zona 13. Updated: Aug 25, 2010.

La Aurora Zoo

La Aurora Zoo is the largest in Guatemala and one of the best in Central America. It was established in 1924 and is home to various animal and plant species. Crowds flock to see "Bomby," an Asian elephant. You can also take a night tour of the zoo and see owls, bats and other nocturnal animals. Tuesday-Sunday 9 a.m.-5 p.m. 5a Ca., Finca La Aurora, Zona 13. Tel: 502-2475-0894, URL: www.aurorazoo. org.gt. Updated: Aug 25, 2010.

CULTURAL CENTERS

Centro Cultural Metropolitano

Located in a historic old postal building in the heart of Guatemala City's historical district, this center hosts exhibitions, plays, musical performances and dance recitals. The center is part of an initiative led by the Municipality of Guatemala and aims to keep alive the country's rich and diverse culture of artistic expression. There are also free art courses available, and the center is home to the Municipal Choir as well as the Youth Symphony Orchestra. 7a Av. 11-67, Zona 1. URL: www. muniguate.com. Updated: Aug 19, 2010.

Centro Cultural de España

Opened in 2003, the Centro Cultural de España is located in the heart of the city's vibrant historical district. The center displays lots of contemporary art and is also very involved in the conservation efforts taking place in Guatemala City's Centro Histórico. It also hosts a variety of exhibitions and workshops, and it encourages interaction with art and Guatemalan culture. The program of events is always changing, so make sure to check out the

Photo by: Guillermo Jacobs

GUATEMALA CITY

website to see what's happening when you are there. It is also possible that the center will move to a larger venue in the near future. Via 5, 1-23, Zona 4. URL: www.cceguatemala.com. Updated: Aug 20, 2010.

Teatro De Cámara

El Teatro de Cámara Hugo Carrillo was named after one of the city's most prolific producers and writers. The theater's décor was inspired by Maya culture, and its wooden interior affords the place fantastic natural acoustics. With a capacity of some 300 people, Teatro de Cámara hosts plays, concerts, lectures and other artistic recitals throughout the year. 24a Ca. and 8a Av., Zona 1. URL: www.teatronacional.com.gt. Updated: Aug 20, 2010.

LANDMARKS

Torre del Reformador

This 70-meter-high (230 ft) tower of galvanized iron was inspired by the iconic Eiffel Tower and is used as a point of reference for those exploring Guatemala City. It was built in honor of General Justo Rufino Barrios, known as "The Reformer" who historically fought to unite Central America and died a hero in battle. The bell at the top of the tower is used every year to officially start Independence Day festivities. 7a Av. and 2a Ca., Zona 9. Updated: Aug 20, 2010.

Avenida La Reforma

Built in 1897, Avenida La Reforma was inspired by the Champs Elysees in Paris, with Guatemala City's upper classes in mind. It is currently the main access point for zones 9, 10, 13 and 14, and visitors can enjoy a leisurely carriage ride down the avenue. Like the Torre del Reformador, which was also inspired by another Parisian attraction, this avenue was named after Rufino Barrios. Updated: Aug 20, 2010.

Zona Viva

Zona Viva is located mainly in Zona 10 but also includes parts of surrounding zones 9, 13 and 14. The area is popular with tourists due to a wide range of restaurants, services, nightclubs, hotels, casinos and malls. Zona Viva is also considered one of the safer parts of Guatemala City. The place is a hive of activity Thursday-Sunday, but there is also plenty of atmosphere during the week. On the December 31, the district overflows with locals and visitors eager to ring in the New Year with lots of dancing and fireworks. Updated: Aug 20, 2010.

Tours

Guatemala City has a wide range of tour operators, and a good place to look into them is at the Chamber of Tourism (URL: www.camtur.org). Tour operators specialize in exploring Maya culture, birdwatching trips, extreme sports, volcano visits, mountain hikes, and popular sites such as Lake Atitlán. Various companies will help you make arrangements for trips to Tikal, Atitlán and Antigua, as well as to other destinations in Central America. Booking with an operator can take a lot of stress out of organizing a trip, and their expertise and experience can make for a much more enjoyable and relaxing time in Guatemala. There are also several companies that cater to large groups, conventions or those attending special events.

Turansa

Established in 1988, Turansa specializes in arranging transportation and guided tours to some of the most popular tourist attractions around Guatemala City. The company is widely recognized and is a member of Guatemala's Chamber of Tourism, so you can be sure of a quality service. They are more frequently used for trips to Tikal, Antigua, Chichicastenango, Lake Atitlán and, of course, Guatemala City itself. Centro Comercial Molino 69, Zona 11,. Tel: 502-2390-5757, URL: www.turansa.com. Updated: Aug 19, 2010.

Clark Tours

With over 70 years experience in travel and tourism throughout Guatemala, Clark Tours have become a reliable and favored choice. They are particularly known for efficiently organizing accommodation and travel arrangements for conferences, conventions and special events. They have a wide network of contacts and are well known in the business, so by handing over the logistics of a trip to a company like Clark, you can save yourself a considerable amount of time and effort. Tel: 502-2412-4700, URL: www.clarktours.com. Updated: Aug 19, 2010.

Lodging

Not surprisingly, Guatemala City's lodging options are numerous and varied (it is the capital city, after all). The cheapest options in Guatemala City are found in Zona 1 and are very close to the airport, a good choice if you have an early flight or are getting in late. You'll get a lot of bang for your quetzal in the cheap to mid-range hotels and hostels in the Old City, or you can splurge on more upscale accommodations in the New Town if you want luxury accommodations and proximity to the bustling Zona Viva (Zona 10).

If you're a backpacker on a budget, you may find that it's hard to find a hostel. Guatemala City seems to have a disproportionate number of hotels to hostels, but don't worry, it doesn't mean there aren't an abundance of cheap options. Updated: Jun 30, 2010.

Zona 1

Guatemala City is divided into 25 zones, and Zona 1 is in the very heart of the city. Zona 1 is also called Centro Histórico (Historic Center), and goes from Avenida Elena to 12 Avenida and from 1 Calle to 18 Calle. There are many historic buildings in this area, such as the Palacio Nacional de la Cultura (National Palace of Culture), where the government of Guatemala used to be headquartered. Now it is a museum, but it is also the spot known as Kilómetro Cero, because all the distances in the roads and highways in Guatemala are taken with this place as the Zero Kilometer. This palace is part of the Plaza Mayor, together with the Catedral Metropolitana and the Central Park (the latter is officially the Plaza de la Constitución). The declaration of independence of Central America was signed here, in what now is Parque Centenario (Centennial Park). You will never find this plaza empty during the day, because it is always crowded with vendors, people coming and going to the buildings and bus stops surrounding it, and there is often a political protest.

Another highlight of Zona 1 is the Mercado Central (Central Market). It is behind the cathedral, and if you are looking for handicrafts, this is the place to go. While there, it is also recommended that you take some time to try the traditional Guatemalan food and tasty treats.

Use common sense and ordinary precautions (as you would anywhere) and avoid walking around unnecessarily at night. If you arrive in town at night, especially if your bus leaves you in 18 Calle, it is better to take a taxi. This area also has a number of pickpockets, usually working the large groups that congregate in this neighborhood. A good way to get the "feeling" of this area is by walking on Sexta Avenida (Av. 6), or as the locals call this activity, sextear. If you come from the south, this avenue will take you to the Plaza Central. Updated: May 04, 2010.

Lodging

Over the past 10 years, Zona 1 has really come to the forefront when it comes to accommodation options, rivaling the established lodging areas in Zonas 9, 10, 13 and 14 with hotels, hostels and rental apartments on offer. Many visitors choose to stay in Zona 1 due to its proximity to some of the more popular tourist attractions in Guatemala City. English is spoken in almost all of the hotels but a few words of Spanish go a long way. Updated: Aug 26, 2010.

Pensión Meza

(ROOMS: $6-13) Pensión Meza is a perpetual favorite among the backpacker set. The dorms and private rooms (with and without private bathrooms) are unspectacular, to say the least, and not exceptionally clean. However, the service at this family-owned place is remarkably friendly, and the hostel comes with quite a history: This is where Ché Guevara stayed during his time in Guatemala. 10a Ca. 10-17. Tel: 502-2232-3177, URL: pensionmeza@hotmail.com. Updated: Sep 08, 2010.

Hotel Chalet Suizo

(ROOMS: $14-44) This small and affordable hostel-like hotel is situated close to many of Centro Histórico's major attractions. Private rooms are available and include hot water, cable TV and free Internet access. There is also dorm accommodation, so it's a popular choice with backpackers and budget travelers. Breakfast and dinner are served in the hotel restaurant, and there is a shuttle service to and from the airport. 7a Av. 14-34. Tel: 502-2251-3786, E-mail: chaletsuizo@gmail.com, URL: www.hotelchaletsuizo.com. Updated: Aug 26, 2010.

Hotel Spring

(ROOMS: $17-45) Hotel Spring offers guests a quiet and welcoming atmosphere in the center of Zona 1. Housed in a colonial building, it features forged iron balconies and garden furniture, and wooden columns and beams. The central courtyard is an ideal spot to relax and unwind. Both private and dorm accommodation is available and the helpful staff speak enough English to help you out. 8a Av. 12-65. Tel: 502-2232-6637, URL: www.unclic.com. Updated: Aug 26, 2010.

Hotel Centenario

(ROOMS: $25-45) Hotel Centenario is located across from Centennial Park and within walking distance of the National Palace of Culture. It has 41 rooms, each with private bath, hot water and cable television. At night, there is also a parking service. The hotel has its own on-site restaurant but there are also plenty of other eateries in the vicinity. The hotel is

GUATEMALA CITY

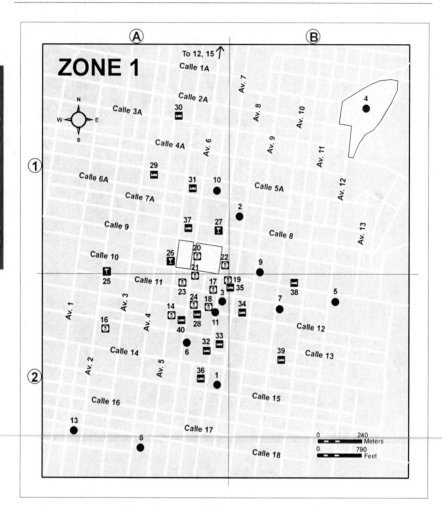

over 80 years old so the décor and facilities are somewhat neglected. 6a Ca., between 5a Av. and 6a Av. Updated: Aug 26, 2010.

Pan American Hotel

(ROOMS: $30) The Pan American Hotel is one of the few hotels that has remained a fixture in the neighborhood since Zona 1's golden years. The on-site restaurant, El Salon Real, enjoys a good reputation and is popular with both locals and visitors. Facilities include parking, safe deposit boxes, Internet and a tour desk where the staff can help you to arrange a tour to the nearby colonial city of Antigua. 9a Ca. 5-63. Tel: 502-2232-6807. URL: www.hotelpanamerican. com. Updated: Aug 26, 2010.

Hotel Tally

(ROOMS: $30-40) With a convenient location in the historic center, The Hotel Tally is an economic yet comfortable alternative to some of the more upscale hotels in the area. The hotel is relatively new and in great condition. Single, double and triple rooms all include their own private bathroom with hot water, cable TV, air conditioning and coffee making facilities. There is also a restaurant serving breakfast and lunch. Hotel Tally is connected to a car rental company so if you decide to rent one while in Guatemala City, you can do so from here. 7a Av. 15-24. Tel: 502-2232-9845. URL: www.tallyrentaautos. com. Updated: Aug 26, 2010.

GUATEMALA CITY

Activities ●

1 Casa Mima A2
2 Catedral Metropolitana B1
3 Centro Cultural Metropolitano A2
4 Cerrito Del Carmen B1
5 Iglesia de Santo Domingo B2
6 Iglesia de San Francisco A2
7 Iglesia San Miguel de Capuchinas B2
8 Museo Del Ferrocarril A2
9 Museo Nacional de Historia B1
10 Palacio Nacional de la Cultura A1
11 Plazuela España A2
12 Teatro De Cámara A1
13 Tipografía Nacional A2

Eating 🍴

14 Altuna A2
15 Arrin Cuan A1
16 Castillo Hermanos A2
17 Ciao A2
18 Katok A2
19 La Fianna A2
20 Los Cebollines A1
21 Picadilly A2
22 Pollo Campero A1
23 Restaurante Rey Sol A2
24 Sand Sand 888 A2

Nightlife 🍸

25 Black and White Lounge Bar A1
26 El Encuentro A1
27 Las Cien Puertas A1

Sleeping 🛏

28 Apart Hotel Continental A2
29 Casa de los Nazarenos A1
30 Hostal De Don Pedro A1
31 Hotel Centenario A1
32 Hotel Chalet Suizo A2
33 Hotel Colonial A2
34 Hotel Fortuna Real B2
35 Hotel Spring A2
36 Hotel Tally A2
37 Pan American Hotel A1
38 Pensión Meza B2
39 Posada BelénB2
40 Royal Palace Hotel A2

Hotel Colonial

(ROOMS: $30) The Colonial Hotel features the type of colonial architecture that attracts tourists to this part of the city. The huge carved doors welcome guests into hallways full of colonial-style furniture, mirrors and antiques dating from various periods in Guatemala's history. The rooms are clean, comfortable, and come with a private bathroom, hot water and a television. There is plenty of parking and if it is full, it will try to accommodate you in a nearby sister hotel. 7 Av. 14-19. Tel: 502-2232-6722, URL: www. hotelcolonial.net. Updated: Aug 26, 2010.

Casa de los Nazarenos

(ROOMS: $30-65) Besides offering hotel accommodation, the Casa de los Nazarenos also serves as a shopping center, a café-restaurant, a boutique and an art gallery. A few years back, a group of young entrepreneurs came together to create this unique hotel in an old colonial building. On the ground floor, you will find the commercial activity, above are the comfortable rooms. Each of the rooms has its own private bathroom with hot water, cable TV and WiFi access. The restaurant also comes highly recommended and serves regional dishes, pastries and freshly prepared desserts. 5 Ca. 3-36. Tel: 502-2332-5013, URL: www.casadelosnazarenos.com. Updated: Aug 26, 2010.

Hostal De Don Pedro

(ROOMS: $35-45) This hotel, housed in a renovated colonial house, is full of old world charm and is considered a part of the city's cultural heritage. Its central location allows guests to get to nearby attractions such as the Central Mercado, the Catedral Metropolitana and the National

GUATEMALA CITY

Palace of Culture with ease. Each of the rooms has a private bathroom with hot water, cable TV, WiFi and a telephone. 4 Av. 3-25. Tel: 502-2285-3434, E-mail: info@ hostaldedonpedro.com, URL: www.hostaldedonpedro.com. Updated: Aug 26, 2010.

Posada Belén

(ROOMS: $39) Posada Belén enjoys a great reputation in the area for its welcoming atmosphere and museum-like ambiance. The comfortable and warm accommodation is adorned with beautiful pieces of art and a collection of authentic Maya pieces. Modern facilities include hot water, a laundry service, WiFi access and a restaurant serving tasty food throughout the day. Tel: 502-2232-6178, URL: www.posadabelen.com. Updated: Aug 26, 2010.

Royal Palace Hotel

(ROOMS: $45) The Royal Palace Hotel is one of the few luxury hotels in the Centro Histórico, and it has over 75 rooms. The accommodation is welcoming, and the hotel has become a favorite for conventions, conferences and special events. There is ample parking, several spacious meeting rooms, and a business center with telephone, fax and Internet. All of the rooms are well equipped with modern conveniences, and there is an excellent on-site bar and restaurant. 6 Av. from 12-66, Historic Center. Tel: 502-2416-4400, URL: www.hotelroyalpalace.com.

Hotel Fortuna Real

(ROOMS: $50) Hotel Fortuna Royal has everything you might expect from a luxury hotel. The warm, inviting rooms are elegantly lit and decorated in a modern style. Each have their own private bathroom with hot water, air conditioning and a laundry service. It also has a convenient café/bar/restaurant serving traditional and international dishes. 12 Ca. 8-42, Zona 1. Tel: 502-2238-2484, URL: www.hotelfortunaroyal.com. Updated: Aug 26, 2010.

Apart Hotel Continental

The Apart Hotel Continental enjoys a great location, close to restaurants, shops, cinemas, museums, a post office, banks and plenty of nightlife venues. Double, triple and family rooms are available and have private bathrooms with hot water, telephone and a TV. There is also apartment-style accommodation, which can be rented for the week or a month. The décor is by no means modern but overall, the hotel is quite comfortable. 12 Ca. 6-10. Tel: 502-2251-8237. Updated: Aug 26, 2010.

Restaurants

Guatemala City has a wide range of restaurants to suit all tastes and budgets. There are plenty of Guatemalan specialties to try, and many restaurants offer a different take on a traditional favorite. Regional dishes include kak'ik, subanik, jocon with tamales and spicy sauce, chuchitos, and paches made from corn. Restaurants like Arrin Cuan, Pollo Campero and Katok offer good examples of the local cuisine. If you want to sample some international food during your stay than there are also plenty of options. Ciao Ristorante serves tasty Italian cuisine, Sand-Sand 888 offers good Chinese food and Los Cebollines serves great Mexican fare. In general eating out in Guatemala City is very affordable and a fantastic way to experience the atmosphere of the city and the local culture. Updated: Aug 26, 2010.

TRADITIONAL GUATEMALAN

Katok

Katok is a restaurant chain that started out in Tecpan, Chimaltenango (a famous Maya archaeological site). As in its outlets in Antigua and other parts of the country, the Centro Histórico branch serves regional cuisine at reasonable prices. Among the more popular dishes are tasty meat stews and its renowned smoked sausage. 12 Ca. between 6 Av. and 7 Av. Tel: 502-2230-5794, URL: www.ahumadoskatok.com. Updated: Aug 26, 2010.

Arrin Cuan

Arrin Cuan is one of the more traditional restaurants in Guatemala's historic center. It serves a mixture of traditional Guatemalan food and international cuisine. There are stews, soups, BBQ dishes, and exotic meats such as deer, turtle and agouti on the menu. At peak times, diners can enjoy some live marimba music while they eat. There is also plenty of car parking on-site, and the restaurant is open for breakfast, lunch and dinner. 5 Av. 3-27. Tel: 502-2238-0242, URL: www.arrincuan.com. Updated: Aug 26, 2010.

VEGETARIAN

Restaurante Rey Sol

(ENTREES: $1-2.50) Rey Sol is a vegetarian restaurant and bakery with a fresh and friendly atmosphere. Rey Sol is open for lunch and dinner Monday-Sunday, and a tasty vegetarian breakfast buffet is served every Sunday morning. At lunch, there is a varied selection of entrées and side dishes, as well as beverages, breads, desserts and soups. Dishes that come highly recommended include the eggplant lasagna and its wholesome vegetable soups. 11 Ca. 5-51, Zona 18; Ca. 5-36, Zona 1. Tel: 502-2232-3516, E-mail: restaurantereysol@yahoo.com. Updated: Jul 09, 2009.

ITALIAN

Picadilly
(ENTREES: $3-5) This restaurant serves a range of international cuisine, but predominantly Italian. It is open for breakfast, lunch and dinner and offers affordable good-quality food. The pizza here is very popular and can be bought whole or by the slice. Spread over two levels, the atmosphere is busy but friendly, and there are TV screens situated on both levels. 6 Av. and 11 Ca., Historic Center. Tel: 502-2429-6436. Updated: Aug 26, 2010.

Ciao
(ENTREES: $8) This restaurant operates under the concept of "Slow Food," and specializes in Italian-style meats, pizza and pasta. According to its owners, it's the only true Italian restaurant in the historic center of Guatemala City. Food is prepared when ordered but is certainly worth the wait. A lunch that includes a salad, main dish and a drink usually costs about $8, and there is a wide selection of seafood on the menu. 11 Ca. and 7 Av. URL: www.ciao.com.gt. Updated: Aug 27, 2010.

CHINESE

Sand Sand 888
(ENTREES: $6) For lovers of Chinese food, Restaurant Sand Sand 888 has a varied and delicious menu, with generous portions and prices starting at around $6 per plate. Some of the most popular dishes include typical favorites such as chow mein, wantons, chop suey and a number of meatless dishes. The restaurant is large and decorated in a traditional Cantonese style. 12 Ca. 6-17, half a block from the Arco de Correos. Tel: 502-2230-5671. Updated: Aug 26, 2010.

MEXICAN

Los Cebollines
Los Cebollines Restaurant offers Mexican food with a hint of Guatemalan flavor. Highlights include the chicken fajitas, tacos and tortas, Tlalpeño soup, and tasty cuts of grilled meat. It also has a lively bar and a breakfast buffet. Do not expect a meal as spicy as in Mexico, but the freshly prepared dishes and the colorful traditional presentation are sure to satisfy. 6 Av. and 10 Ca., Historic Center. Tel: 502-2232-7750, URL: www.cebollines.com. Updated: Aug 26, 2010.

FAST FOOD

Pollo Campero
Pollo Campero is among the more popular restaurants in Guatemala and the only one that has been fully internationalized. Its menu is simple and its prices are low. A walk through the Centro Histórico guarantees a sighting of more than one of these busy restaurants. It gets a bit crowded at lunchtime, when it can be difficult to get a table. It also offers a delivery service. 7 Av. 1911-1949; also on 5 Av. and 9-9, among other locations. URL: www.campero.com. Updated: Aug 27, 2010.

INTERNATIONAL

La Fianna
La Fianna is a restaurant and art gallery specializing in breakfast and lunch. Housed in a remodeled former home, it offers a cheap buffet in a pleasant environment. The cuisine is international with plenty of choice, and there is also a decent selection of desserts. One of the quirks of this place is that the artworks displayed throughout are for sale. There is a VIP area, which can be booked in advance, and there is on-site parking. 10 Ca. 7-24. Tel: 502-2251-1892. Updated: Aug 27, 2010.

Altuna
The food at Altuna is inspired by the famous Iberian gastronomy native to Spain. The warm ambiance is enhanced with wooden furniture and wrought iron ornaments, an ideal setting for a tasty meal of paella or some seafood. The varied menu is accompanied by an extensive wine list that includes both domestic and imported offerings. On Sundays, there is also a children's play area. 5 Av. 12-31. Tel: 502-2253-6743, URL: www.restaurantealtuna.com. Updated: Aug 27, 2010.

Castillo Hermanos
(ENTREES: $20) Stepping inside La Casa del Callejón, Castillo Hermanos is like stepping into a time capsule. Each of the four spacious dining rooms features

furniture dating back to the last century, crystal, silverware, Persian rugs, paintings, old photographs and even a fully intact 20th-century bedroom fully. The menu consists of a selection of pastas, meats and seafood, and there is also valet parking on-site. 2 Av. "A" 13-20. Tel: 502-2366-5671. Updated: Aug 27, 2010.

Nightlife

Las Cien Puertas
This is a great place for a quiet drink with friends. While you're there, don't forget to sign your name on the wall like the thousands of other previous guests. Thursday-Saturday from 7 p.m. Pasaje Aycinena 8-44, between 6 and 7 Av. Updated: Aug 27, 2010.

Black and White Lounge Bar
(DRINKS: $3) The Black and White Lounge Bar is Guatemala City's most well-known gay bar, famous for its wide variety of live entertainment, such as concerts and fashion shows. It even has a secured parking lot. Wednesday-Saturday 7 p.m.-1 a.m. 11 Ca. 2-54. Tel: 502-5904-1758, URL: www.blackandwhitebar.com. Updated: Aug 27, 2010.

El Encuentro
El Encuentro is a bar that guarantees fun and a good relaxed atmosphere. Great pastries and sandwiches also make this an ideal place to grab lunch. Monday-Saturday 11 a.m.-11 p.m. 5 Av. 10-52. Tel: 502-2232-9235. Updated: Aug 27, 2010.

Zona 4

Situated between the Centro Histórico and Zona 9, Zona 4 is one of the most interesting of Guatemala City's zones. It has a wide variety of attractions for the traveler. One of the most popular is Cuatro Grados Norte (four degrees north), which is a pedestrian and green area with restaurants, bars, galleries and cultural centers. The Centro Cultural de España, for example, continuously has exhibitions, workshops for children and adults, and more. Many important buildings are also in Zona 4; in fact, INGUAT (Guatemalan Tourism Institute) has its main offices there. There is also the Centro Cívico and its government buildings: the Banco de Guatemala, Palacio de la Justicia, Municipalidad de Guatemala (City Hall), and others. The largest and most important theater and cultural center in the country,the Centro Cultural Miguel Ángel Asturias (or Teatro Nacional),

is located in the zone. This large and beautiful theater was built by Efraín Recinos, one of the most respected artists in Guatemala today. There are many activities and presentations all year round. It also houses some art schools, and a school of marimba is being built on the premises. Make sure to check the website of this center.

If you arrive by "chicken bus" to Guatemala City, it is highly probable that you will end up in La Terminal de la Zona 4, one of the largest markets in the country. It is an agglomeration of stores, buses and people. Check in advance the cultural agenda of 4 Grados Norte and Centro Cultural M. A. Asturias. Updated: May 04, 2010.

Restaurants

In Zona 4, you will find all types of restaurants, from simple establishments serving regional dishes to fast food outlets and upscale eateries. Highlights in the area include Vesuvio's Pizzeria known for its freshly oven-baked pizzas, La Bandeja buffet restaurant, and Restaurante El Encanto, where you can get some decent typical Chinese food. For those who prefer fast food, there is the expected McDonalds, Taco Bell, Burger King and Subway, among others. It may not be one of the better-known areas for eating out in Guatemala City, but there are still a few hidden gems. Updated: Aug 27, 2010.

Hot Dog Alley
(ENTREES: $1-2.50) Just down the road from the Centro Cultural de España and the Guatemalan stock exchange is Hot Dog Alley, a great budget place in an area of mid-range restaurants. What is actually a group of streets full of hot dog cafés gets super busy between noon and 1 p.m. when the hungry office crowds descend. At Shucos El Chino, on Via 8, 328, Alfredo serves up longaniza, chorizo, beef, bacon and salami hot sandwiches with salad for $1, a double dog for $1.30, or a super grande with five meats for $2.50. It also has great homemade cilantro and hot sauces. The service is quick, so it's great for a fast lunch or a quick snack before hitting the bars nearby. Beers and soft drinks available. Be aware that the bathroom is very basic. Daily noon-7 p.m. Near Ruta 4 and Via 8. Updated: Sep 02, 2009.

La Barra
(ENTREES: $3) La Barra is part of a chain of restaurants that offers a buffet menu for just $3, live music, a bar and a dance floor. You will find two in Zona 4 serving the same menu

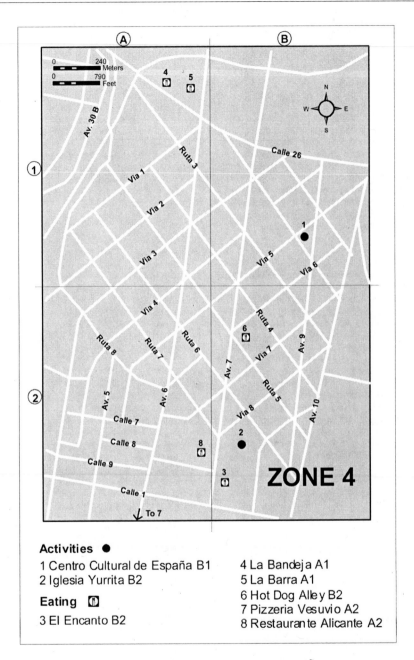

Activities ●
1 Centro Cultural de España B1
2 Iglesia Yurrita B2

Eating 🍴
3 El Encanto B2

4 La Bandeja A1
5 La Barra A1
6 Hot Dog Alley B2
7 Pizzeria Vesuvio A2
8 Restaurante Alicante A2

and playing the same popular music from noon onwards. Both get quite busy at night and are a popular place to start a night out in Guatemala City. Via 2, 4-19, 3rd level of Gran Centro Comercial. Updated: Aug 27, 2010.

Pizzería Vesuvio 🍴

This traditional pizzeria was established by an Italian immigrant who wanted to show Guatemala City's inhabitants what good oven-baked pizza was all about. The restaurant has a friendly atmosphere and is popular with the locals. Vesuvio's also has its own renewable reserve where it gets the fuel for the authentic wood-burning ovens. 6 Av. 6-42. Tel: 502-2334-1017, URL: www.pizzavesuvio.com.gt. Updated: Aug 27, 2010.

La Bandeja

(ENTREES: $4-7) The Bandeja Restaurant serves breakfast, lunch, a dinner buffet, and a range cakes and desserts. Its natural juices of tamarind Rosa de Jamaica and the house horchata come highly recommended by locals and visitors alike. It's pretty busy during the day and is a popular spot for those who work in the surrounding offices and businesses. El Gran Centro Comercial, 6 Av. Tel: 502-2353-2334. Updated: Aug 27, 2010.

El Encanto

(ENTREES: $6-12) Restaurant El Encanto specializes in Chinese food and is a great place to socialize while enjoying some tasty Cantonese dishes. A popular highlight on the menu is the chop suey with cashew nuts. There isn't much parking at the restaurant; it is usually easier to park nearby and walk there. 7 Av. 8-31, near the Torre del Reformador (Tower of the Reformer). Tel: 502-2332-4879. Updated: Aug 27, 2010.

Restaurante Alicante

(ENTREES: $6-15) Alicante Restaurant has been around for many years and serves a varied menu of tasty Spanish food. Decorated with a tasteful maritime theme, this restaurant offers seafood dishes, casseroles and delicious paella. It also has a great selection of wines. 7 Av. 7-46. Tel: 502-233-13647. Updated: Aug 27, 2010.

Zona 9

Zona 9 is one of Guatemala City's more modern districts. Besides banks, office buildings, embassies and government institutions, there are also plenty of entertainment options. The area is home to more than one large shopping center, and there are lots of bars and restaurants offering Guatemalan cuisine, BBQ and oriental food. There are not as many hotels as in other parts of the city but since the area is one of the more modern, the hotels here are generally of a high standard and designed with those visiting on business in mind. It is worth taking note that rush hour traffic is intense around Zona 9 between 7 a.m.-9 a.m. and between 4 p.m.-8 p.m. Updated: Aug 27, 2010.

Lodging

There are plenty of accommodation options in Zona 9, and the area is perfect for those who want to stay within easy reach of the airport, the historic center and the Zona Viva. Zona 9 is generally pretty quiet at night but comes alive during the day with economic activity. Some hotels and the Conquistador Plaza are considered by many to be part of Zona 9, but are technically located in Zona 4. There are plenty of restaurants and shops in the area. In terms of transport, taxis are everywhere, or you can take the public Transmetro ($0.12), which is regarded as quite safe. Updated: Aug 27, 2010.

Hotel Carillon

(ROOMS: $40) The Hotel Carrillon is a small but comfortable hotel situated in the heart of Zona 9. It only has 15 rooms, so it's best to contact them and check availability in advance. All of the rooms have a private bathroom with hot water, and breakfast is included in the rate. Rooms can also be rented for weeks or months at a discounted price. 5 Av. 11-25. Tel: 502-2332-4036, URL: www. hotelcarrillongt.com. Updated: Aug 27, 2010.

Residencia Del Sol

(ROOMS: $60) Residencia del Sol is a great option for those interested in luxury and convenience while staying in Guatemala City. The comfortable rooms have private bathrooms with hot water, cable TV and WiFi, and they afford guests a great view of the surrounding city landscape. The rate includes a tasty breakfast, and the hotel provides a shuttle service to and from the airport for a reasonable fee. There is also on-site parking for guest use. 3 Ca. 6-42. Tel: 502-2360-4823, URL: www.residenciadelsol.com. Updated: Aug 27, 2010.

Hotel Villa Española

(ROOMS: $60-100) The colonial-style Hotel Villa Española is a good choice in terms of price and quality. It is quite a large hotel, with over 60 rooms and suites. Each of the spacious rooms has a private bathroom with hot water, cable TV, telephone and storage space. The hotel also has its own restaurant called El Escorial, which serves good-quality food throughout the day. The on-site bar La Rioja, open noon-10 p.m., is also a pleasant place to relax and unwind. 2 Ca. 7-51. Tel: 502-2332-2515, URL: www.hotelvillaespanola.com. Updated: Aug 27, 2010.

High Conquistador

(ROOMS: $70) El Conquistador Hotel is one of the most traditional hotels in the city. The décor pays homage to some of the great conquerors of America, including Pedro de Alvarado and Hernán Cortés. It has 150 rooms, junior suites and apartments with air conditioning and a private bathroom with hot water. Facilities include a gym, pool, spa, beauty salon, high speed Internet access, parking amenities, a 24-hour taxi rank, a business center, bar and an upscale restaurant. Taking into account the level of service and amenities, the rates here are some of the most competitive in the city. The late night disco/bar hosts a variety of music and dance shows, and there are comedy gigs on weekends. Via 5, 4-68. Tel: 502-2424-4444, URL: www.hotelconquistador.com.gt.

The Plaza Hotel

The Plaza Hotel is a popular one. Located close to several of Zona 9's shopping spots, it boasts over 60 rooms, Internet access, laundry service and a large pool. There is also ample parking for guests and a taxi rank right in front of the main entrance. The La Pergola is a nice place for a drink, and the Las Flores restaurant serves national and international cuisine in a friendly atmosphere. Via 7, 6-16. Tel: 502-2331-6173, URL: www.hotelplaza-guate.com. Updated: Aug 27, 2010.

Restaurants

Zona 9 is a favorite option when it comes to looking for quality dining out options. The choice is varied, but a lot of the city's better BBQ and oriental restaurants can be found in this district. La Media Cancha is a popular BBQ choice, and the Pirex puyazo or lomito comes highly recommended. Chinese restaurant, Queen China, is another Zona 9 favorite with both locals and visitors in search of authentic Asian cuisine at a reasonable price. Updated: Aug 27, 2010.

La Media Cancha

La Media Cancha specializes in BBQ-style dining and offers a range of meat options, a substantial salad bar, and tasty accompaniments or combo specials. The meat is high quality, and the prices are affordable. It's a popular restaurant so make a reservation if possible, particularly on Fridays and Saturdays. Tuesday-Sunday noon-close. 13 Ca. 4-71. Tel: 502-2331-6463. Updated: Aug 27, 2010.

China Queen

China Queen is regarded by many as the best Asian restaurant in the area. It is not the only option in Zona 9, but it has a great reputation

GUATEMALA CITY

for serving tasty typical fare such as sweet and sour pork, chow mein, Cantonese duck and authentic Chinese tea. There is also a bar, ample parking, and the décor epitomizes Chinese style with oriental furnishings and giant live fish tanks. 6 Av. 14-04 and 16 Ca. Tel: 502-233-10519. Updated: Aug 27, 2010.

Zona 10

Zona 10 is a luxury residential area, a commercial center and one of the city's best nightlife areas. The district is considered very safe, and visitors will frequently see civil police patrolling the streets. There is also a high-level private security in the area organized by the local hotels, restaurants and businesses. All of these safety measures are very reassuring, but it is still necessary to maintain a certain level of awareness while out and about. Zona 10 is also known as "Zona Viva," thanks to its vibrant nightlife scene. There are plenty of trendy restaurants, bars, casinos and clubs to choose from. Nightclubs and bars are frequently closing and reopening, so it is best to ask locally where the best places are to go on a night out. Updated: Aug 27, 2010.

Lodging

Zona 10 is one of the best areas in the city when it comes to accommodation. Prices here can be a little bit more expensive than elsewhere in Guatemala City but the quality usually warrants the high price. There and lots of international and smaller hotels to choose from, as well as rental apartments for those planning a longer stay in the capital. Many of the hotels here have a tour desk and will be happy to help arrange day trips, city tours and transport to and from the airport. In terms of hotel facilities, expect gyms, pools, spas, conference amenities and Internet access in the majority of places around Zona 10. Updated: Aug 27, 2010.

MID-RANGE

Posada De Los Próceres

(ROOMS: $40) Hotel Posada de los Próceres is a convenient and economical option. Located right beside the Próceres Mall, it's a great choice for those interested in doing some shopping during their stay. The hotel is also within walking distance of Zona Viva's vibrant nightlife scene. All of the welcoming rooms have private bathrooms with hot water. Shuttles are available to and from the nearby airport,

and there is a 24-hour taxi service right across from the hotel entrance. 16 Ca. 2-40. Tel: 502-2385-4302, URL: www.posadadelosproceres.com. Updated: Aug 27, 2010.

La Casa Grande ♪

(ROOMS: $60) Hotel La Casa Grande is a beautiful French-style mansion, located just a few steps from the United States Embassy. Situated on Avenida Reforma, this affordable hotel is surrounded by bronze statues and monuments, and is a great place from which to explore all that Zona 10 has to offer. The atmosphere is fresh, bright and welcoming, and each room has a private bathroom with hot water. There is also an on-site restaurant, a bar, lounge, Internet access point and a tour desk. Av. la Reforma 7-67. Tel: 502-2332-0914, URL: www.casagrande-gua.com. Updated: Aug 27, 2010.

Hotel Santander Plaza

Santander Plaza Hotel is an excellent choice for both tourists and those visiting Guatemala City on business. Situated in the heart of Zona Viva, this reasonably priced hotel is also conveniently close to the airport. The rooms are spacious and comfortable, and the suites offer panoramic views of the city. The hotel is designed for medium-to-long stays, and hosts a range of amenities, including bottled water, airport shuttle service, gym and a babysitting service. 15 Ca. and 4 Av. Tel: 502-2384-9300, URL: www.santanderplaza.com. Updated: Aug 27, 2010.

HIGH END

The Radisson Hotel

(ROOMS: $120) The Radisson Hotel attracts both tourists and business guests with its high level of service and its elegant, restful atmosphere. The rooms offer guests spectacular views of the surrounding city and are well equipped with modern facilities. There are two on-site restaurants; Hemingway's serves tasty regional and international cuisine, while the Sushi Bar serves both classic and more contemporary varieties of freshly prepared sushi. Guests can also avail of a shuttle service to and from Guatemala City Airport. 1 Av. 12-46. Tel: 502-2421-5151, URL: www.radissonguatemala.com. Updated: Aug 27, 2010.

Mercure Casa Veranda

(ROOMS: $120) The Veranda House Hotel is an ideal choice for people who want to enjoy a prolonged stay in Guatemala City. One- or two-bedroom suites are available and come with a well-equipped kitchen, coffee maker, WiFi access, cable TV, work space, telephone and soundproofed windows. The hotel also has a number of conference rooms and the on-site Spicy Restaurant serves international cuisine throughout the day. 12 Ca. 1-24. Tel: 502-2411-4100, URL: www.accorhotels.com. Updated: Aug 27, 2010.

Hotel Westin Camino Real

The Hotel Westin Camino Real is one of the most renowned hotels in the country. It is a popular venue for international conferences and large social events. Established over 50 years ago, the Westin is decorated with beautiful artworks, antique furniture and features European-style architecture. There are over 200 en-suite rooms, all of which include cable TV, a mini-bar, WiFi, luxurious bedding and a telephone. Amenities include a concierge service, 24-hour taxi rank, a gym, a spa, breakfast buffet and a stylish on-site bar and restaurant. Camino Real Ca. 0-20. Tel: 502-2333-3300 URL: www.caminoreal.com.gt Updated: Aug 27, 2010.

Restaurants

There are plenty of restaurants to suit all tastes and budgets in Zona 10. Casa Chapina serves great regional cuisine and Tamarindo specializes in fusion cuisine. Visitors can enjoy Peruvian fare at the Inka Grill, Spanish food at Mario's or Altuna, or some excellent seafood at the Palmas Del Mar. Whatever you feel like eating, you will have a host of options to choose from in Zona 10. Updated: Aug 27, 2010.

TRADITIONAL GUATEMALAN

Casa Chapina

(ENTREES: $5-9) Casa Chapina Restaurant is a great place to enjoy traditional Guatemalan food and is within easy reach of some of the district's most popular hotels. Favorite dishes include stew, pepian, hilachas and a range of combo plates where you can sample various aspects of the regional cuisine. There is a BBQ area out back where the friendly hostess serves up tasty corn tortillas, hot off the grill. 2 Av. and 14 Ca. Tel: 502-4046-3144/2367-6688, URL: www.restaurantecasachapina.com. Updated: Aug 27, 2010.

PIZZA

Circus Bar

(ENTREES: $7) The Circus Bar Restaurant and pizzeria is a bohemian-style eatery with a circus theme. The tasty pizzas and calzones on the menu are named after various circuses from around the world. There is also an extensive drinks menu and favorites include the Hula-Hula and the Pana-Banana. Guests can enjoy live music while they eat and marvel at the vast collection of circus posters that adorn the walls. 15 Ca. 2-77. Tel: 502-2333-7470, URL: www.circusbar.com.gt. Updated: Aug 27, 2010.

CAFÉ/BAR

Café Dei Fiori

(ENTREES: $4.50) The Café Dei Fiori is located in a quiet area on the edge of the Zona Viva, but within easy walking distance from the center. It is a popular spot for lunch or a coffee on the sunny terrace. There is a varied selection of desserts and WiFi access. 15 Av. 15-66. Tel: 502-2363-5888, URL: www.caffedeifiori.com. Updated: Aug 27, 2010.

INTERNATIONAL

Restaurante De Mario

(ENTREES: $5) Situated in the heart of Zona Viva, Mario's serves tasty Spanish food in a contemporary Mediterranean setting. Specialties include squid, seafood and paella. There is also an extensive drinks list featuring quality wines and liquors. 1 Av. 12-98. Tel: 502-2339-2331. Updated: Aug 27, 2010.

Restaurante Zumo

(ENTREES: $12) Zumo Restaurant welcomes guests with a warm and friendly atmosphere, several intimate dining spaces and fusion-style food. The restaurant has its own cava and is happy to arrange private rooms for larger groups of diners or special events. It also cater sto vegetarians and those with lactose or seafood allergies if you notify them in advance. 1 Av. 12-16. Tel: 502-2334-6316, URL: www.zumo.com.gt. Updated: Aug 27, 2010.

ASIAN

Tamarindo's

(ENTREES: $10) Tamarindo's specializes in fusion food and successfully experiments with cuisines from around the world, including Thai, Japanese and Vietnamese sweet and sour flavors. For lovers of vegetarian food, there are several options available. Guests can dine in the outdoor garden area or in the warmly decorated interior. Tamarindo's Restaurant has been recognized for the high quality of its food both locally and internationally. There is also a sushi menu and a wide variety of drinks to choose from at the bar. 11 Ca. 2-19. Tel: 502-2360-5630, URL: www.tamarindos.com.gt. Updated: Aug 27, 2010.

PERUVIAN

Inka Grill
The similarities between Guatemalan and Peruvian cuisine can be sampled at this popular eatery. The menu includes a number of Peruvian specialties featuring corn, potatoes, poultry and seafood. Guests can also take advantage of a two-for-one offer with the Round Creole menu. 2 Av. 14-22. Tel: 502-2363-3013, URL: www.graninka.com. Updated: Aug 27, 2010.

SEAFOOD

Palmas del Mar
In recent years, Palmas del Mar restaurant has become a firm favorite for excellent seafood and grilled meat dishes. Located in a small mansion, there is both outdoor and indoor dining and a parking area that gets very busy during the weekends. Outstanding dishes include the "Sea and Earth" mixed ceviche and fried shrimp in garlic. 6 Av. 12-24. Tel: 502-2360-5247, E-mail: palmasdelmarsa@gmail.com. Updated: Aug 27, 2010.

Nightlife

William Shakespeare Pub
Known simply as Shakespeare Pub, this one is a favorite with local expats. Featuring live music and cheap drinks, The Shakespeare Pub has been a local fixture for 25 years. 13 Ca. and 1 Av. Tel: 502-2331-2641. Updated: Aug 27, 2010.

Guru
(COVER: $15) This trendy local bar comes with a $15 cover charge and open bar; that's all you really need to know. Has guarded parking. Thursday-Saturday 8 p.m.-1 a.m. 13 Ca. 3-31. Updated: Aug 27, 2010.

Fisher
Staffed by friendly bartenders who know how to pour a drink, Fisher is a great place to come chill out and nibble on nachos and buffalo wings. Late at night, every available space is taken up by people dancing, as the bar does not have a dance floor. 12 Ca. 3-46. Updated: Aug 27, 2010.

Go Deep
Go Deep is a good place to chill and listen to music. It sometimes has DJs and live music. Tuesday-Saturday 6 p.m.-1 a.m. 11 Ca. 3-42. Tel: 502-2360-5078. Updated: Aug 27, 2010.

Esperantos Bar
El Bar Esperantos is a small, popular bar with a bohemian vibe, owned and operated by Pancho, who goes out of his way to ensure his customers have a good time. Service can be a bit slow as the kitchen staff doubles as bar/waitstaff. Tuesday-Saturday 7 p.m.-close 11 Ca. 3-36. Updated: Aug 27, 2010.

Mr. Cocktail
Mr. Coctail has a small and cozy environment with a warm, friendly atmosphere. No cover charge except for big events. Tuesday-Saturday 5 p.m.-close. 3 Av. and 12 Ca. Tel: 502-4918-1290. Updated: Aug 27, 2010.

Bar Deportivo Legends
If you are in Guatemala City and have a craving for karaoke, hot wings, nachos or pizza then Legends is the place to go. With several big screen TVs, it's also a good place to catch a game. Edificio Paseo Plaza, local 108, 3 Av. 12-38. Updated: Aug 27, 2010.

Cocoloco
Cocoloco is a popular local venue for DJs and the occasional dance contest. The crowd can sometimes make it difficult to enter, so arrive early. Be careful, many muggings and robberies have been reported in the area around the club. Tuesday-Saturday 5 p.m.-close. 15 Ca. and 2 Av. Updated: Aug 27, 2010.

Mynt
The Mynt bar is known for its $8 all-you-can-drink special. Good atmosphere and music are additional perks. Thursday-Saturday. Edificio Paseo Plaza Business Center, 2nd level, 3 Av. 12-36. Updated: Aug 27, 2010.

Zona 13
Zona 13 has traditionally been an upper-class residential neighborhood. However, in recent years, a number of hotels, shops and restaurants have begun to appear. Many of the larger houses in this sector have

been converted to hostels and apartments for tourists. The influx of tourists has seen many Internet cafés, supermarkets and gyms spring up in this traditional old neighborhood. Zona 13 is located near the La Aurora airport, the zoo, several museums and a local crafts market. Updated: Aug 27, 2010.

Lodging

From the Hotel Casablanca to hostels, you should have no trouble finding comfortable accommodations to fit any budget. Most are located within walking distance of the airport, but it is highly recommended that visitors take a taxi, especially at night. Updated: Aug 27, 2010.

Hostal Café City

(ROOMS: $15 and up) The Hostal Café City offers dorm rooms with shared bath starting at $10 per night, as well as private rooms starting at $15 with bath. On-site parking and airport shuttle service are available as well. This charming colonial-style hostel has a relaxed, friendly atmosphere and is a great way to meet fellow travelers. WiFi and breakfast are included. 7 Av. A 17-17. Tel: 502-4365-8583, URL: www.hostalcafé city.com. Updated: Aug 27, 2010.

The Airport Inn

(ROOMS: $20 and up) A good bet for those wanting a low-priced private room without sacrificing the community feeling of the hostel. With a social area featuring DVD library, book exchange and board games, this a great place to meet and swap info with other travelers. Private rooms start at $20 per night, with dorms also available for $10. Includes free continental breakfast and airport pickup. 15 Ca. A 7-52, Colonia Aurora I. Tel: 502-2261-3180, URL: www.theairportinn.com. Updated: Aug 27, 2010.

Hostal Villa Toscana

(ROOMS: $40) Hostal Villa Toscana has 12 elegantly decorated private rooms with an array of services and a prime location close to the airport. With rooms starting at $40, it's a bit pricey for a hostel, but you get an on-site restaurant, WiFi, laundry and taxi, as well as tours of the country. Guests have full access to the gym and pool at the nearby club La Aurora at no extra charge. 16 Ca. 8-20, Colonia Aurora I. Tel: 502-2261-2854, URL: www.hostlvillatoscana.com. Updated: Aug 27, 2010.

Hotel Casablanca

(ROOMS: $40) Even the most stressed traveler will have no trouble relaxing in this oasis in the city. All rooms come complete with hot water, WiFi and cable TV. With a friendly staff and a great, reasonably priced restaurant, this is a great value. Rooms start at $40, and free airport shuttle is included in the price. 15 Ca. C 7-35, Colonia Aurora I. Tel: 502-2261-3116, URL: www.hotelcasablancainn.com. Updated: Aug 27, 2010.

AROUND GUATEMALA CITY

El Portal del Ángel

Although it is on the outskirts of the city, El Portal is one of the most famous restaurants in Guatemala. You can soak in beautiful views of the surrounding valleys, thanks to its location on top of one of the hills that surround Guatemala City. The building has a colonial decoration and design. The menu consists mostly of grilled and roasted meats, but you can also enjoy a variety of pasta dishes and Guatemalan favorites like refried beans, plantains, *caldo de gallina* (chicken broth), etc. This restaurant is a little more expensive than other restaurants in its category, mainly because of the "extras" you get, like the fantastic view of the city. Service begins at 6:30 a.m. Although they lack the view, the restaurant's two additional locations are in Zona 10 and Zona 11. Kilómetro 11.2 Carretera a El Salvador; Paseo Miraflores Zona 11, Plaza Fontabela, 12 Ca. 4 Av., Zona 10. Tel: 502-2322-7300, URL: www.elportaldelangel.net. Updated: Sep 03, 2009.

PARQUE NACIONAL VOLCÁN PACAYA

(ADMISSION: $3.50) Part of the Central American Volcanic Arc and regarded as Guatemala's most active volcano, Volcán Pacaya entered its current active phase began back in 1965. The 2,552-meter-tall (8,372 ft) volcano frequently spews lava, hurtles rocks into the sky, lets off steam and disperses large clouds of ash into the surrounding area. Occasionally, ash clouds disrupt flight arrangements at Guatemala City's La Aurora International Airport. Back in 1998, the airport had to temporarily close after the runway was coated with a thick layer of volcanic ash. The most recent eruption at Pacaya took place in May of 2010, causing ash to rain down on Guatemala City, Antigua and Escuintla. Local communities were forced to evacuate the area and a journalist documenting the events was fatally injured by volcanic debris. Scientists expect another spate of volatile activity soon.

Despite the unpredictable nature of Pacaya, it is still a hugely popular destination for tourists to Guatemala. There are a number of reputable agencies based in both Guatemala City and Antigua that organize day trips to the volcano. It is often easier to organize such a trip and take a guide with you rather than attempting to head for the peak on your own. Generally it makes more sense to make the trip from Guatemala City, as it is closer to Pacaya, but the majority of tour operators tend to be located in Antigua. During the 1990s, the area became known for armed robberies, but fortunately, nowadays there are plenty of park rangers patrolling the trails and robberies are virtually unheard-of.

Volcán Pacaya and the surrounding area achieved national park status back in 2001. The park's admission fee goes toward maintaining the park and keeping it safe and tourist friendly. There is a secure parking area at the trailhead in San Francisco de Sales, and there are plenty of rest stops and outhouses along the way. Make sure you wear suitable footwear; volcanic rock is rough. Also, drink plenty of water and bring warm clothing, as it can get quite cold at the top. Naturally, views are better in the morning when the sky is clear. Once you reach the top, the surrounding scenery is spectacular, not to mention seeing an active volcano bubbling with hot lava, flowing lava rivers and shooting jets of steam. Updated: Jul 30, 2010.

PARQUE NATURAL CANOPY CALDERAS

(ADMISSION: $10) This privately owned reserve is situated right on the slopes of Pacaya volcano, just three kilometers (about 2 mi) from San Francisco de Salas. Open daily 8 a.m.-6 p.m., you are free to explore volcanic *calderas* (craters), the rainforest and the picturesque lagoon. Once inside, visitors can also participate in a range of adventure activities including four-wheeling, horseback riding, mountain biking, kayaking, sail boarding, rappelling and zip-lining through the forest canopy. All of the activities are priced individually, allowing you to pick and choose what suits you. You can hire a guide and hike along designated nature trails or up to the volcano. Camping beside the lake is also available for $7 a night, and if you don't have your own tent, you can rent one on-site for another $7. Updated: Jul 30, 2010.

Getting To and Away

If you are heading to Pacaya on an organized tour then most operators will arrange transport from your accommodation. However, if you are traveling to the volcano independently, the easiest way is to follow the CA-9 highway past Amatitlán to a signed turnoff at Kilometer 37.5 and then continue east eight kilometers (about 5 mi) to the village of San Vicente Pacaya. From San Vicente, carry on along the road another 10 kilometers (about 6 mi) to San Francisco de Sales, where you will find the trailhead to Pacaya. For alternatives, check with a tourist information office in the area for bus schedules in the area. Updated: Jul 30, 2010.

MIXCO VIEJO RUINS

The capital city of the Chojoma Maya, Mixco Viejo, fell to Pedro de Alvarado's Spanish conquistadors in 1525 after a three-month siege. The city was once home to about 10,000 Maya, and was fortified by both large stone walls and its location in a steep ravine. It was established in the 12th century as a defensive outpost, and reached its peak population just before the conquistadors arrived. The conquistadors were supposedly led to a secret entrance to the city, and entered the fortified compound virtually unopposed. After the Spanish captured the city, they burned it down and killed many of the Maya living there. There are 120 structures in total, including two courts for *pitziil*, a hybrid of soccer and volleyball. Excavations began by French archaeologists in the mid-20th century, who mistakenly believed the ruins to belong to the Poqomam Maya due to misinterpreted colonial records. Although not quite as spectacular as Tikal or El Mirador, the Mixco Viejo ruins compensate for a lack of grandeur with prime location.

The ancient city is located just 60 kilometers (36 mi) north of Guatemala City, making it a great day trip from town, whereas Tikal and El Mirador are hours, or even days away in the wilderness of El Petén. It is also set amid a very dramatic backdrop, with panoramic views of lushly forested mountains possible due to its mountaintop location. There is also a small museum housing a great deal of information on the city.

There are four daily buses that head to Pachalum (or San Juan Sacatepéquez, which runs much more frequently, but you have to catch a bus that will take you further north to the ruins) from Guatemala City. These will drop you off at the bottom of the hill leading up to the ruins, which requires about a 10-minute walk. The bus shouldn't cost too much (about $0.80 to San Juan, and then a similar fare up to the ruins), and the newly paved road should make for a smooth ride. Updated: Jul 22, 2010.

))))

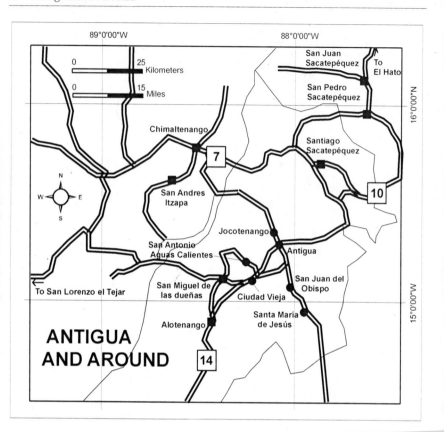

Antigua and Around

It is no wonder why most travelers make Antigua their first destination when coming to the country. The gorgeous colonial city and the volcanoes that ring it make for a wonderful introduction to Guatemala. Once the Spanish capital of Central America, today Antigua is the most popular tourist destination in Guatemala. Updated: Nov 17, 2006.

ANTIGUA

The charming colonial city of Antigua lies in a highland valley, surrounded by three volcanoes. The city is tickled by the skirts of Volcán de Agua to the south, and is within the gaze of two active volcanoes to the southwest: the double-ridged peak of Volcán Acatenango and the smoking Volcán Fuego. Once the seat of the Spanish colonial authority in Guatemala, Antigua oversaw a vast

area stretching from southern Mexico to the impenetrable Darién Gap, the undeveloped swampland that separates Panama from Colombia. The city was originally named "La Muy Leal y Muy Noble Ciudad de Santiago de los Caballeros de Guatemala" ("The Very Loyal and Very Noble Knight's City of Santiago of Guatemala"), and is now La Antigua Guatemala, or simply Antigua.

Today Antigua's status as a UNESCO World Heritage Site has preserved and restored its colonial architecture and old-world appeal. The local government only approves certain shades to paint the exterior walls of buildings and prohibits the display of signs or notices that are out of character with the rest of the city. The cobblestone streets are splashed with colorful house and shop fronts, and old churches and crumbling ruins are dotted throughout. Due to its location, beauty, history, variety of cultural activities and outdoor excursions both inside Antigua and close by, it has become a thriving landing place for

Semana Santa

Semana Santa, or Holy Week, is most likely the most-celebrated holiday in all of Guatemala—but no town puts on a show like Antigua. Thousands of foreigners and vacationing Guatemalans are drawn to Antigua each year to witness the vibrant and elaborate festivities during the holiday.

Although Semana Santa officially runs from Palm Sunday to Easter Sunday, preparation starts weeks before the main event. Local families design and weave elaborate carpets made of flowers, pines, dyed sawdust and leaves. Each one varies in shape, color, and size, with designs influenced by Mayan and colonial traditions. The ornamental carpets, or *alfombras*, blanket the streets on Holy Friday, just in time for a solemn procession where men and boys in purple robes slowly carry giant floats. These floats are so large that some require up to 80 men to carry them, and they hold the most revered items from local churches on top.

Around the robed men, Roman soldiers swing incense burners, creating dense clouds of smoke. Behind them, a float with the Virgin Mary is followed by women dressed in black. The traditions can be very moving, even for people who are not religious. Around 3 a.m. on Good Friday, a band of men on horseback gallop through the streets announcing Christ's death sentence. Over the following days, there are mock crucifixions depicting the 12 stations of the cross throughout the city.

If you plan to visit Antigua during Holy Week, you will want to book your hotel or hostel well in advance. For more information on the details of Holy Week events, pick up a map or schedule at the Instituto Guatemalteco de Turismo (INGUAT) office in the central plaza. Updated: Jul 28, 2010.

globetrotters. Around 47,000 people call Antigua home, and the mixture of locals, travelers and expats gives it a certain worldly air.

If your time is limited in the city, take a walking tour of the main sites, ruins and museums. Wander through the handicrafts market to pick up souvenirs and take a look at how jade is transformed into jewelry or masks in one of the store factories. Get out of town to visit a coffee plantation, or trek up to the edge of a flowing river of red-hot lava on Volcán Pacaya.

VIVA ONLINE REVIEW
ANTIGUA

"You are able to experience colonial history in a very unique way. It is like being transported 400 years back."

Dec 03, 2009

Many travelers hang out here awhile to recoup energy in the peaceful town and recharge on good eats. There is no shortage of restaurants in Antigua. Grab tasty bites from street venders, *comedores* (simple eateries) or restaurants serving cuisine from all corners of the world.

Afterward, there are plenty of bars at which to get a drink to wash it all down.

Many visitors are lured by the well-earned reputation of the city as one of the choice spots to study Spanish, and there are hordes of language schools of all calibers vying for the bucks. Volunteering opportunities are endless both in Antigua and in outlying areas, with NGO organizations and various projects focusing on different social, educational, health and environmental issues. Many students invest their afternoons donating whatever skills they can offer. Forever a popular place to learn salsa, there are qualified instructors running classes for all levels in dance studios around town.

In Antigua, there are infinite options for laying your head at night. The streets are brimming with hostels, guesthouses and hotels of every description and for every pocket—from penny pinching backpackers to luxury travelers. Tourism is the lifeblood of the local economy and language schools are one of the major employers, along with hotels and restaurants. The production of typical handicrafts and fabrics and the cultivation of coffee, macadamia nuts and veggies are other big income earners. Updated: Feb 09, 2010.

ANTIGUA & AROUND

History

Founded in 1543, present-day Antigua is actually the third capital of Guatemala. Spanish conquistadors looked to the Valley of Panchoy after a series of mudslides from Volcán de Agua annihilated the second capital, the town now known as Ciudad Vieja.

For more than two centuries, Antigua—at the time called Santiago de los Caballeros—was the seat of the Spanish colonial government of Guatemala. Spanish rule covered a vast area, including the majority of present-day Central America and Chiapas in southern Mexico. Antigua gradually became the most important city in Central America. In 1773, a colossal earthquake devastated most of Antigua and the government was transferred to the site of present-day Guatemala City. The move did not come without opposition, so a law was passed making it illegal for anyone to live in Antigua. However, not everyone abandoned the town. When the government relocated, the former capital was renamed *La Antigua Guatemala* (Old Guatemala).

The city was on the brink of desertion until the 20th century, when little by little it became repopulated. Antigua was declared a National Monument by the Guatemalan government in 1944 and was designated a UNESCO World Heritage Site in 1979.

Most of the buildings were constructed in the 17th and 18th centuries during the era of Spanish rule and prosperity.

Activities ●

1 Antigua Cooking School A1
2 Arco A1
3 Catedral de Santiago B2
4 Centro Cultural La Azotea A1
5 Iglesia y Convento de Santo DomingoB1
6 Iglesia y Convento la Recolección A1
7 Las Capuchinas B1
8 Monumento a Landivar A2
9 Museo Mesoamericano de Jade B2
10 Nuestra Señora de la Merced
    Church and Convent A1
11 Palacio del AyuntamientoA1
12 Palacio de los CapitanesA2
13 Parque Central A2
14 Proyecto Sitio A2
15 Salsa Dancing - New Sensation
    Salsa Studio A1
16 San Francisco El Grande Church,
    Ruins & Museum B2
17 Santa Clara B2

Eating 🍴

18 Bagel Barn A2
19 Café Colonial A1
20 Casa Escobar A1
21 Comedor Antigua, Central Market A1
22 Héctor Castro A1
23 Kaffee Fernando A1
24 La Antigua Vinera A2
25 La Septima A2
26 Panza Verde A2
27 Ronny´s Tacos A2
28 Sabe Rico A2
29 Sobremesa A1
30 Street Stalls, La Union Park A1
31 Toko Baru A2
32 Travel Menu A2

Nightlife 🍸

33 Café Sky B1
34 Ciudad Vieja A2
35 Funky Monkey A2
36 La Casbah Discoteca and Lounge A1
37 Jocotenango A1

Services ★

38 Cargo Expreso B2
39 D.H.L. A2
40 Enlaces A2
41 Guatex A2
42 Post Office A1
43 Tourism Office B1

Shopping 🛍

44 Artesania Market A1
45 El Reino del Jade A1
46 Museo/Casa del Tejido A1
47 Nim Po't Market A1
48 JADES, S.A. Factory,
    Showroom & Museum B1

Sleeping 🛏

49 Casa Blancas A2
50 Casa Rustica A2
51 Estella´s House A1
52 Hotel Black Cat Inn A2
53 Hotel El Jardin de Lolita A1
54 Hotel Palacio Chico A1
55 Hotel Posada Don Quijote A1
56 Posada del Viajero A1
57 Ummagumma A1
58 Yellow House A1

Transportation 🚌

59 Local Bus Terminal A1

ANTIGUA & AROUND

Today, Antigua is a treasure trove of well-preserved, beautiful, colonial architecture and imposing ruins that remain open for public exploration. Updated: Aug 27, 2009.

When to Go

Antigua is a great place to visit year round; however, November through March are considered the best months. The weather is warm and spring-like (average temperature: 25°C/83°F) during the day, while the evenings are mild. Since Antigua is 1,500 meters (4,920 ft) above sea level, on even the sunniest days, the air is still fresh and humidity is not an issue. Likewise,

throughout the rainy season (May-October), with the wettest months being September and October, the temperature change is hardly noticeable. Rain usually falls only in the afternoon, with occasional overnight thunder and lightening storms. Every year, around July, there is a two-week period of sunny weather that locals call the *canicula*. Unfortunately, no one knows exactly when the heatwave will arrive, so it is impossible to plan for.

If you are in Antigua during *Semana Santa* (Holy Week), you will, without a doubt, witness some of the most spectacular Easter

Pedro de Alvarado

Pedro de Alvarado (1495-1541) was one of the most famous of the conquistadors. Originally from Spain, he set out on a quest for adventure and wealth, and later joined Hernán Cortez in his exploits in Mexico. As an officer in the army, Alvarado distinguished himself by his military ability. Notoriously ruthless, he employed methods of brutality such as hanging or burning men alive, and even feeding men to dogs.

In 1524, he set his sights south and moved his forces into Guatemala. There, he was met with resistance from the indigenous Quiché Nation. By allying himself with historic rival the Kakchiquel Nation, he eventually succeeded in his conquest. In reward, he was named governor of the newly acquired lands and founded the first city of Guatemala, located near to what is now known as Antigua.

Years later, in an attack near Guadalajara, Mexico, the horse that Alvarado was riding lost its footing and he was crushed beneath it. He died from his injuries a few days later and was buried in a church in Tiripetio, Mexico. Upon hearing news of her husband's death, his wife, Doña Beatriz de la Cueva, stained the entire palace (inside and out) black with clay to illustrate the magnitude of her grief. In the midst of her mourning, she appointed herself as the new governor, thus becoming the first woman to rule in the Americas. Her rule was short-lived: On the night of her inauguration, an earthquake caused a mudslide that covered the entire palace, burying her alive and destroying the city. Many believed that her staining of the palace was, in fact, a bad omen that in the end her both predicted and determined her untimely end. She is now known as Doña Beatriz *la sin ventura* (the unfortunate).

More than 40 years after her father's death, Leonor Alvarado Xicoténcatl had her father's remains exhumed and transported from Mexico to Guatemala, where he is now buried in the Cathedral de Santiago in Antigua. Updated: Sep 01, 2009.

celebrations of all Latin America. This is when the town's streets—and hotels—are bursting. Plan ahead and be prepared to pay more for your digs. This also goes for July and August, when the Spanish schools are at their busiest. Updated: Aug 25, 2009.

Highlights

For spectacular views of the city and the surrounding volcanoes, make the easy hike up to **Cerro de la Cruz**.

Visit the haunting ruins of **Iglesia La Recolección**.

Catch a concert or street performance in the historic **Parque Central**.

Climb the iconic **Volcán Pacaya** for a taste of the fiery natural history of the area.

Brush up on your Spanish in one of the city's superlative **language schools**. For a real challenge, try one of the Mayan languages. Updated: Aug 19, 2010.

Getting To and Away

The easiest way to get to Antigua from La Aurora International Airport in Guatemala City is to take shuttle buses from outside the entrance. Until about 10 p.m., many privately run companies vie for your business. The journey is about 40 minutes and costs approximately $10 per person. These mini vans only leave when full, but the wait is not usually long. If you arrive during the day, there are also buses that will take you to the main bus terminal in Antigua, three blocks to the west of Parque Central, near the Mercado Central. Private taxis are also available that cost about $30. There is a useful Tourist Information Desk near the exit where you can check which option best suits your situation and how to pay.

Car rental is available in the airport, or once in Antigua, from $35 a day. Generally, the longer you rent the car the cheaper the rate. Mopeds cost about the same, motorbikes a bit more. Two rental agencies to try are: Avis (5a Av. Norte 22. Tel: 502-7832-2692, URL: www.avis.com.gt) and Hertz (in Aurora airport. Tel: 502-2470-3838, E-mail: aurora@rentautos.com.

gt). Porta Hotel Antigua (Tel: 502-4393-6702, E-mail: Antigua@rentautos.com.gt, URL: www.rentautos.com.gt) also rents autos.

There is currently only one scheduled domestic flight route within the country, from Guatemala City to Flores. There are also charter flights, but not from Antigua.

If you want to take a local bus to or from the east, it is necessary to pass through Guatemala City. Going to or coming from the west, you should change buses in Chimaltenango. Buses go to the following towns from Antigua's main terminal: Guatemala City (1 hr), Cuidad Vieja (20 min), Chimaltenango (40 min), Escuintla (1 hr), San Antonio Aguas Calientes (20 min), San Juan del Obispo (15 min), Santa María de Jesús (30 min), Acatenango (40 min). Check at the terminal for specific times.

More expensive than the public buses, but more convenient, quicker and safer, are the shuttle buses that run all over the country to and from Antigua:

Tikal: $30, 8-9 hr; 7:30 a.m.
Río Dulce: $18, 5 hr; 4 a.m., 7:30 a.m., 9 a.m. 11 a.m.
Panajachel: $8, 2.5 hr; 8 a.m., 12:30 p.m. and 4 p.m.
San Pedro: $9, 2.5 hr; 8 a.m. and 2 p.m.
Chichicastenango: $8, 2.5 hr; 7 a.m.
Semuc Champey: $30, 8 hr; 8:30 a.m.
Monterrico: $10, 2.5 hr; 8 a.m.
San Cristobal de las Casas: $45, 7 hr; 5 a.m.

See agencies for more destinations and details. Updated: Sep 01, 2009.

Getting Around

By foot is by far the best way to see the town; Antigua is small and compact. Around the park you can pick up a ride in a horse-drawn carriage for a tour of the city. Prices vary.

A more exhilarating way to explore the city is by three-wheeled tuk-tuk. What's a tuk-tuk, you ask? Imagine a souped-up golf cart driven by a wannabe Formula One racer. These vehicles also go to villages around Antigua. Tell the driver your destination and negotiate a price. Within town, the standard rate is $1.25. Outside, prices vary, so ask around. Tuk-tuks run 5 a.m.-9 p.m. and are prohibited around Parque Central. After 9 p.m., use a safer but more expensive option: registered taxis. There is no fixed price, but a trip within the city should cost around $3.15. Agree on a price

before getting in. There are taxi stands by near the cathedral at Parque Central and in front of Pollo Campero near the market.

The local buses, *camionetas*, leave from the bus station behind the market and go to all the surrounding villages, as well as to Guatemala City. You can also wave one down in the street. Prices are fixed and vary according to destination.

Travel agencies have shuttles to and from the airport and all the main tourist destinations.

CAR RENTAL

Tabarini

Monday-Friday 8 a.m.-6 p.m., Saturday and Sunday 8 a.m.-1 p.m. and 3-6 p.m. 6a Av. Sur 22. Tel: 502-7832-8107/8109, E-mail: tabarini@tabarini.com, URL: www. tabarini.com. Updated: Jan 30, 2010.

La Ceiba

(CARS: $38/day, 4x4: $86/day) Website prices are cheaper than walk-ins. Monday-Sunday 8 a.m.-1 p.m. and 2-7 p.m. 6a Ca. Poniente 6-D. Tel: 502-7832-4168/5215-8269. E-mail: info@ceibarent.com, URL: www.ceibarent.com. Updated: Jan 30, 2010.

Guatemala Renta Autos

(CARS: $20/day, 4x4: $55/day) Monday-Friday 8 a.m.-6 p.m., Saturday 8 a.m.-5 p.m. 4a Av. Norte 6. Tel: 502-2329-9030. URL: www.guatemalarentacar.com Updated: Jan 30, 2010.

MOTORCYCLE RENTAL

CATours

(SCOOTERS: $36/day, TRAIL BIKES: $45/day) Monday-Friday 7:30 a.m.-6 p.m., Saturday 9 a.m.-6 p.m., Sunday 9 a.m.-1 p.m. 6a Ca. Oriente, 14A. Tel: 502-7832-9638. E-mail: sales@catours.co.uk, URL: www. catours.co.uk. Updated: Jan 30, 2010.

La Ceiba

(SCOOTERS: $44/day, TRAIL BIKES: $55/day) URL: www.ceibarent.com. Updated: Jan 30, 2010.

BICYCLE RENTAL

O.X. Outdoor Excursions

Monday-Friday 10 a.m.-6 p.m., Saturday 10 a.m.-5 p.m., Sunday, noon-5 p.m. 1a Av. Sur 4B. Tel: 502-7832-0074/5801-4301. E-mail: for_the_ox@yahoo.com, URL: www.guatemalavolcano.com. Updated: Jan 30, 2010.

Safety

Visitors should be aware that, however infrequent, crimes against tourists do occur in Antigua. While the most common is petty theft (pickpockets), it should be noted that more violent crimes such as armed robbery, rape and even murder have been reported. Although an increase in tourist police presence in recent years has helped deter such offenses, it is still wise to employ the usual precautions. Avoid walking alone late at night, especially in less-populated areas of the city, such as behind the market and along the outskirts. Be advised that tuk-tuks cease to operate at 9 p.m. nightly, so be prepared to spend a little more to take a taxi between destinations instead ($3 and up).

In addition, keep any valuables concealed when possible. Expensive items such as cameras, cell phones and flashy jewelry can make you a target. For all volcano tours, check the security arrangements before booking. In late 2009, trips to Volcán Acatenango were temporarily suspended due to a shooting incident, so check the current situation with tour operators. You can also arrange for a free escort from the tourist police, which is especially useful for visiting the Cerro de la Cruz and Volcán de Agua.

If you are the victim of a crime, you can call Luis Mich (Tel: 502-5978-3586) for assistance. Mich is employed by INGUAT's Tourist Assistance office and is bilingual and is available around-the-clock. He will accompany you to the police station and will accurately translate your statement before returning you to your hotel. Updated: Oct 14, 2009.

Services

In emergencies, call 1500 toll free within Guatemala to speak to a bilingual operator from ASISTUR (Asistencia Al Turismo), Guatemala's special tourist police force. ASISTUR will connect you to the police, fire department or ambulance service. ASISTUR's bilingual representative, Luis Mich, is also available 24 hours a day, seven days a week with any problems. He will accompany you to the police to report a crime and translate where necessary. Tel: 502-5978-3586.

TOURISM

INGUAT Tourism Office

Pick the brains of the helpful, bilingual staff at the INGUAT Tourism Office, who are happy to answer any question you can think of. At the office, you can grab brochures about Guatemala in English, Spanish, Italian, German, French or Japanese. Useful maps and leaflets cover everything including tours, Spanish schools and volunteering. The website is in eight languages, including English. Monday-Friday 8 a.m.-5 p.m., Saturday-Sunday 9 a.m.-5 p.m. 2a Ca. Oriente, 11. Tel: 502-7832-3783 / 0873, E-mail: info-antigua@inguat.gob.gt. URL: www.visitguatemala.com. Updated: Sep 28, 2009.

MONEY

A cluster of banks surrounds Parque Central, and depending which bank branch, most can help out with money exchange, traveler's checks, money wiring and/or ATM needs.

Banco Agromercantil

Changes U.S. dollars (cash/AMEX traveler's checks) and euros. Monday-Sunday 9 a.m.-7 p.m. 4a Ca. Poniente 8. Tel: 502-7832-0048/0555.

BAC (Credomatic)

This bank has 24-hour VISA/Mastercard ATMs, changes U.S. dollars (cash/AMEX traveler's checks), and gives VISA cash advances. Monday-Friday 9 a.m.-6:30 p.m., Saturday 9 a.m.-1 p.m. 5a Av. Norte 8. Tel: 502-2361-0909. Updated: Feb 22, 2010.

Banco Gandamp

Changes U.S. dollars (cash/AMEX traveler's checks), has 24-hour VISA/Mastercard ATMs and can wire money. Monday-Friday 8:30 a.m.-7 p.m., Saturday 9 a.m.-2 p.m. 5a Av. Norte 2. Tel: 502-7832-0639/6777. Updated: Feb 22, 2010.

Banco Industrial S.A.

Changes U.S. dollars (cash), has 24-hour VISA/Mastercard ATMs and gives VISA/Mastercard cash advances. Monday-Friday 9 a.m.-7 p.m., Saturday 9 a.m.-1 p.m. 5a Av. Sur 4 (half a block south of Parque Central). Tel: 502-7832-0957. Updated: Feb 22, 2010.

KEEPING IN TOUCH

Telgua is the major telecommunications provider in Guatemala. The international dialing code for Guatemala is 502. To make international calls dial (00) before the country code. Payphones only use cards. Ask for una tarjeta Ladatel in any store. Many Internet cafés offer cheap international calls, such as Enlaces, Funky Monkey and La Conexión. Calls from these Internet cafés range from $0.05 per minute to $0.15 per minute to the U.S. and Canada, and $0.15 per minute to

The Quetzal

The quetzal, a beloved symbol of Guatemala, is a bird so breathtaking in its beauty that once upon a time, its tail feathers were traded alongside jade. Locals say the quetzal values freedom so highly that it will commit suicide rather than live in captivity. Visually stunning, the bird captured the imaginations of the ancient Mayans, with its iridescent green body that shimmers gold or violet in changing lights.

In mating season, the male grows twin tail feathers a meter (3 ft) long. Instead of flying, the bird seems to undulate in waves through its home, the cloud forest. To the Mayans, this was the movement of creation. Thus, tail feathers adorned the headdresses of priests and rulers in a symbolic link to Quetzalcoatl, the creator God. For Tecún Umán, a Mayan warrior chief, the quetzal served as protector and spiritual guide.

When conquistador Pedro de Alvarado overpowered Tecún Umán by spearing him in the chest during battle, legend says the quetzal dropped from the sky and bathed its chest in the pool of blood. At dawn, the sacred quetzal arose, its breast no longer green but a vivid crimson; a testament to the death of a ruler and an empire.

The rulers have changed, but the symbolism has not. A line in the Guatemala national anthem states "rather choose death than slavery," and the quetzal and his red chest adorn both the Guatemalan flag and coat of arms. Given that the quetzal has historically symbolized wealth, the government even named its money after the bird.

Seeing as the quetzal is on the threatened list, many Guatemalans have never spotted the sacred bird. Still, the Guatemalan people are proud of their national bird, whose significance is unparalleled. The quetzal is a bridge that ties the past to the present, and serves as a subtle reminder that the heart of the Mayans is still alive today, even in modern Guatemala. Updated: Sep 02, 2009.

ANTIGUA & AROUND

$0.35 per minute to Europe. Cell phones can be rented by guests at the Posada La Merced (7a Av. Norte 3. Tel: 502-7832-3197/3301) for $1 per day, $6 per week, or $20 per month. If you buy a cell phone with Claro, Tigo or Movistar, send free messages from URL: www.sagastume.com.Bear in mind it's not always reliable.

Internet cafés are all over town. The following have good connections, printing capabilities, CD burning, headsets and web cams for Skype. WiFi is also springing up in hotels and restaurants everywhere:

Enlaces

(INTERNET: $0.90/hr, WiFi $1.25/hr) Enlaces offers photocopying, fax and technical support for computers, cameras, iPods and iPhones. Monday-Saturday 8 a.m.-7:30 p.m., Sunday 8 a.m.-1 p.m. 6a Av. Norte 1. Tel: 502-7832-5555/63, E-mail: enlace@pobox.com. Updated: Jan 29, 2010.

Funky Monkey

(INTERNET: $1/hr) In addition to being a popular Internet café and telephone center, Funky Monkey has photocopying and fax services. Monday-Friday 8 a.m.-noon, Saturday-Sunday 9 a.m.-midnight. 5a Av. Sur 6. Tel: 502-7832-7181, E-mail: contact@funkymonkeynet.com, URL: www.funkymonkeynet.com. Updated: Jan 29, 2010.

La Conexión

(INTERNET: $0.60-1.25/hr, WiFi $1.25/hr) To complement its Internet-equipped computers, La Conexión offers scanning services and has a helpful notice board. Monday-Friday 8 a.m.-9 p.m., Saturday and Sunday 8:30 a.m.-7 p.m. Centro Comercial La Fuente, 4a Ca. Oriente, 14. Tel: 502-7832-3768, E-mail: admin@conexion.com.gt, URL: www.conexion.com. Updated: Jan 29, 2010.

If you need to send or receive mail, Antigua's post office (Monday-Friday 8 a.m.-5 p.m.,

Saturday 9 a.m.-1 p.m. 4a Ca. Poniente and Calzada Santa Lucía. Tel: 502-7832-0485) offers shipping and receiving services. Alternative options include privately owned companies such as D.H.L (Monday-Friday 8 a.m.-6 p.m., Saturday 8 a.m.-noon. 6a Ca. Poniente and 6 Av. Sur. Tel: 502-7832-3718/32, URL: www.dhl.com), Guatex (Monday-Friday 8 a.m.-noon and 2-6 p.m., Saturday 8 a.m.-noon. 6a Ca. Poniente, 16. Tel: 502-7882-4583, URL: www.guatex.com.gt) and Cargo Express (Monday-Friday 8 a.m.-noon and 2-7 p.m. Saturday 8 a.m.-noon. 7a Ca. Oriente 3. Tel: 502-7832-3104, URL: www.cargoexpreso.com), which are all in town and specialize in international shipping. Updated Jan 29, 2010.

MEDICAL

There are several public and private hospitals, some with English-speaking doctors, throughout the city:

Public Clinica APROFAM

Monday-Friday 7:30 a.m.-12:30 p.m. 6a. Ca. Poniente 46. Tel: 502-7832-2978. Updated: Feb 22, 2010.

Centro Médico Santiago Apostol

Private hospital with 24-hour emergency service and English-speaking staff. Ca. del Manchén 7. Tel: 502-7832-0884. Updated: Feb 22, 2010.

Hospital Privado Hermano Pedro

Private hospital with 24-hour emergency service and English-speaking staff. Av. de La Recolección, 4. Tel: 502-7832-0420/1197/1190. Updated: Feb 22, 2010.

Hospital Pedro de Bethancourt, San Felipe de Jesús

Public Hospital with 24-hour emergency service. Tel: 502-7832-2511/7831-1315.

Centro de Medicina Bioenergética

Public hospital with 24-hour emergency service. Dr. Licel Figueroa. Carretera a San Felipe de Jesús 118. Tel: 502-7832-7999, 502-5401-7094. Updated: Feb 22, 2010.

Dentist Dr. Gustavo Parada

Monday-Friday 8 a.m.-noon and 3-7 p.m., Saturday 9 a.m.-1 p.m. 5a Ca. Poniente26. Tel: 502-7832-4732. Updated: Feb 22, 2010.

Óptica Santa Lucía

Monday-Friday 9 a.m.-1 p.m. and 2-7 p.m., Saturday 9 a.m.-3 p.m. 5a Ca. Poniente 28. Tel: 502-7832-7945. Updated: Feb 22, 2010.

If in need of a pharmacy, Pharmacy Farmacia Ivori Premium (6a Av. Norte and 2a Ca. Poniente 19. Tel: 502-7832-1559, 502-7832-1560) conveniently has free delivery and several branches around town. The branches are open 24 hours per day, seven days perweek. Updated: Feb 22, 2010.

LAUNDRY

Many hotels in Antigua offer laundry and dry cleaning services at the front desk, but if yours does not, local laundromats and dry cleaners are widely available. Average price for laundry, per load, ranges from about $5-7.50 (both washing and drying).

Dry cleaning prices depend on the number of clothing articles, ranging from $3.50-5 per dress shirt, $5-10 for suits, $14-20 for dresses and $2-$4 for ties. Clothes can be dropped off and picked up at designated times. Home delivery is available at some locations.

Shopping

If you like to shop and prefer to do it all in one place, Antigua is the perfect town. Seemingly designed with shoppers in mind, you can find everything here that Guatemala is famous for, including jade, traditional textiles, pottery, furniture, Mayan masks, coffee and chocolate. Most shops and markets are located with five blocks of Parque Central, and cater to all types of travelers. Credit cards, quetzals and U.S. dollars are generally accepted everywhere.

To avoid unfavorable exchange rates, pay with the currency the price is quoted in. Bartering is normal procedure for anything other than day-to-day items, such as toothpaste or bottled water. The trick is to discover rough prices from other sellers before you start on your chosen item. If you maintain a look of complete lack of interest and even walk away, prices can drop by as much as half! Keep it fun and remember that in the end, both of you should feel like you got a good deal. Even in fixed-price shops, it is worth asking for a discount. Updated: Sep 01, 2009.

Mercado Central

A visit to Antigua's central market is an excellent way to experience local culture firsthand. Rows of wooden stalls come alive with the hustle-and-bustle of vendors peddling their colorful wares. The market is always buzzing with activity. Here, you can find anything from traditional textiles, handicrafts, fresh produce and raw meat to shiny watches, pots, pipes and pirated CDs. Peruse the wide variety of available goods while mingling with the local people. If hungry for a taste of culture, visit one of the many *comedores* (food kiosks) and sample some authentic Guatemalan cuisine. Watch out for pickpockets. Friendly bargaining is acceptable. Daily 6 a.m.-7 p.m. West of Alameda de Santa Lucía between 3 Ca. and 4 Ca. G. Updated: Aug 29, 2009.

Mercado Principal

The *Mercado Principal* (Main Market) is the best place for budget travelers to sample authentic Guatemalan flavors. The market has several eateries to choose from. Although rarely visited by tourists, they are very popular among locals. Located next to the bus terminal, the market is ideal for a quick meal anytime from 6 a.m.-6 p.m daily. Mornings are the best time to visit, as this is when the food is freshest. A wide variety of typical local dishes are available to sample, especially for those interested in Guatemalan culture. Try authentic dishes such as *pepián* (spicy meat stew) and *revolcado* (organ stew)—not for the fainthearted! The market is in front of the bus terminal, where the west end of 4 Ca. Poniente meets Calzada de Santa Lucía.

Artesanía Market

Next to the Central Market, the Artesanía Market is a low-key, relaxed shopping experience. More than 200 stalls sell a wide variety of traditional and modern crafts encompassing *huipiles* (traditional blouses), scarves, glassware, paintings, sandals and candles. Shoppers can browse among the glorious array of handicrafts at their leisure. Despite appearances, all the crafts are handmade; watch out for poorer quality thread and dyes. Friendly bartering can lower prices by as much as half. Facilities on-site include benches, an ATM and toilets ($0.25). Some of the stalls take credit cards, some do not. Find out what the charge is before swiping your card, as fees can amount to up to 10 percent of your total purchase. The market has several entrances and exits that are signposted. Daily 9 a.m.-7 p.m. 4a Ca. Poniente. Updated: Aug 28, 2009.

Nim Po't Market

Conveniently located on the main shopping street, Nim Po't is a warehouse overflowing with local artifacts and crafts, some quite dusty. All prices are fixed. If you have no experience in bartering, this is good place to discover the maximum price of products before heading somewhere else to bargain downwards.

There is a reasonable selection of secondhand books, postcards and a small courtyard café. Daily 9 a.m.-9 p.m. 5a Av. North 29 (Ca. de Arco). Tel: 502-7832-2681. URL: www.nimpot.com. Updated: Aug 28, 2009.

El Reino del Jade

The refined surroundings of El Reino del Jade emphasize the elegance of the jewelry displayed here. The thickness of the window cases is an indication of price. Guatemalan jade is completely different to Asian jade, as it is so tough diamonds are required to cut it. There are 17 green jades, as well as 25 other colors. Lilac and black are the most inexpensive. A jade pendant starts from $30, a mini-mask from $75 and mini-sculptured animals from $30. For those more fortunate, the most exquisite pieces price in the hundreds. Workshop on-site. 9 a.m.-6:30 p.m. 28 5a Av. North (Ca. de Arco). Tel: 502-7832-1597. Updated: Sep 01, 2009.

Studying Spanish

People all over the world come to Antigua for the sole purpose of learning Spanish, and many travelers take classes to brush up on their language skills between hikes. The city has more than 70 Spanish schools for travelers to choose from. Nevertheless, it is important to do your homework before picking a school.

On the Web and at the school's office, ask as many details as possible. A good question to ask is how well prepared the teachers are. Almost all are native speakers of Spanish, but some lack adequate experience or training. Ask if there is a registration fee and if books and other materials are included in the price. Some schools will give you a discount if you take more than a few classes or if you and your friends book together in advance.

If possible, try to visit as many schools as possible before making a decision. Ask locals and other visitors about their recommendations. A number of schools provide additional services, such as guided tours and dancing lessons. All things considered, even if it was not part of your original trip plan, taking Spanish classes in Antigua can be a great addition to your overall experience in Guatemala. Updated: Sep 04, 2009.

Christian Spanish Academy

Located a few blocks from the park, this is the local branch of the Christian Spanish Academy. Headquartered in Florida, this institution was originally created to help missionaries learn Spanish, but now offers a wide range of programs tailored to suit different needs, such as a its "Business Program," "Flight Attendant Program," "Busy People Program," and more. Classes are individual. The building is full of light and some of the classes are given in the interior garden. The school also has a library and can arrange tours and homestays. The registration fee is $20, but there are special prices for long-term studies. 6 Av. Norte 15. Tel: 502-7832-3922/3, Fax: 502-7832-3760, E-mail: information@learncsa.com, URL: www.learncsa.com. Updated: Sep 01, 2009.

Spanish Language Center

Spanish Language Center is less than three blocks from the main plaza. The school works with a local university, so students may earn extra credits. A nice perk is that the school provides free phone calls to more than 40 countries, and textbooks are included in the price. You can also take online Spanish lessons for $9.99 an hour anywhere in the world. The school offers discounts for extended lessons and group bookings, and administrators recommend contacting them before traveling to Antigua because they can help set up hotels, flights and other travel arrangements. 6 Av. Norte 6. Tel: 502-7932-1500 (Guatemala)/1-800-866-6358 (U.S.), E-mail: craig@121speech.com. URL: www.best-spanishlesson.com. Updated: Sep 03, 2009.

Centro Lingüístico Internacional

Located in a large house not far from the bus terminal, Centro Lingüístico Internacional has its own Internet café (with WiFi), laundry service and apartments. Students can take classes in the inner patio or on the second floor, which offers a great view of the volcanoes nearby. The school offers a "Teach and Learn" program that allows you to teach a little of your native language to your Spanish teacher. As is the case with many other Spanish schools, Centro Lingüístico offers dance lessons, tours and other activities.

Av. del Espíritu Santo 6. Tel: 502-7832-1039, Fax: 502-7832-1039, E-mail: info@spanishcontact.com, URL: www.spanishcontact.com. Updated: Sep 03, 2009.

Centro de Español Don Pedro de Alvarado

Unlike other academies, the Centro de Español Pedro de Alvarado lets you decide where you would like to study, be it a park, a café or a market. Classes are one on one, and you can change teacher every week. The school also has free Internet access and a small library. Students at the school can take the FSI and ACTFL proficiency language exams. The staff can arrange dance lessons, tours, bike rental and housing. You can choose to stay in a modest home or in a more luxurious house. 6 Av. Norte 39. Tel: 502-5872-2469/7882-4575, E-mail: donpedro77@hotmail.com, URL: www.donpedrospanishschool.com. Updated: Sep 10, 2009.

Proyecto Lingüístico Francisco Marroquín

Founded in 1969, Francisco Marroquín is the oldest language school in Antigua. It is located less than one block from La Merced Church and is run as a non-profit. It teaches Spanish, Kaqchikel Maya, Quiché, Mam, Q'eqchi and other Mayan languages by special arrangement. Program length is flexible, however, the staff recommends a minimum of four weeks for intermediate-level students. A 30-minute Foreign Service Institute type oral or written exam can be requested to evaluate Spanish competency. Classes can be taken in the lovely garden under ruined arches or in individual mini-classrooms. Facilities include WiFi, an Internet café and a library, and costs for field trips vary according to activity. Students are encouraged to stay with a host family to further their practice. 6a. Av. Norte 43. Tel: 502-7832-1422, E-mail: info@plfm.org, secretaria@plfm.org, URL: www.spanishschoolplfm.com. Updated: Nov 13, 2009.

Spanish School Cooperación

The intimate and affordable Spanish School Cooperación, less than a block from Parque San Sebastian, has a separate location for its office on 7a Avenida. Classes can be taken in the small garden, and are given either individually or in pairs, with a focus on getting the students to speak. Textbooks and salsa lessons are included in the price, but optional cultural activities are charged extra to cover entrance fees and transport. Homestays with local families and discounts for two students sharing one teacher are available. For a change of scenery, the school also has a branch in Panajachel, on Lago Atitlán. 1a Ca. del Chajón 21B. Tel: 502-5812-2482/1887/4147-1686, E-mail: escuela_coop@ yahoo.com, URL: www.spanishschool-cooperacion.com. Updated: Nov 13, 2009.

Academia de Español PROBIGUA

Academia de Español PROBIGUA, less than a block from La Merced Church, offers a wide range of specialized Spanish classes tailored to student needs. These include lessons for business, travel and self growth, as well as medical Spanish classes aimed at doctors, nurses and social workers. PROBIGUA is a non-profit organization that runs Proyecto Bibliotecas Guatemala. The school donates its profits to establish and maintain libraries in rural areas, including two library buses that visit villages daily around the country. The school also provides scholarships to disadvantaged children. There is no registration fee, but the schools requests one book in Spanish as a donation. Discounts are offered for group bookings or extended periods of study. 6a Av. Norte 41-B. Tel: 502-7832-2998/0860, E-mail: info@probigua.org, URL: www.probigua.org. Updated: Nov 13, 2009.

Centro Lingüístico La Unión

La Unión is a reputable setup a few steps from San Francisco Church. In addition to the usual private classes, the school also tailors courses to the specific demands of groups of travelers and professionals. Resources include job-specific vocabulary lists for various fields of work, including teachers, doctors, lawyers, flight attendants and missionaries. Classes for children between the ages of 4-14 can also be arranged. The school also provides opportunities to participate in extra activities and volunteer. Housing options include staying with a local family, or renting a student house or apartment. Special packages for groups are available and discounts are offered for companies, long-term students and groups affiliated with a college/university. A discount on the final weeks payment is an incentive for good test results. 1a Av. Sur 21. Tel: 502-7832-7337/57, E-mail: info@launion.edu.gt, URL: www.launion.edu.gt. Updated: Nov 13, 2009.

Spanish Academy Sevilla

A few doors from Café Sky, Spanish Academy Sevilla has individual cubicle classrooms set around a grassy garden. Sevilla offers programs for all levels and a one-week tourist course specifically for travelers. Classes are normally one on one, but couples can also study together upon request. The school provides textbooks written by its own teachers. Latin American movies play regularly and cultural activities, tours and social projects are available. Accommodation can be arranged in homestays or in private student guesthouses. 1a Av. Sur 17C. Tel: 502-7832-5101, E-mail: espanol@sevillantigua.com, URL: www.sevillantigua.com. Updated: Nov 13, 2009.

APPE Spanish Language School

The popular APPE Spanish Language School offers a good selection of customized courses for teachers, airline personnel, missionaries, diplomats, travel agents, hotel management, foreign correspondents, international business people, health and social workers. If you are planning on staying for a month or more, Spanish classes can be combined with volunteer projects through the school. Most classes are given in the garden or indoor communal area. For more immersion into local life, try the school's branch in San Juan del Obispo, a nearby village. 1a Ca. Oriente 15. Tel: 502-7832-4284/85, E-mail: info@appeschool.com, URL: www. appeschool.com. Updated: Nov 13, 2009.

Centro Lingüístico Maya

The Centro Lingüístico Maya is a well-respected Antigua language school. It offers specialized courses tailored for specific groups, and students can also qualify for university credit. Lessons are given in classrooms or on the rooftop terrace, and twice-weekly excursions and WiFi are also provided. Various volunteer programs are available, and students can choose to lodge with a host family. Discounts are offered for groups and, depending on the season, for extended periods of study. 5a Ca. Poniente 20. Tel: 502-7832-0656/5492/6027, E-mail: clmmaya@guate.net.gt, URL: www. clmaya.com. Updated: Nov 13, 2009.

Escuela de Español Tecún Umán

The administrators of this Spanish institute, somewhat ironically named after a Maya king executed by Spanish conquistadors, have put together some unique offerings. General Spanish classes have eight levels, from beginner to advanced, each one taking about a month to complete. Individual and group instruction is available, as well as classes for kids ages 4-16. Activities, excursions and lectures are available, and lodging options include homestays (some with cable TV and Internet access), rooms in a student guesthouse and apartments. Tecún Umán also provides packages to popular tourist destinations around Guatemala. Discounts for group bookings and those studying more than four weeks are available. 6a Ca. Poniente 34. Tel: 502-7832-2792/7882/4159, Cel: 502-5513-4349, E-mail: suamigodirector@gmail.com, Skype: mariorene1957, URL: www.tecunuman.centramerica.com. Updated: Nov 16, 2009.

Spanish School San José el Viejo

This school has a solid reputation and gorgeous facilities. Set in stunning, landscaped gardens, the school building used to be part of an old church. Individual classes are offered in rooms or cubicles in the garden, and can be customized for doctors, travelers or lawyers if requested in advance. Accommodation is offered in a homestay, or if looking for a touch of luxury, there are 11 beautifully furnished and fully-equipped rooms within the school grounds that grant the use of a swimming pool and tennis court. The spacious Castle Room has a telescope peering out to Volcán de Agua. 5a Av. Sur 34. Tel: 502-7832-3028, E-mail: spanish@sanjoseelviejo.com, URL: www.sanjoseelviejo.com. Updated: Nov 16, 2009.

COINED Spanish School

This friendly school offers a variety of Spanish courses, including intensive, business and medical classes, DELE certificate preparation, and combinations such as language instruction with cultural education, salsa or horseback riding. COINED's custommade itineraries for groups include travel and learning. Classes are one on one, in pairs or in groups of up to four students, and take place in classrooms or on the rooftop study area that has a volcano view. A selection of volunteer and internship programs are also available, and the school rents cell phones and arranges tour bookings. 6a Av. Norte 9. Tel: 502-7832-4846, E-mail: info@cdl.edu, gtkhernandez@intercoined.org, URL: www.coined-guatemala.org. Updated: Jan 29, 2010.

El Mundo del Español

This small, affordable school offers regular classes and specialized courses for travelers, including two-week survival and retiree programs. Classes for children, total immersion and Spanish for business, healthcare and airline staff are available. For those with little free time during the day, El Mundo del Español offers the opportunity to study in the evenings. There is a garden, used as a classroom, at the back, and a salsa studio and travel agency at the front entrance. Prices drop during the low season, so ask for current rates. 1a Ca. Poniente 27. Tel: 502-7832-2711, E-mail: info@elmundodelespanol.com, brendabarrios@yahoo.com.mx, URL: www.elmundodelespanol.com. Updated: Nov 19, 2009.

Academia Colonial Spanish School

Academia Colonial Spanish school is located in the historical monument of Casa Convento Concepción, only four blocks from the central park. It offers one-on-one instruction with the most experienced teachers in an ambiance that is beautiful and conducive for learning. 4a Ca. Oriente 41. Tel: 502-7882-4600, E-mail: info@academiacolonial.com, URL: www.academiacolonial.com. Updated: Apr 29, 2010.

Volunteering

Although Antigua is more affluent than most Guatemalan cities, there is still a significant need for humanitarian aid. Antigua offers countless opportunities for anyone interested in helping out at a nonprofit organization. The majority of the associations in Antigua focus on educating, and providing food for children and orphans. Villages surrounding the city are home to many infants deeply in need of proper nourishment and attention. Most programs are free for volunteers, but they also do not pay or provide any accommodation or food. Some organizations prefer volunteers stay for at least one month, while others are flexible. Your best bet is to visit them personally to see what type of work is needed. All of them arrange public tours on a weekly basis. Volunteering is a meaningful experience that undoubtedly leaves you looking at the world from a different perspective. To be able to contribute effectively, you are expected to have initiative, enthusiasm and a positive attitude. You should also speak some Spanish. Updated: Sep 10, 2009.

Obras Sociales de Santo Hermano Pedro

Volunteers at the Hospital Hermano Pedro mainly care for patients, providing them with hope and companionship. A typical day includes feeding the elderly or playing with the children. This hospital hosts medical missionary groups from abroad, so only social work is needed.

There is no fee or restriction on your period of stay. Anyone with patience and creativity is welcome. To apply, bring two photos and your passport to the hospital, where you will need to fill out a form. Public tours are available on Tuesdays and Thursdays at 3 p.m. 6a Ca. Oriente 20. Tel: 502-7832-0883, Fax: 502-7832-0986, E-mail: voluntarioshp@live.com, URL: www.obrashermanopedro.org. Updated: Aug 20, 2009.

Camino Seguro

Camino Seguro is a non-profit foundation that seeks to improve the lives of children and their families who live in the slums of Guatemala City. Those with specific skills such as gardening, making handicrafts or playing guitar are welcome to help. Anyone over 18 can apply. A minimum stay of one month is required. Registration costs $50. The organization is situated in Guatemala City; expect to spend $1 each way on daily transport. Another way to help is by staying at Hostal Lazos Fuertes, where all profits go to Camino Seguro. Public visits ($12 on private bus) are held every Thursday at 8:30 a.m. Ca. del Hermano Pedro 4. Tel: 502-7832-8428, Fax: 502-7832-8428, E-mail: volunteers@safepassage.org, URL: www.safepassage.org. Updated: Aug 20, 2009.

Common Hope

This non-profit organization looks for both short- and long-term assistance in diverse areas, from dentistry to photography. Situated in a village outside of Antigua, Common Hope provides health care, housing and education for impoverished children. Sponsor a child or provide them with school supplies. Two-hour public tours are available on Thursdays at 2 p.m. There is no program fee. Carretera de San Juan, Km 2. Tel: 502-7922-6600, Fax: 502-7922-6600, E-mail: info@commonhope.org, URL: www.commonhope.org. Updated: Sep 10, 2009.

La Asociación Nuestros Ahijados

Nuestros Ahijados offers short-term volunteer opportunities for travelers looking to help out for a week or two, as well as long-term options for those that decide to stay for awhile. Among other things, volunteers can help at a homeless shelter, distribute clothing or shoes to those in need, or partake in the highlight of the operation, offering care for malnourished infants and children at La Casa Jackson in nearby San Felipe. Carretera a San Felipe 106. Tel: 502-7832-4678, Fax: 502-7832-4679, E-mail: dreamer@conexion.com.gt, URL: www.ana.org.gt. Updated: Nov 12, 2009.

Tours

From individuals in Parque Central offering their services to more professional outfits, there are a plethora of tour operators throughout Antigua. Quality, safety, reliability, equipment and prices vary. It is wise to check out a few before making any decisions. Some specialize in guided historic walks in Antigua, and Mayan cultural tours around local villages and coffee plantations. Others are geared toward the more adventurous types who want to spend their time mountain biking, volcano trekking, kayaking, birding, rock climbing, whitewater rafting or motorcycling. Shuttles, flights and packages are available to all major tourist destinations in Guatemala and beyond. The INGUAT tourist office keeps lists of current tour operators in town. Updated: Oct 27, 2009.

WALKING TOUR

If you have only one day to see Antigua, INGUAT (the national institution in charge of tourism) suggests a four-hour walking tour of the city. You can pick up a map with the suggested tour at INGUAT's office at 4 Calle Oriente 10. The tour will take you on a walking tour of four museums, a cultural center, a few churches and the central park—all in one morning. In reality, the tour is a bit ambitious to accomplish in four hours; it is a better idea to set aside at least half an hour to see each site of interest. However, this map gives you a pretty good idea of which places are best to visit in Antigua. Wear comfortable shoes and take your time. Updated: Sep 07, 2009.

BIKING TOURS

Popular among outdoor lovers, biking tours are a rewarding way to see the countryside. Several tour operators offer easy "Sip and Ride" tours, where you visit coffee plantations, textile villages, and Casa K'ojom, a museum dedicated to Mayan music. Thrillseekers can bike to Almolonga Valley or Volcán de Agua, where challenging terrain and beautiful landscapes await. The reasonably priced tours include a bilingual guide and quality equipment. Trips are three hours, starting at 9 a.m. and 2 p.m. For daredevils, some operators also organize rigorous overnight hike-and-bike trips to multiple active volcanoes. Although costly, they include warm clothing, all meals and professional equipment. Updated: Aug 19, 2009.

ANTIGUA & AROUND

TOUR OPERATORS

Guatemala Ventures

Guatemala Ventures offers a variety of outdoor excursions all over the country. Pedal its "Highland to Island" circuit on a mountain bike, hike the "Maya Trail" or trek the spectacular five-coned "Volcáno Circuit." Guatemala Ventures can also fix you up with less-strenuous options. Birdwatching, horseback riding, caving and whitewater rafting are also available. Its multi-adventure tours are a blend of various activities designed to help the energetic traveler see the highlights of Guatemala. Trips are for all ages and abilities and start from half-day jaunts to multi-day adventures. Daily 8:30 a.m.-6:30 p.m. 1a Av. Sur 15. Tel: 502-7832-3383/4562-3103/5001-8185, URL: www.guatemalaventures.com. Updated: Oct 27, 2009.

CATours

For those looking for adventures of the two-wheeled kind, CATours is the perfect choice. Based inside MOTO Café, Antigua's resident motorcycle experts offer a variety of tours throughout Guatemala, Central America and Mexico. All tastes, experience levels and time commitments are catered for by a medley of itineraries, to be traversed on a wide range of on- and off-road tourer, enduro, trial and quad bikes. Custom-made tours are also available to any destination; just ask for a rate quote. Motorcycle rental and training courses for the inexperienced are also available. Booking your ride online will ensure that a percentage of the fee is donated to charity. 6a Ca. Oriente 14. Tel: 502-7832-9638/5571-7279, Fax: 502-7832-4801, URL: www.catours.co.uk. Updated: Oct 27, 2009.

Old Town Outfitters

If you are up for a bit of exploring, head to specialty outdoor store and adventure travel company Old Town Outfitters, just a block from the park. Take your pick from the wide range of activities on offer, including mountain biking, rock climbing, kayaking, caving, whitewater rafting, volcano hiking, trekking, birding, helicopter tours and Mayan cultural trips. Ranging from day trips to multi-day expeditions, there is something for nearly all skill levels and budgets. The experts will help you create your own custom-made itinerary if you like. Equipment is also available for rental. You can donate school supplies to get a tour discount. 5a Av. Sur 12C. Tel: 502-5399-0440, Fax: 502-7832-4171, URL: www.adventureguatemala.com. Updated: Oct 27, 2009.

Antigua Tours and Travel

Antigua Tours and Travel has its main office next to Hotel Casa Santo Domingo and another one inside Café El Portal facing Parque Central. The agency organizes cultural walking tours of the town visiting colonial buildings, ruins and museums led by historian Elizabeth Bell. Also available are guided trips to coffee plantations, various villages, Volcán Pacaya, and flights and packages to the Mayan ruins of Tikal. Antigua Tours and Travel also provides shared and private shuttle services to popular destinations around Guatemala, and will arrange hotel reservations. Contributions are made to local projects to support the community and restore the cathedral's colonial paintings. Discounts are offered for 10 or more people. 3a Ca. Oriente 22 (Main office)/5a Av. Norte 6, inside Café El Portal (Parque Central office). Tel: 502-7832-5821/2046/9289/7882/4498, URL: www.antiguatours.net. Updated: Oct 27, 2009.

O.X. Outdoor Excursions

O.X. Outdoor Excursions specializes in volcano hiking. Clients can choose from day trips of varying difficulty and overnight excursions, as well as the five-day extreme "Spires of Fire" expedition that takes you to all the active volcanoes in the country. Each one requires good fitness levels and a spirit of adventure. Guides, transport, warm clothing and equipment are included. O.X. also rents out mountain bikes by the hour and is in the process of setting up tours. For those on a mission, try the Outdoor Leadership Skills Development 30-day crash course. Profits go toward the company's "Green O.X. Project," which helps preserve and restore the natural environment and develop sustainable tourism. You can also donate your time as an eco-volunteer. Credit cards are only accepted when booking online. 1a Av. Sur, 4B. Tel: 502-7832-0074/5801/4301, URL: www.guatemalavolcano.com. Updated: Oct 27, 2009.

Things to See and Do

Antigua is a small town by many standards, but the amount of ruins, churches, museums, Spanish schools and hikes make it a unique and engaging place to spend a week, or a year. Students who are learning Spanish in Antigua will probably find their days occupied with hours of study, but their free time can fill up fast.

The museums in this colonial town are rich in culture. Spending a day wandering around the Ayuntamiento and the Museo de Santiago will allow you to experience the truly complex and interesting history of Antigua. Paseo de los Museos, possibly the most impressive museum in town, can be perused in a few hours, but if you have the time, it is nice to linger a little longer. Once a convent, the museum has lovely grounds and is full of little nooks—it could keep you busy for days. If you are itching to get out of town and explore, the area surrounding Antigua has a variety of activities to choose from. Because of the diverse avian population, birders from all over the world are attracted to the four volcanoes that surround the city. Hikers can choose to ascend active volcanoes or climb to the Cerro de la Cruz for a view of Antigua. Updated: Aug 11, 2010.

PLAZAS & PARKS

Parque Central

Surrounded by buildings dating back to colonial times, this central plaza is the main hangout for locals. It is always packed on weekends and festivals, when it is the scene for concerts, parades and processions. Mature trees, gardens and pathways lined with wooden benches radiate from a central fountain where water jets from mermaid breasts. Shoe shiners, indigenous women selling handicrafts and guides offering their services mingle with tourists and locals. This is a no-go area for tuk-tuks, and the south side is closed to traffic, so it is a relatively peaceful place to chill out for a few hours. Updated: Nov 13, 2009.

MUSEUMS

Casa del Tejido

(ENTRANCE: $0.60) Don't be put off by the drab exterior: Casa del Tejido is a must-see for shoppers who want to understand what the designs on their Mayan textiles signify. The unhurried, personal 20-minute tour in English or Spanish opens the door into the symbolism, methods and purpose of Mayan weaving and embroidery in local culture today. An excellent range of textiles, traditional clothes and handicrafts are on sale, each of them handmade by cooperatives throughout the Guatemalan Highlands. Credit cards are accepted, but 7 percent of your total will be added; discounts for use of cash. The entrance fee includes weaving demonstration, coffee and a chocolate taster. Phone for free hotel pickup. Monday-Saturday 9 a.m.-5 a.m. 1a Ca. Poniente 51. Tel: 502-7832-3169, E-mail: alidaperez@itelgua.com. Updated: Sep 01, 2009.

Centro Cultural La Azotea

The Centro Cultural La Azotea is an excellent family-friendly museum detailing local music, costumes and coffee. The interactive exhibition explains how coffee fruits from one tree are transformed into 40 cups of drinkable coffee. The second part of the center is Casa K'ojom, a collection of traditional Mayan instruments, masks and paintings. The displays show the instruments in the context of the ceremonies in which they are used, including a very interesting section on the folk saint Maximón. The last exhibition is the Rincón of Sacatepéquez, a representation of the Kaqchikel villages surrounding Antigua. The displays portray the customs, lifestyles and brilliant costumes of these villages. To get there, you can call ahead and take a free shuttle from Parque Central in Antigua to the museum. Or take any bus going to Jocotenango and stop in front of the church. Cross the street and take the street going to the cemetery. Allow around two hours. Monday-Friday 8 a.m.-4:30 p.m. Ca. del Cemeterio Final Jocotenango. Tel: 502-7831-1120, E-mail: info@centroazotea.com, URL: www.centroazotea.com. Updated: Aug 21, 2009.

Palacio Del Ayuntamiento: Museo De Santiago, Museo Del Libro Antiguo

On the north side of Parque Central is the Palacio del Ayuntamiento, which dates back to 1743. The complex is now home to the *municipalidad*, or town hall, and two museums. Previously the old jail and prison chapel, the Museo de Santiago displays colonial artifacts such as furniture, portraits, religious paintings and weapons. The original stone *sirenas*, or mermaids, removed from the fountain in the central park after the 1773 earthquake are prized exhibits. The site of the first printing press in Guatemala is now the Museo del Libro Antiguo. Exhibits include a replica of the original printing press, a copy of the first book printed in Guatemala, the will of Saint Hermano Pedro and an overview of the history of printing. Climb the stairs to the upper level to enjoy a view of the park, cathedral and volcanoes. Museum information is in English and Spanish. Some information is in Braille. Monday-Friday 9 a.m.-4 p.m., Saturday-Sunday 9 a.m.-noon and 2-4 p.m. Portal del Ayuntamiento 6. Tel: 502-7832-2868/5511, E-mail: museosantiago@mcd.gob.gt. Updated: May 07, 2010.

Museo Mesoamericano del Jade

Just two blocks east of Parque Central, this compact museum displays replicas of some of the most significant jade artifacts ever found. Accompanying the pieces are detailed explanations in English and Spanish of what the objects represent and were used for. The museum is located within the same building as La Casa del Jade, where you can purchase beautiful artifacts made of jade, gold and silver. You can also take a guided tour of the factory in the back room. The factory tour and museum are both free, and it should only take around 30 minutes to do both. Daily 9:30 a.m.-6:30 p.m. 4 Ca. Oriente 10. Tel: 502-7832-3974, Fax: 502-7832-3974, E-mail: sales@lacasadeljade.com, URL: www. lacasadeljade.com. Updated: Sep 04, 2009.

Proyecto Cultural El Sitio

Proyecto Cultural El Sitio is located two blocks west of the Parque Central. The gallery hosts a variety of art expos, performing arts, concerts and movies for evening entertainment. For the musically inclined, it offers guitar and harp lessons. Classes are held during the week and on weekends; prices range $20-30 for a weekly two-hour music lesson. The gallery requests that music students sign up a week in advance. Contact Proyecto Cultural El Sitio for schedules, registration dates and times. Walk two blocks west from the intersection of 5 Ca. Poniente and 5 Av. Sur at Parque Central. Proyecto Cultural El Sitio will be the on your left. 5 Ca. Poniente 15. Tel: 502-7832-3037, E-mail: raquel@elsitiocultural.org, URL: www.elsitiocultural.org. Updated: Sep 09, 2009.

Jades, S.A. Factory, Showroom and Museum

Drop in here for a unique shopping experience, if you go for jewelry, jade or Mayan history. Four blocks from the park, the store has well-presented displays of jewelry, masks and sculptures. An informative museum lays out the facts and history of jade and Mayan cosmology. Check out the craftsmen at work in the factory. Famous visitors include Bill Clinton, who stopped by for a shopping spree. Tours in English or Spanish come with free coffee, or you can browse around alone. Four blocks from Parque Central, on the left just after the gas station. Daily 9 a.m.-6:30 p.m. 4a Ca. Oriente 34. Tel: 502-7832-3841, Fax: 502-7832-2755, URL: www.jademaya.com, 4a. Ca. Oriente. Updated: Aug 20, 2009.

Finca Filadelfia Coffee Farm Tour

Anyone curious about how we get that morning cup of coffee will find the answers at Finca Filadelfia, 10 minutes by tuk-tuk from downtown Antigua. You can visit the coffee fields by mule or aboard a flatbed Mercedes truck with canopy and seats. Part of the tour takes you to the production area. Set aside two hours for the entire experience. After the tour, you can enjoy a cup of the farm's coffee and lunch in Café Tenango, the farm's international-style restaurant. The staff is bilingual, courteous and knowledgeable. From the main square in Antigua, take Calle del Arco north until you dead-end at the La Merced Church. Turn west (left) and go half a block to the corner of 6 Calle. Turn right (north) and continue four blocks, then turn left on Carrete. Daily 8 a.m.-5 p.m. Carretera San Felipe and Jocotenango. Tel: 502-4010-6592, URL: www.rdalton-coffee.com. Updated: Oct 14, 2009.

CHURCHES & RELIGIOUS SITES

San Francisco El Grande Church

For church and ruin enthusiasts, beautiful San Francisco El Grande Church is a must-see. Those who are not fans of crumbling stone can relax on the grassy slopes among the ruins. Chill out with a book or picnic with the kids. There is a museum dedicated to Saint Hermano Pedro, and his tomb rests in a private chapel. Sundays and religious festivals are the best days to browse the stalls selling devotional goods. Photography is allowed in the ruins but is forbidden inside the church, museum and chapel. Tuesday-Sunday 9 a.m.-5 p.m., Saturday-Sunday 1-5 p.m. Walk south to the end of 1a Av. Sur. Entrances are on 7a Ca. Oriente and Ca. de los Pasos. Updated: Sep 01, 2009.

Iglesia de la Merced

A good site to visit if you have a spare 10 minutes, La Merced stands out from other churches in Antigua for its impressive bright yellow and white latticed façade. Inside is basic by comparison, but Baroque lovers will love to take a peek. For less than a dollar, you can also enter the peaceful ruined cloisters next door, with a beautiful tiered fountain, and upstairs, with views of the surrounding mountains. Mosaics, made from recycled magazines by inmates of a local prison are for sale in the courtyard. Try to go on the weekend when, between 4 and 8 p.m., the park outside fills up with locals and tourists alike, all snacking on cheap and tasty street food. Church hours:

Hermano Pedro

One note-worthy historical figure in Antigua who still affects the lives of many Guatemalans today is Hermano Pedro, also known as the Saint Francis of the Americas. He came to Antigua from Spain around 1650, importing with him the tradition of Semana Santa, or Holy Week. He made the first *alfombra*, an intricate carpet of dyed sawdust created for religious processions to traipse along, and led the first procession.

During his life, he helped the poor and less fortunate by opening a hospital, a shelter for the homeless and schools. He was beatified in 1980 and canonized in 2002. Many devout Guatemalans still fervently pray at his tomb in the church of San Francisco El Grande, believing in his divine powers to cure the afflicted and crippled. The messages of gratitude, photographs and abandoned crutches that plaster the walls in the church museum bear witness to his special abilities. Many buildings are named after him, and the Ruta de Peregrino, or pilgrim's route, traces the significant places in his life, including many of the city's churches and ruins. Maps of the route can be obtained from the tourism office. Updated: Jan 29, 2010.

Monday-Friday 7 a.m.-noon and 3-8 p.m, Saturday-Sunday 7 a.m.-8 p.m. Mass: Saturday 6 p.m., Sunday 6 a.m., 9 a.m., 11 a.m., 7 p.m. Corner of 1a Ca. Poniente and 6a Av. North. Updated: Aug 28, 2009.

Iglesia and Convento de la Recoleccion

If you must choose just one ruin to visit in Antigua, this is your best option. Formerly a church, this massive set of ruins is probably the most impressive in town. Inaugurated in 1717, it survived just half a century before being ripped apart by the earthquake of 1773. Most walls, a beautiful archway entrance, and a staircase (to nowhere) still stand. Huge chunks of roof and walls lay scattered all around the site. Daily 9 a.m.-5 p.m. Av. de la Recoleccion. Updated: Sep 10, 2009.

Catedral de Santiago

Sitting proudly on the east side of the Parque Central, this cathedral has an ornate façade and is attractively lit up at night. Built in 1542, it was hit by numerous earthquakes, but is still standing. The inside has suffered and is not as impressive as the outside suggests. 4a Av. Sur, on Park Central. Updated: Nov 16, 2006.

Iglesia y Convento de Santa Clara

The front of this ruin is an impressive archway, which hides a large courtyard inside with neatly manicured gardens. The convent was founded in 1699 by six nuns, but the first building was totally destroyed by an earthquake in 1717. The present building was finished in 1734 and was partially destroyed in the 1773 earthquake. What little that was left standing was destroyed by yet another powerful earthquake in 1874. 2a Av. Sur and 6a Ca. Updated: Aug 14, 2006.

RUINS & HISTORICAL BUILDINGS

Paseo de los Museos

Located on the grounds of Hotel Casa Santo Domingo, the beautifully presented Paseo de los Museos, or Museums Promenade, allows access to the leftover ruins of the Iglesia y Convento de Santo Domingo, destroyed during the 1773 earthquake. Although stone and other materials were taken to reconstruct houses and other buildings, the museum contains old burial crypts and what is left of the ruined church. The complex of museums displays colonial religious art, Mayan artifacts, modern glass sculptures, contemporary international and local art, traditional handicrafts from the region and an antique pharmaceutical collection. Watch craftsmen in the candle and pottery workshops and browse in their store. Each exhibit has detailed information and history in English and Spanish. Ask for a map upon entering; It is included in the entrance fee. Inside Hotel Casa Santo Domingo. Daily 9 a.m.-6 p.m. 3a Ca. Oriente 28. Tel: 502-7820-1220, Fax: 502-7820-1221. URL: www.casasantodomingo.com.gt. Updated: Nov 13, 2009.

Palacio de los Capitanes

The Palacio de los Capitanes, the oldest two-story building in Antigua, lines the entire south side of the Parque Central. Built in 1558, it was the seat of the Spanish colonial government for most of Central America and Chiapas. More recently, it housed the police department, government and tourist offices. It is currently unoccupied due to restoration, but is open to the public for viewing. Tours are offered twice a day, at 10:30 a.m. and 2:30 p.m. You can wander around alone if you wish, but watch where you step. It is expected to fully reopen by the time of publication. Daily 9 a.m.-noon, 2-3:30 p.m. 5a. Ca. Plaza Central. URL: www.palaciodeloscapitanes.com. Updated: Nov 13, 2009.

Las Capuchinas Convento

Founded by five Spanish nuns, this building was completed in 1736, and consists of a circle of 18 small stone rooms, or cells, set behind a bland-looking church. Although it does not look like much from the outside, ruins aficionados may find it worth a visit. If you only have passing interest, it probably will not be worth the admission fee. Corner of 2a Ca. Oriente and 2a Av. Norte. Updated: Aug 14, 2006.

Colegio de San Jerónimo

This ruin site includes a lush garden in front and a fountain at its center. Friars of the Mercedarian Order built the school in 1757, however, it was closed by Spanish King Carlos III just four years later because it did not have royal approval. After a brief stint as the Royal customs house, it was destroyed by the earthquake in 1773. If you are a ruins buff, then it is worth a visit and the entrance fee. However, many travelers may find it sufficient just to peer from the outside fence. 1a Ca. Poniente. Updated: Sep 10, 2009.

Photo by: Douglas J. Klostermann

MONUMENTS

Cerro de La Cruz and El Hato

Overlooking Antigua from the north, Cerro de la Cruz (Hill of the Cross) is the perfect spot to enjoy the beautiful view of Antigua and Volcáno de Agua. This easy walk starts at the end of 1 Av. Norte. Keep walking north until you get to the steps entering the forest. It takes about 20 minutes to reach the cross. For safety reasons, it is not advised to go on your own.

From there, you can hike up to the village of El Hato, where the eco-hostel Earth Lodge is located. The hike will take another hour with no particular difficulties. From the cross, walk uphill to the main paved street and turn left. Keep walking until you get to the village, while enjoying the view on the volcanoes and Jocotenango.

Once you get to El Hato, take the muddy road until you get to the *pila* (water tank). You will see the sign for the Earth Lodge. Enjoy a nice lunch with a breathtaking view on the Panchoy Valley and the Volcán Acatenango. You can hike down to Antigua via the same road or take a bus. You can also stay for a night in one of its tree houses, where you can witness an amazing sunset and sunrise. Tel: 502-5664-0713, E-mail earthlodge@gmail.com, URL: www.earthlodgeguatemala.com. Updated: Jul 09, 2010.

Monumento a Landívar

This large, white monument was built in 1953 in honor of Rafael Landívar, the great poet of colonial Guatemala, who died in 1793. His ashes rest inside. Closed to the public, the monument is surrounded by gardens and can only be viewed through iron railings from the street. Around the corner, on Calle de la Pólvora and Landívar, a plaque marks the only remaining wall of the house where he was born in 1731. Walk along the 5a Calle Poniente toward the market side of town. You will see the monument on the corner when you get to the Calzada Santa Lucía. Corner of Calzada Santa Lucía and Ca. de la Pólvora and Landívar. Updated: Nov 13, 2009.

VOLCANO CLIMBING

With four volcanoes to climb, Antigua is a wonderful place for hikers. Each of the volcanoes is within 25 kilometers (15.5 mi) of the town, which makes Antigua a natural base for those wanting to ascend one, or all four, of the peaks. Each volcano offers something different: amazing views, freshly exposed lava or challenging climbs. If you are looking to climb all four, work your way up from Volcán de Agua, the least challenging of the four ascents. Updated: Aug 11, 2010.

Climbing Volcán De Agua

Located just south of Antigua, Volcán de Agua (3,760 m/12,335 ft) is generally considered to be the least challenging of the four ascents in the area. Unlike its neighbor Volcán Fuego, this volcano has been dormant for the past 500 years. Starting at the village of Santa Maria de Jesús, the trek is considered to be a moderate hike of four to five hours, suitable for most people. The name comes from a 1541 flood when the crater of the volcano was filled with water. Earthquakes originating from the nearby Volcán Fuego caused the rim of the crater to rupture, creating a mudslide that destroyed the original capital city of Santiago de los Caballeros.

In Santa Maria de Jesús, the trail up the volcano starts at the cemetery. From there, you continue up a partially paved road that shrinks to a small trail. Robberies have been known to take place around this area so be extra careful. You can request a police escort at no cost if you feel like you need one. From there, the trail passes through coffee fincas and fields until it ascends into series of steep switchbacks. Once you reach the summit, look to the west; on a clear day, you can see the Pacific Ocean. It is possible to camp at the summit, and there is no fee for doing so. Most people choose to camp inside the hollow cone at the top of the trail. Bring plenty of warm clothes as the temperature drops severely after dark. Updated: Aug 11, 2010.

Climbing Volcán Pacaya

Climbing Pacaya (2,552 m/8,373 ft) is a mind-blowing trek for anyone keen on seeing volcanoes up close and in action. Take the morning trip for a better chance of enjoying clear skies and breathtaking views, but during good weather, you can go in the afternoon for a spectacular early-evening light show. The two-hour climb is tough in certain places, especially at the end, when you must scramble up volcanic scree. However, the payoff is worth the effort. Providing the wind is blowing the sulfurous smoke in the opposite direction, once at the top, you get a close-up view of red lava rivers flowing from the active crater. The tour heads back before sunset, but keep looking to the top on the way down: you may see eruptions. *Note: In May 2010, an*

eruption of Pacaya killed three people. It was closed to climbers. Check with local authorities before attempting the trek. Departures: 6 a.m. and 1 p.m. Updated: Aug 11 2010.

Climbing Acatenango

This is a stunning hike if you are lucky with the weather, but do not attempt without a guide, because you are climbing a serious 4,000-meter (13,000 ft) mountain and the conditions can change in an instant. It is a semi-steep climb, similar to Pacaya, yet slightly longer at five-and-a-half hours. When you reach the summit crater, you can set up camp. The view of the surrounding landscape is nice, but the highlight is getting up in the dark to watch the nearby Fuego erupting, showering fire some 100 meters (328 ft) into the air. Several companies operate this route, but beware of poor standards and check all equipment before you leave. Two reputable companies run trips: Old Town Outfitters (6a Av. Sur and 6a Ca. Poniente) and Mayan Bike Tours (6a Ca. Poniente and 1a Av. Norte). Updated: Aug 11, 2010.

Climbing Volcán De Fuego

At 3,763 meters (12,346 ft), Volcán de Fuego is considered to be a more strenuous climb that its neighbors and is the highest active volcano in Guatemala. It is named for its consistent activity, and it has been spewing lava off and on for decades. Fuego has erupted more than 60 times in the past 500 years. Connected by a ridge to Volcán Acatenango, there are a few different ways to summit. The Alotenago Route has a considerable elevation gain and will offer most hikers a decent challenge. There are several campsites on the trail, so making a two-day summit bid is possible. The second way to the summit is by La Soledad Route. From the base of the volcano, there are several well-maintained trails that lead to one main path to the summit of Acatenango. From there, you can follow the ridge to Volcán Fuego. Updated: Aug 11, 2010.

OTHER HIKING

There are a few options if you want to do some exploration around Antigua but are not interested in hiking up volcanoes. The first, and most popular, is located right in town. Cerro de la Cruz (Hill of the Cross) might be considered more of a walk than a hike, but with several steep stairs that lead to the top, you will get a bit of a workout. The trailhead is within short walking distance (10-20 min) from anywhere in town. Use caution as there have been reported robberies on this path. If you like, you can get a police escort. Other options for hiking around Antigua include tours to cloud forests and coffee fincas. Multi-day trips for wilderness hikes can be arranged with several of the tour companies around town. Updated: Aug 11, 2010.

HORSEBACK RIDING
Travelers to Antigua can visit some of the beautiful surrounding countryside by horseback. Two stables offer horseback riding in Antigua, Centro Cultural La Azotea in Jocotenango and Ravenscroft Riding Stables in San Juan de Obispo. The price is $45 for a three-hour tour. Boots and helmets are provided for you. Minimum age is 6 years old. No experience is required. Updated: Aug 21, 2009.

COOKING SCHOOLS

El Frijol Feliz Cooking School
El Frijol Feliz cooking school teaches in a fun and engaging way. In class, you will learn how to cook Guatemalan cuisine, an exotic mixture of traditional colonial Spanish and local Mayan cooking. Dishes include pepían, chiles rellenos and tamales. Classes are small and hands on, led by a Guatemalan chef named Gabi. 7a Ca. Poniente 11. Tel: 502-7882-4600, E-mail: info@frijolfeliz.com, URL: www.frijolfeliz.com. Updated: May 10, 2010.

DANCE SCHOOLS

Salsa Dreams Dance Studio
(CLASSES: $11/hour) Put your best foot forward and attempt to learn the seductive dance of salsa at Salsa Dreams Dance Studio, located in the Central American Art Gallery. Classes are available by appointment for individuals, couples and groups. Professional instructors speak English, and are enthusiastic and encouraging. The cost is $11 an hour for an individual lesson, with discounts offered for multiple classes. If you are not sure you are ready to commit, drop by on a Monday or Tuesday at 5 p.m. to check out a free lesson. Get ready to sweat! Daily 10 a.m.-7 p.m. 4 Ca. Oriente and 1 Av. Norte 10. Tel: 502-5238-1914. Updated: Aug 29, 2009.

New Sensation Salsa Studio
Salsa dancing is thrilling and flamboyant but most of all, it is just damn good fun. No coordination is required, that is what the teachers are for. New Sensation has top-notch, free workshops at 5 p.m. on Monday and Tuesday that teach the basics and leave you wanting more. Afterward, professional one-on-one or couple-on-one tutoring focuses on completing the moves in style and preparing you for the salsa clubs. Classes in bachata and merengue are also available. Shoes are the tricky part. Flip flops don't cut it and tennis shoes are bulky, but will do in a pinch. Shoes and sandals with some flexibility and grip are perfect. Beginners should avoid heels, but should aim to dance the night away in stilettos by the end! Wear loose-fitting clothes. Monday-Saturday 9 a.m.-7 p.m. 1a Ca. Poniente 27. E-mail: nancylasalsa@yahoo.es. Updated: Sep 01, 2009.

SPAS
Travelers who wish to be pampered will find their desires easily fulfilled in Antigua, with spas equal to—or better than—anything available in larger cities. International-quality reflexology, full-body massages, facials, waxing, manicures and pedicures are all available to the traveler willing to ask questions and do a little research. Consult hotel staffers, other locals and expats to track down the best practitioners. Prices range $8-150, depending upon the services requested. Updated: Oct 04, 2009.

Lodging
Antigua hostels are plentiful and varied. Almost every street is packed with hotels of all descriptions, so you are guaranteed to lay your head somewhere. Unless, of course, you arrive during Semana Santa (Holy Week) when everywhere is chock-full and prices skyrocket. The rest of the year, all budgets and tastes are covered, from backpacker hostels and family-run posadas (guesthouses) to more luxurious boutique and five-star hotels. Many places have rooftop terraces with gorgeous views of the surrounding volcanoes. Most rates include breakfast, Internet and drinking water.

Those wanting to camp or park their camper vans safely overnight can stop for free in the grounds of DISETUR (División de Seguridad Turística), the Tourist Police (Tel: 502-7934-6513/6522-24), south of the artisan market. An alternative if you are seeking a bit of peace is to stay in an eco-lodge tree house or cabin that overlooks Antigua, surrounding villages and volcanoes. New places are constantly arriving on the scene, so it is worth checking out a few before deciding. Updated: Jun 29, 2010.

BUDGET

Jungle Party

(BEDS: $2) This is a great place with a friendly owner and lots of travel information on the blackboard in the buzzing communal area. Rooms are dorm only, varying in numbers of beds, but they are clean, as are the shared bathrooms. The communal area, which is also a bar and restaurant, has a great vibe and makes the place feel fun. 6a Av. Norte between 2a Ca. Poniente and 3a Ca. Tel: 832-0463 E-mail: jungleparty2001@yahoo.com. Updated: Nov 17, 2006.

Estella's House

(ROOMS: $4.25-11) A converted Guatemalan home, Estella's House is a charming alternative to conventional hostels down the road. Five basic rooms cluster around a compact TV salon and adjacent veranda. This quiet and cozy place is kept clean and tidy. Despite its size, it is still easy to meet other travelers. Primarily for long-term stays of at least a week, prices include access to the kitchen, or you can add-on one to three meals a day. Excellent value, especially for the solo traveler, this is also a good spot to practice your Spanish. 41a Ca. Poniente. Tel: 502-7832-1324. Updated: Sep 01, 2009.

La Casa del Huésped

(ROOMS: $5-8) The friendly owner ensures this place is a "family" hostel, and the pleasant central patio with plenty of garden chairs helps develop that kind of community feel. There are seven twin rooms, and the owners offer free tea and coffee, the use of a kitchen and good security. Calzada Santa Lucía Norte between 2a Ca. Tel: 502-832-3422. Updated: Nov 17, 2006.

Ummagumma

(ROOMS: $5-13) Ummagumma is a small, friendly and popular hostel just a few blocks from the market and the center of colonial Antigua. Dorms, single, double and triple private rooms with en-suite or shared bathroom sprawl more than three levels, including the rooftop. A good place to chill, the rooftop terrace has awesome views of volcanoes and city, plus a tiny lounging area with cushions and TV lies in a corner beside one of the two kitchens. There is another communal sitting area below with HBO and free use of Internet. A helpful agent in the entrance meets all travel and tour needs. This is a great spot to hook up with other travelers, and is close to bars and restaurants. 7a Av. Norte 34. Tel: 502-7832-4413/9466/5874-6101/3376, E-mail: ummagumma@itelgua.com, URL: www.ummagummahostel.blogspot.com. Updated: Feb 09, 2010.

Hotel Orquideas

(BEDS: $5.50/ROOMS: $15-25) Hotel Orquideas is an excellent choice for those seeking budget accommodations in Antigua. Located across from the ruins of San Jerónimo, this cozy hotel has got it all for less. The staff is friendly, the beds are comfortable and the bathrooms are clean. Both dorms and private rooms with cable TV are available. All include use of the community kitchen, Internet, free coffee and a hearty breakfast that is served under the covered rooftop patio 8:30-10 a.m. Calzada Santa Lucía Norte 25D. Tel: 502-5219-5406. Updated: Sep 01, 2009.

The Yellow House

(ROOMS: $6-18) A small, quiet, clean hostel with friendly staff, Yellow House is a favorite among budget travelers. Only two blocks from the fruit and vegetable market, and close to ruins and typical eateries. The doubles and single have cable TV. There are various-sized dorms with lockers, shared bathrooms with solar-powered showers and a tiny kitchen. There is a shady patio where an ample breakfast is served, and a relaxing rooftop terrace with hammocks and impressive volcano views. Get there early as beds fill up quickly. 1a Ca. Poniente 24. Tel: 502-7832-6646, E-mail: yellowhouseantigua@hotmail.com. Updated: Nov 13, 2009.

Kafka Hostel

(ROOMS: $6) At Kafka's most recent location there is a beautiful rooftop terrace and garden. Kafka also has a bar and grill that serves American-type food. Ideal for short stays; when you book two nights the third is free. 6a Av. Norte 40. URL: www.kafkahostel.com. Updated: Aug 03, 2009.

The Black Cat

(BEDS: $6) Only one block from Parque Central, the Black Cat Inn would please travelers looking for some comfort without spending too much. With a beautiful garden and a large terrace, it is the perfect place to relax and drink a beer while watching the sunset. The hotel has eight large and nicely decorated private rooms with bathroom and cable TV. There is also a nine-bed dorm. Rate includes a huge free breakfast and WiFi access. Open until

10 p.m., the bar and restaurant offers international cuisine. 6a Av. Norte between 4a Ca. Poniente and 5a. URL: www.blackcatantigua.com. Updated: Sep 01, 2009.

Hostal 5

(ROOMS: $7-50) The small Hostal 5 is a clean, cozy and friendly choice. There are rooms for two and dorms for four or six, each with private bathroom. You can watch cable TV on a big screen in the communal sitting area or kick back and enjoy the volcano views from the little terrace. There is also a tiny bar!, and its board games to keep you entertained. Breakfast and WiFi are include. 4a. Av. Norte 33. Tel: 502-7832-5462, URL: www. hostelfive.hostel.com. Updated: Nov 19, 2009.

Hotel el Jardín de Lolita

(ROOMS: $7.50-12.25) The family-run Hotel el Jardín de Lolita, with its pleasant garden and an aviary, is surprisingly airy for a budget, downtown establishment. Sparsely decorated rooms are clean and have at least two beds. The colorful new building at the back houses travelers sharing a bathroom, while private bathroom-seekers enjoy a rooftop view of Antigua. Guests have use of a small kitchen and off-street parking. Staff are courteous, and children are welcome here. Smoking is not permitted. 31 1a Ca. Poniente. Tel: 502-7832-7000. Updated: Sep 01, 2009.

Base Camp Hostel

(ROOMS: $10-25) This hostel is run by OX Expeditions, an adventure tour operator in downtown Antigua. There are two comfortable TV lounges that serve as great places to unwind and socialize after a day of biking. The rooms are spacious and airy, with triple-decker beds that are custom-made to fit any height. This hostel is good value, with breakfast included. The friendly American owner is happy to provide information. 1 Av. Sur 4B. Tel: 502-5801-4301, Fax: 502-7832-0074, E-mail: for_the_ox@yahoo.com, URL: www.guatemalavolcano.com. Updated: Aug 19, 2009.

Hotel Posada de Don Quijote

(ROOMS: $10-54) The Posada Don Quijote, only three blocks from the bars scene near El Arco and two blocks from the market, is a good budget option for those who don't mind the lackluster décor and less-than-gleaming bathrooms. It also has free Internet and WiFi, cable TV and a fridge in every room, warm-ish water (though not 24 hr), plus unlimited free coffee and purified water.

Book ahead if arriving at the weekend. 1ra Ca. Poniente 22A. Tel: 502-7832-0775, Fax: 502-7832-0726, E-mail: info@ posadaquijote.com, URL: www.posadaquijote.com. Updated: Sep 18, 2009.

Posada El Viajero

(ROOMS: $15) The greatest draw to the cheap and cheerful "Traveler Hotel" is its central location. The 10 rooms are definitely basic, but there is 24-hour hot water as well as free WiFi and purified water. Ask for the top room, the brightest and the only one with a TV. The rooftop terrace may be cluttered and lacking shade, but has superb panoramic views of the surrounding mountains. 7a Av. Norte 18. Tel: 502-7832-6375, E-mail: hotelviajero@hotmail.com. Updated: Aug 16, 2009.

Casa Santa Lucía 2

(ROOMS: $16-40) There is nothing flashy about this place, but Santa Lucía 2 represents good value, with its hot showers and clean, well-maintained rooms. It is located right across from the ruins of Colegio de San Jerónimo and just a few blocks from Antigua's market. Be sure to check out the great *pupusería* to your left as you head out of the hostel. Calzada de Santa Lucía Norte 21. Tel: 502-7832-7418. Updated: Nov 09, 2008.

MID-RANGE

Posada Don Valentino

(ROOMS: $19-39) This is a beautiful budget hotel, only two blocks from the central park. Close to all important sites but far enough away to be a quiet and peaceful location, it offers 18 well-decorated rooms, all with private bath and cable TV. The room options range from singles to quads, and there are also three suites separated from the hotel by a large terrace. The hotel offers an Internet café, international phone calls, a travel agency, laundry service, bag storage, use of a shared kitchen, beautiful terraces with city and volcano views, a very relaxing reading lounge open to a small garden with a fountain, and a very friendly and helpful staff. 5a Ca. Poniente 28. Tel: 502-7832-0384, E-mail: don.valentino@hotmail.com, URL: www.posadadonvalentino.com. Updated: Sep 21, 2007.

Hotel La Sin Ventura

(ROOMS: $23-68) Night owls, look no further than the Hotel La Sin Ventura, less than one block south of Parque Central. The hotel has a little streetside café, an upstairs movie theater, and a popular bar, where you can listen to reggaeton or salsa all night. Next door is the Mono Loco Bar, and plenty of other bars and restaurants are a short walk away. All rooms have private bathroom, some have TV, and breakfast is included in the price. As you may have figured, this may not be the easiest place in town to get a full night's rest, but there is WiFi, a great view from the rooftop terrace and secure parking. Prices fluctuate between the high and low seasons. 5a Av. Sur 8. Tel: 502-7832-0581, Fax: 502-7832-4888, E-mail: 502-7832-4888, URL: www.lasinventura.com. Updated: Nov 19, 2009.

La Tatuana

(ROOMS: $25-52) This is a cozy hotel, two and a half blocks from the main plaza. It has a small inner patio and a terrace. The rooms are clean and comfortable, and the staff is very helpful and kind. It does not offer many amenities because of its small size, however, you will find everything you need, and more in the surroundings. There are two restaurants across the street, Internet cafés and laundromats are also in the neighborhood. 7 Av. Sur 3. Tel: 502-7832-1223, Fax: 502-7882-4336, E-mail: latatuana@hotmail.com, URL: www.latatuana.com. Updated: Aug 31, 2009.

Posada Don Diego

(ROOMS: $28-36) This inn is ideal for those who would rather not be on top of all the bars, but still want to be within easy walking distance of the major attractions. There is an inexpensiv on-site café with a good selection of breakfasts, pancakes, bagels and salads. The guesthouse has only five rooms, set around a small garden. All rooms have a private bathroom, and some of the rooms have cable TV. There is also a sitting area, with a book exchange, overlooking the garden. The price includes breakfast and WiFi access. 6a Av. Norte 52. Tel: 502-7832-1401, 502-5752-2339, URL: www.posadadondiego-antigua.com. Updated: Jan 29, 2010.

Hotel Posada La Merced

(ROOMS: $30-40) This friendly place has rooms around leafy patios and a rooftop terrace with great volcano and town views. There is a little shop in the entrance and the English-speaking staff can help with tourist information. Morning coffee and bread is included in the price, and you can head next door to Fernando's Kaffee for something more substantial. WiFi and cell phone rental are available to guests, and the hotel offers discounts for groups and extended stays. 7a Av. Norte 43A. Tel: 502-7832-3197, Fax: 502-7832-3301, E-mail: 502-7832-3301, URL: www.merced-landivar.com. Updated: Nov 19, 2009.

Hotel Palacio Chico

(ROOMS: $30-57) Small and intimate with only seven rooms, Hotel Palacio Chico is perfect for couples on a romantic getaway. The hotel is well situated on a quiet street, close to the markets and just five blocks from Parque Central. Rooms have private bathroom, cable TV and WiFi. For those traveling without a laptop there is also a tiny Internet café. There are breathtaking volcano views from the balcony and rooftop terrace. Room number three opens directly to a stunning vista of Volcán de Agua. Lush plants adorn the balcony and patio below. The English-speaking staff is amiable and welcoming. 7a. Av. Norte, 15. Tel: 502-7832-3895, E-mail: info@hotelpalaciochico.com, URL: www.hotelpalaciochico.com. Updated: Aug 19, 2009.

Hotel Casa Rustica

(ROOMS: $30-63) A short walk from the best restaurants and monuments, Hotel Casa Rustica is a comfortable hotel with a rooftop terrace and two beautiful gardens. It offers single, double or triple rooms with private or common bathrooms. All have cable TV. Ask for the quiet rooms in the back building with view on the garden. In the lobby, it has two Internet computers, hammocks and a friendly little bar. It also has a friendly common room, a guest kitchen, laundry facilities and free WiFi. 6 Av. Norte 8. Tel: 502-7832-3709, E-mail: casarusticagt@hotmail.com, URL: www.casarusticagt.com. Updated: Aug 21, 2009.

Casa en Familia

(ROOMS: $30-43) This rustic and charming family-run B&B has a beautiful patio offering unobstructed views of the city and the surrounding volcanoes. Thanks to its friendly staff, the hotel feels like home. All rooms have private bathroom and cable TV. The rooms with a balcony have the best views. Ask for a discount if you are staying for more than a week. 7A Av. Norte and Ca. Camposeco 3E. Tel: 502-7832-2465, Fax: 502-7832-6503, E-mail: reserva@casaenfamilia.com. Updated: Aug 19, 2009.

Hotel Posada San Pedro

(ROOMS: $35-50) The main branch of the Hotel Posada San Pedro is a small, quiet inn located three blocks from Antigua's central plaza. The other branch is on the 3a

Avenida Sur, on the other side of the park. The large rooms are on two floors and have a desk and private bathroom. It overlooks a pair of well-manicured gardens, where huge ferns cascade from hanging baskets along the covered walkways. There is a large, fully-equipped kitchen, communal living room with cable TV, and an ample dining room with large windows opening onto the back garden. Climb to the rooftop terrace for great volcano views. 7a Av. Norte 29. Tel: 502-7832-0718, 502-7832-7882, 502-7832-4122, URL: www.posadasanpedro.net. Updated: Nov 19, 2009.

Hotel Casa Santiago

(ROOMS: $35-63) Located on a quiet street, Hotel Casa Santiago has a huge, lovely garden with a polished lawn and fruit trees. There is also a great volcano view from the rooftop terrace. This is a small hotel with individual, double and five-person rooms, each with private bathrooms and cable TV. Breakfast is extra, but there is a large communal kitchen. The hotel is particularly well suited for families. Ask for a discount on stays longer than four days. 7a Av. Norte 67. Tel: 502-2332-7897. Updated: Nov 19, 2009.

Hotel Plaza Mayor Antigua

(ROOMS: $37-61) If you are looking for a place within stumbling distance of the major bars and restaurants as well as the main tourist street with its landmark arch, then the Hotel Plaza Mayor Antigua may be the place for you. It is a small, clean, no-frills hotel with single, double and triple rooms, all with cable TV and private bathrooms. It has a helpful staff as well as good security, with locked gates at the entrance. 4a Ca. Poniente 9. Tel: 502-7832-0055, Fax: 502-7832-1685, URL: www.hotelescentralesdeantigua.com. Updated: Nov 19, 2009.

Santa Clara Hotel

(ROOMS: $50-72) For travelers with a mid-range budget, this is a good choice for keeping the spending within bounds while still enjoying some creature comforts. The staff is friendly and courteous. Both the rooms and common areas are clean and comfortably furnished. For security, the heavy wooden door at the entrance is permanently locked, and each guest is given a second key providing round-the-clock access. There is WiFi in the hotel as well. The hotel is five blocks south from the main square on a quiet street. Cash only;

no credit cards accepted. 2 Av. Sur, 20. Tel: 502-7832-4291, Fax: 502-7832-0342, E-mail: 502-7832-0342, URL: www.hotelsantaclaraantigua.com. Updated: Nov 11, 2009.

Hotel la Casa de Don Ismael

(ROOMS: $53) La Casa de Don Ismael offers comfortable lodging in a family-style setting, and is a great option for those traveling on a more conservative budget. The house is located on a side street less than a block away from Calzada de Santa Lucía, the main street on the western side of town. Don Ismael, who started the family business in 1996, personally makes sure guests are tended to. The rooftop terrace offers majestic views of El Volcán de Agua and the surrounding city, and is a great place to sit and enjoy breakfast (included in room rates). Second side street right off 3a Ca. Tel: 502-832-1932, URL: www.casadonismael.com. Updated: Sep 25, 2009.

El Carmen Hotel

(ROOMS: $55-75) With its central location and attentive service, Hotel El Carmen is a nice choice for travelers on a more comfortable budget. Rooms circle around an inviting, covered courtyard, where breakfast is served 7-10 a.m. This area can also be used for business meetings and informal gatherings. The rooftop terrace is an excellent place for absorbing views of Antigua's rustic rooftops and remains of ruins that dot surrounding volcanoes and hills. 3a Av. Norte 9. Tel: 502-7832-3850, Fax: 502-7832-3852, E-mail: info@elcarmenhotel.com, URL: www.elcarmenhotel.com. Updated: Sep 07, 2009.

Casa Florencia Hotel

(ROOMS: $55-80) Located seven blocks northwest of Antigua's Central Plaza, Casa Florencia Hotel offers colonial-style guest rooms tastefully decorated and furnished with orthopedic beds, private bathrooms, closets with safety boxes, and cable TV. Complimentary morning coffee, high-speed Internet and nearby parking are all available. First-floor rooms open to a garden with a fountain, while upstairs rooms open to a balcony with panoramic views of three distant volcanoes. 7a Av. Norte 100. Tel: 502-7832-0261, Fax: 502-7832-7291, E-mail: casaflorencia@earthlink.net, URL: www.cflorencia.net. Updated: Oct 02, 2007.

Hotel San Pedro

If you are ready to step up from the budget category and gain greater privacy and more amenities, this small, clean hotel is a good choice. Private baths and 24-hour hot water are standard in rooms. There is a kitchenette with all the basics, where you can make your own morning cup of coffee or warm-up that late-night snack you bought. Ask for one of the second floor rooms and you will be treated to $100-view of the volcanoes for half the price. 3 Av. Sur 15. Tel: 502-7832-3594, Fax: 502-7832-3594. Updated: Nov 12, 2009.

HIGH-END

Hotel el Meson de Maria

(ROOMS: $70-155) An elegant and beautiful hotel right in the tourist core of Antigua, the Hotel el Meson de Maria is a solid choice. The rooms are comfortable and tastefully decorated, ranging from standard, superior and deluxe to luxury suites with Jacuzzi, fireplace and private patio. There is a business center with WiFi, in-room massage, and room service from the well-reputed restaurant, La Fonda de la Calle Real. A telescope and binoculars are available in the solarium, and guests can enjoy the view of volcanoes from the rooftop terrace. 3a Ca. Poniente 8. Tel: 502-7832-6068, 502-7832-6069, Fax: 502-7832-6070, E-mail: 502-7832-6070, URL: www.hotelmesondemaria.com.

El Palacio de Doña Beatriz

(ROOMS: $75-255) El Palacio de Doña Beatriz is a sophisticated luxury hotel located in Antigua's best residential area. It is just four blocks from the Art Gallery, the Jade Museum, some of the finest restaurants, typical shops and furniture in town, but away from the commotion of the town center. This boutique hotel is as unique as the people who stay, offering personalized service and luxury accommodations for business or leisure travel. With rich interiors and custom-designed furnishings, guests enjoy a comfortable, residential feeling. Once you stay here you may find it hard to leave! Las Gravileas, Ca. de los Duelos. Tel: 502-7832-4052, Fax: 502-7832-4053, E-mail: info@palaciodebeatrizantigua.com, URL: www.palaciodebeatrizantigua.com. Updated: Mar 02, 2006.

Mesón Panza Verde

(ROOMS: $100-200) Mesón Panza Verde was established in 1986 as one of the first European-style B&Bs in Antigua. The inn is located at the quiet end of famous Fifth Avenue and is just a five-minute walk from Antigua's main plaza and cathedral. Mesón Panza Verde is down a cobblestone street, just past wonderful ruins and delightful shops. The inn has nine suites and three double rooms. Just beyond the entrance, there is an inviting central garden and fountain surrounded by a verand in the quintessential Antigua style. The restaurant is considered one of the finest in the country. Its reputation for "international cuisine with a twist" has made it a favorite with Guatemalans and international travelers alike. Mesón Panza Verde is one of the preferred destinations in beautiful Spanish Colonial Antigua, the land of eternal spring. 15 Av. Sur 19. Tel: 502-7832-1745, URL: www.panzaverde.com. Updated: Feb 19, 2009.

Casa Madeleine Hotel and Spa

(ROOMS: $105-225) Casa Madeleine is a distinctive boutique hotel with an exclusive spa. Nestled in the historical district, Casa Madeleine offers a retreat for those coming to discover the wonders of colonial Antigua. It is a great place to relax and disconnect from the grinds of modern life. Ca. del Espiritu Santo 69. Tel: 502-7832-9348, Fax: 502-7832-9358, E-mail: casamadeleine@aol.com, URL: www.casamadeleine.com. Updated: Jun 12, 2008.

El Convento Boutique

(ROOMS: $133-210) With overexposed stone walls and contemporary décor, this boutique hotel combines old and new. The staff is professional and helpful, and there is a gourmet restaurant on premises. Rooms feature Jacuzzi tubs, giant beds, a fireplace, large bathrooms with towel warmers, cable TV on big screens and WiFi. The rooftop terrace has an amazing view of all Antigua. 2 Av. Norte 11. Tel: 502-7720-7272, E-mail: frontdesk@elconventoantigua.com, URL: www.elconventoantigua.com. Updated: Sep 01, 2009.

Casa Blancas

(ROOMS: $145-270) The Casa Blancas villa is a stunning blend of colonial history and modern luxury, just two blocks from Parque Central. The three-bedroom house provides a uniquely elegant and private stay, which if you have the cash (full villa between $2865 and $4835 per week), is well worth the outlay. Along with the eclectic art collection, the amenities include: large beds, Egyptian cotton sheets, marble bathrooms, housekeeping service and chef, morning newspapers, WiFi, cable TV, iPod shuffle station and film library. Massage and chauffeur services are available for an extra charge. There is also a garden and rooftop views toward Volcán de Agua. 5a Av. Sur. Tel: 502-7832-7166, URL: www.casablancasantigua.com. Updated: Oct 06, 2009.

Casa Santo Domingo

(ROOMS: $150-200) This former monastery will charm you with its dreamy gardens, open archways and immaculate grounds. Parrots perch happily in the trees, and several on-site museums showcase Guatemalan art and history. Each of its 128 rooms come with private bath, flat screen TV and mini-bar. Most have a chimney to keep you warm on those chilly Antigua nights. Groups can take advantage of the hotel's helicopter tours, which can jet two to six passengers off to Panajachel, Chichicastenango or the archaeological site Quiriguá. At night, you can sip a cocktail at the cozy bar. Santo Domingo is within walking distance to the town center; stroll along the cobblestone streets and pastel-painted houses to reach shopping, church ruins and scenic exploration. 3 Ca. Oriente 28A. Tel: 502-7820-1220, Fax: 502-7820-1221, E-mail: concierge@casasantodomingo.com.gt, URL: www.casasantodomingo.com.gt. Updated: Sep 18, 2009.

Posada Del Angel

This exclusive boutique hotel exudes elegance and luxury, and is perfect for honeymooners or those on a romantic getaway. Each chic suite has its own exquisite, individual character and has wood-burning fireplaces, cable TV and large bathrooms. A semi-outdoor living room overlooks a long lap pool, and the Rose Suite opens onto the lovely rooftop terrace with volcano views. Some profits from the hotel go toward helping educate underprivileged children. Royalty, prime ministers and President Bill Clinton have stayed here. 4a Av. Sur 24A. Tel: 502-7832-0260, 502-7832-5244, URL: www.posadadelangel.com. Updated: Nov 19, 2009.

Candelaria Antigua Hotel

A boutique hotel with beautiful woodwork, a great terrace and unique ambiance. Av. Dolores del Cerro 5. Tel: 502-7832-8420, E-mail: service@candelariahotel.com, URL: www.candelariahotel.com. Updated: Aug 03, 2009.

Restaurants

With choices from all over the globe, Antigua is heaven for food lovers. The city is overflowing with dining opportunities. Here you will find cheap comedor eats, café indulgences, pub-style grub and gastronomic delights in world-class restaurants. Budget travelers can savor the flavors of Guatemalan dishes in the market, at street stalls or in local eateries. Those with looser purse strings can splurge on Mexican, Thai, Indian, Japanese, Chinese, Korean, French, Italian, Mediterranean, Peruvian, Spanish, Salvadoran or Cuban. If fast food is your thing, try Guatemala's Pollo Campero, or there is always McDonalds and Burger King. There is something for every palate and pocket. You won't go hungry. Updated: Nov 09, 2009.

TRADITIONAL GUATEMALAN

Comedor Antigua, Central Market

(ENTREES: $1.20-1.50) Travelers on a budget who have a hunger for experience as much as food will appreciate Comedor Antigua. Serving simple meals for more than 50 years, the traditional menu includes local favorites such as pepián, stuffed peppers, stews and roasted meat. Spotlessly clean and artfully decorated, you could be sharing your table with policemen, students, highland traders or an extended family. The ceaseless hum of market life unfolding around you provides ample entertainment. In the far corner of the food stall section at Central Market. Daily 8 a.m.-4 p.m. Updated: Sep 01, 2009.

Street Stalls, La Unión Park

(ENTREES: $1.20-1.50) Cheap and cheerful, quick and tasty, the line of street stalls two blocks south of Parque Central is great for a snack or a meal. The specialty is miniature plates piled high with ham with a choice of salads, sauces, tortillas and BBQ meat or chicken, all for $1.50 or less. Fare varies from stall to stall, so take your time. After buying, picnic in the park surrounded by colonial buildings and local families. Especially popular on weekends. Daily 9 a.m.-7 p.m. 3 Av. Sur. Updated: Aug 28, 2009.

Qui Xampe Asado

(ENTREES: $2) This restaurant's sizzling grill draws in crowds who are hungry for authentic and substantial Guatemalan meals. Economical and centrally located, it is swamped with locals, particularly during lunch hours. This is also a great spot to try out some traditional dishes you may hesitate to taste elsewhere due to hygiene concerns. Try traditional dishes such as pepían (peppery meat stew), or the house specialty: costillas (ribs) drenched in chirmol (tomato and onion paste). The roof terrace has plentiful seats and a view. Daily 8 a.m.-7 p.m. 4 Ca. Poniente 36. Tel: 502-4421-7211. Updated: Aug 19, 2009.

La Vieja Cocina Restaurante

(ENTREES $2.25 and up) If you feel like munching on some typical Guatemalan and Mexican bites while watching salsa dancers go through their paces, this is the perfect place. Cheap and lively, La Vieja Cocina is also the home to El Club de La Salsa Dance Studio, which is open every day 9 a.m.-7 p.m. and offers a free class Mondays at 5 p.m. For a little more than $9, patrons can learn some steps, then cool down with a bucket of beer and nachos. The lunch of the day costs $2.25. The bilingual menu is extensive, as are the offerings at the bar. Daily 11 a.m.-10 p.m., happy hour 7-9 p.m. 6a. Av. Sur, 12B. Updated: Nov 23, 2009.

Caféteria La Taquiza

(ENTREES: $2.50) This place is a cheapie, but it offers a high-quality mix of typical Guatemalan and Mexican eats. Lunch of the day costs $2.50 and a liter pitcher of beer straight from the barrel costs $3.75. The dining area is in a pleasant, shady courtyard, and service is friendly and attentive. Try the carne saltada, a dish of chopped beef with vegetables in a tasty sauce served with rice, guacamole and tortillas. The notice board at the entrance is a useful resource for travelers. There is a bilingual menu. Daily noon-9 p.m. 3a. Ca. Poniente, 14D. Tel: 502-5693-0111 / 1981, E-mail: restaurantelataquiza@gmail. com. Updated: Nov 20, 2009.

La Posada de Don Rodrigo

(ENTREES: $6-15) La Posada de Don Rodrigo Restaurant serves traditional Guatemalan food with a modern twist. The elegant, colonial-style terrace looks out onto a gorgeous flower garden, the perfect place for breakfast or lunch. In the evening, talented local musicians and dancers perform while visitors enjoy local cuisine dinners. 5 Av. Norte 17. Tel: 502-832-0291, E-mail: reservas@corporacionhotelera.com, URL: www.hotelposadadedonrodrigo.com. Updated: Sep 10, 2009.

La Canche ♪

Run by a saintly elderly couple, La Canche is a little-known institution in Antigua among tourists. Directly across from perhaps the most spectacular church in all the city, La Merced, La Canche appears to be like any "mom-and-pop" tienda from the outside (and inside for that matter). But step in,

slip around the register toward the back like you've done it before, and a dimly lit, romantic corridor opens. Aside from the experience of rubbing elbows with people that very rarely serve or eat with gringos, the food is cheap but excellent, and your presence is genuinely appreciated. Can't find the sign for the restaurant? Stop looking, it is not there. The name refers to the owner's light-colored hair. Ask around, you will sound pretty cool. 6a Av. Norte. Updated: Dec 10, 2007.

La Peña de Sol Latino

La Peña del Sol offers wonderful mid-range priced food served like you were in a five-star restaurant and has house drinks to kill for. Great Andean music pours out of a pan flute every night, and there is also a beautiful garden with fountains. This place will not disappoint. 5 Ca. Poniente. Updated: Jul 24, 2009.

Sabe Rico

Also known as the Secret Garden, Sabe Rico is a place to savor food and enjoy the outdoors. The food is freshly prepared from produce from the restaurant's garden and other fresh, organic ingredients. Linger in the delicatessen and chocolatería when entering, and check out the goodies on display. Indulge in decadent chocolate truffles or one of the array of desserts. Sip coffee on the leafy patio, chill out in a hammock in the walled garden, picnic on the lawn or nibble at a shaded table in the fruit and herb garden. On rainy days, relax in the dining alley overlooking the garden or at the single table at the front overlooking the street. Breakfast, lunch and dinner are served here. The menu is varied and wholesome, including antioxidant, light or vegetarian meals, muffins and pastries for diabetics, and gluten-free bread, cakes and cookies. Friendly staff, box lunches for those volcano hikes, party catering and home delivery are also available. 6 Av. Sur 7. E-mail: sisaberico@hotmail.com. Updated: Aug 09, 2009.

Fonda de la Calle Real

This restaurant has three locations in Antigua, each a peaceful place to spend your afternoons/evenings while enjoying Guatemalan cuisine. Many famous visitors have fallen in love with the charm of this restaurant, including Bill Clinton and Princess Cristina from Spain. The menu mostly consists of Guatemalan food, such as pepián (made with chicken or beef), kak'ik (turkey), molletes (a kind of dessert) and more. If you don't feel particularly adventurous, you can try the fried chicken or a steak. The restaurant can host events for up to 80 people. 5 Av. Norte 12. Tel: 502-7832-0507, 502-7832-2629, 502-7832-3749, E-mail: eventos@ lafondadelacallereal.com, URL: www.lafondadelacallereal.com. Updated: Sep 04, 2009.

AMERICAN

JP'S RumBar

(ENTREES: $2.50-5) New Orleans meets Antigua in the mellow JP'S RumBar, two blocks south of Parque Central. This is a welcoming, friendly place to meet locals, expats and travelers, where you can listen to live funk, jazz and blues nightly. Knock one back in the candle-lit bar, chill out upstairs on the cushion-smothered floor or head out to the ample outside courtyard. JP's also has a menu of authentic, inexpensive New Orleans dishes, including a tasty jambalaya. The bar also has a selection of beers, liquors and cocktails; try the bar's original creations, the Obama Nation or the Cuban Missile Crisis. During daylight hours, it is also the home to Academia Colonial Spanish School. Open after 6 p.m. most nights; closed Wednesdays. 7a Ca. Poniente 11. Tel: 502-7882-4244, E-mail: info@rumbarantigua.com, URL: www.rumbarantigua.com. Updated: Nov 19, 2009.

Casa Escobar

(ENTREES: $7-20, DRINKS: $2.40-11) Not just a steakhouse, Casa Escobar offers a more traditional-feeling night out than you would expect from a chain restaurant. There is a very strong colonial theme here, which is aided by the waiters dressed up in traditional costumes. Live music is played on Saturday nights, usually in the form of old-school romantic ballads. Together with the candlelight, this all makes for quite a romantic, if somewhat cheesy, evening out. As well as the house prime cuts of short ribs, skirt steak and rib eye ($18), notable dishes include jalepeño steak, the teriyaki burger ($7) and pasta verde for any vegetarian that does not mind being surrounded by so much meat. Wine by the jug ($11), beers ($2.60) and soft drinks ($2.40) available. Daily 7 a.m.-10 p.m. 6a Av. Norte 2. Tel: 503-7832-5250. Updated: Nov 12, 2009.

Caffé Bourbon

Opened in November 2009, Caffé Bourbon Jazz Bistro has a prime location on the main tourist avenue, a stone's throw from the main plaza. This chic, European-style café and bar is a mellow place to spend a few hours. Succumb to the temptation of the array of pastries and truffles on display, or check out the colorful Spanish menu. Dishes include tapas, sandwiches, organic salads, soups, homemade pasta, and a good variety of international fare with vegetarian options. The tasty Caree de Cordero (roast lamb) or the exotic Flor de Lis salad are worth a splurge. Check out the peacock feather inlaid tables. Daily 8 a.m.-10 p.m., with live jazz at weekends. 5a Av. Norte 16. Tel: 502-7832-7047/3868, E-mail: caffebourbon@gmail.com. Updated: Feb 11, 2010.

Café la Escudilla

(ENTREES: $6-12) This place not only provides a good value, but would be at home in any westernized city. Standard fare includes steak, fish and chicken, served with vegetables and roast potatoes. The layout of the dining area, with trees, candles and twinkling lights, sets a pleasant ambiance. 4a Av. Norte between 3a Ca. Poniente and 4a. Updated Nov 17, 2006.

ARGENTINE

Ni-fu Ni-fa

If you crave a giant, juicy steak when in Guatemala, head to this Argentine steakhouse with a Guatemalan twist. The place has ample space in a large, mainly outdoor setting among lots of greenery. The succulent, mouthwatering *puyazo* (sirloin steak) cooked to perfection will get the saliva flowing. Dig in to the scrumptious salad bar as often as you like. The service is attentive, and the extensive bilingual wine list and menu is pricey but worth every cent. You won't leave hungry. It has WiFi, caters for private events, offers special group prices, and has live music Sundays and during holidays. Sunday-Monday noon-10 p.m., Tuesday-Thursday noon-10:30 p.m., Friday-Saturday, noon-11 p.m. 3a Ca. Oriente 21. Tel: 502-7832-6579, E-mail: nifunifadeantigua@hotmail.com, URL: www.nifunifadeantigua.com. Updated: Feb 11, 2010.

ASIAN

Toko Baru Oriental Fast Food

(ENTREES: $1.35-1.50) Toko Baru's menu contains the East Asian treats you would expect, plus Middle Eastern fare. Roll up and get a super tasty shawarma kebab ($3.50), with juicy beef or vegetarian falafel stuffed into a warm pita pocket, and be sure to douse it in the delicious yogurt dip or the hellishly hot salsa. Chicken satay ($1.35), veggie spring rolls ($1.50), beer ($2) and sodas ($0.75) are also on the blackboard. The café is clean and bright, with enough room to seat about 15 people, or you can get your snack to go. Daily noon-8:30 p.m. 6a Ca. Poniente and 6a Av. Sur. Updated: Nov 12, 2009.

Mida Café

(ENTREES: $1.90) Mida Café serves a mixture of East Asian dishes and typical Guatemalan breakfasts. The decor is simple, with fans, Buddha pictures and Chinese lanterns decorating the walls, and fresh roses on the tables. The café has a relaxed, welcoming feel, with ambient music and an open kitchen visible over the counter. The menu is limited, but is good for breakfast and lunch. The *almuerzo del dia* (lunch of the day) costs $1.90 and includes tortillas and soda, or you can try the Che Yuk Poc Kum, a spicy Korean pork stew. Daily 8 a.m.-7 p.m. 5a Ca. Poniente 23A. Tel: 502-4188-3722. Updated: Nov 20, 2009.

Zen Bar

(ENTREES: $5 and up) East meets west in the Asian-themed Zen Bar. Step inside and you are transported from Guatemala to the Orient. A large Buddha mural greets you, and the rest of the place is decked out in exquisite décor. Zen Bar offers an extensive food and drink menu, including a vast selection of vegetarian options, various daily specials and happy hour 5-7 p.m. Try a generous portion of authentic pad thai ($5), or sample a little of everything from the all-you-can-eat menu ($10). Service is friendly and attentive. Come for dinner and stay for a movie. Selections are shown nightly upstairs on the big screen at 3, 5, 7 and 9 p.m. 7a Av. Norte 16. Updated: Aug 29, 2009.

CAFÉ/BAR

Y Tu Piña También

This laidback, cheerfully bohemian, Caribbean-style café serves up breakfasts, pastas, organic salads, sandwiches, pastries, fresh juices, licuados and more. You can also knock back a few beers or shots of rum before the partying begins. It is a popular haunt for locals, expats and travelers alike. Gather and hang out for a few hours at the rustic bar or on the coffee sacks out back. There is free WiFi if you have a laptop. Monday-Friday 7 a.m.-8 p.m., Saturday-Sunday 8 a.m.-8 p.m. 1a Av. Sur 18C, corner of 6a Ca. Oriente. E-mail: detox@tupinatambien.com, URL: ytupinatambien.com. Updated: Nov 20, 2009.

Kaffee Fernando's

(ENTREES: $1.50-$6) The dining experience at this eatery represents an excellent value, with friendly staff and clean, pleasant surroundings. Located six blocks from the main square, Fernando's is a hangout for the travel savvy. While the cuisine is local, all the ingredients in the dishes are easily recognizable; the only surprises are the bountiful, good-value portions. Eat and run, or sip a cup of Antigua's finest coffee at your leisure. No one is in any hurry to chase you out. 7a Av. Norte 43D. Tel: 502-7832-6953, E-mail: fernando@fernandoskaffee.com, URL: www.fernandoskaffee.com. Updated: Nov 11, 2009.

Café Sevilla

(ENTREES: $2) Café Sevilla is a signless, hole-in-the-wall comedor. Look for the tiny BBQ in the entrance and the poster on the door advertising breakfast and lunch in Spanish. This is a friendly, cheap and simple eatery has no menu. The $2 lunch of the day consists of soda, soup, meat with pasta or rice with some veggies, tortillas, and jelly for dessert. It is always busy at lunchtime so you may have to wait for a seat. Get there before 1:30 p.m. to avoid disappointment. 6a Ca. Poniente 29. Updated: Nov 20, 2009.

La Casa de las Mixtas Café

(ENTREES: $2.25) A lucky few may stumble on La Casa de Las Mixtas, tucked away as it is on a little side street. If the $2.25 *menu del día* scrawled on the whiteboard tickles your taste buds, make your way up the stairs to the rooftop terrace. A favorite among locals, this friendly, laidback place is always busy at lunchtime. The café serves typical Guatemalan fare all day, including grilled meat with tortillas, as well as hamburgers, salads and sandwiches from a Spanish-only menu. Monday-Saturday 9 a.m.-7 p.m. 3a Ca. Poniente 31. E-mail: casadelasmixtas@hotmail.com. Updated: Nov 20, 2009.

The Bagel Barn

(ENTREES: $2.50-8) Just off the south west corner of the Parque Central, this place is good if you need an early breakfast or for the meal deal after 3 p.m. (coffee with bagel or cake $2.50, plus tip). Otherwise it is a little pricey. The bagels are tasty, the free WiFi is fast and there is an easy-going atmosphere. It also shows free movies every afternoon and evening on a big screen. 5a Ca. Poniente 2. URL: www.thebagelbarn.com. Updated: Aug 17, 2009.

Café Sky

Café Sky is THE place to be at dusk in Antigua. Climb the tight winding staircase to the upper terrace and you can watch the sun go down over the town with 360-degree views of the surrounding mountains. The bar underneath, with a covered roof and open sides, is also a nice place to relax with comfortable wooden seats, subtle lighting and a view toward Iglesia San Francisco. The staff is attentive, and there is a full food (including all-day breakfast) and drinks menu. Below it, there is also a travel agency and spa. Daily 8 a.m.-11 p.m. 1a Av. Sur, 15 and 3a Ca. Oriente. Tel: 502-7832-7300. Updated: Oct 06, 2009.

Café Rocio

This small, friendly place has an open kitchen where you can watch your food being prepared while sipping beer, sangria or wine and flipping through a magazine. The café serves a good mix of tasty Asian-style dishes, including Tandoori chicken and Thai satay. The restaurant also has a selection of breakfasts and a typical Guatemalan menu of grilled meats. The menu is in English and Spanish. Monday-Friday 7 a.m.-9:30 p.m., Saturday-Sunday 10 a.m.-9:30 p.m. 6a Av. Norte 34. Tel: 502-7832-1871. Updated: Nov 20, 2009.

Peroleto Restaurante

Peroleto is a great place to check out when you are near the market or visiting the San Jerónimo ruins. This is a simple and funky place, split between a hip little restaurant and a rustic bar-style eating den that opens onto the street. The menu includes sandwiches, a wide selection of mouth-watering fruit smoothies, and great value breakfasts. Specialties include pricier seafood cocktails and ceviches. If you are feeling parched, try the *michelada*, a mixture of local beer, chili sauce and other ingredients; it goes particularly well with the prawn ceviche on a sunny afternoon. Daily 8 a.m-7:30 p.m. Alameda Santa Lucía Norte 34. Tel: 502-7832-9492, E-mail: info@peroleto.com, URL: www.peroleto.com. Updated: Nov 20, 2009.

Café Colonial

Situated three blocks from Parque Central and just across from Ummagumma Hostel, this is a laidback, friendly place for locals and foreigners alike. Good-quality, inexpensive typical Guatemalan food is available throughout the day. In the morning, try the traditional breakfast, which comes with great coffee in little clay cups. Lunch of the day costs only $2.50. There are two adjoining rooms, plus a small bar at the back where national beer signs and

posters decorate the walls. Latin music plays in the background. The menu is Spanish only but the staff is helpful. Monday-Saturday 8 a.m.-10 p.m., Sunday 8 a.m.-5 p.m. 7a Av. Norte 3. Tel: 502-7882-4092. Updated: Aug 19, 2009.

Rainbow Café

(ENTREES: $3-6.50) Enter through the associated bookshop and you will find a funky but pleasant open-air courtyard full of restaurant tables. There is live music every night, including open-mic on Wednesdays. The food—generally a mix of Mexican and Turkish—is fantastic. Even better, the staff is friendly and there is a happy hour. Open until midnight on Sundays. Corner of 7a Av. Sur and 6a Ca. Poniente. Tel: 502-832-1919. Updated: Nov 17, 2006.

FRENCH

Hector Castro

One of Antigua's new favorites, Hector's is an intimate little restaurant without a sign, located across from La Merced Church. A daily specials board sits in the entrance, offering seafood on Tuesdays and Saturdays. Hector, the owner and chef, prepares quality, French-bistro style cuisine in the tiny, open kitchen behind the bar. Several pasta dishes are also available. The beautifully presented grilled duck breast over potato and carrot gratin with roasted grapes tickles the taste buds. The restaurant does not accept reservations, so call 15 minutes before to check if there is space. Monday 6-10 p.m., Tuesday-Sunday 12:30-10 p.m. 1 Ca. Poniente 9A. Tel: 502-7832-9867, E-mail: personalchefantigua@gmail.com. Updated: Nov 16, 2009.

Luna de Miel

This is the place in town to try authentic French crepes, of both the sweet and savory varieties. You can watch them being made on the griddle in the entrance, or chill out on the comfy cushions and sofas. Luna de Miel also serves a good selection of healthy fruit smoothies, fresh juices, local beer and wine. Try the Pasión Maya with a Luna Caprichosa crepe. The restaurant also has WiFi, so it is a great place to hang out while catching up on those E-mails. The menu is in English and Spanish. Monday-Friday 8:30 a.m.-10 p.m., Saturday-Sunday 9:30 a.m.-10 p.m. 6a Av. Norte 19A. Tel: 502-4305 9746. Updated: Nov 20, 2009.

Tartines

The French-style Tartines, just a few steps from the central park, is a great lunch spot. It serves quality, mouthwatering dishes including paninis, salads, crepes, pasta, steak and seafood from a Spanish-language menu. There is also a varied wine list. Sit at one of the little tables inside the entrance facing the bar, or climb the spiral staircase to the rooftop terrace overlooking the cathedral ruins. The delicious *pato con salsa del día* (roast duck with sauce of the day) hits the spot, and is best washed down with a glass of Domaine Bassac-Merlot. Tuesday-Wednesday 11 a.m.-7 p.m., Thursday-Saturday 11 a.m.-10 p.m., Sunday 11 a.m.-4 p.m. 4a. Ca. Oriente 1C. Tel: 502-7882-4606, 502-7882-4607. Updated: May 14, 2010.

INTERNATIONAL

Travel Menu

(ENTREES: $4 and up, DRINKS: $2) From the outside, this Dutch-owned restaurant might look like a run-of-the-mill budget eating establishment. In the evening, however, candle chandeliers set in the wood and brick interior provide an intimate ambiance. The service is relaxed but attentive, and the food is served in big portions. The plato típico is a great value at $4. This atmospheric haunt is also a nice place for a drink at the bar, perhaps a glass of wine or beer. Daily noon-9:30 p.m., often later on weekends. 6a Ca. Poniente, between 6a Av. and 5a Av. Sur. Updated: Nov 12, 2009.

Welten Restaurant

(ENTREES: $6.50-21) This high-end, German-owned establishment has been earning an international reputation since it opened in 1984. The menu combines the finest local, Caribbean and continental cuisines, resulting in an intriguing fusion for your taste buds. Dress casually but nicely. Reservations are a must or you risk being turned away. The clientele frequently includes faces recognizable from the big screen and elsewhere, but pretend that you don't see a thing. Bring both credit cards and enjoy yourself. 4a Ca. Oriente 21. Tel: 502-7832-0630, E-mail: reserve@weltenrestaurant.com, URL: www.weltenrestaurant.com. Updated: Nov 11, 2009.

Meson Panza Verde

Whether you have a date to impress, spare cash burning a hole in your pocket or simply enjoy the good life, Panza Verde is the place to treat yourself. The restaurant offers a sophisticated mix of colonial elegance and modern international flavors. This is a favorite spot to eat lunch, enjoy a mid-afternoon snack or sip drinks before dinner. Choose from an array of exquisitely prepared dishes, vegetarian options, and international specialties to satisfy your palate. The restaurant's bar offers an array of international wines and spirits. Tables are set around an alluring courtyard, and the rooftop terrace has spectacular views of the Volcán de Agua to the south. Children are only permitted for breakfast. From Wednesday to Friday, there is live jazz and Latin music (cover $4), and there is an art gallery on the second floor. Daily 12-3 p.m. and 7-10 p.m. Sunday 10 a.m.-4 p.m. 5a Av. Sur 19. Tel: 502-7832-1745, Fax: 502-7832-2925, E-mail: info@panzaverde.com, URL: www.panzaverde.com. Updated: Oct 12, 2009.

La Septima

At the junction of 7 Calle and 7 Avenida is La Septima, a well-decorated restaurant with solid wood furniture and bright walls. The best time to go is during happy hour (Tuesday-Friday 4-7 p.m.), when there are discounts on buffalo wings and booze. International food, such as Chinese, is also available, as are a variety of salads. There is a pool table room and a TV room, pleasant indoor and outdoor patios large enough to accommodate groups, and a terrace with views upstairs. Delivery and outside catering are available. Tuesday-Friday noon-9 p.m., Saturday-Sunday 11 a.m.-10 p.m. 7a Ca. Poniente 33. Tel: 502-5220-5376, Updated: Nov 12, 2009.

Como Como

Como Como is a stylish European-style restaurant. Run by a Belgian/Guatemalan couple who work as chef and hostess, it has a relaxed and welcoming vibe. The tasty dishes are beautifully presented, and the bilingual menu also offers vegetarian options. Meat-lovers should try the succulent steak with Dijon mustard sauce. Meals are served in an inner courtyard, ideal for groups, or in two intimate dining rooms. The cozy bar has comfortable seating for sipping a cocktail or coffee, and there is a fireplace for cooler evenings. Diners can chill out with WiFi, magazines and board games while they tap their toes to the beat of jazz and world music. Tuesday 7-10 p.m., Wednesday-Thursday noon-3 p.m. and 7-10 p.m., Saturday-Sunday noon-4 p.m. and 7-10 p.m. 6a Ca. Poniente 6. Tel: 502-7832-0478/4010-3612, E-mail: comocomoguate@hotmail.com. Updated: Nov 20, 2009.

Sobremesa: Degustando el Arte

More than a gallery or a mere restaurant, this cultured café allows you to dine and enjoy delightful art at the same time. The manager is a painter who will explain the floor-to-ceiling art displays as you nibble on apple pie and ice cream or sip quality Latin American coffee. This is an intimate spot, a secret hidden away from the tourist crowds. 3 Ca. Poniente 3E. Tel: 502-7832-3231. Updated: May 03, 2010.

La Esquina

The artsy La Esquina is a recent addition to the Antigua scene. The main dining and seating area is located in a leafy courtyard, with a cozy bar nearby. The intimate restaurant serves delicious international cuisine from a bilingual menu. Friday and Saturday nights feature live music, art shows and performances by DJs. Every Thursday, the restaurant hosts La Onda Chapina, an evening dedicated to the tasting of Guatemalan rum paired with typical food. During daylight hours, browse the bazaar of quality handicrafts or use the free WiFi. Happy hour is on Monday, Tuesday, Wednesday and Friday 7:30-9 p.m. Daily noon-10 p.m. 6a Ca. Poniente 7. Tel: 502-7882-4761, E-mail: la.esquina.antigua@gmail.com. Updated: Nov 23, 2009.

ITALIAN

La Antigua Vineria

During the 1700s, taverns were places where travelers quenched their thirst, fed their souls and rested up. Tavern walls were used as message boards for communication between comers-and-goers. In honor of this old custom, the staff of La Antigua Vineria has a tavern wall photo gallery where pictures of modern-day travelers are posted. Hearty Italian food, great wine and beers are offered in this elegant and rustic tavern-in-the-wall. A tiny wine bar on the first floor welcomes visitors, but more seating is available on the second floor and the rooftop terrace. 5a Av. Sur 34. Tel: 502-7832-7370/5206-0446, E-mail: lavineria@conexion.com.gt, URL: www.laantiguavineria.com. Updated: Sep 04, 2009.

MEDITERRANEAN

El Restaurante de Las Mil Flores

This elegant restaurant is situated inside the atmospheric Vista Real La Antigua Hotel. La Mil Flores serves international cuisine with a Mediterranean twist. The bilingual menu has a good selection of appetizers, soups, salads, pasta, meat, seafood and rice dishes, as well as a few Guatemalan classics. The ambiance is tranquil and refined, the dishes are beautifully presented, the staff is attentive and the wine list is hefty. Perhaps not surprisingly, the prices are also a bit steep. The restaurant hosts an an Italian night every Saturday from 6 p.m. with pasta, pizza and Italian wines. Tuesday-Saturday 7 a.m.-3 p.m. and 6-10 p.m., Sunday 7 a.m.-3 p.m. 3a Ca. Oriente 16A Tel: 502-7832-9715, E-mail: infoantigua@vistareal.com, URL: www.vistareal.com/antigua. Updated: Nov 20, 2009.

MEXICAN

Ronny's Tacos

For a quick and cheap snack, you can't beat this Mexican café. The menu has the full range of tasty tacos, tortas, gringas, burritos, quesadillas and sincronizadas. There is a buffet of salsas and condiments to complete the authentic Mexican flavor. Try the Super Gringa, washed down with a cold beer. It is a small place, but there are three tables and a bar to stand and eat at. Cheap lunches, smoothies, hamburgers and sodas are also served. 6a Ca. Poniente and Av. Santa Lucía. Updated: Nov 16, 2009.

SALVADORIAN

El Sapo and La Rana

(ENTREES: $3) This cheap, simple Salvadorian pupusería is tastier than the name ("The Toad and The Frog") suggests. Located on the main drag, the joint's great-value combos include deals such as two pupusas (stuffed corn tortilla) and a soda for about $3, or with a local beer for a dollar more. You can choose from a selection of tasty pupusa fillings such as cheese, chorizo, *chicharrón* (fried pork crackling), chicken and jalapeños. If you feel like something more familiar, you can also try the hamburgers, sandwiches and grilled meat. Radio music plays in the background and the menu is bilingual. Open 10 a.m.-10 p.m. Closed Tuesdays. Calzada Santa Lucía 11. Updated: Nov 20, 2009.

Nightlife

Riki's Bar

(DRINKS: $1-2.60) Reached through Café la Escudilla, you cannot miss this place if you are in town for more than a day. The bar is a hotspot for gringos, but for good reason: The drinks are cheap, the chilled-out music sets the scene and the party goes on well into the night. Happy hour 8-11 p.m. 4a Av. Norte, between 3a Ca. Poniente and 4a Ca. Updated: Sep 10, 2009.

Onis

(DRINKS: $1-3) This two-floor bar is a good spot to sip on a rum and coke while surveying the ruins of San Agustin church, which are lit up at night. The place fills up on ladies' nights, but can lack the crowds on other evenings. Even so, with good Latin music and a nice open-air seating area upstairs, it is a great place to come with or without the crowds. 7a Av. Norte, between 4a Ca. Poniente and 5a Ca. Poniente. Updated: Aug 14, 2006.

Fridas

(DRINKS: $2) Relatively quiet on normal days, this place comes alive with the gringo set on Wednesday when the Ladies' night specials drop prices to $0.25 for a rum and coke. Girls can try to buy drinks for guys but watch out for the eagle-eyed bar staff! A hot and smoky atmosphere comes with the cheap drinks, and DJ music ensures the dance floor fills up early. 5a Av. Norte, between 2a Ca. Poniente and 1a Ca. Updated: Sep 10, 2009.

Café 2000

(DRINKS: $2-5) Straight out of SoHo, this cool lounge bar is the latest in Antigua's upscale Gringoification. Get those strong drinks down while sitting on square, funky-colored chairs and listening to smooth tunes. Hookahs are also available. 6a Av. Norte, between 4a Ca. Poniente and 5a Ca. Tel: 502-832-2981. Updated: Nov 17, 2006.

La Casbah Discoteca and Lounge

(COVER: $3.60-7.25) This is possibly the best place to go for a proper club night in Antigua. With a Middle Eastern theme throughout, there are a lot of different, well-planned seating areas: bar tables right in the middle of the action, with space for bigger groups; cozy booths and private corners with comfy cushions; and, of course, there is a dance floor for getting your groove on. There is also a great rooftop bar, complete with plenty of seats and heaters. It all makes for a fun night out. Tuesday: All you can drink 9 p.m.-midnight, cover $7.25.

Wednesday: Skyy Vodka two for one all night; cover $3.60, includes one drink. Thursday: Ladies night, girls get in free and margaritas and Victoria beer two for one, cover for guys $3.60. Friday and Saturday: cover $3.60, includes one drink. Tuesday-Friday 8:30 p.m.-1 a.m., Saturday 8p.m.-1 a.m. 5a Av. Norte 30 (near El Arco). Tel: 502-7832-2640, URL: www.lacasbahantigua.com. Updated: Nov 12, 2009.

Monoloco (Funky Monkey)

(ENTREES: $4.60-6.50, DRINKS: $2) This is one of the most popular places for the town's Gringo set. Almost exclusively full of visitors, it provides everything you would want: A westernized bar complete with strong drinks, an eclectic collection of European music selected from a massive 700G of tunes and big screen TVs showing sports. There is a lively downstairs bar that is packed most nights, and a more spacious tarpaulin-roofed area upstairs. Good food is also available, including almost certainly the best plate of nachos in town. 5a Av. Sur. Tel: 502-832-4235. Updated: Nov 17, 2006.

La Sin Ventura

Next to the Funky Monkey, this place could not be more eclectic. Things get started in the early evenings, when movies are screened. The vibe switches later on, when the salsa music draws a local crowd. This place is packed on weekends, when things gets hot and steamy—just like a good salsa bar should. 5a Av. Sur, between 5a Ca. Poniente and 6a Ca. Tel: 502-832-0581/4884, E-mail: lasinventura@yahoo.com.mx. Updated: Aug 14, 2006.

Los Arcos Reds Bar and Restaurant

A restaurant you could easily mistake for a typical British football bar, Los Arcos Reds has more than meets the eye. The menu features a huge selection of reasonably priced quesadillas, sandwiches and platters. From tandoori chicken sandwich to Chinese chow mein, the delectable international food is guaranteed to satisfy your craving. The only Guatemalan dish available, chili relleno (stuffed pepper), is exceptionally good. After dinner, kick back with a beer and game of pool while enjoying good music on cozy sofas. WiFi is available. Monday-Saturday 8 a.m.-1 a.m. 1 Ca. Poniente 3. Tel: 502-400-0377. Updated: Aug 19, 2009.

Café No Sé Bar and Restaurant

With three bars inside a long, shotgun-style building, Café No Sé has the feel of a border town dive. The regular crowd consists of expats, wannabe expats, travelers, locals and enough shady characters to make things interesting. The walls are covered in bizarre art and photographs, images of the Virgin of Guadalupe and other eclectic touches. More than 30 kinds of tequila and mezcal are served, plus Gallo and Moza beer on tap. The bar in front features live music every night around 9 p.m. that spills into the other bars and attracts as many locals as it does tourists.

No Sé's tacos and quesadillas are based on *cochinita pibil*, a smokey pork dish from Yucatán. Other tasty selections include tortilla soup, chili, salads and sandwiches. For a quiet meal, you can dine in the back room, where a small garden is illuminated by a skylight. Whether you are in town to party, study, see the sights or just make trouble, Café No Sé is the place to kick off a fun night on the town in Antigua. Daily 12 p.m.-1 a.m. 1a Av. Sur 11. URL: www.ilegalmezcal.com. Updated: Jan 20, 2009.

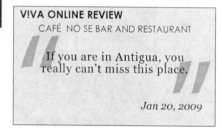

V!VA ONLINE REVIEW

CAFÉ NO SE BAR AND RESTAURANT

" If you are in Antigua, you really can't miss this place. "

Jan 20, 2009

AROUND ANTIGUA

JOCOTENANGO

En route to Chimaltenango, the road out of Antigua passes by San Felipe de Jesús to the north and then moves northwest through Jocotenango. The town's faded pink Baroque church stands out in the scruffy central plaza, which comes alive every year on August 15, when the town celebrates El Día de la Asunción de la Virgin (Assumption Day). There are parades, plenty of food stalls and a fun fair all day, as well as local sports matches and live music in the evening.

The major interest here is Centro La Azotea, a coffee plantation and museum complex that offers guided tours. The cultural center has a museum on Mayan culture and music, weaving traditions and the folk saint Maximón. There is also an equestrian center and on-site café. Groups

are welcome, and it is wheelchair accessible. A shuttle bus runs hourly from the Parque Central in Antigua ($0.60 round trip). Parking is also available. Tel: 502-7831-1120, E-mail: info@centroazotea.com, URL: www.centroazotea.com.

Most travelers just make the day trip from Antigua. That being said, the welcoming Earth Lodge (Cel: 502-5664-0713/5613-6934, E-mail: earthlodge@gmail.com, URL: www.earthlodgeguatemala.com) is a good option for those wanting to stay in the area. Located on the hills overlooking the valley, this eco-retreat is owned by an American-Canadian couple who has been living in Central America for more than 12 years. They have wooden cabañas ($10-19), dorms ($4-5) and tree houses ($11-30). You can also bring a tent and camp ($2.50), or rent one of theirs ($3.50).

There are great views from the community dining room, where they serve home-cooked breakfasts and lunches ($2-5) and an all-you-can-eat dinner every evening ($6). You can go walking, take Spanish lessons, volunteer on the avocado farm in exchange for half-price lodging, or simply relax. All major credit cards accepted.

For a fast food fix, there is Que Dely, a hamburger joint on the southern side of the square. If you are looking for something a little more authentic, browse the street running from the northeastern corner of the plaza, directly north of the church; here you will find a line of *comedores* with good cheap food. On Calle Ancha 27, just out of Antigua on the road to Jocotenango, is Christophe Gourmet Pizza (Daily, 11 a.m.-10 p.m. Tel: 502-783-22732), which also serves steaks, pastas and salads.

If you fancy a two-kilometer (1.2 mi) stroll, Jocotenango is within walking distance from Antigua. To get here, take Avenida del Desengaño, which starts at 1a Calle Poniente between 7a Avenida Norte and Alameda Santa Lucía. Walk north, passing La Merced over on your right, then farther up San Sebastián and a pleasant tree-lined square, from where you can also take a chicken bus. Turn left after the park onto Calle Ancha and follow the road straight for about 20 minutes. The bus takes about five minutes and costs $0.25. You can also take a tuk-tuk for about $1.50-2. Updated: Sep 01, 2009.

ANTIGUA & AROUND

Photo by: Douglas J. Klostermann

SAN JUAN DEL OBISPO

Just about the only thing to see in this otherwise ordinary Guatemalan town is the Palacio del Obispo, one of the first Catholic churches in the country. The Palacio was refurbished in 1939 after centuries of seismic displacement. Once the home of 16th-century bishop Francisco Marroquín, Bethanite nuns still preserve the grounds, which are walled off to the rest of town. Behind the adjacent church, you will find a nondescript door with a bell, which is in fact the entrance to the Palacio. To take a Spanish-only guided tour, ring the bell and a nun will greet you. The complex is beautiful; from the intricately decorated chapel to the European paintings and original 16th-century furniture, you will be brought back in time to colonial Guatemala. Once you are finished with the tour, step outside and take in the gorgeous views of Antigua. There are no official open hours, but the grounds are open throughout the day, so just ring the bell and a nun will probably answer. There are extremely meager eating and sleeping options in town, meaning most visitors choose to just visit just for a few hours.

Getting To and Away

The only form of regional public transportation that will get you to San Juan del Obispo is a bus from the main bus terminal in Antigua (west of El Mercado). The ride takes anywhere from 15-20 minutes, and you can easily catch the bus back to Antigua wherever it lets you off. Taxis are also available, but more expensive. If you are looking for some exercise, it takes an hour to walk north to San Juan del Obispo from Antigua. Updated: Jul 22, 2010.

SANTA MARÍA DE JESÚS

Most travelers head to Santa María de Jesús because it is situated on the lower slopes of Volcán Agua, the easiest to climb of Antigua's volcanoes. For the hike up Agua, you can enlist a guide for about $15 in Antigua, but the climb is doable on your own. Safety has been a small problem, with robberies occurring along the trail. Once you reach the top, there are panoramic views of Antigua and Volcán Fuego. Aside from the volcano, there is not too much to see in the town besides a crumbling old adobe church with a renovated interior.

Gringos are mostly absent from the town, which is known for its textiles and still retains its indigenous Kaqchikel character. There are not really established lodging options, and the town is not known for its cuisine. It is best to keep this to a day trip on your way to the volcano or combine it with a visit to San Juan del Obispo.

Getting To and Away

The cheapest and most reliable way to get to Santa María de Jesús is by bus from downtown Antigua, west of the market. Buses run daily. Taxis are an option, but getting back may be tricky. If you are planning on hiking the volcano, many tour guides offer transportation to Santa María. Updated: Jul 22, 2010.

SAN LORENZO EL TEJAR

Hot springs are the main attraction to the *aldea* (a town smaller than a pueblo) of San Lorenzo El Tejar. Accessible by bus from Antigua, the hot springs are cheap, but the place gets crowded on the weekends. The river that runs through the town is chronically polluted because its residents use it as the communal trash can, however, this does not affect the hot springs. There is not much in the way of lodging or dining here in town, so don't bank on staying overnight. Updated: Jul 22, 2010.

Getting To and Away

The bus that travels between Antigua and San Lorenzo will take you to the hot springs, but you have to ask the driver to drop you specifically at the springs. The bus will leave you at a marked spot by the road, where you must follow a downhill path to the springs. The drive takes about 25 minutes and costs $0.25. Updated: Aug 09, 2010.

EL HATO

High above Jocotenango, the village of El Hato is fairly isolated, meaning lodging and dining options are limited. However, the Earth Lodge ($5-25/night. Tel: 502-5664-0713, E-mail: earthlodge@gmail.com, URL: www.earthlodgeguatemala.com) is a wonderful place to stay, replete with panoramic views of the valleys and volcanoes of southern Guatemala. Despite the Earth Lodge's remote location, there is not a lack of things to do; you can work on the avocado farm for a reduced rate, hike one of the many trails or even enjoy a traditional Mayan spa. Unfortunately that's about it in El Hato, so come prepared to lay low. Updated: Jul 22, 2010.

Getting To and Away

Due to its isolated location, getting to El Hato can be tricky. If you are going to the Earth Lodge, you are in luck: The lodge offers a shuttle service from downtown Antigua for $6. Taxis will charge you exorbitant fees. The chicken buses also run up to El Hato for $0.50, but can be complicated to figure out. You can also hike up from Cerro de la Cruz (Hill of the Cross), which takes about an hour. Safety can be an issue, so do not walk alone. Updated: Jul 22, 2010.

CIUDAD VIEJA

A pleasant four-kilometer (2.5 mi) walk or bike ride from Antigua, Ciudad Vieja is a stress-free little village where you can spend a few hours. The pretty, tree-framed town square has plenty of sturdy park benches. Around the square, you will find a whitewashed 16th-century church and the bright-yellow clock tower of the municipal town hall—just don't try to set your watch to the clock, as the hands never move!

On the south side of the square, you will find the typical Comedor Doña Alís. Nearby is Casa de Veronica, a café offering basic burgers ($1.10), almuerzos ($1.80) and licuados

($1.20). Off the square, you can find the Real Antigua Café at 4a Calle and 1a Avenida. Restaurante Los Volcánes (Monday-Sunday 2-9 p.m. 4a Ca., Zona 4. Tel: 502-4323-0830) is a newly opened family restaurant run by a man name Nicolás. Formerly the head chef at Mono Loco in Antigua, Nicolás whips up some tasty Tex-Mex delights while you relax in the café garden, where you can watch kids playing in the large children's area. For a quicker, cheaper bite, try the takeout from Pizza Mia ($0.55 a slice) at 4a Calle and 5a Avenida.

Internet is available at La Plazuela, next to Doña Alís, as well as at Cyber Conexion and Intercom on 3a Calle, west of the square's southwest corner. Payphones are located on the western side of the plaza. There are some public toilets opposite the church entrance by the sports courts east of the square. The BAM bank (Monday-Friday 8:30 a.m.-6 p.m., Saturday 8:30 a.m.-1 p.m.) is opposite the Real Antigua Café at 4a Calle and 1a Avenida. It does not have an ATM, but it will exchange money. Being so close to Antigua, there is no need to stay overnight. However, you can make a reservation at the town's hotel, Santa Valentina, by calling 502-7831-5044.

Getting To and Away

To reach Ciudad Vieja take the bus south for five minutes from the local bus terminal near the market. It is so close you can also walk, cycle or jog! Updated: Nov 23, 2009.

SAN ANTONIO AGUAS CALIENTES

The town of San Antonio Aguas Calientes lies just six kilometers (4 mi) outside of Antigua, but retains an interesting indigenous vibe. The Kaqchikel people still reside in the area, but an influx of Afro-Guatemalans during the slave trade has added an Afro-Caribbean element. Aside from its diverse ethnic composition, the town specializes in producing crafts, particularly woven textiles and wood carvings, and is therefore a great place to find authentic souvenirs. The town is relatively prosperous because of the craft industry, and has some of the highest literacy rates in Guatemala. Visiting San Antonio Aguas Calientes would make a nice half-day trip.

Getting To and Away

Because it is only six kilometers (4 mi) from Antigua, you can walk to San Antonio Aguas Calientes in about two hours. For those not into two-hour walks, there are also buses that run regularly from the bus station to the west of the market in Antigua. Try to return before evening, because buses run with less frequency as the day goes on. Updated: Jul 22, 2010.

))))

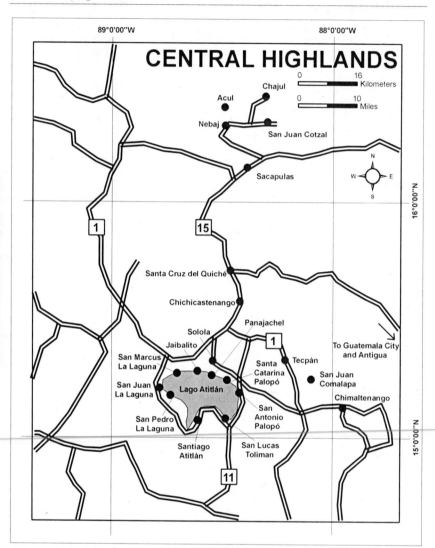

CENTRAL HIGHLANDS

Central Highlands

Guatemala's Central Highlands, which include the provinces of El Quiché, Alta Verapaz and Baja Verapaz, are home to misty forests, traditional cultures, and Guatemala's most important market, the twice-weekly affair at Chichicastenango.

The region has an interesting history. In Verapaz, which means "true peace," the legendary Defender of the Indies, Fray Bartolomé de Las Casas, proved to the Spanish crown in the 16th century that patient missionaries could convert natives to Christianity. In the 1970s and 1980s, Guatemala's brutal insurgency was fought all over the country, but the province of El Quiché was particularly affected.

Nature lovers will want to visit El Biotopo del Quetzal, a protected ecosystem that is home to Guatemala's stunning national bird. It is also known for waterfalls and good hiking trails. The city of Cobán is an attractive provincial capital important to the local coffee industry. The most important visitor site in

Highlights

Chichicastenango Market–Chichicastenango has been a trading post since pre-Hispanic times. Known simply as "Chichi," the Thursday and Sunday markets here are full of traditional culture and handicrafts.

Iximché Ruins–This pre-Columbian archeological site was founded in 1470 by the Kaqchikel Maya. This has been a popular stop on the ruins circuit since German archeologist Jorge Guillemin began exploring and excavating here in 1960.

Lago Atitlán–Volcanoes and tiny indigenous villages ring this clear-blue lake, Guatemala's pride and joy. Take a private boat tour, climb surrounding volcanoes, or just take in the view from a hammock.

Pacaya Volcano National Park–This highly active volcano sprays lava and ash so often that its shape is ever-changing. Designated as a national park in 2001, Pacaya Volcano National Park is a great escape from Guatemala City.

K'umarcaaj Ruins–This archeological site was the ancient capital of the Quiché nation, who once ruled the highlands. Although the town was destroyed by Spanish conquistadors in 1524, the ruins are frequently used by indigenous Mayas for ceremonial purposes.

El Biotopo del Quetzal–This protected ecosystem is named after the quetzal, Guatemala's national bird. If you are looking for good hiking trails and plenty of birdwatching, this is the place to go.

textiles and other locally-made treasures. The market is easily done in a day from Antigua or from many of the towns in the Lake Atitlán region. More adventuresome visitors to El Quiché may want to visit the picturesque town of Nebaj. Updated: Sep 28, 2007.

History
The volcanic chain that stretches from the Mexican border to Antigua has been inhabited since at least 6500 BC. The Maya people who settled here named their homeland Guatemala, which means "land of forests." At one point in time, the Quiché were the principal nation in the highland region, which stretches west from Chichicastenango to Quetzaltenango. Pollen samples uncovered here lead historians to believe settlers began cultivating agriculture in the Guatemalan highlands as early as 3500 BC. In addition, the Maya also developed a hieroglyphic writing system and a complex calendar. The nations who lived here had extensive trading networks but were always continuously at war. The Quiché fortified their cities by building them in inaccessible locations surrounded by ravines.

When the Spaniards arrived in 1523, the Maya civilization was already fragmented, making them fairly easy to conquer. By 1528 Pedro de Alvarado had established rule over the region. The indigenous people were exploited by the new landowners and fell to the bottom of the social hierarchy. It was not until 1821 that Guatemala became independent from Spain.

Unfortunately, the new white ruling class stole huge tracts of land from the natives for the cultivation of tobacco and sugar cane, further exploiting the indigenous people to work the land. In response to protests from landless guerrillas, a civil war finally broke out in the 20th century. It lasted for 36 years (1960-1996). During this time, the highlands were the site of horrific human rights abuses. Guatemala's indigenous people were persecuted by the military, and entire villages were burned. Approximately 200,000 Guatemalans were killed, and 40-50,000 were displaced. Today, you can still explore ruins from highland Maya tribes, mostly the ruins of cities set up for ceremonial or defense purposes. The highlands are a popular pilgrimage destination for the indigenous descendants of the Maya, and many indigenous groups still live in small villages here. Updated: Jul 30, 2010.

the El Quiché province is without a doubt the Chichicastenango market. Visitors come from all over the world to wander in the maze of smoky streets, shopping for masks,

When to Go

The climate in the highlands is quite manageable. There are two basic seasons: rainy (May-October), when it typically rains for a few hours in the afternoon, and dry (November-April). It can get very cold at night, especially in December and January, so come prepared. If you plan on doing a lot of hiking while in the area, keep yourself informed about the weather before you go and while you are traveling around. If you are interested in experiencing Guatemalan highland culture at its best, look into local festivals and when they happen. Many of the villages and towns around Lake Atitlán celebrate Christmas, Holy Week and other regional festivals in style. Updated: Aug 05, 2010.

Safety

People hiking around the highlands have become targets for thieves, so hire a guide where possible. Almost every village or town has them, and hiking with someone who knows their way around can result in a much more enjoyable experience. In the bigger towns, such as Chichicastenango, it is recommended that you avoid walking around late at night, especially on your own. Stay alert and aware of your surroundings, just as you would anywhere else, and you should not run into any trouble. Updated: Aug 04, 2010.

Things to See And Do

Guatemala's Central Highlands offer fantastic hiking opportunities and other outdoor activities. Nature reserves and the area around Lake Atitlán are home to unique ecosystems, and several volcanoes in the Central Highlands are ideal for horseback riding, hiking and dipping in natural hot springs.

There are a number of indigenous villages where you can shop around at big markets for woven textiles and artisan wares, or even watch watch animals being auctioned off by local farmers at smaller markets. You will likely see a decent number of other tourists at these villages.

Maya ruins and old colonial churches tell of Guatemala's rich history. Much of the highland area suffered greatly during Guatemala's civil war, but the people are moving forward optimistically. The stunning scenery and friendly people are bound to leave you with the sense that Guatemala's Central Highlands were well worth the visit. Updated: Aug 04, 2010.

Tours

There are plenty of tour operators offering a range of excursions around the highlands. Depending on your interest, there are day trips to the quaint villages on the shores of Lake Atitlán or to ancient Maya ruins. However, the most popular tours offered in the Central Highlands are the ones that take you up some of the region's many volcanoes. Volcán Atitlán (3,523 m/11,560 ft), Volcán Tolimán (3,152 m/10,340 ft) and Volcán San Pedro (3,024 m/9,920 ft) look out over Lake Atitlán. San Pedro is probably the most popular for hiking, but this hike is pretty steep, so while it is labeled as 'easy,' it does not always feel that way. Volcán Santa María (3,771 m/12,375 ft) is also a popular climb and affords fantastic views of nearby Quetzaltenango. Whatever your experience level, it is recommended that you take a guide and hike in the highlands as part of an organized excursion. The guides know where they are going and while robberies are relatively rare, you are generally better off with a group. Reputable tour companies include Adrenaline Tours and Quetzaltrekkers (based in Quetzaltenango) and tour operator Atitrans (based in Panajachel). Updated: Aug 04, 2010.

Lodging

In the Central Highlands of Guatemala, you will find accommodation options to fit every budget. Hostels in the Central Highlands can be found for as low as $3.50 a night in small towns like Nebaj, but there are also plenty of eco-lodges and ranches for mid-range prices. Two of the most breathtaking places to spend the night (and day) are the lagunas of San Pedro and San Marcos. Accommodations there are cheap, too, even for Guatemalan standards. Chichicastenango, Santiago Atitlán, and Panajachel are also must-sees, and lodging at these sites won't cost you an arm and a leg. Updated: Jul 13, 2010.

SAN JUAN COMALAPA

As the route west from Chimaltenango cuts through pretty corn and pea fields, the scenery begins to change as pine trees appear alongside the climbing and winding roads. At kilometer 63-64 is the turn-off for the village of Zaragosa and the road to San Juan Comalapa.

Rarely visited but worth the detour, the town's major claim to fame is Ricardo Alvarez Ovalle, the music composer for Guatemala's National Anthem, who was born here in 1858. Updated: Sep 14, 2009.

CENTRAL HIGHLANDS

Getting To and Away

Buses leave Chimaltenango every hour for the 45-minute journey to Comalapa. You can also pick up a mini-bus from the highway.

Services

On the high street (numbered as avenue '0'), you will find a BanRural and a Cajero 5B ATM as well as a G and T Continental with Western Union. There is an Internet café at Avenida 2-88 and 2a Calle and a Despensar Familiar supermarket. Updated: Sep 14, 2009.

Things to See and Do

Surprisingly, Comalapa's main draw is its thriving art community. As well as an art museum (3a Ca.), there are smaller art galleries open to the public, like that of internationally renowned artist Iván Gabriel. The Café Galleria is run by his son, Wilder, who offers tours of his father's studio. Gabriel's work has been showcased in over eight countries, including the United States, England and Spain.

Alongside the art, there's a reservation-only restaurant (Av. 2-88, Zona 1. Tel: 502-7849-8168/4224-0789, E-mail: bgabriels@hotmail.com) available for group bookings. It offers a full-course menu for $12 per person.

Works by the famous Maya Kaqchikel painter Andrés Curruchiche, also from Comalapa, can be seen in the Museo Ixchel del Traje Indígena in Guatemala City. Updated: Sep 14, 2009.

Lodging

On the main street is Hotel El Refugio de Dona Catarina (0 Av. 0-72, Zona 1. Tel: 502-7849-8232). Hotel San Juan Los Espera is at 1a Ca. 0-51, Zona 2. (Tel: 502-4146-0807).Updated: Sep 14, 2009.

Restaurants

For a snack there are plenty of food stalls around the main plaza. El Shadai restaurant, next to BanRural, serves up local and international dishes. Nearby is the roast chicken café Pollolandia. Updated: Sep 14, 2009.

CHIMALTENANGO

Chimaltenango straddles the CA-1 highway (Carretera Interamericana Uno), at Kilometer 54 heading west from Guatemala City to Huehuetenango. A grimy, congested place made up mainly of car workshops and basic comedores, there is not much here to persuade any tourist to hang around. It is, however, a transport hub and the place to make a connection for anyone taking a chicken bus west from Guatemala or Antigua. Updated: Sep 14, 2009.

Getting To and Away

To travel east or west along the CA-1 you can flag a bus down along the highway through the center of Chimaltenango. Buses for Antigua exit the highway here, so make sure wait before the turn-off. If you prefer to get a ticket and wait in the terminal rather than on the side of the road, the bus terminal is right by the market. Updated: Sep 14, 2009.

Services

There are more than six banks on the main street (BAM with Western Union, Banco Aztea, BanRural, Banco de Antigua, Banco Proamerica and Citibank), so the town is a good place to stock up on quetzales. Halfway down the high street there is a Bodegona supermarket, Farmacia Los Angeles and Caféspeedy for the Internet. Updated: Sep 14, 2009.

Things to See and Do

The town's high street is 1a Calle, two blocks north of the highway, where you will also find the much calmer central plaza–go here for a break from the chaos if you have some time to kill. There is also a busy market around 3a Calle, two blocks father north of the main street. (It is not a very inspiring place to shop.)

The festival of Santa Ana, the mother of the Virgin Mary and the patron saint of Chimaltenango, is celebrated every year between July 20 and 30, the main day being the 26th. Updated: Sep 14, 2009.

Lodging

If you do want to spend the night here there are plenty of hotels, but most are questionable in quality. A tuk-tuk ride away out of town in Parramos is the country inn La Posada de mi Abuelo (Tel: 502-7849-5930/5510-5973, E-mail: info@laposadademiabuelo.com, URL: www.laposadademiabuelo.com), which offers mid-range rooms for around $27, all with fireplaces, hot-water, TV and a restaurant service. Mountain biking, horse riding and country walks can be arranged from here. Updated: Sep 14, 2009.

In town, Hotel Posada de Don Jorge offers private bathrooms and cable TV for under $10 (3a Av. 2-54). Updated: Sep 14, 2009.

Restaurants

At the eastern end of the main street you will find a drive-in Pollo Campero and nearby a Burger King and McDonalds. On the main strip there are quite a few cafés, such as El Pan Quotidiana and Comidas D'Marta, as well as the Chinese restaurant Jon Wan. Updated: Sep 14, 2009.

TECPÁN

Tecpán should not take up too much space on your itinerary. Its value for tourists lies in the nearby ruins of Iximché. The town itself is non-descript. There are shops on the busy main street, an unkempt square with some stalls and a large white church. It has a friendly-enough feel and if you do need to stay over there are a few options for a meal and a bed.

Getting To and Away

To get to Tecpán, take any bus going west on the Carretera Interamericana, toward Panajachel or Chichicastenango, and get off at the turn-off for Tecpán on the left. The town is about 500 meters (1,640 ft) south of the main highway. You can walk or catch a minibus. Updated: May 03, 2010.

Services

The town has all the services you would usually need. There is an Internet café next to the Hotel Iximché (8 a.m.-9:30 p.m.) that charges $0.75 per hour. On the opposite side of the square to the church there is a bank with an ATM and a Banrural, which will exchange money. Close by is a shopping center of sorts, with Cine Plaza Tecpán, Café Deli, Pasteleria Fina, Sarita Helados and medical and dentist clinics. Updated: May 03, 2010.

Things to See and Do

The word Iximché comes from the Mayan words *ixim*, meaning maize, and *ché*, meaning tree. Founded around 1470, the city was once the Kaqchikel capital. In the shadow of the Ratzamut mountain, and surrounded by the El Molino and El Chocoyos River valleys, the site is considered to be the cradle of historical and archeological Guatemala. Despite there being only foundations left as evidence of the buildings which once provided housing and business and sports facilities for the population of 10,000, it is still a beautiful site, with its mix of wide green plazas and scattered stone ruins.

Things were not always so peaceful. In 1524 Pedro de Alvarado arrived with his henchmen and took the site for his own, establishing the first Spanish capital in Guatemala right here. After years of fighting with their Quiché neighbors, the Kaqchikel leaders tactically aligned themselves with the Spanish when they arrived. However, the Kaqchikel had soon had enough of the excessive demands of Alvarado and fled. Fearing an uprising, Alvarado executed two Kaqchikel leaders in 1540.

Nowadays you can still see some of the pyramids and ball courts of the original town. Where there once would have been adobe and thatched roofs atop impressive stone bases, now only the lower halves remain. The site is still used for ceremonies. In 1980 the Campesino Unity Committee met here to discuss the Declaration of Iximché, after the massacre of some of their leaders the same year as they occupied the Spanish Embassy in Guatemala City.

There are no cafés on-site, but you can buy drinks and it's a great spot for a picnic. All displays are in Spanish and Kaqchikel only. The site is about five kilometers (3.1 mi) southwest of Tecpán. To get there, take a mini-bus or a tuk-tuk from the center of town. The site is open 8 a.m.-4 p.m. Updated: May 03, 2010.

Lodging

There are two hotels just off the main plaza. Posada de Don Martín, by the side of the big white church, has rooms with a private bathroom at $9, and has cable TV and parking. Hotel Iximché has enough space to cater to a coach-load of tourists; there are two buildings with 48 rooms on either side of 1a Avenida, just by the square. Rooms with shared bathroom cost $3.60 and $7.25 with private bathroom and TV. All have hot water. Parking included. Updated: May 03, 2010.

Restaurants

On the square, near the Hotel Iximché, is El Restaurante El Churraquito, serving up churrasco, burgers, sandwiches and cakes for breakfast and lunch. Under Posada de Don Martín is the Lucky Comedor and Cafésandra. On 1a Avenida, going away from the square, you will find the chain restaurants Que Dely (fast food, home delivery available) (Tel: 502-7879-9192) and Holandesa (sweets). Nearby is Pizzaria Napoli (8 a.m.-11 p.m.) Updated: May 03, 2010.

SOLOLÁ

Often hidden high in the clouds above Lake Atitlán, Sololá is a wonderful place to visit. The best time to visit is on market days, which are Tuesday and Friday, as Sololá hosts one of the most impressive markets in all of Central America. The larger market on Friday is a flurry of color, with people coming in traditional dress from all over the highlands. This is the only town with congruent Maya and Ladino municipal governments (the Ladino are a mestizo group in Guatemala). The men adhere fiercely to the traditional fashion code, and you will see them in patterned pants, brown felt skirts (worn over the pants), bright cowboy shirts and cowboy hats. On Sundays the Kaqchikel town elders walk through the streets on their way to church in full regalia and silver-tipped walking sticks.

Getting To and Away

To get to Sololá, take a bus going west on the Carretera Interamericana toward Panajachel and get off as the bus passes through Sololá. If you are coming from Chichicastenango, get off in Los Encuentros and take a bus toward Panajachel. From Quetzaltenango, you can get off on the highway at the turn-off for the lake before Los Encuentros, then catch another minibus. In Sololá there is a bus parking lot at 8a Avenida and 9a Calle, where buses depart every 20 minutes to Panajachel and Los Encuentros. Updated: Feb 28, 2010.

Services

Running south along 7a Avenida from the pastel yellow church you will find Café Internet ($0.75 per hour, 8 a.m.-7 p.m.). There is a dental office and a Banrural bank (Monday-Thursday 8:30 a.m.-5 p.m., Friday 7:30 a.m.-5 p.m., Saturday 9 a.m.-noon) with an ATM and Western Union. Along 6a Avenida there is also a Despensar Familiar supermarket, a Holandesa cake shop and a Que Dely fast-food joint. Updated: Feb 28, 2010.

Lodging

Hotel Cacique Ralon (Rooms: $15 per person. Tel: 502-7762-3138/4657) is a large, clean and well-decorated hotel with WiFi, cable TV, spacious private hot-water bathrooms and big comfy beds. Hotel Angel (Tel: 502-7762-3292) is another option nearby. On the road down to Panajachel, just after the blue hospital, is Hotel Vista Hermosa with views over the impressive steep-sided cliffs that plunge into the lake. Updated: Feb 28, 2010.

Restaurants

Mexican food joint Chileros Taqueria (Tel: 502-7762-5222) cooks up delicious tacos (three for $2). They accept credit cards and do home delivery. Near Chileros are the Comedor y Cafeteria Santa Ana and the bakery Rapi-pan, which has tasty ham and cheese croissants.

LAGO ATITLÁN

The Lake Atitlán basin was created in an immense volcanic eruption 85,000 years ago. Around the basin, volcanoes surged up over thousands of years, leading to the creation of the lake. With its panoramic volcanic views and azure waters, the lake epitomizes tranquillity.

The Lake Atitlán area comprises the provinces of Chimaltenango and Sololá. The area is beautiful and mountainous, and the vast majority of the inhabitants are indigenous, with the Quiché and Kaqchikel people being the most numerous. Chimaltenango province does not have much to offer the traveler, but history buffs will not want to miss the ruins at Iximché and Mixco Viejo. The city of Chimaltenango is a medium-sized provincial capital with an interesting castle that serves as the government building, but the city has little else of interest. In Sololá province is the lake itslef, ringed by several small towns and communities, the most noteworthy of which are Panajachel, Santiago Atitlán, San Pedro and San Marcos. The city of Sololá is also worth a stop as you head down to the lake. Updated: Sep 27, 2007.

Lago Atitlán Crossing

There are two options to see this beautiful volcano-surrounded lake: either take an organized day tour or use the ferry launches. You will not have time to see the place in a day using the ferries, so it is advisable to do a tour. Tours usually cost around $10.50 and go to San Antonio, Santiago de Atitlán and San Pablo. With more time take the ferries, which cost $2.60 per person each way, although you can often bargain down.

Departures can be tricky to work out, but a good plan is to head to San Pedro for the first night, spend the day around there, then take a lancha to San Marcos for the next night. At San Marcos, take in the amazing views of the lake and volcanoes. Take an early lancha past all the bays back to Panajachel and another one out to Santiago, either returning for the 4 p.m. shuttle back to Antigua or staying one night in Santiago. Updated: Nov 10, 2009.

Lodging

The lake's largest town, Panajachel, became a magnet for tourists during the 1960s and since then has seen a large growth in lodging options. Unless you want something more traditional or rustic (in which case, there are a few options in other towns around the lake), Panajachel has the entire spectrum of possible accommodations and is the main hub for tourism and nightlife in the area. Lake Atitlán hotels start at around $10 for a basic, single room and range upwards to $100-150 for the most luxurious options, such as the Hotel Atitlán (home to live peacocks). Another popular, if pricey, spot is the Hotel Posada Don Rodrigo ($75 per night), which lies at the end of the main drag and offers lakefront location and a big waterslide.

Lake Atitlán hostels are difficult to come by, but comparable *hospedajes* abound in Panajachel. Most rooms are under $20, and many are under $10. These hospedajes, which are usually simply a few extra rooms in a family's house, offer cheap, if sometimes dingy, rooms, so make sure you ask to see the room before you commit to anything. Updated: Jun 29, 2010.

PANAJACHEL

Panajachel, called "Pana," is usually the first stop for backpackers in this area. Be warned, if an "authentic Guatemalan" lakeside experience is what you are looking for it is best to catch a boat to another village like San Pedro or Santiago Atitlán. But Panajachel is what it is: full of tourists, hotels, restaurants, Internet cafés, clubs, bars and tourist agencies. The town's bustling nightlife is probably the main draw, since hoards of Guatemalans from the capital mix with tourists on weekends to party until bars close. Mayas from surrounding villages make the trek here to pawn their handicrafts to tourists, and the town's abundance of transport connections to all parts of Guatemala, Mexico and Honduras add to Panajachel's popularity. And the influx of tourism will never spoil the view from the lakeshore. Updated: Aug 02, 2010.

When to Go

The dry season in the highlands runs from November to April, and this is the better time to visit the area. Still, during the rainy season the rains only come down for a couple hours in the afternoons. The temperature drops a bit in the evening so bring a jacket. Panajachel has a weekly market on Thursdays held in the old town near the church that appeals to shoppers looking for fresh fruits and vegetables. Animals are also for sale. Updated: Aug 17, 2010.

Getting To and Away

Buses arrive at and leave Panajachel at Calle Santander and Calle Principal, with direct buses to Antigua (daily at 10:45 a.m. except Sundays, $6). Ten buses run to Guatemala City throughout the day (from 5 a.m.). Additionally, there are eight daily buses that make the trip to Chichicastenango (1.5 hr, $1.50) and six buses daily to Quetzaltenango ($2). The best option when traveling in Guatemala is the shuttle bus. At only a few dollars more per ride ($6 to go from Panajachel to Antigua), shuttles provides the safety not afforded on public transportation. There are numerous agencies throughout Panajachel that offer shuttles, most of which are located on Calle Santander. Be sure to book early on weekends or risk being stranded as the shuttles fill up fast. Updated: Aug 17, 2010.

The nearest international airport is in Guatemala City. Habitat Para La Humanidad (Tel: 502-7762-0408) is in the alley marked by signs for Casa Linda and Hospedaje Montufar. Updated: Aug 17, 2010.

Getting Around

There are two boat docks that ferry visitors to Lake Atitlán's surrounding villages. The first is located at the end of Calle del Embarcadero where boats leave to Santa Cruz (10 min), Jaibalito (25 min), Tzununá (25 min) and San Marcos (45 min). The second dock is located at the end of Calle Rancho Grande. Ferries and lanchas service to Santiago Atitlán. Visitors will barter for a price, which can be between $2-5. It is best to barter directly with the boat captain and not with locals, who may attempt to lead you to the boat and negotiate on your behalf for a $1-2 fee.

Boats depart from here at 6:30 p.m., 9 p.m., 9:30 p.m. and 10:30 a.m., and 1 p.m., 3 p.m., 4:30 and 5 p.m. Return trips from Santiago are scheduled at 6 a.m., 7 a.m. and 11:45 a.m., as well as 12:30 p.m., 1:30 p.m. and 4:30 p.m. Taxi and shuttle service is also an option.

Safety

Visitors to Panajachel do not have a lot of problems with violent crime, as the area's Maya villages generally have a lower crime rate than most U.S. cities. Still, petty theft and pickpockets can happen anywhere at any time. The town has the ability to attract a lot of Guatemalans on a weekend getaway from the nation's capital, including *gringeros*, Guatemalan men on the prowl for foreign women. Instances of drinks being drugged have been reported, so always mind your beverage and refrain from accepting drinks from strangers that could be spiked. Updated: Aug 17, 2010.

Services

Panajachel has many more resources than surrounding villages, including all of the services any tourist would need.

TOURISM
The tourism office is at Calle Santander 1-87.

MONEY
ATMs and banks line Calle Santander, as do tour and adventure agencies. There is a Banco Agromercantil (Monday-Saturday 8:30 a.m.-6 p.m., Sunday 9 a.m.-1 p.m. Tel: 502-7765-1145) on Calle Principal.

KEEPING IN TOUCH
To send or receive mail, head to Panajachel's post office (Monday-Friday 8:30 a.m.-5:30 p.m., 9 a.m.-1 p.m. Tel: 502-7762-2603), which is at A-3 Calle Santander, Zona 2.

Internet access is found readily throughout town. One recommended spot is Mayanet (Ca. Santander, slightly north of Ca. 14 de Febrero).

MEDICAL
Pana Medic (Ca. Principal 0-72, Zona 2. Tel: 502-7762-2174) is a local medical clinic that has 24-hour emergency service.

For emergencies call the police at 502-2421-2810. There is a 24-hour pharmacy called Farmacia Batres at Calle Principal 0-32.

LAUNDRY
If you need to drop off a load of dirty laundry while in Panajachel, Lavanderia Santander (Daily 7 a.m.-8 p.m. Tel: 502-5756-8577) on Calle Santander will help you out.

Things to See and Do

Visitors to Panajachel certainly will not be at a loss for things to do. Study Spanish,

learn of the region's history at local museums, hike, climb, fish, paraglide, swim, cycle or go horseback riding. The biggest problem could be finding enough time to do it all. Updated: Aug 02, 2010.

Museo Lacustre Atitlán
(ADMISSION: $5) Find exhibits that trace the creation and geological history of Lake Atitlán at Museo Lacustre Atitlán. Also on display is Maya archeology that dates from late pre-Classic and Classic times. The museum is located inside Hotel Posada de Don Rodrigo, and costs approximately $5 for entrance for non-hotel guests. Sunday -Friday 8 a.m. to 6 p.m., Saturday 8 a.m.-7 p.m. Updated: Jul 16, 2010.

Museo Raúl Vásquez
Museo Raúl Vásquez has a weird mix of figures from Guatemalan folklore on display on the same shelves as statues of Jesus Christ and other religious figures. There are some interesting watercolor paintings that hang on the walls as well. Daily 10 a.m.-6 p.m. 5a Ca. Peatonal. Updated: Jul 16, 2010.

Reserva Natural Atitlán
This popular reserve, found on the grounds of a former coffee farm, is located slightly outside of town, about a 10-minute walk from Panajachel. To get there, take the road to Solá, and after the first climb, take a left down the valley of San Buenaventura; follow the road for 800 meters (2,625 ft). On-site there is a zip-line among the trees in the forest, a butterfly farm, and nature trails that lead to waterfalls. There are also monkeys on the grounds. Daily 8 a.m.-5 p.m. URL: www.atitlan.com/resnat.htm. Updated: Jul 16, 2010.

Studying Spanish

Learn Spanish near one of the most beautiful lakes in the world. Schools offer numerous one-on-one learning packages, from one-hour daily lessons to full-day sessions. Prospective students need only to walk around to find numerous choices. Be sure to ask around to find the best price, and do not be afraid to negotiate to practice with a native speaker at a fraction of the price one would find at a language school in the United States or Europe. To completely immerse yourself in the culture, do a homestay with a local family. Updated: Aug 02, 2010.

Jabel Tinamit
This Maya-owned and operated Spanish school is one of the more reputable in Panajachel. One-on-one or small group classes

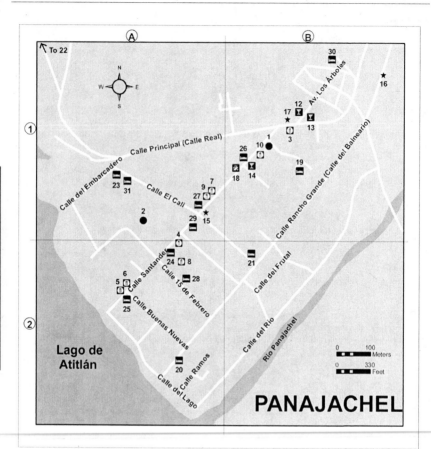

are available. The school's new building is located in the center of town near the main church. The school has a computer lab with eight computers and free WiFi for students with laptops. From the main bus stop (at the cross roads of Calle Principal, Calle Santander and Avenida de Los Árboles) walk up Avenida de Los Árboles for two minutes and the school is located just inside the entrance to Callejon Las Armonias, on the right side. Prices range from $90 for 20 hours per week to $125 for 30 hours per week. Add $5 during the high season months of January, February, June, July and August. Callejon Las Armonias Tel: 502-7762-6056 E-mail: info@jabeltinamit.com, URL: www.jabeltinamit.com. Updated: Nov 17, 2009.

Jardín de America Spanish School

Jardín de America Spanish School offers one-on-one lessons by certified Guatemalan teachers. Lessons run from $95 for 20 hours per week

to $143 for 30 hours per week. All study materials are included, as is coffee, tea and purified water. Homestays with local families arranged by the school cost $75. Volunteer opportunities and tour activities are also set up by the school for its students. Tel: 502-7762-2637, E-mail: nicolas_tr@yahoo.com, URL: www.jardindeamerica.com. Updated: Nov 17, 2009.

Lodging

BUDGET

Hospedaje Sánchez

(ROOMS: $5 per person) The highlight of Hospedaje Sánchez is the pretty view of the surroundings from the rooftop. Rooms are not fancy, but they are clean and quiet. The hospedaje is a one-block walk from the bevy of restaurants, bars and discos found on Calle Santander. Ca. El Chalí. Tel: 502-7762-2244. Updated: May 25, 2010.

Activities ●

1 Jabel Tinamit B1
2 Jardín de América A1

Eating 🍴

3 Atlantis B1
4 Café Bombay A2
5 Deli Jazmín A2
6 El Bistro A2
7 Guajimbo's A1
8 La Lanterna A2
9 Maktub'ar A1
10 Paris Paris B1
11 Porta Hotel del Lago (See 22)

Nightlife 🍷

12 Chapiteau B1
13 Circus Bar B1
14 Pana Arte B1

Services ★

15 Maya Net A1

16 Police Station B1
17 Visa ATM B1

Shopping 🛍

18 Centro Comercial
San Rafael B1

Sleeping 🛏

19 Casa Linda B1
20 Casa Loma A2
21 Hospedaje García B2
22 Hotel Atitlán A1
23 Hotel Cacique Inn A1
24 Hotel Dos Mundos A2
25 Hotel Posada de Don Rodrigo A2
26 Hotel Primavera B1
27 Hotel Regis A1
28 Hotel Utz-Jay A2
29 Mario's Rooms A1
30 Villa Lupita B1
31 Hospedaje Sanchez A1

CENTRAL HIGHLANDS

Casa Linda
(ROOMS: $5-14) This quaint hostel is a nice find off a side street from Calle Santander. Rooms are clean, with suitable beds and balconies that let in a pleasant breeze. The staff is friendly and the cleaning woman keeps rooms in excellent shape. A room with a shared bathroom costs approximately $5 for singles or $7 for doubles. Add another $5 per night to snag a room with a private bathroom. Callejon El Capulin. Tel: 502-7762-0386. Updated: Jul 06, 2010.

Hospedaje Garcia
(ROOMS: $5-20) Here, rooms with shared bathrooms are not only cheaper ($5-$9), but also are bigger and have balconies. If you want a private bathroom, those rooms are fine too and cost $15-20. Ca. 14 de Febrero, Tel: 502-7762-2787. Updated: May 25, 2010.

Casa Loma
(ROOMS: $5-27) Casa Loma has wood-floored rooms with soft beds. There is a nice green area behind the hostel to hang out with friends and have a few beers. A single or double room with a shared bathroom costs $5-10, while rooms with private bathrooms are $20-27 per night. Ca. Rancho Grande. Tel: 502-7762-1447. Updated: May 25, 2010.

Villa Lupita
(ROOMS: $6-10) This family-run option is another excellent cheap choice in Panajachel. There are 18 well-kept rooms, decorated by the family with colorful carpets and funky lamps. The best part of a stay here is the free coffee and drinking water. Singles and doubles with or without private bathrooms are available, and there is hot water. Callejon Don Tino Tel: 502-5511-0541. Updated: May 25, 2010.

Hospedaje El Amanecer
(ROOMS: $8-16) This is a relatively new hotel on the scene in Panajachel. It has two rooms with shared bathrooms and four rooms with private bathrooms and

TV. The showers have hot water, and the rooms are well-kept. Ca: Ramostel. Tel: 502-7762-0636. Updated: May 25, 2010.

Mario's Rooms

(ROOMS: $9-7) Most backpackers walk away from Mario's Rooms with a feeling of satisfaction. The rooms are one of the best deals in Panajachel: petite but clean and with hot showers. While the hostel is not too loud, it is still lively enough that you won't have a hard time meeting a few new friends. Mario's has a nice courtyard, too. Single and double rooms with a shared bathroom are available, as are rooms with private bathrooms that cost a few bucks more. Ca. Santander. Tel: 502-7762-2787. Updated: May 25, 2010.

Hotel Jere

(ROOMS: $12-18) Hotel Jere is a decent, simple hotel. It has nine rooms decorated with local touches and, more importantly, private bathrooms with hot water. Some rooms have a TV. The staff keeps the rooms very clean, and the atmosphere is quiet. Ca. Rancho Grande. Tel: 502-7762-2781. Updated: May 25, 2010.

MID-RANGE

Hotel Casa Ramos

(ROOMS: $22) Located a short walk from the shores of the lake, Hotel Casa Ramos is known for its clean rooms and friendly staff. Employees keep the hotel's 18 rooms sparkling clean. The decor here is traditional, with Guatemalan handmade blankets on the soft beds. Ca. Ramos. Tel: 502-7762-0413. Updated: Jul 06, 2010.

El Chaparral Hotel

(ROOMS: $25) El Chaparral Hotel is one of several new options that have sprung up as the tourist industry continues to expand in Panajachel. It is located only a block from the lake and near all the restaurants along Calle Santander. Rooms are comfortable, with private bathrooms and cable TV. Final Ca. Santander. Tel: 502-7762-0540. Updated: May 25, 2010.

Hotel Utz Jay

(ROOMS: $30) Comfortable rooms and a quiet atmosphere are guaranteed at Hotel Utz Jay. There is a lovely garden that draws interesting birdlife onto the grounds. Rooms are in cottages that are full of traditional Guatemalan designs. There are also fans and private bathrooms with hot water. Services include breakfast, wireless Internet, telephone, parking, mountain bike rental, tourist information, mini-spa and Jacuzzi. 5 Ca. 2-50, Zona 2. Tel: 502-7762-0217/1358, E-mail: reservations@hotelutzjay.com, URL: www.hotelutzjay.com. Updated: Jul 06, 2010.

Hotel Primavera

(ROOMS: $30-50) Hotel Primavera is not another cookie-cutter hotel. All 10 rooms are designed to give guests the comfortable feeling of home. Large windows let in a lot of light and fluffy pillows adorn comfortable, over-sized beds. Rooms also have elegant hardwood floors and are equipped with a private bathroom and cable TV. Single ($30), double ($40) and triple ($50) rooms are available. During the high season, add $10 to the price of each room. Telephone, fax, Internet connection, laundry service, tours and transfers are available. Updated: May 25, 2010.

Hotel Paradise Inn

(ROOMS: $40-45) Not quite paradise, but still an excellent mid-range option. The grounds are manicured with green grass and flowers. The staff will add an additional bed for $5 an evening. Tel: 502-7762-1021, E-mail: panaraquel@msn.com, URL: www.panajachel.com. Updated: May 25, 2010.

San Buenaventura De Atitlán

(ROOMS: $50-243) Venture two kilometers (1.2 mi) out of Panajachel to this extended stay hotel that gives guests all the privacy they need but is still only a short distance from the bars and restaurants in town. San Buenaventura de Atitlán has a private beach, gardens, coffee groves and wooden areas for patrons to enjoy. Rent a kayak at the beach or stroll to the nearby butterfly reserve at the Atitlán Nature Reserve. There are fully furnished townhouses ($243) that comfortably fit up to six people, while single rooms ($50) and two-person suites ($123) are also available. Amenities include a heated swimming pool, sauna, Jacuzzi, phone, cable TV and laundry service. Tel: 1-888-790-5264, Fax: 502-7762-2059, E-mail: info@hotelsanbuenaventura.net. Updated: Jul 06, 2010.

Hotel Cacique Inn

(ROOMS: $62) For whatever reason, this hotel seems to attract tons of Guatemalans on holiday from the capital. This makes for an excellent opportunity to mingle with locals and practice some Spanish. The 34-room hotel features nice beds with warm, handmade Guatemalan bedspreads. Ca. El Chalí 3-82. Tel: 502-7762-2053. Updated: May 25, 2010.

Hotel Regis

(ROOMS: $62) Hotel Regis is a trendy hotel with 25 rooms that stays relatively quiet in the evenings. Rooms are secure and comfortable enough with private bathrooms and hot water. The staff is friendly and there is a hot spring in the garden behind the hotel. Ca. Santander 3-47. Tel: 502-7762-1152. Updated: Jul 06, 2010.

Hotel Dos Mundos

Located one block from the shores of the lake, this hotel has funky, red-tiled rooms. Beds are comfy and private bathrooms have hot water. The on-site café serves excellent cappuccino. Amenities include a swimming pool, restaurant, bar, café and conference room. Ca. Santander 4-72 zona 2. Tel: 502-7762-2078, Fax: 502-7762-0127, E-mail: info@hoteldosmundos.com, URL: www.hoteldosmundos.com. Updated: May 25, 2010.

HIGH END

Hotel Posada de Don Rodrigo

(ROOMS: $90-110) This 41-room hotel has rooms in two separate areas. Some have views of the lake and are more costly, but these rooms are more modern and worth the extra price. All rooms are equipped with a private bathroom, telephone, WiFi, cable TV and room service. Some rooms also have exquisite tubs and chimneys, while there is also an on-site restaurant. Single ($90), double ($100) and triple ($110) rooms are available for reservation. Ca. Santander (at lakeside end). Tel: 502-7762-2326, URL: www.posadadedonrodrigo.com. Updated: May 25, 2010.

Hotel Atitlán

(ROOMS: $120-250) From its humble beginnings as a coffee farm, Hotel Atitlán has easily transformed into one of the finest accommodation choices in Panajachel. Elegantly designed rooms are furnished with fine tables, dressers, and comfortable beds and there are great views from the private balconies. The pool has an excellent view of the lake and volcano. There is also a Jacuzzi, garden, bar and restaurant. Finca San Buenaventura Panajachel and Sololá Guatemala. Tel: 502-7762-1441/2060, E-mail: info@hotelAtitlán.com, URL: www.hotelAtitlán.com. Updated: May 25, 2010.

Porta Hotel del Lago

(ROOMS: $220) This all-inclusive resort is on the shore of the public beach at Lake Atitlán. There are suites, standard rooms and an executive floor. On-site restaurants serve international cuisine. The pool area has a fabulous deck to relax on while drinking cocktails from the bar. Porta Hotel has WiFi, two Jacuzzis, a gym, an art gallery and a kid's club. Additional services such as babysitting or birdwatching, among others, are available for a fee. $220 all-inclusive. Tel: 502-2361-9683, Fax: 502-2361-9667, E-mail: info@portahotels.com, URL: www.portahotels.com. Updated: Jul 06, 2010.

Restaurants

TRADITIONAL GUATEMALAN

Guajimbo's

(ENTREES: $8-12) Head directly to Guajimbo's to fill up on some serious South American parrillas. The barbecued meats here include steak, chicken and sausages that can go head-to-head against any place Argentina has to offer. There are several vegetarian dishes and salads available as well. Friday-Wednesday 7 a.m.-10 p.m. Ca. Santander. Tel: 502-7762-0063. Updated: Jul 20, 2010.

ITALIAN

Restaurante La Lanterna

(ENTREES: $5-9) One of the best choices for authentic Italian food in Panajachel. The homemade pasta—especially the fettuccine—is perfectly complemented with a bottle of Italian wine. The waitresses are friendly. Inside Hotel Dos Mundos. Ca. Santander. Tel: 502-7762-2078. Updated: Jul 16, 2010.

STEAKHOUSE

Órale Steak House

(ENTREES: $8-30) Órale specializes in an array of steak plates; the large sirloins and fillets are some of the best in Guatemala. Mexican dishes are also offered, as well as a variety of chicken and seafood dishes for those that do not want to dine on red meat. Moderate-sized salads can be ordered with your meal. There is a full bar with both national and international drink choices. Also, stop by for an espresso in the mornings to go along with a typical Guatemalan breakfast. Calle Santander next to the Banco Industrial. Tel: 502-7762-0017, E-mail: tacosorale3x10@yahoo.com. Updated: Jul 06, 2010.

CAFÉ/DELI

Solomon's Porch

(ENTREES: $2.50-3.75) This coffee house is a happening hangout in the evenings, a

CENTRAL HIGHLANDS

good meeting place before a night of dancing at a local club. Local acts and traveling hippies with guitars often jam at the small stage area, while pool aficionados flutter around the billiards table or movie buffs view the latest DVD with a plate of nachos ($3.75) or quesadillas ($2.50) at the large-screen cinema area. There is also WiFi and Internet available at no charge to customers. Tuesday-Saturday noon-10 p.m. Ca. Principal and Ca. Santander. Tel: 502-7762-6032. Updated: May 25, 2010.

Atlantis Café And Bar

(ENTREES: $4-8) The decor is delightfully tacky at Atlantis, with stained-glass light shades and a wood-paneled bar. Service is quick. Beers and affordable sub sandwiches are available as well as breakfast, lunch and dinner meals. Have a drink in the beer garden on warmer evenings. Ca. Principal Panajachel. Tel: 502-7762-1015. Updated: Jul 16, 2010.

El Bistro

(ENTREES: $5-11) El Bistro is a relaxing location near the lake shore to sip on a cup of fresh-brewed Guatemalan coffee. Recommended are the chicken sandwich with avocado and peppers, as well as the steak and pasta dishes. Daily 7 a.m.-10 p.m. Ca. Santander, near the lakeshore. Tel: 502-7762-0508. Updated: May 25, 2010.

Maktub'ar Café Jardín

The quiet, open atmosphere of this bohemian restaurant and bar is a the perfect choice if you're looking for a big breakfast, a relaxed afternoon lunch or even an evening drink. Maktub'ar is known for its smoothies, easily the best in town. The music selection includes the owner's own Brazilian tunes and songs by world-renowned musicians. The bar also occasionally has live music. The menu includes a good variety of sandwiches, pizzas cooked on a wood oven, and delicious fruit smoothies. Maktub'ar has tables scattered throughout the restaurant where you can usually start a conversation with other patrons. At night, this is a happening place popular among locals and tourists alike. Happy hour: 7 p.m.-9 p.m.. Tuesday to Friday 10 a.m.-1 a.m., Saturday-Sunday 8 a.m.-1 a.m. Ca. Santander. Tel: 502-7762-2151. Updated: May 25, 2010.

Deli Jasmín

Don't worry about oversleeping and missing breakfast after a night of too much dancing and too many drinks. Deli Jasmín cooks up typical breakfast plates all day, complete with fresh bagels or English muffins you can enjoy in the delightful garden. Unique teas, jams and cookies are hits here. Wednesday to Monday 7 a.m.-6 p.m. Ca. Santander, close to the lakeshore. Tel: 502-7762-2585. Updated: May 25, 2010.

ASIAN

Café Bombay)

(ENTREES: $3-8) At this eclectic vegetarian café, most of the items on the menu are organic, and everything is absolutely fresh. The pad thai and fresh guacamole are the most popular meals. Various dipping sauces served in ceramic dishes accompany the food. The chai goes well with the falafel. Ca. Santander, one block from the lake. Updated: May 25, 2010.

FRENCH

Paris Paris Restaurant

(ENTREES: $6-15) Paris Paris Restaurant touts its 32-centimeter long baguettes, which fill up even the hungriest backpacker, as the best in Panajachel. The restaurant also offers chicken, steak and seafood plates. There is a full bar and live music is played here on weekends. At happy hour (every night 5-7 p.m.) national drinks are two-for-one. Ca. Santander, in the front of the Centro Comercial San Rafael. Tel: 502-7762-0963. Updated: May 25, 2010.

PIZZA

Pizzería Florencia

(ENTREES: $10-20) The cooks at this pizzeria fire up its state-of-the-art steel oven to produce flavors reminiscent of Rome. Pizzas are fairly large and never lack toppings. If someone in the group is not in the mood for a slice, order one of the hamburgers, cheeseburgers or Argentine empanadas. Soda and beers are available as well. There is a delivery option for tired backpackers that do not want to leave the friendly confines of their hostel a moment longer than needed. Ca. Santander. Tel: 502-7762-1055. Updated: Jul 20, 2010.

TEX MEX
Sondra Gail's

(ENTREES: $4-9) Sondra Gail's does Tex-Mex at its finest in Panajachel. The huge plate of nachos is an excellent appetizer to split among friends. Meanwhile, tacos and burritos are popular dinner plates, though the barbecued chicken is probably the best dish. Wednesday to Monday noon-10 p.m. Ca. de los Árboles. Tel: 502-7762-2063. Updated: May 25, 2010.

CENTRAL HIGHLANDS

INTERNATIONAL

Chez Alex

(ENTREES: $10-14) Although considered expensive by Guatemalan standards, $10-14 for a plate of duck or lamb chops at Chez Alex is still a bargain. This diverse menu features escargot and wiener schnitzel, along with more basic chicken and seafood dishes. Atmosphere is friendly. Daily noon-3 p.m., 6 p.m.-10 p.m. Ca. Santander. Tel: 502-7762-0172. Updated: May 25, 2010.

Hotel Atitlán

(ENTREES: $10-20) Early birds should definitely stop here for the expansive Sunday breakfast buffet. For $10, guests can enjoy endless eggs, pancakes, fruit, bread and savory chorizo. The hotel is surrounded by manicured gardens and has a beautiful view of the lake. The lunch and dinner menu offers international options as well. Daily 6:30 a.m.-10 p.m. Tel: 502-7762-1441. URL: www. hotelAtitlán.com. Updated: Jul 16, 2010.

Casablanca Restaurant

(ENTREES: $10-30) Look no further than Casablanca for the best fine dining in Panajachel. This is considered by restaurant connoisseurs to be one of the top places to dine in Central America. Casablanca's knowledgeable staff whip up succulent dishes of chicken, pasta, meat and fresh seafood. Buy a bottle of wine to complete a fine meal at a fraction of the price one would pay for a similar experience in the United States or Europe. Daily 11 a.m.-11 p.m. Ca. Principal. Tel: 502-7762-1015 . Updated: Jul 20, 2010.

Nightlife

Pana Arte

(DRINKS: $2) The classic rock music played at Pana Arte is a welcome change of pace from the continuous blaring of reggaeton at most trendy clubs in Panajachel. A lot of people choose to start the night off here for an early happy hour to take advantage of the $2 mixed drink specials. A lot of other people tend to finish the evening here because bartenders frequently extend happy hour until closing time. Either way, it is an excellent place to save some quetzales while meeting a few new friends. Ca. Santander. Updated: May 25, 2010.

Circus Bar

(PIZZA: $6.50-18) Live bands, gooey cheese pizzas and a long list of imported liquors on the menu draw backpackers and fashion-minded Guatemalans on holiday to this popular establishment. Grab a seat at one of the restaurant's tables, decorated with throwback blue-checkered tablecloths, to have a few drinks and share a Hawaiian pizza, all to the sound of acoustic guitar music. Simple medium pizzas are as cheap as $6.50, while the large and more elaborate meat-packed Americana pizza is $18. The menu also features soups, salads, bruschettas, pasta, seafood and desserts. Daily noon-midnight. Av. Los Árboles. Tel: 502-7762-2056. Updated: Jul 16, 2010.

Chapiteau

If the scene at Circus Bar is a little too mellow, head across the street to dance the rest of the night away or play pool at the discoteca Chapiteau. Backpackers in T-shirts mingle with high-heeled Guatemalan girls on break from city life and the occasional Guatemalan dude with gel-spiked hair, a Miami Vice-style shirt and aviator sunglasses. Two-for-one drink specials are a plus. Wednesday to Saturday 7 p.m.-1 a.m. Av. de Los Árboles, across the street from the Circus Bar. Tel: 502-7762-0374/2056, E-mail: lacarpasa@hotmail.com. Updated: Jul 16, 2010.

AROUND PANAJACHEL

SANTA CATARINA PALOPÓ

Santa Catarina Palopó is a small village full of character located just four kilometers (2.5 mi) from Panajachel. This pretty village has a population of around 1,300 with the majority being of indigenous Kaqchikel Maya descent. Kaqchikel is the native language, but most of the locals also speak Spanish. The local economy is largely based on subsistence agriculture, but with the rise of tourism in recent decades there is now a local market selling artisan wares.

The village locals are easily recognized by the colorful, intricately woven *huipiles*, or blouses, worn by the women. The men also wear a traditional dress of similarly woven trousers and white shirts. The garments are typically turquoise are red, with the latter color being more popular.

Things to See and Do

Must-sees include the colonial church at the center of the town, the artisan market and the village's well looked-after beach. Nearby hot springs can be reached by motorboat or canoe and visitors can also hire a guide to take them around the village or just outside. A viewing point over Lake Atitlán, known as El Mirador, is also popular. There are plenty of festivals in the area, mainly religious. The biggest is November 16th-26th, when locals participate in a series of processions and ceremonies in honor of the village patron saint, Santa Catarina de Alejandría. The most straightforward way to get here is probably by bus from Panajachel, which drops passengers off in the central plaza in front of the colonial church. You can also arrive by boat from Panajachel or other nearby villages, but beware of ticket touts on the docks that might try to overcharge you. It is best to buy your ticket on the boat. Updated: Jul 29, 2010.

Lodging

Options are limited but high-quality: expect luxurious villas set into the hills on the outskirts of the village. Villas and guesthouses tend to have their own on-site restaurants and bars (there are also a few small places in the village where you can sample the local fare).

SANTA CRUZ LA LAGUNA

This little town is actually the closest to Panajachel, but probably the least visited, with most people going to San Pedro La Laguna on the opposite side of the lake. It couldn't be more different from its neighboring towns. Santa Cruz, made up of three villages, has remained rather undeveloped, since the only access is by boat or foot. For foreign visitors, this translates into unspoiled charm and beauty. As with some of the other villages, the shoreline has been mainly bought by wealthy foreigners and Guatemalans, with the local Mayas living in the village high above. For these locals, inaccessibility has meant no phone lines, no commerce and no economic progress. The organization Amigos de Santa Cruz (URL: www.amigosdesantacruz.org) was set up in 1998 by residents of Santa Cruz to help improve the lives of the indigenous villagers through education programs. Updated: Nov 14, 2009.

Getting To and Away

The boat schedule is flexible, with the first lancha to Panajachel usually leaving around 6.15 a.m. and the last one setting off about 6 p.m. From Panajachel there is a less frequent service, which stops at Santa Cruz first before visiting all the other villages. You can also take a fast boat to San Pedro and then go back to Santa Cruz via boat or, for the more adventurous, you can walk around the lake past San Juan, San Pablo, San Marcos, Tzununá and Jaibalito but you have to set off early in day. Updated: Nov 14, 2009.

Things to See and Do

Most people who come to Santa Cruz do so to relax and read. The way of life here is certainly very laid back. Still, there are some activities if you need a little more action. You can walk along the shoreline to nearby San Marcos or take the stunningly high path to Sololá. Swim in the lake (it is usually about 22°C/72°F), or have the Iguana Perdida hotel (see below) organize visits to a local weaving cooperative, among other things. Updated: Nov 14, 2009.

Lodging

You'll see the hotel La Iguana Perdida (Rooms: $5-54. Tel: 502-5706-4117, URL: www.laiguanaperdida.com) just as you get off the boat, right next to the jetty and overlooking the lake. It is a friendly place with various sleeping options, abundant greenery around the cabins and peaceful areas with views of the water. Morning yoga and scuba diving classes are offered and if you sign up before 3 p.m. you can partake in the communal set dinner. This place has a homey feel and a real sense of community.

On the opposite side of the jetty is the Hotel el Arca de Noe (Rooms: $8-37. Tel: 502-7848-1407, URL: www.arcasantacruz.com. Updated: Nov 14, 2009), the first hotel in Santa Cruz. The European owners work hard at keeping the hotel 'green' and also support a group of 18 elderly people from the village through its Los Ancianos program. There are a gym, private beach, and even French boules available.

SAN ANTONIO PAPOLÓ

Eleven kilometers (6.84 mi) from Panajachel after Santa Catarina lies the larger village of San Antonio Papoló. With a population of 2,650, San Antonio feels less touristy than other nearby villages. Altitude varies somewhere between 1,590 and 2,220 meters (5,217-7,284 ft) above sea level, depending on whether you venture to the shore of Lake Atitlán or into the mountains. Before the 1980s, access to San Antonio was either by foot or motor boat, but since then a road linking the village to nearby Santa Catarina and beyond has drawn more tourists to the area. The majority of people here are of indigenous Kaqchikel Maya descent, but they dress uniquely. Here the women wear a navy blue skirt and a blue- or red-striped blouse. The men also wear a version of the red-striped shirt and visitors will note the occasional red turban-like headdress.

If arriving by boat across the lake, it is hard to miss the gleaming white colonial-style church. There are also hot springs nearby and a cave nestled in the mountain behind, which is often used for local ceremonies. There are not many accommodation options, but the standard is quite good. In terms of food, guesthouses usually serve meals, but there are also several places in the town to eat. The local textile co-operative is worth a visit. San Antonio celebrates its patron saint, St. Anthony of Padua, on the 12th of June, so if you are visiting around then, expect a great festival atmosphere. Updated: Jul 29, 2010.

SAN LUCAS TOLIMÁN

At the southeastern tip of Lake Atitlán is San Lucas Tolimán. With a population of some 17,000, the town is quite a busy one. The lake is not a popular destination for tourists, but it is worth a visit if you want to escape the crowds. The largest local market is on Sundays, but you can also buy local goods and produce on Tuesdays and Fridays. Much of the economy is based on onion farming, but there is also a lot of coffee grown in San Lucas. There is even an organic processing plant in the town that you can visit and learn about Café Justicia, an organization dedicated to promoting the fair trade of coffee.

Things to See and Do

The town is flanked by two volcanoes, Volcán Atitlán and Volcán Tolimán, that are good for hikers. Neither climb is too difficult but there are many different paths to choose from. Some guided trips up the volcano depart at midnight and arrive at the summit at around 6:30 a.m. to avoid cloud cover. Updated: Jul 29, 2010.

Parque Chuiraxamoló

This magnificent ecological park is a great way to see Guatemala's beautiful cloud forests. It's the perfect place to enjoy some fresh air and participate in fun activities like mountain biking, birdwatching, trekking and zip-lining over the forest canopy. There are camping facilities in the park with child-friendly zones so the whole family can enjoy all it has to offer. The entrance to the park is located about five minutes

off the International Highway (CA-1), off the road going to Santa Clara. Tour companies offer shuttles, and buses to and from the capital to nearby towns such as Santa Clara and San Pedro pass the entrance on their way. Allow for about 2.5 hours from Guatemala City and an hour from San Pedro. Updated: Jul 29, 2010.

SANTIAGO ATITLÁN

On the southwest shore of Lake Atitlán, nestled between the volcanic cones of San Pedro, Atitlán and Tolimán, is the lakeside village Santiago Atitlán. Constructed by the Maya in the image of the world as they believed it to exist, it is the largest and most significant of the lakeside communities and a visit here on either a Friday or Sunday—when the market is in full swing—will provide you with a vivid insight into rural life in these parts. There is little else to do in Santiago but soak up the tranquillity. Some recommend taking a dip in the lake but others report that it is polluted and only good for kayaking. Also, beware of pesky gangs of kids.

The town holds steadfastly to old traditions, though the western world and tourism are increasingly making their presence felt. Residents continue to wear the customary clothing of the Tz'utujil Maya. For men, this includes embroidered, striped purple-and-white shorts; women, meanwhile, wear a band of red cloth around their heads, although displays of these are becoming increasingly infrequent. Make it here for Holy Week for energetic week-long celebrations.

Santiago has 35 churches, the most notable of which is the old, finely decorated Catholic Church. The church holds a stone memorial commemorating the death of American priest Father Stanley Rother, who was assassinated by a paramilitary group in 1981, after President García branded him a Communist. His body was returned to his native Oklahoma, but his heart was buried in the church.

Santiago Atitlán tends to attract a more hardcore traveler than the party-goers that flood Panajachel and, to some extent, San Pedro. Fantastic nightlife will not be found here, but rather a slower pace of life. Elderly men sport brilliant cowboy hats and and big belt buckles and women congregate on the street to make the all-important flour tortillas. There are excellent views of San Pedro Volcano across the lake in the shadows of the

Atitlán and Tolimán volcanoes. The village is also one of the best spots in Guatemala to find deals on Maya paintings and handicrafts. This small lakeside town still feels the lingering effects of horrific mudslides caused from Hurricane Stan in 2005, which took nearly 1,000 lives. Several international organizations remain in the area.

There is not the glut of accommodation or restaurant options to be found in more tourist-friendly villages. Still, there are gems here, like the fresh fish at El Pescador or the jumbo shrimp at Posada de Santiago. Fine family restaurants offer affordable plates of local cuisine accompanied by tortillas, refried beans and avocado.

When to Go

Semana Santa (Holy Week) is the busiest time of the year to visit Santiago Atitlán, as various rituals and celebrations occur at this time. Fiesta Santiago, which is held every July 25, is another popular time to visit. The best days to come to this village during a normal week are Fridays and Sundays, when the market is in full swing. The market is also open Tuesdays, though it is not as grand.

Getting To and Away

Tourists generally arrive to Lake Atitlán in the touristy town of Panajachel. From there, various ferry crossings can take you to Santiago Atitlán. Locals are quick to lead travelers to lanchas that provide these services. Expect to pay $3-4. It is always best to negotiate directly with the captain. Also be sure to ask whether the boat offers a direct service; otherwise you could be sitting around in the boat as it stops off at several villages first. The final few boats back to Panajachel leave between 4-5 p.m. Buses leave for Guatemala City until 3 p.m. from the central plaza.

Getting Around

Santiago Atitlán is a relatively small village, so walking is the main form of transportation once you arrive. There are a few tuktuks that motor around the island looking for passengers as well. There are no buses that service minor stops in the town, only ones that take you to and from the village.

Safety

Santiago Atitlán itself is pretty safe during daylight hours, though travelers are best served to practice common sense and not sport flashy watches or jewelry. And as always, do not carry large quantities of cash in your pockets. At night it is best to walk in groups. Robberies have been reported while hiking throughout the local trails near town.

Services

It's a better bet to find services and shopping in nearby Panajachel, though there are some options for travelers in a pinch in Santiago Atitlán. There is a MasterCard ATM found in the square, and there is also a post office and bank to change US dollars or travelers checks. Updated: May 26, 2010.

Things to See and Do

Santiago Atitlán has plenty for travelers to do for an afternoon or several days. The market is the highlight for most that come through here, and it is at its best on Fridays and Sundays. The Iglesia Parroquial Santiago Apóstol is an interesting church worth looking at. There are also nice hiking and horseback riding options around the village. Updated: May 26, 2010.

Hiking Around Santiago

Santiago Atitlán is surrounded by hiking trails. Routes lead to the top of each of the three nearby volcanoes, though due to robberies of tourists in the area it is necessary to hire a guide and a couple of tourist police (around $90 per group). Another pleasant hike is to Cerro de Oro, located approximately eight kilometers (5 mi) northeast of town. Updated: May 26, 2010.

Santiago Atitlán Market

The market in Santiago Atitlán is at its best on Fridays and Sundays. Vendors set up shop to sell local crafts and goods to those that pass by, including Maya women dressed in traditional costumes. Stroll past small shops where women and little girls gather to produce tortillas (5 for $0.12). Be sure to ask before snapping a shot of a local—it is insulting to simply treat locals as tourist attractions. Updated: Jul 16, 2010.

Maya Ceremonies

Maya religious ceremonies are conducted throughout the year in Santiago Atitlán. Mayas believe that these practices ensure the sun, stars, moon and planets continue to follow their correct paths. According to legend, if man does not do each ceremony correctly at the appropriate time, the cycle will be broken and the world could end. For useful information about the yearly cycle of celebrations in Santiago Atitlán, check out this website: www.santiagoatitlan.com/Religion/Cycle/cycle.html. Updated: May 26, 2010.

Iglesia Parroquial Santiago Apóstol

The Iglesia Parroquial Santiago Apóstol is one of the most magnificent churches in the Lake Atitlán area. The structure was constructed between 1572 and 1581. There are three altarpieces representing the three volcanoes that tower over the village. Also inside the church are saints dressed in clothing handmade by locals. Updated: Jul 16, 2010.

Museo Cojoyla

(ADMISSION: Free) The Museo Cojoyla is a must-see for those interested in the history of this lakeside village. There is an excellent showcase of the village's weaving past. The museum can be found one block up the street after arrival at the main dock. If you walk past the restaurant El Pescador, you have gone too far. Monday-Friday 9 a.m.-4 p.m., Saturday 9 a.m.-1 p.m. Updated: May 26, 2010.

Lodging

Santiago Atitlán hostels and hotels aren't as abundant as in places like Panajachel or San Pedro. However, there are enough choices, ranging from budget to upscale, for those that want a taste of a more authentic Lake Atitlán village away from the madness of Panajachel. For travelers with enough cash to skip out on the experience of staying in a hostel, the best choice in town is Posada de Santiago. Updated: Jul 13, 2010.

Hotel Chi-nim-ya

(ROOMS: $8-15) Hotel Chi-Nim-Ya is far short of luxury, but it gets the job done for backpackers. The cold concrete floors are hardly inviting, but rooms (available with or without a private bathroom) are OK. There are 22 rooms here that surround a central courtyard. To arrive, walk from the dock to the first intersection and turn left. Tel: 502-7721-7131. Updated: Jul 20, 2010.

Hotel Lago De Atitlán

(ROOMS: $15-19) The best thing about this hotel is the view from the upper levels. Rooms are generally well-lit, with large windows that allow the soft breeze that sweeps across the lake to blow into the room. The hotel is located four blocks uphill from the dock on the left side of the street. There are single, double and dorm rooms available with private bathrooms, TV and showers with hot water. Tel: 502-7721-7131. Updated: Jul 16, 2010.

Posada De Santiago !

(ROOMS: $15-100) Posada de Santiago Hotel provides some of the best rooms in this village. The hotel does a fantastic job of catering to all groups. Backpackers can find a bed in a clean dorm room for approximately $15 per night, while pricier, more private accommodation is also available. There are cottages that range from $50-75, while suites cost $85-100. Services offered include Internet, massage, pool, sauna and Jacuzzi. Tel: 502-7721-7366, Fax: 502-7721 736. Updated: Jul 16, 2010.

Restaurants

Few restaurants are available in this town; there are just three at the entrance to the village. There are a number of food stands and small cafés near the dock that are reasonably priced, but expect only mediocre food here. The hotel restaurants are often your best bet for quality cuisine in the area. Updated: Nov 16, 2006.

El Pescador

Upon arrival to Santiago Atitlán, hop off the boat and head two blocks up the street from the dock to find this restaurant's fresh grilled fish offerings. El Pescador is a fine establishment to grab a drink or sandwich for lunch after a morning of shopping at the Sunday market. The staff is friendly and quick to help, too. Monday-Saturday 7 a.m.-9 p.m., Sundays 7 a.m.-4 p.m. Tel: 502-7721-7147. Updated: May 26, 2010.

Posada de Santiago

(ENTREES: $5-15) This fine hotel restaurant offers savory cuisine. The blue corn pancakes are a popular breakfast choice topped with sweet butter and delicious macadamia syrup. The spicy blackened mahi or jumbo shrimp grilled in butter, garlic and white wine are favorites among patrons. Or, if breakfast at dinnertime is your thing, order up the Chapin Supper special that includes two eggs, refried beans, cream, tortilla, cheese and fried plantains. The smoked turkey sandwiches here are a nice option as well. Tel: 502-7721-7366. Updated: May 26, 2010.

SAN PEDRO LA LAGUNA

Carved into the base of its namesake volcano on the southeast shores of Lake Atitlán, San Pedro La Laguna is a little town with a lot to offer. Although smaller in size than the neighboring towns of Panajachel or Santiago, San Pedro's laidback attitude and breathtaking scenery has put it on the map as an important backpacker destination. The town's approximate population of 13,000 is made up mainly of indigenous Tz'utujil-speaking Mayas, though there is a growing expat community.

The town stretches up from the shores of the lake to the base of the volcano and spreads out between two main docks, the Panajachel dock and the Santiago dock. The upper part of the town, centered around the gleaming white Catholic Church, is home mainly to the locals, while the lakefront is where one will find the majority of businesses and accommodations catering to tourists. Despite this apparent separation between foreigners and locals, there is a pleasant integration of culture. In the town market, backpackers mingle and traditionally-dressed Maya mingle.

The local economy depends upon tourism. Spanish schools, hotels, restaurants, travel agencies, kayak and horse rentals, corner stores and the local street vendors all depend on the tourist dollar. Coffee production is another income source, with Guatemalan coffee being recognized as some of the world's finest. During harvest season, beans are spread out to dry around the town, and the town smells of coffee.

San Pedro has some of the least expensive rates for both Spanish lessons and hotel rooms, with plenty of each to choose from. Similarly, the many restaurants in San Pedro offer a vast selection of traditional and international cuisines. While in San Pedro, there is no shortage of things to do. The more active can seek out hiking and adventure tours, while those looking to relax can simply sit and soak in the spectacular view. Updated: Jul 28, 2010.

Getting To and Away

BY SHUTTLE
For the most up-to-minute shuttle information visit Casa Verde Tours or Big Foot Travel Agency. Shuttle times away from San Pedro are as follows:
To Antigua, Xela: Daily 8:30 a.m. and 1 p.m. (From Antigua: Daily 2 p.m. From Xela: Daily 8:30 a.m. and 3 p.m.)
To Chichicastenango: Thursday and Sunday 8:30 a.m.
To Guatemala City: Daily 8:30 a.m. and noon.
To Tapachula, Monterrico: Daily 8:30 a.m.
To San Cristobal de las Casas: Daily 6:30 a.m.

BY CHICKEN BUS
The bus stop is in front of the Catholic Church. Bus times are as follows:

To Guatemala City: Monday-Saturday 3:30 a.m., 4 a.m., 5 a.m., 5:30 a.m., 6 a.m., 8 a.m., 10 a.m., noon, 1 p.m. and 2 p.m. Saturday and Monday there is an additional bus at 2:30 a.m.
To Xela: Monday-Saturday 4:30 a.m., 5 a.m., 5:30 a.m., 6 a.m., 7 a.m., 8 a.m., 11 a.m. Sunday 4:40 a.m., 5 a.m., 5:30 a.m., 6 a.m., 8 a.m., 11 a.m.

BY BOAT
Boats leave San Pedro around once an hour, or when capacity is reached, from about 6 a.m. to 5 p.m. (check exact schedule at dock), heading for: Panajachel ($3.50), Santa Cruz ($2.50), San Juan & San Marcos ($1.25), Santiago ($2). Updated: Jul 28, 2010.

Getting Around
Everything in San Pedro is easily found and within walking distance. However, for the less athletic or for those who hate hills, a tuk-tuk will take you anywhere you want to go in town for $0.60 per person. Big Foot Adventures Travel Agency also provides tours and transportation. They offer a wide variety of exciting adventures: hiking the Indigino Nariz or San Pedro Volcano, horse riding expeditions, canopy zip-line tours, and now even hanggliding. In addition, they offer information and shuttle services to various destinations in Guatemala. Updated: Jul 28, 2010.

Services

TOURISM
Strangely enough, San Pedro does not have an official tourist office. There is a small wooden shack located by the Panajachel dock which offers some information about the town and employs registered guides, all of whom are willing to offer a service or suggest a hotel. More specific information regarding recreational activities, pricing and transportation services may be obtained from one of the many travel agencies, including Casa Verde Tours or Big Foot Adventures.

MONEY
The bank, Banrural (Monday-Friday 8:30 a.m.-5 p.m., Saturday 8:30a.m.-12p.m.), is located in town just past the market. Getting there on foot requires simply heading straight up the hill from the Panajachel Dock or hopping in a tuk-tuk for a door-to-door service.

There are currently two ATMs in San Pedro; one is located beside the bank, the other beside D'Noz by the Panajachel dock.

When using the ATMs, exercise caution and closely monitor your accounts, as incidents of bank fraud have been reported.

KEEPING IN TOUCH
Like most everything in San Pedro, even the post office (Monday-Saturday 8 a.m.-1 p.m. and 4-6 p.m.) lacks an official address but may be found in the vicinity of the large, white Catholic church in the center or town. A number of Internet cafés are scattered around town, most offering international calls. Although varied, the approximate cost is $1 per hour for Internet and $0.25 per minute for calls to the U.S. and Canada.

MEDICAL
While there is no hospital in San Pedro, there are two Public Health Centers (Centros de Salud): One is located near the Catholic Church, and the other, larger one is on the way to San Juan. Both offer free services, with the exception of prescribed medicines, which patients have to pay for. A number of pharmacies, including the Farmacia La Fe near the market, offer a wide selection of prescription drugs without requiring an official prescription. In addition, there are two private doctors practicing services for a fee. For more serious concerns, the closest hospital is located across the lake in Sololá. Updated: Jul 28, 2010.

LAUNDRY
There are a variety of locations offering laundry services, so take your pick. The average cost is approximately $0.50 per pound.

Things to See and Do
Day planning in San Pedro is simple and there is something for everyone. The more adventurous can kayak around the famous Lake Atitlán, go horse riding, hike the sacred Indigino Nariz or San Pedro Volcano, or explore the lakeside towns by motorbike. Those seeking relaxation can practice yoga, enjoy a professional massage or soak in the hot solar pools overlooking the lake. Weekends at La Piscina, San Pedro's only swimming pool, are host to the Smoking Joe's BBQ and Bocci Ball Tournament. In the evening, enjoy a drink among friends or dance to live music at one of the local bars. Updated: Jul 28, 2010.

Cerro de la Cruz Walk
Facing the lake in the center of San Pedro, head left and stick to the main road all the way to the next settlement, San Juan. Walk through the streets until you are out on the other side of the small village and you will see a well-marked path heading up the hill. A short but slightly steep climb will put you on top to a clearing where you head right to a cross and a small statue. From there you can enjoy a fantastic 360-degree view of the lake, San Pedro and the volcanoes and mountains all around. At the time of writing this was safe to do on your own, but check in town for the latest updates. Updated: Nov 16, 2006.

Indigino Nariz Walk
This is an extension of the Cerro de la Cruz walk and is a bit of a toughie. The climb heads up the same path, but take the left fork at the clearing to start heading up the big hill that towers over you. The route winds around the back of the mountain, offering good views out to the surrounding hills, then climbs to the top to offer fantastic bird's-eye views of Lake Atitlán and its surroundings. It is best to take a guide to show you the paths. Updated: Nov 16, 2006.

Culture Tour of San Juan
This tour gives you a chance to see how life works in these parts. Head to San Juan the same way as for the Cerro de la Cruz walk and meet the guide in town. He will take you to meet local Maya tradespeople, including weavers, people specializing in traditional medicines and painters, and to see churches and many more aspects of the Atitlán culture. Go with a guide from Officina Fundación Solar to Rupalaj K'Istalin in San Juan. Tel: 502-694-3784, E-mail: rupalajkistalin@yahoo.es., Updated: Nov 16, 2006.

Museo Tzu'nun Ya'
(ADMISSION: $4) For a brief lesson in the history of Lake Atitlán and the Maya cultures inhabiting its shores, visit Museo Tzu'nun Ya'. Begin the tour with two short video presentations. The first video depicts life in San Pedro as witnessed by the very first tourist in 1941. The second illustrates the formation of Lake Atitlán through a series of enormous volcanic eruptions. Continue into a series of rooms containing interactive exhibits, ancient artifacts, traditional textiles and antique photos. The whole experience requires less than an hour. Updated: Jul 28, 2010.

Atitlán Adventures
This tour company is owned and operated by a lovely pair: an American man and a Guatemalan women. The two of are very knowledgeable and they arrange some great tours.

Matt (or Mateo, as the locals call him) also leads tours up the volcano and the nearby mountains. This is a very professional and trustworthy business. Updated: Jul 15, 2008.

Studying Spanish

May'ab

May'ab is a long established, centrally located and competitively priced language school. Experienced teachers instruct various levels of classes in a peaceful garden setting. Complimentary refreshments and WiFi are available. Five hours at a local Internet café, one hour of horse riding, and unlimited use of the kayaks are all included in the cost of one week of study. Daily 8 a.m.-6 p.m. 7 Av. 2, Canton Xetawal. Tel: 502-5098-12995. Updated: Jul 28, 2010.

Ixim Achi Casa America

Currently San Pedro's newest and smallest Spanish school, Ixim Achi provides many of the same services as the other schools but at a lower cost. Various volunteer options are available and part of the tuition fees go toward local projects helping impoverished children in the surrounding area. Tel: 502-7772-8173. Updated: Jul 28, 2010.

Lodging

San Pedro is kind of like the cheaper cousin of nearby San Marcos. San Pedro hostel rooms run at around $5-7 a night—pretty cheap, especially considering the lakeside scenery. San Pedro hostels tend to be a bit rustic and rough around the edges, but if you can brave cold showers and concrete floors you'll be just fine. Updated: Jul 13, 2010.

Zoola

(ROOMS: $4-14) In Hebrew, Zoola means to relax, and that is exactly what you are apt to do in this cozy hotel. The eight spacious rooms are tastefully decorated and have comfortable beds (four have private bathrooms). There is also a lounge room for television watching, Internet browsing and a book exchange. Adjacent to the hotel, the restaurant offers a unique dining atmosphere. Low tables centered on straw mats, surrounded by colorful floor pillows, create a very relaxed environment that invites you to savor the experience and forget about the time. Tel: 502-5534-3111, URL: www.zoolapeople.com. Updated: Jul 28, 2010.

Casa Elena

(ROOMS: $4) This three-story terracotta-colored building must be the best value in town. Plenty of clean and tidy rooms run along a plant-filled concrete yard, which leads out to a lake view. Many of the rooms overlook the water, and the shared showers and toilets are tiled and sparkling clean. Arrive early or book ahead to secure a room. Head up from the dock and take the first left for 200 meters (about 650 ft). Tel: 502-310-9243. Updated: Nov 16, 2006.

Hotel Maritza

(ROOMS: $6.50) Nine rooms, colorfully painted from the outside, are lined up along two sides of a lush green garden that has stunning views out over the lake. The downside is that the rooms and showers are maybe a bit too rustic, with ill-fitting doors and concrete floors, but the staff will bend over backwards for you, and a swing on one of the hammocks in the garden is a treat. Head up from the dock and take the first right for 150 meters (500 ft). Updated: Nov 16, 2006.

Hostel Vía del Lago

(ROOMS: $6.50) A popular second choice to Casa Elena, this blue-colored place is set back from the lake but has good views. There is no real communal area, and the large rooms are dimly lit, but the staff is friendly. Head up from the dock and take the first left for 250 meters (820 ft). Updated: Nov 16, 2006.

Restaurants

Alegre Lounge

(ENTREES: $2.60-5.20) This is the place to come if you want your Atitlán experience in English. You could not get further removed from Guatemalan culture than a Sunday roast, filled baked potatoes, live football and a pub quiz. There are daily specials on the menu and there is always something different going on every night of the week. Head up from the dock and it is on the left corner. Updated: Aug 14, 2006.

Shanti-Shanti Café

(ENTREES: $4-5.20) This funky little café must be the coolest place in town. Its menu is unusual and varied, but the best reason to come is the almost all-night happy hour, when Cuba Libres are two for $1.30. The two-level seating area, with bamboo walls, has a really relaxed vibe, there are board games available and the stereo is always playing chilled-out tunes. Happy hour: 9 p.m-1 a.m. Updated: Nov 16, 2006.

Nick's Place

(ENTREES: $3) This place has been around for a while and is justifiably popular for its low prices and its pleasant lakeside seating area. There are good pizza and pasta dishes on offer but go there in the afternoon to sample one of their fantastic juices as the sun sets. It is also a good spot to grab a seat and a drink while waiting for a boat to another town. Updated: Nov 16, 2006.

Chile's Restaurante Latina Café

(ENTREES: $2.10-10.50) This newish place is a little pricier than some of the other spots in town, but it has a good deck looking over the lake and serves fine food and cocktails alongisde hookah pipes. There are free salsa lessons on Tuesdays and Fridays at 9 p.m. and every morning they serve what they call the best fresh ground coffee in town. Tel: 502-594-6194. Updated: Aug 14, 2006.

Restaurante El Fondeadero

(ENTREES: $3) This family-run spot offers good home-cooked food, including curry chicken and beef in wine sauce, in pleasant surroundings. The entrance leads off to a pair of large two-tier dining areas that have fantastic views right over the lake. You are quite likely to have the place all to yourself, because the restaurants at the dock are, for some reason, more popular. Head up from the dock and take first right for 50 meters (165 ft). Tel: 502-863-4276/963-2923. Updated: Nov 16, 2006.

The Buddha

This three-story bar, restaurant, lounge, cinema and cabaret has incredible Asian food and awesome cocktails, as well as a pool table and dartboard. Oh, and don't forget the superb lake and volcano views. On the main trail in San Pedro's Otro Lado. 2-24 7a Av. E-mail: thebuddhaguatemala@gmail.com, URL: www.thebuddhaguatemala.com.

Le Jardín des Saveurs

This place has a cool garden patio, with seating options ranging from candlelit tables to a big group table with pillows for seats. Serves delicious French and Italian food. They use local ingredients and everything is homemade, from bread to pastas. 7 Av. Zona 2. Tel: 502-7721-8154, E-mail: lejardindessaveurs@yahoo.com, URL: http://lejardindessaveurs.zzl.org. Updated: Jul 06, 2010.

Ventana Blue

Ventana Blue is a tiny blue room. The menu presents unique creations of Asian/Guatemalan infusion with plenty of vegetarian options. In addition to great food, they offer a wide selection of martinis. It is the perfect place to take a date. With only four tables, this popular little place fills up quickly, so get there early to assure a seat or call ahead to make reservations. Tuesday-Sunday 6 p.m.-10. Tel: 502-5284-2406. Updated: Jul 28, 2010.

D'noz

Named for its unmatched view of the sacred Indigino Nariz, D'Noz is a well-known establishment providing more than just its delicious European-style food. Enjoy breakfast upstairs while watching the sunrise over the Lake Atitlán, or get comfy with a hot toddy and watch a movie, shown nightly at 8:30 p.m. Downstairs, D'Noz Plaza offers a barista café, gift shop, bakery, media center and San Pedro's only health food store. Open seven days a week, D'Noz has something for everyone. Monday-Saturday 9 a.m.-11 p.m., Sunday 4 p.m.-11 pm. Located right beside Panajachel Dock. Tel: 502-7820-7456. Updated: Jul 28, 2010.

El Barrio

El Barrio serves generous portions of the best-tasting Mexican food in town. The menu also includes the usual bar staples such as burgers and fries, nachos, chili and the famous Chicken Club, big enough to feed two. The kitchen is open until midnight for those with late-night munchies. El Barrio also boasts San Pedro's largest array of spirits and offers creative promotions such as Tequila Tuesdays and Beer and Bacon Night. Daily 5 p.m.-1 a.m. Tel: 502-5474-7580. Updated: Jul 28, 2010.

SAN JUAN LA LAGUNA

San Juan La Laguna may not be one of the more frequented villages or towns on Lake Atitlán, but it is for that very reason that it has managed to retain its traditional charm and appears unscathed by the past few decades of increased tourism to the area. Accommodation is limited to one option, the Ecohotel Uxlabil, a good hotel that has its own private dock on the lake. With a meager population of only 3,000, two co-operatives account for much of the local employment. La Voz que Clama en el Desierto is a 140-member fair trade coffee co-operative that offers guided tours of its growing and production process. Then there is Lema, where many of the town's women create artisan wares and weave beautiful textiles using environmentally friendly dyes. For a spot of culture, visitors can visit not one but two images of the Maya deity Maximón, also known as San Simon. There is a Maximón statue in Atitlán, but there seems to be a more genuine and reverent atmosphere around the one in San Juan. The town is clean, quiet, friendly and lacks the tourist traps of many other towns on the lake. Updated: Jul 29, 2010.

Getting To and Away

The small town of San Juan La Laguna is just a five-minute drive from the larger town of San Pedro. Pick-up trucks pass by regularly, and it is best to wait for one of these if you are heading there in the hot midday sun. The town can also be reached by boat, but an even nicer way to get there is to walk–the views of the lake on the way are spectacular. The best time to walk there is first thing in the morning, when the sky is clear and the air is cool. Updated: Jul 29, 2010.

SAN MARCOS LA LAGUNA

Stepping into San Marcos is like stepping into another world. An idyllic fairyland of forests and valleys, hidden houses and tantalizing glimpses of the lake, San Marcos entices travelers to linger for "just one more day." Al fresco living is the norm and when the surroundings are so beautiful, there is little reason to go inside unless it is raining. A combination of sacred ground and powerful energies have drawn people from around the world to set up non-religious, holistic centers in all manner of healing disciplines. San Marcos is fast becoming the place in Central America to go for yoga, meditation and massage. Taking courses rather than just getting treatments is increasingly popular. Tourist accommodation and services are concentrated in the heart of the village, Barrio 3, by the lake shore. Further back from the lake is the paved part of town, with a few corner stores, the central park and a football field.

The indigenous communities mostly live high up on two hills, either side of the valley. It is common to see traditionally-clad women carrying bundles of vegetables and fruit for sale or walking to church.

An eco-conscience is spreading in San Marcos, as a variety of "green" hotels and cafés crop up. Initiatives to keep the environment and lake clean are ongoing. Have a good look at the brightly painted school wall built from eco-bricks. This is a place to get away from it all–to relax in a hammock, go for a swim and find peace within yourself.

Due to San Marcos La Laguna'a size, there is a limited choice of hotels and restaurants, but the quality is high with options for different budgets. Wholesome, healthy and delicious food is de rigeur, and vegetarians, in particular, will think they have arrived in heaven. As yet there are no street names in San Marcos. Leading up from the dock, through Barrio 3, is the main street and there are signs at the intersections for different restaurants and hotels. Barrio 3 is essentially a delightful, sometimes frustrating, warren of country paths, but sooner or later you should find where you want to go.

The town is filled with ex-pats, who run many of the hotels, restaurants and services. The lake can get very cold at night, so bring warm clothing. Also, there have been a number of recent reports of travelers being robbed and attacked in the area, so extra vigilance is advised. Updated: May 10, 2010

Getting Around

The most atmospheric and enjoyable way to travel around the lake is by lancha. Public lanchas leave Panajachel every half hour from 6:30 a.m. to 7:30 p.m. and take about 40 minutes. Cost is $3. Boats leave San Pedro every half-hour from 6 a.m. to 5 p.m., take 15 minutes and cost $1.20. Some lanchas are direct while some stop at all the villages; ask the captain to find out which is which. A journey between adjacent villages costs between $1.20 and $1.80. If the wind is up and the lake is covered in whitecaps, most lanchas will refuse to leave. A private lancha costs about $12 for the whole boat, one way. Tuk-tuks are available for short journeys. The drive to San Juan has some dramatic views and costs $3. To San Pedro is $5 or $3.60 per person if more than one. To Tzuznuá is $6. Updated: May 17, 2010.

When to Go

San Marcos is good to visit throughout the year. Its mild climate can be cool enough that you'll need a fleece at night but days are warm. Rainy season kicks off in May with occasional showers, the heaviest rains falling in September-October. Mid-November to May is high season. *Semana Santa* (Holy Week, the week before Easter) is hugely popular and there are processions between the villages. The annual Festival of Consciousness, full of creative and enlightening workshops, activities and music, is in March. Updated: Feb 05, 2010.

Getting To and Away

The easiest way to arrive in San Marcos is by tourist shuttle. These run to and from all the major tourist destinations in Guatemala and can be found at any travel agency. There is one morning departure usually leaving at 8 a.m. or 9 a.m. and sometimes an afternoon departure, but this depends on minimum numbers. Prices vary from agency to agency and change constantly, so shop around. A direct shuttle to and from Antigua costs between $4.50 and $7.50 per person and takes three to four hours. Shuttles to or from the airport or Guatemala City cost $15 or more and take four to five hours. Shuttles to Flores cost $37, and the trips last all day or overnight.

Chicken buses to Guatemala City pass through the neighboring village of San Pablo, a $1.20 tuk-tuk ride away from San Marcos. Departures go Mondays to Saturdays at 3:30 a.m., 4:30 a.m., 5:30 a.m., 6 a.m., 8 a.m., 10 a.m., 12 p.m. and 2 p.m. Sunday departures are at 6 a.m., 7 a.m., 12 p.m. and 1 p.m. Cost is $5. Change at Chimaltenango for Antigua. Chicken buses to Xela leave Monday to Saturday at 4:30 a.m., 5 a.m., 5:30 a.m., 6 a.m., 8 a.m. and 11 a.m. from San Pablo. If coming from one of the other lakeside villages, arrival in San Marcos will be by lancha. Updated: May 17, 2010.

Safety
As the popularity of San Marcos continues to increase, it is important for tourists to be respectful to the indigenous population and keep in mind that the village should not be treated one big beach. It is not appropriate to walk around town, even by the lake, wearing bikinis, or to openly drink alcohol in public. The popular swimming area and launch pad known as "the rocks" is actually at the base of sacred ground, so dress accordingly when going to or from. Sunbathing is best done in hotel gardens.

Crime does occur here, so be careful. Do not leave anything unattended while swimming. Hiking alone is usually discouraged and valuables should be left at the hotel. Several businesses in Barrio are funding a security service that patrols at night. These guards will be happy to accompany you wherever you wish to go. Updated: Feb 05, 2010.

Services
Bring cash! And lots of it. There are no ATMs in San Marcos and the majority of businesses do not take credit cards. If they do, fees are high. Quetzales are preferred, but most places will take dollars if pushed. Hotel Aacualax can exchange dollars.

There is a helpful tourist information board and map opposite the San Marcos Holistic Center. The free guide "Sol de Atitlán" has a map of San Marcos and other towns around the lake.

A post office box is located next door to San Marcos Holistic Center, in the hostel El Unicornio, which also sells stamps. Internet is available at Prolink ($1.50/hr) and Blind Lemons ($1.25/hr with an account).

La Blanchisseuse (from $2.5 per 12lb) and El Árbol ($0.75 per lb) provide laundry services and are located on the main street leading from the dock.

The natural clinic (Tel: 502-7723-4912), behind the central park, is open from Monday to Friday, 9:00 a.m. to 5:00 p.m. For more conventional treatment, it is necessary to visit the doctor in Panajachel or the hospital in Sololá. Updated: Feb 05, 2010.

Things to See and Do
At first glance it may seem that there is not a lot to do in San Marcos, so it is doubly amazing how the days can fly by. Relaxation is the primary pastime—swinging in a hammock, swimming, strolling, having a massage or treatment at the Mayan Sauna.

For the body-spirit-mind balance, yoga takes place at La Paz (daily at 8 a.m., $3.75), Las Pirámides (Monday-Saturday at 7 a.m., $3.75) and Xamanek (Monday, Wednesday and Friday at 8:30 a.m., donation). There are numerous courses and treatments in different healing disciplines available at the centers around town.

Adventure junkies will find a thrill in paragliding. Kayaks for rent are available at several places and are a great way to explore; if you're daring, stop off at "the rocks," where you can jump 21 meters (70 ft) into the lake below. Hike over the headland or take a lancha to visit some of the other villages with their own unique charms.

There are also two Spanish schools operating in San Marcos and a handful of volunteer opportunities. Alternatively, different creative courses pop up from time to time, including dance workshops and stained-glass lamp making. Updated: Feb 05, 2010.

Mayan Sauna
This is a must-do if you are staying in San Marcos. The sauna is a concrete dome with a wood-fire-warmed metal drum inside, which you throw water on to heat things up. The

CENTRAL HIGHLANDS

most unique part of the experience is that you can smear sugar all over your body and wait for it to melt into a syrup. Dash into the cold shower to wash it off and you will feel heavenly. Updated: Nov 16, 2006.

Holistic Treatments and Courses

The choices of holistic treatments are astounding. Chakra balancing, crystal healing, shiatsu, past-life regression, emotional freedom technique, reiki, acupuncture, Indian head massage... the list goes on. At any one time, there are at least 10 centers or private therapists working in San Marcos. Depending on the treatment, prices start from $25 for an hour. Generally, the centers are small with no reception staff. If you know what you want, fill your name in on the whiteboard, or look for gaps in the schedule to find out when you can come back for more information. Most places do not take reservations from outside the village. Courses run according to interest and are better (and cheaper) with at least two people, so advance notice is advised. Updated: Feb 05, 2010.

Las Pirámides Meditation Center

The epitome of peace and contemplation, Las Pirámides has a vision to "light the world." The courses here are designed to initiate and reconnect people with their spiritual path, to help them find balance and harmony through the study of philosophy and alternative psychology and the practice of meditation and yoga.

Las Pirámides was founded 11 years ago, based around a temple first built in Guatemala City. The one-month "moon course" starts one day after every full moon. Participants may also join for a single session/class ($4-6), a day ($18), a week ($119), or a month ($480), starting when they wish. Daily sessions are as follows: yoga at 7 a.m., metaphysics at 10 a.m., and meditation at 5 p.m. The fourth week of each moon cycle is a silent retreat. Prices, except for individual sessions, include accommodation and access to a communal kitchen.

The sun course lasts three months and can only be taken after completion of the moon course. The Oracle Spiritual Retreat takes from 21 days to a year. There are also various holistic and massage treatments available. Furthermore, Las Pirámides has a fantastic library that is free for all to use. A two minute walk up the main street leading from the dock, Las Pirámides is signposted to your left. Monday-Friday 2-4 p.m. Tel: 502-5202-4168/5205-7302, URL: www.laspiramidesdelka.com. Updated: Feb 05, 2010.

Paragliding

For those who want to soar like a bird through the crisp air above Lago de Atitlán, paragliding is the answer and Guy is the man who will take you. With eight years of experience in San Marcos under his belt, Guy is passionate, professional and adamant about the fact that this is the best place to paraglide at the lake. Not for the faint-of-heart, flights take off at 2,030 meters, last from 15 to 40 minutes (wind-dependent) and, on a clear day, give you the chance to see six volcanoes at once. The cost is $80 a pop. You can find Guy at Tul y Sol Restaurant, which is on the lake by the Jazmin Therapy Center. It is best to book at least one day in advance. Tel: 502-5854-5365/5293-7979, E-mail: Eltulysol@yahoo.com. Updated: Feb 05, 2010.

San Marcos Holistic Center

One of the oldest centers in town, San Marcos Holistic Center is also one of the biggest. The practitioners here draw on a wealth of experience in many types of massage and holistic therapies to help heal the whole body instead of just treating the symptoms. Treatments start from $27.50 and take place in comfortable rooms at the bottom of a quiet, rambling garden. A variety of courses are available, lasting from one to 21 days, including the internationally recognized Kinesiology course. There is an on-site shop selling homeopathic medicine, incense, natural soaps and other items. Next to Hostel El Unicornio. Monday-Saturday 10 a.m.-4 p.m. URL: www.sanmholisticcenter.com. Updated: Feb 05, 2010.

Therapy Center-Flower House

Intimate and uplifting, Flower House has three treatment rooms set around a sun-drenched courtyard full of flowers and crystals. Teachings flow from a wide variety of disciplines to promote healing, release negative energy and assist the acquisition of knowledge in a supportive and secure environment. Employees here are flexible in their approach to courses, healing sessions and massages based on the needs of the individual customer, and they follow up sessions with practical advice so that patrons can retain these benefits in everyday life. Shiatsu is one of the specialties here. For most massages, it is important not to eat for at least one hour beforehand and to drink lots of water afterward.

If interested in doing a course, try to give as much advance notice as possible so that other participants can sign up. This makes the course more fun and cheaper. A four-minute walk from the dock, the Flower House is on the main street in Barrio 3 next to the Internet shop and opposite a laundry. Monday-Saturday 11 a.m.-4 p.m. Tel: 502-5285-6633/4053-4614, E-mail: Pixyjoke@yahoo.com. Updated: Feb 05, 2010.

Hiking

There are lots of hiking opportunities around San Marcos, from trails in the lush valley to longer treks across the headland to San Juan or Santa Cruz. The three-hour trek to Santa Cruz is quite strenuous, with some steep ascents and descents, but it rewards the hiker with fantastic views and brushes with traditional local life. Follow current advice on safety precautions and leave valuables at home. Jovenes Maya (in Barrio 3) and Luis Chololito (Tel:502-4177-5213) offer guided hikes of the area. Keep in mind that due to the altitude, it can be easy to get out of breath, even if you are in good health. Updated: Jul 16, 2010.

Volunteering

There are four main volunteer opportunities in San Marcos. Soul Projects (www.soulprojects.org) facilitates 10-week programs that include a forest meditation retreat, a Maya family homestay while working on a volunteer project at local schools, a one-week turtle project and a lake clean-up. La Cambalacha (URL: www.lacambalacha.org) is an innovative and creative social project that teaches clowning and performing arts to indigenous kids. Escuela Caracol (URL: www.esceulacaracol.org) is a Waldorf school that provides alternative education to both indigenous and expatriate children. Green New World is building a sustainable community and houses made from the earth of the construction-site. Contact Sam at www.greennewworld.org or through the Flower House. Updated: Feb 05, 2010.

Lodging

San Marcos has accommodation to suit all budgets. Prices range from $4 per room in a house or at Hospedaje Panabaj (behind the central park) to $90 for a private bungalow and all the trimmings. All the hostels and hotels have a garden and most come with a sauna as well. The majority of hotels have an attached restaurant. Payment is in quetzals or dollars, and credit cards are not accepted in many places. It is often necessary to ask for directions when finding a particular hotel, and local boys will frequently wait by the dock to aid you. They might say that a place is

closed or full (not always true) but, when pressed, will take you wherever you wish to go. Any assistance given is in hope of a tip. Updated: Feb 05, 2010.

BUDGET

Hotel Quetzal

(ROOMS: $6 per person) Hotel Quetzal is best known as the local pub, and if you've had one too many, there are plain, clean rooms a stumble away from the bar for $6 per person (shared bathroom). The bar opens at 6:00 p.m. and carries on until the last person leaves. If you fancy a nibble, the French fries are particularly good. Cooked food is available until midnight. There is also a store here and a notice board that advertises up-and-coming events. Hotel Quetzal is one of the few businesses with a generator, so if all the lights go out, you know where to come. Tel: 502-4146-6036, URL: www.hotelquetzal-gt.com. Updated: Jul 01, 2010.

Casa La Paz

(ROOMS: $6.60) Set in lush gardens with a nice communal area at its center, there are double and dormitory rooms in traditional-style bungalows. The vibe is chilled-out and there is a Maya sauna on-site as well as massages. Tel: 502-702-9168. Updated: Nov 16, 2006.

Hostel El Unicornio

(ROOMS: $6) A quirky collection of huts dotted around an overgrown patio and garden, El Unicornio offers back-to-basics living alongside nature (don't be surprised to come in contact with bugs). This hostel is popular with backpackers who, for $6 per person, get their own room, a free pancake breakfast, use of the kitchen and a hammock to lounge in. There are shared bathrooms only. Located in Barrio 3, a short walk from the main dock, El Unicornio doubles as the local post office. Hostel El Unicornio is next to San Marcos Holistic Center in Barrio 3, a five minute walk from the dock. Updated: Jul 01, 2010.

Hotel La Paz

(ROOMS: $7-25) The sprawling, beautiful gardens of La Paz are full of treats for a seeker of inner balance and harmony. Daily yoga sessions, a superfood juice bar, massages, a sauna, and a vegetarian restaurant combine with rustic private bungalows or a cottage-style dormitory to create the perfect ambiance for getting away from it all. Spanish lessons can be arranged here. The restaurant, open daily 8 a.m.-8 p.m., has a menu for breakfast and lunch but dinner is set and should be booked in advance. Tel: 502-5702-9168, URL: www.sanmarcoslapaz.com. Updated: Feb 05, 2010.

Hotel, Restaurant and Bar Paco Real

(ROOMS: $10-25) Paco Real is a respectable choice in the heart of Barrio 3. Comfortable cabins come with balconies overlooking a well-kept garden. There are shared bathrooms only. The cozy restaurant (open daily, 7:30 a.m. to 9.00 p.m., bar till 11.00 p.m.) has a comprehensive choice of dishes, large portions and a warming fire in the evenings. This is also the place to come for lessons from San Marcos Spanish School. From the dock, follow the main street into the heart of Barrio 3. At the second "major" crossroads, turn left and Paco Real is on your right. Updated: Jul 01, 2010.

Hostal del Lago

(ROOMS: $15) Hostal del Lago is the only budget accommodation situated directly on the lake. The rooms (with private bathroom, unless you choose a bed in the dorm) are average, but the long garden has awesome views of the lake and surrounding volcanoes. You can sweat in the sauna, then jump off the private dock into a moonlit lake. The $12 daily rate includes breakfast, coffee, drinking water, kayak rental, and access to the sauna and the poorly-equipped kitchen. There are cheaper options as well and a mixed dorm. Kids have lots of room to run around in here. Tel: 502-5898-9872/9660, URL: www. hostaldellago.com. Updated: Feb 05, 2010.

HIGH END

Retreat Lake Atitlán Guatemala

(ROOMS: $150) The Retreat is a luxury property created for those seeking a sabbatical from our chaotic daily lives. It is a gated one hectare (2.4 ac) community straddling its own mountain with a main lodge and three thatched little stone guesthouses, each with its own personality. These stone houses have double beds with fine linens of pure cotton and protected by mesh mosquito nets. They also each have their own private patio with a cane gate, hammock, table and chairs. A short walk away at the lodge, guests will find a full kitchen, fireplace, salon, and multiple verandas and hammocks. The views of the lake and volcanoes are stunning. Outdoor baths are cordoned off by stucco walls

with flowering vines hanging overhead. A full-time gardener, who is also the caretaker, handyman and gatekeeper, lives on-site. The villas are available on a weekly basis for $700 for two people. Retreats for individuals that include other services are available. Inquire for the price of the penthouse. Tel: 502-5857-6397, E-mail: darlenalake@ yahoo.com. Updated: Dec 14, 2007.

Restaurants

There is a relatively small number of cafés and restaurants in Barrio 3, but a surprising diversity of food types is offered, including French, Italian, Indian, Mexican and North American cuisine. With an emphasis on fresh produce, several cafés are vegetarian only, serving up delicious salads, tofu, falafel, hummus and other treats. You can also find an abundance of homemade, melt-in-the-mouth baked goods: chocolate brownies, cakes, biscuits and breads. For Guatemalan food, you have to venture out to the popular Comedor Mi Marquensita, Comedor Los Abrazos or the cluster of street stalls near central park. Prices vary. For a filling breakfast and a cup of real coffee, expect to pay $3-5. Lunch costs $3-7, dinner and a drink about $10. Updated: Feb 05, 2010.

Moonfish Café

(ENTREES: $3-5) En route to "the rocks," the Moonfish Café is a down-to-earth place for chilling by the lake while enjoying a treat. The locally-sourced and homemade menu items (the owners even roast their own coffee) is mostly vegetarian and includes tofu and tempe, as well as nachos, pizzas and juices. A small shop sells natural peanut butter, soy products, and honey alongside handicrafts. Committed to protecting the environment, this eco-friendly place even has composting toilets. A San Marcos favorite, especially for the coffee. It is possible to pay in quetzals as well as U.S. dollars. Wednesday-Monday 7:30 a.m.-6 p.m. Updated: Jul 01, 2010.

Blind Lemons

(ENTREES: $4-6) Heavily influenced by the blues, Blind Lemons is a mellow place to eat yummy food. All the favorites are here, including burgers, burritos, steaks and pastas. The service can be slow, so put your order in quick. There is a small well-stocked bar. Fridays are live blues nights. Movies and sports are shown regularly on a giant projector with a great sound system. WiFi and computers with Internet available. Daily 8 a.m.-11 p.m. Updated: Feb 05, 2010.

Restaurant Il Forno
(ENTREES: $8) Recommended by locals as having "the best pizza in the world," Italian-run Il Forno is the real deal. The décor is understated; the focus here is pizza. Pizzas are cooked in a traditional wood-burning, brick oven. (Salads are also available). Sit outside in the garden to be sociable or sit back inside and watch a movie. Films are shown nightly at 7 p.m. Open Monday to Saturday, from midday to 9 p.m. Updated: Feb 05, 2010.

Restaurant Tul y Sol
(ENTREES: $10) Accessible from the lakeshore or through town, Tul y Sol has the best French cuisine in town. Delectable rich sauces, excellent cuts of meat and a range of tempting seafood options make it tough to squeeze in a dessert, but it's hard to resist banana suzette flambéed in rum. The veranda seating area has an enchanting view of the lake. Breakfast and sandwiches are also available. Daily 8:30 a.m.-9 p.m. Updated: Jul 01, 2010.

Las Mañanitas
The open-air restaurant Las Mañanitas is perfect for a lingering breakfast. Located in the grounds of Hotel Aaculaax with terrific views of the gardens, the ambiance is relaxed and the soundtrack soothing. Slightly more expensive than other cafés, Las Mañanitas has a select menu featuring homemade bread and jams, pancakes, shakshuka (eggs cooked in tomatoes) or eggs cooked your way. For lunch, there are tasty sandwiches. Daily 8 a.m.-4 p.m. Updated: Jul 01, 2010.

TZUNUNÁ
A small, traditional village, Tzununá is a pleasant 30-minute walk from San Marcos, though the last bit of the trail is something of an uphill slog. The village was originally located on the lakeshore, but mudslides caused by Hurricane Stan in 2005 destroyed it, and the villagers decided to rebuild on high ground. This is a peaceful village that tourists rarely visit, where children fly their kites in the street and women wash clothes by the river. Tzununá is one of a couple of places at the lake that has canopy tours. Available through the Hotel Xocomil (www.hotelxocomil.com), it costs $7.50 per person for the 325-meter-long (1,060 ft) zipline.

Afterward, if you feel inclined to spend the night, check out the simple rooms, which seem a tad expensive at $25 even after you take into account the swimming pool and basketball court. The restaurant serves local and international fare. Lomas de Tzununá (URL: www.lomasdeTzununá.com) has much fancier accommodation. Rooms here start at $75 for one person or $85 for two including breakfast. Updated: Jul 05, 2010.

Getting To and Away
Most public lanchas will stop at Tzununá dock. Wave at the passing lanchas so they know to come over and pick you up. Point in the direction you wish to go. The cost is $1.20 to San Marcos or Santa Cruz. It is possible to take a tuk-tuk from San Marcos for $6, but if you wish to take one back again, best ask him to wait for you. Updated: Feb 05, 2010.

JAIBALITO
Jaibalito is a tiny, tucked-away village whose inhabitants primarily speak the Mayan language of Kaqchikel, though many locals also speak Spanish. During the day, men take to their boats to fish on the lake while women head to the fields or settle down to some weaving. Few tourists stay overnight, but those who do will have the chance to appreciate the charming change of pace that happens when the sun sets and the day of work is done. Apart from services available through the hotels, there are no other tourist amenities. Advertised tours, Spanish lessons or activities are usually based in Santa Cruz. Next to the dock, two small café huts sell snacks and drinks. Updated: Jul 05, 2010.

Getting To and Away
Lanchas leave Panajachel for Jaibalito every half hour from 6:30 a.m. to 7:30 p.m. (20 min, $2). Boats leave San Pedro for Jaibalito every half hour from 6 a.m. to 5 p.m. (20 min, $2). The nearest village is Santa Cruz, a 30-minute walk away or five minutes by lancha. There is no access to Jaibalito by road. Updated: Jul 05, 2010.

Lodging

Vulcano Lodge
(ROOMS: $25-60) Set in the valley, Vulcano Lodge is surrounded by mountains and facing volcanoes. Comfortable rooms and al fresco sitting areas are scattered around the exotic gardens. There is one suite with two bedrooms, great for a family on vacation. At the four-course dinners ($12), everyone sits together, a chance to meet other

guests. Non-guests are welcome but should book ahead. Tel: 502-5410-2237, E-mail: info@vulcanolodge.com, URL: www.vulcanolodge.com. Updated: Jul 05, 2010.

La Casa del Mundo

(ROOMS: $35-74) Perched on the side of a cliff, Casa del Mundo is a little slice of heaven. Popular with honeymooners and couples, the hotel has vabulous views at every turn (and lots of steps; decent mobility is a must for guests). The staff anticipates your every need. There is a private swimming area, a hot tub, and a popular restaurant as well as secluded gardens. Breakfast and lunch are served from the menu; dinner is served family-style and by candlelight. Quiet time starts after 9:30 p.m., so party animals be warned. If you ask the lancha driver, he will drop you off at the hotel's private dock. Walking from Jaibalito or Santa Cruz, the entrance is clearly signposted at the top of the hill. Tel: 502-5218-5332/5558, E-mail: casamundo@gmail.com, URL: www.lacasadelmundo.com. Updated: Jul 05, 2010.

Posada Jaibalito

Posada Jaibalito is an adorable, small guesthouse with weekly and monthly rates. Set around an overflowing garden full of plants and trees, verandas and hammocks, accommodation is in much-sought-after double rooms or a spacious dormitory. The excellent restaurant has cheap dishes from around the world, but the gold star goes to the bread, homemade by Hans, the German baker. Free Internet, kitchen and friendly local staff make this posada every budget traveler's dream. Updated: Jul 05, 2010.

Restaurants

Club Ven Acá

(ENTREES: $15-20) Decadent luxury is the only way to describe this lavish bar and restaurant. Sip a mojito, take a languid swim in the infinity pool and feast your eyes on the picturesque beauty of Lago de Atitlán. Gourmet sandwiches for lunch warm the stomach up for a delectable three-course dinner. Dinner is served at 6 p.m. and has a fixed menu. Reservations must be made by 3 p.m. at the latest. Club Ven Acá has a private dock for arrivals by lancha. Dress up. Cocktails start from $5 and bottles of wine from $22. If you ask the lancha driver, he will drop you off at the private dock. Otherwise, turn right at the main dock and follow the

lakeside path until you reach Club Ven Acá. The public lanchas stop at 7 p.m., so book a private lancha for the return trip. Club Ven Acá can help you with this. Open Wednesday to Sundays, 11 a.m. to 5 p.m. Tel: 502-5051-4520, URL: www.clubvenaca.com. Updated: Feb 05, 2010.

Quiché Province

The Departamento del Quiché is located right in the center of Guatemala, between the Highlands and Verapaces. It is home to Chichicastenango, the K'umarkaaj Maya ruins, and the Ixil Triangle, making it an important destination on most visitors' itineraries.

The south, where Chichicastenango and its famous market are found, is more accessible and heavily populated than other parts of Quiché. At the center of the province is Santa Cruz del Quiché, the administrative capital and site of the former Quiché capital Utatlán.

To the north, at the source of the Río Negro, is Sacapulas. Continuing north from here, the landscape becomes increasingly desolate, rising to meet the dramatic Cuchumatanes mountain range. Beyond are the lowland plains of the Ixcán.

The area has a rather dark history. It was here where locals finally turned to guerrilla warfare to fight against shocking state repression, as government forces continued to target and kill thousands of Maya locals until the 1990s. Catholic priests, who were often linked to the rebels, were also killed and the church withdrew all its representatives from the region in 1981.

Quiché remains a Maya stronghold to this day and is full of traditional villages with distinctive fiestas and costumes.

Getting To and Away

The roads around Quiché can be very quiet, particularly on the lonely routes up into the Cuchumatanes. It is advisable to travel in a group and plan your route beforehand.

Quiché is at the crossroads of many places of interest to travelers, meaning that once you have sampled the province's delights you can cross east toward Uspantán and on to to the ruins at Cobán; north to the remote towns of Nebaj, San Juan Cotzal and Chajul for some trekking; or west to Huehuetenango and up to Todos Santos via Aguacatán. Updated: Nov 14, 2009.

CHICHICASTENANGO

Chichicastenango is a medium-sized town in the Quiché region about two to three hours away from Guatemala City. It is home to an artisan market that is among the most extensive of its kind in the world and is certainly the largest in Central America. The visitor can bargain for a wide array of hand-carved wooden masks, finely woven tapestries, ceramics, paintings and more. There is even a section of the market still used by the locals to buy and sell fruit, vegetables, meat, and other daily necessities. Market days are Sundays and Thursdays, although a visitor is likely to find someone willing to sell on any day.

There is more to Chichicastenango than the market, however. The area has long been a stronghold of indigenous culture. The locals still speak regional dialects that differ little from what they spoke before the arrival of the Spanish, and many of them—particularly the women—still wear their colorful traditional clothes. On the steps of the 400-year-old cathedral of Santo Tomás, native shamans bless the faithful with incense and incantations in Quiché. Not far away from the center of town, a stone idol that somehow managed to escape the Spanish destruction of native statues draws many visitors. The cemetery, with its large mausoleums, is also worth a visit.

Because of its relative proximity to Guatemala City, Antigua, and Panajachel, Chichicastenango has less facilities for the traveler than it might otherwise. Most visitors come for a day trip and return to one of these more comfortable towns. There are, however, a growing number of restaurants, hotels, and even Spanish schools for the visitor who wishes to get to know Chichicastenango a little bit better.

At 2,021 meters (6,630.5 ft) above sea level, the average temperature doesn't go much above 18°C (64.5°F), dipping down to 5°C (41°F) at night.

Chichi was founded in 1540 by some K'iche' fleeing nearby Santa Cruz del Quiché. After their home was destroyed by Alvarado's men, the Quiché set up camp here, near Chaviar, a commercial center at the time. Spanish settlers followed, and as a result, the area has a wealth of cultural, historical and anthropological treasures, both colonial and indigenous, to match its natural beauty. Chichicastenango's many charms have transformed this traditional, quiet town of narrow cobblestone streets into a major tourist attraction.

Around the square you'll find the enigmatic Iglesia de Santo Tomás, which not only demonstrates a striking mix of indigenous and ladino (Guatemalan mestizo group) spiritualism, but is also the place where the Popol Vuh, the Maya holy book, was unearthed by a Spanish priest. Nearby is an archeological museum with displays on the region's history. Just a 20-minute walk from the town center is the Maya ceremonial site of Pascual Abaj (dedicated to the God of stone), also known as Turcaj. The tourist information office may also be able to direct you to lesser-known, less-visited sites. Chichi is a fascinating town where Maya traditions and Catholicism blend and local culture is standing the test of time. It is a place that rewards some digging and exploration. Updated: Dec 09, 2009.

When to Go

Chichi is good to visit any time of year. The Santo Tomás fiesta and Easter celebrations reveal the townsfolk of Chichi at their most religious. December 14 to 21 the festivities include street parties, screeching fireworks, the Palo Volador (men hanging from ropes form a very, very high pole), and, of course, lots of drinking and dancing. On September 1, locals celebrate the first day that treated tap water became available to the town. The day starts with gun shots sounded from 5 a.m.—which can be quite a shock if you're not expecting them—and there are street parties in the evening. Updated: Nov 14, 2009.

Getting To and Away

To get from Guatemala City to Chichicastenango, you can catch one of the chicken buses headed toward Santa Cruz del Quiché. Coming from Antigua to Chichicastenango, you can catch one of these buses on the Carretera Interamericana highway in Chimaltenango or take a shuttle bus from one of the many agencies. The day trip shuttles from Antigua arrive about 10 a.m. and go back about 3 p.m. Shuttles going to Panajachel also make a stop here on market days, so you can pick up a few goodies and then carry on. The return from the lake makes the same stop. There is not an official bus terminal in Chichi. Mini buses to Panajachel, Quetzaltenango and the south leave from a parking lot near the Telgua office on 7a Avenida and 11a Calle. Buses to Santa Cruz del Quiché and the north leave from the other side of town on 5a Avenida near the Arco Gucumatz. Updated: May 03, 2010.

CENTRAL HIGHLANDS

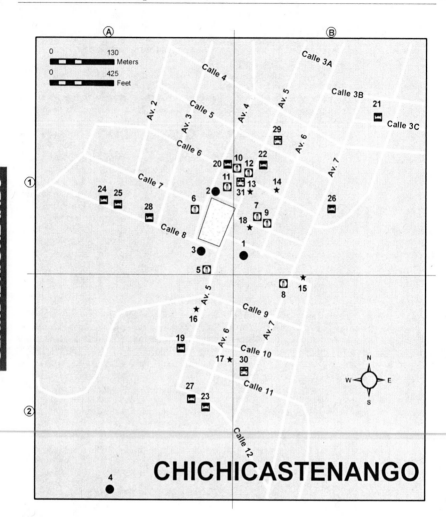

Getting Around

In Chichicastenango itself, you can walk pretty much anywhere you want to go. If you would like to take a tuk-tuk, there is always a line of them waiting for your business along 6a Avenida, opposite the Tziguan Tinamet restaurant. To walk from one side of the town to the other would takes around 30 minutes. You can also walk out to Pascual Abaj or up to Arco Gucumatz for a nice view of the town. Updated: Nov 14, 2009.

Safety

Chichicastenango is a quiet town, and is more or less safe. There are not many street lights after dark, and not many people out and about after 8 p.m., so take care to keep to the better-lit, busier streets. The market presents the perfect opportunity for pickpockets, so take great care. Even children, however cute they are, are often involved in pickpocketing. Updated: May 03, 2010.

Services

There is a BAM branch with an ATM and a Western Union (Monday-Friday 9 a.m.-6 p.m., Saturday 9 a.m.-1 p.m. and Sundays 9 a.m.-6 p.m.) on 5a Avenida and also a Banrural with an ATM on 6a Calle, opposite the square. There are some clean public toilets down the hill from the Iglesia Santo Tomás, which cost Q2, and around the square there are some payphones. The Tourist Information Office (Daily 8 a.m.-6 p.m., closed

Activities ●

1 Iglesia Santo Tomás B1
2 Market A1
3 Museo Rossbach A1
4 Pascual Abaj A2

Eating

5 Cantina Tres Estrellas A1
6 Casa San Juan A1
7 El Mesón de Don Miguel B1
8 La Cocina Tipica B2
  Helados Marco Polo
9 Panaderia El Corazon de Jesús B1
10 Restaurante Las Brasas B1
11 Restaurante Tipico A1
  La Villa de Don Tomás
12 Tziguan Tinamet B1

Services ★

13 BAM B1
14 Banrural B1
15 Despensar Familiar supermarket B2
16 Public toilets A2
17 Telgua office A2
18 Tourist Information Office B1

Sleeping 🛏

19 Hospedaje El Salvador A2
20 Hospedaje Girón A1
21 Hotel Chalet B1
22 Hotel Chuguila B1
23 Hotel Posada Belen A2
24 Hotel Posada El Teléfono A1
25 Hotel Mashito A1
26 Hotel Santo TomasB1B1
27 Hotel y Restaurante Tutto's B2
28 Maya Inn

Transportation 🚌

29 Buses to Santa Cruz del Quiché, north B1
30 Mini buses to Panajachel, A2
  Quetzaltenango, south
31 Tuk tuk stop

CENTRAL HIGHLANDS

noon-2 p.m. for lunch) is located opposite the Panadería El Corazón de Jesús, on the side of the pink municipal building. There is Internet available and maps for $0.60. The Despensar Familiar supermarket is on 7a Avenida and 10a Calle. Updated: Nov 14, 2009.

Things to See and Do

Chichicastenango Market 🎵

No visitor should come to Chichicastenango without seeing the weekly market. The town becomes a different place on Sundays and Thursdays, when the usually quiet highland settlement is overrun by chaotic, colorful crowds. There are a lot of wonderful things to buy for your home and your loved ones (and a fair bit of tacky junk, too). Just as impressive as the wares are the people who come from all around to sell them; the market is a brilliant display of traditional dress from the various towns in the region. Indeed, there has been a market held here for thousands of years. Today you'll find a mix of people, from serious traders, groups of weavers and tourists on day-trips from Antigua to buyers for chic European stores. To make the most of your day, make sure you are at Chichi early. With all the extra traffic, the town's narrow streets become blocked, a situation complicated by a confusing one-way system. The market also starts to get busy after 10 a.m., once the day-trippers arrive from Antigua, so shopping is easier early in the morning. Bargains are easiest to find early in the morning or late in the day, but inspect whatever you're buying to make sure you aren't getting a bad deal.

The day-trip shuttle buses from Antigua arrive about 10 a.m. and leave again about 4 p.m. Shuttles going to Panajachel also make a stop here on market days, so you can pick up a few good fruits and vegetables or a quick bite of hot food, or take a break at one of the cafés nearby. Updated: Nov 26, 2009.

Museo Rossbach

This archeological and anthropological museum has three rooms exhibiting historical pieces from Chichi and the surrounding region that date to the pre-Hispanic, colonial and modern periods. There are ceramic artifacts, pieces of jade, copies of the Popol Vuh manuscript and typical local textiles. There is also an interesting display on the Mayan dialects spoken across the country. You need only about 20 minutes to tour the museum.

Loved it? Loathed it? Write a review and help other travelers.

5a Agenda 4-47, Zone 1. Tuesday-Saturday 8 a.m.-12:30 p.m., 2 p.m.-4:30 p.m., Sunday 8 a.m.-2 p.m. Updated: Nov 26, 2009.

Iglesia Santo Tomás

Dating from the mid-16th century, and rebuilt in the 18th century, this atmospheric church is a great introduction to the fascinating highland blend of Catholicism and Maya spiritualism. It is believed that the locals converted to Catholicism after a resident Spanish priest was seen reading the Mayan sacred book the Popol Vuh, which he had discovered in the monastery next door. Incense and a fire burn constantly on the front steps, and it is customary to make an offering here before entering. The spirits of deceased loved ones are said to reside in special places within the church and sit alongside Catholic saints. Updated: Nov 26, 2009.

Pascual Abaj

A short walk south of the town center is the Maya ceremonial site of Pascual Abaj, a shrine which is still very much in use today. There are some small altars and a pre-Columbian idol, and if there has recently been a ritual you will no doubt see burned incense, empty liquor bottles and flowers laying around. Chickens may also be sacrificed. Located so close to Chichi, Pascual Abaj attracts its share of tourists, but it is still important to be respectful of worshippers and to be careful when taking photographs. To get to the shrine, walk down 5a Avenida past the church, then turn right on 9a Calle and follow the path and the signs up through pine forest. Updated: Nov 26, 2009.

Lodging

If you want to stay the night in Chichicastenango before or after visiting the markets, accommodation can be found for as little as $4 per night. However, you only get the bare minimum for this price. More comfortable hotels are also available. Updated: Jul 13, 2010.

Hotel Posada El Teléfono

(ROOMS: $4-10) El Teléfono offers modest accommodations, but there are few extras here: Guests can use the *pila* to wash clothes and there is also a small shop that sells coffee, sodas, beer and snacks. The upper rooms are reached by steep stairs. One double room has a TV. This is a good budget option with mountain views and a garden patio. Head to the southwestern

corner of the main plaza and walk down the hill toward the cemetery. It is on your right after Hotel Mashito. 8a Ca. 1-64. Tel: 502-7756-1197. Updated: Sep 14, 2009.

Hospedaje El Salvador

(ROOMS: $6.50-18) The Salvador is a large hotel that is a five-minute walk south from the marketplace. The hotel looks a little worse for wear, and the rooms are meager. However, there's lots of space, and if you're on a tight budget you can save even more money by opting for a shared bathroom. All rooms have a TV, and those on the top floor have more natural light and views of the town. Walk down 5a Avenida, pass the church and keep going for five minutes. 5a Av. Arco Gucumatz 10-09. Tel: 502-7756-7329. Updated: Sep 17, 2009.

Hotel Posada Belén

(ROOMS: $5-10) The Belén's 18 rooms are split evenly between those with private bathrooms and those without, but all are reached by steep and narrow staircases. The outside door is locked at 9 p.m. and the place feels more secure this way, especially being down a quiet street away from the main square. But the hotel is manned 24/7 in case of late or early arrivals so access is no problem. There is a nice view of Pascual Abaj from the courtyard. Laundry service is available. To get there, walk down 5a Avenida, past the church for about five minutes. 12a Ca. 5-55. Tel: 502-7756-1244. Updated: Sep 12, 2009.

Hotel y Restaurante Tutto's

(ROOMS: $12-15) At the quiet southern end of town, this family-oriented hotel is bright, open and welcoming. All rooms have cable TV and 24-hour hot water. There is a dorm room available, accommodating six to eight people, which has a lounge area and is wheelchair accessible. Tutto's Restaurant, open for breakfast, lunch and dinner, has big windows overlooking the Pascual Abaj hill. Children under 12 stay for free. Longer stays preferred. 12a Ca. 6-29. Tel: 502-7756-1540, E-mail: hoteltuttos@yahoo.com. Updated: Sep 18, 2009.

Hotel Chuguila

(ROOMS: $12-30) Hotel Chuguila has been around for quite a while, but recently, a new complex has been built on the upper level of the building that has a shopping center, an Internet café (free for guests) and a fair trade gift shop. The 15 rooms are decorated with patterned floor tiles and local fabrics and have hot water and TV. You can also pay extra for a room with a fireplace. There are seats out front of each room and there is ample parking in the courtyard. 5 Av. 5-24. Tel: 502-7756-1134. Updated: Sep 18, 2009.

Hotel Chalet

(ROOMS: $24-27) This lovely, bright hotel on a quiet road northeast of the plaza is decorated with local fabrics and typical clothes. All rooms have private bathrooms, lots of daylight and warm, colorful blankets. There is a common breakfast area where coffee and books are available, as well as a tidy rooftop terrace with clear views. The owner, Manuel, and his staff are very accommodating. Internet is available for a small charge. 3a Ca. 7-44. Tel: 502-7756-2286, E-mail: manuelchalet@yahoo.com, URL: www.chalethotel-guatemala.com. Updated: Sep 15, 2009.

Hotel Santo Tomás

(ROOMS: $95-140) Santo Tomás is as good as it gets in Chichicastenango. Located in an attractive white building centered around two delightful courtyards, it comes complete with bilingual parrots. There is even a heated swimming pool. All the rooms have a fireplace, a big bathroom with bathtub, and solid wooden furniture. There is a restaurant and full lounge-bar open 7 a.m.-10 p.m., as well as a bookshop with tourist information. Santo Tomás is often booked for tour groups so it's wise to call ahead for a reservation. 7a Av. 5-32. Tel: 502-7756-1316, E-mail: hst@itelgua.com. Updated: Sep 15, 2009.

Mayan Inn

(ROOMS: $90-146) This comfortable and slightly old-fashioned hotel off the southwest corner of the square has well-furnished rooms, some with bathtubs and all with large beds, TV and impressive collectors' items such as paintings, chests, mirrors and benches. There are three dining rooms, a pleasant garden, and a cocktail bar where live music sometimes plays. Each room is assigned an attendant, so there are no locks on the doors. Internet is $1.50 for 30 minutes and there is a laundry service available. 8a Ca. A 1-91 and 3a Av. Tel: 502-7756-1176/4753, E-mail: info@mayaninn.com.gt, URL: www.mayaninn.com.gt. Updated: Sep 15, 2009.

Hotel Mashito

Despite having been painted entirely fluorescent green, this hotel is still easy to miss, tucked away on a quiet street. All the rooms use local fabrics and some have a TV. Unfortunately, the rooms with outside windows are also those with shared bathrooms. The rooms with private bathrooms are quite dark, but the vivid décor certainly helps to brighten the place up. There is a central garden for all guests to enjoy. No food is available, but the hotel is not too far from the market. Overall, Hotel Mashito is a nice and quiet place to relax. 8a Ca. 1-72. Tel: 502-7756-1343. Updated: Sep 16, 2009.

Restaurants

Chichicastenango is not a town for night owls, so be sure to not wait too late before heading out to eat at night. During the day there are lots of food stalls around the main square selling tortillas, kebab-style sandwiches, stews, and fried chicken with fries and fruit. Right by El Calvario church, next to the little park, there is a take-away pizza stand open all day, every day. There are also a few restaurants, such as Buena Aventura and Kieq'Ik Steak House, in the pink *centro comercial* next to the square. If you prefer something more upscale, head to the restaurants in the nicer hotels, like the Santo Tomás. Updated: Sep 14, 2009.

Tziguan Tinamet

(ENTREES: $1.50-12) Tziguan Tinamet's specialty is pizza, and you can make your own from the extensive list of meats, veggies and cheeses, from a personal five-inch to a shareable 14-inch for $1.25-11. Typical breakfast is also served, in addition to soups, salads, steaks and chicken, which go from $2.50-9. There is plenty of space and you can watch the street scene from the table at the window, which is a good place to sit, as the low lighting can make the place seem a little dark. Find it on the corner opposite the tuk-tuk stand one block north from the plaza. 5a Av. 5-67. Tel: 502-7756-1144, E-mail: crusigam@hotmail.com. Updated: Sep 15, 2009.

Restaurante Las Brasas

(ENTREES: $3-9.50) This large family-run steak house one block north of the plaza, located on a second floor, is eclectically decorated and has long tables for big groups. Restaurante Las Brasas serves up an excellent steak, as well as a variety of other good meat and fish dishes, for around $6. If you're not in the mood for steak, try the *longaniza* (a spicy sausage). Specials include *lomito adobado* (marinated loin) for $9.50, which comes with soup, vegetables, rice and tortillas. There are pasta and salad options for vegetarians and a choice of burgers and sandwiches for the kids. Full bar. Reservations are recommended on the busy market days, but home delivery is also an option. Daily 7 a.m.-10 p.m. 6a Ca. 4-52, Comercial Girón, 2nd floor. Tel: 502-7756-2226, E-mail: frans1089@ yahoo.com. Updated: Oct 02, 2009.

Casa San Juan

Right on the main plaza, with an upper floor overlooking the square, Casa San Juan is a great place to take a break from the stress of the market while still feeling like a part of the action. There is a pretty courtyard downstairs and a large open restaurant and bar upstairs, making this one of the best choices in town for a drink. There is a full menu that includes nachos, chili relleno, churrasco and fish and a range of hamburgers, sandwiches and salads, plus a list of delicious desserts. Tuesday-Sunday 9 a.m.-9 p.m. 4a Av. San Juan, 6-58. Tel: 502-7756-2086/5134-8852, E-mail: csjcomidayarte@gmail.com. Updated: Sep 18, 2009.

La Villa de Don Tomás

(ENTREES: $3-6) Don Tomás is similar to Las Brasas but has more fish and seafood on offer. The spaghetti comes with a choice of different sauces and the crepes are a great vegetarian option for just $3. The restaurant is somewhat lacking in atmosphere, but the owners are planning renovations. Reservations are possible, as is home delivery. Daily 7 a.m.-9 p.m. 6a Ca. 6-45, Plaza Comercial Utz Raju, 2nd floor. Tel: 502-5217-9820/4783, E-mail: restaurantelavilladedontomas@gmail. com. Updated: Oct 02, 2009.

El Meson de Don Miguel

Right opposite the tourist information office and just one block east of the square, Don Miguel dishes up no-nonsense local and international fare, including breakfasts, pizzas, burgers, Mexican tortillas, salads and basic *comida tipica*. The atmosphere is relaxed, with good lighting, pleasant furnishings and a view of the municipal theater. Don Miguel is a good place for an early evening beer, with enough room for a reasonably sized group. Sodas and wine are also available. Daily 7 a.m.-8 p.m. 7a Ca. 5-64, 2nd floor. Updated: Sep 15, 2009.

Panadería El Corazón de Jesús

This clean eat-in or take-out bakery, below El Meson de Don Miguel, sells great cakes and juices. It's just one block from the market, so it makes a good place to refuel while shopping, although it can get very busy on market days. There are quite a few tables, and with open arch doorways it's bright with a pleasant breeze. Open 6:30 a.m.-7 p.m. 7a Ca. 5-64, corner of 6 Av. Updated: Oct 15, 2009.

Cantina Tres Estrellas

This bar is a rough-and-ready drinking hole down the hill past the church. No snacks are served, and it is only open during the day, but it's a decent spot to rest your legs and grab a quick drink. Beer ($2.50 per liter of Gallo), hard liquor ($0.90 aguardiente) and soft drinks served. Open 7 a.m.-7 p.m. 5a Av. and 9a Ca.. Updated: Oct 15, 2009.

Helados Marco Polo

This small café opposite the supermarket serves ice cream, sundaes, milkshakes and other savory snacks. It is right next to the shuttle bus stop for Quetzaltenango/Xela, and it opens early for breakfasts. Daily 7 a.m.-7 p.m. 7a Av., by the Telgua office. Updated: Sep 18, 2009.

SANTA CRUZ DEL QUICHÉ

At 2,012 meters (6,061 ft) above sea level, in the southwestern Sierra de Chuacús, Santa Cruz del Quiché is the capital of the El Quiché region. The population of around 21,000 is made up mainly of the Quiché and Ladinos. The town serves as a central market point for the surrounding villages, which produce maize, beans and livestock. The University of San Carlos Guatemala City and the Academy of Mayan Languages both have campuses here.

The town was founded in 1539 by Pedro de Alvarado, right-hand man of Hernán Cortés. At least 100 years before that, the Quiché King Gucumatz had chosen an area four kilometers (2.5 mi) west of town for the site of the Maya capital Ku'markaaj (or Utatlán in Nauatl). Alvarado burned down the entire city, reducing the Quiché rulers to peasant status. It is said that the church in the town plaza was built by Dominican friars out of the Ku'markaaj stones. More recently, Quiché, as it is known, and the surrounding area suffered years of internal conflict. The army barracks in the center of town is a reminder of those times.

Santa Cruz del Quiché is a small town, so restaurants, cafés, shops and hotels are all within walking distance. There are a few hotels to choose from, most in the budget category, and mainly comedores or cafés for food. Once it gets dark some food stalls around the square stay open for a while, but the town center does get quiet, and there isn't much to do in the evening. The main attraction for tourists visiting Santa Cruz del Quiché is, without a doubt, the nearby Maya ruins. As the regional capital, Santa Cruz has good transport links to the north and south and serves as a transport hub for the Ixil Triangle. Updated: Sep 18, 2009.

When to Go
The big festival in Santa Cruz del Quiché is held August 14-19, the main day being the 18th, with traditional dancing and other typical activities. Market days in Santa Cruz del Quiché are Thursday and Sunday, when the town square becomes packed with buyers and sellers from the region; otherwise the town is rather unexciting. Two nights here would be enough time to arrive, wander around town, visit the ruins and take in the market before moving on. Updated: May 04, 2010.

Getting To and Away
The bus terminal is about one kilometer (0.6 mi) southeast of the plaza, near the permanent market and not far from the Hotel San Pascual. Due to its central location and its status as provincial capital, Santa Cruz is well-connected and it is easy to get buses going north and south. Chicken buses to Guatemala City leave every half an hour until approximately 5 p.m. (3.5 hr). Buses go first to Chichicastenango, which takes 30 minutes, and then on to Los Encuentros, which takes another half hour. Buses also go to Quetzaltenango (3 hr), Nebaj (2 hr, 15 min), Uspantám (2 hr, 45 min), and nearby Totonicapán. Santa Cruz is also a hub for travelers bound for the Ixil Triangle. Mini buses wait around the main plaza and leave when full, which is more frequently than the public buses. Updated: May 04, 2010.

Getting Around
Minibuses wait around the north and south sides of the plaza. You can pick up a minibus going to K'umarkaaj and back for $0.15 each way. There are red tuk-tuks and taxis floating around, too. It is easy to see Santa Cruz's sites on a leisurely stroll through town. Updated: May 04, 2010.

Safety
Santa Cruz del Quinche is quite safe. As usual, take care of your possessions, especially in the market, where pickpockets may be at work. The streets are quite dark and very quiet after about 7 p.m., so it would be wise to stick to the well-lit streets. Updated: Nov 14, 2009.

Things to See and Do
Santa Cruz del Quiché is a pleasant enough town in which to spend a day or two, although it is a little dirty. The town center, dominated by a grand white church, has quite a buzz about it when everyone gathers around the square in the late afternoon. There is also a small plaza in front of the former military barracks. Of course, you can't miss the Ku'markaaj ruins. Market days in Santa Cruz del Quiché are Thursday and Sunday, but there is a general market selling everyday goods around 7a Calle. On the road south back to Chichicastenango, amid pine forests, is the pretty Laguna Lemoa. Updated: Sep 21, 2009.

K'umarkaaj
(ADMISSION: $3.50) K'umarkaaj, or 'Place of Reeds,' is the ancient Maya capital, renamed Utatlán (a Nauatl word) by the Spanish. These ruins are the main draw for tourists stopping off in Santa Cruz del Quiché, 2.5 kilometers (1.6 mi) away. Covering 120,000 square meters (1.3 mil sq ft) and surrounded by deep ravines, which once served as natural defenses, the city must have been truly impressive in its heyday. Today, however, the buildings are mostly hidden under grass, with only the odd rock outcrop or stone marking to remind you that there was once a temple or a palace here. Archeological excavations were carried out in the 1950s and 1970s but little subsequent restoration work has been done. Today the site's center is a square around which three pyramid-shaped temples topped by thatched platforms once stood: the temple of Tohil, the jaguar God; Awilix, the patron goddess of one of the noble house; and Jakawitz, a mountain deity.

At its height, the city, led by king Gucumatz, housed around one million Quiché, including the clan's nobility. There were 23 palaces, houses and ball courts. By the time the Conquistadores reached Kumarkaaj, the Quiché were weakened by war. When leaders invited Alvarado to stay in the city, Alvarado thought it was a trap, so he instead tricked two lords, Oxib Quej and Belejep Tzí, into visiting his camp on a nearby hill, where they were captured and burned to death. The Spanish took control of the city and then razed the town completely (as described at the Iximché ruins near Tecpán). There is a 100-meter-long (330 ft) tunnel which stretches underneath the ball court from an opening. It's a little difficult to find, so ask the friendly clerk at the entry-gate for directions. Look out for empty bottles of alcohol and freshly burned incense sticks laying around in the opening; these are the signs of a recently performed religious ceremony.

There are no food stalls on-site, but the grounds make a nice spot for a picnic, so a little preparation would serve you well. Also, a flashlight would be handy for going into the tunnel. To get to K'umarkaaj, catch one of the mini buses for Totonicapán at the plaza. These pass by the ruins. A return trip costs Q2 ($0.50). You can also take one the red tuk-tuks floating around. Daily 9 a.m-5 p.m. Updated: May 07, 2010.

Lodging

Santa Cruz del Quiché is only about 30 minutes from Chichicastenango, making it possible to visit as a day trip. However, if you decide to stay the night, there are a few accommodation options, none of them spectacular. Most Santa Cruz Del Quiché hotels are standard backpacker and budget places, but they are very close to the town center, so at least they are convenient. On the road north from Chichi, before you arrive at Quiché, there is the Hotel Casa de Campo (Tel: 502-5868-7553), which is of a higher standard than any of the Santa Cruz Del Quiché hotels. If you come across the bright pink Hotel Centenario, it is actually a "love motel." Updated: Jul 13, 2010.

Hotel San Pascual

(ROOMS: $4-14) This verdant family-run hotel doesn't look much from the outside—indeed, it's a little hard to find the entrance—but it is a good money saver, especially if you opt for a shared bathroom. There is a garden courtyard, rooms have hot water and cable TV, and there is a large car park a block away included in the price. It's between the bus terminal and the plaza. 7a Ca. 0-43 and 1a Av., Zona 1, Tel: 502-7755-1107. Updated: Sep 14, 2009.

Hotel Las Vegas

(ROOMS: $7-18) The Hotel Las Vegas, formerly the Hotel Maya Quiché, has something of an out-of-town motel feel, and the courtyard might have better been designated a garden rather than a car park. But the rooms are big, with

hot-water showers and cable TV. The road-side rooms tend to be a little noisy. Parking is included in the price and there is free purified water. The reception is attended 24 hours. 3a Av. 4-19, Zona 1, Tel: 502-5540-8895. Updated: Sep 14, 2009.

Hotel Acuario

Not even one block from the square, this is a well-placed hotel if you want to be close to the action. It is found on the second floor overlooking 5a Calle and is a stone's throw from Rock Café. Being so close to the square (and the a church's belltower), this place might be one to avoid if you're a light sleeper. The free Internet, TV, parking and rooms with private hot showers, however, make an enticing package. 5a Ca. 2-44, Zona 1, Tel: 502-7755-1878, E-mail: café acuario@hotmail.com. Updated: May 03, 2010.

Restaurants

The heart and soul of Quiché is found around the double plaza. Mid-afternoon to early evening, the squares fill up with locals milling around, filling up the benches and snacking on hamburgers, hot dogs, and tacos at the many food stalls. There is also fruit for sale if you desire something healthier. For fast food there's the ubiquitous Pollo Campero and if you fancy buying a bottle La Taberna, Cantina is close by. 2a Av. and 8a Ca., Zona 1. Updated: Sep 15, 2009.

San Miguel Panadería

Facing the plaza from the western edge, this is a great place to relax and quench your thirst with a juice, café americano, mochaccino or even a café amaretto. Hamburgers, sandwiches, tostadas, pizza and plenty of cakes are also available to satisfy your hunger. Daily 8 a.m.-8 p.m. 2a Av. And 5a Ca. Updated: Sep 21, 2009.

Comida Típica

A basic and authentic Guatemalan comedor, Comida Típica serves all the usual favorites, including desayuno tipíco and churrasco, as well as mojarra—a fish dish typical of the area. There are tables to sit down inside and a take-out liquado and milkshake bar on the street. Daily 8:30 a.m.-11 p.m. Updated: Sep 21, 2009.

Zona Rock Café

By way of evening entertainment, there isn't much to speak of in San Cruz del Quiche, but the Rock Café is open from 4 p.m. until 2 a.m. should you fancy a beer ($1.60), a Cuba

Libre ($2.50) or a few hours of dancing (although the place is rather quiet mid-week). There is occasional live music but with no specific schedule, so ask at the bar. 3a Av. and 5a Ca. Updated: Sep 18, 2009.

SACAPULAS

Sacapulas, seated at the base of the Cuchumatanes on the banks of the Río Negro, is a fairly non-descript little town with lovely views. Most will just pass through en route to other destinations, this being the gateway to the Ixil Triangle as well as a junction between the Central to the Western Highlands on the route east to Uspantán. However, if you reach Sacapulas late in the day, this is as good a place as any to take a break from traveling. There are a couple of hotels and places to eat but not much to do apart from sit and relax.

Getting To and Away

To get to Sacapulas, take a bus or mini-bus from Santa Cruz del Quiché heading north (1.5 hr). Moving on, there are several buses a day to Nebaj (1 hr, 15 min) and to Uspantán (1 hr, 45 min), from where you could continue on to Cobán. From here you can also get minibuses to Aguacatán (1 hr 30 minutes) and then onto Huehuetenango. Updated: Sep 18, 2009.

Services

There is a Banrural bank on the north side of the square. The gas station on the road east to Nebaj and Uspatán has a store stocked full of snacks and a decent bathroom. There is a Red Cross (Cruz Roja) station on the left before the bridge.

Things to See and Do

There isn't much to do in Sacapulas, so do as the locals do and while away the afternoon sitting under one of the two huge cieba trees in the pretty town square. Here you should be able to spot the women of Sacapulas wearing their traditional pom-pom headdresses. The market is held on Thursday and Sunday. The Tourist Center Nelly (left over the bridge on the road to Aguacatán) has a swimming pool, and nearby there are some basketball and five-a-side soccer pitches, which usually generate a lot of local activity.

Lodging

The Comedor y Hospedaje Tujaal (Tel: 502-5550-9051) is a bright and clean hotel on the south bank of the Río Negro, right before the bridge. Rooms have views of the river and cost around $10. At Hospedaje

Río Negro (Next to Red Cross. Tel: 502-5410-8168), rooms are basic and have shared bathrooms but are about half the price of rooms at Tujaal.

Restaurants

The Tujaal hotel has a pleasant restaurant with big windows looking toward the Cuchumatanes. There is a string of comedores as you go right over the bridge, which is something of an informal truck stop. This part of town is well-lit and there are usually plenty of people around, even after dark.

USPANTÁN

Uspantán is a rather remote highland town, and for a long time it was dismissed by travelers for being too difficult to reach. The poor road conditions, often caused by severe landslides from the steep faces of Cuchumatanes, meant journeys here were long and arduous. However, since the roads between Sacapulas, Nebaj and Cobán (partially completed) are now paved, stopping off in Uspantán on your way to the Maya ruins and the Verapaces makes sense. The town itself is unremarkable, but the cultural traditions and customs of the area may be of interest to tourists, and lovely rivers and abundant wildlife can be found in the surrounding countryside.

Getting To and Away

Getting to and away from Uspantán is much easier than it used to be, now that the roads are paved and there are more mini buses traveling between Sacapulas, Nebaj and Cobán via Uspantán. Mini buses park around the plaza, just opposite the church. Buses to Quiché and Cobán leave every 30 minutes between 4 a.m. and 4 p.m. and costs $3-3.60. The ride to Cobán takes about two and a half hours, with the second half of the journey on a dirt road. Updated: Jan 10, 2010.

Services

At the center of town is the usual market and plaza, which has a park in the northern half and a ball court in the southern. Nearby you'll find: Internet (7a Ca. and 6a Av., next to the market), with printing, Skype, and scanner; BAM (Monday to Friday 9 a.m.-5 p.m., Saturdays 9 a.m.-1 p.m.); a police station (6a Av. and 5a Ca.); tuk-tuks opposite the police station; and public restrooms south of the square.

Photo by: Ricardo Valdéz

The tourist office (Tel: 502-7951-8125/5635-5943. E-mail: visituspantan@gmail.com/maresperanzao027@gmail.com) is located in municipal buildings on the east side of the square and is attended by a mix of local and VSO (Voluntary Service Overseas) staff members. The enthusiastic staff runs various guided tours with transport, lunch and entrance fees all included from $7-20 per person.

Day trips offered are: **Pena Flor:** the old Uspantán capital city, also known as Tz'unun Kaab; **Laj Chimel:** birthplace of Nobel Prize winner Rigoberta Menchú (see www.lajchimelecoturismo.com); **Balenario Sechum Chola:** local co-op farming village with spring-fed swimming pool; **Cerro Sagrado Xoconeb':** a sacred ceremonial site in honor of the God Ajaw Catarata de Los Regadillos-a stunning waterfall accessed along a mountain path; and **Laguna Danta:** a lake mysteriously full in the dry season and empty in the rainy season.

Lodging

Hotel Don Gabriel

(ROOMS: $4.80-15.60) The newly-built and well-looked-after Hotel Don Gabriel is right in the center of town, and with its grand sweeping staircase and spotless 39 rooms, it is arguably the best place to stay. There is also a lovely garden roof-terrace with views directly to the mountains, pretty pagodas to sit under and lighting for evening drinks. Standard single rooms are $4.80-8.40 and doubles are $9.60-15.60, or nicer rooms are availalbe for $12 per person with bathtub, hot water and TV. There is secure parking and wheelchair-accessible rooms are available. No credit cards. 7a Av. and 6a Ca. Tel: 502-7951-8540/5196-6892, E-mail: hoteldongabriel@yahoo.es. Updated: Jan 10, 2010.

Hotel Uspanteka

(ROOMS: $4.80-9.60) The Hotel Uspanteka is not far from the northeastern end of the square and is a good budget option: single rooms are $2.40-3.60 and doubles $4.80, with four-bed rooms going for $9.60. All rooms have shared bathrooms. There are no modern TVs or towels, only some rooms have windows, and the mattresses are quite thin, but there is hot water and the hotel is clean. 5-18 6a Ca. Tel: 502-7951-8078.Updated: Jan 10, 2010.

Dona Leonor

(ROOMS: $9-20) Dona Leonor is another hotel which seems to be popular, with cable TV, WiFi, parking, laundry service and a comedor. Single rooms cost $9, doubles $15.60 and triples $20, all with private bathrooms. 6a Ca. and 4a Av. Tel: 502-7951-8045/8041.Updated: Jan 10, 2010.

Restaurants

There are a few cafés in the town center and some food stalls around the square. Café Portal de la Villa is on 6a Avenida, between 6a and 7a Calles, with a Sarita ice cream shop nearby. Updated: Jan 10, 2010.

Restaurante y Pizzeria Picadelly (Daily 8 a.m.-9 p.m. 7a Av., between 7a Ca. and the plaza. Tel: 502-5055-3881) is great for breakfast; the 'tipico' is very generous, with chorizo, plantain, eggs, beans, cream and tortillas. Also on the menu are burgers, pizza, sandwiches, steak, chicken and seafood. Coffees and licuados are available but no beer. Updated: Jan 10, 2010.

Ixil Triangle

The Ixil Triangle is the name given to three towns in the very north of the Quiché department: Santa María Nebaj, San Gaspar Chajul and San Juan Cotzal, which form a triangle shape on Guatemala's map. Being isolated by the Cuchumatanes, the population are majority Ixil, one of the smallest ethnic groups in Central America, and speak the Ixil Mayan dialect. Many people use Spanish only as a second language. The rolling green hills are beautiful, the locals welcoming and the pace of life relaxing.

The towns and remote villages in the region were the site of bloody battles between the 'Ho Chi Minh' front of the Ejército Guerrillero de los Pobres (The Guerrilla Army of the Poor) and the government army during the 1970s and 80s. Indeed, Rigoberta Menchú, the Nobel Prize-winning campaigner for indigenous rights, born in nearby Uspantán, wrote about the atrocities committed by the Government forces in the Nebaj town square. During the years of fighting, many locals were killed or tortured, while many others fled north or to Guatemala City. Maya locals began to trade in their colorful indigenous dress for less conspicuous clothing to blend in. Since the 1996 Peace Accords were signed, many Ixils have been returning, despite the painful memories, to set up businesses, farm the land and resume their traditional cultural practices.

Getting To and Away

North from Sacapulas to the Ixil Triangle, the steep first stretch of the road is buttressed by mountains, and there are some superb views of the Cuchumatanes. The road drops down the other side of the mountains into the valley where the Ixil Triangle rests. From Santa Cruz del Quiché, buses go directly to Nebaj and take about two hours and 15 minutes. From Nebaj, you can take shuttle buses to the neighboring towns of Chajul and Cotzal as well as to the small village of Acul. There are also buses to Nebaj from Cobán and one direct bus from Guatemala City. The roads are now paved, although there are already plenty of pot-holes and speed bumps to slow you down. Updated: Nov 30, 2009.

NEBAJ

Far from the gringo-hippie circuit around Lake Atitlán or the Spanish schools and backpacker bars of Antigua, you will find the remote town of Santa María Nebaj. This unspoiled mountain village with adobe-walled houses, cobblestone streets and charming inhabitants is known as the gateway to the Ixil and is a great jumping-off point for trips.

Nebaj has something to offer almost every traveler. It is a great place to settle in and improve your Spanish or study Maya culture in a laidback rural atmosphere, especially if you stay with a local family. It also provides easy access to both easy and difficult hikes of the big surrounding hills, from which the vistas are impressive.

Nebaj was the site of atrocities perpetrated by the government during the civil war (1960-1996). Although Nebaj's citizens are now the keepers of many sad memories, you will not hear much talk of the war unless you probe. Many people are returning to their homeland after fleeing decades ago, and the town and surrounding area is now a hive of business and development activity. The Nebajeños are famous for their weaving (look out for the embroidered huipiles with geometrical designs in greens, yellows, reds and oranges), observance of traditional customs and environmentally conscious way of life. They are also serious about their fiestas—especially saints' days. Updated: May 03, 2010.

When to Go

Nebaj is at an altitude of 1,900 meters (6,234 ft), so it can be quite cool in the evenings or when the sun is not out. Temperatures range between 7-27°C (45-80°F). The rainy season generally runs from May to September and dry season from October to May, but you can still get rain in December. It is therefore a good idea to pack a few layers of clothing to prepare for warm, cold and wet weather. In mid-August is the festival of Santa María de Nebaj, celebrated around the 7th-16th.

Getting To and Away

Nebaj is well-served by mini buses and some chicken buses from Santa Cruz del Quiché (2 hrs 15 min) and Sacapulas (1 hr). The bus terminal in town is one block south of the market, off 7a Calle and 2a Avenida, but you can also pick up mini-buses on the roads out of town: the northeast route, Calzada 15 de Septiembre, for Chajul and Cotzal, or the road going south, 5a Avenida past the hospital, for Sacapulas.

If you're heading west you can take a bus to Sacapulas and change to a bus going toward Huehuetenango. Going east, take a bus to the turn-off for Uspantán and change to one for Cobán. There is also one daily early-morning direct service to Cobán. Transport tends to start early and finish not long after dark. The last mini bus from Santa Cruz del Quiché leaves at about 7 p.m., and the last bus going south from Nebaj leaves at about 5:30 p.m. There is one direct bus to Guatemala City, which takes five to seven hours and leaves very early in the day. You can also arrange private buses through Pablo's Tours. Tel: 502-4090-4924, E-mail: pablostours@hotmail.com.

Getting Around

Outside the town center, you can stroll around and leisurely soak up the highland atmosphere. For slightly longer journeys you can pick up a tuk-tuk on the street or from around the square. Mini buses travel the now-paved roads to Cotzal and Chajul regularly throughout the day and leave from a few blocks southeast of the square. Buses leave more often to Acul but the road is a little rougher, so you should allow more time for that journey. Updated: Jul 06, 2010.

Safety

Nebaj is a safe town and you are unlikely to have problems walking around during the day or evening. Of course, usual safety precautions should still be taken. Also, if you are going out hiking but are not with an organized group, it is best to set off early and time your walk to be back in town before sun-down. Updated: May 04, 2010.

Services

MONEY

The Banrural is impossible to miss: opposite the church on the plaza before the square.

KEEPING IN TOUCH

The post office is on 4a Calle and 5a Avenida, the road running behind the bank. Internet is available at El Descanso for $1.20 per hour and at the Internet Café in the big yellow building along the west side of the square. Both have printers.

MEDICAL

Dr Rudy Cabrera's surgery (Daily 9:30 a.m.-1 p.m. and 3-6 p.m. 4a Av. Tel: 502-7756-0129/5763-9478) is located on the first floor of Hotel Santa María. If your teeth need seeing-to there is the Laboratorio Dental San Juan (Daily 7 a.m.-12 p.m. and 1-5 p.m. 4a Av., 2-30. Tel: 502-5183-5731). There is also a hospital on the road coming into the town from south and there are plenty of pharmacies around the square.

SHOPPING

The Mercado de Artesanías, on 3a Avenida, is one block south of the bus terminal and is where you'll be able to buy your own Nebajeño huipile, among other highland souvenirs. At the regular market, east of church, you'll find a mix of second-hand western clothing and fruit and vegetables from the surrounding area. The busiest days are Thursdays and Sundays. Updated: May 04, 2010.

Things to See and Do

Nebaj and the surrounding area has a lot of activities to offer, depending on the amount of time you have and what interests you. The town square is often quite lively and is a good place to see some excellent examples of the Nebaj women's traditional dress. Foodies should sample *boxboles*, a traditional meal from the Ixil made from folding guiskil leaves inside a maize dough. Those looking to unwind should try a *temascal* sauna to cleanse the mind, body and soul. If you have more time, you can organize a homestay with an indigenous or ladino family, help them collect and cut firewood, make tortillas and learn about local agriculture. There are a number of volunteer opportunities, as well. Updated: May 04, 2010.

HIKING IN AND AROUND NEBAJ

One thing you must do, and it may be the very reason why you came to Nebaj, is go hiking to some of the most enchanting villages in highland Guatemala. Short or long, easy or strenuous, you can choose a hike to suit your needs and tastes.

There are two hiking agencies located right next to each other on 3a Calle between 5a and 6a Avenida (hikes range from $15 to $80):

El Descanso has its own guide crew, known as Guias Ixiles. They speak English and Spanish (as well as Ixil) and run the very useful website www.nebaj.com.

Pablo's Tours can organize various hikes, such as those below as well as to the villages of Chechocum, Xexocom and Checua, plus horseback riding, home-stays and saunas. Tel: 502-4090-4924, E-mail: pablostours@hotmail.com.

It is worth getting a guide for numerous reasons. First, though it is safe around this area, if you get lost, the distances between isolated villages could prove a serious problem. Also, Spanish is the second language here, and if you don't speak Ixil, having a guide can help you cross language barriers. Further, local knowledge can really enrich your experience, giving meaning to the Maya customs you will see in the villages. And finally, supporting locals employed in tourism is a way to give something back to the communities.

One-Day Hikes

Cataratas: The hike to the *cataratas*, or waterfalls, is a pleasant two-hour, three-kilometer (1.86 mi) walk from the north of Nebaj. It goes through green pastures following the river.

Acul: To reach this traditional Maya village six kilometers (3.7 mi) out of town, the hike takes five hours, which includes walking time up and through the mountains, stopping for lunch at the Hacienda San Antonio and time in the village itself. Return journey is by bus.

Cocop: This peaceful three- to four-hour, nine-kilometer (5.6 mi) hike follows the narrow Nebaj river valley up to this mountain-top hamlet. There are awesome views high over the surrounding area.

Sacred sights: Get a two-hour insight into Maya worship and tradition from a local expert and see sights you probably never would have found yourself.

Multiple-Day Hikes

Todos Santos: If you have three days to spare and don't mind breaking into a sweat, you'll be rewarded by this 10-18 kilometer (6.2-11.1 mi) hike all the way into the Western Highlands. Avoiding major roads, the route snakes through the mountains, crossing pretty fields full of wildflowers, passing La Laguna Magdelena and heading up into the rocky altiplano. On the second night, you'll stay in Capellania, where you can trek over to El Mirador for some superb views out over Huehuetenango and across to the San Marcos volcano. The route continues onto La Ventosa, where you can catch a bus if your feet are tired; otherwise you'll follow the Río Limón on to Todos Santos for your third night. Remember to take warm clothes on this one, as the hike goes over 3,000 meters (9,843 ft) and the nights are chilly. Harder routes are also possible.

Las Aventuras: This hike goes to Acul, ending there the second night after staying the first night at Las Majadas, but covers a lot of territory: 25-36 kilometers (15.5-22.3 mi). The route starts out through the dense forest which surrounds Nebaj, which can be tricky to penetrate

(the reason why this was the hideout of the "Guerrilla Army of the Poor"), but when it opens out, the views of the Cuchumatames are worth it. You can also visit three neighboring lagoons near Las Majadas and the cheese factory at Acul before trekking back to Nebaj on the third day.

Xeo-Cotzol: This is a popular two- to three-day hike due to its relative difficulty compared to the other hikes around Nebaj and the opportunity it provides for contact with the Maya communities in the surrounding villages. There is quite a lot of going up and down the steep mountain sides, covering about 37 kilometers (23 mi), but the views are splendid and so are stop-offs at Xeo, Cotzol, and Finca la Vega, where cheese, cream and mushrooms are produced. You can visit other villages, such as La Pista, where a lot of the guides from Guias Ixiles live. ⚡ Updated: Dec 28, 2009.

Studying Spanish

On top of tourist information, tasty food and an Internet café, you can also arrange for language classes at El Descanso. Three packages are available: the most cheap is $80 a week, which gets you four hours daily in group class, while the most expensive is$145, for which you get a home-stay, four hours a day of private classes, five hours a week of free Internet and two arranged hikes at $145. Students are assigned an English-speaking buddy, so even novices can have a smooth transition to life in Nebaj. 3a Ca. Tel: 502-7832-6345, E-mail: ttrusz@gmail.com. URL: www.nebajlanguageschool.com. Updated: May 04, 2010.

Volunteering

After years of suffering from war and poverty, Nebaj is now the center-point for community development in the Ixil areas. Two organizations providing opportunities for travelerss to do their bit are Proyecto Mosaico (URL: www.promosaico.org) and Social Entrepreneur Corps (URL: www.socialentrepreneurcorps.com). The former offers both short- and long-term placements for a donation of $55-270 and organizes home-stays, language classes and pre-trip orientation. The latter was founded by the guys who set up El Descanso and has a mix of programs for individuals as well as groups. Updated: May 04, 2010.

Lodging

There are a number of accommodation choices in Nebaj, and most are not too far from the main square. As a general rule, hotels in this region do not include breakfast in the price of the room, nor do they have restaurant facilities on-site. However, they do usually have hot water and clean facilities, and staff are friendly. Nearly all budgets are catered to, and there are family-friendly options as well as dorm rooms for groups. Updated: May 04, 2010.

Media Luna Medio Sol

(ROOMS: $4-22) Media Luna Medio Sol is Nebaj's only hostel-style accommodation, offering mainly dorms and a couple of private rooms. This place would appeal more to backpackers looking for a comfy (and cheap) night's sleep, or perhaps a family with children traveling on a budget. This is a fun and relaxed place with a ping-pong table and lounge area with TV. There's also a basic communal kitchen and there are discounts for longer stays. It is run by El Descanso just down the road, so if no one is around, stop by there. There is an Evangelical church next door, which often has loud singing—a heads-up for those who prefer a quieter stay. Ca. 6-15. Tel: 502-5749-7450. Updated: Sep 21, 2009.

Hotel del Centro Naab'a'

(ROOMS: $7-21) Naab'a' is a small, simple three-level hotel next to Taco Express. There's not much to see from the outside, but walk through the alley under the sign to see the three pink levels. The rooms are simple but have big beds and clean bathrooms. Despite being just off the road, the hotel is quiet. With cheap prices and friendly owners, this is definitely a good-value option. 3a Ca. 3-18. Tel: 502-4145-6243/4029-3404. E-mail: naabacentro@yahoo.com. Updated: Sep 21, 2009.

Hotel Café Maya Ixil

(ROOMS: $9-17) The Maya Ixil is a long-standing Nebaj hotel and restaurant with plans for some major improvements, including a roof garden, Internet café and bar. For now, it provides a somewhat dull place to eat but offers good budget rooms in the center of town, all with big beds, private bathroom, hot water and TV. The café and front rooms have views from the north side of the plaza. 5a Calle. Tel: 502-7755-8168. Updated: Sep 14, 2009.

Hotel Turansa

(ROOMS: $9-16) Turansa has 16 rooms decorated with pine furniture and equipped with private bathrooms, hot water and cable TV. Rooms are situated around a parking lot courtyard. The lower level rooms lack

sunlight, so opt for one on the upper level. You can pay extra for a double bed and there is secure parking. 5a Ca. and 6a Av. Tel: 502-4144-7609. Updated: Sep 21, 2009.

Hotel Shalom

(ROOMS: $9-29) There are actually two Shaloms in town. Shalom One, in the center of town, is the older sister of Shalom Two, just out of town on the road south. The older hotel has two levels of spacious rooms with private bathrooms, hot water, cable TV and wood-paneled walls. This motel-style option is just one block from the square. The lower level is wheelchair accessible but the bathrooms are narrow. Number Two is much newer, with a sauna and a country inn feel, but is too far away for a quick stroll into town. Shalom One: Calzada 15 Septiembre and 4a Ca. Tel: 502-7755-8028. Shalom Two: Tel: 502-4404-4233/4202-4506. Updated: Sep 18, 2009.

Hotel Villa Nebaj

(ROOMS: $10-35) Impressive or on the garish side—depending where you stand—with a folk-artsy exterior and entrance hall, Hotel Villa Nebaj is a step up from the other hotels in town. The rooms are painted bright yellow, with nice tiled floors and locally made quilts on the comfortable beds. The best rooms are upstairs and at the back of the building, as the lower rooms are a little dark and the road can be noisy. Calzada 15 Septiembre. Tel: 502-7756-0005/7755-8115. E-mail: villanebaj@yahoo.com. URL: www.villanebaj.com. Updated: Sep 21, 2009.

Hotel Santa María

(ROOMS: $15-24) Hotel Santa María is the newest (and probably best) place to sleep in town. The rooms and bathrooms are spacious, and the beds are big. All the furniture is locally made and the bedspreads have patches of recycled huipils. The bright white sheets are fresh and changed every day (if you think this is not environmentally friendly, speak to the owners, as they are very flexible). There is free WiFi available in every room and secure parking out back. 4a Av. Tel: 502-4212-7927/4621-9890, E-mail: hsmnebaj@gmail.com, URL: www.hotelsantaMaríanebaj.com. Updated: Sep 21, 2009.

Restaurants

There are plenty of bakeries around the main square, where you can get yourself a snack and then people-watch while resting on one of the benches in the plaza. The town center is full of your typical Guatemalan eateries, all more or less the same. La Casona, a new restaurant in town, is worth a try (8a Ca. and 4a Av. Cel: 502-4015-3360). For a really authentic Nebaj culinary experience, guests staying at the Hotel Santa María are invited to eat in the family dining room, where the mother of the house rustles up boxboles, pepián and traditional sauces from age-old family recipes. Updated: Sep 21, 2009.

Taco Express
(ENTREES: $1.50-2.50) As the name suggests, this is a Mexican fast food joint. It's small but has a few tables to sit down. All the food is prepared in front of you and the menu above the counter has pictures so that you can see what you're supposed to be getting: tacos or super tacos with chicken or beef, burritos, roast chicken amd hamburgers. There is a fridge full of soft drinks but no beer. 3a Ca. 3-18. Updated: Sep 18, 2009.

Pizza Genio
(ENTREES: $1.50-12) This place is a bit of a strange mix, offering pizza and Chinese food as well as the usual burgers (veggie option available) and sandwiches. There are the usual toppings to choose from, plus you can get chop suey on the side. The decor is definitely basic and it could do with a revamp, but the food is tasty and they do take-out. 4a Av. and 2a Ca. Tel: 502-4608-1098. Updated: Sep 18, 2009.

El Descanso
Founded by a Peace Corps volunteer back in 2001 to provide sustainable employment for youngsters in Nebaj, El Descanso has become something of a unofficial traveler/tourist information hub as well as a great place to eat and hang out. The funky fabrics and sofas give it a relaxed, bohemian feel and the menu has everything: breakfasts (including the backpacker's favorite, yogurt and granola), salads, sandwiches, burgers, Italian and Mexican meals and some good desserts. The regional boxboles special is available at Thursday lunch. 3a Ca., Zona 1. Tel: 502-7756-0202/5749-7450. Updated: Sep 18, 2009.

Tienda y Comedor Central
A very basic eatery right on the northwest corner of the square, with a mini-store attached from where you can order any drink you want, including beer and aguardiente. It is mainly frequented by locals, including the police from around the corner, so it is good for basic local meals or a quick drink. Ask to use the bathroom, which is out behind the family kitchen. 5a Ca. and 5a Av. Updated: Sep 21, 2009.

SAN JUAN COTZAL
Making up the Ixil Triangle's southeastern point, San Juan Cotzal is an appealing little town, relaxed and happy beneath the towering Cuchumatanes. Nothing much happens here and the pace of life is slow. The locals, when not out tending their fields, pass the time in the pretty town square, sitting on benches under flowery trellises. Wednesdays and Saturdays are good days to visit, as the town awakes with the arrival of the market.

Getting To and Away
To get to Cotzal, you can take one of the many mini-buses that run from Nebaj all day from early till about 7 p.m. The journey takes about 30 minutes. Updated: May 04, 2010.

Things to See and Do
Of interest is the community tourism group Tejidos Cotzal (URL: www.tejidoscotzal.org), which supports local back-strap weavers. Guided tours are offered to see the weavers at work. You can find their office on a corner of the square to the left of the church. The Banrural on the square is open Monday to Friday 8 a.m.-4 p.m. and 8 a.m.-12 p.m. on Saturdays. However there is no ATM, so plan accordingly or change money during bank hours. Updated: May 04, 2010.

Lodging
Hotel Maguey is the only place to stay in town. What it lacks in luxury it makes up for with its homey and welcoming feel; the family owners are proud of the business they have built. All rooms are doubles with shared hot-water bathrooms and cable TV, all for the price of $5.40. Upstairs is a roof terrace with hammocks. There is no wheelchair access, as the rooms are up a narrow staircases on two floors. This is a budget hotel, so there is no heating for those cold, misty nights, but just ask and you'll receive lots of extra blankets. The owners don't like alcohol on the premises.

The Maguey hotel also has an unpretentious comedor on its ground floor that offers typical breakfasts, churrasco, menú del día, soft drinks and coffee. It is basic but clean and cared-for and definitely offers the travelers the feel of a family restaurant. Being the only hotel/restaurant in the village, if there are any other travelers in town you will most certainly bump into them here. Updated: May 04, 2010.

CHAJUL

San Gaspar Chajul is the northern point of the three towns in the Ixil Triangle and has a very distinctive feel. On the road coming into town, you'll pass some great examples of adobe houses with the red cloths of the women's skirts hanging out to dry. The locals tend to spend a lot of their time outside: kids play their games on the street and the women do their back-strap weaving on the front porch. You will also see them doing their washing down at the stream, which runs through the village. Traditionally, they wear earrings made of old coins hung on woolen-string, and their huipiles are fantastic shades of embroidered animals. However tempting, remember that taking photographs is frowned upon here and you should respect people's privacy. Updated: Dec 27, 2009.

Getting To and Away

From Nebaj take one of the regular mini buses that come this way. Baltazar Lines (Tel: 502-5721-7863) run buses from Chajul to Santa Cruz del Quiché. Updated: Dec 27, 2009.

Things to See and Do

The square is pretty filthy and definitely lived-in, but has a very interesting colonial church, the site of a pilgrimage during Lent. It is also in this square where Rigoberta Menchú claims she saw her brother and other suspected anti-government sympathizers publicly executed by the army, as described in her book. Although this terrible event did definitely take place, the date of the killings and whether Rigoberta Menchú was even actually there have been called into question by the research of American author David Stoll.

The Museo Maya Ixil de Chajul, a block down from the square, holds some interesting displays on local hunting and weaving techniques. There's an arcade on the square too, if you fancy a go at old-school space invaders games. There is a Banrural bank on the square that does not have an ATM but will change dollars. There is a pharmacy nearby. Updated: Dec 27, 2009.

Lodging

Hotel Gaspar (Tel: 502-4038-5623), a couple of blocks west from the square, has a fresh feel. It appears quite new and

clean. The rooms, at $6-8.40 per person, are bright and clean with hot water, TV, and locally crafted heavy wooden doors. There is a center courtyard with greenery, street parking and a laundry service available (if you ask). Updated: Dec 27, 2009.

Another option is the Hotel El Descanso (Tel: 502-7755-4001/4478), a little farther away from the square but on the road into the center by the bridge. Along the road is the turn-off to the Posada Vetz K'aol (Tel: 502-7765-6115), whose owner serves up tasty home-cooked meals. Updated: Dec 27, 2009.

Restaurants

Food options are definitely lacking in Chajul, so if you're coming for the day you might bring a packed lunch. You could try Comedor Mary, which cooks up basic breakfasts and set meals. There are some food stalls around the plaza. Updated: Dec 27, 2009.

AROUND IXIL TRIANGLE
ACUL

As you explore the mountain scenery and countryside around Nebaj, the traditional Maya village of Acul is worth at least an extra day's stay on your itinerary. Acul was one of the many 'model villages' built in 1983 after government raided the countryside, burned down the original settlements and packed people into controlled areas in the hunt for revolutionaries and sympathizers. Families speaking as many as five different languages and practicing various religions were forced to live together under constant surveillance.

This now-peaceful countryside village shows a very different face today, and since the Peace Accords were signed in 1996, projects led by NGOs have helped Acul forge a path for the future.

At the entrance to Acul is Finca San Antonio, run by the Italian Azzari family (here since the late 1930s), who produce wheels of cheese on-site against a backdrop of mountains reminiscent of Switzerland, lending a European feel to the village. Updated: May 07, 2010.

Getting To and Away

Getting to and from Acul is pretty straightforward. If you take a guided trekking tour to the village from Nebaj (6 km/3.7 mi), it will take you about five hours; if you want to make your own way, it will take about two hours.

Catching a 4x4 will take less than an hour, giving you more time to soak up the atmosphere in Acul. Ask at El Descanso for walking directions or a ride. Public mini buses and trucks also leave from the square. Updated: May 07, 2010.

Lodging

When weighing accommodation options, consider staying at the Finca in wood cabins ($12/15 per person for rooms with shared/private bathroom). It also owns Hacienda Mil Amores, a group of four delightful stone cottages with private bathrooms for around $50 per room. Meals are extra, but they are tasty and wholesome. You can arrange horseback riding, hikes or visits to see the farm animals through either place. Tel: 502-5704-4817. Updated: May 07, 2010.

Posada Doña Magdalena is an excellent place to stay and popular among tourists, perhaps due to the friendly owner, a local lady who speaks Spanish, Ixil and English. There are dorm rooms available for $5 per person and doubles around $8 per person, all with shared bathroom. Meals are served in the family dining room with a flower garden out front. Tel: 502-5782-0891.

SANTA AVELINA

The village of Santa Avelina, about 10 kilometers (6 mi) from San Juan Cotzal, rests at approximately 1,310 meters (4,300 ft) above sea level, and its 2,000 inhabitants are of predominantly Maya Ixil descent. From the village you can take a 15-minute walk along a bridle path to some spectacular waterfalls good for swimming. Ask at the Tienda Lux for access and directions. The village's primary school was built by a charity group from Texas, HELPS, which also collects donations to pay the teachers' wages, runs a health program and sets up pen-pals. There is also a local coffee co-operative and honey farm, both of which produce fair trade certified products. If you would like to visit the coffee fields, contact Andrés Cruz Martínez (Tel: 502-5171-7904). Updated: May 17, 2010.

IXCÁN

The Ixcán is formed by an expanse of forest and planes below the steep and spectacular Cuchumatanes. It is a sparsely populated area and rarely sees foreign visitors besides Mexican workers crossing the border to the north. During the 1960s and '70s, many people migrated here from the Quiché and Huehuetenango provinces looking for untamed land to claim as their own. Later, this area became the site of much vicious fighting, when the government's army clashed with the 'Commander Ernesto Guervara' front of the Ejército Guerrillero de los Pobres (The Guerrilla Army of the Poor).

The new villages were razed to the ground, pushing the inhabitants even farther north. Only recently has the Ixcán seen some of its former inhabitants return from exile from either Mexico or the United States. Being so remote and devoid of any real tourist attractions, the area only attracts adventurous travelers going between Alta Verapaz and northern Quiché or upper Huehuetenango.

If you choose to travel this way, there are some hotels in Playa Grande, a rudimentary frontier settlement with some basic comedores and a Banrural with an ATM. The same is true of Barillas. The area's fiesta is celebrated May 15-17. The local Mayan languages of Uspantek and Q'eqchi' are spoken in Ixcán, as is Spanish.

Getting To and Away

Travel through the Ixcán can be a very difficult task, but the scenery is rewarding. Playa Grande is the transport center, where you can join a pick-up truck going west toward the town of Cantabla or southeast to Cobán. The road, really nothing more that a dirt track, passes through the remote Ixcán towns of Puente Xabal, Veracruz, Mayalan and Altamirano before reaching Barillas. From here you can move onto San Mateo Ixtatán and into Huehuetenango.

Going north from Nebaj, the roads are very poor, and travel times can easily double during the rainy season. Playa Grande to Barillas takes about five hours on a good day. There are no regular public buses running here. There are occasional chicken buses, but your best bet is to arrange to take pick-up trucks in town or to flag them down en route, as the locals do. This should only be attempted in daylight hours; at night this is a very lonely area. Updated: Nov 30, 2009.

)))))

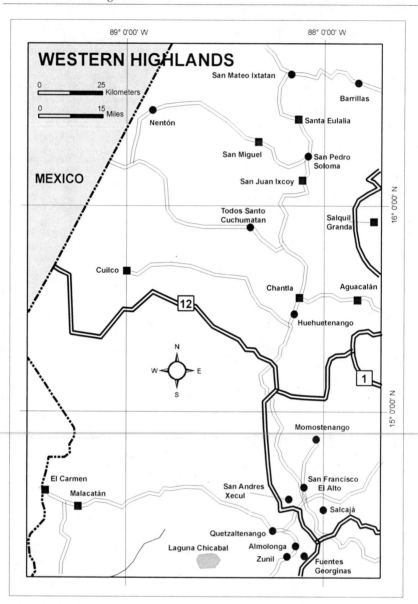

Western Highlands

Comprising the provinces of Huehu-etenango, Totonicapán, Quetzaltenango and San Marcos, Guatemala's Western Highlands are mostly for die-hard travelers who are looking to get off the gringo trail and look for some adventure.

Crossed by the picturesque Cuchumatanes mountain chain, Guatemala's western highlands are rugged and beautiful, and home to a largely indigenous population. Away from the main cities, local women still wear *huipiles* (native blouses) and more people speak traditional languages such as Mam, Jacalteco and Quiché. Travelers who stay in the region for a while will be able to identify where a person is from by their clothing.

There are several towns, cities and sites of interest for visitors in the region. The city of Quetzaltenango, also referred to as Xelajú or Xela ("SHAY-la"), is Guatemala's second largest city and a popular spot for visitors who want to learn Spanish in a more authentic or less touristy place than Antigua or Panajachel.

Todos Santos Cuchumatán is a traditional Maya village, located in the remote mountains above bustling Huehuetenango. It is known for its traditional lifestyle, men who still wear native clothing, and its annual festival of Todos Santos on October 31-November 2.

The province of Huehuetenango is also home to the ruins of Zaculeu, a Maya stronghold that fell to the Spanish early in the conquest. The province of Totonicapán is noteworthy for having genuine native markets in both the city of Totonicapán and Momostenango. Visitors who have already visited the larger and more famous market in Chichicastenango may want to see these smaller, more authentic markets.

CUATRO CAMINOS

Cuatro Caminos, located in the department of Totonicapán, is basically an important intersection in which the four roads or "Cuatro Caminos" head off to different cities. From Cuatro Caminos, the road to the southeast goes to Guatemala City. To the southwest, Quetzaltenango. To the northwest, Huehuetenango and the Mexican border. The last road, to the northeast, leads to Totonicapán. There is not much to see or do in Cuatro Caminos. There are some shabby restaurants where you can get a bite to eat and several vendors selling fruit, candy, and other snacks. Mainly it is a place to change buses. Be careful as petty crimes are common in Cuatro Caminos. Updated: Oct 19, 2007.

QUETZALTENANGO/XELA

The second-largest city in all of Guatemala, Quetzaltenango is an important commercial hub in the highlands. The city is a sprawling conglomeration of districts and neighborhoods that seems to go on endlessly in any direction from the center. Although its population is estimated to be about 300,000, it often seems larger.

To the Quiché people who lived in the city for centuries before the arrival of the Spanish, the city was called "Xelajú," or "Under Ten Mountains." Quetzaltenango, or "Place

of the Quetzal bird" was the name given to it by Conquistador Pedro de Alvarado's Mexican allies during the conquest. Although the name stuck as far as the Spanish were concerned, the locals still more commonly refer to the city as Xelaju, or Xela for short.

The city was the capital of the Quiché people at the time of the Spanish conquest. They fought valiantly against Pedro de Alvarado and his men, but ultimately the city fell. The Quiché leader, Tecún Umán, bravely went to battle with the Spanish, but died in battle outside of town. According to tradition, he fell in single combat with Alvarado himself, although there is little historical evidence to support this notion.

The city remained important during the colonial and republican periods, and when coffee was introduced in the nineteenth century, the city boomed. The fine houses and buildings of the coffee boom can still be seen in the colonial center of town, and the region still produces a good deal of coffee. Although, insiders will tell you that the coffee grown in Alta Verapaz and Huehuetenango is of higher quality.

There are some tourist attractions in Xela, making the town worth a visit. The colonial center has some interesting architecture, and the hills and mountains around the city are good for hiking. The central market has some traditional crafts for sale, and they're generally cheaper than you'll find them in Antigua or Panajachel. The city is convenient to other places of interest such as San Francisco el Alto and Momostenango. There are an abundance of Spanish schools in Xela, which mainly attract the serious students who don't want to study in Cuba-libre-soaked Antigua or hippie heaven Panajachel.

These students in general sacrifice two-for-one margaritas for a more authentic homestay and less distractions. Updated: Sep 02, 2009.

Economy

Xela is a university town, with one large state university (San Carlos de Guatemala) and six private universities. As such, education is the most important income for the local economy. Agriculture is in the second position and tourism comes in the third. Updated: Aug 28, 2009.

When to Go

At 2,330 meters (7,644 ft) above sea level, Xela's climate is variable. Temperatures year-round average 25°C (77°F) during the

Highlights

If you have limited time in Xela, spend a day visiting the yellow church at **San Andrés Xecul**, followed by some relaxation at the hot springs **Fuentes Georginas in Zunil**. On your second day, try hiking the **Santa María Volcano** or **Laguna de Chicabal**.

If you're able to spend more time in the area, you can take a two-day trip to climb the highest volcano in Central America, **Tajumulco** (4,220 m/13,845 ft). Browse the colorful local market of **San Francisco del Alto** (Fridays) and the blanket market in **Momostenango** (Sundays).

To learn about sustainable and ecotourism, spend a day or two at **La Comunidad Nueva Alianza** learning about coffee and macadamia production. Updated: Sep 02, 2009.

daytime and 7°C (45°F) at night. During the coldest months (December-February), temperatures can sometimes drop to freezing. Neither heating nor air conditioning are provided in buildings. It's best to dress in layers. Bring a heavy sweater for early morning, and plenty of T-shirts to wear in the afternoon. Updated: Sep 03, 2009.

Holidays and Festivals

Feria de la Virgen del Rosario (Independence Festival), held during the week of September 15th, is Xela's big annual party, with a week-long fair outside town. The most important day is the 15th, on which day the students parade around town.

Although not as big as in Antigua, the Quetzaltenango Semana Santa (Easter Week) celebration is a good opportunity to see the elaborate processions. The most important day is Good Friday. Updated: Sep 03, 2009.

Getting To and Away

First-class bus companies operating between Quetzaltenango and Guatemala City have their own terminals. Note that timetables can change without notice. The trip takes around four hours.

Transportes Galgos

($7) Rodolfo Robles Monday-Saturday 4 a.m., 8:30 a.m. and 12:30 p.m. Sunday 12:30 p.m. and 3 p.m. 17-43, Zona 1. Tel: 502-7761-2248.

Transportes Alamo

($7) Monday-Saturday: 4:30 a.m., 6:30 a.m., 8 a.m., 10:15 a.m., 12:45 a.m. and 2:30 p.m. Friday: extra bus at 4:45 p.m. Sunday: extra bus at 3 p.m. and 4:45 p.m. 14 Av.5-15, Zona 3. Tel: 502-7763-5044.

Línea Dorada

($9) Nonstop. Monday-Saturday 4 a.m. and 2:30 p.m. 12 Av. and Ca., Zona 3. Tel: 502-7767-5198.

Fuente del Norte

($7) Daily: 9:30 a.m. and 3:30 p.m. 7 Av.3-33, Zona 2. Tel: 7761-4587.

For second-class buses, head to the Minerva Terminal behind Minerva Market, on 7a Calle in Zona 3. Buses leave frequently for highland destinations, the Pacific Coast and Guatemala City. Buses run every day, but with less frequency during the holidays.

Almolonga and Zunil

($1, 15 minutes) every 15 minutes between 6 a.m. and 7 p.m. You can take the bus at the petrol station at the corner of 9 Avenida and 10 Calle in Zona 1.

Antigua

($4.50, 4 hours): every 30 minutes, 3 a.m.-5 p.m. Take a bus heading to Guatemala City and change at Chimaltenango.

Chichicastenango

($3, 3 hours): Buses leave at 5 a.m., 6 a.m., 9:30 a.m., 11 a.m., 1 p.m., 2 p.m. and 3:30 p.m. Or take a bus heading to Guatemala City and change at Los Encuentros.

Ciudad Tecun Uman

($3.50, 4 hr): Every 10 minutes, 5 a.m.-7 p.m.

El Carmen/Talisman

($5, 4 hours) Every 30 minutes. Take a bus to Coatepeque, then a bus to El Carmen.

Guatemala City

($5, 4 to 5 hr) Every 30 minutes. 3 a.m.-5 p.m.

Huehuetenango

($3, 2 hours) Every 15 minutes, 4 a.m.-6 p.m.

La Mesilla

($4, 3.5 hr) Buses leave at 5 a.m., 6 a.m., 7 a.m., 8 a.m., 1 p.m. and 4 p.m. Or take a bus to

Huehuetenango and change there.

Momostenango
($2, 2 hr) Every 30 minutes, 6 a.m.-5 p.m.

Panajachel
($2.50, 2.5 hr) Buses leave at 5 a.m., 6 a.m., 8 a.m., 10 a.m., noon and 3 p.m. Or take a bus heading to Guatemala City and change at Los Encuentros and Sololá.

Retalhuleu
($2, 1 hr) Every 30 minutes, 4:30 a.m.-6 p.m. Look for the sign Reu on the bus.

San Andrés Xecul
($0.80, 40 min) Hourly, 6 a.m.-3 p.m. Or take any bus heading to 4 Caminos and let the ayudante (helper) knows you want to go to San Andrés. When they drop you at the junction, flag a pick up.

San Marcos
($1.50, 1 hr) Every 30 minutes, 6 a.m.-6 p.m.

San Pedro La Laguna
($3, 2.5 hr) Buses leave at 8 a.m., 11 a.m., 12:30 p.m. and 4:30 a.m.

San Francisco El Alto
($1, 1 hr) Every 15 minutes, 6 a.m.-6 p.m.

Totonicapán
($1, 1 hr) Every 20 minutes, 6 a.m.-5 p.m. Buses depart from the Toto Terminal in 2 Calle in Zona 2 or you can take a bus from La Retonda. Look for the sign Toto on the bus.

Major tour operators offer daily shuttle service to Guatemala City airport ($35), Antigua ($25), Panajachel ($15), San Pedro La Laguna ($15) and San Cristóbal de Las Casa in Mexico ($25).

Getting Around
Once you arrive at the Terminal Minerva, walk south through the market to the Templo de Minerva. From there you can catch any minibus to the Parque Central ($0.20 for the 20 minute drive). Going from the city center to Minerva, you can catch a minibus at the corner of the 4 Calle and 14 Avenida in Zona 1. Minibuses run between Hyper País Supermarket and La Retonda every day between 7 a.m. and 10 p.m., passing through the market La Democratia, Parque Central and Parque Bolivar.

A taxi from the bus terminal to the Parque Central should cost $3. If you need a taxi, just head to Parque Central during the day or ask your hotel to call for one. At night, only take a taxi service that someone has recommended to you. You can rent a car at Tabarini. 9 Ca. 9-21 Zona 1. Tel: 502-7763-0418, tabarini@centramerica.com. URL: www.tabarini.com. Updated: Sep 03, 2009.

Safety
Xela is a fairly safe city, but the crime rate has been increasing, especially around Christmas. During the day, you can walk around without any problems. At night, walk in groups or take a taxi to go home. It's better to use a taxi that has been recommended to you. It's wise to only carry with you the minimum amount of money you need. If you get robbed or need to contact the authorities, you can call Asistur 24-hours per day at 1500 or 502-2421-2810. Updated: Sep 03, 2009.

Services
The main post office is located at 4 Calle 15-07 Zona 1. It opens 9 a.m. to 5 p.m. Monday to Friday and 9 a.m. to 1 p.m. on Saturday.

TOURISM
The Inguat Tourism office is housed in the same building as the former Casa de la Cultura. However, the staff is not particularly friendly and they don't have much information or any maps. Open Monday to Friday 9 a.m.-5 p.m. and Saturday 9 a.m-1 p.m.

If you want good information and service, head to the Casa de Los Altos. They provide tourist information, city tours and talks about Guatemalan history and culture. They even have a poetry club. There is also a café and souvenir shop on-site. Monday-Saturday 7 a.m.-7 p.m. 6 Ca. 12-32 Zona 1. Tel: 502-7765-2226, URL: www.casalosaltosxela.com. Updated: Sep 03, 2009.

MONEY
There are a few banks around Parque Central. Banco Industrial, in the beautiful building on the north side of the Parque, is the place to go if you want to change traveler's checks or dollars. Monday-Friday 9 a.m.-7 p.m., Saturday 9 a.m.-1 p.m. .

For visa, you can find an ATM on the east and west side of the Parque Central, and on 14 Avenida. For MasterCard, only the ATM on the west side accepts it. If the ATM is not working you'll have to go to the shopping mall, La Pradera, close to the bus terminal in Zona 3. You can also find ATMs close to La Democratia market,

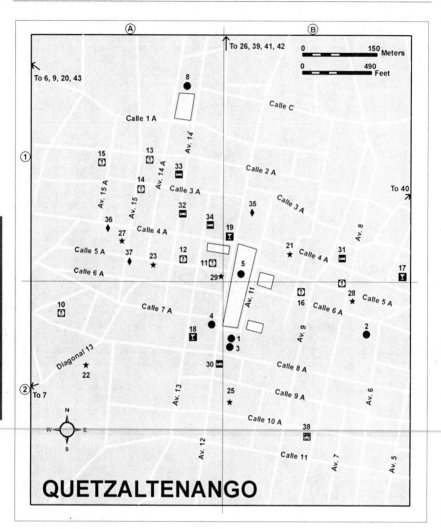

QUETZALTENANGO

around Parque Buenito Juarez. ATMs are open daily 8 a.m.-8 p.m. If you need cash after 8 p.m., La Pradera shopping mall is the only place open until 9 p.m. Updated: Aug 28, 2009.

KEEPING IN TOUCH

You can make international phone calls from many Internet cafés in town. The price is around $0.15 per minute to call land lines in the USA, Canada and Europe. The cheapest is to open a Skype account. There are many Internet cafés around the Parque Central that charge between $0.40 and $0.50 an hour. Most of them offer Skype and high speed connection.

Celas Maya Internet Café

($0.75 per hour) They charge a bit more than other places but offer Skype, phone calls and Fax services. Daily 10 a.m.-6 p.m. 6 Ca. 14-55, Zona 1.

Art Place Internet Café

($0.50 per hour) They offer Skype and phone services. Daily 9 a.m.-7 p.m. 12 Av. 3-35, Zona 1 Updated: Sep 03, 2009.

MEDICAL

There are a large variety of health professionals practicing in Quetzaltenango. Many of them are US, Canadian, Mexican, Cuban

Activities ●

1 Casa de la Cultura B2
2 EntreMundo B2
3 Museo de Historia Natural B2
4 Museo del Ferrocarril A2
5 Parque Centroamérica B1
6 Parque Zoológico A1
7 QuetzaltrekkersA2
8 Teatro Municipal A1
9 Temple Minerva A1

Eating 🍴

10 Blue Angel Video Café A2
11 Casa Babylone A1
12 Café Baviera A1
13 Restaurant and Bar Bamboo A1
14 Royal Paris A1
15 Sabor de la India A1
16 Tacos Dona Berta B2

Nightlife 🍸

17 Bajo La Luna B1
18 El Cuartito A2
19 Salon Tecun B1

Services ★

20 Asociación Pop-Wuj A1
21 Banco Industrial B1
22 Casa Xelaju A2
23 Celas Maya A1
24 Celas Maya Internet Café (See 23)

25 Hospital San Rafael B2
26 La Democratia B1
27 Post office A1
28 Sakribal B2
29 Tourism Office A1

Sleeping 🛏

30 B&B Miguel de Cervantes A2
31 Casa Mañen B1
32 Hotel Los Olivos A1
33 Hotel Modelo A1
34 The Black Cat Hostel A1

Tours ♦

35 Altiplano's Tour Operator B1
36 Diversity Tours A1
37 Icaro Tour A1

Transportation 🚌

38 Buses to Almolonga and Zunil B2
39 Buses to Guatemala City B1
40 Buses to Totonicapan B1
41 Linea Dorada B1
42 Transportes Alamo B1
43 Transportes Galgos A1

WESTERN HIGHLANDS

or Guatemalan trained. Quetzaltenango has multiple private hospitals and one large public hospital. There are also dozens of private clinics offering health services around town.

Hospital Privado Quetzaltenango

Ca. Rodolfo Robles 23-51, Zona 3. Tel: 502-7761-4381.

Hospital San Rafael

This hospital has a 24-hour emergency. 9 Ca. 10-41, Zona 1. Tel: 502-7761-4414.

Cruza Roja

It has a 24-hour service and you pay a donation. 8 Av. 6-62 Zona 1. Tel: 502-7761-7591/502-7761-2746 Updated: Aug 29, 2009.

LAUNDRY

It costs around $2.20 to wash and dry a one kilogram (2.2 lb) load of clothes. Most of the hotels offer laundry service so ask at the desk. Planeta Unido (Monday-Friday 8 a.m.-noon and 2-6 p.m., Saturday 8 a.m.-1 p.m. 9 Ca. 9-38), Run by the women of shelter of the NGO Nuevos Horizontes, a load costs $2.50 for washing and drying. Updated: Aug 28, 2009.

SHOPPING

You can find anything in Xela, from used clothes to souvenirs. If you want to taste the real Guatemalan shopping experience, head to the market La Democracia in Zona 3. Open every day from early morning to late afternoon, fruits and vegetables are cheaper than in Zona

1. Bargain hard. If you're looking for pirated DVDs, clothes, electronics or even furniture, you'll find it there. Updated: Oct 02, 2009.

Trama Textile

If you're looking for beautiful woven souvenirs, go to Trama Textile. One block north of Parque Central, inside Santa Maria, Trama is a women's weaving association representing seventeen cooperatives from five regions. Created in 1988 to support the families after the Civil War, its mission is to offer training, support and work for fair wages to women and to maintain and develop their art, design and culture. Open Monday to Saturday 9 a.m.-6 p.m., the shop has a large selection of bags, scarves, tablecloths and other souvenirs. Weaving classes are offered for $4.50 per hour and there are volunteer opportunities. Monday-Saturday 9 a.m.-6 p.m. 3 Ca. 10-56, Zona 1. Tel: 502-7765-8564, E-mail: rama. textiles@yahoo.com, URL: www.tramatextiles.com. Updated: Oct 02, 2009.

Market Sunday

The first Sunday of every month there is a handicraft market at the Parque Central. There are also a few souvenir shops on the first floor of the Centro Commercial next to the Park. Always bargain. Parque Central. Updated: Oct 02, 2009.

Bake Shop

For delicious cakes and breads, go to the Bake Shop in Zona 3. Run by American Mennonites, this bakery sells everything from healthy whole wheat breads to glazed donuts and delicious cookies. Tuesday-Friday 9 a.m.-6 p.m., it's best to go early. 18 Ca. and 1 Ca., Zona 3. Tel: 502-7761-5367. Updated: Sep 18, 2009.

Al-Nature Shop

To buy fair-trade products, go to Al-Nature. Two blocks from Parque Central, this coffee shop supports local cooperatives by selling granola, organic coffee, jams, peanut butter, chocolate and natural medicine. Do your shopping while enjoying a good cup of coffee and a delicious piece of pie. Monday-Saturday 9 a.m.-8 p.m., Sunday 3 p.m.-7 p.m. 13 Av. 8-34A, Zona 1. Updated: Oct 02, 2009.

Things to See and Do

Apart from the Parque Central and the theater, there is little to see in Xela. You will have to get out of the city to visit the different villages, hot springs and local markets. If you're into hiking, there is a large choice. You can climb either Volcán Tajumulco, Santa María or Laguna de Chicabal. Another option is to go cycling along Guatemalan's bumpy roads. Xela is a great place to learn salsa dancing and do some yoga. Visitors who have more time can take Spanish and Quiché (Mayan language) lessons in one of the numerous language schools, or volunteer for an NGO. Updated: Aug 29, 2009.

Parque Centroamérica

Like most Guatemalan cities, Xela is built around a central park. The Parque Centroamérica gives a European feel with the presence of Greek columns. On the south side, stands La Casa de la Cultura and the Museo de Historia Natural. On the eastern end of the Parque is the original façade of the Iglesia del Espíritu Santo which was built in 1535 by the Bishop Francisco Marroquín. This is all that's left of the original church which was severely damaged in the earthquake of 1902. A new church was erected behind the façade. The Municipalidad (City Hall) was also reconstructed after 1902 in grand neoclassical style. On the west side is Pasaje Enrique, a pedestrian and commercial arcade, home to several bars and restaurants. Updated: Aug 29, 2009.

Casa de la Cultura

When the Espíritu Santo Church and Franciscan convent were built, a cemetery was built at the location of the present Casa de la Cultura. In 1872, after the triumph of the Liberal Revolution, the governor converted the cemetery and convent into a prison and warehouse for flour. At the end of the 1800s, City Hall was located in this building. In 1955 it ceased to function as a prison and in 1962 the Casa de la Cultura was officially inaugurated. On 10 November 1977, it was declared a "National Building." Parque Central. Updated: Aug 29, 2009.

Museo de Historia Natural

This museum has an interesting collection covering the Maya, the liberal revolution in Central American politics and the Estado de Los Altos of which Xela was the Capital. Marimba, the weaving industry, stuffed animals and other local artifacts that are exhibited in the museum. Casa de la Cultura, Parque Central. Monday-Friday 8 a.m.-noon and 2-6 p.m., Saturday-Sunday 9 a.m.-noon and 2-5 p.m. Updated: Aug 29, 2009.

Teatro Municipal

At the northeast of Parque Central, the theater was built in 1894 by the architect Enrique Jones. On July 19, 1895, General Justo

Rufino Barrios celebrated the completion of the Municipal Theater. But during the earthquake of 1902, it suffered serious damage, to the extent that the Official Commission of Engineers recommended its demolition. Instead, a decision was made to restore the building. On 21 November 1908, the second façade was inaugurated. Today the theater holds regular performances. 1 Ca. between 14 Av. and 14 Av. A, Zona 1. Updated: Aug 29, 2009.

Parque Zoológico

Inaugurated in 1956, this small zoo is a favorite place for Guatemalan families during the weekend. There are a few monkeys, coyotes, raccoons, deer, sheep and birds in small cages. And there is a playground for the kids. Tuesday-Sunday 9 a.m.-5 p.m. Av. las Americas 0-50, close to the supermarket Hyper Pais and the Minerva Temple. Tel: 502-7763-5657/5672-8230. Updated: Aug 29, 2009.

Temple Minerva

Outside the Zoo and in the middle of 4 Calle stands the Temple Minerva. It was built in 1900 by the dictator Estrada Cabrera, to honor the Roman goddess Minerva. In Roman legend, she was born, fully grown and armed to the teeth, from the forehead of Jupiter. Associated with wisdom, commerce and progress, she symbolized Estrada Cabrera's plans to modernize the country and promote it as the cultural heavyweight of Central America. Take a mini-van which goes to the supermarket Hyper Pais and get out at the market Minerva. 4 Ca., Zona 3. Updated: Aug 29, 2009.

CYCLING

Cycling is a great way to discover the surroundings of Xela if you're not afraid of dusty, bumpy roads. You can go to Zunil and Fuentes Georginas, Los Vahos or Salcajá and San Andrés Xecul in a day trip. More adventurous travelers can go to the Pacific Coast or to Lago Atitlán on a multi-day trip. Vrisa Bookshop (Monday-Saturday 9 a.m.-6 p.m. 15 Av. 3-64 Zona 1) and Monte Verde tours (13 Av. 8-34, Zona 1. Tel: 502- 7761-6105 rents bike for $5 per day and $13 week. They both organize biking day trips if you want to go with a guide. Updated: Aug 29, 2009.

Santa María

Climbing Santa María (3,772 m/12,375 ft) can be easily done from Xela. You can start walking at the village Llanos del Pinal, 5 kilometers (3.1 mi) south of Xela. The trip to the summit takes about four hours. The last 20 minutes are

quite steep, but, once at the top, you'll have a beautiful view of the volcanoes around Xela. To the south, you can see the volcanoes of Lake Atitlán. To the north, on a clear day, you can see Tajumulco and Tacana. You can take a guide or go on your own. Take a taxi to Llanos del Pinal to start the hike. Updated: Mar 13, 2009.

Volcano Climbing

There are many volcanoes to climb from Xela and the variety will please hikers at all levels. Volcano Tajumulco (4,220 m/13,845 ft) is the highest point in Central America and is a challenging two day-trip from Xela. On the first day, you'll travel by bus to the starting point Huitan and walk about five hours to get to the camping area. After a night in the cold mountains, you'll awake at 4 a.m. to get to the summit and watch an amazing sunrise. You can see the volcanoes of Santa Maria, of Lake Atitlán and even Tacana at the Mexican border. Bring some warm clothes.

With an early start, Volcano Santa María (3,772 m/12,375 ft) can be done in a day trip from Xela. Starting at the village Llanos del Pinal ($6 in taxi), it takes about four hours to get to the summit. It's advised to be in a good physical condition and to start early. The view at the top is beautiful with Xela on the east side, the volcanoes of the Lake Atitlán on the south side, the active volcano Santiaguito and its eruptions on the west side and Tajumulco on the north side. The total trip will take about eight hours.

La Laguna de Chicabal (2,712 m/8,897 ft) can be done in half a day, leaving Xela early. A beautiful lake is nestled in the crater. The volcano and the lagoon are considered one of the most important sacred sites with ceremonies. The Maya Mam spirituality is captured in the natural mountainous landscape, the lagoon and the environs. Chicabal is one of the last cloudy woods of this region of Guatemala, with its own flora and fauna. To get there, take a bus ($0.75) two blocks north of Benito Juarez, at the intersection of 15 Avenida and 6 Calle Zona 3. Look for the bus to Chile Verde (30-min drive). Buses start running at 7 a.m. Tell the attendant you want to go to Chicabal. From the village, it's a good one hour steep hike to the park. Entrance fees: $2. Then it's another 30 minutes hike to get to the view point from which you can see the lake, Santa Maria and Santiaguito if it's not misty. Be sure to arrive early as it's usually misty after 10 a.m. You can then climb down the 615 stairs to walk around the lake. Because the lake is sacred, swimming is not permitted.

WESTERN HIGHLANDS

For your safety, it is not recommended to go on your own to do the hikes around Xela. Tour operators offer trips to the different volcanoes. Updated: Aug 29, 2009.

Horseback Riding

Saddle up for a horseback adventure in the Quetzaltenango valley. Feel the magic of freedom and infinite space, the intense blue of the sky, the vertigo of the ravines with carpets of crops on the bottom and the surprise of the locals while riding through the fields and the indigenous villages. You can ride in Almolonga through the fruit fields with amazing views of the surrounding countryside, and visit a family making fruit jelly. Or ride through corn fields from Salcaja to San Andres Xecul. Tour operators offer tours for beginners and people with very little knowledge of horseback riding through to experienced riders. Rate is $35 for a four-hour trip including transport, guide and equipment. Updated: Aug 29, 2009.

Museo del Ferrocarril

The Museo del Ferrocarril is a must-see for train enthusiasts or simply those interested in learning a bit more about Guatemala's history. This well put together museum features several old locomotive trains that once traveled between Xela and Retalhuheu, a replica waiting room and intact administrative offices with all the old equipment and decoration that they would have had back in the 19th century. There is even a replica of a room at the Hotel Zacapa, which would have been frequented by train travelers at the time, and some modern art on the upper floors. Daily 8 a.m.-6 p.m. 12 Av. and 7 Ca. Zona 1. Updated: Aug 03, 2010.

Studying Spanish

Attending a Spanish school in Quetzaltenango is a great way not only to learn the language, but to have an intimate, thorough introduction to the local culture. Most of the classes are one-on-one, taught by competent, friendly locals who often become good friends with their students. All of the Spanish schools offer guided cultural and social activities, and many of them can also arrange for their students to volunteer with local organizations. Most private lessons cost under $200 a week, and a few schools put the majority of your tuition toward a worthy cause, such as a local school or a scholarship fund. The schools take very good care of you, most of them arranging housing with a family or in a safe, comfortable apartment. Updated: Aug 25, 2010

La Democratia

Run by the energetic owner Flory, this small school is five blocks north of Parque Benito Juarez in a quiet part of Zona 3. You'll feel like you're at home and the highly qualified teachers will help you progress rapidly in Spanish. Part of your tuition goes toward building classes in local schools around Xela. You can volunteer and teach English in local schools with a minimum commitment a month. 9 Ca. 15-05 Zona 3. Tel: 502-7767-0013, E-mail: info@lademocracia.net, URL: www.lademocratia.net. Updated: Oct 02, 2009.

Casa Xelaju

A five-minute walk from Parque Central, Casa Xelaju offers Spanish and Quiché classes for beginners, Spanish for educators and healthcare professionals, and Spanish literature classes. They also offer a semester abroad for students who want to earn college or university credits. Volunteer work is available at La Pedrera, an indigenous community close to Xela. Callejon 15, Diagonal 13-02, Zona 1. Tel: 502-7761-5954, URL: www.casaxelaju.com. Updated: Oct 02, 2009.

El Mundo en Español

This very friendly family-run school is close to the bus terminal. They offer 20 or 25 hours of classes a week and homestay. A portion of the tuition goes to the Guarderia Canton Choqi, a daycare center for disadvantaged children and women who are victims of domestic violence. Volunteer opportunities are available at the Guarderia or other projects. 8 Av., Ca. B A-61, Zona 1. Tel: 502-7761-3258. E-mail: gladiolalife@yahoo.com, URL: www.elmundoenespanol.org. Updated: Oct 02, 2009.

Sakribal

Founded and run by women, this school gives a part of the tuition to a scholarship program for young indigenous girls who wouldn't otherwise have the opportunity to study. Sakribal offers volunteer work in health, social work, education and ecology. 6 Ca. 7-42, Zona 1. Tel: 502-7763-0717, E-mail: info@sakribal.com, URL: www.sakribal.com. Updated: Oct 02, 2009.

Proyecto Lingüístico Quetzalteco

Voted the best school in Xela and second in Guatemala, PLQ is very professional and politically minded. It was established to support groups and projects working toward solutions for Guatemala's social and economic problems. They have been working with human rights and popular organizations. Participation in local cultures and volunteering are strongly encouraged. The school also runs La Escuela de la Montaña on a coffee farm run by ex-guerilleros in Colombia, an hour and 15 minutes from Xela. 5 Ca. 2-40, Zona 1. Tel: 502-7765-2140, E-mail: hermanda@plqe.org, URL: www.hermandad.com. Updated: Oct 02, 2009.

Asociación Pop-Wuj

Asociacion Pop-Wuj is a cooperative owned by five experienced teachers. The school has a very strong social commitment and most of the students volunteer in social projects. They have specialized medical and social courses. 1 Ca. 17-72, Zona 1. Tel: 502-7761-8286, E-mail: info@pop-wuj.org, URL: www.pop-wuj.org. Updated: Oct 02, 2009.

El Nahual Language Center

Located on the outskirts of the city, El Nahual is an NGO that runs a Spanish school and some great community projects. Students are encouraged to volunteer for Manos de Colores, a free after-school program for local children and adults; or help out in the community garden. 27 Av. 8-68, Zona 1. Tel: 502-7765-2098, E-mail: cdl.elnahual@gmail.com, URL: www.languageselnahual.com. Updated: Oct 02, 2009.

Celas Maya

One of the biggest school in Xela, Celas Maya offers Spanish and Quiché classes with highly qualified teachers. The school can arrange volunteer placement if you have an intermediate level of Spanish and commit to a minimum of one month. 6 Ca. 14-55, Zona 1. Tel: 502-7761-4342, E-mail: celasmaya@gmail.com, URL: www.celasmaya.edu.gt. Updated: Oct 02, 2009.

Volunteering

Xela has many nonprofit social organizations that are looking for volunteers. Volunteering possibilities are endless, ranging from teaching English to children to building stoves in local villages. You can volunteer anywhere from a week up to a year, part-time or full-time, but most of the organizations prefer if volunteers stay for at least a month. Skills in fields such as medicine, nursing, teaching and computers are in high demand, but there are possibilities for anyone willing to help. Volunteers must normally pay their own living expenses. To start, you should go to EntreMundos, an NGO connecting volunteers with local organizations. Check their website for volunteer opportunities or stop at their office (Monday-Thursday 1 p.m.-5 p.m. 6 Ca. 7-31, Zona 1). Updated: Oct 02, 2009.

Asociación Nuevos Horizontes

This NGO supports the rights of women and children, working with them in situations of personal difficulty and social risk. They own the only shelter for abused women in Guatemala and run programs focused on the health and personal development of these women. They also own a laundry run by the women of the shelter. Volunteers work in the shelter's daycare center. A minimum commitment of three days a week for four weeks is required. 3 Ca. 6-51, Zona 2. Tel: 502-7761-6140, E-mail: nhcoordinadoras@gmail.com, URL: www.ahnh.org. Updated: Oct 02, 2009.

Voces de Cambio

This NGO works with teenage girls in Xela. Through writing and photography, they are encouraged to challenge the deeply ingrained and destructive social norms that exclude them from contributing to the development of a democratic society. It is the only all-girls after-school program in Guatemala. Volunteers can help with the photo workshop. 12 Av. 3-35, Zona 1. Tel: 502-5893-5646, E-mail: info@vocesdecambia.org, URL: www.vocesdecambio.org. Updated: Oct 02, 2009.

Quetzaltrekkers

Quetzaltrekkers is a trekking company that employs volunteer guides and supports La Escuela de La Calle, a school for street children. To volunteer as a guide you must make a minimum three-month commitment, and have trekking experience and first aid certification. A three-month commitment is also required to volunteer in the EDELAC school as an English or computer teacher, social worker, or health care worker. Casa Argentina 12 Diagonal 8-37, Zona 1. Tel: 502-7765-5895, E-mail: quetzaltrekkers@gmail.com, URL: www.quetzaltrekkers.com. Updated: Oct 02, 2009.

Tours

Kaqchikel Tours

Close to the Cultural Center los Chocoyos, Kaqchikel Tours is a Guatemalan family-run business. Small and friendly, founded in 2003, it offers hikes and tours around Xela and operates a small hostel. The guides speak Spanish and English. 7 Ca. 15-36, Zona 1. Tel: 502-5010-4465, URL: www.kaqchikeltours.com. Updated: Oct 12, 2009.

Altiplano's Tour Operator

Half a block from Parque Central, Altiplano's Tour Operator is the best one in town. With great service and experienced guides, they offer hikes, tours, shuttles and packages. They organize 1-2 day ecotours to the finca Nueva Alianza close to Retalhuleu. All the guides speak English fluently. 12 Av. 3-35, Zona 1. Tel: 502-7766-9614, E-mail: info@altiplanos.com.gt, URL: www.altiplanos.com.gt. Updated: Sep 18, 2009.

Diversity Tours

With ten years of experience, Diversity Tours offers hikes and treks around Xela, shuttles, plane tickets and packages to different destinations in Guatemala and Mexico. All the guides speak English. 15 Av. 3-86, Zona 1.Tel: 502-7765-8954, URL: www.diversitytours.com.gt. Updated: Sep 18, 2009.

Icaro Tour

Founded by the owner of the school Celas Maya, Icaro Tours offers hikes and tours around Xela. Every month they organize multi-day group tours at fixed dates to Tikal and Semuc Champey. All the guides speak fluent English. 15 Av. 6-75, next to Celas Maya School, Zona 1. Tel: 502-7765-8205, E-mail: info@icarotours.com, URL: www.icarotours.com. Updated: Sep 19, 2009.

Comunidad Nueva Alianza

The Comunidad Nueva Alianza is a fair trade, organic coffee and macadamia plantation owned and operated by a cooperative of 40 Guatemalan families. The cooperative is located in a temperate area, 1,000 meters (3,281 ft) above sea level, in the Guatemalan municipality of El Palmar and is about 45 minutes north of the coastal town of Retalhuleu. The community is nestled among a 121-hectare (300 ac) plantation of organic coffee and macadamia trees where large tracts of natural tropical forest have been preserved as well. A walk through the plantation will bring you to waterfalls with crystal clear water and breathtaking views of volcanoes Santa María (3,772 m/12,375 ft) and Santiaguito. The cooperative can organize tours during the weekend for Spanish students and for travelers who want to visit the community and learn more about coffee and macadamia nuts. 12 Av. 3-35, Zona 1. Tel: 502-5047-2238, E-mail: ecotours@café conciencia.org, URL: www.comunidadnuevaalianza.org. Updated: Mar 13, 2009.

Monte Verde Tours

Inside the Spanish School Madre Tierra, Monte Verde Tours offers hikes, tours and bike trips around Xela. They organize day trip to Santa Anita and Nueva Alianza coffee farms. 13 Av. 8-34, Zona 1. Tel: 502-7761-6105, E-mail: info@monteverdetours.com, URL: www.monte-verde-tours.com. Updated: Sep 19, 2009.

Lodging

From dorms to high-end rooms, Quetzaltenango hostels and hotels are varied in price to meet any traveler's needs. Prices are cheaper than in Antigua but a bit more expensive than smaller towns. There are some basics things to look for in these hotels. Quetzaltenango has some cold nights, so be sure the hotel has hot water and thick blankets. Most of the hotels are a maximum 10 minutes walk from Parque Central, so you can enjoy the nightlife. If you stay for a week or more, many hostels offer weekly or monthly discounts. Updated: Jun 29, 2010.

BUDGET

La Casa de las Amigas

(ROOMS: $3-4) The cheapest hostel in Xela will please people traveling on a very strict budget. Run by a cooperative of teachers from the Proyecto Linguistico language school across the street, it feels like home. There are four dorms and two private rooms, only one has a bathroom. There is a communal kitchen and a small patio. 5 Ca. 2-59, Zona 1. Tel: 502-7763-0014/0108, URL: www.snino.com. Updated: Aug 29, 2009.

Guesthouse El Puente

(ROOMS: $5-10) Neighbor of the Spanish school Celas Maya, this small budget hostel has five good-sized rooms and a large, well-equipped kitchen. The grassy garden area is a great place to laze on the grass in the sun, read, chat and study your Spanish. The one room with a private bathroom is spacious with closet space and the necessary furniture. The rooms without bathrooms are comfortable and quiet, the best having garden views. Discount for extended stays. 15 Av. 6-15, Zona 1. Tel: 502-7765-4342. Updated: Aug 29, 2009.

B&B Miguel de Cervantes

(ROOMS: $6) On 12 Avenida, only two blocks south of Parque Central, this Guatemalan-owned B&B is small and cozy. They have eight basic private rooms with shared bathrooms and a fully-equipped kitchen. Rates include a continental breakfast and Internet access. There is a discount per week and per month. Works by local painters decorate the hotel. The small restaurant is open Monday-Friday 8 a.m. to 5 p.m., and Saturday 8 a.m.-1 p.m. 12 Av. 8-31, Zona 1. Tel: 502-7765-5554/5688-4694, E-mail: xelacervantes@yahoo.com, URL: www.learn-2speakspanish.com. Updated: Aug 29, 2009.

Hostal Don Diego

(ROOMS: $6-9) Just three blocks from the Parque Central, this hostel has a number of cozy but dark dorms and privates with shared bathrooms. The tiled courtyard area is ideal for studying Spanish or socializing with yours fellow travelers. You will also find sofas and arm chairs for relaxing after a long day of exploring the local area. There is an on-site travel desk with all the information of what you can do around Xela. Daily rates include a small breakfast. Weekly and monthly rates include the access to the kitchen. There is WiFi access in the hostal. 6 Ca. 15-12, Zona 1. Tel: 502-5308-5106, E-mail: info@hostaldondiego-xela.com, URL: www.hostaldondiegoxela.com. Updated: Aug 29, 2009.

The Black Cat Hostel

(ROOMS: $7-30) Just one block from Parque Central, the Black Cat hostel is a fun place to meet other travelers. In addition to dorm accommodations, single, double and triple rooms are available. One private room and one dorm have their own bathroom. You can enjoy the sun in the patio and the upstairs corridor, or watch a movie in the comfortable TV room. It fills quickly during the weekend so make sure to arrive early or book in advance. A huge and delicious à la carte breakfast is included, don't miss it! Open every day from 8 a.m. to 10 p.m, the restaurant offers delicious international cuisine with huge portions. An on-site travel agency offers tours and shuttle. There is WiFi access. Payment by visa accepted with 6% extra tax. 13 Av. 3-33, Zona 1. Tel: 502-7761-2091, E-mail: xela@black-cathostels.net, URL: www.blackcathostels.net. Updated: Aug 29, 2009.

Casa Tete

(ROOMS: $8-14) Half a block from Parque Bolivar, this Casa Tete is a good place to meet fellow travelers. Rooms are basic but are equipped with cable TV and bathroom. There is a large guest kitchen, sunny patio, WiFi, parking and laundry service with one free load per week. If you're planning to park here for awhile, Casa Tete offers discounts on longer stays. Diagonal 2, 1-33, Zona 1 (Parque Bolivar). Tel: 502-7765-0217/5208-0999. Updated: Sep 09, 2009.

Hotel Andina

(ROOMS: $8-19) Only five minutes' walk from Parque Central, this is a good place for people traveling on a budget and looking for basic but clean accommodation. The hotel offers small rooms with a lack of furniture but with bathroom. They have a restaurant with local food open every day, and free parking. There is a cable TV on the sunny patio. 8 Av. 6-07, Zona 1. Tel: 502-7761-4012. Updated: Aug 29, 2009.

Los Chocoyos Centro Cultural, Casa Siguan

(ROOMS: $10) Two blocks from Parque Central, Casa Siguan is inside the Chocoyos Centro Cultural. They have six private rooms, tastefully decorated, with bathroom and cable TV. The large and sunny patio is the perfect place to relax, surf the net on your computer, or have a beer. Guests have full access to the community kitchen and free WiFi. Rates include tea, coffee and laundry service. There is a discount if you stay a week or a month. The bar serves drinks, sandwiches and pizza from 8 a.m. to 8 p.m. during the week and until 12 a.m. on Friday and Saturday. Special events are held during the weekend with a DJ so be ready for some noise. They also sell souvenirs in a small shop at the entrance. 7 Ca. 15-20, Zona 1. Tel: 502-7761-6497/5514-0399. Updated: Aug 29, 2009.

Casa Doña Mercedes

(ROOMS: $11-23) Run by a friendly Guatemalan family, Casa Doña Mercedes will please travelers looking for comfort and a quiet environment. The hotel is minutes away from Parque Central, as well as numerous restaurants and bars. The hotel's nine rooms are clean and spacious, with cable TV; some have private bathrooms. There is WiFi, laundry service, and a fully equipped community kitchen with a cute little patio. The sunny rooftop terrace is the perfect place to relax and enjoy the view of the city. 6 Ca. 13-42, Zona 1. Tel: 502-5687-3305. Updated: Oct 12, 2009.

Hostal 7 Orejas

(ROOMS: $12) A five-minute walk from the Parque El Calvario, this beautiful six-room hotel provides a charming alternative for travelers looking to go back in time. Each room has comfortable wooden beds, bathroom and cable TV. The common lounge and kitchen are decorated in a 1950s style. Rates include continental breakfast, WiFi, parking and free laundry for every three nights of your stay. There is a café as well, open everyday from 5 to 10 p.m. offering coffee, drinks and sandwiches. 2 Ca. 16-92, Zona 1. Tel: 502-7768-3218, E-mail: info@7orejas.com, URL: www.7orejas.com. Updated: Oct 05, 2009.

Ecohospedaje Ranchitos del Quetzal

(ROOMS: $13) From Guatemala City or Antigua, Ranchitos del Quetzal is about 30 minutes before Cobán and a few hundred meters from the entrance to the Biotopo del Quetzal. Quaint and rustic, Ranchitos offers simple rooms, which each have two or three beds, a balcony and private bath. A private trail on the premises, helpful staff, delicious food and its proximity to the Biotopo del Quetzal make this an excellent choice at an affordable price. Some visitors report more luck spotting the rare quetzal at Ranchitos than in the Biotopo. While V!VA was there, there were four quetzals spotted at Ranchitos in less than 24 hours and none in the Biotopo. Approximately 150 meters (492 ft) beyond the Biotopo del Quetzal entrance at the curve in the road. If traveling by bus from Guatemala City, take a Monja Blanca bus to Cobán and ask the driver to let you off at Ranchitos del Quetzal, right after the Biotopo del Quetzal. Updated: Aug 27, 2009.

Casa Real del Viajero

(ROOMS: $13-23) Casa Real del Viajero is a 10 minute walk from Parque Central, and has 17 private rooms for up to four guests each. It's a hotel for families or travelers looking for somewhere quiet. Ask for a room with an exterior window because the others have little light. Simply decorated, each room has a closet, a cable TV and a bathroom. Rates include free parking. Guests can use the kitchen or eat in the restaurant ($2.50 per meal). The large and sunny patio is a good place to read a book or surf the Internet on your computer. There is WiFi for an extra cost of $2.50 per day. 9 Ca. 9-17, Zona 1. Tel: 502-7761-4594, URL: www.hotelcasa-realdelviajero.com. Updated: Oct 12, 2009.

MID-RANGE

Hotel Los Olivos

(ROOMS: $22-60) Across the street from The Black Cat Hostel, Los Olivos offers large rooms with bathrooms and cable TV. The rooms accommodate up to five guests, are sparsely decorated and furnished, but clean. Open every day 7 a.m.-9 p.m., the restaurant serves Guatemalan breakfast ($1.50-5), lunch ($3-7) and dinner ($3-7). Rates include parking. 13 Av. a 3-32, Zona 1. Tel: 502-7761-0215, URL: www.xelapages.com. Updated: Oct 12, 2009.

Villa de Don Andrés

(ROOMS: $28-77) Just minutes away from Parque Central, this small B&B is the perfect place for travelers looking for luxury accommodations at an affordable price. Its charm, elegance and comfort will make your stay enjoyable. There are four spacious rooms which can accommodate up to six guests each, with bathroom and cable TV. You can choose between the deluxe package, which includes breakfast and laundry, or the basic package, including only the room. The cozy lounge and dining room are perfect for sitting back and relaxing after a long day. There is WiFi, free parking and an Internet room with 30 free minutes per day. 13 Av. 6-16, Zona 1. Tel: 502-7761-2014. Updated: Oct 12, 2009.

Casa San Bartolomé

(ROOMS: $25-40) One block from Parque Bolivar, located in a colonial house, this charming B&B will please travelers looking for peace and quiet. San Bartolomé's six rooms are small but tastefully decorated with Maya fabrics, pieces of contemporary art and carved wood furniture. A visit to the terrace, filled with flowers and with a view of the surrounding mountains, is a must. Breakfast à la carte is included and can be taken outside your room on the cute little patio. All rooms have bathroom and cable TV, and can accommodate up to three guests each. Rates include WiFi and parking. There are also two apartments that can be rented monthly. 2 Av. 7-17, Zona 1. Tel: 502-7761-9511, URL: www.casasanbartolome.com. Updated: Oct 12, 2009.

Hotel Modelo

(ROOMS: $40-86) Only a block from the theater, Hotel Modelo has been around since 1912 and is set in a beautiful old colonial

WESTERN HIGHLANDS

house. The rooms are clean and large with colonial furniture. There is a nice flower court in the back for sunny days. Rates include breakfast à la carte, parking and WiFi. The restaurant is open for breakfast (7:15 a.m.-10 a.m.), lunch (12 p.m.-3 p.m.) and dinner (7-9 p.m.). There is a business center too. Payment by credit card accepted. 14 Av. A 2-31, Zona 1. Tel: 502- 7761-2529, URL: www.hotelmodelo1892.com. Updated: Oct 12, 2009.

Casa Mañen
(ROOMS: $49-100) Beautifully decorated, the B&B Casa Mañen will please honeymooning couples looking for a romantic and comfortable place to stay. The eight spacious rooms are decorated with local handicrafts, handmade wool blankets and rugs. All have hand-carved furniture, tiled floors, cable TVs and bathrooms with hot water. Three rooms have a fireplace for the chilly evenings. Ask for a room upstairs with balcony. The rooftop terrace has a beautiful panoramic view of Xela and the mountains. Rates include WiFi, parking and a huge breakfast served between 7 and 11 a.m. The restaurant is open between 11 a.m. and 9 p.m. and serves Guatemalan food for lunch and dinner. 9 Av. 4-11, Zona 1. Tel: 502-7765-0786, URL: www.comeseeit.com. Updated: Oct 12, 2009.

Restaurants
Quetzaltenango offers everything from the comedores with lunch at $1 to elegant restaurants with live music. Most of the restaurants are in Zona 1 but you can find some in Zona 3. If you like Indian, Italian, French or more local specialties you will find a restaurant for you. Prices vary between $1 to $30. There is also a large selection of coffee shops offering delicious coffee and hot chocolate and with live music one or two nights a week. Updated: Oct 12, 2009.

TRADITIONAL GUATEMALAN

Street Food in Parque Central
(ENTREES: $1) Food stalls can be found on the southeast corner of Parque Central along the market. You can try the papusas (corn tortillas filled with cheese, bean and/or pork skin), enchiladas (tostadas, covered with mixed vegetables, soy product or beets), elote (corn that comes in a variety of sizes and colors) or rellenos de plátano (plátanos that are sliced, filled with beans, and coated in cream). To drink, try the arroz con leche (rice with milk) or the atol de elote (a wheat and thick corn-based drink). Parque Central, Zona 1. Updated: Aug 29, 2009.

Econo Comidas
(ENTREES: $1.50-3) Two blocks from Parque Central, this small restaurant serves economical breakfast, lunch and dinner options. Better than fast-food places, you can eat a big burger or sandwich for only $2.50. Alternatively, more traditional food like eggs and frijoles (black beans) or chorizo (sausage) are available. Monday-Sunday 7 a.m.-9 p.m. 14 Av. 4-48, Zona 1, at the corner of 5 Ca. and 14 Av. Updated: Aug 29, 2009.

Café and Restaurant Utz'Cana'
(ENTREES: $2-3) Next to the supermarket Despensa Familiale, this restaurant serves typical Guatemalan food with a vegetarian option, hamburgers and sandwiches at a very cheap price. The lunch of the day costs only $2 including a drink and tortillas. Relax in a cozy atmosphere while listening to the local music and enjoying free WiFi. Monday-Saturday, 8 a.m.-8 p.m. 13 Av. 6-20, Zona 1. Updated: Aug 29, 2009.

Casa Ut'z Hua
(ENTREES: $2-3) Open since 1980 and run by a native family of Xela, they serve delicious authentic Guatemalan and Quetzalteco dishes for budget prices. While dishes such as el pepián (meat with a sauce made from pumpkin seeds, sesame, cinnamon, Castile pepper, cumin, cherry tomatoes and white bread crumbs), el quichom (pork with a spicy sauce made from tomatoes, garlic, pepper, seeds of the corn, Coban chili peppers and white bread crumbs) and el jocom (beef with sauce made of cherry tomatoes, Castile pepper, cumin, cilantro, spicy green chiles and white bread crumbs) are found in many parts of Guatemala, each has been adapted to local preferences. Open every day 7 a.m.-9 p.m. 12 Av. 3-05, Zona 1. Tel: 502-7768-3469. Updated: Aug 29, 2009.

MEXICAN

Tacos Doña Berta
With two locations close to Parque Central, Tacos Doña Berta is the place to go if you want to eat tacos. Try their famous beef, chicken or mixed tacos with vegetables. They have a special offer of three tacos for $1.50. As for drink, their natural fruit juices are delicious. Open every day noon-9 p.m. Corner of 10 Av. and 6 Ca., Zona 1 and 3 Ca. between 14 Av. and 14 Av., Zona 1. Updated: Aug 29, 2009.

WESTERN HIGHLANDS

INTERNATIONAL

Restaurante Balalaika

(ENTREES: $3-6) Small and with friendly staff, Balalaika serves lunch and dinner with a selection of burritos, nachos, sandwiches and hamburgers with vegetarian options too. Try one of their crepes for dessert, they are delicious. Well decorated and with local music, it makes you want to stay longer for another beer. Open Monday to Saturday 12 p.m.-12 a.m. and Sunday 8:30 a.m.-12 a.m. WiFi. 14 Av. A 3-26, Zona 1. Updated: Aug 29, 2009.

Casa Babylone

(ENTREES: $4-15) With the biggest menu in town, Casa Babylone has food for all tastes and budgets. They serve all types of cuisine, from local to Middle Eastern, and have the only sushi bar in town. If you're vegetarian, they have tofu, salads, soups and cheese. Try the falafel or hummus, they're delicious. There is WiFi, and payment by Visa is accepted. Open every day noon-11 p.m. Babylone is on the corner southwest of Pasaje Enrique. 5 Ca. 12-54, Zona 1. Tel: 502-7761-2320. Updated: Oct 12, 2009.

La Casa del Prado

(ENTREES: $5-15) La Casa del Prado is an old mansion on the hill with a beautiful view of Xela. It offers a variety of Chinese and international food for all budgets, and is a 20-minute walk from the Parque Central. To get there, you need to go east on 8 Calle until you get to the end of the street. Just look for the green house on the hill. Open Tuesday to Sunday 11:30 a.m.-10:00 p.m., it's a perfect place to come on a sunny day to enjoy the flower garden and the view. 8 Ca. 0-95, Zona 4. Tel: 502-7763-2292. Updated: Oct 02, 2009.

Parrillada Rincón Uruguayo

Opened in 2001 by Uruguayan Richard Raffo, Parrillada Rincón Uruguayo serves delicious, beefy national and South American dishes. Choose from an international wine list, then enjoy your meal while listening to folk music. The restaurant is located in Zona 3, close to the Alamo bus terminal. 14 Av. 7-10, Zona 3. Tel: 502-7767-4745, URL: info@parrilladarinconuruguayo.com. Updated: Oct 05, 2009.

CAFÉ/BAR

Blue Angel Video Café

(ENTREES: $2-6) In front of the Chocoyos Cultural Center, Blue Angel is very popular among Spanish students. This economical café offers excellent healthy vegetarian food and fruit juices. It's Xela's longest running video cinema. They show films in two rooms every night at 8 p.m. and it only costs $1.25. Or you can come anytime during the day to watch the film of your choice. Monday-Saturday 1 p.m.-10:30 p.m., Sunday 3 p.m.-10 p.m. 7 Ca. 15-79 Zona 1. Updated: Aug 29, 2009.

Coffee Company

(ENTREES: $2.5-4) On 14 Avenida A, this two-level coffee shop serves fair trade coffee and natural fruit juices. If you're hungry, you can try one of their crepes or sandwiches ($2.50-4). It's a quiet and comfortable place with free WiFi. Monday-Saturday 7 a.m.-8 p.m, Sunday 3 p.m.-8 p.m. 14 Av. A 3-16, Zona 1. Updated: Sep 20, 2009.

Café Baviera

(ENTREES: $3-4) On the southeast corner of Pasaje Enrique, this new coffee shop serves one of the best cappuccinos in town. On two levels, elegance meets modern cool. Head to the second floor for the comfortable couch or stay on the first floor to watch the activity in the Parque Central. Open Tuesday to Sunday 8 a.m.-8 p.m. (until 11 p.m. Thursday-Saturday), the café has WiFi and serves breakfast, sandwiches, burgers and pastries. Friday is Ladies Night and Saturday there is live music. 12 Av. 4-52, Zona 1. Updated: Oct 05, 2009.

Coffee Shop Time

(ENTREES: $4-5) At the southeast corner of Pasaje Enrique, this new coffee shop is a good place to come for an afternoon coffee. On 2 levels, elegance meets modern cool. Head to the second floor for the comfortable couch or stay on the first floor to watch the activity of the Parque Central. They serve one of the best cappuccinos in town. Open Tuesday to Sunday 8 a.m.-8 p.m. (until 11 p.m. on Thurs-Sat.), they serve breakfast, sandwiches, burgers and pastries. Friday is ladies night and Saturday is live music. 12 Av. 4-52, Zona 1. Updated: Sep 20, 2009.

A Cupa Café

(ENTREES: $4-6) Inside the Spanish school Eureka, just a block south of Parque Central, the Cupa Café's specialty is pizza. It also serves sandwiches. Try the pizza Napolitano or Capriccioso—crispy and delicious. Tuesday is Ladies' night, Wednesday there are Poker and Ping-Pong tournaments, and Thursday is Live Music night. Tuesday-Saturday 2 p.m.-11 p.m. 12 Av. 8-21, Zona 1. Tel: 502-7766-9836. Updated: Oct 02, 2009.

Restaurant and Bar Bamboo

(ENTREES: $5-10) This brand new restaurant is only a block south of the theater. Decorated with bamboo, it serves delicious vegetarian meals, soup and a large selection of sandwiches and hamburgers. Try the Coffee Bamboo (coffee with Baileys). Open Monday to Wednesday 11 a.m.-10 p.m., Thursday to Saturday 11 a.m.-1 a.m. and Sunday 3 p.m.-10 p.m. 2 Ca. 14A-32, between 14 Av. A and 15 Av., Zona 1. Tel: 502- 5565-3698, E-mail: wieland52@hotmail.com. Updated: Oct 02, 2009.

Café La Luna

This coffee shop specialty is hot chocolate–definitely the best in town. The halls are decorated with fascinating old photos and objects, and while the food is nothing special, go for some cake or a snack if you're really hungry. Open Monday to Friday 9:30 a.m.- 9 p.m. and Saturday 4- 9 p.m., Café La Luna is two blocks east of Parque Central. 8 Av. 4-11, Zona 1. Updated: Oct 05, 2009.

INDIAN

Sabor de la India

(ENTREES: $6-10) This Guatemalan-Indian owned restaurant serves authentic Indian cuisine. There is a good selection of vegetarian and non-vegetarian meals, which are served in large portions. For delicate stomachs, the food is not too spicy. Try the poori or the naan with peas, lentils or vegetables. Tuesday-Sunday 12 p.m.-10 p.m. Ca. 15 2-34, Zona 1. Tel: 502-7761-9957. Updated: Oct 02, 2009

ITALIAN

La Genovese

(ENTREES: $7-15) Two blocks south of the Municipal Theater, La Genovese is one of the best Italian restaurants in Xela, with reasonable prices. They serve dishes such as penne with black truffles and smoked salmon, and penne a la Gorbachov (with a creamy vodka sauce). They have a large selection of pastas and pizzas for all budgets. If you're still hungry, try the delicious tiramisu for dessert. To drink, choose one of their fine Italian wines. Open Monday-Friday 1 p.m.-10 p,m, Saturday and Sunday 1 p.m.-9 p.m. 14 Av. A 3-38, Zona 1 Tel: 502-4041-2366. Updated: Oct 02, 2009.

FRENCH

Royal Paris

(ENTREES: $5-20) The Royal Paris is a very popular authentic French restaurant, that is one block south of the theater. The food, bistro ambiance and café/theater spirit has seduced Guatemalan and foreign tourists alike. Dishes include crepes, baked camembert and onion soup as well as meat and fish, which you can enjoy accompanied by French wine. There is live music every Wednesday, Friday and Saturday night. Don't miss the salsa and rumba night with Sombrero Negro on Friday night at 8 p.m. Arrive early to ensure that you get a seat. The Royal Paris shows French films with Spanish subtitles every Tuesday night at 7 p.m. Daily noon-midnight 14 Av. A 3-06, Zona 1. Tel: 502-7761-1942, E-mail: royalparis@yahoo.com. Updated: Oct 02, 2009.

Nightlife

Xela's Zona Viva is growing bigger and better. Tourists frequent bars and restaurants around Parque Central, while the locals hit the streets surrounding the theater. By law, bars must close at 1 a.m., but most of them just shut their doors and let people party for another hour. Most bars have a theme every night, like Salsa Night, Ladies' Night, Game Night–or feature live music. Often there are special parties or benefits. To know what is going on, check the magazine Xelawho or the flyers around town. Updated: Oct 05, 2009.

Ojalá Patio y Cultura

Ojalá has a beautiful, comfy patio, and often organizes special events. Tuesday is Cinema Night, Wednesday is Trivia Night, Thursday there is live music, and Friday and Saturday there are DJs, concerts and party nights. Open Tuesday to Saturday 5 p.m.-1 a.m. 15 Av. A 3-33, Zona 1. Tel: 502-7763-0206. Updated: Oct 05, 2009.

La Rumba

La Rumba is very popular among travelers and locals alike. Close to the supermarket La Despensa, the bar is open Tuesday to Saturday 5 p.m.-1 a.m. and has a theme every night, from reggae to hip hop and 80s music. There are free salsa classes on Fridays at 7 p.m. and happy hour happens every day between 5 and 10 p.m (two drinks for $2). Entrance is free except for special events. 13 Av., Zona 1. Updated: Oct 05, 2009.

La Parranda

La Rumba's main competition, La Parranda is a favorite place to go on Wednesday for its free salsa classes. There is a class for beginners at 9 p.m. followed by an intermediate class at 10 p.m. Open Wednesday to Saturday 5 p.m.-1 a.m. There is a $2 entrance fee on Friday and Saturday nights. 14 Av. 4-41, Zona 1. Updated: Oct 05, 2009.

Salón Tecún

Attracting both travelers and locals, Salón Tecún claims to be the country's longest-running bar. Located in Pasaje Enrique, you can sit outside even when it's raining, Tecun is quiet during the day but busy at night when people come to have a drink after work. Daily 11 a.m.-1 a.m. Inside Pasaje Enrique.

Pool and Beer

A five-minute walk from Parque Central, Pool and Beer is one of the only places in town where you can play pool. Small and cozy, it offers Italian food and six varieties of microbrewed beer. Saturday is Karaoke Night and Sunday DJs spin from 8 p.m. until 12 a.m. Open Tuesday to Sunday 6 p.m.-1 a.m. 12 Av. 10-21, Zona 1. Tel: 502-7765-8916. Updated: Oct 05, 2009.

Bajo La Luna

Set in a cellar beneath Café La Luna, this small bar is the perfect place to enjoy good cheese and wine. Open Thursday to Saturday 8 p.m.-1 a.m. 8 Av. 4-11, Zona 1. Updated: Oct 05, 2009.

Carluccio's Pub

Three blocks from Parque Central, Carluccio's has a good selection of microbrewed beer and hard alcohol. The small, two-level pub plays a mix of Latin music, reggae, dance, funk and hip-hop. There's also a DJ on Friday nights. Open Wednesday to Saturday 6 p.m.-1 a.m. 14 Av. A 3-32, Zona 1. Updated: Oct 05, 2009.

El Cuartito

Just around the corner of Parque Central, this small, friendly café is a favorite among Guatemalans and travelers alike. It serves the best mojito in town as well as organic coffee; gourmet, herbal and chai tea; hot chocolate and more. Try a delicious homemade dessert or veggie snack. There is free WiFi, a nice patio for sunny days, and live music every night. Don't miss the Trova music group on Saturday, but arrive early because it fills quickly. Cuartito is just around the corner from Parque Central. Open every day (except Tuesday) 11 a.m.- 11 p.m. 13 Av, 7-09, Zona 1. Updated: Oct 05, 2009.

AROUND QUETZALTENANGO

LOS VAHOS

Situated about 3.5 kilometers (2.17 mi) from the Parque Centroamérica are the modest saunas and steam baths of Los Vahos. If you are interested in a hike out of Quetzaltenango, then this is great option. The journey from town can take two to three hours and is mostly uphill, but the views of the city behind you get better and better. The steam baths themselves are two very simple stone rooms but occasionally the vents are lined with eucalyptus leaves, creating a magnificent herbal scent. Another way of getting there is to take a bus in the direction of Almolonga and ask the driver to drop you off at the road to Los Vahos. From there it's a steep walk of about 2.3 kilometers (1.43 mi). Alternatively you can take a taxi from Quetzaltenango which usually costs around $25 for a round trip including waiting time. Updated: Aug 09, 2010.

ALMOLONGA

Almolonga is a small agricultural town located just five kilometers (3.11 mi) southeast of Quetzaltenango. This pleasant town produces lots of the region's fresh vegetables and holds a busy market on a Tuesdays, Thursdays and Saturdays. Thanks to its well irrigated location in the base of the valley, it cultivates some of the finest produce you'll lay your eyes on while in Guatemala. There isn't much else to see in the town and so it isn't a very popular place to stay in or stop for a meal. However, there are two churches, Iglesia de San Pedro's bright yellow and blue façade is one of the more unusual that you will see and the more frequented Iglesia Evangélica El Calvario sports a massive modern auditorium and outdoor speakers. The annual Festival de San Pedro y San Pablo is celebrated June 27-29. Updated: Aug 02, 2010.

LAS CUMBRES

Located half a kilometer (1,640 ft) south of Quetzaltenango is Las Cumbres; a small highland resort that serves as the perfect spot to relax and unwind while traveling around Guatemala's Western Highlands. The very comfortable accommodations are housed in quaint red-tiled cottages and there is an on-site restaurant that has a great reputation. Room prices range somewhere between $33-47 a night and the rustic rooms feature modern conveniences such as cable TV and a CD player. If you get tired of the steam baths, sauna or hot tub, you can always occupy yourself in the small gym, with a game of pool or on the squash court. Updated: Aug 02, 2010.

ZUNIL

This pretty market town is a typical example of a small, Guatemalan highland town. Situated in a lush valley and overlooked by a huge volcano, Zunil is ideal for those who want to experience an agricultural community steeped in indigenous culture. As you travel to Zunil from Quetzaltenango you are met with a picturesque scene of low red-tiled and rusted tin roofs surrounding a gleaming white colonial church, Iglesia Santa Catarina. The church itself is certainly worth a visit. The ornate façade, serpent-like columns and the intricate altar of silver are beautiful examples of the importance that churches have historically held in Guatemala. The town also has its own effigy to San Simón, or Maximón. Images of this non-Christian deity are highly regarded throughout Guatemala. Zunil's Maximón moves from house to house every year after the October 28th festival held in his honor. Unlike the Santiago Atitlán version, visitors to this Maximón can actually pour Quetzalteca down the effigy's throat. You will have to inquire with a local to find out where he is. Children from the village will take you to him for a small fee and you also pay the caretakers to see him, and a few cents per photograph.

Another worthwhile visit is to the Cooperativa Santa Ana. More than 500 local women work with the cooperative. At their base located just a short walk from the church, visitors can see them work, buy their elaborate textile wares and even take a weaving lesson. Public buses from Xela and Fuentes Georginas frequently pass by the village which is situated just 10 km (6.2 mi) from Quetzaltenango. Accommodation options are quite limited but there is a fantastic eco-lodge within easy reach of the town. Built on natural steam vents, the rooms feature their own fireplace, sauna and Jacuzzi. If it is some laid back relaxation that you are after, Zunil is certainly an option. Updated: Aug 02, 2010.

Getting To and Away

If you are heading to Zunil on an organized day trip the tour operator or guide will usually organize all transportation to and from the town. However, if you are visiting Zunil independently then it is also quite easy to get there. Apart from car rental or a taxi, camionetas and pickups frequently pass through Quetzaltenango on their way to Zunil. Generally one will pass every half an hour and the best place to catch it is on the corner of 10a Ca. and 8a Av., Zona 1. Updated: Aug 02, 2010.

FUENTES GEORGINAS

Situated high in the hills above Zunil is one of Guatemala's finest hot spring resorts, Fuentes Georginas. It makes a popular day trip for both locals and tourists from Quetzaltenango or Zunil. One of the country's more affordable resorts at about $2.75, the springs are more temperate than they used to be but the temperature is still quite hot near the pool's rocky source. Hurricanes and consequent landslides have damaged the pools and the general area in recent years. However, the pools have now been fully refurbished and are in good condition.

Thanks to its location at the base of dormant volcano Cerro Quemado, there are plenty of pleasant hiking trails for visitors to take. You can hire a guide for $10 at the restaurant and explore the tropical plants and surrounding scenery. Hikes can take anywhere between 3-5 hours one way, so consider this if you want to hike and enjoy the springs in the same day.

The accommodation at Fuentes Georginas is quite basic and not frequently used but there is a great on-site restaurant that serves local cuisine and tasty cocktails. There are also a few sheltered picnic areas where you can barbeque your own food, but you will have to bring fuel and your own supplies to use this facility. Updated: Aug 03, 2010.

Getting To and Away

Buses leaving from the Minerva bus terminal in Quetzaltenango for Zunil travel frequently and will drop you off about eight kilometers (5 mi) from Fuente Georginas. From there you can take a pickup the rest of the way to the springs. It is also possible to walk to Fuente Georginas and usually takes about two hours. Take the road to Cantel from Zunil's plaza and after some 60 meters turn right downhill and you will soon find a sign for the hot springs. Alternatively you can book a trip via a tour operator in Zunil which generally costs around $10 and they arrange entry and transport for you. Updated: Aug 03, 2010.

CANTEL

Cantel is a small industrial town located east of Quetzaltenango and Zunil. It became one of the more important industrial suburbs when it contributed significantly to Quetzaltenango's late 19th-century period of prosperity. The Fábrica de Hilados y Tejidos de Cantel, which still exists today, started out in 1883 and began to combine European technology with the already popular weaving tradition to create good-quality textiles.

However, nowadays the town is better known for the Copavic Glass Factory. All of the beautiful hand blown glassware produced at the factory is made from recycled materials and much of it is exported around the world. As a place to visit there isn't very much else to do but Cantel makes for a pleasant excursion out of the city. Updated: Aug 03, 2010.

EL PALMAR VIEJO

El Palmar Viejo is one of the more unusual tourist attractions to visit around Quetzaltenango. Back in the 1990s the infamous Hurricane Mitch caused havoc in this little village and forced the inhabitants to resettle in a new village, El Palmar Nuevo. Since then, many of the ruins have become overgrown but it still makes for an interesting walk around. Just passed the old village cemetery is a Maya altar and a deep ravine that cuts El Palmar Viejo in two, and runs directly over the church that used to serve the villagers of this small town not so long ago. The ravine can be crossed via some slightly unstable swing bridges. It is recommended that you take a guide with you rather than venture there alone as the area is quite remote. El Palmar Viejo is signposted off the road to Retalhuleu from Xela and is roughly four kilometers (2.5 mi) west from the main road. Updated: Aug 09, 2010.

SALCAJÁ

Of all the small towns in the area, Salcajá is a rather uneventful place to visit. However, if you are passing by on your way to Quetzaltenango there are a couple of things for which the town is known for. The first is the fact that it is home to Central America's first Christian Church. Iglesia de San Jacinto is a typical old colonial church situated just two blocks west from the main road. Dating back to 1524, it boasts a pretty carved façade, an ornate altar and several paintings from the colonial era.

The other things for which Salcajá is known for and are worth sampling are two fermented beverages. The first, caldo de frutas, is made from a combination of pears, apples, peaches and white cherries. The other popular drink, rompopo, is similar to eggnog and is made with egg whites, rum, sugar, crushed almonds, spices, vanilla and cinnamon. If you like them both enough to take with you, they can be bought in bottles from several of the local shops. Updated: Aug 02, 2010.

Getting To and Away

Access to Salcajá is via the Pan-American Highway, so if you are traveling there yourself it is very easy to get to by following the signs off the highway. Located just a short distance from Quetzaltenango itself, many of the transport options that leave the town in that direction make a stop in Salcajá. Of course, there is always the possibility of renting a car in Xela or if there are enough of you it can be viable to take a taxi. However, pickups are frequent so there is usually little need for added expense. Updated: Aug 02, 2010.

SAN ANDRÉS XECUL

If you head west off the Pan-American Highway at a crossroads between the turnoff for Salcajá and the Cuatro Caminos junction, you will find San Andrés Xecul. This small highland town of steep cobbled streets and adobe houses with tiled roofs is home to one of Guatemala's most photographed churches, Iglesia San Andrés. Its ornate and colorful façade features some 250 carved enameled characters on a canary yellow background. Angels, saints and cherubs can be seen alongside tropical fruits sprouting from vines that adorn its many columns. Extracts from the façade are replicated in the woven huipils that many of the indigenous local women wear. At first, the church can appear somewhat bizarre but it is certainly worth a look.

The town holds a decent market on a Thursday, which takes place in the plaza outside the church and spreads into nearby streets. It isn't a tourist-orientated market as in many other highland towns, but it's nice to walk around it for an hour and see how the locals trade. Besides a few marimba bands, there isn't much else to see in San Andrés Xecul. Visitors usually spend an hour or two on their way elsewhere or on an excursion out of Quetzaltenango. Updated: Aug 03, 2010.

Getting To and Away

Buses to San Andrés Xecul leave Minerva bus terminal in Quetzaltenango about every half hour. However, many people find it easier to take a bus from La Moría midway between Salcajá and the Cuatro Caminos junction and then take a pickup for the short remainder of the journey to the town. Of course, if you choose to visit the town through a tour operator in Xela, they will usually organize all transportation to and from the San Andrés. Updated: Aug 03, 2010.

TOTONICAPÁN

Situated northeast from the Cuatro Caminos Junction and through 30 kilometers (18.6 mi) of pine forests, lies the department capital of Totonicapán, known locally as Toto. This modest town is known for producing some of Guatemala's finest crafts, particularly textiles and wooden toys and carvings. A large market is held on a Saturday and is certainly worth a visit. For those who want to stay the night, there are a few accommodations and dining options in the town. Hospedaje San Miguel and Hotel Totonicapán are comfortable and La Hacienda serves decent regional dishes.

The town also celebrates several festivals throughout the year, including the Feria de San Miguel Arcángel from the 24th-30th of September and the Fiesta de las Danzas on the last Sunday of June. Updated: Aug 03, 2010.

SAN FRANCISCO EL ALTO

Located just north of the Cuatro Caminos junction, the highland town of San Francisco El Alto is home to one of Guatemala's largest markets. Unlike the more tourist orientated version in Chichicastenango, San Francisco's Friday market treats visitors to a truly authentic highland experience. You won't find a wide array of artisan textiles and souvenirs, but if it's the experience you are after then it is certainly worth a visit. There is also a large animal section at this market, where bleets, neighs and the clucking of hens are intermingled with loudspeaker auctions and advertisements for unusual remedies, such as shark oil.

Another worthwhile place to see in San Francisco El Alto is the town's baroque style church, Iglesia San Francisco de Asís. Its possibly dull façade belies an elegant interior with beautiful retablos and frescos on the arches and ceiling. By paying a small fee, visitors can climb up the church's spiral staircase and get an even better view of the large market and the town. While most venture to San Francisco for a day trip, there are a couple of accommodation options for those who want stay a little longer. The Hotel Vista Hermosa is quite comfortable for around $5-8 a night, as is the Hotel Galaxia for $7, with secure parking. However, when it comes to dining out there is even less choice. Restaurante y Café tería La Fuente, situated beside the butchers, serves a tasty hot chocolate and a fine sandwich. Updated: Aug 02, 2010.

Getting To and Away

As with most towns around Quetzaltenango, there are frequent pickups to San Francisco that can usually be taken every half hour to an hour. If you are with a group or book a tour through an operator then they will usually organize all the necessary transportation. There is of course the option of renting a car or taking a taxi but unless you are traveling in a group that option can work out to be a bit expensive by Guatemalan standards. Updated: Aug 02, 2010.

MOMOSTENANGO

Momostenango, which means "Fortified Place of Many Idols," is a small indigenous town located in the foothills of the Cuchumatanes mountains in the department of Totonicapán. A very old town, it is mentioned in the Popol Vuh by its old name, Chuvá Tzac, as well as in some other ancient texts. The town is mostly indigenous, and traditional Maya religions are still practiced in Momostenango, which still unofficially adheres to a 260-day calendar that dates back to before the arrival of the Europeans.

Most visitors to Momostenango are there to shop for the warm, heavy woolen goods (especially blankets) that are produced and sold there. The best day to visit is Sunday, when the market takes over the main squares of the town. There is also a hot springs outside of town. Tourist facilities such as hotels and restaurants are limited, but do exist. Buses leave regularly from Quetzaltenango and pass through San Francisco el Alto. Updated: Oct 16, 2007.

Getting To and Away

Buses for Momostenango, or 'Momo' as it is locally known, leave Quetzaltenango's Minerva bus station throughout the day. You can also catch buses to the town at the Cuatro Caminos junction and from San Francisco El Alto. Many visitors prefer to visit Momostenango as a day trip rather than staying there overnight. As with many towns around Quetzaltenango, tour operators offer day trips that include a guide and your transportation to and from Momostenango. Updated: Aug 25, 2010.

LAGUNA CHICABAL

Just a two hour walk from the village of San Martín Sacatepequez is beautiful Laguna Chicabal. The lake sits within a volcanic crater at an altitude of about 2,712 meters (8,900 ft) and is surrounded by a lush cloud forest. There is something tranquil about a visit to the lake and the cloudy mist that lies close to the water's surface only adds to its calm atmosphere. There usually aren't very many tourists there on the same day and often you might be the only visitor. As you approach the lake area you will come across the ranger's station where you pay roughly $2 for park entry. If you arrive by car, parking is an additional $1.30. There is some cabin accommodation close to the lake but you will need to bring your own sleeping bag if you want to stay, and there is no hot water in the shared bathroom.

People with their own camping gear often camp near the tourist center or down at the lagoon for another $1.30. There is a lookout point about 45 minutes uphill from the center but there is often too much cloud around the lake for a decent view. Once you get down to the shore the scenery is just as picturesque. Bathing in the lake is strictly forbidden at all times. Laguna Chicabal is considered sacred by the local community and many traditional ceremonies are held there. Usually, access to the lake is restricted when ceremonies are taking place, but if you do happen to stumble upon one on a visit it is important to respect the local culture.

Do not interrupt the ceremony and refrain from taking photographs of the people without their permission. The locals are generally extremely friendly so once you are considerate and don't impose you'll get a warm welcome. Updated: Aug 05, 2010.

Getting To and Away

Walking is one easy way of reaching the lake. The hike from the nearby village of San Martín Sacatepequez only takes two hours and isn't very difficult. You can of course drive

WESTERN HIGHLANDS

there yourself but there is a parking fee at the tourist center of $1.30. If you get dropped off the bus from or into town, then just follow the signed path from the side of the road. As always, guided tours booked in advance will organize all transportation to and from Lake Chicabal for you. Updated: Aug 05, 2010.

HUEHUETENANGO

Meaning "Place of the Ancients" in Nahuatl, the departmental capital of Huehuetenango, or 'Huehue' as it is known by many, is a relaxed and friendly town, serving as the access point for the Western Highlands. Despite this, it is only 1,901 meters (6,237 ft) above sea level and actually occupies the valley at the foot of the Cuchumatanes. From the steep winding road out north of Huehuetenango, toward Todos Santos, are some spectacular views from the Mirador looking out over the whole town.

With its relatively low altitude, Huehue is less chilly and less traditional than the altiplano towns rising above it, boasting average temperatures ranging from 16°C (61°F)-24°C (75°F). The town has an unhurried atmosphere and a friendly, open vibe and although there is not much here by way of tourist attractions it is nevertheless a pleasant place to spend a couple of days.

In the center of town is the main square with the town hall, the colonial church and other Neoclassical buildings around its edges. It also contains a 30 square meters (100 sq ft) relief map of the area. The market is to the east of town, three blocks from the square. Only four kilometers (2.5 mi) away are the ruins of Zacaleu, a Maya heritage site. Indeed the Mam have inhabited this land for centuries, and a trip up to the highland towns north of Huehuetenango will immediately demonstrate this.

Huehuetenango, with a population of 57,289, is located about six hours from Guatemala City, and 275 kilometers (170 mi) from the Mexican border at La Mesilla, making it the center of transport and commerce in the area. Many visitors never make it this far up into the Western Highlands, opting instead for day trips to Chichicastenango or some other spot by the lake. However, making the effort to get up here is rewarding. The craggy, mountainous landscapes and isolated villages harboring unchanged Maya traditions transport you to a very different Guatemala than the one you will find in Antigua or the Eastern Highlands.

If you are only in Guatemala on a short vacation, it might not be worth heading all the way up here. However, if you are on an extended trip, you could do a lot worse than to soak up some highland spirit on your way from or to Mexico. The route from the border skirts around the uplands but does not delve into the true highlands, so you'll need to jump off in Huehuetenango in order to get onward buses to places like San Mateo Ixtatán. Alternatively, you can stop off in the Western Highlands while traveling from Quezaltenango on your way east to Sacapulas or Nebaj via Aguacatán, and then even onto Cobán via Uspantán. Updated: Dec 01, 2009.

When to Go

Huehuetenango is situated in the valley below the Cuchumatanes mountain range, and it therefore enjoys mild, warm weather all year round. Local festivals with dancing, drinking and traditional offerings are celebrated in Huehuetenango July 12-17 and December 5-8. Market days are Thursdays and Sundays, with a variety of food, pottery, leather goods and textiles offered for sale. Huehue is also an alternative place to enroll in a summer language school when Antigua's schools are busy or full, as is often the case. Updated: Nov 30, 2009.

Getting To and Away

Most travelers get to Huehuetenango by bus. Huehue's bus terminal is out of town near the Carretera Interamericana, 2 kilometers southwest of the center. If you arrive into this terminal there are mini buses and tuk-tuks which will ferry you in to town. The terminal is messy, but well organized, with ticket offices for all the companies from which to buy your ticket before boarding.

From Huehuetenango you can take buses in all directions: Mesilla takes 1.5 hours; Quezaltenango takes three hours; Guatemala City takes six hours. To get from Huehue to Antigua, take a bus going to Guatemala City and change in Chimaltenango. When traveling to Atitlán and Chichicastenango change at Los Encuentros. To the north: Todos Santos takes two hours 30 minutes, Barillas takes six hours, Nentón takes three hours, Gracias a Diós takes four hours. You can also pick up buses to the villages in the north from Calle 1a. To go to Soloma or San Mateo Ixtatán take buses going to Barillas. To the east buses to Aguacatán take 40 minutes, from there, onwards connections are available. Updated: Nov 30, 2009.

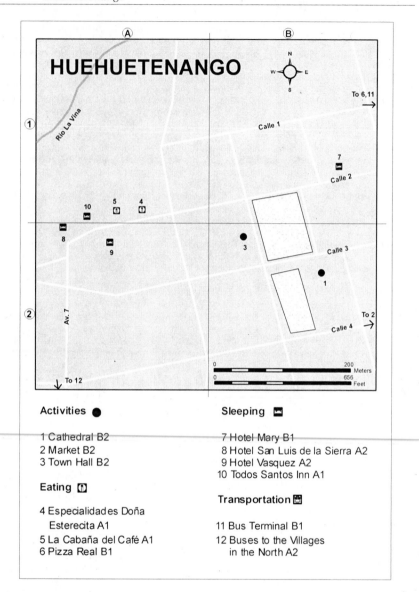

WESTERN HIGHLANDS

Activities ●

1 Cathedral B2
2 Market B2
3 Town Hall B2

Eating ⓘ

4 Especialidades Doña
   Esterecita A1
5 La Cabaña del Café A1
6 Pizza Real B1

Sleeping ⌂

7 Hotel Mary B1
8 Hotel San Luis de la Sierra A2
9 Hotel Vasquez A2
10 Todos Santos Inn A1

Transportation ▣

11 Bus Terminal B1
12 Buses to the Villages
   in the North A2

Getting Around

The bus terminal in Huehuetenango is about a mile outside the city center, close to the Pan-American Highway. The buses that go from the terminal to "El Centro" are frequent and cheap at $0.40. During the day the buses leave from the east side of the station, and after dark (before 11 p.m. and after 2 a.m.) they leave from the street outside. A taxi from the terminal to the town center will cost about $4, a pretty high price for only a mile. Downtown is very compact and easy to walk around. However, there are also plenty of taxis and tuk-tuks waiting to be hailed. Updated: Aug 24, 2010.

Safety

Huehuetenango is a small, relatively quiet town, and visitors will find it less intimidating than some larger Guatemalan cities.

However, tourists are occasionally the targets of petty crimes such as pickpocketing and robbery, so some precautions should be applied: keep valuables concealed, wear bags in front of you in crowded places such as markets or buses, and avoid walking alone after dark. Updated: Aug 24, 2010.

Services

TOURISM

Huehuetenango's Centro de Información Turística is located on 2a Calle, inside the Gobernación Departamental building. The staff speak English and offer a variety of printed information about the town and nearby attractions. Tel: 502-7694-9354. Updated: Aug 24, 2010.

MONEY

The two main banks in Huehuetenango are G&T Banco Continental (located on the north side of the plaza along 2a Ca.) and the Banco Industrial (6a Av., 1-26, Zona 1). The ATM at G&T accepts both Visa and MasterCard; the one at Banco Industrial is Visa/Plus. Both banks can cash traveler's checks and exchange dollars. Updated: Aug 24, 2010.

KEEPING IN TOUCH

The post office is located just east of the plaza (2a Ca. 3-54.) There are also several Internet cafés nearby that have payphones and international calling, including Telgua (next to the post office), Genesis Internet (2a Ca. 67) and Señor Xplorer (5a Ca. 5-97) Internet access costs around $0.60 per hour. Updated: Aug 24, 2010.

MEDICAL

La Hospital Nacional de Huehuetenango is located on Las Lagunas, Zona 10 (Tel: 502-764-1849). There is also a private hospital in town, Hospital Privado López, on Calle del Costado to the right of the Iglesia del Calvario. Updated: Aug 24, 2010.

Things to See and Do

Huehuetenango is more frequently visited as a pit stop on the way to or from Mexico. Thanks to its convenient location close to the Mexican border, there are plenty of lodging and dining options in the town. However, when it comes to things to do or see there isn't very much on offer. There are of course the ruins at nearby Zaculeu or the town's parque central but generally that's about it. Despite the lack of sightseeing or activities in the town, it does however serve as a

comfortable base for exploring nearby coffee plantations or the surrounding Sierra de los Cuchumatanes. Updated: Aug 09, 2010.

Parque Central

At the heart of Huehuetenango is the parque central. Carefully tended gardens surround an old colonial-era fountain, making this park one of the country's prettier central plazas. Visitors can enjoy more than just the plaza itself as there are several important buildings surrounding it that boast fine architecture. To the south is a beautiful old Neoclassical church, the Catedral Templo de la Inmaculada Concepción. To the west is the 19th century Municipalidad or City Hall and to the east is the Gobernación Departmental building that is home to a splendid 20th century clock tower. Updated: Aug 06, 2010.

Zaculeu

Zaculeu lies just four kilometers (2.45 mi) west of Huehuetenango's central plaza. In October 1525, the historical Mam ceremonial site fell to Spanish conquistador Gonzalo de Alvarado after a two-month siege. Dating as far back as the early classic period, these ancient ruins underwent some modest restoration during the 1940s. Although the typical colorful decoration of similar Mam temples wasn't replicated, graying plaster was used to try and bring them closer to their original form. Admission is around $4.50 and there is a small museum on-site displaying skulls and other artifacts found in a tomb under one of the temples. There are a few places across from the main entrance selling snacks and refreshments. You can hire a cab from town for about $8, including an hour's wait at the site, which is plenty of time, or hop on a cheap local bus from outside the school at the corner of 2a Ca. and 7a Av. Updated: Aug 09, 2010.

Adrenalia

Adrenalia Tours no longer has an office in Huehuetenango, but its long-time driver, Mario Martínez can be hired to take you around on half, full, and two day tours of both Huehuetenango and surrounding areas. Tours generally begin in the city center and branch out into nearby towns and natural sites. The price of the tour includes door-to-door pickup, entrance fees and guide. See the company's detailed website for more information. Tel: 502-7768-1558, URL: www.adrenalinatours.com. Updated: Aug 24, 2010.

WESTERN HIGHLANDS

Altiplano

Altiplano is a proudly "100% Guatemalan" operator that is based in Quetzaltenago, but offers a full-day tour in Huhuetenago. The tour begins in the city center and ends with a two-hour walking tour of Zaculeu, a small Maya archeological site and park a few minutes outside the town. Altiplano also offers longer "adventure" hiking and biking tours in beautiful nearby natural areas. Tel: 502-7766-9614, URL: www. altiplanos.com.gt. Updated: Aug 24, 2010.

Studying Spanish

La Academia de Español Xinabujal is Huehuetenango's only language school. It offers one-on-one Spanish courses at about $150 for 20 hours of study and can arrange homestays with families. 4a Av., 14-14, Zona 5. Tel: 502-762-7730, E-mail: academiaxinabul@ hotmail.com. Updated: Aug 24, 2010.

Lodging

Huehuetenango's accommodations range from dank and depressing to moderately charming. Even the nicer options are a little worn and ramshackle, but it is not difficult to find a safe and fairly comfortable room. Most of the hotels in the area range from low to mid-range in price, with very few high-end places. Hostels are difficult to come by as well, but budget travelers will find hotels that offer the same sort of rooms and costs. Almost all the hotels are conveniently located close to the bus terminal or the central plaza. Updated: Aug 24, 2010.

BUDGET

Hotel Central

(ROOMS: $4-8) Hotel Central is primely located in the central plaza. It is safe but plain, with large rooms a little on the dark and damp side. Double and single rooms are available, all bathrooms are shared. 5A Av. 1-33, Zona 1, Tel: 502-7764-1202. Updated: Aug 24, 2010.

Hotel Guatemex

(ROOMS: $10-20) Hotel Guatemex is located right in front of the bus terminal, so it is a good option for late arrivals to Huehuetenango. It is safe and clean, with cable TV in each room. Singles and doubles available, expect to pay more for private bath. Tel: 502-7769-0398. Updated: Aug 24, 2010.

Hotel La Sexta

(ROOMS: $14-$17) Hotel La Sexta is about a block from the central plaza. It is plain, but safe and clean, with cable TV in each room and

free storage for backpacks. Single, double, and triple rooms available; expect to pay more for a private bathroom. 6 Av. 4-29, Zona 1, Tel: 502-7764-1488. Updated: Aug 24, 2010.

Hotel Mary

(ROOMS: $15-16) Hotel Mary can be found just east of the main square, opposite the Post Office. It is a clean, safe place to stay, but without any fancy extras. The staff is efficient and accommodating and the interior is plain but bright. The beds are big and comfortable and there is hot water, non-electric showers and cable TV. Free, secure parking is also available. 2a Ca. 3-52 and 4a Av., Zona 1. Tel: 502-7764-1618. Updated: Sep 21, 2009.

Hotel Gobernador

Hotel Gobernador is about a five-minute walk from the central plaza in Huehuetenango. Its rooms are large and clean, if a little worn. Some are older and damper than others. Since all rooms are accessed through the lobby, they are quite safe. The staff is friendly and the steaming hot showers will be welcomed by many travelers. Double and single rooms are available, with private bathrooms at slightly higher prices. 4A Av. 1-45, Zona 1. Tel: 502-7796-0765. Updated: Aug 24, 2010.

MID-RANGE

Hotel Vasquez

(ROOMS: $19) Hotel Vasquez is as colorful on the inside as it is on the outside; the pink exterior goes with the turquoise walls and the 1970s-style patterned bed covers, all working to give the place a happy vibe. There are no double beds—only twins—but all are neat and clean and have private bathrooms, tiled floors and cable TV. The owner is easy-going and there is parking on-site. 2a Ca. 6-67. Tel: 502-7764-1338. Updated: Sep 21, 2009.

Hotel San Luis de la Sierra

(ROOMS: $25-40) The San Luis is a modern hotel with a smart dining room serving breakfast and dinner. It has a large secure parking lot around the back and well-furnished rooms. Some rooms have views toward the mountain and others can be a little small, so ask to see a few. All are carpeted , well-lit and comes with cable TV and private bathrooms with hot-water showers. The reception also has a fridge with cold drinks and beers, and is open late. 2a Ca, 7-00, Zona 1. Tel: 502-7764-9217, E-mail: hsanluis@ intelnet.net.gt. Updated: Sep 21, 2009.

Hotel Zaculeu
(ROOMS: $28-32) One of the oldest hotels in the area, Hotel Zaculeu is a short walk from both the central plaza and the bus station. It is well-kept by a friendly staff. The rooms in the newly remodeled section of the building are slightly more comfortable than the ones in the older section. Its lovely courtyard is a great place to sit and relax with a book. Single and double rooms are available, with cable TV and private bathrooms. 5A Av. 1-14, Zona 1, Tel: 502-7764-1086. Updated: Aug 24, 2010.

Restaurants
Almost all of Huehuetenango's restaurants are located close to the central plaza, so it is easy to pick and choose. Rarely will you find an entree priced at more than $8 or so; most of the meals cost far less. The fare is typically generously portioned and ranges from traditional Guatemalan to the more familiar burgers, pizzas, and pastas. There are also a few cafés that serve up exceptional local coffee and fresh-baked pastries. Many of the restaurants are open Monday-Sunday, so you won't have to worry about going hungry. Updated: Aug 24, 2010.

Café Bougambilias
(ENTREES: $1-4) This charming café is a great place to sample cheap, hearty local cuisine. The two upper floors offer diners a great view of the central plaza below, while the ground floor is crowded with cooks busily preparing heaping platefuls of meat, rice, salad, and tortillas. Monday-Sunday 6:45 a.m.-9:30 p.m. 5a Av., north of 4a Ca. Tel: 502-7764-0105. Updated: Aug 24, 2010.

Especialidades Doña Esterecita
(ENTREES: $2.50) The local history behind this restaurant justifies its rightful place on anyone's list of eateries in Huehuetenango (see the menu for the full story). Breakfasts and the menu of the day are a very good value (Q22/$2.50 for your choice of meat, rice, vegetables, tortillas, soup, drink and dessert) but the real draw are the baked goods: pies, cakes, tarts, crepes, croissants, empanadas and puff pastries. Most are displayed in a glass case so you just have a look and take your pick; if you can decide which one to have, that is. Monday-Saturday 8 a.m.-10 p.m. 2a Ca. 6-40, Zona 1. Tel: 502-7764-2212. Updated: Sep 18, 2009.

Hotel Casa Blanca
(ENTREES: $2.50-8) One of the nicest places in town, the restaurant at the Hotel Casa Blanca offers both inexpensive set breakfasts and lunches as well as elegant dinners. The seating is very scenic, both inside overlooking the hotel courtyard and outside in a lush garden. Breakfasts and lunches consist of large portions of tasty local fare, and dinner features a range of grilled meats, pastas and salads, including a decadent $6 filet migon. Monday 6 a.m.-10 p.m., Sunday 8 a.m.-9 p.m. 7a Av., 3-41. Tel: 502-7796-0777. Updated: Aug 24, 2010.

Mi Tierra Café
(ENTREES: $3-5) A popular spot with the locals, Mi Tierra serves up tasty, homemade burgers, nachos, and sandwiches. It is a great place to grab a cheap, filling lunch or dinner. There is also a wide array of delicious baked goods that are best paired with a cup of their fantastic coffee, always freshly brewed from locally grown beans. Monday-Saturday 7 a.m.-9 p.m., Sunday 2-9 p.m. 4a Ca. 6-46, Zone 1. Tel: 502-7764-1473. Updated: Aug 24, 2010.

Lekaf
(ENTREES: $5-8) Lekaf is typically packed with lively families. It serves up a wide variety of food, including pizza, pasta, and grilled meat. Their delicious fruit and yogurt smoothies are particularly worth sampling. There is live music on the weekends, and it is also a good place to grab a drink after dinner. Saturday-Sunday 10 a.m.-11 p.m. 6 Ca., 6-40. Tel: 502-7764-3202. Updated: Aug 24, 2010.

La Cabaña del Café
Looking like something transported straight from an Alpine ski resort, this cozy logwood cabin looks inviting, especially on a dark evening in Huehue. An entire page of the menu is dedicated to coffee: espresso, café mocha, cappuccino, Irish coffee and, the one not to miss, café tres leches. Sandwiches are the house specialty, but there are also breakfasts (the muffin breakfast is delicious), burgers, pastas, tortillas, salads and yummy crepes for dessert. The staff is very friendly and Saturday night there is often live music. Daily 8 a.m.-9p.m. everyday. 2a Ca. 6-50, Zona 1 Tel: 502-7764-8903. Updated: Sep 21, 2009.

AROUND HUEHUETENANGO
The road north from Huehuetenango toward Paquix passes right through the middle of Chiatla, 5 kilometers (3.1 mi) from Huehuetenango. It is a pretty village with a large plaza and two parks around

WESTERN HIGHLANDS

which are the town hall with its clock tower to the east and the church to the west. Everything you need is around the square: Banrural with Cajero 5B (7A Ca.), Internet café (5a Av. and 7a Ca.), Hospital Privado (6a Ca. Tel: 502-7764-5396, E-mail: cepromediccuchumatanes@hotmail.com), Casa de la Cultura (south side of church) and a Despensar Familiar supermarket (7a Ca.). For food there is Café Rosales (7a Ca.), Comedor Salmeri (6a Av. and 7a Ca.) and Comedor La Bendición (7a Ca.) with the Pinky Pool House next door. There is also a small café in the central park.

A peek inside the Iglesia Nuestra Señora de Candelaria church is well worth it. See the murals depicting the Spanish watching over the Maya working in the fields and their conversion to Catholicism, and the special glass-encased altar. Take a minute to listen to the prayers being said outloud in Mam, the local Mayan dialect.

Buses leave from 1a Calle and 1a Avenida in Huehuetenango about every 20 minutes. Updated: Sep 18, 2009.

CHIANTLA

The road north from Huehuetenango towards Paquix passes right through the middle of Chiatla, five kilometers (3.1 mi) from Huehue. It is a pretty village with a large plaza and two parks around which are the town hall with its clock tower to the east and the church to the west. Everything you need is around the square: Banrural with Cajero 5B (7A Ca.), Internet café (5a Av. and 7a Ca.), Hospital Privado (6a Ca. Tel: 502-7764-5396, E-mail: cepromediccuchumatanes@hotmailcom), Casa de la Cultura (south side of church) and a Despensar Familiar supermarket (7a Ca.). For food, there is Café Rosales (7a Ca.), Comedor Salmeri (6a Av. and 7a Ca.) and Comedor La Bendición (7a Ca.) with the Pinky Pool House next door. There is also a small café in the central park.

EL MIRADOR

If you are driving or with a private tour group make sure you stop off at El Mirador, just before Kilometer 280 north of Chiantla. Winding up the steep road cut into the cliffside, there are some unbeatable views back across the valley with Huehuetenango far away below and the Cuchumatanes mountain range across the

other side. On a clear day you can see the conical shape of the Volán Santa María, part of the chain of volcanoes to the south of Quetzaltenango. It is after this point that you notice the scenery beginning to change, often with cloud mist in the air and even snow on the peaks. Updated: Sep 18, 2009.

LAGUNA MAGDELENA

Known as the 'other Semuc Champey' (the high mineral content gives the water its stunning emerald green color), Laguna Magdelena is rarely visited by tourists due to its inaccessibility. Thirty-five kilometers (21 m) north of Huehuetenango, on the high road to Paquix and El Mirador, look for the sign saying 'Magdalena 18 km,' where the paved road ends and the 4X4 (or your feet) starts to work. There are no shops or hotels around here but you could ask for permission to camp. It is about 3,200 meters (10,500 ft) above sea level so remember to pack warm clothes if you do and bring enough food and water. The air is beautifully fresh up here and if you stay you'll be rewarded with stunning views of the night sky. Only attempt to hike to the Laguna if you're in good shape. Updated: May 04, 2010.

UNICORNIO AZUL

Continuing on the road north to Paquix and the village of Chancol, about 1 kilometer after El Mirador, a sign indicates the turn-off to the Unicornio Azul lodge and equestrian center. The Posada Rural is a tranquil place to stay, with spectacular views and great opportunities for horseback riding, whether pro or beginner. Packages are available covering accommodation, transportation, riding across the mountains, camping and food, local guides and park entrance fees.

To get there, you can take the bus from Huehuetenango, either from the bus terminal or by waiting on the road to Chiantla in the direction of La Cumbre or Todos Santos for about 50 minutes and ask to be dropped off by La Capellanía. From there it's about another 6 kilometers (3.7 mi), which you can walk, take a taxi or arrange beforehand for the center to pick you up (Q45/$5.60). Alternatively, the center can meet you in Huehuetenango and bring you all the way by car for a fee of $28 (Tel: 502-5209-5328, E-mail: unicornioguatemala@hotmail.com, URL: www.unicornioazul.com). Updated: Sep 18, 2009.

AGUACATÁN

Aguacatán doesn't appear to be much more than a town built around the through road which cuts east to west across the base of the Cuchumatanes from Sacapulas to Huehuetenango. It is, however, the source of the Río San Juan and also an important part of history. Forged by Dominican friars out of two opposing villages, even now the Chalchitek still live to the east and the Awakatek to the west of town. Gold and silver were mined here during colonial times but today the town survives on the growing and selling of vegetables, mainly garlic. The traditional dress is distinctive with the women wearing elaborate headdresses.

It is quite a lively little town especially in the late afternoon and early evening with plenty of people out in the square, walking around and eating snacks from the many food stalls. Market day is Sunday, although it often gets going Saturday afternoon. Running from east to west from the point where you enter the town on the main road to the plaza in the center you will find the Centro Comercial, Hotel Emperador, Comedor Frances, Restaurante Campo Alegre, Hotel y Restaurante Ray (Tel: 502-7766-0877), parqueo (opposite Ray's), Banrural and Farmacia Galicia. On the other side of the square there is a pizza take-out joint.

Buses leave Huehue every half-hour until about 7 p.m. The journey takes 40 minutes.

TODOS SANTOS CUCHUMATÁN

Todos Santos is a very closed indigenous community located high in the barren, rocky Cuchumatanes mountain range. The nearest city is Huehuetenango. The men and women still wear their traditional, brightly colored clothing and speak Mam, the local language that has not changed since before the arrival of the Spanish. They do not trust outsiders, but have learned to tolerate tourists. The people survive on subsistence farming, tourism and textiles: the men knit finely-made shoulder bags and the women make huipiles (a sort of colorful blouse). There only about 30,000 members of the community living in town and the surrounding areas. Every year, thousands of visitors descend upon the village in order to see the famous festival, which begins in late October but culminates on the first of November. The community is sort of going forward and backward at the same time in terms of traditional culture; although more and more people are abandoning traditions by wearing western clothes. There is a new era of religious tolerance in Guatemala and long-repressed local religions are making a comeback.

The village is at an elevation of about 2,500 meters (9,000 ft) and the mountain pass to get there from Huehuetenango goes higher than that. The bus trip takes almost two hours, even though Todos Santos is only about 45 kilometers (30 mi) away. It gets quite chilly in the evenings, so dress accordingly. Food and lodging are relatively cheap in Todos Santos. There are no deluxe hotels or fancy restaurants in town. Updated: May 03, 2010.

When to Go

Being 2,740 meters (8,990 ft) above sea level, Todos Santos can get pretty cold in winter, so it is advised to take some warm sweaters and also rain gear, especially if you want to go hiking. The weather can be damp and foggy all-year-round. The obvious time to visit is for the annual All Saints' Day festival on November 1. The raucous fiesta turns a peaceful, quiet place into an unrecognizable party town. The three-day celebrations include horse racing, music and dancing at the cemeteries and lots of drinking. Visiting on the weekend is a good choice, as you will experience the lively Saturday market as well as the usual relaxed pace of life here. Updated: May 12, 2010.

Getting To and Away

It is an interesting journey up to Todos Santos form Huehuetenango. The ride is bumpy and arduous, but don't let that put you off. The scenery is fantastic and the views over the mountains magnificent, especially if you travel in the morning, before the mist sets. Chicken buses run about 10 times a day from the main Huehuetenango bus station and will only set you back $1. The journey takes about two hours and 15 minutes. You can hire a shuttle bus for one to six people from Todos Santos direct to Huehuetenango for about $10 per person, to Huehuetenango and Panajachel for $30 per person, and to Quetzaltenango or La Mesilla for $18. There are also group mini buses available for rent, leaving at 7 a.m. everyday totheusual places, as well as to Cobán ($200 for 6/8 people), Tikal ($730), and even the Esquipulas border ($390) and Livingston ($430). For more information ask at the Internet café next to the Hotelito Todos Santos Inn. Updated: May 12, 2010.

Getting Around

For what there is to see in Todos Santos, you can walk, stroll and relax, soaking up the Mam culture. As with other towns in Guatemala, there is a one-way system governing the route through town; the road in from Huehuetenango passes along the main street to the plaza and church, then loops back around to the exit. Once you arrive, there is nowhere nearby to really go, unless you get your walking boots on and go hiking to other remote villages. Updated: May 17, 2010.

Safety

Todos Santos is a quiet mountain town, and is one of the safer places in Guatemala; it is good advice to remain respectful at all times, as it is anywhere when traveling. Avoid taking photos of people, as this may deeply offend or prompt the person you're pointing the camera at to ask for money. It is best to stay away from children. In April 2000 a Japanese tourist and the bus driver who tried to defend him were killed by an angry mob of locals when he tried to comfort a crying girl by picking her up. Days earlier the bodies of two children had been found with their organs missing (organ trafficking occurs in the area), leading to the radio station warning residents to stay away from strangers in town. Despite these words of warning, this was an isolated incident and Todos Santos is usually a very friendly town. Updated: May 17, 2010.

Services

Despite being small and seemingly disconnected, Todos Santos actually has most of what you might need, except for an ATM. The Banrural (Monday to Friday 8:30 a.m.-5 p.m., Saturday 7:30 a.m.-11 a.m.) is impossible to miss on the main street before the square. Important to bear in mind is that you are a long way from anywhere else if you run out of cash but at least the bank will change dollars. The Post Office is on the other side of the square to the bank to the left of the Palacio Municipal and by the church. There is a great Internet café next to Hotel Mam which charges $0.85 an hour, and also doubles as a tourist info office (see entry on hiking). Updated: May 17, 2010.

Things to See and Do

Todos Santos is a mellow place (except for November 1st) so do not come here looking to party. It is a great place to organize some hiking, brush up on your Spanish or

Mam, buy some original textile souvenirs or relax with a good book and get away from it all, literally. There is a great handicrafts shop run by local women's cooperative, housed in the Casa Familiar, which sells embroidered shirts, bags, belts, throws which all have the name attached of the person that made the item, ensuring that each worker gets their fare share of the profits. The Internet café up the hill by Hotelito Todos Santos Inn has information on weaving classes (10 hours a week for $25), as well as Spanish classes (25 hours a week for $60), and homestays. Updated: Feb 16, 2010.

Museo Balam

This family run museum showcases a collection of typical local dresses, holiday and ceremonial outfits, shoes and masks, all lovingly passed down from generation to generation. This place doesn't see many tourists, so it's good to go in and give it some attention. It's open all day every day and you can contact Fortunato Pablo Mendoza for a personal guided tour. Tel: 502-5787-3598. Updated: May 17, 2010.

Maya Sauna

You can try a traditional Maya sauna, or *temazcal*, at the Academia de Español y Mam Hispanomaya or the Casa Familiar. These are small stone-built or adobe structures, called *a chuj*, which you crawl into and sweat out any impurities. Wooden fires with stones onto which water, sometimes with herbs, is poured provide the steam. Many families have their personal versions, good for keeping healthy they say during the particularly chilly months of December and January, so ask your host family if you're staying with one. Updated: May 17, 2010.

Cumanchúm/Tojcunenchén

Taking the track that climbs up behind the church will lead you to the ceremonial site of Tojcunenchén. There are only a few grassy mounds here but it is still used for traditional Maya rituals and you will no doubt find incense and evidence of sacrificed animals around. It is a pretty place offering fantastic views of the Chemel mountain peak (ruined only slightly by the radio mast on top). Remember to be respectful as this is not a tourist site. The citizens of greater Todos Santos are among the few who still keep to the Maya 260-day Tzolkin calendar. Updated: Feb 03, 2010.

Horse Races

The Spanish conquest swept across two continents and countless islands, leaving death, destruction and disease in its wake. By the time it was over, everything from Texas to Chile was under Spanish rule. Some native populations resisted longer than others, but they all were defeated eventually.

Located up high in the windswept, rocky Cuchumatanes mountain range, in a remote corner of northwestern Guatemala, the tiny village of Todos Santos was one of the ones that held out the longest. Even today, the townspeople believe that the Spanish were able to conquer them for only one reason: the Spanish had horses. Locals are still passionate about the subject, and every November first, they ride horses all day to prove that the Spanish no longer have that equestrian advantage and that they never would have defeated them in the first place without it.

Thousands of tourists descend upon this remote village every year, to see the famous festival. Travelers will usually arrive and late October and stay to watch the festival through the first or second of November. Despite the rise of tourism in the region, present day Todos Santos remains an extremely closed indigenous community, devoted to ancient traditions. The men and women still wear their traditional, brightly colored clothing and speak Mam, the local language that has not changed since before the arrival of the Spanish.

A big part of the festival is devoted to riding horses. Despite being called a "race," this portion of the festival really stretches the traditional sense of the word—there is no competition and no winner—just men riding back and forth on the same stretch of road all day. Most of them are drunk and have been for days. It's part of the ritual. Many fall from their horses and fatalities have been known to occur.

The races have religious significance, and if someone dies during the race it is considered an offering to the Maya spirit world, and the community will have good luck in the coming year. The members of the community save money all year in order to spend it on food and alcohol during the festival.

Another fascinating part of the festival is the "Dance of the Conquistadores" in which local men dress up as Spanish conquistadores, complete with hand-carved wooden masks depicting blond haired, blue eyed men. They dance in the central square in an elaborate, intricate ceremony, depicting the conquest. The Devil even makes an appearance, in a bright red suit and painted mask.

The outfits are elaborate and colorful. But you don't have to wait for November first to visit Todos Santos: it's fascinating on any day of the year, and if you're interested in traditional native culture, you may want to check it out quickly before the modern world makes it to this remote corner of Guatemala. As with the Spanish arrival centuries ago, the town is currently riding out a tumult of cultural currents.

Long ago, the people of Todos Santos exhibited bravery in the face of cultural adversity. They steadfastly preserved local traditions and managed to master the very object once used to by the Spanish to defeat them: the horse.

Today, this noble beast has become a symbol of their independence and freedom, high in the rocky Guatemalan mountains. The festival itself—with its flamboyant costumes and equestrian flair—places the town firmly in the saddle of tradition, riding into the future steadily grasping the reigns of cultural change. Updated: Nov 22, 2006.

WESTERN HIGHLANDS

WESTERN HIGHLANDS

HIKING IN AND AROUND

TODOS SANTOS

When you find yourself in Todos Santos, look for the Internet café by the Hotelito Todos Santos Inn. It serves as an informal tourist information point and from there you can organize guided hikes for about $15 per person, or less if you're in a group. The Swiss husband of the woman who runs Casa Familiar and the women's cooperative is also a keen guide, speaking French, German, English, Spanish and Mam. Alternatively, you can ask around, get some directions and go walking yourself.

La Torre

At 3,837 meters (12,589 ft) above sea level, this is the highest non-volcanic peak in Central America. A 90-minute hike through pine and cedar forest and past farm houses will take you to the lookout, where there is an unbeatable view stretching all the way from the mountains of Mexico down to Antigua and including Tacaná, Tolimán and the Volcán de Agua. Tuilam is the village at the end of a three-hour hike atop the mountain range, with views of the volcanoes surrounding Quetzaltenango, Panajachel and San Marcos Tuicoy is a village about five hours outside town. The trek takes in some amazing scenery. You can take a bus back and also add in a detour to Puerto del Cielo. Puerto del Cielo is located four hours from town, but your efforts will be rewarded at "heaven's gate." At 4,210 meters (13,812 ft) above sea level, you get an awesome view across to the mountains of Mexico. Piedra Cuache is reached by an easy three-hour walk, mostly on flat ground passing historical rock formations.

Las Cuevas

A pleasant two-hour walk leads to this group of caves, used for Maya rituals. Begin at La Macta, the tree growing out of a rock.

San Juan Atitán

This trek goes through an ancient cloud forest to a village over the other side of the hills from Todos Santos through a beautiful isolated valley, where traditional dress is purple and white. Thursday is a good day to go for the market, but otherwise the village is pretty quiet.

Tzunul Village

With birds singing and the water flowing, the walk to Tzumul is a relaxing three hours along the river. You can usually see people sitting out on their porches weaving.

Rosario Village

This is a great opportunity to see the Friday animal market. You'll see young boys herding their sheep to sell during the three-hour trek.

Las Letras

If you don't have much time, this is a good and quirky walk to do by yourself. On a hillside overlooking the town, its name is spelled out in rocks, sort of a Guatemalan version of the Hollywood sign. The views are nice too. Updated: May 12, 2010.

Lodging

Todos Santos, Guatemala; yet another town whose altitude outnumbers its population. However, the town is home to a vibrant market, weaving cooperatives and a thriving indigenous culture where men wear red and white striped pants. If you're looking to stay here, your options are limited, but cheap. One of the cheapest places you can stay only costs $2.50 a night, but you get what you pay for. Updated: Jul 19, 2010.

Hospedaje La Paz

(ROOMS: $2.50) Hospedaje La Paz is very much at the austere end of the accommodation spectrum. The beds are in very basic dorm-style rooms (though, except when it is unusually busy, you will not need to share) and all with shared bathrooms. There is hot-water but you'll need to bring your own blankets for the chilly nights as well as a pad-lock for your room. Being a family-run place it is child-friendly but has an 8:45 p.m. curfew. Check out is also early at 9 a.m. Updated: May 04, 2010.

Hotelito Todos Santos

(ROOMS: $5-15) Along the narrow alley up above the main street, just past the Hotel Mam, you'll find the inviting Hotelito Todos Santos. The single, double and triple rooms are comfortable and extra blankets are available upon request and the private bathrooms have hot water and towels. There is a cozy communal living room, as well as a dining room where breakfast is served (not included in the room price). The outside door is locked at 10:30 p.m. but there is a bell for late entries.

Up the hill from the main square toward Casa Familiar look for the sign to turn left. Updated: May 04, 2010.

Casa Familiar

(ROOMS: $5-25) Casa Familiar is much more than just a place to rest your head for the night, with a cooperative weaving

Photo by: Amigo Latino

center, a restaurant, a hotel and a private house for rent. Currently in the middle of renovations, the hotel part of the house will eventually have 12 rooms split between: budget rooms with shared bathrooms, and more commodious digs. All guests can use the communal fully-stocked kitchen. The owners also have a lovely traditional wooden house with single and double, dorm rooms to rent that is just a 10 minute-walk from the village center. There is use of the kitchen and pila and you can either stay with the family or rent the entire house. Tel: 502-5580-9579/7783-0656. Updated: Jul 16, 2010.

SAN PEDRO SOLOMA

San Pedro Soloma, about half way between Huehue and San Mateo Ixtatán, is a small village that will appeal to visitors looking for a glimpse into the local indigenous culture and access to some incredible hiking. The town, which dates back to pre-Columbian times, occupies a flat valley once a large lake known as El Valle del Ensueno.

Most the community's residents are engaged in farming maize, coffee and beans as well as raising cattle. Traditional textiles are woven and sold locally as well as exported to Mexico along with other produce, a trade which has halted the trend of locals moving to work in farms in the south.

Many people still wear typical dress. Men wear the white cotton capixay (knee-length pants and long tunic), with a belt round the waist and a beige palm-leaf hat. Only the town's mayor can wear a black overcoat. Women typically used to wear red huipiles but now often wear shorter blouses in various colors.

The town's fest day is celebrated July 24-30 in honor of Saint Peter. For more information on Soloma visit the town's website www.sanpedro-soloma.com where, among other information, you'll find a link to a site with poems about Soloma and also a Flickr page full of photos written and complied by the patriotic Zacarias brothers.

The people of the local Canjobal culture are very friendly and welcoming to foreign travelers. There are a number of hotels in town and being only three hours from Huehuetenango it is a good place to break your journey if you plan to continue up past San Mateo Ixtatán. There are a few places to eat as well as Internet café s and a Banrural with ATM. Buses leave hourly from Huehuetenango on the route north toward Barillas until around 5 p.m.

HIKING IN AND AROUND SAN PEDRO SOLOMA

Hiking in this remote corner of Guatemala is a great opportunity to take in the wild and intensely beautiful landscape of the Cuchumatanes mountains and the panoramic scenery. You can set out yourself to walk between the towns, but you should make sure you are prepared with warm clothes and good directions before you do. Or you can also take advantage of local knowledge and tour agencies' itineraries. Adrenaline Tours offers some great tours in this region with buses, food and accommodation taken care of so all you need to do is walk and take in the beauty of Guatemala's natural world. It offers a one-day tour from Huehuetenango leaving at 8 a.m. and visiting San Juan Ixcoy, San Pedro Soloma and Santa Eulalia. It goes to the Aldea Chuzcap lookout point, which has some awesome views of the surrounding mountains and the Bacau Mayan alter built above a hidden Mayan temple.

Here, local religious men perform shamanic rituals every Thursday. Nearby the Bacau is the Pajaj waterfall, an hour's walk from Soloma. While beautiful and worth visiting it is not as impressive as the Pepajaú waterfalls two hours south of Soloma. The route follows a mountain path crossing river bridges and at times is quite a difficult trek. See also Quetzal Trekers (URL: www.quetzaltrekkers.com) for more info on organized tours. Updated: May 11, 2010.

SAN MATEO IXTATÁN

The small village of San Mateo Ixtatán, at 2,540 meters (9,678 ft), is certainly worth your time if you are looking to visit a traditional community near Huehuetenango. Here most speak the Maya dialect Chuj, not Q'anjob'al as in Soloma, and the town has kept to its customs more fiercely than some of the other nearby villages. Here the majority stay home, employed in sustainable and commercial agriculture; raising cattle, sheep and goats or growing coffee and cardamom, beans, maize, wheat and potatoes. Many villagers also make and sell huipiles (long embroidered tunics often with lacy collars worn by women) and capixay (brown woolen poncho-style tops worn by men).

It gets pretty cold between November and January, with the warmest months being April and May. The town festival celebrating the Saint Matthew (San Mateo) is held September 19-20th. The town merits your attention having its fair share of points of interest.

From the town salt wells (from which the town's name if thought to derive; 'ixtat' meaning salt in Nahuatl) women boil water to make the famous sal negra (black salt), said to have curative powers as well as being delicious. There are a number of unrestored pre-Columbian ruin sites around the village, but the most impressive are Wajxaklajunh, which are thought to have an astrological significance. The Catholic church, with its obviously pagan images, is also very interesting.

Furthermore, The Ixtatán Foundation, which set up the first high school and now works to improve the illiteracy rate here, is open to visitors. From Huehuetenango the chicken bus takes five or six hours to San Mateo Ixtatán on its way to Barillas. The last afternoon bus sets off about 3 p.m.

There is a late evening bus but this is not advised. E-mail: info@ixtatan.org, URL: www.ixtatan.org. Updated: May 07, 2010.

BARILLAS

Barillas is a scruffy ladino frontier town with a population of around 14,000 and at 1,554 meters (5098 ft) above sea level it is also warmer. This ladino frontier town on the edge of the Ixcán wilderness doesn't offer very much in the way of tourist attractions, accommodations or restaurants. However, it does serve as a convenient pit stop for those heading east to Playa Grande or north to the picturesque Laguna Maxbal. Situated about 18 kilometers (11.2 mi) north of Barillas, this aquamarine lake is surrounded by lush forests and, although not the most popular, the area around it is a great adventure option.

As a traveler the only reason to visit Barillas is to pass through on your way between Alta Verapaces and the Highlands. That said, if you do decide to come this way and need to stay over there are a few hotels, such as the Hotel Quetzal near the square, and a few places to eat. Furthermore, it is still an interesting place to see, if only in contrast to nearby traditional Mam towns and will help to complete your picture of Guatemala.

There are around seven buses daily from Huehuetenango. The trip takes about six hours as the roads are in poor condition and the bus stops at every village on the way. To Playa Grandes unscheduled pickups make the five-six-hour journey. In the rainy season journeys take longer or are impossible. Updated: Aug 06, 2010.

NENTÓN

If you are traveling east of La Mesilla along the Pan-American Highway, you will see a turn off for the small town of Nentón. Like many towns off the highway, there isn't a lot to do here, but if you want to see something a bit more unusual than your typical tourist attraction it might be worth a look. Located 35 kilometers (21.7 mi) north of Nentón, El Cimarrón is a 300-meter-deep (385 ft) limestone sinkhole with a forest at its base that has only been explored in recent years. Other nearby places to see include Laguna Yolnabaj and the beautiful Río Azul. It can often be easier to take a guide with you around this area, than trying to figure it out yourself. Updated: Aug 06, 2010.

Getting To and Away

Turning north off the Carretera Interamericana before La Mesilla a rough road travels up the lime-stone plateau to Nentón and the northern border crossing with Mexico at Gracias a Diós.

In this area you will find a couple of natural attractions worth visiting if you have made it this far. La Cimarrón is a sink hole with a huge forest and lake at the bottom which has just recently been explored for the first time. You can get transport from La Trinidad to La Cimarrón. Furthermore, La Laguna Yolnabaj is a magnificent lake, which you can get to from Yalambajoch, and to visit Río Azul. You may ask at agencies in Quetzaltenango for organized trips to this remote area. Updated: Dec 28, 2009.

GRACIAS A DIÓS

Gracias a Diós is a pretty ordinary town offering very little in the way of accommodation and sightseeing. It isn't a popular place for tourists to stay but it is a relatively straightforward border crossing into neighboring Mexico. The friendly immigration authorities might even grant you a day pass to hop across the border to the nearby Lagunas de Montebello. These emerald lagoons are renowned for stunning scenery and the rich dense forests that surround them. Updated: Aug 06, 2010.

Getting To and Away

Turning north off the Pan-American Highway, before La Mesilla, a rough road travels up the lime-stone plateau to Nentón and the northern border crossing with Mexico at Gracias a Diós.

At La Trinidad, 35 kilometers (21.7 mi) farther north of Nentón and nine kilometers (6.9 mi) east of Gracias a Diós, a dirt track goes down to Yalambajoch and carries east onto San Mateo Ixtatán. Some pick-ups and 4X4 vehicles pass this way so you should be able to thumb a ride. There are also two early-morning daily buses from Yalambajoch to Huehue.

It is not advisable to cross the border at Gracias a Diós. Mostly Mexican and Guatemalan migrant workers use this gateway and it is not an area frequented by many western travelers. If you do wish to use this crossing get your exit stamp first in Huehuetenango. On the other side, you can get your entry stamp in the town of Carmixán and find some onward transport. Updated: Dec 28, 2009.

LA MESILLA

Chicken buses hurtle along the Pan-American Highway west from Huehuetenango and arrive in La Mesilla around 80 kilometers (50 mi) and two hours later. Despite the busy highway it is a pretty drive through mountain scenery, past highland villages such as La Democracia. There are a couple of hotels in La Mesilla, which are basic but acceptable, and there are plenty of food stalls and street vendors. There is no real reason to stay here, however, you make the crossing into Mexico in about an hour and 30 minutes if you arrive during the day.

From Huehuetenango, buses leave more or less every 30 minutes until 6 p.m., with the buses leaving the border for the return journey following the same pattern. There are also privately-run mini buses plying the same route.

The border on the Guatemala side can be quite hectic, so be prepared. There are no exit charges leaving Guatemala but have spare cash in case you need to pay any penalties for over-staying and to pay the $20 fee for a Mexican Tourist Visa. It is a good idea to arrive during banking hours; there is an ATM in La Mesilla but it not guaranteed to be fully-stocked. And you need some change to get yourself a ride between the two border-gates, as they are actually three kilometers (2 mi) apart. At all border crossings there are currency exchange guys ready to take your old cash out of your hands. They may appear sketchy but you can get a good deal if you know your exchange rates before you arrive.

At the border you must make sure you check-in and check-out of each country, to avoid having to trek between the checkpoints or problems exiting the country later on. If you have a car you'll need to cancel the permit on one side and get a new on one the other. Always check the paper work at customs there and then, if anything as been completed incorrectly it will be your headache later on. For more information on crossing the border in a vehicle see: www.drivetheamericas.com/wiki/Mexico-Border_Crossing.

On the Mexican side, the border town itself is called Ciudad Cuauhtémoc in the state of Chiapas, where there is one basic hotel. There are mini buses and shared taxis to the next major town, Comitán or it's a three and half hour bus ride to San Cristóbal de las Casas, which costs around $10. Updated: Jan 07, 2010.

!!!!!

WESTERN HIGHLANDS

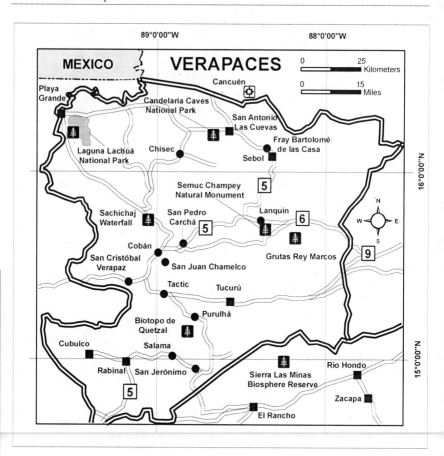

The Verapaces

The geographical heart of Guatemala known as the Verapaces—in fact, the two departments of Alta Verapaz to the north and Baja Verapaz to the south—is a beautifully green area. From the drier valleys around Salamá, the land rises into low mountains covered with misty cloud forest, then north of Cobán, its only real city, evens out into cardamom-planted hills, from which bulge curious limestone bumps. It is a land of hidden waterfalls, gently rushing rivers and mysterious caves, and it offers lots of outdoor adventures, from spelunking to underground river tubing and quetzal-spotting hikes.

If you like to know where your caffeine comes from, you can also visit one of the many coffee plantations, or even a tea plantation. Indeed the region is a very agricultural one; Alta Verapaz concentrates 80 percent of Guatemala's cardamom production, Guatemala being the number one exporter of the aromatic seeds, and Baja Verapaz exports vegetable seeds and ornamental ferns around the world. The area is also an indigenous stronghold, where many people in the rural areas speak Q'eqchi' before Spanish and still practice ancient Maya rites.

Although the region is home to one of Guatemala's major attractions, the spectacular pools of Semuc Champey, it is still not overly touristy. Enough visitors come that the infrastructure is there, from shuttles to hotels, but you are not swamped by tourists as in Flores or Antigua. In fact, as a foreigner wandering the colorful small-town markets, you will more likely attract shy giggles and friendly smiles. Updated: Dec 11, 2009.

Highlights

Las Conchas—For a very off-the-beaten-path alternative to Semuc Champey, take the trip to Las Conchas, where you can swim in the pools formed by a series of waterfalls pouring through tropical forest.

Parque Nacional Laguna Lachuá—In one of Guatemala's best-preserved parks, hike down to the quiet lake and take a swim in its warm waters, camp or stay at the rustic hostel, and wake up to the sounds of the jungle.

Cuevas de Candelaria—Walk through the intricate speleological formations and tube down the rivers of one of Central America's largest underground natural complexes. Updated: Dec 11, 2009.

History

Verapaz is the only Guatemalan region that was conquered by the cross and not by the sword, earning it the name of *verdadera paz*, which translates to "true peace" in English, later shortened.

The first inhabitants of the area were Pipil-speaking nomads from what is now Mexico, who cultivated cacao for trade and corn for subsistence. They were conquered by the Quiché, but rebelled and eventually resettled nearer to the Pacific, where they were subjugated by the Spanish conquest. The mainly Q'eqchi' population who lived in the central mountains area, on the other hand, fought the conquistadors so fiercely that the name of their territory, Tuzulutlán, became known as the "land of war."

By 1528, Pedro de Alvarado, the governor of Guatemala, had suffered enough defeats to try inviting Dominican friars to try to convert the natives. The first three friars to foray into Tuzulutlán—Luis de Cancer, Domingo Vico and Pedro de Angulo—followed local trade routes, accompanied by indigenous translators. Following the proposal of Fray Bartolomé de las Casas, they began peacefully evangelizing the area, carrying with them gifts as well as crosses and images. They succeeded in winning over the ruler of the area, the cacique known as Aj Pop Baz. He was baptized as Don Juan Matalbatz and encouraged the construction of churches.

The warrior-sounding name of Tezulutlán was changed to Verapaz in 1547, the original full moniker being "Vision de paz de la nueva Jerusalem de las Indias," proving a bit too much of a mouthful. Then in 1573, Padre de las Casas obtained from the Audencia of Mexico a capitulation by which the indigenous people, though Christianized and now under the authority of the King of Spain, could not be subjected to the encomienda system of forced labor that prevailed elsewhere in the colonies. Indeed, Verapaz grew pretty much as an independent territory, until it was annexed to Guatemala in 1608. The friars' religious presence left a strong mark on the area, as they founded villages and convents, planted crops and raised cattle over the two following centuries.

When General Francisco Morazán took power in 1829, he initiated a secularization process. In short, he appropriated the clergy's lands and squeezed the religious orders out of their dominant position. One of the liberal government that followed in the late 1870s, that of Justo Rufino Barrios, encouraged foreigners to settle in Guatemala—but as civilians this time.

Many Germans came to Alta Verapaz and took advantage of the favorable climate to create coffee plantations—and even one tea plantation—to the point that two thirds of the department's coffee production were in German hands by the late 1890s. It is also around that time, in 1877, that Verapaz was divided in two departments: the smaller Baja Verapaz to the south, with Salamá for capital; and the larger Alta Verapaz, with Cobán as its capital. But this European colony came to an end during the two world wars, as the Germans were deported from Guatemala, under pressure from the U.S.

Yet the coffee and cardamom plantations, the many colonial churches, and, of course, the names of such towns as Fray Bartolomé de las Casas remain a legacy of the Verapaces' distinct history. Updated: Dec 11, 2009.

VERAPACES

Bartolomé de Las Casas and The Verapaz Experiment

In north-central Guatemala, there are two departments named Alta and Baja Verapaz, or Upper and Lower Verapaz. The word Verapaz is a contraction of two Spanish words that means "true peace," and there is an interesting story behind it.

In 1537, the great Defender of the Indies, the Dominican friar Bartolomé de Las Casas, was horrified at the brutality of the Spanish conquest. At the time, the most common justification for the conquest was the somewhat illogical notion that in order to "save" the natives—that is, to bring them to Christianity—it was first necessary to pacify or subdue them with military force. Massacres, mass burnings and enslavement of entire populations were, according to this logic, in the best interests of the natives (at least in the long run).

Las Casas didn't buy it. He was determined to show that evangelization of the New World could take place peacefully. He proposed an experiment: If the Spanish crown would grant him a region, he would bring the natives into the fold peacefully. The crown agreed to the experiment (much to the consternation of the conquistadors) and gave Las Casas a region of north-central Guatemala that had been notoriously difficult to subdue: The local Q'eqchi' people were warlike, defiant and killed any Spaniards who attempted to enter their territory.

Las Casas hand picked a team of brave and patient friars, and together they slowly began to make peaceful contact with the Q'eqchi' people. They translated Bible verses into Q'eqchi' and sent gifts to the local rulers, one of whom agreed to let them come in. Within a few years, the region had been Christianized and Las Casas' experiment was a success.

The story ends badly, however. Once the region was pacified, Spanish fortune hunters, slave owners and conquistadors swarmed in, looking for treasures and slaves. The Q'eqchi' rose in bloody revolt, which was brutally quashed. By the late 1540s, the Verapaz project was in tatters, a victim of European greed.

The region still has the name, however, and local residents are proud of their unique place in colonial history. Today, one of the towns of Alta Verapaz is named Fray Bartolomé de Las Casas in honor of the brave friar who tried to put an end to the senseless violence of the conquest. Updated: Nov 23, 2009.

When to Go

Most of the sights in the Alta and Baja Verapaz, being outdoor, are best visited in the summer, which begins in November-December or January-February, depending on the area, and ends in May. But don't shy away from winter wetness, as showers tend to fall in late afternoon, leaving you plenty of time to enjoy the day. As in the rest of Guatemala, Semana Santa (Holy Week) is the height of excitement, with colorful processions and festivities; all towns also hold celebrations for their own patron saints. Updated: Dec 11, 2009.

Getting To and Away

Taxis are plentiful in Purulhá and will take you around town for $1.25 and to the nearby reserves for $1.50 to $2. Buses to Guatemala City can be caught on the highway roughly every hour (4 hr, $4.25). Buses and microbuses to Cobán (1.5 hr, $1.25) leave from near the market every 30 minutes, as do buses to Salamá (1.5 hr, $1.25), with service respectively at 6 a.m., 9 a.m. and 5 p.m. Updated: Dec 08, 2009.

Safety

While criminality is a serious problem in Guatemala as a whole, the Verapaces are far enough from Guatemala City and from the narcotraffic of the Caribbean and of the Mexican border to be considered relatively safe. Also, in this indigenous area, traditional forms of social control are still strong, meaning lower levels of delinquency. Still, the roads are not exempt from highway robberies, especially the Cobán-Petén section (which the police have been patrolling after a recent spate of incidents), so be careful if driving your own vehicle and don't travel by night. In the larger towns, take taxis at night, and always ask at your hotel where it is safe to walk on your own. Updated: Dec 11, 2009.

Things to See and Do
The Verapaces are a fantastic destination if you like to be outdoors, exploring the many natural parks that cover the emerald hills of the Sierra de las Minas and other low mountain ranges. To catch sight of the beautiful quetzal, Guatemala's flagship bird, hike in any one of the dozen reserves along the Corredor Biológico del Bosque Nuboso in the cloud forest of Baja Verapaz. As you continue north toward Cobán, more adventures await you in the form of ziplining over coffee plantations, and caves and underground rivers in Lanquín or Candelaria to explore. Spectacular turquoise waterfalls and quiet rivers with swimming holes are also yours to discover, unless you prefer an easy jungle hike to Laguna Lachuá. The indigenous culture is also very strong in the Verapaces, and a stroll through the market of any small town, like Purulhá or San Jerónimo, will bring you in direct contact with the ancient languages, colorful crafts and traditional dresses that make Guatemala so unique. Updated: Dec 11, 2009.

Tours
While most major attractions such as Semuc Champey or the Biotopo del Quetzal can easily be done independently, it does take some resourcefulness to figure out the local transport and lots of time to suffer through hours of bone-grinding bus rides squeezed with 25 people in a vehicle designed for 16. In short, if you like your comfort and can spare the cash, tours are a simpler way to see the Verapaces. Many reliable operators in Cobán (or the only one in Salamá), including hotels and hostels, offer a whole variety of packages that in the most popular sights, and can usually customize one-day or multiple-day tours. While community tourism is taking off around Chisec and the Cuevas de Candelaria, the few local organizations mostly offer simple guided tours that do not include meals or accommodation. Updated: Dec 11, 2009.

Lodging
While most decent-sized cities and towns offer a full range of accommodation options, from backpacker hostels to fancy hotels with pools and WiFi, as soon as you hit rural places such as Fray Bartolomé de las Casas, Raxruhá or Purulhá, the choice will

be significantly reduced. It does not mean that the hotels will not be comfortable; in fact you will almost always find either air conditioning or a fan, and often a TV, but they might serve nothing but beans and eggs for breakfast. Near and in parks such as Laguna Lachuá or the Corredor Biológico del Bosque Nuboso, you will find plenty of hotels, from rustic to high-end, more used to catering to foreign tourists and offering all-inclusive deals. Updated: Dec 11, 2009.

SALAMÁ
The capital of the department of Baja Verapaz, Salamá lies at the bottom of a pretty valley, between the green folds of the Sierra de las Minas and of the Sierra Chuacús, in a region of tropical dry forest. It is mostly an agricultural region, which benefits from mild temperatures, and produces cattle, fish, flowers, fruit and vegetable seeds for export.

The city of Salamá was founded by the Dominicans between 1550 and 1560, during their so-called "pacific conquest" of this central area of Guatemala. Its original name comes from the predominant indigenous language Quiché, "tzalam já," meaning board of water, or perhaps "tzalam á," meaning tranquil river. The Dominican friars built the church of San Mateo, patron saint of the town, and in the 17th century, they established a convent in Salamá to govern the smaller convents of the region, Rabinal, San Miguelito, Cubuilco and others. But after independence in 1829, General Morazán expelled the religious orders from the state of Guatemala and secularized their possessions. In 1877, the state of Guatemala divided the region of Verapaz into two departments, Alta and Baja Verapaz, and Salamá became capital of the latter. The population, though it maintains its strong Maya culture (predominantly Achi'), is still heavily Catholic, and religious celebrations are still important. Although it is a departmental head, Salamá is pretty much a small town in a rural region, and market days, Mondays and Fridays, are particularly busy days, as farmers from the entire municipality come to sell their goods.

There are few actual tourist attractions in town, but Salamá offers good infrastructure if you want to base yourself there to explore the smaller towns nearby or the biological reserves higher up in the cloud forest. Updated: Dec 07, 2009.

VERAPACES

When to Go

It is more pleasant to visit Salamá in the summertime (November-May). Of course, Semana Santa is also spectacular, as in the rest of Guatemala, with processions and sawdust carpets leading up to the Calvario. On May 3, a traditional dance is held for the Día de la Cruz. The patron saint of Salamá, San Mateo, is celebrated September 17-22, with horse events, processions ,and lots of food and drinking. 8a Av., east side of Parque Central, Zona 1.

Getting To and Away

Buses of the cooperative Rutas Verapaz go to Guatemala City (3 hr, $4.25) every hour 4 a.m.-2:30 p.m., and leave from the southern corner of Parque Central. Microbuses to Cobán (2 hr, $2.50) leave every 20 minutes from 6a Avenida, just off 5a Calle near the restaurant Carreta, as do microbuses to Rabinal and Cubulco. Buses to Purulhá (1.5 hr, $1.25) leave every hour and a half from 5a Calle beyond the market. Buses to San Jerónimo (30 min, $0.75) leave every half-hour from the hospital, honking their way down 5a Calle. Updated: Dec 07, 2009.

Getting Around

Most of the services you will need can be found within a tight central perimeter, perfectly manageable on foot. Otherwise, taxis will take you around for $1.20-3; you can find plenty by the western corner of Parque Central and near the Despensa Familiar on 5a Calle, as well as at inter-city bus stops. Updated: Dec 07, 2009.

Safety

It is safe to walk around most parts of Salamá until about 8 p.m.; as in any other part of Guatemala, just be careful with your personal possessions and don't flaunt expensive objects. If you visit during the fair in September, be cautious about drinking and risks of brawls. If you want to hike up to Cerro de la Cruz, go as a group and never alone. Updated: Dec 07, 2009.

Services

Since Salamá is a sizable town, there are plenty of financial and health services, as well as shops. There is no tourist information office here yet, but an INGUAT delegate has been named for Baja Verapaz. The woman at the information desk of the municipality is helpful if you have specific questions. Otherwise check out www.guatemala-tourisme.info, for a good overview of the town.

The police (Tel: 502-7940-0050) is one block north of the Parque Central at 7a Avenida 6-37, and there is a post office (Monday-Friday 8:30 a.m.-5:30 p.m., Saturday 9 a.m.-1 p.m.) across the street, at 7a Avenida 6-18.

There are plenty of banks, including Banrural on the Parque Central. It has a ATM that accepts the main international cards (Visa, Mastercard, Cirrus). Banco Agromercantil is half a block away on 6a Avenida and does money exchange; it has an ATM too. Western Union is everywhere in town.

There is a hospital a bit out of town (Tel: 502-7940-0125) as well as plenty of small clinics (most around 7a and 8a Av. and 4a Ca.), and lots of pharmacies, including Farmacia San Mateo 30 meters (98 ft) from the western corner of the Parque Central.

You can use all manners of communications services at the cybercafés Matrix (8 a.m.-8 p.m. 5a Ca. 6-26) and Garna (8 a.m.-8 p.m. 8a Av. 6-70,), where Internet costs $1 per hour and Skype is installed on most computers.

There is a supermarket, Despensa Familiar, halfway down 5a Calle, just before the market. Updated: Dec 07, 2009.

Things to See and Do

The city of Salamá may not be a major tourist draw, but there are enough attractions, churches and other historical remains to keep you busy for a day. Updated: Dec 07, 2009.

Salamá Market

Salamá's market bubbles with life every day, and is a good place to stroll, taking in the smells, the colors and textures of all manners of fresh fruit and vegetables, weighed on handheld scales, or perhaps to buy a *refresco* (soft drink)on the go. Bigger market days are Mondays and Fridays. Updated: Dec 08, 2009.

Mirador Cerro de la Cruz

If you follow the paths leading from behind the Calvario up the Cerro de la Cruz for 30-45 minutes, you will reach the mirador atop the mountain, at 1260 meters (4,134 ft). From there, you will be offered a 180-degree view of the valley of Salamá. There is a small chapel and cross there, and on May 3, celebrations of the Día de la Cruz, with folkloric dances and marimba music, take place there. If you are lucky, you might also watch (from a distance) a Maya Achi' rite performed with burning of candles, incense and sweets. Updated: Dec 07, 2009.

Temple of Minerva

This slightly unimpressive replica of the structure of a Greek temple was built in 1916 by liberal president Manuel Estrada Cabrera in honor of Minerva, the goddess of knowledge, in the hope of encouraging culture in Guatemala. The temple can make for a quick stop on your way to the Iglesia del Calvario. End of 6a Av., from south of Parque Central, Barrio del Calvario. Updated: Dec 08, 2009.

Villa Deportiva

Once the Alcatraz of Guatemala, the former maximum-security prison of Salamá now serves as an area for fútbol matches and other sports. There is not very much to see nowadays, but the impregnable walls and watchtowers are still intact, a chilling reminder of the recent violent history of the country. 6a Ca., between 2a Av. and 3a Av., up the hill from the market. Updated: Dec 08, 2009.

Iglesia del Calvario

The Neoclassical Calvario church, built in 1899 on the site of an ancient Maya cemetery, is reached by a climb up 120 steps. It houses a Señor de Esquipulas or Black Christ, which is celebrated on January 15. If you climb up the narrow ladder (with no safeguards) to the left of the entrance, you can crawl into the bell niche and catch a view of the city. End of 5a Av., Zona 4, up the hill. Updated: Dec 08, 2009.

Iglesia San Mateo

The 16th-century colonial church sits just on the Parque Central, and its pretty Baroque façade looks best at the end of the afternoon, as the rays of the setting sun hit it. Inside, there are a dozen massive Rococo-carved altarpieces, among the best preserved in the country. Also check out the statue of the friar holding a broom, on the right of the aisle, and the blue cupola painted with stars. The first bishop of the Verapaz, Fray Pedro de Angulo, was buried here in 1625. Updated: Dec 08, 2009.

Tours

Only one tour agency operates from Salamá: Eco Center Tours, better known as Quetzalito Tours, run by the friendly and chatty José Guzman out of his house on the far side of the bridge. He offers packages around all the Verapaces, from half-day tours to Rabinal and San Jerónimo to full-day or multi-day tours to Semuc Champey, Lanquin and the biological reserves nearby. Prices depend on the package and on the size of the group, but start at $60 per day per group, and include transportation and guide. Mr. Guzman senior, Francisco, studied the quetzal for 30 years and is very knowledgeable about the lovely bird; he will also give you an impromptu marimba concert on the ancient instruments he keeps in his house, which he plans to turn into a Quetzal and Marimba Museum. 8a Av. 3-20, Zona 2. Tel: 502-7940-0459/4519-7111. E-mail: ecocentertours@gmail.com. Updated: Dec 09, 2009.

Lodging

Most accommodation options in Salamá offer more or less the same types of rooms at a similar price, except for the fancier Tza'Lama and Lily's Inn, both on the outskirts of town, which are inconvenient unless you have your own vehicle. Updated: Jul 19, 2010.

Hotel Rosa de Sharon

(ROOMS: $9) Tucked away in a quiet alley off the market street, the bright yellow Rosa de Sharon offers 15 double and triple rooms, which are spacious but somewhat spartan, and you can tell the sheets have gone through years of use. Each room comes with a small TV, a ceiling fan and private bathroom with hot-water showers. 5a Ca. 6-39, Zona 1. Tel: 502-5081-9031. Updated: Dec 07, 2009.

Posada Don Maco

(ROOMS: $9.75) Some of the 28 rooms have recently been redone, equipped with firm mattresses and fluffy towels, so try to choose one of the newer ones in the building on the far side of the courtyard. The rooms are equipped with cable TV and showers with hot water in the private bathrooms. If you are traveling with children, they will love the family of huge squirrels in the cage by the reception area. 3a Ca. 8-26, Zona 1. Tel: 502-7940-0083/1683. Updated: Dec 07, 2009.

Hotel San Ignacio

Rooms here are pretty small, with a private bathroom squeezed in. The ground floor ones open onto a dark indoor corridor, so make sure you get a brighter one that looks onto the terrace, a shaded area with plenty of plants. A traditional chapin breakfast can be served for $3, and guests can use the kitchen to save on meal expenses. 4a Ca. 7-09, Zona 1. Tel: 502-7940-0186. Updated: Dec 07, 2009.

Restaurants

While official restaurants are few and far between, dozens of cafeterias serve cheap grub (a basic dinner of eggs, beans, tortillas with coffee costs about $2) and bakeries at every corner

VERAPACES

send delicious aromas of bread and cake wafting down the streets. Updated: Dec 07, 2009.

Las Cabañas

While this little hole-in-the-wall cafeteria may not look too promising from its bright orange façade, it is an excellent place to sit down for a cheap, delicious lunch. For the lunch of the day, you can chose from three or four meat, poultry or sometimes shrimp options, with a side of rice, salad and tortillas plus juice for under $2. Daily until 4 p.m. North side of the Parque Central, 10a Av. 7-50, Zona 1. Updated: Dec 07, 2009.

Las Cascadas

(ENTREES: $7-15) This white-tablecloth restaurant is one of the better ones in town, and its patio filled with plants make it a pleasant one too. Its extensive menu features seafood ($12-15), pastas and all the usual poultry, beef and pork dishes. 10a Av. 4-98 (Ca. de los Naranjos), Zona 1. Tel: 502-7940-0819. Updated: Dec 07, 2009.

Café Deli Donas

(ENTREES: $2-3.60) This pleasant little café serves breakfasts of eggs, beans, bread or waffles ($2.50-3.60), sandwiches ($2 to $3), as well as the whole gamut of coffees, cappuccinos and other drinks. And, of course, there is a huge selection of cakes, including tiramisu, to choose from in a refrigerated display, which you can savor on the patio. 5a Ca. 6-61, Zona 1. Tel: 502-7940-1121. Updated: Dec 07, 2009.

AROUND SALAMÁ

From Salamá, you can easily visit the towns of Rabinal and San Jerónimo, as well as the municipal park Los Cerritos, just three kilometers (1.86 mi) out of town. It is a dry tropical forest, with various types of cacti, and contains a few small archeological ruins. Updated: Dec 07, 2009.

SAN JERÓNIMO

Only around 18,000 people live in San Jerónimo, an isolated valley town in the Verapaces region of Guatemala. The town used to be home to a booming business: Central America's first brown sugar mill, which you can still tour today. King Carlos V found the region perfectly suited for the production of sugar, and in 1549, demanded that a large mill and intricate roman-style aqueduct to supply it be built. Later, San Jerónimo also began producing cochineal dye, tobacco, wine, and moonshine—industries that came under fire from a new government in 1829.

Today, the remains of the 124 aqueduct archways that still dot the tiny town give San Jerónimo a unique feel unlike other places in the highlands of Guatemala. Although there isn't really much to do here besides look at the ruins or visit the town church, you may find yourself wanting to stay the night. On the outskirts of town, you will find Hotel Hacienda Real del Trapiche (Tel: 5027940-2542), which offers good beds, home-cooked meals, private baths and cable TV for $20 per night. Another option is the colonial-style Hotel Posada de los Frayles (Tel: 502-7723-5733), which has all the same amenities, plus a swimming pool and beautifully landscaped gardens for $28 per night. Both of these hotels have their own restaurants, which are some of the best options for food in San Jerónimo. Another option is to stay in nearby Salamá, a town many travelers prefer to use as a home base when exploring the smaller towns throughout this region. Updated: Aug 06, 2010.

Getting To and Away

San Jerónimo is located about 10 kilometers (6.2 mi) from Salamá, toward the La Cumbre Junction. Between 6 a.m. and 5:30 p.m., minibuses depart every half-hour from Salamá to San Jerónimo. If reaching San Jerónimo from Guatemala City, you must first take an hourly bus leaving from in front of Café Deli-Donas (15 Ca. 6-61) between 3 a.m. and 8 p.m. headed to Salamá, and then hop on the minibus for the rest of the route. Updated: Aug 06, 2010.

Things to See and Do

Museo Del Trapiche

Behind San Jerónimo's church is the Museo del Trapiche, located on the grounds of Central America's first brown sugar mill. King Charles V demanded the mill be built in 1549, and soon after, 1,000 workers were producing 90 tons of processed sugar each year here. Inaugurated in 1999, the Museo del Trapiche has a huge wheel—seven meters (23 ft) in diameter—on display. You can also see ruins from the aqueduct with 124 arches, which was built to bring water to the farm. Also available for viewing are archaeological relics, popular art and handicrafts. On site, there are BBQ grills where you can cook lunch. The museum is free to visitors. Monday-Friday 8 a.m.-4 p.m., Saturday-Sunday 10 a.m.-4 p.m. Tel: 502-5514-6959. Updated: Aug 06, 2010.

VERAPACES

Los Arcos

Just a few minutes walk from the town center you will find a series of 124 arches, once a Roman-style aqueduct system that powered the old sugar mill of San Jerónimo. Since the arches are hundreds of years old, today they lie in varying states of decay. To find them, follow the main road east (away from Salamá). Wander right and slightly downhill until you reach a sign reading "Barrio El Calvario." Look closely to the right and there they are. There is also another set or arches if you turn right at the second dirt alley on this road. Updated: Aug 06, 2010.

RABINAL

To the west of Salamá, along a scenic road, is the colonial town of Rabinal, famous for pottery and citrus harvest. Founded in 1537 by Fray Bartolomé de Las Casas, Rabinal adheres to many pre-Colombian traditions. Market day in Rabinal is Sunday, but the best time to visit is during the annual fiesta of San Pedro, at the end of January. Corpus Cristi is another festive time to stop by. Rabinal also has a colonial-era Baroque church and a small museum that is of interest, especially if you want to learn about the massacres that happened here during Guatemala's civil war. Updated: Aug 06, 2010.

CUBULCO

Continue climbing further west to a high mountain pass and then dip into another valley to find yourself in the town of Cubulco. The Achi' Mayas live here, and as in most small towns, the main attraction is the annual fiesta, which peaks each year on July 25. Stick around and you might be able to catch sight of the acrobatic *palo volador*, a tradition where dancers tie a rope around their legs and spin down a pole upside down until they reach the ground. Updated: Aug 06, 2010.

SIERRA DE LAS MINAS BIOSPHERE RESERVE

Sierra de las Minas is a magnificent Biosphere Reserve situated in eastern Guatemala, bordered by the valleys of the River Polochic to the north and Motagua River to the south. It was officially designated a biosphere reserve by UNESCO back in 1992, due to its varied land cover types, rare fauna, and valuable jadeite and mineral reserves. With a population of some 44,000, there is a significant amount of indigenous communities living in the reserve, including Q'eqchi' Maya and Pocomchí. There are also a lot of conservation workers, biological researchers and miners to be found in the Sierra de las Minas. It is from centuries of mineral resource exploration that the Sierra de las Minas got its name. Altitude can vary from anywhere between 150-3,000 meters (492-9,842 ft) above sea level. The region is extremely popular with nature lovers eager to encounter rare animal species and a tropical environment. There are a few nice hotels and lodges located around the reserve for visitors to stay in. They are generally very comfortable, but remember that some areas can get cold at night. A lot of accommodation options also serve food, and help organize hikes, birdwatching trips and other excursions around the reserve. Updated: Jul 29, 2010.

SAN RAFAEL CHILASCÓ

San Rafael Chilascó is a small agricultural community situated about 12 kilometers (7.5 mi) from Cobán. The people here have chosen to take charge of tourism in the area, focusing on ecotourism and education in their tours. The Chilascó Community Tourism Organization (Tel: 502-5301-8928/5776-1683) charges $2 for entry to the visitor center, from where you can rent horses, borrow rubber boots, hike to the nearby waterfall or hire a guide. Opinions differ on whether the Salto de Chilascó is Central America's highest waterfall at an impressive 130 meters (427 ft). Either way, the scenery is spectacular, and it is certainly worth a visit. In terms of accommodation, the tourism organization will try and accommodate you in its own basic lodge or with a local family for around $5 a night, and there are several comedores in the area where visitors can eat. Buses traveling between Salamá, Cobán and Guatemala City pass the Highway CA-14 turnoff, from where visitors can travel into Chilascó. Updated: Jul 29, 2010.

Getting To and Away

The roads leading into the north of the reserve are quite difficult, particularly in rainy weather, so this mode of access is generally avoided by most visitors. Roads to the west and south of the park are in much better shape, and vehicles usually have no issue reaching the part of the Sierra de las Minas this way. Along the road from Cobán to Senahú (CA-14), there are plenty of entrances, and entry to the south of the park is via the San Agustín Acasaguastlán road. However, in bad rain, these usually better entrances also get messy and difficult and are best attempted in a 4x4 vehicle. Updated: Jul 29, 2010.

VERAPACES

Things to See and Do

El Salto De Chilascó

El Salto de Chilascó attracts hundreds of visitors to San Rafael Chilascó every year. This spectacular waterfall towers at some 130 meters (427 ft), and is regarded by many as the highest waterfall in all of Central America. The local ecotourism association provides guides to the waterfall and will also rent out rubber boots and ponies for the hike. It charges $4.30 per person for the hike, and the guide will cost you an additional $4.50. From the tourism center to the waterfall, it's about five kilometers (3.12 mi), and the hike usually takes somewhere between two and three hours. The first two kilometers (1.24 mi) can be traveled by bicycle or vehicle, but after that, it's either on foot or by pony. Be sure to bring suitable clothing; sneakers are fine in summer, but for rainy weather, bring rain boots if you have them and a waterproof jacket. About 500 meters (1,640 ft) in, there is a much smaller waterfall called El Saltito, which is a nice spot if you want to get in the water and relax for a while. Updated: Jul 29, 2010.

BIOTOPO DEL QUETZAL !

In 1976, biologist Mario Dary Rivera decided to create the Biotopo del Quetzal in order to protect and study endangered plants and animals. At that time, he convinced the municipality of Salamá to donate part of its lands to his project. Nowadays, the Biotopo de Quetzal is one of the main natural reserves in Guatemala. This 1,044-hectare (2,580 ac) site, situated about an hour from Cobán, is an ideal spot to fully enjoy the cloud forest ecosystem.

The reserve is also the obvious place to go if you want to observe Guatemala's national bird, the quetzal. Even here, though, only lucky visitors will get a chance to catch a glimpse of the bird. For the best chance of seeing one, visit the reserve between March and June (when females lay their eggs), and wake up early. The Biotopo has two major trails, both very well-maintained: Sendero los Helechos, which is two kilometers (1.2 mi) long, and Sendero los Musgos, which is twice as long. Walking through the humid atmosphere of the reserve, you will be able to observe several varieties of air plants (epiphytes, mosses, ferns, orchids) and different species of animals, including spider monkeys. Both trails will lead you to waterfalls

and small pools where swimming is allowed. If you go deep into the forest, you may find Xiu Gua Li Che, a 450 year-old tree. Maps of the Biotopo are available for $0.75 at the Visitors Center (daily 7 a.m.-4 p.m), where both trails start. Admission to the reserve is $2.50.

If you plan to camp in the reserve, stop by the Visitors Center to get information: Camping is not always allowed. The camping site also offers a BBQ area, and a shop selling snacks and drinks. Several accommodation options exist besides camping in the reserve. Several lodges are situated along the road just outside of the Biotopo. You can try the Hotel y Restaurante Ram Tzul. Situated in a private 150-hectares (370 ac) forest, it offers rooms in wooden cabins and private bathrooms (price per night starts at $40).

The Hotel y Comedor Ranchito del Quetzal, located 200 meters (656 ft) away from the reserve's main entrance offers a choice of simple rooms and family bungalows, starting at $36 a night. Updated: Jul 29, 2010.

Getting To and Away

The reserve is located on the highway to Cobán. If you are going to or from Cobán, it is definitely worth stopping at Biotopo del Quetzal for a few hours. By car, take Highway 14 until Kilometer 161 (east of Purulhá). Another option is to take a bus from Guatemala City. It will drop you right in front of the entrance of Biotopo de Quetzal. Updated: Jul 29, 2010.

PURULHÁ AND THE CORREDOR BIOLÓGICO DEL BOSQUE NUBOSO

The small, friendly village of Purulhá, set snugly amid the steep mountains of the Sierra de la Minas, is not really a tourist destination by itself. But it sits right in the middle of the cloud forest of the Corredor Biológico del Bosque Nuboso, a 28,000-hectare (69,190 ac) protected area, which contains 15 private reserves. These are definitely worth a visit for at least one day, to wander through coffee fincas and ancient forests toward hidden waterfalls, and, of course, to spot the quetzal, Guatemala's star feathered inhabitant. A good time to visit is February, March and October-December for better chances of quetzal-spotting, and during the fiesta patronal of Purulhá, from June 6 to 13, in honor of San Antonio de Padua.

If you decide to base yourself in the village, where you might be the only foreigner, you will be absorbing the quiet atmosphere of small-town Guatemala: Passersby will greet you with a polite "buenos días," children will giggle, youngsters will swagger in front of your camera, but mostly people will be happy to ask you lots of questions about yourself and your country. A good place for a stroll and colorful photo opportunities is the market, which runs almost the entire length of the village, toward the back when you come from the highway.

There are a few basic services, several comedores and one hotel. The Banrural bank, located between the city hall and the church, has a ATM that accepts international cards. There are a couple of cybercafés, including KpNet on the street leading from the highway to the market, and there is a health center in Barrio La Cruz as well as Dr. Berta Ramos' private clinic in the Barrio El Centro. The one and only hotel (not counting one truck-driver joint outside of town) is El Descanso de San Antonio in the Barrio El Centro (Tel: 502-5514-1640/7941-7426). The rooms may be a bit dark, but they are clean and have TVs and comfortable beds. A room with shared bathroom costs $6, and one with a private bathroom costs $9.60. Attached to the hotel is a friendly cafeteria, which serves a large variety of breakfasts of eggs, cereal, oatmeal or pancakes for $1.20-2.40, sandwiches and lunches for $2.40-3.60. There are little comedores and street food stalls scattered about, but the one real restaurant, which sits on the highway, is Montebello (Tel: 502-7941-7418, E-mail: ecomontebello@yahoo.com). It serves BBQ for four to six people ($40), all types of meat (churrascos, lomitos, hams and ribs of pork) for $6.60, as well as breakfasts.

The Montebello, which contains a private reserve with coffee finca, is also a good place to inquire about packages in the surrounding private reserves since the manager, Brenda Lemus, is also the president of the Asociación del Corredor Biológico del Bosque Nuboso (Tel: 502-4877-7431, E-mail: corredorbosquenuboso@gmail.com, URL: www.corredorbiologico.org), which counts the main reserves along the road and fosters sustainable ecotourism in the area. It offers two- and three-day packages ($277/$437), which include transport, food, lodging in the hotels of the reserves, and visits to waterfalls, Maya caves, orchid nurseries, weaving workshops and quetzal conservation parks. You can also go to one of the reserves independently, since nearly all of them offer lodging, restaurants and activities. They are all set along highway CA-14, and if you are traveling by bus, ask to be dropped off there. A few accommodations are: Country Delight (Km 166.5. Tel: 502-5709-1149; rooms $40 per person), Finca San Rafael (Km 164. Tel: 502-2365-7229, E-mail: fincasanrafael@yahoo.com; rooms $18 per person), Hacienda Río Escondido (Km 144. Tel: 502-5208-1407, E-mail: ecorioescondido@yahoo.com; cabins from $78), Posada Montaña del Quetzal (Km 156. Tel: 502-5976-7689, E-mail: hpquetzalcoban@hotmail.com; rooms from $20). The more backpacker-oriented one is Ranchitos del Quetzal (Km 160.5. Tel: 502-5368-6397, E-mail: ranchitosdelquetzal@yahoo.com; rooms from $7.25).

Another great source of information about ecotourism is the Fundación Defensores de la Naturaleza in Purulhá (2a Av. 2-17, Barrio El Carpintero. Cel: 502-5881-6077, E-mail: dmatanzas@defensores.org.gt, URL: www.defensores.org.gt). The foundation also welcomes volunteers who speak Spanish and are interested in projects preserving natural resources and educating local communities. Updated: Dec 08, 2009.

COBÁN

Sitting at more than 1,320 meters (4,331 ft) above sea level, the mountain air and coffee aroma of Alta Verapaz's capital city lure you into a world of misty forests and Maya culture. A small, laidback town, Cobán has many surprises in store for those who have a thirst for unexplored terrain and ancient civilizations.

Founded by friar Bartolomé de las Casas, the town had voluntarily converted to Christianity thanks to the friar's approach toward the natives. When a local chief, Juan Matalbatz, refused to kneel before the Spanish Emperor Carlos V, he was brought before the king, to whom he said, "A king should not bow before another king." Cobán was then given the prestigious title as "the Imperial City" in 1538. Since then, Cobán plays a significant role not only in the Verapaz region, but also in the country.

As a major gateway into the region's natural wonders, Cobán is moving forward in the ecotourism industry. From canopying to rafting, adventure-seekers will find endless opportunities to get off the tourist trail. Set in a treasure trove of untouched reserves, it is within proximity to remote Maya tribal villages and famous sites such as Lanquín and

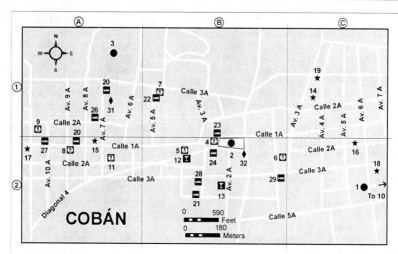

COBÁN

Activities ●

1 Museo El Príncipe Maya C2
2 Parque Central B2
3 Templo El Calvario A1

Eating 🍴

4 Café Fantasía B2
5 Café La Posada B2
6 Comedor Reynita B2
7 El Peñascal B1
8 Kam Mun A2
9 La Parrillada A1
10 Restaurante Pocomchi C2
11 X'kape Kob'an A2

Nightlife 🍸

12 Duende's Music and Bar B2
13 Bok'atas B2

Services ★

14 Farmacía Batres C1
15 Internet Pamáczimo A2
16 Lavandería Berty C2

17 Lavandería Monja Blanca A2
18 Muqb'ilb'e Spanish School C2
19 Policlínica Galeno C1

Sleeping 🛏️

20 Casa Cacao A1
21 Casa d'Acuña B2
22 Casa Luna B1
23 Hostal Casablanca B1
24 Hotel La Providencia B2
25 Hotel Los Faroles A1
26 Hotel Minerva A2
27 Hotel OxibPeck A2
28 Posada de Don Pardo B2
29 Posada de Doña Victoria B2

Tours ♦

30 Aventuras Turísticas (See 23)
31 INGUAT office A1
32 Guatemala Story B2

VERAPACES

Semuc Champey. With good infrastructure, Cobán serves as an excellent base to recharge and obtain information about the region. A few kilometers away is the Biotopo del Quetzal, one of the few places in the country to spot the rare bird. The turquoise waters of Laguna Lachuá and the mystifying Candelária caves are also within a few hours from Cobán.

With a population of 65,000 inhabitants, this town is relatively prosperous and optimistic. Generating most of its income from producing and exporting coffee and cardamom, Cobán owes its success to the favorable weather conditions. The early 19th century saw a major migration of German coffeeplanters in a bid to reap profits from the export industry. When World War II struck, the U.S. government coerced Guatemala into deporting the Germans back to their country. These days, German influence is still evident in Cobán and its surrounding villages.

Compared to the rest of Guatemala, this region puts more emphasis on the preservation of the Maya heritage. Many women in Cobán still dress in their distinct *huipils*, and most residents speak Q'eqchi' as their first language. Although most cobaneros can also speak Spanish, the Maya descendants from some surrounding villages are only fluent in their native dialect. Visit these rural communities to get a taste of the past and how it connects to the present.

These days, Cobán's wide choices of authentic restaurants and country-style hotels make visiting it a comfortable and insightful encounter. Dining in Casa D'Acuña and El Peñascal can be a unique gastronomic experience. Don't forget to sample the town's specialties such as *kak'ik* (a spicy turkey stew) and *tiú* to tease your taste buds. Updated: Sep 28, 2009.

When to Go
Set amid the cloud forests, Cobán is blessed with a cool, temperate climate. A misty drizzle, known among the locals as *chipi chipi*, occurs almost year round and drenches the city in gloominess. Thanks to the annual rainfall of 3.5 meters (11.5 ft), the hills are green and lush. The dry season (March-May) sees high temperatures, while the winter season (December-January) gets very cold and wet. With an average temperature of 19°C (66°F), it is generally warm during the day. Temperatures drop drastically in the evenings, so bring a jacket.

The most important festival in town, known as the Rabin Ajau folkloric festival, takes place in late July or early August every year. Maya beauty queens from all over the country descend on the town to compete in their traditional outfits. An annual national orchid show is held here every December, when the country's national flower, Monja Blanca, is in full bloom. Updated: Sep 28, 2009.

Getting To and Away
There are frequent departures between Guatemala City and Cobán on one of the country's best transport services, Transportes Monja Blanca (Tel: 502-7952-3571, URL: www.tmb.com.gt). Buses leave from

The Rabin Ajau Festival

Considered the largest and most important Maya festival, Rabin Ajau is celebrated on a grand scale in Cobán, with firecrackers, *cofradia* (brotherhood) processions and traditional dances. Meaning "the daughter of the king" in the Mayan Q'eqchi' language, the Rabin Ajau festival is the crowning of the country's Maya beauty queen. Held on the last Saturday of every July, this is a great opportunity to learn about Guatemala's Maya heritage and to become immersed in local celebrations that have been preserved for centuries. The contenders for the role of *Reina Indigena* (indigenous queen) are not only judged by their looks, but also on the languages they speak, their knowledge of traditional customs and ceremonial presentations.

Maya beauties from all over the country travel to Cobán for this once-in-a-lifetime opportunity. Parading in their traditional huipil and headdress, they flaunt their skills in weaving baskets and handicrafts. An annual event since 1947, the cobaneros are proud to call this feisty and spirited occasion their own. The event is usually scheduled to commence at 7:30 p.m., but typically does not start until 8:30 p.m. Attendees are entertained by marimba performances and thank-you speeches before the contestants are unveiled. Held in the Instituto Nacional de la Juventud, Alta Verapaz (INJAV), next to the stadium, seats are sold for $7.25, and a standing-room ticket costs $5.50. Try to squeeze into one of the side balconies for a better view. Book your tickets in advance at the Palacio de Gobernacion to avoid disappointment. Updated: Sep 29, 2009.

the terminal, at 2a Calle 3-77, Zona 4, every half-hour between 1:30 a.m. and 5:30 p.m. for the four-hour journey. Pullman standard and special buses are available.

Several terminals are scattered around town serving routes to different destinations, which can be rather confusing. Microbuses to Lanquín (3 hr) depart regularly between 6 a.m. and 3 p.m. from the terminal along 3a Calle, between 1a and 2a Avenida, Zona 4. From the terminal near Rossi stadium, you can get buses to Tactic (1 hr), Biotopo El Quetzal

VERAPACES

(1.5 hr) and Fray Bartolomé de las Casas (3 hr). Those heading into Petén can catch the bus to Flores via Sayaxché at 5:30 a.m. and 6:30 a.m. from the Terminal del Norte (near INJAV), Zona 4, and then change buses there. The five-hour journey costs $6.25 each way. To venture into Northern Verapaz, buses to Chisec (1.5 hr) and Laguna Lachuá (4 hr) depart every half hour across the street from INJAV. They cost $1.75 and $5, respectively. For full bus schedules departing from Cobán, check www.cobanav.net/bus.php.

Daily direct shuttle buses can be arranged through most tour operators, including Maya'ch Expeditions (1a Ca. 4-11, Zona 1. Tel: 502-5658-6778, URL: www.mayachexpeditions.com). Casa D'Acuña (4a Ca. 3-11, Zona 2. Tel: 502-7951-0482) provides direct shuttles to Tikal and Antigua for $18.50 and $15 each way. They might be considerably costlier than public transport, but is safer and faster. Updated: Oct 14, 2009.

Getting Around

The town of Cobán is small enough to get around by foot. To get out of town, the cheapest and most efficient local transport is the microbus. Most journeys on these mini-vans do not cost more than $1. Last buses usually leave from nearby villages at 6 p.m. to return to Cobán. Be prepared for a squeeze, as they usually try to fit in as many passengers as possible. There are plenty of yellow-topped cabs in town, with many concentrated around Parque Central and along 1a Avenida, Zona 1. A taxi ride around town costs $2.50-3.75. To book a cab in advance, call 502-5058-4577. For car rentals, there are a few agencies in town that have 4x4s for hire. Check out Tabirini (7a Av. 2-21. Tel: 502-7952-1504) or Inque Renta autos (3a Av. 1-18, Zona 4. Tel: 502-79521431). Updated: Sep 29, 2009.

Safety

The town center of Cobán is relatively safe, as not many crimes against tourists have been reported. That said, travelers should avoid walking alone at night or flashing jewelry and valuables. Streets are usually deserted after 10 p.m. The outskirts of town should be avoided, as they tend to be more prone to crime. Isolated mugging incidents have been reported in Parque Las Victorias, so check with the tourist office before visiting alone. Alternatively, contact the Tourist Police, DISETUR (Tel: 502-5551-3992), located behind the Palacio de Gobernacíon,

for assistance. When taking public transport, always keep an eye on your valuables. It is important to only take a registered taxi (with yellow sign). Updated: Sep 29, 2009.

Things to See and Do

Since Cobán serves as a jumping-off point for most visitors to the region, few actually stay and explore the town. Those who do, however, might find Cobán an intriguing and diverse place to visit. Exploring the city can be relaxing and simple. Visit the town's remarkable Maya museum, or climb the steps up to the town's most important church for a bird's-eye view. Test the zip lines and learn about roasting processes at coffee fincas. The town is relatively compact; allow two to three days to see all of it. From Cobán, you can also conveniently visit surrounding traditional Maya villages, nearby natural caves, swimming holes and waterfalls. From cultural tours to thrilling adventures, you just need to look deeper to find more. Updated: Sep 29, 2009.

Parque Central

This relatively small triangular park represents the heart of the city, where major activities take place. The park is flanked by the cathedral, the Palacio de Gobernacíon and the Municipalidad (Town Hall). Built on higher ground, all roads leading to the park are steeply inclined. Frequented by locals, it is a leisurely meeting point, especially on Sunday mornings. In the middle of the park stands a statue of the Father of Independence, Manuel Tot. An important figure in Guatemala, he fought for the country's liberty and was incarcerated by the government. Updated: Sep 29, 2009.

Templo El Calvario

Built atop a hill overlooking Cobán, the temple is 137 steps away from the city center. At the start of the long stairway, visitors are greeted by a shrine where locals pray and leave offerings. Many Q'eqchi' religious rituals are also held at altars of the temple. Dating back to 1810, its simple white façade has been restored to its original glory. Candlelight illuminates the interior of the church, where a glass crucifix enclosing a figure of Jesus Christ stands. During Holy Week, processions reach the top of the church. Get a panoramic view of the city and its surrounding greenery from the church's entrance. Daily 6 a.m.-6 p.m. Av. el Calvario, Zona 1. Updated: Sep 29, 2009.

Parque Las Victorias

Further north of Templo El Calvario is a densely forested nature reserve that acts as a retreat from the city. This 84-hectare (208 ac) national park is close to the city center, and has extensive walking trails, a campground ($2.50/person for camping) and BBQ facilities. You might find peace at the calm lagoon and lookout point. There are also shaded picnic areas and a playground for the young ones. The park is rather quiet, even on weekends. Always try to go in a group, as mugging incidents have been reported here. Daily 8 a.m.-4:30 p.m. 11 Av. and 3a Ca., Zona 1. Updated: Oct 15, 2009.

Museo El Príncipe Maya

For history and culture buffs, this private museum is a must. Despite its small scale, it showcases an impressive display of Mayan artifacts, ceramic ritual plates, weapons and jade jewelry. With explanations in English and Spanish, this museum places its collection within the context of Maya culture and traditions. The centerpiece of the museum is a burner depicting an ancient god reviving from the netherworld. Another highlight is a complete hieroglyphics panel from 656 AD, illustrating the royal history of Cancuén. No photo-taking is allowed in the museum. Daily 9 a.m.-6 p.m. 6a Av. 4-26, Zona 3. Updated: Oct 15, 2009.

Finca Santa Margarita ♪

Cobán is home to the best coffee in Guatemala. Set up by one of the region's pioneering German coffee planters, Erwin Paul Dieseldorff, this working coffee farm brings you behind the scenes of coffee-making. The informative 45-minute tour by the bilingual guide walks you through the history, technique and step-by-step process of producing world-class coffee. At the end of the tour, you get to taste a cup of freshly roasted coffee. Admission, including the guided tour, costs $3.75 per person. Monday-Saturday 8:30 a.m.-11 and 2-4 p.m. 3a Ca. 4-12, Zona 2. Tel: 502-7951-3067. Updated: Oct 15, 2009.

Vivero Verapaz

A visit to this orchid haven is interesting whether you are a plant-lover or not. The nursery is home to more than 400 of the 770 orchid species found in Guatemala. The best time to visit is between December and February when most of the flowers (including Guatemala's national flower, Monja Blanca) are in full bloom. Besides orchids, you can also observe other plants such as heliconia, bonsai and ceiba. The knowledgeable guide will show you the oldest plants in history. Situated one kilometer (0.62 mi) outside of town, it is a 40-minute walk or five-minute taxi ride ($2.50). Carretera Antigua de Entrada a Cobán. Daily 9 a.m.-noon and 2-4 p.m. Tel: 502-7952-1133. Updated: Oct 16, 2009.

Studying Spanish

Although there are not as many language-learning options in Cobán as in Antigua and Quezaltenango, there are several Spanish schools that offer cheaper prices and closer interaction with the locals. You can also find better options to learn Maya language here due to the greater presence of traditional tribes in the area.

Muqb'ilb'e Spanish School

Muqb'ilb'e Spanish School arranges one-to-one Spanish and Q'eqchi' classes along with a full-board homestay and two excursions a week. Cost is $145 for 20 hours of classes and one week of lodging. 6a Av. 5-39, Zona 3. Tel: 502-7951-2459, E-mail: contact@spanishschoolscoban.com, URL: http://spanishschoolscoban.com. Updated: Sep 29, 2009.

Active Spanish School

Active Spanish School is the most popular academy in town, thanks to Nirma Maez, a gregarious teacher. For $145 a week, including 20 hours of classes and homestay, you can also choose to be involved in volunteering opportunities provided by the school. 3a Ca. 6-12, Zona 1. Tel: 502-7941-7123, E-mail: contacto@activespanishschool.com. Updated: Sep 29, 2009.

Tours

With Cobán being the gateway to adventure spots in the region, tour operators are plentiful here and most offer similar tour packages at standard prices. Travel agencies are concentrated around Parque Central. Take your time to shop around and negotiate prices. Day trips to Semuc Champey and Grutas de Lanquín are most popular among travelers, with overnight stays as an option. For a different experience, some operators arrange hikes to the cloud forest, where you can interact and stay with a Q'eqchi' Maya family. Tours include all meals; vegetarian food is available. Operators also offer shuttle services to destinations across the country Updated: Sep 29, 2009.

Aventuras Turísticas ♪

This operator, with a wide range of tours, is not the cheapest in town, but it is reliable and established. It has a good reputation among travelers and is popular especially among adventure-seekers. Full-day rafting tours along Class III rapids of Río Cahabón cost $75, including safety instructions and equipment. Check out the half-day Coffee Adventure tours ($18) that bring you on walking trails through coffee plantations as well as birdwatching and canopying along the zip lines. It has two offices in town. 1a Ca. 3-25, Zona 1 and 3a. Ca. 2-38, Zona 3. Tel: 502-7951-4213/7952-1143, URL: www.aventurasturisticas.com. Updated: Sep 29, 2009.

Guatemala Story

This operator specializes in ethnotourism, bringing travelers to the Chicacnab village deep in the cloud forest, where native Q'eqchi people reside. An indigenous guide will explain the history, traditions and cultures of the Maya descendants. During the hike, you might even get an opportunity to see the quetzal (depending on season). These tours include an overnight homestay in the community and cost $38-50. Participants should understand minimal Spanish and be physically fit for the two-hour hike. 1a Ca. 1-36, Zona 1. Tel: 502-7951-4628/4403-6531, URL: www.guatemalastory.com. Updated: Sep 29, 2009.

Maya'ch Expeditions

Offering similar tours as the other agencies, this operator stands out for its excellent service and bilingual agents. It offers some of the lowest prices in town. If you book more than one tour, you will be entitled to one free night's stay in Semuc Champey. Trips to sites further afield (Laguna Lachuá and Candelaria) can also be arranged. The office is located on Parque Central. Check its website for detailed itineraries. 1a Ca. 4-11, Zona 1. Tel: 502-5658-6778/5166-3484, URL: www.mayachexpeditions.com.

Lodging

Cobán has a long imperial history, stretching back from the Maya to the Spanish, and then on to the German plantation owners. However, its current lodging options are a little less varied. Most places offer the same sort of cheap rooms for similar prices. Many Cobán hotels pride themselves on characteristic colonial architecture and lush gardens. Most have their own restaurants, though breakfast is usually not included in the room rate. The majority of the hotels are located around Parque Central. Several hostels organize tours and provide laundry services. Advanced booking is usually not necessary. Cobán is a great stepping-off point for many other places of interest, so if you're on a budget and looking for a home base, it's a good place to look. Updated: Jul 19, 2010.

BUDGET

Hotel Minerva

(ROOMS: $3-7) This cheapie is a decent choice for those on a strict budget. With prices for double rooms (with private bathroom) as low as $7, this hostel is the cheapest in the area. Just a 15-minute walk from the city center, it is close to eateries and Internet cafés. Rooms are small and dark, with not much ventilation. For $3 more, you can get a room with cable TV. You are free to use the *pila* in the backyard to wash your clothes by hand. Ca. 13-65, Zona 1. Tel: 502-5562-6377 .Updated: Oct 16, 2009.

Hostal La Paz

(ROOMS: $3.80-4.50) Basic but spotless, this hostel offers excellent value for the budget-conscious backpacker. Situated 1.5 blocks from the city center, it is just a hop away from most attractions and activities in town. Despite its old interior, the rooms are airy and bright, and the warm and friendly host will make you feel at home. There is no TV in the entire hostel, though there is a comfortable lounge to hang out in. The hostel only has double rooms, no dorm beds. 6a Av. 2-19, Zona 1. Tel: 502-7952-1358. Updated: Nov 11, 2009.

Hotel La Providencia

(ROOMS: $4.20-6.30) Right on the edge of Parque Central, this hostel is down to the bare basics with no hot water or TV. The double rooms here are among the cheapest in town. The shabby, crumbling interior and the dark corridor can be depressing. Its only saving grace is the view of the city from the rooms; ask for the rooms facing the back of the building. All rooms have private bathrooms. There is also parking available. Diagonal 4, 2-43, Zona 2. Updated: Nov 11, 2009.

Posada de Don Pedro

(ROOMS: $5-9.30) This hostel is not the best deal in town, but the family who runs it is welcoming and enjoys interacting with guests. Those who prefer a local experience to hanging out with other travelers will appreciate this hostel. The hostel's entrance is not conspicuous as you have to pass through a grocery store to enter. Laundry service here costs $0.75 per

VERAPACES

pound. The cheaper rooms do not have private bathrooms or TVs. 3a Ca. 3-12, Zona 2. Tel: 502-7951-0562/4509-3604. Updated: Nov 11, 2009.

Hostal Casablanca

(ROOMS: $5.60-$9.35) No other hostel has a better location than the Casablanca, which is situated right in the heart of the city. Despite its proximity to the city's hustle and bustle, the hostel is surprisingly tranquil and calm. Spotless and orderly, the hostel is kept in good shape. The welcoming outdoor lounge is a great spot to enjoy a beer and a view of the night sky. The hostel also organizes affordable tours to nearby coffee plantations and Semuc Champey. 1a Ca. 3-25, Zona 1. Tel: 502-5900-5064, URL: www.aventurasturisticas.com. Updated: Oct 16, 2009.

Casa D'Acuña

(ROOMS: $6.25) With inexpensive rooms and an attractive setting, Casa D'Acuña is highly recommended for its great value and reliable reputation. An exotic orchid garden welcomes you as you follow the alluring walkway into the hostel. The colonial architecture combined with the wooden furnishing creates a little Eden right in Cobán. Its popular restaurant, El Bistro, will win you over with its ambiance and modern cuisine. All rooms have bunk beds and shared bathrooms. Internet WiFi is available in the lounge. 4a Ca. 3-11, Zona 2. Tel: 502-7951-0482/0484. Updated: Oct 16, 2009.

Casa Luna

(ROOMS: $6.35-10) Popular with budget travelers seeking comfort and a homey environment, Casa Luna has rustic, clean rooms and a grassy patio lined with hammocks. Located two blocks away from Parque Central, it is a short climb away from restaurants and travel agencies. None of the rooms have private bathrooms, but cable TV and Internet WiFi are available. Hot water is only available at night. The hostel's helpful tour operator provides information and organizes tours to nearby areas. 5a Av. 2-28, Zona 1. Tel: 502-7951-3528, E-mail: casaluna@cobantravels.com, URL: www.cobantravels.com. Updated: Sep 29, 2009.

MID-RANGE

Hotel Rabin Ajau

(ROOMS: $9.30) Within a five-minute walk from Templo de Calvario, this hotel building is prominent and pleasant on the outside, though its entrance is rather obscure. Rooms are bright and airy, and equipped with private baths and cable TV. With only double and triple rooms, the hotel is a better value for couples and families. Its restaurant serves up big breakfasts, not included in the price of the room. 1a Ca. 5-37, Zona 1. Tel: 502-7951-4296. Updated: Oct 21, 2009.

Hostal de Doña Victoria

(ROOMS: $11.80-13.40) With some of the most tastefully ornamented rooms in town, this artsy hostel is a haven for the spiritual ones. This characteristic hostel is definitely worth your buck. Transformed from an old convent, the air smells of history. Its garden is paradise, where a well and crawling vines create a poetic spot to while the day away. Inside the rooms, satin draped across the ceiling and wrought-iron candle chandeliers add a romantic touch. The hotel has its own restaurant. WiFi is available in the lounge. 3a Ca. 2-38, Zona 3. Tel: 502-7951-4213/4034-8723, URL: www.hotelescoban.com/eng_hostal.htm. Updated: Oct 20, 2009.

Casa Cacao

(ROOMS: $12.20) From the outside, this hotel's beautiful colonial-style exterior covered in green vines seems to create a sanctuary for those seeking a peaceful environment. Situated at the start of the stairways to Templo de Calvario, it is also within comfortable walking distance from Parque Central. The room décor might not live up to the exterior, but their spaciousness and the facilities in the hotel make up for it. Ample parking space and WiFi are available. Rooms are charged at a standard price per person, whether you are in a single, double or triple room. Av. del Calvario 2-18, Zona 1. Tel: 502-7951-3822. Updated: Dec 10, 2009.

Hotel Oxibpeck

(ROOMS: $13.70) Entering this pet-friendly hotel, you are greeted by a dozen mischievous parrots. They definitely make your stay an interesting one, but unless you are a genuine bird-lover, you might not appreciate parrots chirping right outside your bedroom day and night. Rooms are standard, though you could find better rooms at these prices. All rooms come with a private bathroom and cable TV. WiFi is available in the lobby and lounge area. 1a Ca. 12-11, Zona 1 Tel: 502-7951-3224/7952-1039. Updated: Oct 21, 2009.

Hotel Los Faroles

(ROOMS: $12-22) This modern four-story hotel is gleaming with a fresh and contemporary look. Strikingly different from other hotels in town, it stands out with its clear-cut design and affordable prices. Its clean and well-kept rooms are moderately-sized, and are equipped with TVs and private bathrooms. WiFi is available in the lounge. There is only one suite in the hotel, with double the space and ample sunshine pouring in through the small veranda. 2a Ca. 3-61, Zona 1. Tel: 502-7951-1140/4136-3490. Updated: Oct 21, 2009.

HIGH-END

Hotel Villa Ancestral

(ROOMS: $16.60-23) Elegant and tastefully designed, this colonial hotel provides guests with a classy abode to rest in. With a medieval-style interior, the hotel's charming garden and restaurant turn its sophistication level up a notch. Rooms are small and pleasant, with a fan and cable TV. Ask for the rooms with patios. WiFi is available in the rooms. For $0.62 extra, a typical local breakfast is included. 6a Av. 3-11, Zona 1. Tel: 502-7951-1348/7952-1141, URL: www.hotelancestralcoban.com. Updated: Oct 21, 2009.

Casa Duranta ♪

(ROOMS: $19-27) Iron-cast antiques and high ceilings give an aristocratic air to this refined hotel. The hotel is built to cater to the needs of luxury travelers in search of style and comfort. All the rooms look out into the garden where vines weave around the walkways and hummingbirds roam freely. Sparkling clean rooms are equipped with a safety-deposit box and WiFi. An events room is also available for meetings. Book early as it fills up fast. 3a Ca. 4-46, Zona 3. Tel: 502-7951-4188/3596, E-mail: info@casaduranta.com, URL: www.casaduranta.com. Updated: Sep 29, 2009.

Restaurants

From inexpensive comedores to upscale restaurants, there are endless opportunities to indulge in local cuisine in Cobán. The most typical cobanero dish has to be the kak'ik (sometimes written as 'cack-Ik'). A rich turkey stew cooked with spices, it is always served hot and steamy, with rice and tamales on the side. Easily found in major restaurants, this is usually the most expensive dish on the menu. Unlike other major cities in Guatemala, there are not many international restaurants offered here. However, sandwiches and pastas are part of every restaurant's menu. Street food stalls cluster around the central park in the evenings. Updated: Sep 29, 2009.

TRADITIONAL GUATEMALAN

Comedor Reynita

(LUNCH: $2) The budget traveler hungry for a taste of local flavor will find eating here a genuine experience. Sit with the locals, have some home-cooked food and enjoy the *ranchero* (folklore) music. Set lunch includes meat, rice and a tortilla for $2. The menu is limited, though, with only two platters to choose from. The dishes are simple and small but scrumptious. Don't leave without trying *pollo encebollado* (chicken and onion stew). Monday-Saturday 11 a.m.-8 p.m. 1a Av. 2-50 Zona 1. Updated: Sep 29, 2009.

La Parrillada

This restaurant serves up juicy and meticulously prepared grilled meat at unbelievably economical prices. Entering the restaurant, a humble and upbeat atmosphere engulfs you. Many flock to this locals' favorite haunt for late-night supper. Perfect for meat lovers, this restaurant serves up a substantial *parrillada* (assortment of grilled meat and organs), which is enough for two. For $3, you can enjoy a complete meal of a sizable pork skewer or succulent beef steak with beer. A small portion of honey-glazed ribs comes complimentary with drinks. Tuesday-Saturday noon-11 p.m., Sunday-Monday 4:30-11 p.m. 11a Av. 2-11, Zona 1. Tel: 502-5629-9503. Updated: Sep 29, 2009.

Restaurante Pocomchi

Known as the "home of kak'ik," this simple restaurant provides a cheaper alternative to the otherwise pricey dish. Serving other distinctive platters such as *tiú* (turkey in thick rice broth) and *sak-ik* (specialty of San Cristóbal Verapaz), its menu is distinct. The huge servings are enough for two. The restaurant's friendly owners take pride in their culinary competence. Sandwiches and fried chicken are also available, prices starting from $1.80. Daily 8 a.m.-9 p.m. 4a Ca. 10 and Av. B 4-40, El recreo, Zona 3. Tel: 502-4061-2749. Updated: Oct 23, 2009.

PIZZA

Pizzería Bambino

This cheapie has the lowest prices in town, suitable for budget travelers looking for nothing more than tummy fillers. It is located right across the road from the Monja Blanca bus terminal. There are very limited choices, with only hamburgers and pizzas on the menu. With beef patties freshly

Kak'ik

Cobán's pride and joy is the limelight-grabbing celebrity on every restaurant's menu: kak'ik. Ask some locals and you will quickly find out that they are awfully proud of this wildly popular dish, which features a fat turkey leg dipped in red, steamy soup, and sprinkled with coriander leaves and the remnants of chilies and spices. The word "ik" means spicy in Q'eqchi', and the main ingredient of the stew is the dried cobanero chili. It is used alongside cilantro, mint and various varieties of herbs, with the most prominent one being achiote. Other ingredients for brewing this savory stew include *samat*, an herb found in Alta Verapaz, and several heads of garlic. Served with tamales steamed in banana leaves and a small portion of rice, the turkey stew is dished out hot, right from the stove. The dish is a concoction of long history and living traditional spirit.

Some Mayas say that kak'ik's red coloring evokes memories of blood used during rituals and ceremonies by their ancestors. Today, Mayan Q'eqchi' women keep their traditions alive by killing and cooking the turkey as it has been done for generations. Deemed national cultural heritage by the Ministry of Culture and Sports in November of 2007, and considered by many to be the unofficial national dish of Guatemala, kak'ik can be found in many restaurants all over the country, especially in its hometown of Cobán. Restaurante Pokomchi, also known as *la casa de chunto* (house of turkey), is one of the best places to try this traditional dish. Updated: Sep 29, 2009.

made on the spot, you are sure to get your food fast and hot. Daily 8 a.m.-9 p.m. 2a Ca. 3-40, Zona 4. Updated: Oct 21, 2009.

El Peñascal

(ENTREES: $3-9) A rustic folkloric restaurant with soothing background music, this is the best place to try cuisine unique to the region. Its fine dining standards ensure quality service and exquisite taste. The house specialty, kak'ik ($8.75), is highly recommended. Other typical dishes worth trying are the *tepezcuintle* (a wild rodent known as lowland paca) stew and turtle soup. To save some pennies, try its economical

set lunch ($3.65), which is equally rich and filling. Live marimba performances start at 8 p.m. every Saturday. Daily 7a.m.-11p.m. 5a Av. 2-61, Zona 1. Tel: 502-7951-2102, E-mail: elpenascal@restaurantescoban.com, URL: www.restaurantescoban.com. Updated: Sep 29, 2009.

CAFÉ/BAR

Café Fantasía

Ideal for a lazy afternoon, Café Fantasía has an undeniably country cottage feel thanks to its leafy garden, pastel walls and vintage décor. Breakfasts here are a great value, with a choice of continental, typical and American breakfasts. The wide selection of sandwiches makes it hard to decide what to order. Main courses are slightly costlier here. Don't leave without trying the appetizing cakes and meringue pies. Daily 9 a.m.-7:30 p.m. 2a Ca. 3-08, Zona 3. Tel: 502-7951-4097. Updated: Oct 21, 2009.

X'kape Kob'an

(ENTREES: $4-5) The restaurant's name literally means "Cobán's coffee" in Q'eqchi'—and its home-grown coffee is the best in town. Enjoying coffee or lunch here is undoubtedly a true gastronomic and cultural experience. Besides sipping a cup of tea in its ethnic-centric café, you can also visit its coffee plantation in the backyard. Meals here are affordable (though small), with regional, international and vegetarian food to choose from. The French owner does a mean quiche ($4.30), and an authentic *b'achlancha* (chicken cooked in leaves and spices). The restaurant uses 100 percent natural products, which come from the local communities. Daily 7.30 a.m.-9 p.m. Diagonal 4, 5-13, Zona 2. Tel: 502-7951-4152. E-mail: xkape.koban@gmail.com. Updated: Sep 29, 2009.

Café La Posada

Café la Posada is located at the far end of the hotel, overlooking the central park. With a relatively economical menu, the café is simple yet endearing. On its

VERAPACES

veranda, there are only tables for two, lit up by candles. Inside, there is a cozy sofa area warmed by a fireplace. Be prepared to be sweetened up by the special selection of wine and desserts. Daily 1-8:30 p.m. 1a Ca. 4-12, Zona 2. Tel: 502-7952-1495/7951-0588. Updated: Oct 23, 2009.

CHINESE

Restaurante Kam Mun

Those craving international food might find their answer at this Chinese restaurant. Although food is not exactly authentic, the big portions and exotic touch are its saving grace. Its old-fashioned oriental interior almost brings you back into the 1980s. Conveniently located along the city's 1a Calle, its big red signs are easy to spot. Try the exclusive *palomita* (pigeon) or *pato en curry* (duck curry). Daily 11:30 a.m.-9:45 p.m. 1a Ca. 8-12, Zona 2. Tel: 502-7952-1109/7951-3061. Updated: Sep 29, 2009.

INTERNATIONAL

El Bistro

This classy and atmospheric restaurant is part of the budget hostel Casa D'acuña, though the pricey menu might not cater to the standard backpacker. Ask the locals, and they will all agree this is the finest restaurant in town. Those who are looking to splurge will surely be fond of its exquisite European dishes and candlelit setting. Dip into unique dishes such as *weinwurst* (Munich sausage marinated in beer) and grilled whiskey prawns. Daily 7 a.m.-11 p.m. 4a Ca. 3-11, Zona 2. Tel: 502-7951-04827/951-0484. Updated: Oct 23, 2009.

Nightlife

Bok'atas

With all-red furnishings and a disco ball, this pub gives off both casual and pumping vibes. A great spot to chug down some beers, Bok'atas has plenty of tables to hang around but no dance floor to boogie on. Besides its lip-smacking *boquitas* (tapas) and juicy steaks, there is a wide array of liquor and reasonably priced beers. Popular with people of all age groups, the crowd starts packing in around 10 pm. Beware, the loud '80s music can be deafening. Monday-Saturday 4 p.m.-1 a.m. 4a Ca. 4-34, Zona 2. Updated: Oct 23, 2009.

Duende's Music and Bar

Just one block away from Parque Central, this local favorite is grooving with energy. Blasting Guatemalan folk music, it is the best place to mingle with locals and observe how they party. Although not your typical hip disco, this bar is still a hopping joint to put on your dancing shoes. The dance floor is small but packed with locals pairing up and bopping to fast-beat music. Get ready to share your first dance with a cobanero; they sure will make you feel at home here. Monday-Thursday 4 p.m.-1 a.m., Friday-Saturday 4 p.m.-4 a.m. 2a Ca. 3-12, Zona 2. Tel: 502-4135-5409. Updated: Sep 29, 2009.

AROUND COBÁN

SAN CRISTÓBAL VERAPAZ

Lying in the highlands, 19 kilometers (18 mi) west of Cobán, this Poqomchi' Maya village is the best place to find out more about the tribe that remains one of the smallest and oldest Maya groups alive.

Just off the main square, you can find Museo Katinamit (Admission: $1.20), where their traditions, festivals and musical instruments come to life. Explanations of their costumes and hieroglyphics are in English and Spanish. The museum is set up by a non-profit organization, CeCEP (Centro Comunitario Educativo Pokomchi; URL: http://cecep.iponetwork.org), which also runs the Aj Chi' Cho Language Center (URL: www.ajchicho.50g.com). Learn Poqomchi' or Spanish and stay with a local family for $120 a week. The best time to visit is on January 20, when the entire village celebrates the Feria de San Sebastián with masked processions and fire-ball games.

To get there from Cobán, catch a bus ($0.65) from the corner of 7a Avenida and 2a Calle, Zona 2. Updated: Sep 29, 2009.

TACTIC

Set in a valley of green rolling fields, the town of Tactic is not exceptionally striking, except for the beautiful local huipiles and the colorful market. The town's activities are focused around the square where the Iglesia de Asunción stands. From there, you can see the respected Templo El Chi'Ixim (Church of the Corn God) on the distant hilltop. On January 14, the day of Jesus Cristo Chi'Ixim, processions take place on the steep slopes, reaching the temple.

At the north end of town is Turicentro Chamché (Daily 7 a.m.-5 p.m. Admission: $1.20), where families frequent the complex's zoo and swimming pools. For a place to stay, check out Hotel Villa Linda (Private room: $6.25/person), just one block away from the center. Buses ($0.85) to Tactic leave from the terminal next to Estadio Rossi in Cobán. Updated: Sep 29, 2009.

SAN PEDRO CARCHÁ

Situated six kilometers (3.73 mi) from Cobán, this sizable town is expanding so quickly that it is almost forming a part of the city. Affectionately known as Carchá among the Q'eqchi' locals, it is built on a gentle rise overlooking the surrounding mountains. Buses from Cobán will drop you off at the corner of the square, where the town's simple white church stands proudly. In the Parque Central, a monument of the town's founder is overshadowed by the tall pine trees. Beside the church is the Museo Regional (Monday-Friday 9 a.m.-noon and 2-5 p.m. Admission: $1.25), which showcases Alta Verapaz's Maya cultural artifacts, and stuffed animals and birds, including the quetzal. Another interesting attraction is Balneario Las Islas, a natural swimming hole formed by the Río Chikoy.

An excellent alternative to staying in Cobán's city center is to check-in at the Mansión Santo Domingo de Guzmán (Km. 216 Carretera a San Pedro Carchá. Tel: 502-7950-0777). A high-end lodge set in the thick forests, this hotel has brightly lit and luxurious rooms, and a restaurant that serves chic modern cuisine.

To get to Carchá from Cobán, take the microbus from the corner of 2a Calle and 4a Avenida, Zona 4. Many public buses that go toward Lanquín and Uspantán leave from the terminal next to the Carchá fire station in the morning, with connections to Nebaj and Quiché. Updated: Sep 29, 2009.

Services

The INGUAT office (Av. del Calvario 1-17, Zona 1, Edificio Los Arcos) is located 15 minutes from the city center along the road leading to the Calvario church. The helpful bilingual guide provides maps and brochures, and is happy to answer any questions. Banks and ATMs are in abundance, with most located within blocks from Parque Central. Exchange your foreign currency and traveler's checks at the bank. Most banks are open Monday-Friday 8:30 a.m.-7 p.m. and on Saturdays 8:30 a.m.-5:30 p.m. Banco Industrial has an office and Visa ATM at 1a Calle and 2a Avenida, Zona 1. Mastercards can be used at Banco & T Continental, at the corner of 1a Calle and 4a Avenida.

The town's post office is located at the junction of 2a Avenida and 3a Calle, Zona 2. Card phones are available all around the central park. Internet service is fast and accessible all over town. Internet Pamáczimo (1a Ca. 10-21, Zona 3. Tel: 502-7951-3044) offers high-speed Internet at $0.75 per hr, as well as printing and CD burning services. Laundry service is available in most hostels. Lavandería Monja Blanca (Daily 8 a.m.-6 p.m. 1a Ca. 13-37, Zona 4) charges $4.75 per basket for both washing and drying. Lavandería Berty (2a Ca. 5-10, Zona 3. Tel: 502-7951-4880) has 24-hour service, including ironing and dry cleaning.

There are several pharmacies around the central park, a few of which have 24-hour services and accept credit cards. Farmacia Batres (3a Av. 1-04, Zona 4. Tel: 502-7951-1503) is one of them, with a wide range of medical products on sale. Policlínica Galeno (3a Av. 1-47. Tel: 502-7951-2913) has outpatient services. Most businesses, including tour operators, are closed on Sundays.

To bag some unique and quirky souvenirs, check out the range of recycled products at the little gift shop in the backyard of X'kape K'oban. All items are hand-crafted by local communities, and a percentage of the profits go directly to them. The Centro de Artesanía behind the Palacio de Gobernación is small and has the standard souvenirs on sale; you are better off getting your mementos in the market of Chichicastenango. Those craving a taste of home can seek solace in the modern mega-mall, Plaza Magdalena (1a Ca. 15-20, Zona 2). Situated two kilometers (1.24 mi) from the main plaza, you will find anything you need here, from cinemas to giant electronics stores and a food court. Updated: Oct 14, 2009.

Things to See and Do

Balneario Las Islas

An oasis hidden in the outskirts of San Pedro Carchá, this best-kept secret is definitely not your typical tourist trap. The cool waters of the Río Chikoy provide a welcome respite from the heat, while the shady grass patches are ideal for picnics and BBQs. Thanks to its isolated location, it is never overcrowded, even on Sunday afternoons. The main area of the balneario opens up to a series of gushing rapids, beside which are manmade pools converted from natural swimming holes. The upper section of the river is set amid a Tarzan-like jungle environment. The safety ladders, slide and rocky platform are tastefully constructed, retaining the river's natural beauty. Plentiful seating areas and facilities make this an excellent family retreat. To get there, walk one kilometer (0.62 mi) north from the town center, or catch a taxi for $1.85. Updated: Sep 29, 2009.

SAN JUAN CHAMELCO

Within eight kilometers (5 mi) southeast of Cobán is the biggest Q'eqchi' Maya village in the area. The most prominent landmark in town is Iglesia San Juan, said to be the first church built in Alta Verapaz; German influence can be seen from the Hapsburg eagle on the church's façade. In front of the church stands a statue of Don Juan Matalbatz, a local chief who had refused to bow before Spanish King Carlos V. He believed that a king should not stoop before another king. Carlos V respected him and named Cobán "the Imperial City."

Walking one kilometer (0.62 mi) east from the central park, you will find a starkly different landscape of pine trees, plush houses and ranches. Popular with families, El Pueblito (Barrio Santa Ana, Zona 2. Tel: 502-7951-4162) makes a great vacation place, with charming cottages and activities such as mini-golf and go-karts to indulge in.

Further down the road is Rancho Santa Fe (Tel: 502-7950-0365, E-mail: ranchosantafeguate@hotmail.com) with opportunities to go horseback riding and fishing. Restaurant Nim-Peck (Friday-Sunday noon-8 p.m. Tel: 502-7950-0377, E-mail: nimpeck@gmail.com) is a gorgeous oasis of greenery. There is outdoor seating in a garden veranda; eating under hanging orchids and vines makes this gastronomic experience a surreal one. To get there from Cobán, take a microbus ($0.30) from the terminal at 4a Calle Zona 3.

GRUTAS REY MARCOS

Discovered only in 1992, this cave system is home to several intriguing stalagmite and stalactite formations. The journey through the caverns is an easy walk, suitable for all ages. Expect to creep through a narrow tunnel and wade through a stream of rapids before getting to the impressive cave galleries. Giant formations here have been dubbed names like "the Twin Towers"

and the "Leaning Tower of Pisa." After the walk, visitors can dip into the refreshing waterfall nearby, Balneario Cecilinda.

The caves stretch one kilometer (0.62 mi) into the earth, but don't expect to reach the end during the one-hour guided tour. Admission costs is $4.35, including a guide, helmet and boots. The only way to get there by public transport is to catch a microbus ($0.25) from San Juan Chamelco, followed by a 400-meter (1,312 ft) walk uphill. Alternatively, get a taxi from Cobán ($9.35 oneway), or join a day trip ($18.50) organized by the tour operators. Updated: Sep 29, 2009.

SACHICHAJ WATERFALLS

This 15 meter-high (50 ft) waterfall is not the highest in the country, but its natural beauty makes it worth a visit. Cascading gently from a cave into a pool of emerald water, this retreat is wonderful for swimming and a picnic. If you're up for a hike off the beaten path, this place fits the bill. To get there on your own, catch a microbus toward Chisec and ask to stop at Tienda y Comedor Reina. From there, it is a 40-minute walk. You can hire a guide here, which is highly recommended, as it is easy to get lost in the maze. Adrenaline Tours arranges half-day trips to the waterfall, leaving at 9:30 a.m. and 2 p.m. The tour costs $30 per person, including transport, guide and entrance fees. Updated: Oct 13, 2009.

GRUTAS DE LANQUÍN

Although not as captivating as neighboring Semuc Champey, the caves of Lanquín still make for great excursions from Cobán. Those traveling north to Petén can stop by here en route to Tikal.

Sixty-one kilometers (38 mi) east of Cobán is the un-striking town of Lanquín, and a short distance away is the mystifying cave system that stretches deep into the earth. Its discovery date is unknown, though locals have been using it for religious purpose since before 1650.

Although a walkway and electric lights have been installed near the opening of the cave, much of it has yet to be explored. In 1950, several local villagers explored deep into the cave for six hours and miraculously found a lagoon. Their attempts to venture deeper in were hindered by the long stalactites that prevented swimming or passing through on a boat. The actual depth of the cave is still unknown.

VERAPACES

Photo by: Fernando Reyes

VERAPACES

Entering the cave, you will be awed by the sheer size of it. Some parts of the cave reach a height of 60 meters (197 ft). Impressive formations of gigantic stalagmites and stalactites are astonishingly surreal. At the highest point in the cave, you will find an area where locals still make their sacrifices to this day. Especially from April to May, and November to December, many natives make these sacrifices to pray for a good harvest. Some communicate with the dead, while some practice witchery through these sacrifices. The cave is home to thousands of bats. When sun sets, they fly out of the cave in an eerie sort of wave, almost darkening the skies.

Watch out for the slippery floors, and be sure to wear shoes that have a tight grip. Admission is $5.65. Opening hours are from 8 a.m.-5 p.m.

To stay in the area, El Retiro (Tel: 502-7983-0009) is an excellent choice to get away from the urban sprawl and completely unwind. Set in a verdant surrounding, the guesthouse sits right along the Lanquín River, making swimming a daily activity when staying here. Price ranges from $4 for a dorm bed to $6 for a private room. Excellent and affordable food is served at its restaurant, including vegetarian food. Be warned, you might not want to leave this backpacker's paradise! In the town of Lanquín, the Rabin Itza

hotel (Tel: 502-7983-0055) is located close to the bus terminal and has spacious rooms with balconies. This option has easier access to transportation, though it lacks that spiritual touch. A night's stay here costs between $3.50 and $8 per person.

Getting to Lanquín by public microbus is straightforward. Buses leave regularly between 6 a.m. and 3 p.m.. However, the last bus returning to Cobán is at 1 p.m., leaving little time to explore the area. It is best to stay a night here. Updated: Sep 29, 2009.

SEMUC CHAMPEY !

One of the country's spectacular natural wonders, Semuc Champey captures the hearts of many, owing to its phenomenal beauty and jungle setting. The site is formed by the Río Cahabón, which flows under a 300-meter (984 ft) limestone bridge, above which the famous series of turquoise-colored pools have formed. These pools shimmer in various shades of green, ranging from light turquoise to dark emerald. Perfect to cool off from the smoldering heat, the refreshing waters are crystal clear. Underwater, you will find many tiny fish swimming past and nibbling at your feet. Because of its remote location, nine kilometers (5.6 mi) south of Lanquín, Semuc Champey's pristine pools are yet to be swamped with tourists. Although the pools are surrounded by thick forests, wooden walkways have been constructed to allow easy access. Follow the walkway toward the upper end of the pools, where the river starts flowing under the limestone bridge. The dangers of the rocky bottom and fast-flowing river have caused a couple of deaths. Swimming is prohibited in this area.

Some tour guides will lead you down, one pool at a time, until you arrive at the part where the river gushes ferociously from under the limestone bridge. From the last pool to the river, guides will bring you down a rope ladder through a waterfall. The rocks are extremely slippery here, and conditions are dangerous. Those who do attempt the descent should be warned of the risks involved. For a picture-perfect view of Semuc Champey from above, there is a steep walkway that leads to the lookout point. The climb takes around 35 minutes each way, and can be somewhat difficult. Bring a bottle of water and boots for the climb. Admission is $6.50 per person. Camping is allowed in the grounds, though not advised due to possible flash floods.

There are no restaurants or food stalls in the park, so be sure to bring your packed lunch if you are coming on your own.

Hotel Jam Bamboo (Tel: 502-4549-9735, E-mail: cabralmariano@hotmail.com), located two kilometers (1.24 mi) from the pools, has a relaxed hippie vibe to it. Basic wooden bungalows house private rooms that are decent and clean. Prices here range $3.75-7.50 per person. There is no hot water or TV, but Internet is available. The staff jams on drums at night, which you will probably find either enchanting or incredibly annoying. Another popular option is Las Marías (Tel: 502-7861-2209) with similar lodging standards, but nearer to Semuc Champey. Built right along the river, you can take in the view while lounging at its restaurant. Prices here range from $3 for a dorm bed to $7.50 for a private room with bathroom.

Getting To and Away

To get to Semuc Champey, catch a microbus from the plaza in Lanquín, which runs more frequently in the morning. The bus schedule is flexible, so ask around for a better idea. Many tour operators in Cobán arrange

day trips ($37.50) that are excellent deals, considering the entrance fees and meals are included. Updated: Sep 29, 2009.

LAS CONCHAS DE CHAHAL!

A bit like Semuc Champey but with a fraction of the tourists, Parque Natural Las Conchas is a set of waterfalls on the Río Chiyú tumbling into tranquil green pools amid tropical rainforest. While the highest of the waterfalls forms a white curtain several meters high, the currents beneath are not so strong and you can swim across the pools. A series of boardwalks lead off to viewpoints above the whole river and if you climb all the way up the final ladder to the mirador atop a tree on a small island, you will find that it was worth every minute of the long, bone-jarring ride. Indeed, one of the reasons that the balneario is such a great uncrowded getaway is that it is out of the way, where the hills of Alta Verapaz roll into the Petén and Izabal. The park itself is fitted with picnic tables, BBQs, changing rooms and bathrooms, but there is nowhere to buy food (except during Semana Santa) and if you come on a weekday, there might not even be anyone manning the ticket booth (in which case you can just walk right in).

To reach the park, you need to get to Chahal, an hour and a half from either Fray Bartolomé de las Casas or Río Dulce on bumpy dirt roads (the trip costs about $2), then from the market in Chahal, catch a microbus to Las Conchas (1 hr, $1). The park entrance is marked.

Because microbuses to Las Conchas only go every hour and a half and service ends early (3 p.m.), you want to get an early start. While you could go on a day trip from Fray Bartolomé de las Casas, Río Dulce or Chahal (where the infrastructure is very basic), a better plan is to spend the night at Oasis Chiyú, a rustic hostel in the community of Las Conchas, a 30-minute walk from the park on a jungle path. The spacious wooden hostel, built and operated by a friendly American-Japanese couple, offers basic rooms for $7 and home-cooked meals for $5-6; there is a huge deck with hammocks, a good book exchange, you can dip in the Río Chiyú at the bottom of the garden, and the owners

VERAPACES

offer adventure tours to caves and Maya communities starting at $10. While "rustic" here means no electricity and compost toilets, it is truly an oasis of tranquility, perfect for the most nature-oriented souls. E-mail: tierramadretours@yahoo.com, URL: www.naturetoursguatemala.com. Updated: Dec 08, 2009.

CANCUÉN

The ruins of Cancuén are an important Maya site of the classical period (300-900 AD). Although they are technically part of the southern area of Sayaxché, Petén, they are accessible from Raxruhá in the Alta Verapaz. The port city of Cancuén, which was populated by nobles and craftsmen, played a strategic role in the control of the trade route between the highlands and lowlands of Guatemala. It was founded around 656 AD on a meander of the Río de la Pasión, effectively controlling navigation. It reached the height of its splendor in the late 8th century, as king Tajal Chan Ahk commissioned most monuments and made Cancuén prosper via political alliances, and via the trade of jade, obsidian, quetzal feathers and other exotic goods. But in the year 800, a massacre, possibly perpetrated by a rival dynasty, wiped out the rulers and destroyed the city, leaving it to be slowly covered up by the jungle.

The ruins of the ballcourt markers were discovered in the early years of the 20th century and in 1967. Thanks to investigations by a Harvard archeologist, the first mapping of Cancuén was conducted. Subsequent excavations, led jointly by the American University of Vanderbilt and the Guatemalan Universidad del Valle, uncovered the ruins of a palace, a water reservoir and several houses. These were restored (maybe a little bit too neatly), involving the local communities in the preservation and touristic exploitation of the site. A visit through the site takes you from the visitors' center to the reconstitution of a thatched hut, then to the ballcourt where the game of pelota was played (using knees and elbows to pass a ball), then to the palace and its staircase with well-preserved murals. Several carved altars lying about the site are still used by nearby Mayan communities to celebrate traditional rituals.

As you follow the footpaths and boardwalks through the forest, you may see toucans, monkeys, agoutis, parrots, iguanas and butterflies. Unfortunately, habitual residents of the jungle also include bloodthirsty mosquitoes, who come in largest numbers August-January, so try to visit outside of those months.

It is possible to camp at Cancuén if you bring your own tent; the fee is $3.10 per person. Meals (roughly $6.20 per dish) can also be prepared by the local community, if you give them advance notice of a few days. Admission to the site is $4.35. Daily 8 a.m.-3 p.m. Tel: 502-5042-1161. Updated: Dec 07, 2009.

Getting To and Away

From Raxruhá (which is about two-and-a-half hours from Cobán and one hour from Chisec), get a microbus headed to the community of La Unión, 45 minutes away on a dirt road, ($1.25, every hour 7 a.m.-3 p.m.). There, get the little shop by the Cancuén sign to contact a *lanchero* who will take you by boat to the site, a pleasant 20-minute ride on the jade-green waters of the Río de la Pasión. It is best to reserve by calling ahead (Tel: 502-5935-2604). The boat rental (up to 20 passengers) costs $37.20, so if you are traveling in a very small group, you might want to hike to the site instead (40 min); you will need to pay a village youngster to show you the way, but the villagers warn that the buffaloes on the way can be aggressive. Updated: Dec 07, 2009.

PARQUE NACIONAL CUEVAS DE CANDELARIA

The Cuevas de Candelaria are a complex of natural caves and subterranean waterways running through the limestone hills of Alta Verapaz. With the Candelaria river running 22 kilometers (13.7 mi) underground (80 km/50 mi including all the branches), they form the longest such system in Central America. Exploring the caves either on foot or on an inflatable inner tube is a great adventure: Your lantern will reveal dripping stalactites, bulbous stalagmites and roofs of shining droplets, while bats flee screeching. Gliding down the underground river makes for good family fun too, as you splash in cool dark pools, then emerge in the middle of the forest. But a guided tour through the caves will also reveal to you how they were (and still are) a sacred site for the Maya. As described in the Popol Vuh (the Maya equivalent of the biblical Genesis), these caves were an access to the underworld, and religious rites have been performed here for centuries. The caves were first explored using spelunking equipment in 1974, and was fully mapped by scientific expeditions in the following years. Now the local communities have organized tours and accommodation.

Different caves can be explored from four different visitor centers: Candelaria Camposanto, Candelaria Muqbila, Complejo Cultural y Ecoturistico Cuevas de Candelaria and Los Nacimientos, all accessible from the Chisec-Raxruhá road, or else on a tour from Cobán or Chisec. The cheapest way to visit the caves is to base yourself in nearby Raxruhá, staying in Hotel El Amigo (Tel: 502-5368-5616; simple rooms with private bathrooms: $7.25) or in the friendly Hotel Cancuén (Tel: 502-7983-0720; from $4.25 basic rooms to $27 suites), which also runs tours to Los Nacimientos. From Raxruhá, microbuses run every 20 minutes and will drop you at any of the caves for $0.60.

Los Nacimientos

This private reserve, which holds the final leg of the Candelaria river, belongs to the retired doctor who owns the Hotel Cancuén in Raxruhá. He organizes day tours for $18, including transport, a couple of hours through dry caves and three hours of tubing. He takes good care of his guests, gladly sharing his knowledge of the area, in particular of the Cancuén archeological site. Tel: 502-7983-0720/0792, E-mail: hotelcancuen@gmail.com, URL: www.cuevaslos-nacimientos.com. Updated: Dec 08, 2009.

Complejo Cultural y Ecoturistico Cuevas de Candelaria

Managed jointly by one of the French speleologists who explored the caves in the 1970s and by the local community, this center is perhaps the more upscale one. While the cave and tubing tours are similar to those offered elsewhere (caves: 1.5 hour, $4.25/person; tubing: $9/person or $42 for the three-hour tour with lunch), accommodation here is in a pretty lodge, where a night costs $36 (single) to $48 (double). Tel: 502-4035-0566, E-mail: reservaciones@cuevasdecandelaria.com, URL: www.cuevas-decandelaria.com. Updated: Dec 07, 2009.

Candelaria Muqbila

Also run by a local community, this center situated a 20-minute walk (or five-minute drive) off the main road offers cave tours (1.5 hr, $5/person) and tubing ($5.50/person) as well as accommodation in wooden cabins for $7/person. 7 a.m.-4 p.m. Tel: 502-5340-5671.

Candelaria Camposanto

The community of Camposanto runs cave tours ($4.25/person, 45 min) and tubing ($5/person) from the little shop Tucan by the side of the road, which unfortunately is rarely staffed by anyone competent or informed. They also offer very spartan accommodation in the rustic Hotel Pito Real for $3 per person. Tel: 502-5747-7401. Updated: Dec 08, 2009.

CHISEC

A small, unattractive indigenous town in the middle of cardamom country, Chisec itself is of little interest to the traveler. It can be used as a base to visit Laguna Lachuá, and has a few nice caves and lakes nearby. If you are going to the Caves of Candelaria, you are better off basing yourself in the even smaller, but friendlier town of Raxruhá, just one hour further to the northeast. Chisec was founded in 1813 by groups mostly from the Q'eqchi' highlands of Alta Verapaz. No proper road actually connected the town with the rest of Guatemala until 1976; before that, people had to walk more than one day through the jungle to get anywhere reachable by vehicle. In the early 1980s, it suffered from the war between the guerrillas and the army and its militias, and many people were displaced. Now it is little more than one paved road, surrounded by a few shops and residential lots, and many very rural villages set in the nearby hills where crops spring from a rich, red soil.

If you must stay in Chisec, you can use the services of the two banks, Banrural and Banco Agromercatil, both equipped with ATMs; buy a few basic products in the shops and at the market; or use the slow Internet for $1 per hour in one of the two cybercafés (Superación, down by restaurant Don Miguel, or La Huella Digital, also on the main street, one block north of the central park). There are plenty of cheap eateries around, the best one being Cafeteria Mishel, half a block north of the central park, which serves decent dinners for $2. The one proper and clean restaurant in town is the Mini-Restaurant Don Miguel, housed in a funny orange hexagonal building, on the main street toward the exit to Raxruhá (Tel: 502-5156-7470). It serves a wide variety of breakfasts of eggs, waffles or traditional chapin for $2-3, chicken and meats for $3-4, as well as juices and soft drinks.

Unless you want to spend the night in the kind of place that looks like a truck-driver hotel, your only semi-decent option is the Estancia de la Virgen (Tel: 502-5514-7444, E-mail: hotelestanciadelavirgen@gmail. com). You can hardly miss its massive bilious-yellow façade, since it is the only three-story construction in town, towering over the main road at the exit to Raxruhá. It offers 50 rooms with private bathrooms and fans or air conditioning (singles $11.40, doubles $18), some already begging for a paint job and more zealous cleaning. There is a swimming pool surrounded by three-meter (9.8 ft) high statues of tyrannosauruses, probably its idea of a kid-friendly park. If you are on a shoestring budget and can close your eyes to stained walls and dank showers, the Hotel-Restaurant Los Nopales (Tel: 502-5514-0624), on the east side of Parque Central, offers eight basic rooms in a low building for $5.

Chisec is manageable on foot, but if you feel lazy, tuk-tuks will take you around for $0.60. One local community tourism association, the Agretuchi (Asociación Gremial de Turismo de Chisec) (Tel: 502-5978-1465, E-mail: agretuchi@yahoo.com), hidden away in a simple wooden house on lot 135 of the Barrio Centro, one block west behind the Distribuidora La Económica, can help organize tours to nearby caves and can give you brochures. They can also find guides or call ahead to reserve accommodation, but their packages do not usually include transportation. Among the tours offered are Sepalau (1 day, $38 per person), B'omb'il Peq and tubing on Río San Simon ($45), Cuevas de Candelaria ($50), Cancuen ($36). Updated: Dec 07, 2009.

Getting To and Away

Fortunately, microbuses run through Chisec very frequently. Buses to Cobán (1.5 hr, $1.80) leave every 20 minutes from the car park one block south of the municipality from 4 a.m. to 6 p.m. Microbuses to Playa Grande (which drop you at the entrance to Laguna Lachuá park) in theory go every half-hour from the street corner two blocks south of the Parque Central, while microbuses to Raxruhá go every 20 minutes (1 hr, $1.80), a little less frequently to Fray Bartolomé de las Casas; they can drop you at the entrance of one of the Candelaria caves complexes. Buses north to Sayaxché and the Petén (2 hr, $6) are frequent throughout the day, going hourly up the main street. Updated: Dec 08, 2009.

Things to See and Do

Cuevas de B'ombi'l Peq

This cave system can be explored on a proper rappelling and speleological adventure, squeezing into the narrow holes that lead into a chamber with wall paintings. You can organize a tour through Agretuchi in Chisec, or you can go on your own and just climb down a series of rudimentary ladders and gaze up at the overhead leaves filtering sunlight. On the way, you will pass the smaller cave of Jul Iq'. To get there, ask any northbound bus to drop you off at the Puente San Antonio ($0.25), three kilometers (1.86 mi) out of town, then follow the clearly marked path for 25 minutes. The walk to the caves takes you through cow pastures, fields and up through the forest. Updated: Dec 08, 2009.

Lagunas de Sepalau

The three pocket-sized lagunas of Sepalau, whose waters are emerald green from reflecting the surrounding forest, are a lovely spot to swim or even kayak. There are tables to picnic at, bathrooms and a parking area. While the ride to get there is lovely, taking you through hilly farmland and tiny communities, the bumpy dirt road is in such poor condition that the 10 kilometers (6.2 mi) take 45 minutes to cover. You can try to catch one of the packed pickups that go out there, but they are few and far between, with the last ones leaving early in the day. Therefore, unless you have your own 4x4, you need to hire a van from Chisec, for approximately $12. Updated: Dec 08, 2009.

PLAYA GRANDE

Although translating as "big beach," Playa Grande is neither by a lake nor by the sea; its name refers to the plains fertilized by the river Chixoy, where corn, beans, cardamom and coffee are grown. Playa Grande is also the head of the municipality of Ixcán, a name which means "yellow woman" in Q'eqchi', "snake woman" (referring to the form of the rivers winding across the territory) in Kaqchikel, and "convergence of the sky and land" in Qanjobal, the third local indigenous language. Playa Grande is technically in the department of Quiché, but it is a convenient base for visiting Laguna Lachuá in Alta Verapaz or to cross over into the Highlands, and it is just a couple of hours away from

VERAPACES

the sharp angle of Mexico's border. Some shops will even change Mexican pesos.

While most of the municipality's population is scattered in small agricultural communities in the surrounding countryside, Playa Grande is large enough to make a good stopover to refuel on money, food or other supplies. But its muddy streets lead to no other attraction than the wild bazaar of a market and the microbuses honking down the main street, so you will likely be heading out pretty fast. There are several banks: a Bancoagromercantil on the main street of Zona 1 as well as a Banrural farther down, both with ATMs accepting Visa, Mastercard and Cirrus. There are a few cybercafés around, including Tecnicentro La Selva, four blocks up 2a Avenida from the market.

Should you need to spend the night, the dark, wood-paneled La Reina Vasty (Av. Principal, Zona 1, above Ferretería La Pala. Tel: 502-5514-6693/0385) offers what are the nine neatest rooms in town, with clean tile floors, comfortable beds, private bathrooms, air conditioning and TV for $15.

Just around the corner is the Hotel España, hiding its green façade behind heavy bougainvilleas. While the cheaper rooms with shared bathrooms ($6) tend to share every noise from the corridor and other rooms, the rooms with private bathrooms, in the wing buildings, are better ($15 single, $24 double). Attached is the El Hangar restaurant, where the potentially annoying cascade of exuberant hanging plants and surly waitresses serving liter beers to the locals actually give a touch of character. The menu at El Hangar extends from breakfasts ($5.50) —the stack of fruit pancakes is excellent—to full meals including *tepezcuintle* (a type of agouti), venison ($6), and all manners of beef, chicken and seafood ($4.80-$12), as well as tacos ($5). 2a Av., Lote 51 and 52. Tel: 502-7755-7645 (hotel)/7755-7646 (restaurant).

If you prefer a cheaper and greasier fare of fried chicken, there is a Pollolandia on the corner of 2a Avenida, and a string of comedores offering basic dishes for just over $1. Updated: Dec 08, 2009.

Getting To and Away

From the parking lot at the far end of the main street in Zona 1, you can catch microbuses that go to the Mexican border every 45 minutes (2 hr, $2.50) and to Cobán every hour (5 hr, $6.50). There is also direct service to Guatemala City (9 hr, $14.50) and to Varillas in Huehuetenango, should you want to follow the back route to the highlands. There also are dozens of microbuses serving all the nearby villages; hop on any bound for Playitas or Chisec to be dropped off at Parque Laguna Lachuá (45 min, $0.60). Updated: Dec 07, 2009.

PARQUE NACIONAL LAGUNA LACHUÁ

Named after the almost perfectly circular lake in its mist, the Parque Nacional Laguna Lachuá is a 14,500-hectare (35,830 ac) park of subtropical rainforest and is worth an overnight stay if you like to combine quiet wildlife watching with relaxing swims. The larger eco-region of Lachuá is a RAMSAR site (wetlands of international importance), home to 40 species of amphibians, 170 species of birds, and 130 species of mammals including tapirs, ocelots and pumas. Among those denizens, the easiest to spot are the hundreds of butterflies, the shy agoutis and squirrels, or maybe a boa constrictor.

The highlight of the park is the lake, whose crystalline waters turn a turquoise green under the sun. You can take a refreshing dip, or simply enjoy the silence on the deck by the visitor center, watching tarpons leap dolphin-like in the distance. While the original name Lachuá comes from the Q'eqchi' for "smelly water" because of the high sulfur content of the lake, only a few swampy areas actually emit smell; in fact, the park is maintained strictly clean of any form of pollution or agricultural exploitation. Come in the summer, between February and May, to face fewer mosquitoes; choose a weekday to avoid local weekend crowds.

At the visitor center by the lake, there are BBQ areas and picnic tables, as well as a rustic hostel with small but clean single, double and family rooms ($6/person). The toilets are impeccably maintained latrines, and there are real showers as well as a generator providing electricity. There is neither shop nor restaurant, but you can cook your own food in the communal kitchen, shared with the friendly park rangers. The area is an hour's walk (4.2 km/2.49 mi) from the ranger station at the park entrance on a well-maintained path. Admission to the park costs foreign adults

VERAPACES

$4.80, children $1.40 and nationals $0.60.
Camping is possible for $3; you can rent tents
for $1.80. Daily 7 a.m.-4 p.m. Tel: 502-4883-
3821, E-mail: info@lachua.org, URL: http://
lachua.org. Updated: Dec 08, 2009.

Getting To and Away

To get to the park from Cobán (4 hr, $5.50)
or from Chisec (3 hr), it is a long and bumpy
microbus ride on a pothole-infested road
with irregular buses. Try to get an early start,
as you will need to hike an hour after reaching the park itself. Alternatively, you can take
a beach-bound bus from Cobán, spend the
night in Playa Grande, then hop onto any
local microbus the next day, when you are
fresher for the hour-long hike. If you prefer to
have all transportation taken care of for you,
just book a day tour from Cobán, with prices
starting at $60. Updated: Dec 07, 2009.

RÍO IKBOLAY

While not strictly in the national park, the
river Ikbolay is just outside its bounds, in the
larger Lachuá eco-region. The aquatic ride
up to the *renacimientos*, or renaissance, of
the river, where the water spurts from the
rocks in a series of cascades, is a nice one, but
it is a bit logistically complicated. You must
first take a microbus, which only runs once
a day to the community of Rocja Pomtila,
on a turn-off from the Chisec-Playa Grande
road, then hire the 12-person boat for $18.
The simplest way of visiting is by getting
the Agretuchi in Chisec to organize the tour.
Rocja Pomtila. Tel: 502-5315-1962/5806-
4183. Updated: Dec 07, 2009

VERAPACES

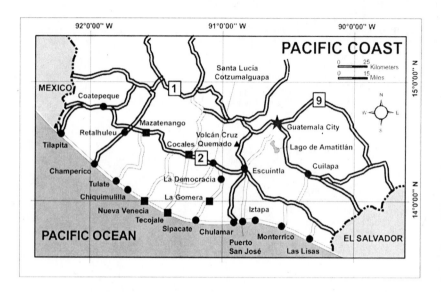

Guatemala's Pacific Coast

Because of Guatemala's orientation, its "western" coast—that is to say, its Pacific coast—is actually for the most part to the south, and most Guatemalans refer to it as the "southern" coast. It consists of the provinces of San Marcos, Retalhuleu, Suchitepequez, Escuintla and Santa Rosa.

These provinces are similar in that they comprise the land between a string of inland volcanoes and the coast. The rich soil in this region has fostered the rise of thriving agricultural and livestock industries as well as a booming fishing industry. Home mostly to working-class Guatemalans with little or no indigenous blood, these provinces tend to be somewhat rough-and-tumble, and more than a little dangerous. The main towns, such as Escuintla and Puerto San José, have little to offer visitors.

The biggest draw on the southern coast is almost certainly the small beach town of Monterrico. As beaches go, it's not too impressive—head north to Mexico if that's what you're looking for—but it's probably the best Guatemala has to offer. Ruins buffs will want to visit some sites along the southern coast, most notably Takalik Abaj, near the city of Retalhuleu. A relatively small site with only about 80 structures, Takalik Abaj is most interesting due to several impressive stone carvings and possible links to the ancient Olmec culture.

For Guatemalans, the Pacific Coast starts once you pass over the volcanic mountain ranges that divide the rest of the country from these western flatlands. The actual coast is still a several-hour journey away but already the air changes from cool and crisp to hot and steamy, the dramatic landscape turns into rolling farmland, and time seems to slow down to match the languid pace of life along the waterways and canals. Unless, of course, it's the weekend in one of the tourist towns, when life is jumping to the energetic and loud rhythm of the best *ladino* (local mestizo culture) pop music.

The Pacific Coast offers a little bit of everything: ancient archeological ruins, surfing, farm-stays, adventure parks, volcanoes, mangrove tours, turtle watching, volunteering projects, deep sea fly fishing and more. You can stay in a tiny village that rarely sees a tourist, one that has built to cater to tourists, or an exclusive lodge. Accommodation varies from the divine to the squalid but invariably comes with a swimming pool. Fresh fish and seafood can be found in abundance, but there are few alternative options. Transport is local-style, but in a part of Guatemala that is predominantly visited by locals, what better way to understand the heart of its people? Updated: May 10, 2010.

Highlights

Monterrico–Managing to hold onto its small-town charm, Monterrico offers the breadth of choice tourists would expect from a coastal resort within a unique ecosystem of volcanic beaches and freshwater mangroves.

Sport Fishing–Catch one sailfish, or catch 10, on a section of coast near Iztapa, famous as one of the best places in the world to reel in this awesome creature (Xocomil, Xetulul and Autosafari parks).

Chapín–Take your pick from a water park, an amusement park and a safari park, all widely acclaimed and considered by foreigners and locals alike to be brilliant fun whether you are aged 8 or 80.

Sea Turtles–Watch a mother lay her eggs or a baby make the dash for freedom, best seen from September to January in Monterrico, Las Lisas or Sipacate, where turtle hatcheries work to ensure the continuing survival of the species.

Serious Down Time–Those on a budget should head to Tilapa for a taste of local life while those looking for an unforgettable weekend getaway may prefer the idyllic hotels of Las Lisas.

Historical Ruins–The draw of the Olmec- and Mayan-influenced archeological park of Takalik Abaj cannot be ignored, but there is something quite remarkable about walking through the cane fields near Santa Lucía Cotzumalguapa only to find an enormous sculpted head, still used by Mayan descendents in rituals and ceremonies.

Fincas–Stay at a finca near Retalhuleu and experience waterfalls, birdwatching and life on an eco-friendly working farm. This is a convenient alternative base to visit the nearby ruins of Takalik Abaj.

Surfing–Guatemala does not have the same quality of surf beaches that can be found in other Central American countries; however, there is a decent enough break at Sipacate, and experienced surfers might like to try out the break at Iztapa. Updated: Mar 10, 2010.

History

The majority of the Pacific Coast's long and glorious history is lost to the past. Archeological sites have been destroyed or are hidden among extensive farmlands, and from what has been found, experts argue as to what can be concluded about the past. However, there is still hope, as continued excavations at sites like Takalik Abaj reveal structures buried several feet underground.

The Olmecs had a thriving civilization during the Preclassical period, the most notable remnants of which are several big heads and one of the earliest forms of writing found in Guatemala; then again, these accomplishments could be attributed to the Maya, depending on whether these groups intermingled or not. The legendary symbol of the Jaguar God, which represents Santa Lucía Cotzumalguapa, definitely first appeared in Olmec art and was later adopted by the Maya as a representation of earth and night.

After the Olmecs came, the Ócos and Iztapa cultures arrived, followed by the Pipil, who moved in sometime between 400 and 900 AD. The Pipil were the ones who fought the Spanish, and many of the indigenous people of the Pacific Coast today descended from them, but Pedro de Alvarado conquered all and continued up to Xela (Quetzaltenango). Pedro also established the first seaport of Guatemala in Iztapa, where he harbored his fleet.

The modern Pacific Coast is a hodgepodge of farmland, coastal villages and inland towns displaying various degrees of development. The farms have mostly turned to sugar-cane and the large factory just outside of Santa Lucia is the main aggregator in the area. However, coffee, bananas, rubber and maize are still popular crops and there are a small number of eco-conscious fincas on the outskirts of Reu.

Largely overlooked in the past, except as a source of agriculture, the Pacific Coast is beginning to show the benefits of increased investment as town squares are renovated and infrastructure is improved. More towns and villages are starting to actively encourage tourism, both resident and overseas, but the impact on the environment is rarely considered. Monterrico is more aware than most and their efforts to develop within a fragile ecosystem, by keeping businesses small and local, should be encouraged. Updated: Mar 10, 2010.

PACIFIC COAST

When to Go

The coast can be visited year round. The rainy season runs from August to October, but generally it only rains for a couple of hours a day. The sticky heat can be quite taxing, but the spectacular lightening storms go a long way in making up for it. The hottest time of year is actually January to March but the heat is not as oppressive in these drier months. Busy season runs from November to mid-May, with Christmas and New Year's seeing all the hotels fully booked. Otherwise, it is often very quiet, almost deserted, during the week, while on weekends, day trippers flock to the beach for a dose of sea and sand. Turtle spotting is best from September to January. Updated: Mar 10, 2010.

Getting To and Away

Apart from infrequent shuttle buses traveling between Antigua and Monterrico, there are only three ways to get around the Pacific Coast: hired car, local buses or incredibly long and expensive taxi rides. Realistically, most trips will be by bus.

The bus routes, while bumpy, appear to be more daunting than they actually are. The highway is long, straight and much faster than the one running parallel to it on the other side of the mountains. However, for most of the coast, it is not possible to travel next to the ocean because of the mangroves and canals. Cutting out to the coast from the highway can take from twenty minutes to two hours, depending on which coastal town you wish to visit.

Traveling on the Pacific Coast may involve up to four bus changes and a boat ride, but invariably the last bus will deposit you at the door of the next one or a paltry two-minute walk away from it. Always tell the ticket collector your final destination so that he knows what crossroads to drop you off at. Often this will result in a speedier journey with less backtracking. It is rare that the buses are so full that you don't get a seat, although on occasion you may have to wait ten minutes. Trying to squeeze in your luggage can be tricky so the smaller the bag, the better.

As the entire length of the Pacific Coast is covered in canals and mangroves, the last part of the journey is frequently by boat, easily the best way to arrive in any village. Except for a couple of secluded hotels, it is not necessary to charter a boat unless the ferries have finished for the day. The ferries generally run from sunrise to sunset. Last buses back from coastal towns tend to finish at around 3 p.m., though, as they are used to serving a day tripper crowd. Don't forget on your bus trip to take a look out the window. Most of the fields on the coast are sugar cane fields. It is the fences that are most interesting. The ground here is so fertile that if a farmer plants a log or branch in the earth it will roots and turn into a new tree, creating these amazing 'living fences' that you can see all over Guatemala. Updated: Mar 10, 2010.

Crossing into Mexico

On the Pacific Coast, there are two border crossings to choose from, one at Ciudad Tecún Umán and the other at El Carmen. Border formalities are fairly standard at all Guatemala/Mexico crossings. There are no fees to enter Guatemala or Mexico; all you need is a passport valid for six months after your date of arrival.

BORDER CROSSING AT CIUDAD TECÚN UMÁN

Most travelers prefer to cross at Ciudad Tecún Umán because a bridge directly links Ciudad Hidalgo in Mexico. The border is open 24 hours a day; however, it is always advisable to cross with plenty of daylight hours left to get to your next destination. If necessary, there are also several hotels and restaurants on both side of the Mexico/Guatemala border, although they tend to be a bit seedy. From Ciudad Tecún Umán, it is easy to catch a bus to your next destination, although the last of them usually depart around 6 p.m. Buses can take you to Guatemala City, Quetzaltengo, and a number of smaller cities for only a few dollars. If the city you are looking for is not listed, you can also take a bus to either Retalhuleu or Coatepeque, where another roster of buses is offered. On the Mexican side of the border, buses travel to Tapachula every 20 minutes from 7 a.m. to 7:30 p.m.

BORDER CROSSING AT EL CARMEN

About 39 kilometers (25 mi) north of Ciudad Tecún Umán, there is another bridge that connects El Carmen in Guatemala with Talismán in Mexico. Crossing the border here is much quieter than in Ciudad Tecún Umán, and the border is also open 24 hours a day. Services here are

PACIFIC COAST

more basic than at the at the other Pacific Coast border crossing, including less lodging, restaurants, and buses.

Buses run from El Carmen to Retalhuleu and Coatepeque, and sometimes you can catch a bus to Quetzaltenango. Across the border in Mexico, you hop on a bus between Talismán and Tapachula (30 min) until around 10 p.m. Updated: Jul 28, 2010.

Crossing into El Salvador

There is a fairly quiet border crossing to La Hachadura, El Salvador at Ciudad Pedro de Alvarado along the Pacific Coast Highway (CA-2). Buses run frequently from here to Escuintla and then further to Guatemala City. On both sides of the border, you will find basic accommodations and eateries. Another, more heavily-trafficked crossing into El Salvador lies further north at Valle Nuevo/Las Chinamas. Updated: Aug 06, 2010.

Safety

The Pacific Coast is a fairly safe part of Guatemala, as far as this country goes, especially in the small seaside villages. As always, though, be careful with valuables, cash and cameras. Be especially mindful after dark. Crime is generally opportunistic and therefore could occur anytime and anywhere, but the majority of tourists are unlikely to encounter any problems. Three trouble spots are the towns of Coatepeque and Puerto San José, which have a somewhat dodgy reputation after dark, and the Bilbao Stones in Santa Lucía Cotzumalguapa, which should not be visited by lone travelers. Updated: May 10, 2010.

Things to See and Do

The Pacific Coast has a lot more to offer than most tourists give it credit for. Apart from surfing in Sipacate or marveling at the unique ecosystems that have built up around the mangroves and volcanic sand beaches in Tilapa and Monterrico, there are several significant Maya and Olmec archeological sites around Retalhuleu, Santa Lucía Cotzumalguapa and La Democracia; a couple of awesome, fun parks; and a section of coastline that hosts one of the best places in the world to catch a sailfish.

For those seeking some adrenaline kicks, there are a couple of volcanoes to be climbed as well as kayaking, mountain biking and rafting adventures. Surprisingly, finding a place to swim is harder than you would think, as undertows and rips prowl the coastline.

The best places to swim are in the pleasant seaside village of Tulate or the towns of Puerto San José and Champerico. If getting away from it all is what you are looking for, there are a couple of acclaimed luxury hotels in these spots. Updated: Mar 09, 2010.

Tours

Reuextreme, which is based out of Guatemala City but also has an office in Reu, offers tours of Manchón Guamuchal Wetlands and a variety of activities, including river rafting, kayaking and mountain biking. Several *fincas* (estates) in the area around Retalhuleu include tours of the coffee farm, hiking and birdwatching. At Monterrico and Tilapa, there are boat tours of the mangroves and waterways, nesting turtle tours and horse rides up the beach. Otherwise it is a question of doing it yourself or coming with one of the tour operators in Antigua, Quetzaltenango and Guatemala City, who include the Pacific Coast on their list of attractions. Updated: Mar 10, 2010.

Lodging

The best choice of accommodation is in Monterrico, the only town on the Pacific Coast to have everything from attractive budget hostels to luxury resorts and bungalows. Otherwise it is best to pick your destination on the basis of the type of accommodation you desire.

The city day-tripper towns of Puerto San José, Iztapa, and Champerico have basic, unappealing hotels unless you stay in one of the luxury out-of-town lodges. Tilapita and Sipacate have rustic but atmospheric hotels, Tulate is small but serves an ever-increasing number of visitors on the weekend, and Las Lisas has a couple of renowned up-market hotels. All the towns on the Pacific Highway itself have a small and unremarkable, but acceptable, selection of hotels. Retalhuleu, though, has some lovely places to stay.

In Monterrico it is possible to find a room at a beachside hotel with a swimming pool from $5 per person, but everywhere else it generally starts at $10 per person if traveling alone and $6 per person if in a couple. Air conditioning adds at least $10 to the room price per night. Generally, fans and private bathrooms come as standard. Sipacate has the only official campsites, but in many places locals would be happy to let you set up camp for next to nothing. How safe all your gear would be is another matter. Updated: May 10, 2010.

TILAPA AND TILAPITA

The town of Tilapa is friendly and laid-back but unremarkable, so it's best to head straight for the beach. If the rains have not washed the wooden bridge away, you can walk over the canal to La Isla el Tular Tilapa; otherwise, take a *lancha* (public motorboat). The island is incredibly narrow (standing in the middle, you can see the canal and the beach at the same time) and very tranquil. There are no hotels, but Ronny has started renting out a room on his family's property for $6 a night and intends to build a couple more. (Just ask around for Ronny.)

Travelers looking to experience real life on an isolated island will love this place. There is nothing to do here except walk on the beach, watch the dogs chasing the pigs and learn how to climb a coconut tree. Ronny has fishing rods (bring line and hooks with you) and will happily teach you how to throw a net. There are some hammocks in a shady, breezy spot to laze away the day when it all gets too much. Simple meals are available.

Tilapa has a couple of hotels in town, near the bus stop, which would do for a night but not for a holiday: recommended is Hotel Misapa ($10 doubles with private bathroom, $6.50 singles or $5 doubles with shared bathroom).

Tilapita is the long spit next to La Isla el Tula and is only accessible by lancha. There are almost 1,000 houses here and the town is well looked-after by locals. Houses on the canal side are set back, but rather than clearing the land for access to the waterway, residents have cut channels through the mangroves to reach the docks. The same has been done on the beach side, so the natural tree line still exists. There is a small and vitally important *tortugario* (protected turtle hatching site) in operation opposite the only hotel, Pacific Mar. Pacific Mar has simple but adequate rooms with private bathrooms ($12.50 doubles, $7.50 singles). The restaurant prepares local fare and seafood dishes from $5. They also have a pool, which is useful since days are hot and swimming in the sea can be unsafe.

Getting To and Away

Buses leave to and from Coatepegue every fifteen minutes (4 a.m.-6:30 p.m., $1.25, 1 hr). Buses to and from Tecún Umán also depart every fifteen minutes (4 a.m.-3 p.m., $1.25, 1 hr). There are occasional buses to Guatemala City but it is usually faster to go to Coatepegue first and change there. To reach La Isla el Tular Tilapa, walk straight ahead from the bus drop-off across the concrete bridge through the swamp to the dock. If the bridge is there you can walk to the island or take a *lancha* (motorboat) across the canal for $0.30. A lancha from the same dock to Tilapita costs $1.25 per person and runs whenever there is the need. Updated: Feb 10, 2010.

Things to See and Do

Apart from doing little, the only key tourist activity in Tilapa or Tilapita is visiting Manchón Guamuchal Wetlands. The wetlands encompasses 13,500 hectares (33,359 ac) of different ecosystems, including swamps, mangroves, rivers and volcanic sand beaches. It is also a protected site, according to the Ramsar Convention on Wetlands. The best time to visit is from October or November to March, as the most migratory birds arrive then to stay during the winter. At all times of year, it is possible to see pelicans, herons, egrets, ducks, sparrow hawks, buzzards and falcons. Crocodiles do live here, but they are rarely spotted. The mangroves act as a nursery for juvenile fish and other aquatic creatures. One of the mud-skippers is called "boca de oro," or mouth of gold, because it looks like he has a piece of gold in his mouth.

Tourism in the wetlands is largely undeveloped. Reuxtreme can organize kayaking trips, which, if you have the energy, are the best way to explore the area because they make it much easier to get close to nature, in particular the birds. Otherwise, trips by *lancha* (motorboat) can be arranged from $6.25 for a short visit to $38 for three hours. For the most part, the guides are new to this, so you may need to be quite explicit about what you want. You can ask to glide down the waters with the motor off for a while, which is considerably more atmospheric and less disturbing to the wildlife.

If going by yourself, then arrange a trip once you arrive in Tilapa or Tilapita. Otherwise, tour operators will usually pick you up and return you to Retalhuleu.

Cover up your arms and legs, wear mosquito repellent and bring water and a snack with you if you have not arranged any alternatives. The earlier in the morning that you venture out, the more birds you are likely to see. Updated: Feb 10, 2010.

COATEPEQUE

Bus connections from the border to other towns are pretty good, so there is little reason to have to spend a night in Coatepeque. This hot, busy town is clogged with traffic fumes and has nothing in the way of tourist attractions. It does have a reputation for being something of a trouble spot after dark.

If you find yourself here for the night, it's worth finding a comfortable hotel. Hotel Santiago is opposite the Santa Lucia bus terminal on the edge of town and has pleasant rooms for $21.25 for two people or $12.50 for one person. There is an attached restaurant. Hotel Europa is opposite the central park and has surprisingly great rooms with a balcony and cable TV for $11.25 per person.

The park is where it's all at: restaurants, fast food joints, ATMs and Internet cafés are all there. One block up from Hotel Europa, opposite Hotel Baechli, is Lei Lei, a good Chinese restaurant with large meals from $5. Updated: Feb 10, 2010.

Getting To and Away

Santa Lucia Terminal on the east road into town has five-star, fast buses to Guatemala City three times a day, at 3:30 a.m., 5:30 a.m. and 2:45 p.m. for $8.75. The main terminal is on the other side of town, a $0.30 microbus ride away or a $1 taxi ride. From here there are departures every fifteen minutes to Quetzaltenango (4 a.m.-5:15 p.m., $2, 2 hrs), Guatemala City (4 a.m.-3 p.m., $6.25, 5 hrs), Retalhuleu (4 a.m.-6 p.m., $1, 1 hr) and Mazatenango. Leaving from a corner of the bus station, microbuses head to Tecún Umán (for the border) every 10 minutes (5 a.m.-8 p.m., $1, 40 min). There are buses to Tilapa every 15 minutes (4 a.m.-6:30 p.m., $1.25, 1 hr). Updated: Feb 10, 2010.

RETALHULEU

Retalhuleu, or Reu as it is called for short, has hints of the colonial charm of Antigua, but you will probably be the only tourist in town. Despite the rich historical heritage in the surrounding area, the tourists who do visit usually come on long day trips from Quetzaltenango.

However, there are some excellent hotels in Reu and many activities and sights nearby, including Takalik Abaj, the Olmec and Maya Preclassical archeological park. It is a pleasant place to use as a base for a few days, as it is also close enough to the coast for day trips to the beach (though beaches a little further away are more enticing).

Once you have left the Pacific Highway, entry to Reu is via Calzada las Palmas, a grand Avenida of palm trees dotted with some impressive houses. The streets fringing Reu are nothing to write home about, but once you reach the central park, the town reveals its vibrant heart. The church is named for Saint Antonio of Padua, a town in Northern Italy, and the Italian love of beautiful architecture seems to have spread to the buildings surrounding the square. There are even Roman-style sculptures in front of the church.

The square is filled all day with people resting in the shade and watching the world go by. When the sun goes down, the noise of birds nesting in the trees is almost deafening and lovers come out to stroll hand-in-hand. It is a lovely place to spend some time, and near most of the best hotels and restaurants.

Reu is the capital of the region, but feels more like a small town. Many of its inhabitants are Quiché, and while it is unusual to see native dress, they still follow the old customs. I Reu is in the process of modernizing, though, and its latest effort is a new pedestrianized shopping center at the end of 5a Avenida. The climate here is subtropical and the land is extremely fertile. There are many *fincas* (estates) across the region that grow coffee, macadamias, sugar cane, mangoes and coconuts. Some of these fincas have added lodges, enabling visitors to experience life on a working plantation. Updated: Feb 10, 2010.

When to Go

Reu is a good town to visit all year round, as it does not get quite as hot as coastal towns, nor is it plagued with mosquitoes. Rainy season is between July and November, but it is rare for the rain to last for long. Reu celebrates a town festival on December 8th, but the fiesta lasts from December 5th-14th. Updated: Feb 10, 2010.

Getting To and Away

The town's bus station is a patch of road at 8a Avenida and 10 Calle. From here, buses leave every 20 minutes from 5 a.m. until 6 p.m. to Quetzaltenango, Guatemala City (via Escuintla and Santa Lucía Cotzumalguapa), Coatepegue, Tecún Umán and Mazatenango. Buses for Champerico leave from an area of the marketplace on the other side of town.

Getting Around

Taxis normally wait by the market, opposite Pollo Camperero on Calzada las Palmas, and can be hired to visit Takalik Abaj or the fincas. Your hotel will be able to arrange one. Few tourists visit here, so prices are not set in stone. Agree on all prices and times first. *Tuk-tuks* (small vehicles with a bench seat for passengers) putter around the town and charge $0.60 for a trip. Buses for El Astinal (Takalik Abaj) depart every half hour from behind the marketplace and cost $0.60. Ask repeatedly and you'll find it eventually. A daily bus at 11 a.m. to Comunidad Alianza departs from the same place (it leaves the Comunidad at 6:30 a.m.). You can also take a tuk-tuk to Quatro Caminos (the Pacific Highway junction) and wait for it there or try and hitch a lift. Updated: Feb 10, 2010.

Safety

Reu is a relaxed, safe town and tourists need take no more than usual precautions with their valuables or their person. The greatest annoyance is most likely the boy racers charging around the streets at night while you are trying to sleep. Few people actually live in the center of town, so be mindful that the streets can get pretty deserted at night. Updated: Feb 10, 2010.

Services

INGUAT (Guatemalan Institute of Tourism) does not have an office in Reu yet, but there is a representative based here who is very helpful. Contact Rony Soto (reuasistur@gmail.com). There are numerous banks and ATMs around the central park. The police station, the supermarket and Cinterview Internet ($0.75, Daily 8 a.m.-9 p.m.) are also on the central park. The air-conditioned Internet Antigua ($0.60. 8 a.m.-7 p.m.) is on 4 Calle. The National Hospital of Retalhuleu is on Boulevard Centenario, 3a Avenida in Zone 2. There is a laundromat on 5 Calle. Updated: Feb 10, 2010.

Things to See and Do

Depending on what tickles your fancy, there are quite a few things to do in the area around Reu and a couple in town as well. The archeological park Takalik Abaj is high on most visitors' list, as is the small museum on central park. For a fun-filled day, there is the acclaimed Xocomil water park or Xetulul amusement park. To relax in nature and learn more about traditional farming methods, there are several fincas that can be stayed in. There are also opportunities to go mountain biking, rafting, kayaking or hiking. Finally, the beach is only a couple of hours away. Updated: Feb 10, 2010.

Reuxtreme

This is the only tour company that has a base in Reu as well as in Guatemala City. The shop is next to Casa Santa Maria, and they will call Alejandro for you, who speaks good English, if he is not there already. It would be best to try and organize any trip a few days in advance. The family is from this area, so they know it very well. Apart from standard tours to Takalik Abaj, they can also arrange rafting trips on the Rio Nahualate, kayaking in Manchón Guamuchal Wetlands, birdwatching tours and mountain biking. Trips require minimum numbers but if you are alone, the best bet is to aim for a weekend when more excursions are taking place. Multi-day trips also possible. At Hostal Casa Santa Maria, 4 Ca. 4-23, Zone 1. Tel: 502-5205-1132, E-mail: reuxtours@reuxtreme.com, info@reuestuyo.com, URL: www.reuxtreme.com, www.reuestuyo.com. Updated: Feb 10, 2010.

Museo de Arqueología y Etnología

Located in a colonial house on the central park, the small museum holds some interesting artwork and pottery. Rooms are divided into time periods such as Preclassic, Classic and Postclassic to enable easy comparisons, while the upstairs floor is dedicated to Retalhuleu and the surrounding area. This includes a section on the local soccer team and a map of historically significant places. Sometimes music events are held on the grounds in the evenings. This museum is worth a look but it will probably only take half an hour at most. Tuesday-Saturday 8:30 a.m.-12:30 p.m. and 2 p.m. to 5 p.m., Sunday 9 a.m.-12:30 p.m. 6 Av. 5-68, Zona 1. Tel: 502-7771-0557. Updated: May 14, 2010.

Casa Samala–Casa de Cultura

Two blocks behind the museum, the Casa de Cultura is a pleasant place to come afterward for a cup of filtered coffee and a break. There are several different rooms containing traditional arts and crafts, paintings, some old photographs and a small library that you are allowed to use while at the house. The café is set around an indoor courtyard and also serves simple breakfasts, lunches and dinners for $3. Acting as an unofficial tourist information center, the staff is helpful and polite. Monday-Saturday 8 a.m.-7 p.m. 8 Av. 5-84, Zone 1. Tel: 502-7771-0513. Updated: May 14, 2010.

Lodging

The standard of hotels in and around Retalhuleu is comparatively high, but there is little in the low-budget range. Prices generally start from $10 per person. All rooms have cable TV and private bathroom. Some have air conditioning, others just a fan. If you are struggling with the heat, then consider air conditioning a must. A couple of hotels have swimming pools as well. It is possible for non-guests to use the pool at Don José and Hotel Astor for a fee. Updated: Feb 10, 2010.

Hotel América

(ROOMS: $11-13.75) Conveniently located a two-minute walk from the bus station or a ten-minute walk from the central park, Hotel América may be on the run-down side of town, but it's the cheapest hotel here and perfectly agreeable. Accommodation is simple, clean and includes cable TV, fan and private bathroom as standard. The rooms are a tad on the small size, but if you ask for one upstairs then at least you'll get lots of light and a great window for watching the street. The management is very friendly. 8 Av. 9-32, Zone 1. Tel: 502-5820-6570/5360-1483. Updated: Feb 10, 2010.

Hotel Genesis

(ROOMS: $15-28.75) The sign says three stars, and Hotel Genesis lives up its rating without being very memorable. Rooms are clean and comfortable with a big TV, hot water and air conditioning. This is a great bargain for singles longing for that ice cold breeze instead of a fan. If you are looking to while away some time, the ample lobby also has table football and pool. The central park is a minute away on foot. 6 Ca. 6 - 27, Zone 1. Tel: 502-7771-2855. Updated: Feb 10, 2010.

Hotel Posada Don José

(ROOMS: $14-42) Built in the mid-19th century, Posada Don José is a lovely colonial house on two floors and set around a large swimming pool. The spacious rooms come with cable TV and air conditioning, and you can choose between having carpet or a balcony. This is the most expensive hotel in town and is extremely popular. The staff is very attentive and the restaurant is well worth a visit even if you stay elsewhere. The Annex down the road is cheaper with less attractive rooms, but you are allowed to use the facilities in the main house, including the gym. 5 Ca. 3-67, zone 1. Tel: 502-7771-0180/4182, E-mail: posadadonjose@hotmail.com, URL: www.hotelposadadedonejose.com. Updated: Feb 10, 2010.

Hotel Astor

(ROOMS: $18.75-34.50) Located in a colonial house just off the central park, Hotel Astor looks more grandiose than it is. The faux rock garden, swimming pool, Jacuzzi and patio area are lovely places to relax, but rooms are pretty much regulation modern hotel rooms. Air conditioning is included in the price. The dark wood bar is open till 1 a.m. and there's a stuffed crocodile for company. It is possible to access the pool if staying elsewhere, and it's worth asking for the latest promotion. Sometimes they offer $3 entrance with a free hamburger, fries and drink. 5 Ca. 4-60, Zone 1. Tel: 502-7771-2559/0475/2562. E-mail: hotelastor@intelnett.com, hotelastor_reu@hotmail.com. Updated: Feb 10, 2010.

Hostal Casa Santa Maria

(ROOMS: $16.25-34) An inexpensive boutique hotel, Casa Santa Maria is a wonderful find. The beautifully decorated rooms surround a small inner courtyard, garden and swimming pool. You have a choice of fan or air conditioning, and the price includes a continental breakfast. WiFi is also available, but the signal does not reach most of the rooms. The best reception is on the patio. There is a selection of games and a collection of Spanish books that may be borrowed. Reuxtreme is based next door. 4 Ca. 4 - 23, Zona 1. Tel: 502-7771-6136/5205-1132, E-mail: info@hostalcasasantamaria.com. Updated: Feb 10, 2010.

Restaurants

For a decent sized town, the restaurant options in Reu are surprisingly limited. The fare is inexpensive, tasty and typically Guatemalan with some seafood influences. Vegetarians will struggle to find variety in their meals and might want to consider a trip to the supermarket. Alternatively, there are always licuados. At the end of 5a Avenida, in Centro Comercial La Trinidad, there is a drive-thru McDonald's, a Pollo Camperero and a line of fast food stores with al fresco dining on a shady, pedestrianized street. In the center of town, facing Hotel Genesis, there is a row of ceviche stands, and on the opposite corner of the square, you can find the ubiquitous taco stands. Updated: Feb 10, 2010.

Restaurante La Luna and Licuados

(ENTREES: $2.5-4.5) La Luna may not be winning prizes for food presentation, but the homemade Guatemalan or Chinese meals are tasty and the service is quick.

Photo by: K. Heredia

Combined with an excellent central location and a breezy ambiance, this place is popular with locals and visitors alike. The cafeteria maintains its standards by enforcing a strict quota of three beers per person. After that you'll have to head to Lo de Chaz across the road. If you fancy a *licuado* (smoothie) instead, they can bring you one from the top-notch licuado bar next door. Monday-Saturday, 8 a.m. to 1 p.m. Sundays. 5 Ca. 4-97, Zone 1. Tel: 502-7771-0194. Updated: Feb 10, 2010.

Restaurante Lo De Chaz

(ENTREES: $2-4) Huge, blue, wooden gates welcome you into a down-to-earth local restaurant with wooden tables and plastic chairs. A variety of chicken dishes in different sauces are available for $4 or fillet mignon for the bargain price of $5. They also serve breakfast, soups and snacks. Restaurante Lo de Chaz doubles as a bar: the bar stays open until 11 p.m. during the week and until midnight on weekends. Apart from a selection of whiskeys, they whip up a number of cocktails at $2 a pop. Monday-Wednesday 7 a.m.-11 p.m., Thursday-Saturday 11 a.m.-11 p.m. 5 Ca. 4-65. Tel: 502-7771-4749. Updated: Feb 10, 2010.

Restaurante Posada Don José

(ENTREES: $3-14) For a choice of mixed European and Guatemalan cuisine, Posada Don José is the best place to eat. The food is delicious, there are some very tempting desserts and the coffee is filtered. Vegetarians will be thrilled to discover that they, too, have some options, even if these are just pasta, salad, a panini sandwich and soup. Breakfast also brings something a bit different, including eggs benedict or a dish called 'divorciado.' Surprisingly, considering the locale, the restaurant is very reasonably priced. Guests can sit poolside, in the bar or in the air conditioned restaurant. Daily 7 a.m-10:30 p.m. Updated: Jul 20, 2010.

Restaurante Super Redd

(ENTREES: $3.75-15) There are several pizza places near the central park on 5a Avenida, and Restaurante Super Redd is the best. Apart from serving semi-authentic American pizza with a variety of toppings, mostly meaty ones, guests can also have salads, sandwiches, burgers or pasta. There are a couple of vegetarian options as well. This is a pleasant café with indoor or outdoor seating areas and the staff is very amenable. All meals are made to order. Super Redd is open from Mondays-Saturdays 7:30 a.m-9 p.m.,. 5a Av. 6-58, Zone 1. Tel: 502-7771-0172. Updated: Jul 20, 2010.

AROUND RETALHULEU

Parque Acuático Xocomil

Xocomil stands high above other water parks, and that's not just because it has the longest water slide in Central America. This park competes with the best water parks in the world. It is terrific fun for the whole family, and there is so much to do that it's hard to fit it all into one day. Tube down a Maya river, take on your friends in a mammoth water fight, go crazy in the wave pool and get fit climbing up stairs for yet another of the 14 different water slides. There is also a beach to chill out on when it's time for a break. There are several restaurants, kiosks and shops around the park serving meals, snacks and drinks. To reach the park, any bus traveling between Quetzaltenango and Reu can drop you off or there are frequent microbuses running from Reu (the ride is about 30 minutes long) between Thursdays and Sundays. Catch a park microbus from the roundabout. Thursday-Sunday 9 a.m.-5 p.m. Tel: 502-7722-9400, URL: www.irtra.org.gt.in. Updated: May 14, 2010.

Parque De Diversiones Xetulul

Winner of the prestigious Applause Award in 2008 for the best amusement park, Xetulul sets high standards for an adrenalin-packed day out. The park is divided into seven themed areas that take visitors on trips around Europe as well as Guatemala. You can take an exhilarating gondola ride and see the Trevi fountain in Italy, watch the Moulin Rouge in France, take to the skies in a Spanish Galleon or explore a German town. Naturally three of the zones are dedicated to Guatemala, including one on the Maya. Xetulul also has Central America's largest roller coaster. Each area has themed restaurants offering traditional cuisine. To reach the park, any bus traveling between Xela and Reu can drop you off, or there are frequent microbuses running from Reu (the ride is 30 minutes or so) between Thursdays and Sundays. Catch a park microbus from the roundabout in front of the new shopping center. Thursday-Sunday 9 a.m.-5 p.m. Tel: 502-7722-9400, E-mail: eventos@irtra.org.gt, URL: www.irtra.org.gt. Updated: Feb 10, 2010.

Finca El Patrocinio

The 140-hectare (345 ac) Patrocinio Reserve includes a variety of different habitats and is dedicated to conservation and restoration of the natural environment. The reserve is also involved in agrotourism, working with and supporting a local community of 10 families. Visitors can hike or birdwatch from the observation tower. A variety of tours are available, including ziplining, mountain biking and a general tour of the area. Accommodation is in one of three rooms, with private bathrooms, in the comfortable lodge. The reserve can be reached by a combination of walking, the Comunidad Alianza bus, pick-up trucks and hitchhiking. Otherwise take a taxi from Reu. Any stays or tours should be booked a few days in advance. Tel: 502-7771-4393/5203-5701, URL: www.reservapatrocinio.com. Updated: May 14, 2010.

Parque Arqueológico Takalik Abaj

The main reason most visitors come to Reu is to see Takalik Abaj. While not as famous as Tikal in the North, it is considerably older and just as important. The site covers 6.5 square kilometers (4 sq mi) with ten terraces and 13 pyramids, which are is divided into four groups: North, West, Central and South. Unfortunately, most of the groups are on private land and cannot be visited, so the national park focuses on the Central group. At the entrance, a guide is assigned to accompany visitors, and while not obligatory, a tip is advised at the end, as it is the guides' stories and information that bring Takalik Abaj to life. Tours last from two to three hours.

The name Takalik Abaj means 'standing stones' after the massive stone monuments on the site's grounds, which are made of granite and marble. The closest place where this material is found is 30 kilometers (18.64 mi) away, and carrying it can't have been an easy job.

Digs and restorations are still carrying on all over the park, and the present findings indicate there is much more to be found. Parts of the causeways, the cobbled roads that linked the temples, have been uncovered, as have parts of the water drainage system.

There are numerous stone sculptures around the park. The *barrigons* (pot-bellies) represent humans, although some look more like monkeys, and are thought to symbolize fertility. A variety of frogs also symbolize fertility: some face east and some face west. Temples,

PACIFIC COAST

sculptures and the profiles on monuments always face a certain direction: to the north toward the ancestors; to the east toward the sunrise, or life; to the west toward the sunset, or the end, death or evolution; and to the south towards knowledge and experience. The ball court was positioned strategically to face the east and west.

This site is significant because of the mix of styles, Olmec and Maya in particular. The area is undoubtedly Preclassic and a date of 300 BC is widely considered as accurate. However, it is not known for sure if the Olmecs and the Maya mixed or if they were both here at different times. One sculpture that isclearly Olmec is of a man raising a stick inside the open mouth of a jaguar. Also in the park is a small wildlife sanctuary, which has crocodiles, turtles, a single big cat (a jaguar relative), boars, raccoons, deer, birds and other animals. It is possible to feed them for $0.25.

To reach the park, take a camioneta from the marketplace in Reu to the town of El Asintal for $1.20. From here regular pickups run to the park for $0.60. Daily 7 a.m.-5 p.m. Updated: Jul 20, 2010.

Tak'alik Maya Lodge

This lodge and farm is located on Terrace 9 of the Takalik Abaj national park. A 10-minute walk through the sub-tropical forest takes you to airy, all-natural bungalows, with fantastic views of the surrounding nature from the balcony. For the package price, you get a two-day, one-night stay, which comes with three meals, use of both the swimming and waterfall pool, and tours of the national park, plantation and coffee fields. It is also possible to just spend a day here for $28, including all tours and lunch. The lodge is 2.5 kilometers (1.6 mi) past Takalik Abaj on the same road. Tel: 502-2369-7206/5616/9055, URL: www.takalik.com. Updated: May 14, 2010.

Comunidad Alianza Coffee Farm

Up in the hills with a commanding view of the active Volcán Santiaguito, which still lets out regular smoke clouds, Comunidad Alianza is a wonderful place to come and relax for a few days or volunteer on a traditional finca. The locally-run enterprise involves forty families and produces coffee, macadamia nuts, items made from bamboo and biofuel. Different packages can be arranged, including tours of the plantation and the facilities. There is a refreshing waterfall at a 20-minute walk from the main house, and birds can be seen

all over (sunrise is the best time to spot them). Meals can be arranged but the food is basic and portions are small, so you might want to bring something extra. Volunteers can cook their own meals in the kitchen. Electricity is provided via hydro-power or a generator and usually runs till 10 p.m. To reach here, a Ciufuentes (blue and cream) bus with a sign saying 'Hocken' leaves the marketplace in Rue daily at 11 a.m. for Comunidad Alianza and returns at 6:30 a.m. in the morning. There is no mobile phone reception up here. Updated: May 14, 2010.

CHAMPERICO

Thirty-four kilometers (21 mi) from Reu, and the closest beach to Quetzaltenango, Champerico is one of the most popular beaches on the northern end of Guatemala's Pacific Coast, though it is hardly the most attractive. Many visitors choose to stay at better quality hotels in and around Reu, but there are a couple of good ones at the beach too. At the end of the central road leading to the beach, Hotel Maza has clean, comfortable rooms with TV, private bathroom and awesome views from the terrace for $25. Opposite Hotel Maza and actually on the beach, Hotel Sub-marino has cramped, basic rooms for $10 (1 person) or $14 (2 people). Both hotels are in the thick of the action and for most visitors that's what this place is all about: getting down and partying, at least on the weekends. During the week, the scene is much quieter, but the existence of some beach-goers means that not all of the restaurants close. They line the beachfront, serving similar seafood dishes from $5 a plate. Champerico feels like a giant seedy pick-up joint, and nightclubs abound. The beach is broad, with little rubbish and a long, ugly pier. A stone wall cordons off the main beach area and lifeguards are usually on duty, so swimming is pretty safe. The beach is prettier, though, the further you walk away from town. At the end of the day, unless an all-night party is what you are looking for, it's probably better to head to one of the other coastal towns for that welcome beach break. Updated: May 14, 2010.

Getting To and Away

Buses to Champerico leave from one of several terminals hidden in the marketplace. The easiest way to find it is to turn left just past the big yellow Malcora building on the Calzada Las Palmas or take a tuk-tuk (motorized vehicle with a bench for passengers). The bus trip takes 45 minutes and costs $0.75. Buses leave (and return) every 15 minutes from 5:30 a.m. till 6:30 p.m. Ten kilometers (6.2 miles) from Cuatro Caminos (crossroads to Reu), take road to left at Cuatro Caminos. URL: www.comunidadneuvaalianza.org. Updated: Feb 10, 2010.

EL TULATE

The beautiful beach at Tulate gently slopes into the ocean, creating the perfect setting for long walks and refreshing dips. The low-key surf is safe for children or weak swimmers to venture out and have a splash around. On the weekends, there are lifeguards on duty. Unlike many other beaches on the Pacific coast, Tulate is surprisingly rubbish-free, although the canal side of the beach cannot make the same claim.

To reach the beach, take a *lancha* (motorboat) for $0.55 across the canal. A short paved street, lined with comedores and tiendas, leads to the beach.

Only a handful of accommodation options exist in Tulate, but they are agreeable ones. Villa Victoria is a tourist center that is rather busy and noisy on the weekends but deserted during the week. Rooms cost $18.75 with shared bathroom or $31.25 with private bathroom. There is one on both sides of the canal. Prices are the same. It is a difficult toss-up between a two minute walk to the beach or a breezy room that opens onto a glorious canal view. Hotel Sol y Mar is on the wrong side of the canal but has cheap, acceptable rooms starting from $11.50. Playa Paraíso is a ten minute walk along the beach (toward the left) and has a more sophisticated set-up with a restaurant, swimming pool, spacious rooms and hammocks in the gardens. Rooms cost $41.

Playa Paraíso has the only restaurant that is open every day. Otherwise there are plenty of restaurants serving seafood and typical local food, but during the week most of them are closed. There is no ATM in Tulate. The nearest one is at the halfway town where the bus stops for a while. Updated: Jul 06, 2010.

Getting To and Away

Regardless of whether you are coming from the east or the west, if you are already on a bus then stay on it and change at Cuyotenango (20 minutes from Retalhuleu at the junction with the Pacific Highway, $0.55). Buses for Tulate originate in Mazatenango ($1.50), where they leave on the hour from 5 a.m. till 5:30 p.m., and then make a frustrating stop in Cuyotenango for half an hour. The bus will fill up but even if no seats are available immediately, one will come free within 10 minutes or so. Frequent stops are a fixture on this route, so the whole journey takes at least two hours. This includes another 20 minute stop halfway. If you can, grab the bus driver before he exits to find out how long you've got so you can stretch your legs or get a snack. Buses end at the lancha dock in Tulate. Updated: Feb 05, 2010.

SANTA LUCÍA COTZUMALGUAPA

The run-down appearance of modern Santa Lucía belies its distinguished historical importance. A 10-square-kilometer (6.2 sq mi) area called the "Cotzumalguapa nuclear zone" contains within it the sites of Bilbao, El Baúl and El Castilo. More than 200 structures and 180 sculptured monuments have been discovered here, dating from somewhere between 500 to 800 AD.

The predominant tribe throughout the years were the Pipil, although the Quiché and Kaqchikel also took their turn in charge before the Spaniards came. Life changed dramatically and the old ceremonial grounds were lost, first to nature and then to coffee. Ironically, it was while land was being cleared for a coffee plantation that some ruins were discovered and the search for more began. Nowadays the coffee plantations have all given way to sugarcane plantations. In the town itself there is little to show for the history immortalized in the surrounding area. A massive stelae that used to be in the central square, next to the church, disappeared when the park was remodeled in 2003.

The Bilbao stones, a 15 minute walk from the center of town, are famous more as a place where tourists are attacked than for the story they tell. It is strange that Santa Lucia makes little fuss about something which most towns would fuss too much about.

Modern day Santa Lucía Cotzumalguapa is named after the lady Santa Lucía, a beautiful virgin who had caught the eye of the invading Spaniards. Fearing that she would be taken against her will, she chose instead to take out her eyes with a pen, correctly guessing that they would no longer be interested. In the main church, above the center altar, there is an effigy of her holding a pen and a box (containing her eyes) in her right hand.

The latter part of the town's name, Cotzumalguapa, means 'place of the comadrejas,' which is an animal, similar to a weasel, that used to be found all around this region. Updated: Feb 09, 2010.

History

Experts are divided as to the exact time period that the area of Bilbao flourished. Some put it at middle Classic (400 to 550 AD) while others consider it to be late Classic (550 to 700 AD). There is no doubt though that the area was inhabited as early as the Preclassic period because one monument from 37 AD is the oldest known in Guatemala and includes one of the earliest Hieroglyphic texts ever seen.

It is generally considered that from approximately 500 AD the area was inhabited by the Nahuatl-speaking Pipil, who migrated from Central Mexico and could have owed their allegiance to the city of Teotihuacan. One of the reasons why the ancestral links are unclear is because the area developed a unique artistic style evident in the ceramics and, more significantly, in the sculptures. The realistic representations of human figures could have been portraits. There is a preoccupation with death, sacrifice, and interactions with supernatural beings.

Influences of this style spread over a wide area, indicating that Santa Lucia was a place of power. It is also assumed, because of many architectural pieces found, including carved stairs and pillars and the open platform design of Bilbao, that the site may have served as a palace, as housing for the privileged, as an administrative center or as a place of worship.

Many of the stelae display plants, fruits and vines as symbols of fertility and cacao as a symbol of wealth. Cacao and quetzal feathers were considered 'money' for a long time. Scenes depicting decapitated bodies are common and there are sculptures of skeletons and torn-off limbs. On a less macabre level, potbellied sculptures were also popular, as well as giant heads who possibly represented different gods. At some point the Quiché and Kaqchikel came from the northwest to defeat the Pipil and take over their land. They were, in turn, defeated by the Spaniards, who

abandoned the monuments to nature. It was not until 1860, when land was being cleared to create a coffee plantation, that Pedro de Anda found some partially buried stones with carvings and so began the uncovering of this settlement. Updated: Feb 09, 2010.

When to Go

Rainy season is between July and November and can make the going a little soggy when traipsing around, but it's nothing that a pair of wellies and a poncho couldn't sort out. Semana Santa is a popular time of year, as there are processions up to El Calvario church, on the road near the Bilbao stones. Prayers for Santa Lucía begin on November 29th, but her day is actually celebrated from December 12-13. If there is a choice, then visiting on the weekend could be marginally more interesting because locals will visit the stones to make pagan offerings. Market day is on Sunday. Updated: Feb 09, 2010.

Getting To and Away

Despite the building of a ring road around Santa Lucía, most buses along the Pacific Highway still pass the edge of town on what is confusingly also called the Pacific Highway. Therefore, the bus station in town (on the east end of 5 Calle) is only really useful for buses toward La Democracia and Sipacate. On the Santa Lucía part of the Pacific Highway, there are some bus stops at intervals, but the most popular place for picking up a bus is outside the Esso station at the end of 4a Avenida if heading toward Guatemala City or El Salvador or on the opposite side of the road if heading toward Mexico. The best bet is to take any bus and change at Escuintla (for the east) or at Cocales (for the west) as needed. Updated: Feb 09, 2010.

Getting Around

The taxi rank is on the east side of the central park. Your hotel can also you a cab. Santa Lucía is small enough to be able to walk everywhere by foot, but the traffic fumes make it rather uncomfortable. For a tour of the major sites and museums, a taxi will charge between $20 and $25 for the trip, taking as much time as you like. There are no tuk-tuks (motor vehicles with a bench seat for passengers) in Santa Lucía. Updated: Feb 09, 2010.

Safety

Santa Lucía is a fairly safe town, so applying normal precautions when going about should be enough. As for visiting the stones, it is hard to tell whether a danger of theft still really exists or if it is just that no tourists go by themselves anymore so the problem no longer presents itself. Ideally, find out about the latest before leaving, but independent travelers should definitely avoid visiting the Bilbao Stones alone. This is where most of the problems have occurred in the past. As for the other sites, walking around alone should be avoided, as these places are quite remote and the chances of getting lost are high. It is more likely that travelers will be befriended by a sugar cane worker than robbed, but you never know. Leave all unneeded valuables and cash at the hotel. Updated: Feb 09, 2010.

Services

There is no tourist office in Santa Lucía but the Municipality Office (north side of the central park) can help out with guides. Numerous banks and ATMs are located around the central square on 3a Avenida and 4a Avenida for changing money or withdrawing cash. The banks are not used to seeing many tourists with dollars so you may have to try a few. The security guard on the door usually knows what's up, helping you avoid wasting time in long queues. Pharmacies abound but Hospital IGSS is a couple of kilometers west of town. Internet Cre@ is halfway up the colonial building to the west of central park and has air conditioned, reasonably fast Internet for $0.55 per hour. Updated: Feb 09, 2010.

Things to See and Do

The only reason to spend a night in Santa Lucía is to make the most of this region's interesting history. Key hotspots are the two museums and the massive stone carvings at Bilbao and El Baúl Hilltop. An unhurried tour of all four sites would take about half a day. While maps indicate that there is much more to be seen in the area, exploring is not welcomed and much of the land is on private property.

The church next door to the central park is worth passing by, if only to view the virgin holding her eyes (unfortunately, you can't see them, since they're in a box), but aside from that the town center holds little of interest. For a post-sight-seeing refreshing dip, tourists with a car could drive to Siquinalá to look for the waterfalls; otherwise head to Hotel Santiaguito and chill out by their pool. Updated: Feb 09, 2010.

Museo El Baúl

The free, open-air museum of El Baúl is a collection of sculptures found from all over the sugarcane plantation's estate. At the entrance, visitors are greeted by a massive stone jaguar that is, coincidentally, the symbol of Santa Lucía Cotzumalguapa. Some of the sculptures have perplexed experts, such as the giant head with a full beard. An excellent preserved stela of a ballcourt player is sandwiched between two 3-D sculptures of a unique style. There is also a collection of heads with open mouths, and you can see from the way the backs of the heads were designed that they were supposed to fit into walls as 'bricks.' Elsewhere on the grounds, archeologists have found a ball court, a sweat bath and an obsidian workshop, but these are not open to visitors. The sugarcane factory itself is no longer in operation but visitors can see an old German steam tractor and two steam engines that used to run on a system of private tracks. These are to the left of the museum. Reaching El Baúl is easiest done by taxi as part of a tour, but there are worker buses in the morning and afternoon and occasional micro buses to a town further along the road. Otherwise, it may be possible to hitch. It is possible to walk to the El Baúl hilltop site from here, but be prepared to get lost. Realistically, it is simpler to go the hilltop site first and head to the farm afterward. When arriving at the plantation, skip the first gate and make for the second one, which has a sign for the museum. A guard will sign and let you in. Monday-Friday 8 a.m.-4 p.m., Saturday 8 a.m.-noon. Updated: Jul 16, 2010.

El Baúl Hilltop

This site with a glorious half-buried giant head and a well preserved monument is popular with descendents of the Pipil, who come to honor their ancestors and their Gods in the old ways. At the weekend, it is possible to see a ceremony taking place, but it is more common to find the remnants of a smoking fire, melted candles, flower petals scattered around the head and monument and the butt of a broad cigar on the ground. The site is surrounded by fields and forests and volcanoes Aqua and Fuego form a lovely backdrop.

However, it is not easy to find these carvings. On the road from Santa Lucía to El Baúl, take the signposted right fork to Los Tarros (the left fork leads to Finca El Baúl). After a few minutes of driving, turn onto the last dirt road to the right before the line of houses finishes. Just down this road, another paved road heads to the left. Park at the end of this road and the carvings are in the fields beyond. After leaving the dirt track, instead of turning left to return to the fork, carry on up the road until reaching San Juan Perdida, an old church now stunningly reclaimed by nature. This is the cemetery for the Maya and the tombs are strewn with colorful streamers and decorations, as if in preparation for a party. Among the tombs are some simple mounds of dirt with trees or flowers growing from them. This seems, in many ways, to be a far more fitting tribute to life and death than a concrete box and an appropriate reminder of the importance of living in harmony with mother earth. Updated: Feb 09, 2010.

Bilbao Stones

It is a surreal walk to leave the hustle and bustle of town, enter the cane fields and seemingly discover by chance the existence of carved boulders. Dating from the late classic period, there are three sets of stones here, some of which are still well preserved. Copies of a couple of the stones, including the impressive Monument 21, can be seen at the Museo Cultura Cotzumalguapa. Due to assaults on tourists, the Bilbao stones should not be visited alone. Local kids sometimes volunteer to show the way, but are not likely to be much of a deterrent to a would-be thief. On the outskirts of Santa Lucía Cotzumalguapa. Updated: Feb 09, 2010.

Museo de Cultura Cotzumalguapa

In the mid- to late-1800s, land in Cotzumalguapa was cleared to make way for a coffee plantation. Many stelae, ceramics and artifacts were discovered and are on display at the Museo de Cultura Cotzumalguapa, including a copy of the famous Bilbao Monument 21 from the cane fields.

The copy of Monument 21 is superb. The original rock had been artificially flattened before the carving began and it depicts a central figure in a headdress, a shaman (to the left) with a hand puppet and a god (to the right). All around the monument are carvings of vines, birds (9 in total) and cacao beans, a symbol of wealth. The original is part of the Bilbao stones just outside of town. Other highlights of the museum include a sacrificial altar inspired by the crocodile and a carved skeleton. Rubbings of many of the carvings are hung on the walls and make it considerably easier to decipher the often intricate and faded detail than looking at the stones themselves. Apart from the larger carvings, there is

also a collection of ceramics, obsidian and smaller sculptures. Some fragments of the yoke that the ball players wore can be seen here and a fantastic diagram illustrates how the game would have been played. Augusto Fernandez is the museum's custodian. He is usually happy to show you around and give explanations in Spanish with the occasional odd word of English, provided that you don't turn up in his lunch hour (1 to 2 p.m.). If he is not to be found at the office, ask for him at the store almost directly opposite the church. To reach Finca Las Illusiones, turn at the sign off the Pacific Highway, 2 kilometers (1.24 mi) east of town, then carry on up the track and over the crossroads. Mondays to Fridays 7 a.m.-4 p.m., Saturday 7 a.m.-11. Updated: Feb 09, 2010.

Lodging

Accommodation options are limited in Santa Lucía. The best hotels are on the Pacific Highway, which cuts through the south end of town. Most hotels come with a private bathroom and cable TV. Just off the central square on 4a Avenida, Hospedaje Reforma has the cheapest rooms ($4 per person) but they are not particularly clean. For those on a budget, this would be a good time to treat yourself to something better. Updated: Feb 09, 2010.

Hotel Internacional

(ROOMS: $11-17.95) The cheapest decent hotel in Santa Lucía, Hotel Internacional has clean, reasonably-sized rooms with TV, private bathroom and fan. The staff is friendly and courteous. As the hotel is set back from the main road, down a side street, it is quiet at night. Reception is open 24 hours but this is not the sort of hotel that rents rooms by the hour. The restaurant offers the usual run of Guatemalan hotel cuisine. Take the side-street off the highway at km 90. Look for the Hotel Internacional sign. Km 90 Pacific Highway, Callejón de los Mormones. Tel: 502-7882-5504/5496/8919. Updated: Feb 09, 2010.

Hotel El Camino

(ROOMS: $17-26.25) Popular with businessmen, Hotel El Camino has a pleasant lobby, reception and restaurant area, although the rooms themselves are somewhat soulless. Ask for a room upstairs, as they are brighter and airier. The rooms are large and come with air conditioning, hot water and cable TV. There is free WiFi. There is also ample parking available or it is 10-minute walk downhill from the main bus stop on the Pacific Highway.

Km 90.5 Pacific Highway. Tel: 502-7882-5316/5951/5954, E-mail: hotelelcamino@hotmail.com. Updated: Feb 09, 2010.

Hotel Santiaguito

(ROOMS: $41-54.25) Santa Lucía's take on a luxury hotel, Hotel Santiaguito is modeled on a typical European-style hotel, with twin double beds and a charming décor. Inside the grounds is an attractive and enormous swimming pool which could prove very welcome after a sweltering hike around the Maya sites and museums. Visitors may use the pool at a small charge of $2.50. The on-site restaurant serves up meals from a menu and a delectable buffet. Km 90.4 Pacific Highway. Tel: 502-7882-5435. Updated: Feb 09, 2010.

Restaurants

Around town, there are a number of *comedores* (dining halls) and fast food joints and some pretty good bakeries. Most hotels have attached restaurants, the best of which are at Hotel El Camino and Hotel Santiaguito, or there are a couple of appealing options located near them on the Pacific Highway. At Km 87.5, there is a small shopping mall that is home to a supermarket, Pollo Camperero and McDonald's. Updated: Feb 09, 2010.

Julio's

(ENTREES: $1.50-2) Located opposite Hotel El Camino, Julio's is where the businessmen come to get decent food at prices considerably lower than in the hotel's restaurant. The food is typical local fare: beans, cheese, eggs, plátanos and tortillas for breakfast or dinner, a set menu for lunch, hamburgers for a snack and *licuados* (smoothies) to wash it all down. There is a cozy atmosphere and a North American diner feel to the green and white staff uniforms. Daily 7 a.m. to 8 p.m. Km 90.5 Pacific Highway. Tel: 502-7820-0375/5536-9496. Updated: Feb 09, 2010.

Robert's Steakhouse

(ENTREES: $5-20) Meat lovers should not miss out on Robert's Steakhouse. Pride of place on the menu goes to 8- or 16-oz steaks, cut and cooked as you like. There are seafood alternatives as well. Vegetarians are almost out of luck except for a cooked cheese dish or the obligatory salad. The spacious restaurant is open-air and the staff is keenly attentive. Roberts is open till 10 p.m. and has a well-stocked bar for

a couple of after dinner drinks—purely as an aid to digestion, of course. Tuesdays-Sundays 11 a.m.-10 p.m. Km 87.5 Pacific Highway. Tel: 502-7882-6675. Updated: Feb 09, 2010.

Costa Linda

(ENTREES: $7-20) A local favorite as much for the specialty seafood and ceviche dishes as for the lively atmosphere, Costa Linda stays open till at least 10 p.m. and doubles as a rancho pub. Decorated with gusto, your first instinct on arrival could well be to look for a place to tie the horses up. The food is not cheap, but comes highly recommended. Strict vegetarians will find their choice limited to a salad. Daily 11 a.m.-10 p.m. Km 89.5 Pacific Highway Tel: 502-5849-5223. Updated: Feb 09, 2010.

LA DEMOCRACIA

From the outskirts, La Democracia appears to have seen better days. However, it has one major draw: a number of large, crudely done Olmec-style heads that were discovered at a farm on the edge of town. Nearly all of the heads now surround the pleasantly decorated central square under the shade of an enormous ceiba tree. The origin of the heads is still somewhat of a mystery. Some of the sculptures have flattened heads pointing to the skies, their arms encircling extended bellies, while others just show somber faces with bulging eyes. At one corner of the square is a museum, in which three rooms display archeological artifacts, paintings and jade. The museum is open from 9 a.m. to 4 p.m. Tuesday-Saturday and costs $4.

For anyone other than the most dedicated of historical aficionados, La Democracia is best treated as a stop-off on the way to somewhere else rather than a destination in and of itself. The delightful Antojitos Mary, tucked away in the new building opposite the square, has smoothies or tasty meals and is a good place for a break. Otherwise you can find an ice-cream shop, a bakery, a fried chicken joint and burger shops all right next to each other. There is an ATM on the square and an Internet café. The one guesthouse in town, Paxil y Cayalá, is pokey and over-priced ($7 for a room with shared bathroom, $15 for private bathroom). Updated: Jul 06, 2010.

Getting To and Away

All buses up and down the road leading from Siquinalá to Sipacate pass by the square in La Democracia. There are regular direct buses from Guatemala City and frequent buses from Santa Lucía Cotzumalguapa; otherwise take any bus along the Pacific Highway and change at Siquinalá. Leaving La Democracia, buses depart every 20 minutes in either direction from 6 a.m. to 6:15 p.m. and it is fastest to get on the next one that is heading the way you wish to go and then change at either Siquinalá ($0.50, 15 min) for Escuintla, Guatemala City, Santa Lucía Cotzumalguapa or at La Gomera ($1.20, 30 min) for Sipacate. Updated: Feb 05, 2010.

SIPACATE AND LA PAREDÓN

An unremarkable little town on the bank of the Canal de Chiquimulilla, Sipacate is best known as the surf beach in Guatemala (although top surfers might prefer the break at Iztapa). Access to the beach is a lancha ride across the canal ($0.55 per person). Also on the beach here is MarMaya (URL: www.marmaya.com), a secluded resort with luxury, beachside rooms ($47) and bungalows ($100 for up to 6 people).

There are a couple of cheaper places to stay in Sipacate town, but with a dearth of activities in the evenings, or even open restaurants, tourists would probably be happier elsewhere. Eating-wise, the choice is not exactly extensive; Comedor Natalia and Restaurante Familiar on the main street offer standard local dishes or licuados and are open daily for breakfast, lunch and dinner. There is no ATM here. The closest are in La Democracia or Siquinalá.

Travelers on a budget should head east to La Paredón, a 15-minute tuk-tuk drive from Sipacate ($2.50 per ride) or a pretty 10-minute lancha trip ($1.20 per person). This humble village, on a narrow stretch of sand between the canal and the sea, is home to Surf Camp El Paredón (URL: www.surf-guatemala.com). A rustic, friendly surf camp (or campemente as the locals call it), El Paredón charges $2.50 per person for tents, $5 for a dorm bed or $20 for a cabin, all set in a garden right on the beach. Large meals are cooked to order and cost from $3 to $4.50. Unsurprisingly, most of the clientele are interested in surfing so there are boards to rent and lessons available. The surf breaks further out to sea on this stretch of the coastline, making for a less noisy place to sleep at night compared to Monterrico and creating good conditions to learn

or practice surfing. The area in front of the Surf Camp is popular with local youngsters who come to splash around in the late afternoon sun or to show off their surf skills.

The best time of year for surf is between December and April. The village itself would be beautiful, except for the massive piles of rubbish that can be found strewn about. The beach is not the cleanest, either. However, the people who live here are genuinely friendly, and it is hard to go a few steps without being greeted by a big smile. Inside the village are a number of small tiendas and Comedor Antojitos Mary that sells cheap meals and licuados. Another eating or sleeping option is Hotel and Restaurant Rancho Bocabarra, a 10-minute walk down the beach (canal to the right). Basic cabins are $25.

The area surrounding Sipacate and La Paredón is designated a national park but appears to be so in name only. A mangrove trip can be arranged around the canal on an ad hoc basis or the Surf Camp has kayaks for rent. Most of the weekend visitors here are more interested in taking a ride on a banana boat for $1.20. Turtles do come and nest on the beaches between July and November (peak months are August to October) but the turtle nursery in town is in dire need of funds and has essentially closed. Updated: Feb 05, 2010.

Getting To and Away

Direct buses to Sipacate run from Santa Lucia Cotzumalguapa and Guatemala City via Escuintla. Otherwise if on a bus running along the Pacific Highway you should change at Siquinalá. Walk one minute down the road toward Sipacate and wait outside BAM bank for a direct bus or take one that departs from here for La Gomera, the licuado capital of the Pacific Coast ($1.50, 45 minutes) and change there for Sipacate ($1, 20 minutes). In Sipacate, a tuk-tuk ride costs $0.55 per person. To find the lanchas for the beach, walk down the central road, turn left along the last paved road before the canal and turn right at the sign for Rancho Carillo. To reach La Paredón, take a tuk-tuk ($2.50 per ride) to the lancha dock out of town and then a lancha for $1.20 the rest of the way. Lanchas depart in both directions, from 5 a.m. to 7 p.m. in the evening. The Surf Camp is only a five-minute walk from the dock but not well sign-posted so it is easier to ask for directions. When leaving La Paredón, microbuses wait for passengers and leave every hour or so for La Gomera ($2, 20 minutes). Updated: Feb 05, 2010.

ESCUINTLA

The largest city in the Pacific Coast and a major crossroads, Escuintla provides excellent transport links running from 6 a.m. to 6 p.m. in all directions (some have longer hours), meaning there is no excuse to get stuck here unless arriving late in the day. Escuintla has no tourist attractions and a simple pass through should be more than enough to satisfy any curiosity.

Most travelers' first taste of this hot, bustling city will be the bus triangle, a handy place to make onward connections. On the corner of 1 Avenida and 9 Calle, all buses pass through here, and it is the main Escuintla drop-off and pick-up point outside of the bus station. The bus station is seven blocks south of the central fort-like police station. If arriving here, take a taxi to 4 Calle for $1. Once there, everywhere is within a five-minute walk. If disembarking at the bus triangle and not carrying onwards, head up the hill to 4 Calle and turn right (opposite McDonald's). Down this street is Internet Cyberhouse, an air-conditioned Internet café (9 a.m.-9 p.m.) and Casa del Abuelo, a courtyard restaurant good for a Guatemalan-style breakfast or lunch for about $4 (8 a.m.-6 p.m.).

Next to the small park on 3 Avenida and 4 Calle is the motel-style Hotel and Restaurant La Villa, complete with pool and off-street parking. A reasonable deal for couples at $13 per person, singles might find $19 a little steep (Visa credit cards accepted at no extra charge). The restaurant is open from 6:30 a.m. till 10 p.m., serves alcohol and has an extensive menu. Snacks cost $2 to $3 and meals from $4 to $7.50.

Around the corner on 3A Avenida, between 5 and 6 Calle, Hospedaje Idris has possibly the cheapest deal in town. Here you will find clean, basic rooms with fan, TV and shared bathroom for $6.25 per room. However, they also rent rooms by the hour, and the room is only available from 5 p.m. till 9 a.m. The manager is happy to look after bags in the meantime. Hostal Real Antigua at 6 Calle 3–22, the street opposite Hospedaje Idris, is a good in-between choice and has spacious rooms, including private bathroom, TV and fan for $9.50 per person. The hub of Escuintla is on 4 Avenida, a stone's throw from all the hotels. Numerous banks and ATMs can be found between 3 and 6 Calles. The main market and police station in

a fake-looking fort (worth a look) are on this Avenida, while the central park and dilapidated church are just off it at 8 Calle. There is a taxi rank at the base of the park. Another Internet café, Compunet, is at 4-55 on 4 Avenida (Monday-Friday 8 a.m.-6 p.m., Saturday 8 a.m.-2 p.m.), $0.60 per hour.

On and around 4 Avenida there are plenty of comedores, pizza places and street stalls. Café Jardín, at the corner of 3 Avenida and 5 Calle, is a likable restaurant that offers attentive, friendly service and that actually stays open late enough for dinner, but only until 8 p.m. (opens at 11 a.m.). Thursday through Saturday, the joint turns into a disco at 8 p.m. The menu is small but food is well-prepared; options include sandwiches or burgers with beans, guacamole and fries for $4 or a big plate of meat for $10. This is a good place to escape the traffic. Updated: Feb 05, 2010

Autosafari Chapín

Central America's only safari park, Autosafari Chapín is a wonderfully different day trip in Guatemala and one that kids will love. The drive through several enclosures brings encounters (sometimes surprisingly close) with lions, rhinos, leopards and some species native to the country such as white-tailed deer and tapirs. Afterward there is a large, refreshing pool to cool off in. There are also snack vendors, a restaurant and picnic areas on site. If visiting here, it's worth hiring a car for the day, but the entrance fee does include a minibus tour for those arriving by local transport (an hour's bus ride from Escuintla). Tuesday-Sunday 9:30 a.m.-5 p.m. Carretera al Pacífico, Km 87.5. Tel: 502-2363-1105, URL: www.autosafarichapin.org. Updated: Jul 16, 2010.

Lago De Amatitlán

Lago de Amatitlán will leave most tourists wanting more, even though the lake is too polluted for swimming; it is possible to navigate the lake on a pedal boat, or take the chairlift up to a pretty viewpoint on the hillside. The lake is easy to reach, as buses pass the turnoff every five minutes traveling between Escuintla and the capital. The main road is about a 15-minute walk from the lake. There are some small stores and lakeside comedores. Updated: May 10, 2010.

Getting To and Away

At the bus triangle, there is a perfectly located licuado stand (great fruit shakes, but ask them to go easy on the sugar) next to the commercial center. Waiting here,

PACIFIC COAST

buses will pass going downhill to Taxisco, Chiquimulilla and the El Salvador border or uphill to Antigua and Chimaltenango (every 20-30 min, 6 a.m.-6 p.m.). Across the road, a line of buses head to different towns on the way to Mexico (every 20-30 min, 5 a.m.-7 p.m.). The assistant will help you find the right one. A little uphill, on the right-hand side, buses stop on their way to Guatemala City (every 15 min, 4 a.m. to 8 p.m.) There is a minibus stand here with buses for Puerto San José (every 15 min, 6 a.m.-7 p.m.; $1.25, 25 min). A second Puerto San José minibus stand is at 4 Avenida and 11 Calle, opposite the not-so-rosy Hotel Rosario. The bus station has frequent departures to the same destinations as the bus triangle. If beginning a journey in Escuintla, the bus station is the best place to start when heading east, and the bus triangle for everywhere else. Updated: Feb 05, 2010.

PUERTO SAN JOSÉ

Two hours from Guatemala City, Puerto San José is the closest beach to the capital and a scruffy seaside resort. This was once the great port of Guatemala, but now the cargo ships visible on the horizon depart from Puerto Quetzal, a few kilometers to the east. Two bridges over the dirty canal provide access to the ocean. The beach is black volcanic sand and lined with wall-to-wall seafood comedores.

Apart from the restaurants there is little shade. The sea is relatively calm here, so even kids can play in the water. A lifeguard is on duty during the weekends, when the town is overrun by day-trippers. Dogged by violence and gang trouble, Puerto San Jose is a less-than-desirable place to wander around at night. The bright green Papillion Hotel is in the action, on the main strip parallel to the beach, with adequate rooms (fan only) for $12.50. Hotel Costa Real, in a quieter setting, on 9 Calle between Avenida del Comercio and Avenida 30 de Junio, has better rooms with air conditioning and cable TV for $32. Each has a swimming pool.

Internet, markets, banks and ATMs can be found on the streets on either side of Parque Central. There are numerous places to eat scattered throughout town, the most appealing of which are on the beach. If walking is too much work, a tuk-tuk ride around town will cost $0.60. On the main road leading

to the beach (Avenida del Comerico), intriguing bottles of amber liquid can be seen for sale. They look like honey but are actually *aceite de tiburón* (shark oil).

A pleasant spot to hang out for the day is the beachside water park Aqua Magic (Wednesday-Friday 9 a.m.-5 p.m., Saturday-Sunday 9 a.m.-6 p.m.). Aqua Magic has multiple pools, waterslides, snack vendors and picnic areas. Entry is $8 (adults) and $5.60 (children). There is an ostrich farm on the outskirts of town (Km 100) where visitors can pet a bird and eat a lean ostrich steak. Entry is $3 (adults) and $2.50 (children over 10). Updated: Feb 05, 2010.

Getting To and Away

Direct buses leave to Guatemala City, Zone 4 station (Every 15 min 4 a.m.- 6 p.m.; $2, 2 hr) from the junction of Avenida 30 de Junio and 9 Calle. The direct bus to Antigua passes through here at 2 p.m. Microbuses to Escuintla (Every 10 min 4 a.m.-6 p.m.; $1.25, 25 min) leave from further up Avenida 30 de Junio (away from the beach).

Camionetas ($0.25) or microbuses ($1.25) to Iztapa and Puerto Viejo pass up Avenida 30 de Junio (every 15 min 6 a.m.-6 p.m) and arrive at Parque Central, just off Avenida del Comercio. The microbus from Puerto Viejo to Monterrico takes one hour and costs $1.20. Updated: Feb 05, 2010.

CHULAMAR

Balneario Chulamar is the stretch of beach five kilometers west of Puerto San José and almost deserted in comparison. It is important to bring everything you might need with you, as there are no services available on the beach itself. Soleil Pacific has a very exclusive club-style hotel, complete with theater, restaurants, games areas and various swimming pools. All-inclusive packages start from $120 on weekdays for two people and from $160 on the weekends (URL: www.gruposoleil.com). Updated: Feb 05, 2010.

Getting To and Away

There is no public transport to Chulamar. Taxis can be hired from Parque Central in Puerto San José for $1.20. There is security at the road entrance to Chulamar where Soleil Pacífico Hotel is located. Updated: Feb 05, 2010.

IZTAPA

A small collection of slowly rusting boats is testament to the dying legacy of the first seaport in Guatemala. Established by the conquistador Pedro de Alvarado, who in the mid-16th century found safe harbor for his fleet here, Iztapa was used for 300 years before a decision was made to move the port to Puerto San José. The coast around Iztapa is known as one of the best in the world for deep-sea fishing. Sailfish are the prime target. However, the hotels that cater to these aficionados tend to be all-inclusive and are located out of town on the road to Puerto San José. Iztapa itself is hot and unattractive, catering primarily to the day-tripper crowd. There seems little reason for most tourists to venture here unless in dire need of an ATM, which is on the main square. Die-hard surfers who may want to consider staying here for the fast break, best caught on a low to rising tide. Keep in mind, there is no direct access to the beach, you have to take a boat across the canal for $1.20 each way.

There are four hotels in town. Hotel Villas de Michatoya ($10 per person), two blocks back from the park, just off 4a Avenida, has the best rooms including fan and TV. Hotel Club Sol y Playa ($12.50 per person), on the main square, has a clean-ish swimming pool. The cheapest rooms in town are at Hotel Brasilia and Hostel Posadje Familiar Maria del Mar (starting from $2.50 per person). Iztapa has a large number of comedores scattered around. For something different, try Cafeteria Mei-Ko on 6a Avenida, which specializes in Chinese food. Lanchas can take you across the canal to basic restaurants on the beach, but they only open on the weekend. Perhaps the most pleasant places to eat at are near the road bridge, on a broad swathe of the Canal de Chiquimulilla that gives them a riverside feel. Rancho San Rafael serves the usual run of Guatemalan seaside fare and is open between 7 a.m. and 8 p.m. Updated: Mar 09, 2010.

Getting To and Away

Microbuses to Monterrico, costing $1.25, leave every 20 minutes (6 a.m.-6 p.m.) across the bridge in Pueblo Viejo, a 15-minute walk from the center of town. Microbuses and camionetas to Puerto San José pick up here but also pass through Iztapa town and the petrol station in the town center. Buses to Guatemala City leave every half hour or so from outside the bar Abarroteria Emir on the main square. Updated: May 11, 2010.

Things to See and Do

Sport Fishing

Sailfish, the holy grail of deep sea fishermen, are found in such numbers off the coast of Iztapa that it is possible to actually get a little bored of them. However, there are also large numbers of tuna, dorado, roosterfish and blue, black and striped marlin to keep the game interesting. The reason for this prime hunting ground is a glorious, bait-rich eddy where the currents from Mexico turn back after hitting the coast of El Salvador. This fantastic gift of nature has turned the coast off Iztapa into the sailfish capital of the world.

Caught sailfish are normally in the 31-40 kilogram (70-90 lb) range, but there are regular releases of fish over 45 kilograms (100 lb) as well. A year-round average of 15 to 20 bites a day reaches a regular 40 bites in peak season, with top boats averaging 2,000 releases per year. All sailfish and marlin are fished on a catch-and-release basis, but the others you are free to keep, within reason.

Weather-wise, it is rare that conditions are so bad that it is not possible to put to sea, and while certain times of the year are better for different fish, sailfish can be caught throughout the year, including during rainy season (late June-September). It usually rains for a couple of hours each day. Most of the fishing takes place 24-32 kilometers (15-50 mi) offshore. The lodges may have a boat available. Fly fishing is the order of the day and novices are as welcome as the experienced.

The best seasons to fish are:

Sailfish: November-May (30-55 kg/70-120 lb)
Marlin: October-December (160-360 kg/250-800 lb)
Yellow Fin Tuna: Summer (7-14 kg/15-30 lb)
Dorado: May-December

Lodging

Most tourists to Iztapa are gunning for sailfish and stay at exclusive lodges near the Puerto Quetzal marina, a two-hour drive from Guatemala City. Tours of popular sites in Guatemala are available for those not so keen on reeling in a 90-pounder. As a standard, most lodges have swimming pools, a Jacuzzi and a bar for some chilling-out time. A deposit

PACIFIC COAST

Photo by: Corrie Wingate

of up to 50 percent is normally required. Tips, alcoholic drinks, equipment rental and laundry are not usually included in the package price. All the lodges employ security personnel. Peak times of the year are over Christmas and Easter when the lodges fill up sometimes as much as a year in advance. Updated: May 11, 2010.

Guatemalan Billfishing Adventures

(ROOMS: $721) Award-winning Captain Brad Philips runs a popular outfit. Philips' nine years of experience in Guatemalan waters with an average release rate of 15 sailfish per day, coupled with his small fleet of only two boats, mean that this charming lodge is often fully booked. Brad and wife Cindy pride themselves on the personal touch of their business and have tried to think of everything, including US cable TV, so guests can catch the latest sports as well as some fish. And if that is not enough, the delicious home-cooked meals are sure to have even the toughest of customers longing for more. Billfish Inn, Marina Pez Vela. Tel: 502-7880-4152, E-mail: info@guatbilladv.com, URL: www. guatbilladv.com. Updated: Mar 09, 2010.

Sailfish Bay Lodge

(ROOMS: $848) Situated on a barrier island in the Pacific Coast, the deluxe and professionally-run Sailfish Bay Lodge is well set up for large groups of big-game fly fishermen. The two air-conditioned bungalows can take from 16 to 19 anglers each, spread over four rooms and two floors. Otherwise there are eight private beachfront bedrooms. Also in the ample grounds are a swimming pool, Jacuzzi, open-air restaurant and gift shop. Corporate fishing programs are available and popular with repeat clients. There is a contact form on the website. Day charters also possible. Sailfish Bay, near Iztapa. Tel: 513-984-8611/800-638-7405 (U.S.), E-mail: info@sailfishbay.com, URL: www.sailfishbay.com. Updated: Mar 09, 2010.

Pacific Fins Resort

At Pacific Fins Resort, it is all about the fishing. Boasting a team of experienced and determined captains, six boats ready for the deep blue and a panga for catching roosterfish inshore, the staff is as eager to put to sea as you are. Back on land, most of the accommodation is in self-contained, air-conditioned villas with sun decks, but there are two private rooms as well. After a hard day's fishing, guests can forget about the real world enjoying a sundown in the open air Jacuzzi or pool. Tel: 888-700-3467/727-896-3467 (U.S.), 502-7881-4788 (Guatemala), URL: www.pacificfins.com. Updated: May 10, 2010.

Buena Vista Resort

Despite its large size, Buena Vista still manages to make you feel at home, largely due to the efforts of the accommodating staff and the personal involvement of the owners Jody and Suzy. Fishing is, of course, the main draw, but there are enough other activities to keep the interested non-anglers, too. At the end of the day, fishermen can enjoy the fruits of their labor and a cold beer while soaking up the soothing ocean breeze. Large groups are also well-accommodated at the lodge. Ca. Bajamar Lote 19, Buena Vista Island. Tel: 866-699-3277/305-735-2387 (U.S.), 502-7880-4203 (Guatemala), E-mail: info@buenavistasportfishing.com, URL: www.buenavistasportfishing.com. Updated: May 10, 2010.

MONTERRICO

On the face of it, Monterrico appears to be your typical sultry beach town, but dig a little deeper and contrasts soon start to emerge. From its humble beginnings as a fishing village, Monterrico is re-inventing itself as the premier destination on the Pacific Coast. Guatemala City day-trippers mix with European vacationers, older back-to-basics hotels mingle with new resorts and among the numerous comedores are a handful of truly great restaurants.

However, Monterrico is much more than just a beach town. A barrier island, Monterrico is surrounded by water: the Pacific Ocean on one side, the Chiquimulilla Canal on the other. This creates a unique environment, allowing species which have died out in the rest of the world to survive here amid the mangroves and lagoons of the protected Biotopo de Monterrico.

The beach itself is a 22-kilometer (13.7 mi) long strip of black volcanic sand bordered by the white foam of crashing waves.

PACIFIC COAST

During the midday heat, the black sand is unbearably hot, but it cools down quickly in the late afternoon when sun-seekers come out to lie on towels, stroll along the water's edge or fit in a game of volleyball.

For six months of the year, Monterrico is the nesting site of three types of turtle. The commercialization of beaches usually means turtles become scared off; however, the development in Monterrico is low-key enough that tourists coming here August-December or January still have a chance to see a nesting turtle near their hotel.

The streets of Monterrico are laid out in the form of a cross. Calle Principal is the long, paved road that leads from the canal docks and through the center of town to the beach. Just before it reaches the pedestrianized zone near the beach, one sandy street, called Calle de los Hoteles, goes to the left and another sandy street, Calle Cementerio (after the cemetery) heads to the right. At the crossroads, there is a helpful signpost listing many of the hotels and their distances from that point. There are two paved roads that lead off Calle Principal. One travels west past Hotel Utz-Tzapa on a scenic route to the towns of Itztapa and San José, eventually finishing at Escuintla on the Pacific Highway. The other road goes east toward Hotel Dos Mundos and Parque Hawaii. Updated: Feb 06, 2010.

When to Go

Monterrico is hot all year round. Slow season is from August-October, coinciding with rainy season. It can rain for anywhere from a few minutes to all day. The mosquitoes are at their worst in rainy season. High season is November to mid-May. Otherwise, when to go depends a lot on what you want to see. Nesting turtles can be seen from August to January, while baby turtles are released every evening from mid-September to February. From November to March, whales, orcas and dolphins are passing down the coast and can sometimes be seen from shore.

It is worth taking into account the huge differences between weekdays and weekends. During the week, the town can seem deserted. Room rates are often cheaper and visitors may have the beach to themselves. Starting from Friday night, hordes of Guatemalans descend from the capital to spark the town into action, bringing with them coolers full of drinks, high spirits and lots of noise. Updated: Feb 06, 2010.

Getting To and Away

The simplest way to arrive may be by tourist shuttle, but it is not necessarily the easiest. Agencies in Antigua are notorious for selling tickets and leaving customers waiting on the pavement for a minibus that never shows. Also, the buses only leave if they have a minimum of five customers, so if the agency is not honest about that, then it might be better to go to another one. Shuttles departing Monterrico (10 a.m. and 4 p.m.) are more reliable. A direct bus runs from Antigua. It leaves Antigua at 5 a.m. and 3 p.m. and departs from Monterrico (from Ca. Principal) at 6 a.m. and 3 p.m. (2.5 hr, $4.50).

Otherwise travelers have two options: to come via San José and Iztapa or via La Avellana. For travelers coming from Lake Atitlán or the west, Escuintla is the crossroads where this decision must be made. Travelers from El Salvador or Chiquimulilla will hit Taxciso first, the jumping off point for La Avellana and the original route.

A bus from Escuintla to Taxciso takes one hour 30 minutes and costs $2.50. At Taxciso, take a tuk-tuk for $0.30 or walk a few minutes downhill to the minibus stop (outside Soda la Fuente Adriana) and catch a bus to the dock at La Avellana ($0.60, 30 min).

From here, you will take a lancha through the mangroves to Monterrico ($0.60, 20 minutes). Lanchas generally depart when the main buses arrive (roughly every hour, between 5:30 a.m. to 4 p.m.). The dock in Monterrico is at the far side of town; follow the road for 15 minutes until it hits the beach and hotel area. Direct buses from Chiquimulilla (via Taxciso) to La Avellana leave every hour from 6 a.m. till 6 p.m. but the last public lancha leaves La Avellana at 4 p.m. Private lanchas to or from Monterrico can be hired 24 hours a day for $6.

Traveling by local transport to Monterrico from anywhere other than Antigua involves several changes but, in most cases, the drop-offs are right next to the pick-up points, so connections are smooth.

Leaving Monterrico, lanchas depart at 3:30 a.m., 5:30 a.m., 7 a.m., 8 a.m., 9 a.m., 10:30 a.m., midday, 1 p.m., 2:30 p.m. and 4:30pm. Arrival in La Avellana coincides with a bus departure for Taxciso. See Getting Around for information on microbuses to Iztapa and San José. Updated: Feb 06, 2010.

PACIFIC COAST

Photo by: Ryan McCoy

Getting Around

Although you may wish for some motorized transportation in this heat, in Monterrico it is all about the feet. The key is to walk slowly. Bicycles are available for hire at Café del Sol ($6 for half a day, $10 for the whole day). The business next to the Internet shop rents out quad bikes but at $25 for an hour, they are unlikely to be practical for long-term use.

Microbuses leave from the west junction for Puerto Viejo and Iztapa every 20 minutes, from 6 a.m. to 6 p.m. ($1.20 for the hour drive). From here, camionetas ($0.25) and microbuses ($1.20) depart for the half-hour ride to Puerto San José.

Microbuses to Parque Hawaii depart from the Hawaii junction (east) in Monterrico, and from Parque Hawaii at 7 a.m., 9 a.m., 11 a.m., 1 p.m. and 3 p.m. An additional microbus leaves Monterrico at 4 p.m. The microbuses drive around for a long time to pick up passengers and might not actually leave until 45 minutes after the scheduled departure time. The cost is $0.90. Otherwise, it is common to hitch-hike along the road and pay the driver a few quetzales. Updated: Jul 16, 2010.

Safety

On the whole, Monterrico is a fairly safe village. Opportunistic crime does occur, but rarely, and it is more likely to happen on weekends when the numbers in town swell. It is wise to take the usual precautions regarding keeping belongings safe. Walking around or looking for turtles at night is generally fine, but as always, staying in groups is preferable.

A far bigger danger here is the ocean itself, which has deceptively strong currents. The beach cuts away sharply, causing a fierce undertow—especially at high tide. If caught in an undertow, breathe when you can, relax and let it take you. Fighting it will only exhaust you faster. Eventually, you will be deposited at the surface; rest for a moment and then start the swim back, all the time keeping a sharp lookout for the next big wave. The most important thing is not to panic. If in doubt, ask someone who knows when is a good time to swim.

There is a lifeguard on weekends and flags are posted to indicate the condition of the sea. Green is OK, yellow means be careful and red means danger. Under no circumstances should even the strongest swimmer consider going into the ocean after a few drinks. It's too dangerous. Updated: Feb 06, 2010.

Services

At the entrance of the supermarket, there is an ATM, but it doesn't always work; the next-nearest one is in Iztapa. There are lots of problems with electricity here so even those places that accept credit cards might struggle sometimes. A 5-10% charge is usual for credit cards. Banco Rural, just off Calle Principal on the road to Hawaii, changes U.S. dollars.

There is one Internet café in town, next to the football field near the dock ($1.50/hr). Hotel Atelie del Mar has WiFi for $1.50 / hr. Hostal Gecko runs a laundry service for $5 a big bag. The post office and police station are both on Calle Principal and the pharmacy is on a side road just before the church. Updated: Jul 16, 2010.

SHOPPING

Monterrico is not known for its shopping, but there are a couple of special places to see. Violeta has an art gallery is at Hotel Atelie del Mar, where she sells watercolors painted on silk; her work is sold internationally. The artesanias at Dasú (excellent ice cream café) make jewelry and some awesome lamps using natural products only. Otherwise, shopping in Monterrico is limited to the run-of-the-mill beach flip-flops, caps, shell jewelry and such. It is possible to buy insect repellant and sun cream from small shops and the main supermarket on Calle Principal. Updated: Feb 06, 2010.

Things to See and Do

The most obvious things to do are lie by the pool or take a walk on the beach. Horseback riding on the beach is available at $8.75 per person for one hour or quad-biking for $37.50 an hour. To experience the Biotopo Monterrico, take a boat tour through the mangroves and lagoons, visit the wildlife sanctuary and museum at Tortugario Monterrico or head up to Parque Hawaii to visit their sanctuary.

Monterrico has a relaxed attitude toward activities. Guides or facilitators will frequently approach you to boost numbers and it makes no difference to price if booked directly or through a middle-man. Guides should have an official ID. Invariably it will be a kid who accompanies horseback riders. During turtle nesting season, simply walking up and down the beach at night can result in the discovery of a female laying her eggs. Guides will

offer to accompany you for $3 to $5 per person, and while informative their services are not absolutely necessary. Bring a flashlight, walk around and look for non-moving flashlights–they will have found a turtle. However, women should be careful about going in ones or twos.

Two companies are currently offering whale watching trips. Pacific Whale Watching (Web: www.whale-watching-guatemala. com), has regular departures on Saturdays and Sundays from December to April. These can be joined from Antigua or at the marina near Puerto San Jose. Guests of the other company, Productos Mundiales (Web: www. productos-mundiales.com), have reported terrible trips including seven hours out to sea in a boat with no toilet or shade.

There is one Spanish school in town. Twenty hours of lessons per week costs $90 at El Proyecto Linguistico. Homestay and accommodation options also available. Updated: Feb 06, 2010.

Biotopo Monterrico-Hawaii

Covering 2,800 hectares (6,920 ac), the Biotopo Monterrico-Hawaii was set up in 1977 to protect the delicate ecosystem that has evolved along the coast, the estuarine channel and the coastal mangroves and lagoons. The area is home to caimans (a small alligator), green iguanas, freshwater tortoises and several endemic species including an amphibian with four eyes (two up, two down) that is now extinct in the rest of the world. There are 250 species of birds that live here and another 250 pass by on their migratory route between North and South America. Until the construction of a bridge at Iztapa in 2008, this isolated area was only accessible by water, thus ensuring the survival of so much wildlife and native flora and fauna. As Monterrico's popularity as a tourist spot is set to increase, it is important that the conservation of the Biotopo is not put at risk by heedless large-scale development. Updated: Feb 06, 2010.

Tortugario Monterrico

(ADMISSION: $5) In operation since 1976, Tortugario Monterrico breeds and releases several animal species, including turtles, caimans, green iguanas and a pre-historic freshwater fish. A dilapidated museum displays a hodgepodge of pickled specimens, photos and newspaper articles relating to mangrove conservation, plants, fauna, whales and turtles. All is in Spanish, but a knowledgeable guide

PACIFIC COAST

The Turtles of Monterrico

Three species of turtle come to Monterrico to lay their eggs. The leatherback (baule) is an awesome turtle with a soft, leathery skin that grows up to two meters long and nests here between mid-October and January. At birth, tiny male turtles head out to sea to spend the rest of their lives in the open ocean. Scientists are still unsure as to exactly where they go but leatherbacks are known for their long migration routes. After 200 million years on this planet, this magnificent creature is seriously near extinction. During the 2007 to 2008 season only 75 of nearly 40,000 eggs rescued by ARCAS belonged to the leatherback.

Another turtle found here, whose population numbers are also dwindling rapidly, is the East Pacific Black Turtle, a subspecies of the beautiful green turtle. This quirky turtle begins life as a fish eater but becomes vegetarian as an adult, preferring to munch on sea grass instead.

Visitors to this region are most likely to see the heart-shaped Olive Ridley (parlama) Turtle that nests along this stretch of the coast between July and December in large numbers. Positive conservation measures mean that Olive Ridleys are one of the few species of turtles not currently on the endangered list. Female turtles always return to the beach where they were born to lay their eggs. Once sure it is safe, they crawl up the beach, dig a hole with their flippers and deposit approximately 100 ping-pong ball sized eggs. The female enters a trance during this time and is completely unaware of anything else happening around her. After burying her eggs, she returns to the ocean, leaving them to fend for themselves.

Monterrico has numerous egg collectors. They dig an entrance way from the back of the nest and invariably remove the eggs before the exhausted female even has a chance to cover them with sand. Egg collecting is illegal, but an agreement has been struck that if 20 percent of the clutch (in practice 12 eggs) is donated to the hatcheries, the hatcheries will offer to buy the rest of the eggs. The reality is that if a hatchery representative is not on site when the eggs are harvested, the donation is not made. When donations are made, a receipt is given to the collector so they can legally sell the rest of their eggs. It takes 45 to 55 days for the eggs to incubate. The temperature of the nest affects the gender: males want 25 to 30 degrees, females 35 degrees plus. To ensure a good mix, the temperature is kept at approximately 32 degrees so the deeper eggs are male (cooler) and the eggs on top are female (hotter). When the turtles hatch, they are still blind as they dig their way out of the egg and onto the sand. Usually they would now begin their dash to the ocean but the hatcheries put chicken wire around the nest to collect them. The turtles are then all released together to increase their chance of survival. The first few days of a turtle's life are not happy ones. If a bird has not picked them off before reaching the ocean, there are many larger fish and predators hoping to do so then. Baby turtles swim continuously for the first 24 hours before stopping to find a safe haven. Only one turtle in a thousand eggs will grow to be an adult. Turtles can live up to 100 years old. Updated: Feb 06, 2010.

Conscientious Turtle Behavior

Tourists should refrain from touching the turtles, interrupting their behavior, shining lights in their eyes or using flash photography. Lights disorientate and confuse the turtles as to what direction they should be heading in. When releasing baby turtles, it's important to release them above the high-tide line, which is where the nest would normally be. They need to run themselves down into the surf to help strengthen their muscles and prepare them for the big swim ahead. The sight of egg collectors can be quite distressing, but it is better for tourists not to try to stop the practice; they will not be successful and will only create animosity. However, tourists may encourage collectors to make the 12-egg donation to the hatcheries. Updated: Feb 06, 2010.

can be hired for a tour in Spanish for an extra $6 per person. A separate section on the beach is devoted to turtle conservation, with an egg hatchery, some pens for baby turtles and a small trail that briefly informs why turtles are dying in such great numbers and how to help prevent it. The entrance is 10 minutes on foot down Calle des Hoteles. In season, baby turtles are released at 5:30 p.m. daily on the beach outside the Tortugario. Visitors can sponsor a turtle for $1.20 and let it go in a mock race. This race has attracted some criticism in the past, as turtles were saved up to race on Saturdays only. It is best for the turtles if they are released as soon as possible after hatching. Like many conservation measures, creating a local interest in preservation may or may not be in line with the best ecological practices; protecting species is a balancing act. Daily 7 a.m.-7 p.m.Updated: Feb 06, 2010.

Lodging

Once a quiet fishing village with a single hotel, Monterrico has been grown in popularity over the years for beach-seeking tourists. Accommodation varies dramatically but breaks down into two basic groups: beach-break motels and more luxurious hotels with their own unique vibe. Prices and quality vary considerably. Roughly half the accommodation is on the beach and the other half is one sandy street back. The more luxurious accommodation tends to be located outside of Monterrico, and there are some high-end hotels in Parque Hawaii as well.

Swimming pools are standard, and essential when the sea is so frequently off-limits. Another trend here is the traditional *rancho* (palm leaf) roof, which is not only atmospheric but keeps rooms cooler than the tin roofs. However, they do drop debris, so keep that in mind if a room seems dirty.

All but the most basic of rooms are equipped with a fan and a mosquito net; many hotels have rooms with air conditioning as well. Check-in times vary between 1 p.m. and 3 p.m., check-out times between 11 a.m. and 1 p.m. Most hotels pump their water supply directly from the ground, so depending how close you are to the ocean, it may have a salty quality to it. Some hotels do pump fresh water; really, it's in the luck of the draw. Only the most expensive hotels have hot water showers but in these temperatures, you're not going to miss them.

Many hotels raise their prices on weekends, but if you're staying for a while, a package can be arranged. During Semana Santa and New Year's, prices often double and hotels are packed. Single room prices are only a fraction lower than doubles, except at budget hotels. Groups, on the other hand, have their pick, as rooms with up to four double beds are common.

During weekends in high season it can be difficult to find a decent room, so better book ahead or arrive on a Thursday. Weekdays you might find that you are the only people staying at your hotel. If hotels are filling up, travelers can head to Calle des Hoteles: Hotel El Mangle or Hotel El Baule are both full of character, but rooms vary considerably in quality (you may want to ask to see a few), or the nearby Hotel San Gregorio and Hotel Long Beach are adequate but bland. The cheapest accommodation in Monterrico at $5 per person is the run-down Hotel El Delfin (on the beach, good pool) and the funky Hostal Gecko, one street behind. Hostal Gecko has no pool, but it does have a tiny kitchen that guests may use. Updated: Feb 08, 2010.

BUDGET

Johnny's Place

(ROOMS: $5.50-25) Ever popular, Johnny's Place compensates for some tattered edges with its upbeat and friendly vibe. With multiple pools, an oversized chessboard in the grassy garden, a beachside café and a cushioned lounge area, this place is designed to relax and entertain. There is even a late-night bar and club (weekends only). There are daily late-afternoon football or volleyball games, regular movie and poker nights and a number of hammocks for those less active moments. The bungalows include kitchen access but the dormitory does not. Rooms have air conditioning or fan. Johnny's Place is a five-minute walk past Brisas del Mar on Calle des Hoteles. Johnny's Place also rents out Casa Carina, a beautiful house on the beach with a private swimming pool and BBQ ($140 per night, sleeps a maximum of 8 people). Restaurant and bar hours: Daily 7:30 a.m.-10 p.m. Tel: 502-4369-6900/5812-0809, E-mail: reservations@johnnysplacehotel.com, URL: www.johnnysplacehotel.com. Updated: Feb 08, 2010.

Eco Beach Place Hotel

(ROOMS: $7.50-12) Managed by the friendly father and son team, Luis and Juan, Eco Beach Place is a large, rustic wooden house topped by a rancho roof. Basic rooms have up to three beds and private bathroom, but with a maximum occupancy of 16 people, this is not a busy hotel. At the front of the house, a bar and shady verandah overlook the beach, while in the back is a swimming pool surrounded by a small garden. There is a restaurant as well. Tel: 502-4500-4646/4223-2088, E-mail: ecobeachplace@hotmail.com. Updated: Feb 08, 2010.

Hotel Brisas Del Mar

Possibly the best budget deal in Monterrico, Brisas del Mar has clean, simple, motel-style rooms with fan or air conditioning. All rooms face the garden and ample swimming pool, but what really makes this hotel a winner is the open-air restaurant and hammock area upstairs, with ocean views. The restaurant (entrees: $3-7) is open daily 7:30 a.m.-8 p.m. Tel: 502-5517-1142. Updated: Feb 08, 2010.

MID-RANGE

Hotel and Restaurant Atelie Del Mar

(ROOMS: $22-41) In a village built on volcanic sand, the flourishing gardens at Atelie del Mar are a testament to the work ethic and caring touch that the hotel's owners put into their business. Owned and managed by Stig (Finnish) and Violeta (Guatemalan), no trouble is too big or query too small. Beautifully decorated throughout, the hotel has 10 comfortable rooms, an outside seating area and a huge pool. Singles or couples will appreciate the good conversation, serene surroundings and home-cooked food (as well as the WiFi). The restaurant (entrees $5-15) is open Monday-Thursday 8 a.m. to 9 p.m., Friday-Sunday 8 a.m.-10 p.m. Tel: 502-5752-5528, E-mail: info@hotelateliedelmar.com, URL: www.hotelateliedelmar.com. Updated: Feb 08, 2010.

Hotel and Restaurant Café del Sol

(ROOMS: 25-41) Befitting the hotel's name, the rooms here are painted a welcoming yellow. Most of the spacious rooms are one street back from the beach in a garden next to the pool and hot-water Jacuzzi. The excellent restaurant, however, opens directly onto the beach. Complete with hammocks and lounge chairs, this is the perfect spot to toast another glorious sunset with a cold beer. Good deals for groups. Restaurant and bar (entrees $6-15, plus 10% service) Monday-Thursday 7:30 a.m.-8 p.m., Friday-Sunday 7:30 a.m-10 p.m. Tel: 502-5810-0821, URL: www.café-del-sol.com. Updated: Feb 08, 2010.

La Palma B&B

(ROOMS: $25-63) Unlike any other accommodation in Monterrico, La Palma B&B is exclusive, intimate and charismatically Italian. Just six rooms are available around the twin courtyards, and neither owner is shy about their policy of selectivity. This is their home and maintaining a harmonious environment matters to them. Patricia makes divine Italian meals that are, unfortunately, only available for guests (except for take-out desserts). Philippe, a long-time traveler, is passionate about the unique habitat of Monterrico and is a fascinating person to talk to. Spanish and Italian are the languages of choice, with some English spoken. Tel: 502-7848-1622/5452-0890/5817-3911, URL: www.lapalmahotelmonterrico.com. Updated: Feb 08, 2010.

Hotel and Restaurant Pez de Oro

(ROOMS: $43.75-55) Hotel Pez de Oro makes a bold minimalist statement with its colored cabins, bright yellow deck chairs and treeless black-sand gardens. While the external appearance is modern, the cabins are furnished with traditional woodcraft. At the high end of the mid-range hotels, Pez de Oro has a sophisticated, resort-style set-up and a well-known Italian restaurant (Monday-Friday 7:30 a.m. to 8 p.m., weekends until 9 p.m.) Tel: 502-2368-3684, E-mail: pezdeoro@intelnett.com, URL: www.pezdeoro.com. Updated: Feb 08, 2010.

HIGH END

Hotel Utz-tzaba

(ROOMS: $65-159) Five kilometers to the west of Monterrico, Hotel Utz-Tzaba is a down-to-earth holiday resort for couples, groups or families. Situated around the edge of a large square garden, rooms are comfortable and equipped with air conditioning and hair dryers, while the bungalows sleep six people in two separate rooms and have a kitchen. The pool complex includes numerous bathing areas (some with shades), Jacuzzis, a kiddie pool, a poolside bar and a fantastic infinity pool. Food-wise, the restaurant offers a standard selection of Guatemalan and international meals and snacks. A 50 percent discount during the week turns this place into a real bargain. WiFi. 5 km west of town, toward Iztapa. Tel: 502-5318-9452, E-mail: info@utz-tzaba.com, URL: www.utz-tzaba.com. Updated: Feb 08, 2010.

Hotel Dos Mundos
(ROOMS: 90-169) To the east of Monterrico (1.5 km/0.93 mi), the luxurious Dos Mundos Pacific Resort is set in extensive grounds on a largely deserted stretch of beach. This highly-acclaimed hotel is popular with those looking to get away from it all. Spacious, rustic bungalows are air conditioned and designed with a touch of Guatemalan flair. There are two pools: a children's pool and a vast infinity pool for adults to gaze out over the ocean, the latter appropriately situated next to the bar. The beachside open-air restaurant (daily 7 a.m.-9 p.m.) serves authentic Italian fare at prices that reflect the quality of the hotel. Tours of the area and shuttles can be arranged. Tel: 502-7848-1407/1771, E-mail: dosmundospacific@hotmail.com, URL: www.dosmundospacific.com. Updated: Feb 08, 2010.

Restaurants
Monterrico is full of restaurants and comedores, but many have little to differentiate themselves; however, there are a few standouts. There are also several respected Italian restaurants at Hotel Dos Mundos (the priciest), Hotel Dulce y Salado, Hotel Pez de Oro and Hotel El Mangle. Eating out can be a tad more expensive here than at other tourist hotspots, especially if you stick to the hotel restaurants.

For prices, expect to pay $2.50-6 for breakfasts, snacks and sandwiches, while main meals cost between $4 and $15. During the weekend, street stalls set up at the corner of Calle Principal and Calle des Hoteles, selling chicken and chips or meat, salad and tortillas for $1.50 to $3. A hot dog stand is open most nights at the start of Calle des Hoteles.

Nearly all restaurants (including hotel ones) close by 8 p.m. on weekdays and by 9 p.m. or sometimes 10 p.m. on weekends. If you find you've missed the boat, Johnny's Place is always open till 10 p.m. Most restaurants open between 6:30 a.m. and 8 a.m. for breakfast. During low season, restaurants sometimes close at random times as they feel like it. A standard Monterrico menu is fish (friend, steamed or grilled), shrimps, fried chicken, pastas, soups, burgers, salads, *ceviche* (seafood or fish cooked in lime) and *caldo de mariscos* (seafood stew). Meals usually come with chips or rice, salad and tortillas. Vegetarians will find they are often limited to salad, pasta or a sandwich. This close to the ocean,

seafood is naturally popular. Commonly served fishes are sierra (meaty, few bones), mojarra (very boney and not very flavorful) or dorado (otherwise known as mahi-mahi or dolphin fish and excellent for eating). Sierra or mojarra are served whole.

Some places offer shark. Sharks are a misunderstood and essential predator in the ocean. They reproduce slowly and should not be eaten any more than a turtle, ray, dolphin or whale should. Lamentably, they have yet to be offered the same levels of protection as these species.

A quick fish tip: to get rid of that fishy smell on your hands after eating, ask for a lime (or save a half during the meal), smear the juice all over your fingers, and then either rinse off with water or wipe it off with napkins. Updated: Feb 08, 2010.

TRADITIONAL GUATEMALAN

Restaurant Calle Real
(ENTREES: $2-8) A two-minute walk down Calle Principal away from the beach, Calle Real is a pleasant open-air restaurant serving local food at low prices. Dishes have a slight European feel, as fish is served fried, grilled or breaded and pasta is served with garlic and olive oil. As well as the usual round of sandwiches and salads, Calle Real also has burritos and desserts. The licuados here are particularly good and so big that they are almost a meal in themselves. Daily 7:30 a.m.-7 p.m. Updated: Jul 16, 2010.

Comedor Aurnelia
(ENTREES: $4-5) At the start of Calle Cementerio is Comedor Aurnelia (not well-marked at the time of this review, due to a blown-away sign), named after the owner. Aurnelia puts a lot of effort into making good food but at the end of the day, the major difference between this place and other comedores is the price: This is some of the cheapest food in town and the comedor is frequently busy because of that. Try the garlic shrimp or chicken and wash it all down with Aurnelia's refreshing lemonade. Updated: Feb 08, 2010.

INTERNATIONAL

Taberna El Pelicano
(ENTREES: $5-22) Creative, delicious cuisine and a mellow, candle-lit ambiance combine to make El Pelicano the finest restaurant in Monterrico. For 12 years now

the Swiss chef has been delighting guests with her cooking, and choosing from the extensive menu is so difficult that you might just have to come back. If money is an influencing factor, then try the pasta; the half portion is enough to fill almost anyone up. It seems a pity, though, to miss out on the mouth-watering steaks, risottos and fabulous sauces. A few years ago, they adopted a grumpy pelican with a bad wing who will sometimes moodily show himself. Wednesdays-Saturdays noon-2 p.m., 5:30 p.m.-10 p.m., Sundays noon-3 p.m., 6 p.m.-10 p.m. Calle des Hoteles. Tel: 502-4001-5885. Updated: Feb 08, 2010.

Las Hamacas

(ENTREES: $8-11.50) Las Hamacas looks like all the other restaurants on Calle Principal, but the food is a cut above most. Its popularity arises from their tasty pizzas, including vegetarian pizzas and the house special with shrimp and ham. The menu is small but they also have seafood, ceviche and pasta dishes and a variety of beers or juices to drink. Surprisingly, there are not many hammocks. Daily 11 a.m.-8 p.m. Updated: Feb 08, 2010.

CAFÉ/BAR

Las Mananitas

(ENTREES: $3-10) Café-bar Las Mananitas, with its fresh vibe, awesome upstairs chill-out deck and enticing meals, looks like it should be in Bondi Beach rather than Monterrico. Visitors bored with the same menu choices listed everywhere else will be thrilled to discover dishes such as bagels and eggs, Peruvian ceviche, chorizo pinchos, pesto ciabatta and Cajun chicken nuggets. A great spot at the beach to hang out in, day or night, Las Mananitas also has a fully stocked bar, regular drinks specials and happy hours that are perfect for sundowners (Friday-Sunday 5 p.m.-6 p.m., Monday-Thursday 11 a.m.-7 p.m.). On the beach at end of pedestrianized zone, Ca. Principal. Tel: 502-5771-7768, E-mail: mananitas.monterrico@gmail.com. Updated: Feb 08, 2010.

Dasú Helados y Artesanía

(ENTREES: $3-5) Dasú is worth every second of the 20-minute walk up the beach to reach it. The Italian-style ice cream is homemade using all natural ingredients and tastes divine. Among the usual favorite flavors are intriguing options such as a refreshing Rosa de Jamaica, almond,

tiramisu, Bailey's and seasonal fruit. Dasú also has cocktails, licuados, cakes and sandwiches. Located on a secluded part of the beach and surrounded by palm trees, this is a good as spot as any to help you believe in paradise. Tuesday-Sunday 11 a.m.-7 p.m. East of town 1.5 kilometers (0.93 mi), next to Dos Mundos Updated: Feb 08, 2010.

ITALIAN

Hotel and Restaurant El Mangle

(ENTREES: $6-10) The traditional wood-fired pizza oven draws the hungry into this restaurant, but there are other options, such as sandwiches, seafood and pasta. The pizza is relatively expensive, at $12-14 for a pizza for one, but it's also the best in town. Situated at the beach end of the hotel, the restaurant of El Mangle has a quirky, Romanesque, antique-shop feel with an odd mix of wooden cabinets, columns and nooks holding statues of the Madonna. The soundtrack is distinctly chilled out. Daily 8 a.m.-8 p.m. Ca. des Hoteles. Tel: 502-5514-6517. Updated: Feb 08, 2010.

Restaurant Pez De Oro

With wooden tables and blue and white checkered tablecloths, walking into Pez de Oro feels like walking into an Italian countryside restaurant, except for the stunning ocean views. The traditionally-prepared meals include pasta, shrimp, fish, steaks, chicken, an excellent homemade ravioli and some very tempting Italian desserts. Prices here are a cut above the rest but then so are the ingredients. Pez de Oro is a pleasant place to come for a romantic dinner for two. Monday-Thursday 7:30 a.m.-8 p.m., Friday-Sunday 7:30 p.m.-9 p.m. At the hotel Pez de Oro, on Ca. des Hoteles. Tel: 502-2368-3684, E-mail: pezdeoro@intelnett.com, URL: www.pezdeoro.com. Updated: Feb 08, 2010.

Nightlife

The best places to go for a drink are Johnny's Place, the cozy El Caracol, or the upstairs deck at Las Mananitas. On weekends these places get busy and the nightclubs at El Kaiman and Animal Conocido open. Places start to pump at 10-11 p.m.

A note on nightlife etiquette for women: On weekends, Monterrico is primarily a beach hang-out for city dwellers who want to let loose. It can be quite intimidating for female tourists to walk around at night and be faced with a barrage of comments from groups of young men, purely because they have blond hair or are dressed up. The rules are different here. Ladies: If a guy says "hola," even suggestively, it's more effective to give a bored "hola" back and keep going than to ignore him. Guatemalan men are used to being sexually assertive and pursuing women, but no harm is usually intended. In the clubs, unless you stay hidden among a group of tourists, men are going to ask you to dance. They can be incredibly pushy and it won't necessarily matter that you have a boyfriend or a husband unless you can immediately point him out. Guatemalan men can take rejection very personally; sometimes it is more effective to say good-bye after relenting to one dance. The fact that you've given him a shot is more acceptable than a blanket "no."

Watching the local women strut their stuff is also quite the experience. They flaunt their bodies, dance suggestively with different men and have no qualms about demanding respect if a man stands out of line. If in doubt, take a cue from them and have some fun. At the end of the night, that's what it is all about. Midnight strolls along the beach with a guy indicate a different sort of action. If that's not what you're after, keep it light-hearted and public. Updated: Feb 08, 2010.

El Kaiman

El Kaiman is where the Guatemalans come to bump and grind. A large open-air dance floor is packed with sweating bodies dancing to Latino pop music. From here, revelers spill out onto the beachfront to cool down or take the edge off any hunger pangs at the grilled meat stand. On Fridays and Saturdays, it starts to get busy from about 10 p.m. and closes when it closes. A beer or rum and coke costs $2. El Kaiman is next to Johnny's Place, so you can switch between the two. The easiest way to arrive is by walking along the beach.

El Kaiman is just past Johnny's Place. If you walk along Calle des Hoteles, you have to cut through the hotel (El Kaiman also has rooms) to get to the club. Don't worry if it seems deserted. Daily from 9 p.m. Updated: Feb 08, 2010.

Playa Club

Johnny's Place kicks it up with their own nightclub, open on the weekends. Here you can dance on the tables to an eclectic mix of pumping dance oldies and modern Latino pop. When tired of that, there is a lounging area for chatting or just watching the flow. You are more likely to find tourists here as well as Guatemalans, and it's also the favorite spot of town teenagers to practice their break-dancing moves. Playa Club opens at 8 p.m. and closes when the party's over.

Happy hour is 10 p.m.-11 p.m. with two-for-one bottles of beer for $2.50 and double shots of rum and coke for $2. Ca. des Hoteles. Daily from 8 p.m.Updated: Jul 16, 2010.

PARQUE HAWAII

Parque Hawaii is a picturesque stretch of beach seven kilometers (4.35 mi) from Monterrico, which is fast turning into an alternative destination on this part of the coastline. A handful of luxurious hotels have set up shop, but there are no additional services to speak of as yet. The area's key appeal is that it is underdeveloped. This area is also the home to ARCAS Parque Hawaii, a well-run conservation and community development project. Updated: Jul 16, 2010.

Parque Hawaii Arcas

(ADMISSION: $1.75) Parque Hawaii is actually the stretch of beach east of Monterrico but also refers to the respected Guatemalan NGO, ARCAS, who has a base here and runs conservation and community development projects. In addition to the turtle hatchery, they also look after unwanted pet iguanas, caimans, Jesus lizards and fresh water tortoises. Any offspring are released into the wild at an appropriate age. The creative and interesting displays are in Spanish, but one of the volunteers will be happy to show you around and explain everything in English. On the way to the beach, there is a delightful trail relating the importance of turtles to different cultures across the world as well as advice on how to preserve turtle populations. A big part of the work by ARCAS is to help develop sustainable and environmentally friendly habitats within the local communities.

Tourists can assist in a fun way by learning how to make bracelets and hammocks for $6, which goes to support a village that has eroded into the ocean and is left without resources. The entrance fee is a requested donation of $1.25, although any amount is appreciated. ARCAS is popular with volunteers, who participate in various

PACIFIC COAST

projects depending on the time of year. These projects included collecting eggs for the hatchery, wildlife breeding and release programs, local environmental education and mangrove conservation. The cost is $70 per week including lodging and kitchen access. When there is space, tourists can come to stay for $10 a night and go with the volunteers on an egg hunt. There is not a great deal of shade so wear a hat and sunblock and don't forget the insect repellant. Daily 7 a.m.-8 p.m. URL: www.arcasguatemala.com. Updated: Feb 06, 2010.

Mangrove Swamp Tour

Waking up at 5 a.m. might not be everyone's cup of tea, but the early bird catches the worm and there are a lot of birds to be seen in the mangroves. Watching the sunrise from a pristine lagoon is not half bad either. Paddle boat trips take approximately two hours (engine noise scares off the wildlife) and are the best way to experience the wonder of mangroves. Caimans, iguanas, herons, kingfishers, jacanas and pelicans may be seen. Don't forget your binoculars or your mosquito repellant. Cost is $5.25 per person. Guides can be found everywhere, and usually they will find you (make sure they have ID). You can also pop up to the Tortugario and ask there. Sunset tours are possible. Talk to your guide about exactly how the trip will work, as there are several possible start points. Updated: Feb 06, 2010.

Lodging

Hotel Casa Bella

(ROOMS: $150-300) Casa Bella is in a private, secluded world of its own. Deluxe bungalows sleep up to either four or nine people, dependent on size. All come with air conditioning, cable TV and a kitchenette. Casa Bella occupies a picturesque section of the beach and is surrounded by palm trees, having no immediate neighbors. The center of the garden is taken up by a large, cool swimming pool, and sun-wary guests can relax on the shaded deck by the beach. Restaurant (meals $5-12) open for breakfast, lunch and dinner. Tel: 502-7821-3088, E-mail: bramishka@yahoo.com, URL: www.casabellamonterrico.com. Updated: Feb 08, 2010.

Hotel Hawaiian Paradise

(ROOMS: $94-275) The grand Hotel Hawaiian Paradise has several spacious luxury apartments, which are perfect for families or groups of up to seven people, while dotted around the grounds are double or twin rooms. If hanging out in the swimming pool becomes too much, there are also hammocks, a Jacuzzi and a games area on a shaded part of the rooftop. From here, there is a stunning view of Parque Hawaii and guests can play pool or table football while admiring it. Complete with an inexpensive restaurant, there is little reason to leave this hotel. Restaurant (main meals $5-12) open for breakfast, lunch and dinner. Tel: 502-5361-3011, URL: www.hawaiianparadise.com. Updated: Feb 08, 2010.

CHIQUIMULILLA

In the past, Chiquimulilla was something of a cowboy town with good leather products for sale, but nowadays it is just another town. You can still find a couple of shops selling cowboy boots or saddles. For most travelers, Chiquimullia will only be a staging area on the way to or from El Salvador.

The bus station at the Mercado Terminal is in the south end of town, seven blocks from Parque Central. Buses will often drop off here and then carry on further into town, a little closer to the accommodation options; otherwise a tuk-tuk around town costs $0.30. The main road leading up from the Mercado Terminal is called Colonia Vista Hermosa or 4a Avenida. A couple of blocks up this road, on 5 Calle, is Hotel Vital, which has unremarkable rooms ($6 per person). Two blocks past here, on 3 Calle, is Hotel San Carlos, with a cafetaria and considerably more comfortable rooms with cable TV (singles $10, doubles $12.50). Internet cafés, banks and ATMs can all be found on 1a Avenida around Parque Central. The street market is up here as well and is as good a place as any to wander. There is a medical clinic around the corner from Café Don Carlos. Updated: Feb 05, 2010.

On the corner of 4a Avenida and 5 Calle is Café Don Carlos, a lovely, inexpensive European-style café serving breakfast, lunch, dinner and cappuccino (Monday-Saturday 7:30 a.m.-8 p.m.). Restaurant El Bambu (Daily 7 a.m.-9:30 p.m) is on the main road coming into town, next to La Fontaine Pizza, and has typical Guatemalan dishes, including lots of meat and seafood specialties.

PACIFIC COAST

Getting To and Away

The Mercaro Terminal is next to the indoor market, on the southern edge of town, and has buses for Las Lisas (every half hour 6 a.m.-6 p.m.), Guatemala City (via Taxciso and Escuintla, every 10 minutes 2 a.m.-5 p.m.), La Avellana (every hour 6 a.m.-6:30 p.m.) and the border at Ciudad Pedro de Alvarado (every hour 8 a.m.-6 a.m.) All these buses will pause outside Restaurant El Bambu to pick up passengers, which is a more agreeable and convenient place to wait.

A better place to catch a bus to the border is outside Refac. Patrimar, on the corner opposite Restaurant El Bambu. Border-bound buses pass here every half-hour from 5:30 a.m.-7 p.m.

Buses for Cuilapa leave from the Mercado Terminal every half hour between 5:15 a.m. and 4:15 p.m., but it is worth taking them from the street opposite Gasolinera Doña Abby on the corner of 4a Avenida and 5 Calle. Wait outside Tienda Mimer. The bus always stops here for at least 15 minutes before continuing on to Cuilapa. Updated: Feb 05, 2010.

LAS LISAS

Cut off from the rest of Guatemala by the Canal of Chiquimulilla, the pace of Las Lisas is slow. A quiet fishing village with a population of just 1,000 people, Las Lisas is a town that travelers who are looking for "the real Guatemala" will adore. Although the town is on the whole not used to tourism, most of the visitors here are weekend day-trippers from the city so there are few hotels and many places close mid-week.

The best hotel is the attractive Hotel Canal View (rooms from $25), a few minutes from the dock on foot, with a swimming pool, restaurant and hammocks in a sheltered garden. The rest of the hotels are on or near the beach and have basic concrete rooms. Hotel Las Lisas ($18.50 for a room with fan, $31.25 with air conditioning) has a restaurant. Both places are open mid-week and may give a discount. Hotel Puerto del Mar has rooms for $5.50. Travelers are welcome to sling a hammock under a *palapas* (palm-leaf shelter) on the beach for next to nothing.

Apart from the beachside comedores, only open on the weekend, there is little choice for eating out. Stands around the village have licuados, sandwiches, burgers and fried chicken; otherwise hotel restaurants are the only other option.

There is no Internet or bank in Las Lisas. The closest are in Chiquimulilla.

The beach and canal are separated by a one-kilometer (0.62 mi) strip of land, so it is possible to watch the sunset over the waves before darting across to see the colors change over the smooth waters of the canal. A lovely walk is to pass by the dock, keeping the canal on your left, until you reach the last house. Follow the path to your right for as long as you like; eventually it passes through the palm trees and out onto the beach, which will take you back to the village. The whole loop takes about 80 minutes but can be made shorter by cutting through to the beach sooner.

From August to December, Las Lisas is an excellent place to watch nesting turtles at night. Because there is no light on the beach, you may only have to walk a few minutes before seeing one.

Las Lisas has two amazing hotels, Caleta Azul and Isleta de Gaia, both apart from the village itself. These hotels can only be reached by hiring a private lancha. Sometimes the hotel may be able to pick up guests on a supply run. Updated: Jul 02, 2010.

Getting To And Away

Buses leave every hour for the 60- to 90-minute trip from Chiquimulilla (6 a.m.-6 p.m.) to the dock of Las Lisas. Lanchas for the final stretch cost $0.50 and depart every 15 minutes from 5 a.m.-7 p.m. in both directions. At the main dock, lanchas can be hired to go to Caleta Azul and Isleta de Gaia for $25. Updated: Feb 05, 2010.

Lodging

Las Lisas hotels are few and far between. In fact, there are really only two worth mentioning, listed below. Both Las Lisas hotels offer quiet and secluded bungalows, usually for between $50-70 a night. The hotels are more like resorts, with swimming pools and private restaurants.

Caleta Azul

(ROOMS: $59-148) One of two peaceful retreats on the Barra del Jiote, Caleta Azul is the perfect place to unwind and indulge in some serious relaxation time. On a secluded stretch of beach, guests have a choice of two-, three-, and four-person bungalows with hammocks and fans (four-person bungalows have air conditioning). The prices include all meals and they have spiced up the menu with a distinctly Caribbean flavor. Apart from boat trips to the mangroves, the hotel also organizes scuba diving on two small wrecks or deep-sea fishing excursions. Buses leave every hour for the 60- to 90-minute trip from Chiquimulilla (6 a.m.-6 p.m.) to the dock of Las Lisas. Lanchas for the final stretch cost $0.50 and depart every 15 minutes from 5 a.m. to 7 p.m. in both directions. Barra del Jiote. Tel: 502-5715-2849/4101, URL: www.caletaazul.net. Updated: Feb 05, 2010.

Isleta de Gaia

(ROOMS: $77-162) On an island of sand in the Canal de Chiquimulilla, Isleta de Gaia is a beautiful and isolated boutique hotel. Gaia is the Mother Earth, and in her honor, the French American owners have designed an eco-friendly hotel that fits in perfectly with the rich and diverse environment of the pacific coast and mangrove swamps. All the accommodation is in comfortable bungalows, with balcony or terrace, for between two and six people. Kayaks and boogie boards are available and visits to the mangroves can be arranged. The restaurant offers a mix of traditional and Mediterranean fare. Reservations should be made through the website at least four days beforehand. Barra del Jiote. Tel: 502-7885-0044. URL: www.isleta-de-gaia.com.

CUILAPA

Up in the hills on the way to Guatemala City, Cuilapa has a refreshingly cooler climate compared to the lowlands below. This small, non-descript town with one distinctive claim to fame: this is the absolute center of the Americas, and at the end of a dusty car-park, there is a map to prove it. You can find the monument next to the central market at the top of 1a Avenida.

A couple of hotels in town are good for a night. Hotel Shekina, two blocks down the street behind the market, has clean rooms with private bathroom, cable TV and a pool for $10 (one person) or $15.50 (two people), while Posada K-Lily, three blocks uphill of the park and just off 2a Avenida, has similar rooms for $9.50 (one person) or $12.50 (two people), but no pool. A

tuk-tuk around town costs $0.30.

Near the central market or on 2a Avenida, there are clusters of food stalls, fast food vendors and comedores. The main streets in town are 1a Avenida and 2a Avenida, which run either side of the central park. Both have a couple of banks with ATMs and Internet cafés (8 a.m.-8 p.m.). Updated: Feb 05, 2010.

Getting To and Away

There is no bus station in Cuilapa as it is essentially one big crossroads. Buses to Guatemala City pass up 1a Avenida and down Calle 1. Buses to Chiquimulilla and two border points with El Salvador pass down 2a Avenida. There are buses to Las Chinamas (every hour, 5:30 a.m.-6 p.m.) and Ciudad Pedro de Alvarado (via Chiquimulilla; every half hour, 5:30 a.m.-6 p.m.), so make sure you are heading to the border crossing you actually want. Updated: Feb 05, 2010.

VOLCÁN CRUZ QUEMADA/TECUAMBURRO

Tecuamburro is a dormant volcanic complex consisting of three peaks: Cerro La Soledad (1,845 m/6,053 ft), Cerro Peña Blanca (1,850 m/6,070 ft), and Cerro de Miraflores (1,945 m/6,381 ft). Out of the three, Cerro La Soledad is the easiest to climb with a better trail, great views and places for camping below it, while the hike up Cerro Peña Blanca is considered the most beautiful. Hot rocks venting thermal gases can be seen on all the peaks. The slopes are thickly forested so it is a good idea to wear long trousers. Ascents take two to three hours.

The Laguna de Ixpaco was formed 2,900 years ago and is a popular place to come and relax in the hot mud baths. At the base of the Tecuamburro volcanic complex, the laguna is one of the start points for hiking the volcanoes. Another is from the village Tecuamburro, nine kilometers (5.6 mi) further along the road.

Cruz Quemada, accessible from Santa Maria Ixhuatán, is another easily scaled volcano (three hours up), surrounded by coffee plantations and next to a small milky-green lake. At 1,690 meters (5,545 ft) high, the summit is covered in radio antennas. None of these volcanoes are climbed regularly, so be prepared and bring all supplies with you. Guides for any of these hikes can be hired at the village Los Esclavos (at the junction five minutes from Cuilapa, onto the road to Chiquimulilla). Halfway up the road between Chiquimulilla and Cuilapa is a turn-off for the Laguna de Ixpaco at the village of El Vainillal. Nine kilometers (5.6 mi) past the lagoon is the village of Tecuamburro at the base of the volcano. Updated: Feb 05, 2010.

)))))

PACIFIC COAST

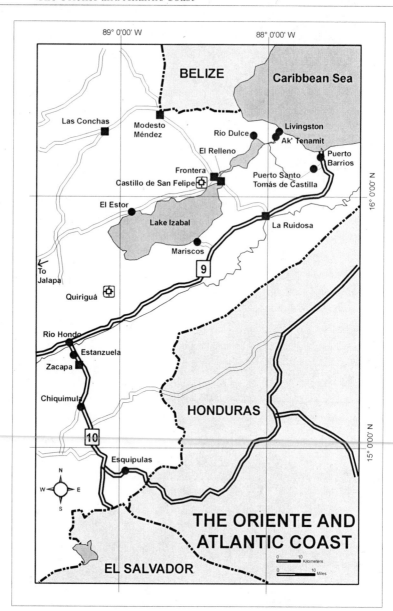

The Oriente and Atlantic Coast

Guatemala's Oriente, or eastern region, is home to the low, dry, hot provinces of El Progreso, Jalapa, Jutiapa, Zacapa, Chiquimula and Izabal. The population of this region is mostly ladíno, or mestizos with little or no indigenous ancestry. There are a few small pockets of indigenous populations, as well as some West African descendents (Garifuna) on the Caribbean coast, notably in the village of Lívingston. Visitors will want to check out the impressive Maya site of Quiriguá, Guatemala's most important ruins outside of the Petén. You may also want to take a boat trip on the Río Dulce to

Highlights

Quiriguá–Outside of the Petén, the Quiriguá ruins are the most important in Guatemala. Along the Motagua River sit around 20 stelae, or Maya statues, on a three-square-kilometer (1.2 sq mi) site. One of them is 11 meters (35 ft) tall and weighs an estimated 60,000 kilograms (130,000 lb).

Livingston–This tiny Guatemalan town is full of Caribbean charm. Most locals are descendants of escaped slaves and natives of the Lesser Antilles. The best time to visit is during the Wanaragua Festival (around Christmas and early January), when you can expect to see native costumes and white masks.

Río Dulce–The "Sweet River," a popular sailboat destination, begins at Lake Izabal. On its banks you will find the Río Dulce National Park, a 130-square-kilometer (80 sq mi) protected area.

Castillo de San Felipe–Built in 1595, this Spanish fortress was constructed to protect Izabal from Caribbean pirates. The well-preserved site was added to the UNESCO World Heritage Tentative List in 2002. Updated: Aug 18, 2010.

or from Lake Izabal, and visit lively Livingston. While you're visiting ruins, hop over the border and into Honduras to see the magnificent site at Copán, not far from Guatemala.

The city of Esquipulas is home to the *Cristo Negro*, or the Black Christ, a dark-skinned wooden carving of Christ that draws thousands of visitors and pilgrims every year. The festival of the Cristo Negro, on January 15, is packed. The Cristo Negro makes its home in the impressive Basilica de Esquipulas.

On the northern shore of Lake Izabal sits the Castillo San Felipe, a more-or-less preserved Spanish fortress built in 1595. It protected Izabal from Caribbean pirates and served as a military prison. Not far from the castle is the Parque Nacional Río Dulce, a large protected natural area home to many species of birds and animals. The small town of El Estor is of little interest, but it is a good place to explore the lake region. On the coast, the town of Livingston is worth a visit, as

it is home to a pocket of black Caribs and their Garifuna culture. There is a local festival of dancing and partying in late November, but the town is lively any time of year. Updated: Aug 18, 2010.

History

Quiriguá, an ancient Maya site from the classic period, is one of the oldest clues as to what life was like in the Oriente of Guatemala. There is some evidence that suggests the area was occupied as early as 400 BC, but it is generally accepted the area was an important trade route from 200-900 AD. Today, you can find some of the finest carvings made by the Maya here—around twenty towering statues dot the landscape. Diego García de Palacios, sent out by Spanish King Felipe II, was the first known European to discover the ruined cities of the Maya. In 1576, Palacios wrote to the King to describe the ruins and explain there were only around three families living in the valley, none who knew much about the ruins. It would be 300 years before they were mapped.

When the Spanish came to Izabal, they built Castillo de San Felipe to protect the area from Caribbean pirates. Before the fortress was constructed, pirates eagerly stole products and attacked ships in the area. Armed with cannons, the castle was involved in many bouts. At one point, it was even totally destroyed. However, by 1855 it was completely abandoned.

The town of Livingston also has an interesting history that today makes the beach town Guatemala's most intriguing cultural melting pot: a mixture of Garifuna, Maya, Native American and Ladino people live here together. The town has a unique Caribbean feel, mostly due to the fact that many locals are descendants of slaves who escaped to this area. Since around 1795, their culture has been preserved through native language and traditions, including music, religion, dress and food. Updated: Aug 18, 2010.

When to Go

The rainy season from mid-May to mid-October makes it difficult to travel in this region of Guatemala, however it is by no means impossible. Travelers usually prefer to visit Guatemala during the country's holidays and festivals, which usually center around Christmas and Easter. One of the largest attractions in the area is when Livingston hosts the Wanaragua Festival around Christmas and early January. Updated: Aug 18, 2010.

ATLANTIC COAST

Safety

Tourism is a huge source of income in some towns in the Oriente and along the Atlantic Coast, which means many locals who make their living this way can be quite aggressive. For example, the only way to reach Lívingston is by boat, and once you arrive you will be approached by a crowd offering you—or possibly harassing you about—a place to stay. Your best option is to be polite but firm: say you have reservations (even if you do not). No matter which hotel you end up staying at the proprietor will be much happier not having to pay one of these street vendors a fee for bringing you to the door. As always, although most towns in this area are generally safe, it is also never advised to walk around alone especially at night. Updated: Aug 18, 2010.

Things to See and Do

Most travelers visiting the Oriente and Atlantic Coast in Guatemala stay around the Río Dulce area. The river flows out of Lake Izabal, the largest lake in Guatemala, where a Spanish fortress called Castillo de San Felipe was built in the 1500s to protect the lake from pirate invasions. Today, the river is spanned by one of the largest bridges in Central America. The town of Fronteras is to one side of the bridge and on the other is Rellenos. East of these two towns are several resorts and marinas. Río Dulce flows into another lake called El Golfete, which has a handful of houses and tiny business on the shore. A large gorge surrounded by wildflowers and animals alike—howler monkeys is the Río Dulce's next stop until it enters the Caribbean Sea near Lívingston, a town of Garifuna people. The Río Dulce National Park is located on the banks of the Río Dulce, covering an area of around 130 square kilometers (80 sq mi). Other attractions in this part of Guatemala include the Quiriguá ruins along the Montagua River, where around 20 sandstone monuments from the Maya Classic Period (200-900 AD) have been unearthed. Updated: Aug 18, 2010.

Tours

While visiting the Oriente and Atlantic Coast in Guatemala, you can explore Maya ruins, take a sailboat along the Río Dulce to the Caribbean, or have a guide show you the ins and outs of the area's flora and fauna. By land and by sea, there are plenty of adventure-related activities to partake in, including hiking, climbing, biking and various water sports. By far the most popular

place for an archeology tour in this area is through the Quiringuá ruins, famous for their sandstone monuments constructed during the Maya Classic Period (200-900 AD). Sailing is a popular activity along the Río Dulce, but if you are looking to hop aboard a boat you could also visit the Caribbean-influenced town of Lívingston, only reachable by water.

There are also several eco-lodges deep in the Oriente that can take you on wildlife tours and organize other activities. No matter what your style of travel, there is something for you to do in this part of Guatemala. Updated: Aug 18, 2010.

Lodging

If you're looking to escape Guatemala City and have already crossed Antigua and Tikal off your list, visit the Atlantic Coast of Guatemala. Along the Atlantic Coast, you will find a handful of sleepy towns on black sand beaches. There is a lot to see and to do in this part of Guatemala, where Caribbean and Guatemalan cultures mix together. However, you will need a place to stay.

In tiny towns like Jutiapa and El Estor, hostels are dingy and hard to find, whereas in Lívingston, Chiquimula, and Esquipulas, hotels are a dime a dozen. Along the Río Dulce you will also find a whole host of options. Updated: Jul 13, 2010.

Restaurants

Restaurants in the Oriente and along the Atlantic Coast of Guatemala range from low budget hot dog stands to elegant beach-side marinas. Taco stands intermingle with more modern, air-conditioned eateries, but almost all have a casual atmosphere and are relatively cheap. If you are looking for international cuisine, just about every town has its very own Chinese restaurant and it is common for fancier establishments to serve spaghetti. If you are looking to taste some authentic Guatemalan food (which you should!), be sure to try *pepián*, a meat dish smothered in rich tomato gravy. Updated: Aug 25, 2010.

RÍO HONDO

At first glance Río Hondo appears to be not much more than a string of basic *comedores* (dining halls) and motels flanking the Carretera al Atlántico, used mainly as a truck stop. At the Río Hondo junction, reached by bus traveling from Guatemala City to the east coast in about three hours, you'll find the turn-off for Zacapa, Chiquimula and Esquipulas and further south the border with Honduras and El Salvador. However, don't miss the less obvious minor road on the opposite side of the highway, just by the Coffee garden, which winds up to the charming village of Río Hondo proper: a great place to make a pit stop. It is a pretty and well-finished village, with a gleaming white church and a well-groomed park offering some shade from the unforgiving sun. Around the small central plaza there are a couple of spots to eat at, such as Antojitos Río Honduranos and the Antojitos La Bendición, and a general store where you can stock up on supplies for your journey. There is also an Internet café ($1 per hour 8 a.m.-9 p.m.), a couple of ATMs at the Banrural, Banca Red and Banco Reformador, the Farmacia Candelaria and a post office.

Back on the main road you will drive past a few places to sleep, such as the big yellow Hotel Hawaii (Tel: 502-7934-0504) just at the junction, which is an okay option if you just need somewhere to rest your head ASAP. Before the junction, going west to east, is the Hotel El Atlántico, a better choice all round offering rooms with air conditioning, private bathroom, hot water, cable T.V. as well as a pool and gym, restaurant, and private parking. Km 126, Ruta al Atlántico, Río Hondo.Tel: 502-7933-05933, E-mail: hotel_elatlantico@hotmail.com.

The Hotel Longarone is another option, adverting itself as 'A little bit of Italy in the heart of Guatemala.' The tagline is debatable, but it is definitely a very nice hotel with a pool and slides, gym and restaurant. There are three levels of rooms for one to three people: Type A $65-95, Type B $55-65, and Type C $43-73, with family rooms for four people costing $117. Km 126.5, Ruta al Atántico. Tel: 502-7933-0488, E-mail: hotellongarone@hotmail.com, URL: www.hotel-longarone.com.

Traveling east toward the coast there is the thatched Comedor El Paraíso (Km 139) and the El Meson de la Sierra restaurant (Km 143), both large and relaxing places to have a quiet meal. At Km 149 is the well-run Valle Dorado water park and hotel complex. Guatemalans in the city often make the trip out here to relax in the sun, on the slides, and in the pools. Day rates are available (open everyday 9 a.m.-5 p.m. except Monday). Packages, which include accommodation, meals

and drinks, entertainment and access to the parque aquático, are a good value and range from $60 for adults and $25 for children. There are also some souvenir stores and an ATM. Tel: 502-7933-1111, URL: www. hotelvalledorado.com.

Getting To and Away

Your best bet is to take a bus to Chiquimula and, from there, catch a minibus to Río Hondo. The trip only costs $1 and lasts about 40 minutes. Minibuses leave every half hour or so. Updated: Aug 25, 2010.

ESTANZUELA

A turn-off on the road between the Río Hondo junction and Zacapa leads to the sleepy village of Estanzuela, one kilometer (0.6 mi) from the highway. This quiet town with quaint cobblestone streets has a pretty square at 1a Calle where local ladies serve up tasty snacks in the shade of the large azalea bushes. There is a post office, stationery shop and pharmacy around the square. On 2a Calle, there is a small *tienda* (store), a meat restaurant called Churrascos Sarita and the Comedor Familiar, the best place in town for a bite to eat and a game of pool. Incongruously, this small town of no real significance has its own museum of paleontology, which may be the only reason to spend any time here. El Museo de Paleontología Bryan Patterson, also known as El Museo de Estanzuela, exhibits some interesting fossils, like the whole skeleton of a 50 thousand-year old mastodon, and pieces from Maya tombs. Back on the main road there is a hotel, the Turicentro La Estancia, and plenty more restaurants. Updated: Jun 12, 2010.

ZACAPA

Smack in the middle of the Montague Valley is Zacapa, a dry and dusty town trapped in the blistering sun and searing heat of the Sierra de las Minas; the average temperature is 38°C (92°F) and the climate is reflected in the fiery personality of the inhabitants. There isn't much to grab your attention here, even the world-famous rum of the same name is not made in town (distillation requires cooler temperatures); but, you could break your journey and refresh at one of the many restaurants on 4a Calle. The bus station is on the left after the big bridge. Buses from Guatemala City to Chiquimula stop here, but you can also catch a minibus from other local towns. The roads are a bit of a maze but wandering around you should find: several pharmacies,

ATLANTIC COAST

dentists and opticians, an Internet café, Magic Café Sports Bar (Chinese, grilled meats and seafood, Tel: 502-7941-4080), and the Don Jorge sandwich shop on 17a Calle. Additiionally, there is a pleasant plaza and a nice little café on 16a Avenida and 5a Calle; a Pizza and Burger Diner on 13a Avenida and 3a Calle; a Hotel Wong on 7a Calle, Miramundo Hotel and Restaurant on 17a Avenida and Hotel De Leon on 16a Avenida and 11a Calle. Several banks with ATMs exist on 4a Calle, and nearby the town hall and church on 12a Avenida and 3a Calle. Updated: Jun 12, 2010.

CHIQUIMULA

Chiquimula is a hot, dry departmental capital located at the junction of highways CA-10 and 12. The local economy is mainly focused around mining and tobacco farms. Unless you have pressing business with the local municipal authorities, your time spent in Chiquimula will most likely consist of transferring buses en route to Copán or Guatemala City. However if you are feeling curious, or simply want to get out of the bus to stretch your legs, there are enough interesting sites in town and in the surrounding areas to make this an interesting day trip.

The nearby village of Ipala features the 1650 meter (5,413 ft) Volcán de Ipala, an extinct volcanic crater with a clear 3.5-kilometer (2.17 mi) wide lake. Although much of the water from the lake has been siphoned off in recent years by nearby villages, it still makes for a spectacular site. The ascent up the volcano will take you about two hours by foot. Buses leave every half hour or so from Chiquimula. The town itself features a couple of interesting sites including the now abandoned Estación de Ferrocarril at 4a Calle, deserted since the mid-80s, and the ruins of a colonial era baroque church which was destroyed during the 1765 earthquake.

Although there is nothing in town to warrant a five-star Michelin review, Chiquimula does offer enough choices in the low- to mid-price range that you shouldn't find yourself subsisting on Oreos or sleeping in the street during your (probably) brief stay in Chiquimula.

When to Go

Chiquimula is hot and sweaty more or less all year round but even more so in the summer months when there can also be flash rainstorms. In mid-August there is the departmental *Feria del Tránsito,* the Transport Fair, with horse parades, carnival parades, food stalls and games. In May, there is a festival celebrating the importance of tamales, a food that should not be underrated when it comes to the Chapines. The locals here also support the January saint's celebrations in nearby Esquipulas. Updated: Aug 23, 2010.

Getting To and Away

To the east of the large market at 11a Avenida and 1a Calle there is a large and pretty useless bus terminal as the vast majority of buses seem to pick passengers up on the side of the road. It is best to ask at the ticket office to be sure or to ask the helpers standing around about the destination you require. There are coaches to Guatemala City (3 hr, 30 mi) and Puerto Barrios (5 hr) every hour until about 6 p.m. Minibuses go regularly to Esquipulas, Ipala, Angiuatú (El Salvador border)until about 8 p.m. All are an hour away. You can get to Copán from the El Florido border (1.5 hr) until to 4:30 p.m. Updated: Aug 23, 2010.

Getting Around

Chiquimula is usually blocked by traffic circulating via the one-way system. This means it can be quite unpleasant to walk around on some of the roads due to the pollution. However, the town center is quite small and you can walk everywhere, unless, for example, you arrive by bus and wish to take a taxi to Hostal Maria Teresa or Hotel Poasada Perla de Oriente. Updated: Aug 23, 2010.

Safety

Chiquimula is a relatively safe town but you should follow the general dos and don'ts regarding your safety. The streets are not well-lit and are quite quiet at night, so take care when walking around, especially if you're on your own. A lot of people hang around the central square so be careful with your bags and watch out for pickpockets here as well as in the markets. Updated: Aug 23, 2010.

Services

There are two Internet cafés quite close to each other. Powernet, on the northeastern corner of the square, is $0.40 for 15 minutes, $1 for an hour, 9 a.m. – 9.45 p.m. They have Skype installed but you need your own earphones. There is also an Internet café inside the small shopping mall, next to Café Martell. The Post Office is near the larger market hall, in the north east corner of the town, on 10a Avenida and 2a Calle.

ATLANTIC COAST

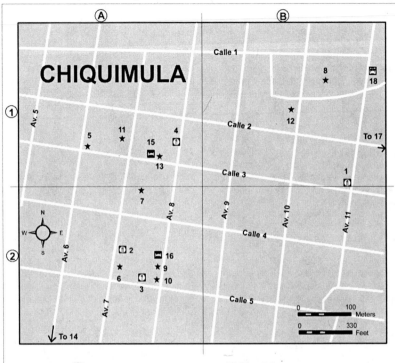

Eating 🍴

1 Joe's Pizza B1
2 La Parillada de Calero A2
3 PROA Seafood Restaurant A2
4 Taqueria A1

Services ★

5 Banrural, BAM A1
6 Banco G&T A2
7 Church A2
8 Market B1
9 Medical Pharmacy A2
10 Oasis Supermarket A2

11 Piaz A1
12 Post Office B1
13 Shopping Center (Café Martell, Internet Café, Supermarket) A1

Sleeping 🛏

14 Hostal Maria Teresa A2
15 Hotel Hernández A1
16 Hotel Posada Don Adán A2
17 Hotel Posada Perla de Oriente B1

Transportation 🚌

18 Bus terminal and local buses B1

There are a number of ATMs in Chiquimula: you'll find a Banrural and a BAM on the northwestern corner of the square, as well as a Banco G&T on 7a Avenida next to La Parillada de Calero, so you should not struggle to get cash.

If you're sick there is a good 24-hour pharmacy on 8a Avenida, between 4a and 5a Calles (Tel: 502-7942-5353). There is also a doctors' office on 3a Calle, between 10a and 11a Avenida. Updated: Aug 25, 2010.

Things to See and Do

There isn't a great deal to do here by way of tourist activities. Chiquimula is a working town and it is hectic, dirty and very hot. One thing you can do is sit in the shade of the trees in the central plaza and people watch the local chiquimultecos. The church is opposite the square and behind the square is the smaller of the two markets where you can wander through and delight in the kitsch gear on offer, as well as the usual culinary treats and see what delights are on offer. Half a kilometer (0.3 miles) east of town there is the old Baroque church, which was destroyed and abandoned after the 1765 earthquake but is now being restored. Updated: Aug 25, 2010.

Ilpala Volcano, Crater Lake and Cueva de la Leona

The scenery en route between Jalapa and Chiquimula, whether you take the backroad shortcut via San Luis Jilotepeque or the longer route via Progresso and Agua Blanca, is just spectacular. The sun and heat is countered by the lush sub-tropical mounds, which just seem to sprout up out of the valley bottom, and the pretty patchwork of cultivated fields.

For some amazing views out across the plain you can hike up Volcán de Ipala. It looks just like another big hill more than a volcano and subsequently it is not so easy to spot. However, there is one large green road sign along the smooth black-top road between Agua Blanca and Ipala indicating a turn-off to a parking lot and where the trail begins. As you pass by cows being herded to and from their fields, it takes about an hour and a half to reach the summit via a somewhat steep and narrow path. It can be a challenging trek but it is not dangerous.

Before reaching the top there is a side path leading to the Cueva de la Leona, where legend has it a lioness and her cubs used to live, feeding on the white-tailed deer that still live there. Emerging from the trees at 1,650 meters (5,413 ft) above sea level you'll find the beautiful crater lake about 3.5 kilometers (2 mi) in diameter, which takes about an hour to walk around. You can camp here but you would need to bring your own equipment and provisions as there are no stores or no real shelter. Always check the weather forecast before pitching a tent as the rain and thunder storms can come in rather quickly. The area is administered by CONAP, which charges at $1.50 entrance fee. There is a visitors' center and a basic lodge but these may not be open. To get here take a bus from Jutiapa or Progresso toward Ipala/Chiquimula and asked to be dropped off at the sign for the parking lot, or take a bus/taxi from Ipala. Updated: Aug 23, 2010.

Lodging

Chiquimula hostels are actually basic guesthouses on the streets around the main square. Used mainly by Guatemalans on the road, you'll never be short of a bed here in Chiquimula. Hostels aren't your only option. By Guatemala's standards, there are also a few mid- to high-range hotels. Most places have a 10 p.m. curfew but also have bells for late entry. It's often hot and sweaty in this busy working town and you'll pay more for pleasure of air conditioning, but at least you don't need hot water. All have free parking space on-site. Updated: Jul 13, 2010-

Hotel Posada Perla de Oriente
(ROOMS: $10-40) The Perla de Oriente is a large hotel with plenty of rooms at a wide range of prices, a restaurant and a swimming pool surrounded by lounge chairs and tropical plants. It's a mid-range hotel that could do with a bit of care and attention and the pool definitely needs a cleaning; but, it's good enough for a few nights. The rooms have T.V., fan or air conditioning. 2a Ca. 11-50, Zona 1. Tel: 502-7942-0014/0152. Updated: May 11, 2010.

Hotel Hernández
(ROOMS: $10-30) The long-established Hotel Hernández is deceptively big, and its small shop-front opens up to corridors of 30 clean rooms and a swimming pool (though the pool is not really for lounging around). The bonuses here are the free breakfast and Internet availability in the lounge. Also, it's fairly quiet for being so close to the square. 3a Ca. 7-41 Zona 1. Tel: 502-7942-0708/5412-2313. Updated: May 11, 2010.

Hotel Posada Don Adán
(ROOMS: $12-24) Just one block from the main square but quiet enough to get a good night's sleep, this is a nice budget option. The family that runs this place is very accommodating and will turn on the hot water at your request. Although with the heat of Chiquimula, it's doubtful you'll need it. All rooms have private bathrooms and fans (there's an extra charge for air conditioning) and there's lots of veranda space for relaxing with a book or a beer. 8a Av. 4-30 Zona 1. Tel: 502-7942-0549. Updated: May 11, 2010.

Hostal Maria Teresa
(ROOMS: $23-55) This hotel is away from the center. It's on the road coming into town from the south, opposite the small El Calvario park. Don't let the title "hostal" fool you; this

Photo by: Don Sampson

is one of the better hotels in Chiquimula. Its colonial-style decor and green courtyard make it a fine place to escape the Oriente's hot sun. Rooms have cable TV and private bathrooms with hot water; but, the rooms are on the small side. Internet is available. 6a Ca. 6-21, Zona 1. Tel: 502-7942-0177. Updated: May 11, 2010.

Restaurants

Gastronomy is definitely not what you come to Chiquimula for but there are enough places to eat to keep you full even if your taste buds are not blown away. The market, right next to the church, is open during the day and you can pick up a fried snack from the comedores or some fruit. Taco stalls are around the main square that are open later. 7a Avenida has a number of eateries including Pizza Burger Diner, La Parillada de Calero, Holandesa, D'Café, Telepizza a

and the ubiquitous Pollo Campero. Out on the exit road south, down 6a Avenida, there is a Dominoes pizza in a nice little square with a park and coffee shop and even a Dunkin Donuts stand. Also, there are a couple of supermarkets open until 9 p.m. Updated: Mar 13, 2010.

Taquería Picate

(ENTREES: $1-5) This Mexican taco joint is just a short walk from the main square and is great for a delicious budget feed. The tacos, burritos and *gringas* (quesadillas) cost from $1-5 with a variety of fillings, and there are burgers and nachos, as well as quesadillas for vegetarians. There is a self-service toppings bar so you can pile on as much guacamole or spicy salsa as you like. During the day the place is more family-orientated but gets quite noisy with late-night groups. Beers as well as sodas are on the menu. There is a patio out back which is also wheel-chair accessible. Parking is available too. 8a Av. between 2a and 3a Ca. Updated: May 10, 2010.

Proa Seafood Restaurant

(ENTREES: $6-10) This is a nice mid to high-end family restaurant with a play area for kids and a maximum two beers per person policy. Some dishes seem a little over-priced but the food is tasty. Along with *ceviche* ($7.50), *mojarra* ($6.50) and fishburgers ($6), there are also meat dishes such as *caldo* ($10) and *churrasco* ($6). Unfortunately for vegetarians, there is nothing purely vegetable-based. There is a pleasant outdoor patio area and parking. Credit cards can be used for a 7 percent fee, and dollars are accepted. Home delivery is available. Breakfast includes typical Guatemalan fare as well as French toast and cereals. Daily 7 a.m.-11 p.m. 5a Ca. 7-61. Tel: 502-7942-7934. Updated: May 10, 2010.

Joe's Pizza

(ENTREES: $6-14) There are two Joe's Pizza locations: one is a basic take-out joint, and the other is a more substantial restaurant just a block away. Pizzas range from ($6) for a 'personal' pie and ($14) for 'grande' but there are also sandwiches, calzones, burgers, pastas and salads available for about ($4). The restaurant is air conditioned. They also do frapuccinos, which are a refreshing change in Chiquimula's sweltering heat. Daily 9 a.m.-11p.m. 10a Av. and 3a Ca. Take-out: 3a Ca. and 11a Av. Tel: 502-7942-7530/502-7723-6113. Updated: May 10, 2010.

La Parillada De Calero

(ENTREES: $7-13) This is another good value hangout that will appeal principally to meat-eaters, although there are also some lighter options such as salads. The restaurant has a friendly vibe about it: lots of buzz as waiters zip around the patio, kids laughing and travelers enjoying their plates of roast chicken and kebabs. *Puyaso, chorizo, lomito* and *pollo* are sold by the pound at $26-31, or you can order grilled shrimp or fish ($7-13). To wash it all down, a pitcher of refreshing lemonade goes for $6.50. Dollars and all credit cards are accepted for no additional fee. 7a Av. 4-83. Tel: 502-7942-5639. Updated: May 10, 2010.

JALAPA

Marooned amid the spectacular Eastern Highlands, you'll find Jalapa, a fairly well-off town with plenty of shops and restaurants but nothing much to see by way of tourist attractions. Nor is there much else around Jalapa since it's mainly surrounded by farming fields of cattle, *maize*, tobacco and sugarcane. Stopping here is only really necessary if you're looking for somewhere

ATLANTIC COAST

to take a break from a long journey. If you do stopover in Jalapa, it is a pleasant enough place to pass time with friendly locals, a stroll around and a good meal.

Getting To and Away

There are regular buses to Jalapa from Guatemala City which take three hours and travel one of two different routes either passing by Sanarate in the north or Jutiapa in the south. Buses also go to Chiquimula via Ipala which also takes three hours. Jalapa's grimy bus terminal is behind the market on 1a Calle A.

Crossing into El Salvador

It is a picturesque 33-kilometer drive (20.5 mi) out to the border crossing with El Salvador at Anguiatú. The majority of nationalities can purchase a visa at the gate but always check before setting off. The border gate is open 24-hour,s but since it is rather remote, for safety reasons, it is advisable to arrive there well before sun-down to make sure you are not stuck on the other side. There are a few restaurants near the border and along the road. A coffee shop and a Banrural (no ATM) is located six kilometers (4 mi) away from the border, and Joe's Pizza is 10 kilometers (6 mi) away. Tel: 502-7942-8752. Buses from Esquipulas leave about every 30 minutes, or sooner if full, and the journey takes an hour. Updated: Jun 12, 2010.

Services

The street names used here are very confusing so the best thing to do is start on the main street, called 1a Calle, and from there, you'll come across what Jalapa has to offer: Mr. Cool Internet café ($0.60/hr, closed Saturday); Banco de Antigua, Ban Trab and Banrural; Farmacias Batres (open 24 hours—look for the small service window); Post Office; dentist; hospital; market; plus plenty of places to eat and a few hotels.

Lodging

Family-friendly Hotel Casa del Viajero ($3-15 1a Av. 0-64, Tel: 502-7922-4086/2371) is a satisfactory budget option. Some rooms have private baths and TV. There is a basic cafétería on the premises. The Casa Real ($14-20. Av. Chipilapa A 1-03. Tel: 502-7922-2804/7417) is Jalapa's mid-range option. It is a full-fledged hotel complete with room service, restaurant and roof terrace. Rooms have free WiFi, plasma TVs, private bathrooms, fans and even swan-shaped towel arrangements. Dollars and quetzales are accepted, as well as credit cards (with a 7 percent fee). The restaurant ($2-6.50)

serves typical Guatemala fare and some international dishes in a typical, hotel-restaurant setting. The restaurant has a relaxed family-friendly feel and is wheelchair-accessible, as are some rooms in the hotel.

Restaurants

Along Jalapa's main street, 1a Calle, there are a number of eateries including a great churros bar painted bright pink, a frozen yogurt bar, the Cafétería Casa Contenta Chinese restaurant, Los Amigos on the corner near Hotel Viajero and 'Taco Central' by the square. Pizza Burger Diner serves breakfasts, pastas, salads, chicken, fish and churrascos as well as its namesake dishes. It's a clean and bright American style diner with a children's play area, free WiFi and two-for-one pizza Wednesdays and Fridays. Daily 7 a.m.-10 p.m. 1a Calle, between Chipilapa and Chipilapa A. Tel: 502-7922-7798. Updated: May 11, 2010.

ESQUIPULAS

If you've had your fill of Chiquimula and would like to start making your way toward Copán, try jumping on Highway 10 and heading south toward the Honduran border. Follow Highway 10 as it veers east into the mountains and you will find yourself in the picturesque town of Esquipulas. Named for a Maya lord who welcomed the Spanish conquistadors into his realm, today Esquipulas is well-known throughout the region for its sparkling white basilica which contains a tiny statue of Jesus called El Cristo Negro. The basilica is a popular pilgrimage site for people from all over Latin America, with thousands making their way there every year.

If you plan to visit try and make it during the week when the church will be almost deserted. Weekends are a bit hectic with the devout descending on the town in droves, spoiling the tranquil calm of the basilica with shouting and shoving. Outside the church gift shop a priest armed with a bucket of holy water stands ready to bless your things free of charge.

Activities for the non-faithful are a bit limited, but the Cueva de las Minas cave complex just outside of town and the Chatun nature park on the road to Honduras might make for entertaining jaunts. The park features canopy tours and a petting zoo. But really, as beautiful and serene as it is, there's not much to keep ones attention after visiting the basilica and the adjacent market. Being a tourist town, the selection of accommodations tends to be a bit higher quality and higher priced than in other similar sized towns like Chiquimula. Also be advised that prices rise dramatically on the weekends and holidays, especially during the devotional festival held the week of January 15. Cheaper rooms tend to be found in the streets immediately north of the basilica, but you are safer paying a bit more and rooming elsewhere. Gang members and illegal immigrants from Honduras have been known to frequent these places. Updated: Aug 25, 2010.

When to Go

Being the "number one religious destination in Central America," Esquipulas gets packed not only during the main pilgrimage period in mid-January but also every weekend, as well as a second minor pilgrimage in early March. While the pilgramages are going on, you must book your hotel in advance and get up early if you wish to get a glimpse of the revered Black Christ. The parades in honor of the saint happen over 10 days with the main day being January 15. At this time of year the climate is quite pleasant. During the summer months, the town heats up and there are less pilgrims so this is a good time to negotiate room prices. The rainy season lasts from May to October with an average temperature of around 25°C (77°F); although, temperatures can drop down to 10°C (50°F) at night so bring a light coat. Updated: Aug 25, 2010.

Getting To and Away

The Rutas Orientales office (for longer distances) is on 11a Calle and 1a Avenida, opposite La Rotonda restaurant. Buses run every hour to and from Guatemala City between about 2 a.m. and 6 p.m. The minibuses at the end of 11a Calle and 6a Avenida go to the border-crossings with Angiuatú/El Salvador (one hour) and Agua Caliente/ Honduras (30 minutes) every 30 minutes, or when full, until about 6 p.m. To go to the El Florido border, for the Copán ruins in Honduras, you need to meet the buses that are coming from Chiquimula at the road crossing that leads to Jocotán. Updated: Aug 25, 2010.

Crossing into Honduras

There is a very small border crossing from El Florido, Guatemala to Copán, Honduras. The crossing is mostly traversed by people looking to visit the Copán Ruins, an archeology park with Maya ruins that is just one kilometer (0.6 mi) outside of the town. The checkpoint it open 24 hours, but it is wise to allow plenty of time to cross the border during daylight hours.

The easiest way to cross into Honduras is by public transportation. A bus or private van will unload passengers just before the checkpoint so you can walk across the border. At the immigration office, you will have to show your passport but it will not be stamped. There is no fee for leaving Honduras or to enter Guatemala; however, you may be asked to pay unofficial fees—which can amount up to $20 per person. The best way to avoid fees is to pay attention to whether or not travelers in front of you are paying and what amount they are spending. If you are asked to pay, ask for a receipt and your fees may be magically dropped. If not, remember that a proper receipt will have the country's emblem on it. Updated: Aug 25, 2010.

Getting Around

Everything there is to see in Esquipulas is more or less in walking distance. If you need to get a taxi just ask in your hotel or get one on the street. During high season, there is a tourist train which takes tired visitors around the streets, and sights, of Esquipulas.

Safety

When in Esquipulas use the same common sense procedures you would use when traveling through any Latin American country. Don't wander the streets with your giant backpack looking for a hotel; choose a hotel next to the bus station; or, grab a taxi to your destination. Avoid walking alone at night and avoid public intoxication at all costs. Robberies usually don't turn violent as long as you don't resist; immediately handover whatever is being demanded. Remember, anything that you have can be replaced.

Secure any documents including credit cards in a money belt along with most of your cash. Keep a small wad of cash in your pocket so you have something with which to placate a robber.

Anything electronic including cell phones, cameras and laptops should be kept with you at all times. Do not allow a backpack containing these items to be checked into the baggage compartment on a bus.

If at all possible avoid the lower end accommodations in Esquipulas. There have been reports of gang activity and illegal immigrant smuggling. Updated: Aug 25, 2010.

Services

There are plenty of banks with ATMs in town: Banco G&T is on 9a Calle and 3a Avenida; Banco Industrial is on 10a Calle and 3a Avenida next to Hotel Legendario; and, Cajero 5B ATM is on 2a Avenida, next to the Hotel Payaqui. There isn't an Internet café or a post office in town, but, if you're staying at a mid-range plus hotel, most offer WiFi. The reception desk may be able to help you with posting items. Also ask the hotel about laundry service.

For your health needs, there is a Farmacia Batres and a Farmacia Don Bosco opposite each other on 11a Calle and 2a Avenida. In the same building, on 9a Calle between 5a and 6a Calles, there is the Clinica Dental and Clinica Medica. For up-to-minute information, see www.esquipulas.com.gt. Updated: Aug 25, 2010.

Things to See and Do

There are a few non-religious activities in Esquipulas. The park in front of the basilica is a nice place to rest in the shade, although this can get pretty busy on the weekend and during the pilgrimage. As well as the modern shopping mall La Perla (2a Av., opposite the Restaurante Santa Fe) there is a huge market area filled with kitsch Jesus candles, jewelry, candy and t-shirts. At the end of 11a Calle there is a "hands of peace" monument as it was here the Esquipula II (Peace) Accord was developed in the mid 1980s, a framework of conflict resolution for Central America.

La Basilica

The Esquipulas basilica was voted by Guatemalans as being the premier wonder of Guatamala (according to survey by Banco Industrial) and it certainly pulls in the crowds. As the center piece of the town, its gleaming white façade is very impressive. Inside, the air is heavy with incense, murmured prayers and belief, as devotees demonstrating their commitment to the saint by approaching on their knees. There is a separate side entrance to a special viewing circuit. Mass times are at 6:30 a.m., 11 p.m, 5 p.m. Monday to Saturday and at 6:30 a.m., 8 a.m., 9:30 a.m., 11 a.m., 12:30p.m., and 5 p.m. on Sundays, with extra blessings in between (times may change during the fiestas).

Parque Chatun

(ADMISSION: $8 adults, $6 children) Parque Chatun is an all-round family entertainment park about three kilometers (1.9 miles) out of Esquipulas. It's not quite Six Flags but it's a fun day out. There you can go zip-lining, boating on the lake, plays in the pools and on the slides, go bungee jumping, use the climbing wall, play soccer, basketball and volleyball (if there are enough of you to make up two team) visit the mini-farm or just walk and sit and enjoy the fresh air. You can even camp overnight if you wish. The space is also used for events. Entrance to the park, includes unlimited use of the attractions (except zip-lining is extra).

Volcán De Quetzaltepeque

This little-visited volcano, probably due to not being located close to other groups of volcanoes, is an interesting climb (plenty of interesting flora and fauna on the way, such as sweet gum trees) and is not too strenuous (taking about one hour 30 minutes). However, it is quite easy to get lost as the trails are not marked out. The peak is around 1,900 meters (6,234 ft) high but the views are not the best due to the dense vegetation at the top but there is one spot where you can make out the basilica. And remember to take long pants and a coat as it can get quite cold at the top. You can reach the base by taking a road from Quetzaltepeque to Caserío Los Planes where you can park, but you should ask in Esquipulas for further directions or a taxi.

Lodging

One thing is for sure, you do not have to walk far or search long to find Esquipulas hostels or hotels. Unless you arrive at the height of the pilgrimage period (January to March), in which case you'd be wise to make a reservation well in advance or arrive very early in the day, hostels and hotels are readily available. If you're on a budget head to 2a Avenida and 9a/10a Calle in Esquipulas. Hostels are so numerous here they've started to name them Hotelito 1 and Hotelito 2. In the low season or on weekdays, you can negotiate on prices or opt for a fan rather than air conditioning to save pennies. Generally breakfast is not included in the room price and most have a check-in time of 1 p.m. and check-out time of 3 p.m. Practically all of the hotels and hostels have secure parking. Updated: Jul 13, 2010.

BUDGET

Hotel de Los Angeles

(ROOMS: $4-28) Another good budget option on the western side of 2a Avenida, for $4-9, is Hotel de los Angeles. You can get a spacious room with a private bathroom, hot water, a fan and a TV. There

ATLANTIC COAST

is also a family room for $24-28. There are common areas for relaxing and a restaurant on site which serves up delicious typical Guatemalan dishes. Dollars are accepted but credit cards are not. 2a Av. 11-94. Tel: 502-7943-1254/0607/1343/0103. Updated: Jul 07, 2010.

Hotel La Favorita

(ROOMS $6-12) Hotel La Favorita is a favorite with low-income Guatemalan families on a pilgrimage to the basilica. This no frills hotel may not have a pool or any other luxuries, but the rooms do have hot-water, sheets and towels and there is a TV providing some evening entertainment. This is a good option if you're on a tight budget and/or traveling alone. Rates are $6 without a bathroom and $12 per person with bathroom. Open 24 hours and with flexible check-in, check-out times. 2a Av. Updated: Jul 07, 2010.

Hotel Posada De Santiago

(ROOMS: $9-38) Nearby Hotel Posada de Santiago is a little dark but, for the price, the rooms are a good value and spacious with T.V.s, hot-water showers, ceiling fans, a restaurant and on-site parking. Singles to quadruples, all with private bathrooms, are between $9-38. This hotel is at the upper end of the budget category but there is no Internet available. 2a Av., Zona 1. Tel: 502-7943-2023. Updated: Jul 07, 2010.

MID-RANGE

Hotel Payaqui

(ROOMS: $23-31) This place may not look like much from the outside but it might be the best value of all the hotels in Esquipulas, plus it is literally on the basilica's doorstep. Walk past the rather dull café out front to the reception area and further on to the large swimming pool with a café, bar and spacious poolside area for lounging about. There is also a hotel spa and beauty salon and a games room for the kids. But the best choice would be one of the themed rooms looking out over the pool. There is also free WiFi Internet access, a mini bar in some rooms and a souvenir shop. All credit cards are accepted but a fee is charged. 2a Av. 11-56. Tel: 502-7943-1143, E-mail: info@hotelpayaqui.com, URL: www.hotelpayaqui.com. Updated: Jul 07, 2010.

Hotel Portal de la Fe

(ROOMS: $25-80) This is a well-finished mid-range hotel with a friendly staff. There is a pool on the roof, albeit small, and some pretty nice views of the cathedral dome. There is also a café open in high season. Free WiFi covers the whole hotel and a range of rooms costing from $25 for a single to $80 for a quadruple. Rooms have comfy beds, cable TV, hot water and good showers. Unfortunately the room windows only look onto the corridors so they lack natural light. Rooms do have the all-important fan however. There is secure underground parking which also provides wheelchair access. 11a Ca. 1-70. Tel: 502-7943-4124. Updated: Jul 07, 2010.

Hotel Peregrino !

(ROOMS: $30-50) Hotel Peregrino is one of four hotels on 2a Avenida directly facing the basilica. This is a very respectable lower to mid-range hotel (no Internet), offering basic but comfortable rooms with shared and private bathrooms, T.V., hot water, parking, a courtyard for sitting outside (good if it's a particularly sticky evening), and even a rooftop pool with a view of the basilica and surrounding mountains. Rooms on the first floor are also wheelchair accessible from the secure car park. Doubles cost from $42. 2a Av. 11-94. Tel: 502-7943-1054/1859, E-mail: info@hperegrino.com, URL: www.elperegrinoesquipulas.com. Updated: Jul 07, 2010.

Hotel Gran Estefania

(ROOMS: $30-52) The three hotels, Hotel Gran Estefania, Plaza Maxine and Villa Zona, all in different locations around the center of town, are all owned and run by Dr. Quijada, a very welcoming and enthusiastic hotelier who speaks English and Spanish. All rooms have private bathrooms, hot water and cable T.V. but there are a range of prices available, with Villa Zona being the cheapest (in the 2a Av. budget zone). The Gran Estefania has two pools and two kitchens for client-use, as well as a restaurant if you're not planning on doing your own cooking. Dollars and credit cards are accepted. 1a Av. A, Plaza Santa Fe. Tel: 502-5943-5215/4412/0648. Updated: Jul 07, 2010.

Hotel Gran Chorti

(ROOMS: $30-150) This large white hotel on the road coming into town is hard to miss and is the most resort-like hotel around. It is well-run and spacious, with a big bar and restaurant serving good seafood dishes at reasonable prices. If you're looking for somewhere to escape and cool down, the pool and pool-side area are a pleasant distraction. Doubles, triples and quadruples range between $34-70 and the presidential suite is $150, but be sure to check the room first as some are definitely better than others. There is also Internet and free parking, cable TV and no charge for all credit cards. Being a kilometer (0.6 mi) out of town is a slight draw-back but the hotel runs a free shuttle bus to the basilica 8 a.m.-7 p.m. Km 222, the road into Esquipulas. Tel: 502-6685-9966, E-mail: rgranchorti@ grupo-predinsa.com, URL: www.realgranchorti.com. Updated: Jul 07, 2010.

Hotel Villa Del Rosario

(ROOMS: $37-52) Hotel Villa del Rosario is only half a block from the basilica and, being one of the newer additions to the hotel scene in Esquipulas, has a fresher feel. There is a medium-sized rooftop pool, bar and café (although the restaurant is not open in low season), free Internet and parking. The well-appointed rooms are all en suite with hot water and air conditioning. Doubles, triples and junior luxury suites cost between $37-52. Dollars and all major credit cards are accepted with no fee charge. A nice touch is the room-service delivery deal which the hotel has with the La Rotunda restaurant (ask at reception for a menu). 11a Ca. (next to Portal de la Fey). Tel: 502-7943-4511/4512, E-mail: hotelvilladelrosario@hotmail.es, URL: www.hotelvilladelrosario.com. Updated: Jul 07, 2010.

HIGH END

Hotel Legendario

(ROOMS: $125-150) This is perhaps the most expensive hotel in town but it seems a little much for what it offers. It does have all that you would usually expect from a high-end business-style hotel. There is a large, well-attended reception complete with international flags, two bars, a restaurant, pool, large rooms and it is cleaned regularly. There is a babysitting service, laundry service and tour-operator on site. It's just a shame that it's a little dated and lackluster; a spot of renovation would maybe justify the high prices. 9a Ca. 3-00 and 3a Av. Tel: 502-7943-1824, URL: www.portahotels.com. Updated: Jul 07, 2010.

Restaurants

There are lots of places to eat in Esquipulas. For local atmosphere and a good view, the restaurants on 2a Avenida, staring directly at the basilica, cannot be beaten – but you'll have to fight for a table in any one of them during high season (January through March, July, plus weekends). Your fast-food needs are catered to with a Pollo Campero, a pizza place, burger joint and a diner very close to each other near the back of the basilica. Additionally, there are often taco stands around as well as comedores on the eastern and western sides of the basilica. Don't miss the fresh juice stands usually found on the northern side of 2a and 3a Avenidas, or the bakery at 4a Avenida between 9a and 10a Calles. Updated: Aug 03, 2010.

Restaurante Los Angeles

(ENTREES: $3-7) The menu at Los Angeles might not be extensive or international but it largely caters to a domestic crowd, and it is definitely a pleasant place to soak up the family atmosphere of Esquipulas within view of the basilica. Often times live marimba music is being played which adds to the feeling of being apart of real, everyday Guatemala. There are three choices of cooked breakfasts; there is grilled meat; the chicken dinner is a good value; seafood and fish meals; and, soups and salads. 2a Av. 11-94. Tel: 502-7943-1254/0607/1343/0103. Updated: Aug 03, 2010.

Restaurante Santa Fe

(ENTREES: $3-10) The Restaurante Santa Fe has a modern appearance and a casual atmosphere. The tables are set smartly but it's the sort of place to have lunch rather than dinner. It provides air conditioned dining close to the action but sufficiently cool and clean so you can eat your shrimp in peace. The menu offers full meals, such as mixed grill (two people), chicken, spaghetti Bolognese, as well as menu del dia and breakfasts. It is large enough to accommodate groups and will fill up with visiting Guatemalans. There is no parking provided. 2a Ca./Plaza Santa Fe (around the corner from the Hotel Los Angeles). Updated: Aug 03, 2010.

Restaurante Payaqui

(ENTREES: $6-12) Although it has more of a cafeteria feel and is not quite in-keeping with the comfort level of the hotel, Restaurante Payaqui is pretty similar to the other restaurants along 2a Avenida. It does get busy, serving the hotel guests and the tourists visiting the Basilica. So, the reataurant is full of activity and, with the flat screen TV on, noisy. There is the usual shrimp, churrasco, chao mein, chicken and soups and salads. 2a Av. 11-56. Tel: 502-7943-1143. Updated: Aug 03, 2010.

La Rotonda

La Rotonda, on the left as you drive into town on the main road, is modern and fresh and a good place to escape the streets if it is high season. There's no terrace but the canopy roof and big windows let in the breeze and a lot of light. Breakfast served from 7a.m includes: cereal, typical Guatemalan fare and porridge. The cuisine is a mix of local and international foods with seafood, burgers, pizza and burritos, as well some great salads served in huge portions. The desserts are also good. Delivery is available. Dollars are accepted as well as Visa (with no fee). Open until 10 p.m. 11a Ca. (opposite the Portal de la Fey hotel). Tel: 502-7943-2083/2361. Updated: Aug 03, 2010.

Restaurante La Hacienda

With the look of an Argentine steakhouse, this is one of the more high-end places to dine in Esquipulas, although the prices are similar to La Rotonda. Out of season it can look pretty forlorn but its three dining rooms get packed when the tourists are in town, so reservations are recommended. There is a good selection of wines to accompany the delicious grilled meats and the service is attentive. You should try the local favorite here, *Punta de Puyaso*, a tender and flavorful sirloin cut. Dollars and credit cards accepted but some credit cards have fees. Daily 8 am.-10 p.m. 2a Av. (northern end) and 10a Ca. Updated: Aug 03, 2010.

QUIRIGUÁ

The town of Quiriguá is small and unremarkable. The only reason to come by here is perhaps to pick up transport or to pass some time after visiting the ruins and before moving on. Along the road, it is a three-kilometer (1.9 mi) walk back from the ruins and then you follow the disused train tracks west to the town. It would be preferable to visit the ruins earlier in the day and then move on to stay in Denny's Beach in Mariscos, Río Dulce or Puerto Barrios, for example, where there are more accommodation choices and a lot more to do.

If you do want to stay in Quiriguá, there is one decent hotel and a few eating options. A steep cobbled stone road winds off the CA-9 Highway into Quiriguá town center, about three kilometers (1.86 mi) from the ruins. If you follow the road on the opposite side of the grassy square to the church you will find: Librería Karen; Hotel y Restaurante Royal; Farmacia Eloi; Antojitos Benyelf; Pan y Pastel Lido; a couple of beauty salons; and, Librería Joseth with Internet, phones, faxes and a video games room. The red and yellow Hotel y Restaurante Royal is a good place to stay. The owners are very welcoming and as there is no specific restaurant menu they will make you what you want from the fresh produce available that day, including veggie options, seafood, meat and pasta, and they will and even deliver your dinner to your room. The rooms have private bathrooms with hot water, fans, big beds and TVs. There is a nice terrace outside the rooms with views of the church, chairs to relax in and a laundry service available. There are also some cheaper rooms at the back of the hotel but without windows. Rates are negotiable but around $9.50 per person. Dollars but not credit cards are accepted. Ca. Principal. Tel: 502-5797-8788/7947-3639.

All buses going between Puerto Barrios and Guatemala City, traveling on the CA-9, pass by the turn-off for Quiriguá town, which is a different turn-off than that which goes to the Quiriguá ruins and the banana plantation (2 km/1.24 mi closer to Puerto Barrios). There are usually minibuses and motorbikes at this junction for lifts to the town. Updated: Aug 31, 2010.

Getting To and Away

Quiriguá is located around the 203 kilometer mark on the Carretera Atlántico or 220 kilometers (136.7 mi) from Guatemala City, and relatively easy to visit as it is not far from the highway that links the city to the coast. All buses that travel the highway between Guatemala City and Puerto Barrios pass near the town and the adjacent ruins. From the town you can take a pick-up truck or walk through the nearby banana plantation.

Getting Around

Quiriguá is about 220 kilometers (136.7 mi) from Guatemala City, and relatively easy to visit as it is not far from the highway that link the city to the coast. There is a small town nearby by although facilities are limited. Quiriguá is better done as a day trip.

Things to See and Do

Ruins of Quiriguá

Cauac Sky was the greatest ruler of the city of Quiriguá during the Maya classic period. He is depicted on Stela E at Quiriguá, the most impressive of the Maya stelae, or tall, carved standing stones. The largest of the Maya stelae, Stela E stands 11 meters (35 ft) tall and weighs an estimated 60,000 kilograms (130,000 lb). Archeologists estimate the stela was finished around 771 AD.

It is one of 20 or so at the Quiriguá archeological site, once an important Maya city. The glyphs (Maya picture-writing) on the stela show Cauac Sky receiving the trappings of power from the ruler of the nearby city of Copán, 18 Rabbit. Later, Cauac Sky would defeat the forces of Copán in battle and order the beheading of 18 Rabbit, one of the greatest of Copán's rulers.

The Maya empire wasn't really an empire at all, but a collection of city-states that were unified by language and commerce. The Maya were great builders, warriors and astronomers, and their culture peaked around 600-800 AD before mysteriously disappearing. Historians have a number of theories for their decline, including too much warfare among the city-states, natural disasters and disease. Whatever the reason, by the time the Spanish arrived in the sixteenth century, the descendants of the Maya were scattered into smaller pockets of civilization spread out over southern Mexico, Belize, Guatemala and northern Honduras.

The Quiriguá archeological site is noteworthy for several reasons. Besides Stela E and the other magnificent carved standing stones, the area is one of the few places which features "full-figured glyphs", which is a certain intricate form of Maya writing into stone. It also features "zoomorphs," which are great stones carved into animal shapes. Much of the site has yet to be excavated: it is managed jointly by the University of Pennsylvania and the Guatemalan government. Admission to the site costs about $3. It is a UNESCO World Heritage site. Updated: Apr 20, 2007.

Lodging

With only two options to choose from you can't be too picky. Hotel El Edén offers single or double rooms for around $7 per night or you could try the nearby Hotel Royal which has an attached restaurant for around the same price. Updated: Aug 19, 2010.

PUERTO BARRIOS

Puerto Barrios is a port city that serves as a landing point for nearby attractions such as Lívingston, the Punta de Manabique Wildlife reserve, the Maya ruins of Quírigua and the Río Dulce. Once Guatemala's main Caribbean shipping port, the town is named for President Justo Rufino Barrios, a reformist leader who initiated construction in the 1880s. A railroad linking Puerto Barrios to Guatemala City was finished in 1908, and the area became the shipping center for United Fruit Company, the former plantation-owning banana giant. In the 1970s, United Fruit was sold to Del Monte and one of the worst earthquakes in the history of Guatemala destroyed most of the port facilities at Puerto Barrios. A twin port town was constructed across the bay to the southwest: Santo Tomás de Castilla. The area is still the main Caribbean seaport in Guatemala, mostly due to the fact it remains a hub for Dole and Del Monte. Updated: Aug 19, 2010.

When to Go

Puerto Barrios is typically hot and humid. You will probably want to avoid visiting during the rainy season, generally from May to October, when the waters at nearby beaches and rivers are murky and the weather is miserable. Updated: Aug 19, 2010

Getting To and Away

In Puerto Barrios there isn't a specific bus terminal so all the buses leave from around the market. Litega Pullman buses, for stops along the Carretera al Atántico, leave from 6a Avenida between 9a and 10a Calles. Over 20 buses a day go to Guatemala City between midnight and 4 p.m., taking five to six hours. First class direct costs $10, snack included. Second class costs $6.20 and makes stops, including at Morales. Around the market: for buses to Chiquimula and Esquipulas go to the south-western corner of the market; for buses to Honduras go to the west side; for buses to Río Dulce you can take any bus along highway CA-9 and change at the La Ruidosa junction.

Public *lanchas* (boats) leave from the dock at the end of 12a Avenida. To Lívingston, boats leave about every 40 minutes but they often wait until they are full, which can be a little frustrating. These private boats cost $4 and take 30 minutes. The slower public ferry takes triple the time, is slightly cheaper and leaves once in the morning and once in the evening. Check at the dock for the most accurate schedule.

If you want to charter a private boat it will cost about $20. For Punta Gorda in Belize, there is only one lancha in the morning, for around $20 and takes one hour 30 minutes. Remember to clear immigration, for a $10 fee, at the office on 12a Avenida between the dock and Hotel Europa. Updated: Aug 26, 2010.

ATLANTIC COAST

Getting Around

Puerto Barrios is a sprawling town and the restaurants and services of interest to travelers are spaced out. The best way to get around Puerto Barrios is by bus or taxi. Both options are relatively cheap, but be aware that taxi drivers often try to charge tourists more. Be sure to only ride in taxis that have an identification number on both doors. As for public transportation, the main bus line runs the most common route, from the Central Market in Puerto Barrios to San Agustín in Santo Tomás de Castilla. Minibuses for short distances convene around the north-eastern corner of the market, at 9a Calle and 7a Avenida. Bus stops do not have signals most of the time, so pay close attention or ask someone to let you off. Updated: Aug 26, 2010.

Safety

Puerto Barrios is not used to a lot of tourists and, although not unfriendly, it is worth being aware. Chose carefully where you stay. Be aware of your possessions when you're walking around and even in your hotel room if you're traveling on a budget. If you go out at night, plan where you're going first and don't walk down poorly-lit streets. Barrio Rastro, where some of the bars and clubs are, is full of local flavor and is a cool place to hang out. But be sensible: Take taxis instead of walking in the dark, always look for a registration number and ask the driver not to pick up anyone else. Updated: Aug 26, 2010.

Services

The banks are mostly near the center, by the market. Banrural with a Cajero 5B ATM in on 8a Avenida and 9a Calle. CitiBank is on 15a Calle and 7a Avenida, but there is no ATM. There is also a Cajero 5B ATM at the Despensar Familiar supermarket on 8a Calle and 5a Avenida.

If you need a pharmacy, Farmacia la Doce is on 12a Calle and 5a Avenida (Tel: 502-7948-5205). Not too far away, there is a doctors' office on 15a Calle and 6a Avenida and there is also one on 16a Calle between 8a and 9a Calles. There are a couple of dentist offices, one on 7a Avenida and 16a Calle and another on 8a Avenida and 11a Calle, Tel: 502-5600-5360, E-mail: joseangelm@turbonett.com.

There are at least three Internet cafés in Puerto Barrios: Global center is on 8a Avenida and Gecko's, opposite the cathedral, is a cool oasis of peace open every day 9 a.m.-7 p.m., 30 minutes ($0.50). 10a Ca. and 8a Av. There is also an Internet Café near the Safari restaurant on the end of 5a Avenida (not open Sundays).

The police station and the post office are around the corner from each other on 6a Avenida and 6a Calle. For package delivery to the US there is also Tito Express on 6a Avenida and 14a Calle.

You can get camping supplies from Marleny's on 6a Avenida between 12a and 13a Calles. Updated: Aug 26, 2010.

Things to See and Do

Puerto Barrios is a working town and subsequently does not hold much attraction for travelers, unlike neighboring Lívingston. You will probably not be here unless you're passing through on your way to Honduras. However, if you do have a few hours or an evening to spend here there are a few things to do. You could spend a few hours browsing the large market in the middle of town. Instead of a shady plaza there is the cathedral, opposite Gecko's Internet Café, a peaceful place to sit and contemplate. Otherwise, eating and drinking to pass the time is a pleasant choice, particularly by the glimmering ocean of the Gulf of Honduras at Safari or Cangrejo Azul or the historic Hotel del Norte. In front of the Hotel del Norte there is a new park and malecón, or promenade, for walks along the waterfront in the sun and the breeze. Further out, there is an air-conditioned mall called La Pradera on the way to Santo Tomás. Updated: Aug 31, 2010.

Jardín Botánico y Restaurante Ecológico El Hibiscus

The Hibiscus garden and restaurant, located at Km 284 on the CA-9 highway just outside of Puerto Barrios, is a peaceful place to stop for a meal, to shop for gifts, to learn about Guatemalan textiles at the Museo del Traje Típico Contemporáneo, or to pick up travel and tour information for Punta Manabique and Cerro San Gil. The restaurant is surrounded by a lush tropical garden where butterflies, birds and lizards roam free. The restaurant itself is a wooded dining room with wicker furniture and colorful, Maya textiles. On the menu are traditional Guatemalan foods, plus other seafood, steak, and chicken dishes. Outside are pleasant, botanical gardens with many species of tropical plants. You can eat on the patio and then take a stroll through the tropical gardens. The complex also has a handicrafts shop, as well as a costume museum that displays a variety of traditional clothes and describes contemporary folklore and the history of

ATLANTIC COAST

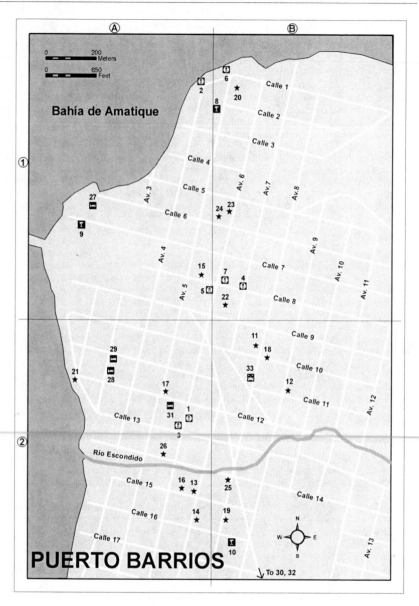

Bahía de Amatique

PUERTO BARRIOS

To 30, 32

Guatemala. Daily 6 a.m.-6 p.m. Tel: 502-5206-8890, E-mail: hibiscus@intelnet.net.gt, URL: www.hibiscusprojectizabal.com. Updated: Aug 31, 2010.

Tours

Chiltepe Tours

Chiltepe Tours will take you around the city in an open-sided truck for $34 per adult or $29 per child, which includes two beverages. The company is based in Antigua, so call to arrange. Tel: 502-5907-0913. Updated: Aug 26, 2010.

Lodging

In Puerto Barrios, being the port town it is, many of the budget hotels are frequented by prostitutes and their customers. You are therefore recommended to either opt for one of the mid-range hotels, of which there a number,

Eating	
1 Antojitos Doña Mari A2	16 Doctors' surgery A2
2 Cangrejo Azul A1	17 Farmacia La Doce A2
3 Charlie's Snacks A2	18 Gecko's Cafe Internet B2
4 Pollo Campero B1	19 Global Center Internet B2
5 Restaurante Maxim Express A1	20 Internet café B1
6 Safari B1	21 Lancha dock A2
7 Taco Contento Express B1	22 Market B1
	23 Police B1
Nightlife	24 Post Office B1
	25 Telgua B2
8 Canoa Club B1	26 Tito Express Delivery A2
9 Jeffery's A1	
10 Planeta Azul B2	Sleeping
	27 Hotel del Norte A1
Services ★	28 Hotel Europa A2
	29 Hotel Miami A2
11 Banrural B2	30 Hotel Puerto Libre B2
12 Cathedral B2	31 Hotel Valle Tropical A2
13 Citi Bank A2	32 MarBrissa B2
14 Dentist A2	
15 Despensar Familiar	Transportation
Supermarket A1	33 Buses B2

ATLANTIC COAST

usually with pools which are ideal for the sweltering heat. Or, if you really need to save your pennies, you should thoroughly check out your hotels first and make sure you feel comfortable and safe staying there. Even if you don't stay at the Hotel del Norte on the sea front, it warrants a visit. Updated: Aug 01, 2010

BUDGET

Hotel Europa
(ROOMS: $10-12) This is a budget hotel but family-run and definitely not an excuse for a brothel. It has recently been re-decorated and fitted with mosquito nets on the windows and the owners are house-proud as well as being very helpful. If you arrive late give them a call from the bus station and they'll pick you up.

There isn't a restaurant but you can order take-out delivery. It is very close to the lancha dock and also very close to the immigration office if you need a visa for Honduras. Rooms have private bathrooms, TV and fans. 3a Av. between 11a and 12a Ca. Tel: 502-7948-1292/502-5975-1785. Updated: Aug 01, 2010.

Hotel Miami
(ROOMS: $15-21) It doesn't look like much from the outside, but the Hotel Miami is centered around quite a nice green courtyard and, like the Europa next door, this budget hotel is also being renovated. The bathrooms are well-done, there are new nets on the windows and air conditioning and T.V.s in some rooms. Rooms are $15-21 with private bathrooms, T.V.s and firm beds. There is no restaurant on

site but beer and cold drinks are stocked. Less than two blocks from the public dock, this hotel is convenient for onward travel to Livingston/ Río Dulce. 3a Av. between 11a and 12a Ca. Tel: 502-4064-4090. Updated: Aug 01, 2010.

MID-RANGE

Hotel Valle Tropical

(ROOMS: $22-57) Similar to Marbrissa but closer to town and down the road from the public lancha port, this hotel also has a pool and conference rooms. However, it is in a rather unexciting and lackluster concrete building painted a garish shade of green. Rooms are basic but clean and cost $22 for a single, $41 for a double, and $57 for a triple. The breakfast buffet is $4.35 extra. It also has WiFi and cable TV and the check-out isn't until 1 p.m. Credit cards are accepted but carry a 5 percent fee. 12a ca., between 5a and 6a Av. Tel: 502-7948-7084, E-mail: reservaciones@ hotelvalletropical.com. Updated: Aug 01, 2010

Hotel Puerto Libre

(ROOMS: $36-41) A large hotel, mainly used for conferences and events such as local weddings, with 31 premium rooms at $41 and 10 standard at $36, plus a medium-sized pool and a palapa-style restaurant serving mainly seafood and a mix of local and international dishes. There's an online booking system via the website. It's located at the crossroads of the CA-9 and the road to Santo Tomás de Castilla. Km. 292 Ruta al Atlántico. Tel: 502-7948-4739/4740/4741, E-mail: ventas@hotelpuertolibre.com. Updated: Aug 01, 2010.

Hotel Marbrissa

(ROOMS: $90-150) Outside of town, this large resort-style hotel has two pools, one with slides for the kids and one large enough for laps, a tennis court, gym and pool tables. It's a great place to escape the high temperatures and searing sun and definitely one of the better hotels in Puerto Barrios. There is a bar and a very good restaurant by the pool, and the room price includes a buffet breakfast. Rooms come with air conditioning, cable TV, mini-fridge, and there is WiFi and a laundry service. 25 Ca. and 20 Av., Col. Virginia. Tel: 502-7948-1450/6190, E-mail: informacion@marbrissa.com, URL: www.marbrissa.com. Updated: Aug 01, 2010.

Restaurants

Tapado, the fish soup that is famous in these parts, and *pan de coco* is the thing to try here. If you're wandering around town try going south on 6a Avenida and between 12a and

13a there are two other restaurants to try, Antojitos Doña Mari, a grilled meat shack, and Charlie's Snacks, a Mexican place with a terrace. In town, there are a group of comedores by the market and the ever-present Pollo Campero. A couple of pretty nice restaurants can be found on the seafront in the Barrio Rastro, the place to go if you're looking for a night out. Updated: Aug 19, 2010.

Taco Contento Express

(ENTREES: $1.20-4) On the same corner of the market as Maxim Chinese restaurant but on the other side of the road, the 'happy' taco is a good spot for a grabbing a quick snack. You can eat in, taking the weight off at the picnic benches as you watch the busy world go by, or take away. There are all the usual Mexican favorites, with a three tacos for $1.20 deal, and the super gringa ($2.85) is particularly sloppy and satisfying, though not for anyone on a health kick. Corner of 6a Av. and 8a Ca. Updated: Aug 01, 2010.

Restaurante Maxim Express

(ENTREES: $5-12) Opposite the market on the northwestern corner, this place claims to serve the best Chinese food in Puerto Barrios, and that maybe because it is the only Chinese restaurant in Puerto Barrios. There is the usual chow mein, chop suey and sweet and sour dishes as well as duck, seafood and pigeon. It is well-priced and a good place to fill up if you're on a small budget as bread and salsa is offered at no extra charge. Tuesday-Sunday 10:30 a.m.-10 p.m. 6a Av. and 8a Ca. Tel: 502-7948-8779/7963. Updated: Aug 01, 2010.

Safari

(ENTREES: $5-17) This is a great place on the waterfront with a lovely sea breeze and pleasant views. This is a nice spot to while away the afternoon with a bottle of wine ($17). It gets quite busy on a Sunday afternoon as it's a favorite with locals for family lunches. The menu includes filet mignon, ($7), ceviche ($10), pasta dishes ($8) and salads ($5) for vegetarians. Dollars and credit cards accepted but with a 7 percent fee and 10 percent service charge is added to your bill. Parking is available and the restaurant is wheelchair friendly. Daily 9 a.m.-9 p.m. 1a Ca. and 5a Av. Tel: 502-7943-0563. Updated: Aug 01, 2010.

Cangrejo Azul

Cangrejo Azul is the place to come for seafood in Puerto Barrios. The *tapado* ($9) is very good and the lobster ($12) is not bad either. Meat dishes, such as pork chops

($5), are available and there is green salad ($2.50) if you are vegetarian. Like Safari, there's a lovely terrace looking out over the water. There is also live music Thursday to Sunday. The only downside is that it is quite a ways out of town. It is best to get a taxi and definitely do not walk there after dark. Parking is available and wheelchair access is possible. Dollars, Mastercard and Visa are accepted. Daily 10 a.m.-12 p.m. 7a Av. and 1a Ca. Tel: 502-7948-4863. Updated: Aug 01, 2010.

Nightlife

For a place to dance head to the Barrio Rastro: Canoa Club (5a Av. and 2a Ca.) and Twins Disco (6a Av. and 2a Ca.) are two clubs near to each other playing Reggaeton and punk rock, though this is the not the safest place to hang out so don't take any valuables with you or get too dressed up. A little farther south, around 6a Avenida and 6a Calle (not far from the police station), is where a lot of the strip bars are located so be careful around this area too. Planeta Azul (16a Ca., between 8a and 9a Avenida) is another nightclub. For something more relaxed the Hotel del Norte is a good place to have a beer and a snack and enjoy some faded splendor. It's pretty dilapidated but it has a certain charm and you really feel like you're in the Caribbean sitting on the wooden terrace, taking in the sea air. Nearby is Jeffery's, a shack-style bar good for a beer or two. Otherwise, the Safari and Cangrejo Azul restaurants are good options for an evening of drinks by the bay. Updated: Aug 01, 2010.

Container

On the water across from the Hotel del Norte you will find two steel shipping containers that have been converted into a simple bar. This is a great place to sit back and enjoy a few beers, or sample some bar food such as burgers and tacos. Daily 10 a.m.–10 p.m. 7a Ca. Price. Updated: Aug 19, 2010.

Hotel del Norte

The seafront Hotel del Norte is a sloping, wooden structure that houses a restaurant serving international and local cuisine. If you are looking for a place to sit back and enjoy a drink, stop by the colonial-style bar where you can take in the views of the bay from a century-old structure. If you stay the night at the hotel, there is air conditioning and a cable TV. The hotel also has a swimming pool and is surrounded by gardens. 7a Ca. Tel: 502-7948-2116. Updated: Aug 19, 2010.

AROUND PUERTO BARRIOS
PUERTO SANTO TOMÁS DE CASTILLA

Across the bay from Puerto Barrios is Puerto Santo Tomás de Castilla, a port that has been in operation since colonial times. Although abandoned in the 1600s, a doomed Belgian colony took root here in 1843. In the 1960s, the Guatemalan Navy made this their base, and finally a major seaport was built in 1976 after an earthquake destroyed much of Puerto Barrios.

Today, the seaport at Santo Tomás de Castillo is one of the busiest in Central America—nearly 1,400 ships come in here every year, and counting. The port also started receiving cruise ships in 2004, dropping off passengers bound for nearby attractions such as Río Dulce, the Maya ruins of Quiriguá, and Lívingston. It is normal for four cruise ships dock here a month, however, Carnival Cruise Lines recently announced construction of a $40 million terminal at the port, which is expected to bring 200 cruises and 200,000 passengers here every year. Updated: Aug 19, 2010.

Cerro San Gil

One popular excursion from Puerto Santo Tomás de Castilla is to a rainforest park that centers around Cerro San Gil mountain. The preserved area is home to more than 350 species of birds, as well as jaguars and other mammals. Río Las Escobas is also in the park. In Río Las Escobas, you can swim in the cool waters of the watershed that supplies Puerto Barrios and hike several nature trails that take you past waterfalls and natural pools. To organize a visit, contact FUNDAECO (Tel: 502-7948-4404. URL: www.fundaeco.org. gt), the private conservation group that looks after the park. Updated: Aug 19, 2010.

Punta de Palma

Also nearby Puerto Santo Tomás de Castilla is Punta de Palma beach, a popular local spot for weekend getaways along the coast. The beach is not very large, and all that it has in the area are a few tiny refreshment stands. So, if you are really looking to hit the sand, you would be better to visit the Caribbean town of Lívingston. Updated: Aug 19, 2010.

Green Bay Hotel

If you are looking for a private beach retreat near Puerto Santo Tomás De Castilla,

ATLANTIC COAST

the 50-room Green Bay Hotel is the perfect option. From the outside, the thatched-roof bungalows look unassuming, but inside you will be treated to a modern hotel room with all the standard amenities: air conditioning, hot water, TV, and bay windows that look out into the jungle. You can dine in the Green Bay Hotel's restaurant, or book a tour to any nearby attraction. Tel: 502-7948-2361. Updated: Aug 19, 2010.

PUNTA DE MANABIQUE WILDLIFE REFUGE

Around 20 kilometers (18 mi) north of Puerto Barrios is a peninsula that separates Amatique Bay from the Gulf of Honduras. The area, covered with mangrove swamps, white sand beaches, and tropical rain forests, was declared a wildlife reserve in 1999. Save for the rich marine life and bird and mammal species that live in the park, the area is largely uninhabited—a fact that may soon change with the promise of new cruise ships docking in Guatemala's Caribbean port. For now, however, you can come explore the amazing biodiversity of the secluded 50,000 hectare (123,500 ac) park.

The reserve is managed by a conservation group called Fundacíon Mario Dary (www.guate.net/fundarymanabique), who works with locals to make every effort to conserve the ecosystems of the area. These locals—mostly fisherman and farmers—are becoming more and more involved in ecotourism efforts, which have been greatly helped by USAID. One achievement is the introduction of solar-powered energy to the area, providing electricity which allows luxuries such as refrigeration.

Inside the reserve, there are many species of fauna, including manatees, tapirs, jaguars and howler monkeys. In addition, 235 species of birds have been identified in the park, including the endangered yellow-headed parrot. As for marine wildlife, you may be able to spot the four species of sea turtles that inhabit the park, as well as sea bass, lobster and conch, which are abundant. There is also a 10-kilometer (6.2 mile) canal, Canal Inglés, along which you will find the small community of Santa Isabel. This is where the visitor center for the reserve is located, which is the place to arrange a fishing trip with the locals through the mangrove forests and lagoons. Further north, on the outskirts of the reserve, is another community called Estero Lagarto, where you can rent a kayak

to explore swamps and canals. East, near the border with Honduras, is El Quetzalito, a good place for crocodile-spotting and birdwatching.

Getting To and Away

Getting to the reserve is not easy, as there is no regularly scheduled service. The best option is to book a package with Fundacion Mario Dary, who runs a small lodge in the community of Punta de Manabique near the tip of the peninsula. The lodge, El Saraguate, offers dorm-style beds and the food is prepared by local families. At the lodge, you can explore nature trails or snorkel in shallow waters. The Fundacíon also maintains the Julio Obiols Biological Research Station on the cape of Cabo Tres Puntas. For $100 per person (double occupancy), you will be transported from Puerto Barrios to the research station for a two-night stay that includes meals. There is a lighthouse on the cape. The other option is to try and hitch a ride with a group leaving Puerto Barrios, or hire a boat to take you from the municipal dock. Transportes El Chato (Tel: 502-7958-5525) charges $180 for the one-hour trip. It is also possible to hire a boat from Lívingston, which may be cheaper. Updated: Aug 19, 2010.

LÍVINGSTON

Lívingston is a small town located where the Río Dulce empties into the Atlantic Ocean at the Bay of Amatique. Historically isolated, Lívingston is becoming an important visitor destination as travelers journey there to relax, dance and soak up a Caribbean vibe.

The inhabitants of Lívingston are the descendents of escaped slaves and natives of the Lesser Antilles, who made their way to parts of the Central America coast by means of the Bay Islands in Honduras. They recognize their slave heritage with the *wanaragua* or John Kunnu dance, in which dancers clad in ornate costumes and white masks make fun of slave-holders. The wanaragua festival takes place around Christmas and in early January.

Lívingston's greatest natural attraction is Los Siete Altares, or "the seven altars." It is a series of waterfalls and pools along a small river through a lush forest. They are located to the north about an hour's walk from town along the beach. Updated: Nov 21, 2006.

When to Go

Many travelers prefer to center their trips to Lívingston around the towns fiestas and festivals. The most popular is the Wanaragua Festival, which happens around Christmas and early January. Other popular holidays include Semana Santa, or Holy week, and Garifuna National Day on November 26th. Keep in mind the rainy season in this part of Guatemala is from mid-May to mid-October, making travel much more difficult (but not impossible). Updated: Aug 19, 2010.

Getting To and Away

There are several options to reach Lívingston, all of them by water. Ferries leave the Muelle Municipal in Puerto Barrios and travel across the bay to Lívingston at 10 a.m. and 5 p.m. from Monday to Saturday. It is also possible to take a smaller boat, which departs once they have enough people aboard. These smaller boats, called lanchas, take about half the time as the ferry (30 minutes), but are twice as expensive. International boats also leave Honduras and Belize, most notably from Punta Gorda, Belize on Tuesdays and Fridays. To leave from Belize, you will have to pay a departure tax at the immigration office on the dock. Make sure to check in with immigration if you arrive from another country. Updated: Aug 19, 2010.

Getting Around

Getting around town in Lívingston is only done by foot or by taxi. Even if your cab ride is short, expect to pay around $3 per ride. However, Lívingston is extremely small and easily navigable, especially if you stick to the main street, Calle Principal. Updated: Aug 19, 2010.

Safety

The hustlers in Lívingston can be a bit dodgy, so be aware once you get off the boat you may be bombarded with people asking you if you need taxis or accommodations. These men merely escort you to a hotel and then demand the owner pays them a fee, so it is better to just find accommodations on your own—or book in advance, if possible. Also be wary of anyone who strikes up a conversation with you on the street. You may also be asked to pay up front for tours or even if you can "lend" money to a local, which are obvious scams. Furthermore, Lívingston is used as a bridge for northbound drug traffic, so it is best to stay away from sticky situations. Updated: Aug 19, 2010.

Services

There is a good 'OGC' Internet café, Organisación Garifuna Guatemalteco, on the main street going toward Playa Barique,

charging $0.80 an hour and it is open until late. Just down the hill at Café Gotay, Internet is available as well as tasty meals. The Telgua office and the post office are next to each other, on the right opposite the municipal building, by Hotel Villa Caribe. The Tourist Information office is west of the dock on the other side of the sports courts. Banrual is close-by but the ATM is often out of order so it is wise to take enough cash with you for your stay, or take money you can exchange at the bank. There are two communal clothes-washing 'pilas' which are free to use alongside the locals. One is down the hill toward Playa Barique and the other is along Calle Marcos Sanchéz Dias. There is a laundry service on the hill up from the dock, in a little cabin on the right. There is a small fruit stall next to Ríos Tropicales hotel. Nearby Ríos Tropicales hotel is a pharmacy and a bakery selling delicious pan de coco. Updated: Aug 30, 2010.

SHOPPING

There are some souvenir shops on the main street. A shop next to the Restaurant El Malecón sells souvenir clothes, textiles, beads, hats etc. There are also stalls set up along the Calle Principal in late afternoon and early evening selling hand-crafted jewelry and CDs. There are lots of stores along the high street selling supplies you might need, such as toothpaste, telephone cards, washing detergent, snacks, drinks and liquor. Nearby Ak' Tenamit, along the Río Dulce, hand-made gifts made my Q'eqchi Maya locals are sold. Updated: Aug 30, 2010.

Things to See and Do

Lívingston is a place to slow down, relax and unwind as the locals do. There isn't a great deal to do here, but it is a fascinating place to experience the mix of Garifuna (Black Crib) and Q'eqchi' Maya culture. You'll have enough to keep you busy if you spend a few days soaking up the chilled-out vibe, visiting a beach and the waterfalls, and throwing in a tour to, for example, the Belize barrier reef or Punta Manabique. There are some bars on the high street, where there is often live music, as well as a couple of clubs, but beware of the locals begging for a beer. Updated: Aug 31, 2010.

Los Siete Altares

Even farther around the coast from Hotel Ecológico Salvador Gaviota, pass Playa Quehueche, five kilometers (3 mi) west of the town center, is the very impressive set

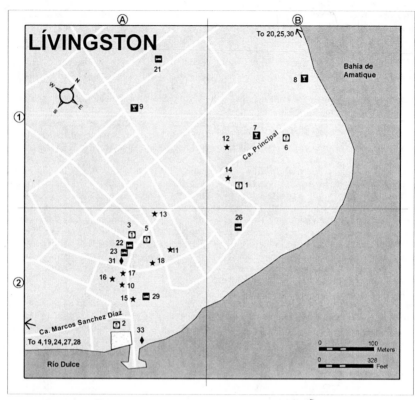

of waterfalls called Los Siete Altares. There are peaceful green pools to relax in, away from the hustle of town, and you can have lunch or a beer at the café where you pay to enter. You can walk here yourself by following the beach around the coast and just before the beach ends take the left path up the hill. If you prefer, you can take an organized group tour with Happy Fish Travel for $10 per person, which includes town sights and a jungle walk. Entrance closes at 5 p.m. Updated: Aug 30, 2010.

Beaches

Despite being on the Caribbean coast, the beaches in Lívingston are not the greatest. They are quite narrow and gray so you will need to take a tour to Playa Blanca, Punta Manabique or the cayes in Belize to find anything like the photos in tourist brochures. However, the Playa Capitania (turn left off the Calle Principal by the OCG Internet café) and Playa Quehueche (by Vecchia Toscana and Hotel Ecológico Salvador Gaviot) rarely get busy so you can always find a little strip of sand to relax on. The water away from town is clean and deep enough for at least a dip. Updated: Aug 30, 2010.

Zapotillo Cayes

If you have a day to spare while in Lívingston, but no time to go to Belize itself, a trip to the Zapotillo Cayes is well-worth the money ($50 plus $10 entry fee). Zapotillo Cayes is part of the Belize barrier reef. Depending on the sea conditions, the journey out to the reef can take between one and two hours. Once there you can relax on the white sand beaches (watch out for the biting sand flies), or you can snorkel in clear, gorgeous turquoise seas around beautiful coral while spotting colorful fish and nursing sharks. Trips typically include transport, lunch and equipment. There are no hotels here, as the islands are protected, but you are allowed to camp. If you want to camp speak to the travel agency for advice and the Belize entry guards for permission. Updated: Aug 30, 2010.

Río Sarstún

Serving as the natural border between Guatemala and Belize, Río Sarstún is a nationally protected area managed by FUNDAECO. FUNDAECO is an environmental NGO. Río Sarstún is home to a number

Eating 🕮

1 Antojitos Los Tres Garifunas B1
2 Buga Mama A2
3 Happy Fish A2
4 Malena's A2
5 McTropic A2
6 Tilingo Lingo B1

Nightlife 🍸

7 Cafetín Brisas del Mar/
   Café Gotay B1
8 Long Beach Disco/
   Disco Playa 8 B1
9 Ubafu A1

Services ★

10 Bakery A2
11 Banrural A2
12 Communal Pila B1
13 High street stores A2
14 Internet OGC B1
15 Laundry A2

16 Municipal/
   Immigration Office A2
17 Pharmacy A2
18 Post Office A2

Sleeping 🛏

19 Casa de la Iguana A2
20 Hotel Flowas B1
21 Hotel Garifuna A1
22 Hotel Río Dulce A2
23 Hotel Ríos Tropicales A2
24 Hotel Rosada A2
25 Hotel Salvador Gaviota B1
26 Hotel Solidario B2
27 Hotel Viajero/Hotel Beresford A2
28 Posada Delfin A2
29 Villa Caribe A2
30 Vecchia Toscana B1

Tours ◆

31 Exotic Travel A2
32 Go with Gus Tours (See 27)
33 Public lancha office A2

of local families, a visitor's center (where guests can stay overnight), and a great place to experience nature at its best. There are hiking trails, mangroves and lagoons to explore as well as bird-watching and sport fishing. Contact the travel agencies on the Calle Principal in Lívingston to organize transport here. Updated: Aug 31, 2010.

Río Dulce Tour

The tour begins in Lívingston at 9:30 a.m. This trip along the river is organized with Exotic Travel Agency. The boat costs $12 per person one-way, and you visit The Canyon, Tatin River, Ak' Tenamit Project, Finca Tatin, The Island of Birds, Flower Lagoon, Little Lagoons and The Castle of San Felipe de Lara. The tour makes two stops, one at Ak' Tenamit Project and the other at the Hot Springs, where you can swim. The tour ends in Fronteras Town, Río Dulce. If you choose to take the round-trip tour then you will return to Lívingston. Ca. del Comercio. Tel: 502-7947-0133, Fax: 502-7947-0049, E-mail: info@bluecaribbeanbay.com, URL: www.bluecaribbeanbay.com. Updated: Dec 14, 2007.

Tours

Exotic Travel Agency Nature and Adventure Tours

The "Ecological Tour" walks you through the town of Lívingston, up to the lookout point and then on to a small Garifuna village. We then go to Rio Quehueche, where you will travel along the river in a canoe for half an hour. From here we take a lazy stroll along the beach, where we rest for a short time before walking through the jungle to the Seven Waterfalls. Ca. del Comercio, inside Bahia Azul Restaurant. Daily 7 a.m.-11 p.m. Tel: 7-947-0151, Fax: 7-947-0136, E-mail: info@bluecaribbeanbay.com, URL: www.caribbeanguatemala.com. Updated: Jan 04, 2008.

Tour Siete Rios

Hotel and tour operator Rios Tropicales offers trips along the seven rivers that flow into the Río Dulce. Travel by kayak and explore the biodiversity and local communities. Tel: 502-7947-0158, Fax: 502-2442-1787, URL: www.mctropic.com. Updated: Oct 13, 2009.

Go with Gus Tours

Go with Gus Tours, run by a local couple, organizes tours in the area which aim to give something back to the local people and environment. The full-day Lívingston-Río Dulce Humanitarian tour, costing $130, takes in a visit to one of the schools in the area, a short city walking tour (optional), a walk into the jungle and a trip to a Maya village. Travel is mainly by water-taxi. There is also a beach tour during which you can spend an hour of the tour helping to clean the beach, and an 'agricultural' tour, which includes horse-back riding and hiking. Hotel Posada El Delfín, Ca. Marcos Sanchéz Dias. Tel: 502-7-947-0694, E-mail: GoWithGusTours@turcios.com, URL: www.gowithgustours.com. Updated: Aug 30, 2010.

Happy Fish Travel

Happy Fish restaurant and travel agency, on the high street, runs daily tours to various nearby locations, such as Playa Blanca ($14), Río Dulce ($17), Belize cayes for snorkeling ($50 minimum six people), Punta Manabique ($120 1-7 people private tour) and to Lívingston for a bike tour ($5). They can also arrange complete tour packages, for example: the 'archeological' tour includes transfer from the airport in Guatemala City to Antigua, transfer to Lívingston, visits to Quiriguá, Copán in Honduras and Tikal, and all hotel accommodations for four nights. Ca. Principal Comercio. Tel: 502-7947-0661/5510-3772, E-mail: info@happyfishtravel.com, URL: www.happyfishtravel.com. Updated: Aug 30, 2010.

Exotic Travel Agency

Located within the Bahía Azul restaurant, Exotic Travel Agency runs tours to the Zapotilla Cayes and Placencia in Belize; to Río Dulce and all the stops along the way ($12); to a Garifuna village fro a jungle walk; and, to the Los Siete Altares waterfalls ($10). Diving courses and water sports are also available. It can also book onward travel tickets to Antigua, Tikal, Flores, Copán in Honduras, Punta Gorda in Belize etc. Tel: 502-7947-0133, E-mail: exotictravelagency@hotmail.com, URL: www.bluecaribbeanbay.com. Updated: Aug 30, 2010.

Lodging

Lívingston has a range of hotels to suit all needs and tastes. However, even the mid-range hotels can be quite basic compared to hotels in Antigua, for example. For super cheap digs try the Hotel Beresford or Hotel El Viajero, they are right on the water front, west of the dock, but are very basic and $3 a bed. There are a couple of nice hotels round the northern coastline but it is worth mentioning that it can be quite difficult to get a taxi into and from the town center, especially at night. For a first rate stay Villa Caribe is the best choice. Check out in Lívingston is usually about 11 a.m. although at some places it is as late as 1 p.m. Reservations are recommended from May through August and during festivals. Updated: Aug 21, 2010.

BUDGET

Hotel Viajero

(ROOMS: $3) A budget choice at the water's edge, this place rolls out over the water and offers you the chance to listen to the waves as you sleep. There are 45 beds in different sized simple tile-floored rooms, each with adjoining bathrooms. The decor could do with freshening up but the place is perfectly clean. On the waterfront. Tel: 502-7884-0249. Updated: Nov 21, 2006.

Hotel Solidario

(ROOMS: $4-5) The Hotel Solidario is more like a communal house. It's quite basic but a good place to stay if you might stick around for a while: there's a nice laid back feel and it's only $4/5 a night with WiFi, a shared lounge and kitchen, great views across the Amatique Bay, and a lovely breeze off the sea. There are no frills however, which means no TV, no bed sheets and no hot water. Ivan, the Chilean who manages the hotel, uses the profits to run a community library for the kids in Lívingston, as well as providing some tourists services, such as a guided tours and bike rentals. Playa Capitania. To get there, turn right off the main street by the OGC Internet café. Updated: Aug 21, 2010.

Hotel Río Dulce

(ROOMS: $5-18) If you like being in the center of the action, the location of the Hotel Río Dulce couldn't be better. Right on the main street and just uphill from the dock, this recently renovated hotel does not have a phone, a TV, Internet or air conditioning but it does have tons of old school Caribbean charm. The bungalows, which are more like wooden chalet-style rooms, have their own bathrooms and cost $18 for 2 people; private rooms are $8; and, dorm beds are $5 both with shared bathrooms. All have fans. Ca. Principal. Updated: Aug 21, 2010.

Casa de la Iguana

(ROOMS: $5-19) La Iguana is a nice place to chill out in a hammock during the day, as it is away from the hectic main street, but it is known for being a big party place at night. It is a very welcoming place and if you're a single traveler it is a great place to meet people. The dorms and rooms, $14-19 per person for doubles, $5 for a dorm, are in well-built wooden cabins with chunky wooden beds, pretty flower details painted on the walls, fans, and colorful sheets. The top floor rooms have more light and some have sea views. There is a lounge area, where the family-style dinners are served, with WiFi and cable TV. There is also a Spanish school and tours can be organized. Plus, there's even a laundromat down the road ($3 per piece). Ca. Marcos Sanchéz Dias. Tel: 502-7947-0064. Updated: Aug 21, 2010.

Hotel Rios Tropicales

(ROOMS: $9-25) This is a nice smart choice for the money, offering clean well-appointed and well-decorated rooms around a pleasant, if a little cluttered, courtyard. Bathrooms are tiled and clean and there is a good communal area in which to relax. It is not on the water, but it is just a two-minute walk uphill from the dock and the owners are helpful as long as you speak some Spanish. From Livingston's Main Pier to the hotel you have to walk 300 meters (1,000 ft) to the gate. The hotel is situated in front of the bank and Municipality on the left side of the main street. Tel: 502-7-947-0158, E-mail: hotel_riostropicales@yahoo.com, URL: www.mctropic.webs.com. Updated: Jun 03, 2010.

Hotel Ecológico Salvador Gaviota

(ROOMS: $10-70) Located on a narrow stretch of beach, the Salvador Gaviota is the perfect place to stay if you're looking for some peace and quiet and a supply of good food and good service. There are four charming thatched bungalows, ($70), as well as rooms with private bathrooms ($18/person) and rooms without private bathrooms ($10/person). All have nice big beds with clean white sheets. There is also WiFi available and a jetty with hammocks out on the water. It is quite a ways out of town on Playa Quehueche, so it is best to get a taxi form the dock when you arrive. All credit cards have a 10 percent fee. You can E-mail the hotel to make a reservation

through the website. Playa Quehueche. Tel: 502-7947-0874, URL: www.hotelsalvadorgaviota.es.tl. Updated: Aug 21, 2010.

MID-RANGE

Hotel Casa Rosada

(ROOMS: $20) The Casa Rosada is an appealing and homey guesthouse run by a welcoming Q'eqchi' and Belgian couple. It's a great location with lovely gardens and a private terrace right on the water. All rooms have shared bathroom facilities but the thatched bungalows ($20) are delightful, very clean and well-kept. The owners also cook and the on-site restaurant is very popular: dinner is served from 7-9 p.m. but you must make your dinner reservation before 6 p.m.; breakfast is also available at $4. There is WiFi and a book and magazine exchange. Ca. Marcos Sanchéz Dias. Tel: 502-7947-0303, E-mail: info@hotelcasarosada.com, URL: www.hotelcasarosada.com. Updated: Aug 21, 2010.

Hotel Doña Alida

(ROOMS: $25-37.50) A no frills hotel located right on the water. Rooms are bright and roomy with private bathrooms (tiled, clean, no hot water) and spectacular views. No communal area or restaurant. It is not on the main strip of town, but just three minutes walking distance from the town's center. Leaving the docks, turn right at the first street and the hotel is a little more than halfway down the street. Ask for rooms 10 or 11 for the best views. Owner speaks English and Spanish. Barrio Capitania. Tel: 502-5667-4898, E-mail: hotelalida@yahoo.es. Updated: Jul 06, 2009.

Vecchia Toscana
"The Italian in Lívingston"

(ROOMS: $60-150) This hotel and restaurant right on the beachfront is run by a family of Italians—just taste the pasta or the coffee and you will know it's authentic. The hotel has comfortable rooms as well as bungalows set in the gardens and a swimming pool. Breakfast is included. Although it is right by the beach, the place feels very private. Barrio Paris, beachfront. Tel: 502-7947-0884, Fax: 502-7947-0884, E-mail: contactanos@vecchiatoscana-Lívingston.com, URL: www.vecchiatoscana-Lívingston.com. Updated: Dec 12, 2008.

Hotel Posada El Delfín

(ROOMS: $65-120) There's a hint of faded grandeur about El Delfín but it is still one of the better hotels to stay at in Lívingston and does get booked up by tour groups. There is a restaurant and bakery on site, yoga classes, and a tour agency that organizes excursions out to Playa Blanca and Río Dulce as well as scuba and fishing trips. There are 24 rooms, some with bath tubs and mini-fridges, and one honeymoon suite. All have private bathrooms, telephones and ceiling fans. Ca. Marcos Sanchéz Dias. Tel: 502-7-947-0694, E-mail: eldelfin@turcios.com, URL: www.posadaeldelfin.com. Updated: Aug 21, 2010.

HIGH-END

Hotel Villa Caribe
(ROOMS: $130-180) With a prime location on the point looking out over the Bahia Amatique, Villa Caribe is a lovely hotel and probably the best in town. There is a great pool right next to the sea and an attractive restaurant serving international cuisine—the breakfast buffet is very good. The best rooms are the seven cabins which have great furnishings, private balconies, air conditioning and cable TV at $180. The 40 standard rooms and two junior suites also have balconies and views, fans and cable TVs, for $130-150. There is also WiFi, a computer available for use and a laundry service. The one non-positive thing that can be said about this hotel is that, occasionally, the service is disappointing. Ca. Principal. Tel: 502-7947-0072, E-mail: info@villasdeguatemala.com, URL: www.villasdeguatemala.com. Updated: Aug 21, 2010.

Restaurants
If there's one thing you won't do in Lívingston it is go hungry. Indeed, there are at least five restaurants within two small blocks along the main street, known simply as Calle Principal, all good places to try the local specialty tapado, a stew made with coconut milk, plantains, fish, and other ingredients. Many restaurants on high street serve similar dishes at a similar price, so it doesn't hurt to share the wealth and try a different one every night. The more expensive hotels also have nice restaurants and it's worth taking a trip out to Playa Quehueche for the authentic Italian at Vecchia Toscana. For good coffee try the little bar in Hotel Rios Tropicales. Updated: Aug 15, 2010.

TRADITIONAL GUATEMALAN

Bahía Azul
(ENTREES: $1.75-5) This is uphill from the waterfront so do not come here if you are looking for a view but do go there if you want some good value food with a tasty twist. Breakfasts

are good and varied while main dishes offer everything from pasta to a special aromatic spiced fish traditional to the local Q'eqchi' culture. Atmosphere is relaxed with smart wood tables and burning incense, and there is also a travel agency on site. Av. de Commercio (main road). Tel: 502-7947-0133, E-mail: chewian@hotmail.com. Updated: Nov 21, 2006.

Bocas del Río
(ENTREES: $5-9) A simple eatery offering simple food done well. The owner knows how to cook so if you are looking for a no-frills piece of perfectly grilled fish or some succulent shrimp with rice, bread and salad at low prices then this is the place to come. Beers are cheap too. So head here to watch the sun go down from the circular restaurant area. Bocas del Río is located on the waterfront left out of the main dock, adjoined to Hotel Viajero Tel: 502-7884-0149. Updated: Nov 21, 2006.

Antojitos Los Tres Garifunas
Follow the main street down toward the beach and this cheap and cheerful but oh-so-authentic eatery is just on your right before the crest of the hill, next to the Internet café where all the locals hang out. It barely sees a tourist so it's a top spot to sample Garifuna food made by Garifuna for Garifuna. There is the classic rice and beans, sopa de mariscos, frita de banana verde and tapado, among other dishes. A good thing to try here is the Guifiti local drink. Barrio La Capitania. Tel: 502-5682-4925. Updated: Aug 15, 2010.

Malena's
Malena's is, or at least was, one of the more upscale restaurants in Lívingston; nowadays its décor looks a little dated. Upstairs at the Hotel Posada El Delfín is a charming wooden jetty overlooking the Río Dulce. The menu includes all the usual local and international dishes served elsewhere in town; but, come for the views, the tropical mood and the romantic Caribbean ambiance. The owners also have the Sandwich Shoppe down the road, which is a classy diner only open in the evenings. Ca. Marcos Sanchéz Dias (Posada Delfin). Tel: 502-7-947-0694, URL: www.posadaeldelfin.com. Updated: Aug 15, 2010.

INTERNATIONAL

Restaurante McTropic
(ENTREES: $3-11.25) On the other side of the road, across from Happy Fish, McTropic specializes only in good food. You can get a coco

loco fresh coconut cocktail for only $2 and all the traveler dishes you could shake a fork at: yogurt, granola and fruit, Thai green curry, guacamole and nachos, rice and beans, chai tea and espresso as well as local fish dishes. The restaurant is housed in a rustic but charming Caribbean-style building, which is cool enough to sit in if the few tables on the terrace are taken. Daily 7 a.m.-10 p.m. Ca. Principal. URL: http:// mctropic.webs.com. Updated: Aug 15, 2010.

Happy Fish

(ENTREES: $9) In a cool and shady wooden building, Happy Fish serves not only your travel needs but also has an extensive menu. Try a fruit smoothies (although not the best in town) or iced coffee while you wait for your tour. Also on the menu are pancakes, fresh ham and egg salad or ceviche and *conch a la plancha* ($9). The staff is very helpful and don't seem to mind if you only buy a beer while you use their free WiFi. All credit cards as well as US Dollars, Quetzals and Belize Dollars are accepted. Daily 7 a.m.-10 p.m. Ca. Principal. Tel: 502-7947-0661. E-mail: info@ happyfishtravel.com, URL: www.happy-fishtravel.com. Updated: Aug 15, 2010.

Tilingo Lingo

Painted in cozy shades and resembling a cute cottage with tables at the windows looking out toward the beach, the warm glow emitted from this quirky and welcoming restaurant won't fail to draw you in, either for a pre-dance cocktail or to sample the tasty international fare. The Mexican owner has spent time living in India and even has her own cook book on sale. Options include Israeli breakfasts, French toast, Vietnamese spring rolls, Thai curry and Mexican quesadillas. Daily 7 a.m.-10:30 p.m. Ca. Principal, Playa Barique. Updated: Aug 11, 2010.

Nightlife

Nightlife is everywhere in Lívingston. In the balmy heat people hang out on the streets, drinking, talking, joking round and jamming to impromptu drumming sessions. The high street can get very hectic with people promenading up and down or sitting to people-watch in front of the many cafés. The cafés on Calle Principal all serve beer and spirits and often have live music. If you want to escape the sometimes over-powering buzz of the center head to the bars at the Villa Caribe, Toscana or Posada Delfín for a more relaxed evening. Updated: Aug 15, 2010.

Long Beach Disco and Disco Playa 8

The scruffy stretch of beach at the end of 'Main Street' is nothing to bother about during the day; but, come night-time this is the place to get your groove on. There are a couple of discos here, nothing much more that shacks with a dance floor, but there is a bar serving cans and spirits and usually plenty of people dancing to the very very loud tunes. Some of the music is pretty hardcore but if you don't fancy joining in you can sit back under the palm trees and watch. Be careful, however, as the lighting is extremely poor so you should watch your possessions and perhaps keep away from the water's edge. Updated: Aug 15, 2010.

Ubafu

Although this could be the coolest place to hang out in late-night Lívingston, it can be a bit hit or miss, especially when it's the low season, so make sure you try it more than once. And don't arrive too early. When there's a crowd and the live music is rocking it has a great atmosphere. It is a labor of love for the local musicians who entertain the throngs of people, serve the drinks, stock the bar and close up once the night is over. Ubafu is near Restaurtante Margoth on the main street heading west from Calle Principal. Updated: Aug 15, 2010.

Casa de La Iguana

You may not find much local spirit here but if you fancy a night socializing with fellow travelers, there is fun to be had at La Iguana. Most nights there are some games in store, including the drinking variety as well as big screen sports. The owner, Rusty, is very welcoming, plus the guests as well as the people who work here are a fun crowd so the bar stays open as long as you stay up. Movies are also shown here and there is sometimes live music. Ca. Marcos Sanchéz Dias. Tel: 502-7947-0064. Updated: Aug 15, 2010.

Cafétín Brisas del Mar

Las Brisas is a little out of the way, down the un-lit road leading to the beach, but with *coco locos* for only $0.62, beers and *tortilla de harina* snacks and if you're heading for the beach clubs anyway, this place is a good spot for a pit-stop before hitting the dance floor. Stop in for a late-night drink if you need a breather from the loud tunes. Café Gotay, next door, also stays opens late for drinks and serves full meals as well. Ca. Principal, Playa Barique. Updated: Aug 15, 2010.

ATLANTIC COAST

AROUND LÍVINGSTON
AK' TENAMIT

Set up in 1992, this non-profit organization provides basic health care, vocational training and community solutions for the indigenous Q'eqchi' Maya in and around the rain forest in eastern Guatemala. It is exceptional because this democratically-elected board is entirely indigenous. The charity works to improve equality for Maya women and girls and to promote cultural pride and youth empowerment. Many of the students educated by Ak' Tenamit gain valuable hospitality and tourism work experience at its site and in the restaurants in Lívingston. On the Río Dulce/Lívingston trip many of the public lanchas make the detour to the site and it is worth taking a look round, especially its souvenir shop for some great handmade crafts. You can also donate online or arrange to sponsor a student. Tel: 502-2254-1560, URL: www.aktenamit.org. Updated: Jul 20, 2010.

FINCA TATÍN

Hidden in the jungle and reachable only by boat, this place is for those who want to experience the natural wonder of the steamy Guatemalan Caribbean rather than being in-town. Birdwatching is a usual pastime, visits can be arranged to indigenous villages, as well as trips to hot springs and kayaking or hiking in the national park. Accommodation is in dorms ($5.50) and bungalows ($8 for shared bath, $15.50 private, $20-42 riverfront). Tel: 502-5902-0831, E-mail: fincatatin@yahoo.com, URL: www.fincatatin.centroamerica.com. Updated: Jul 06, 2010.

Rancho Corozal

(ROOMS: $82-250) The Rancho Corozal, run by the same people who own Quinta Maconda Inn in Antigua, is not a guest house but a lush two-acre villa set within 8 hectares (20 ac) of privately-owned rainforest just a 20-minute boat ride from Lívingston. The house sleeps 10 in 5 double beds under thatched roofs with nets. There is a hammock and living room, kitchen, private bathrooms, which use rain water collected from tree run-off (so, there is no hot water or electricity), and a wooden deck that looks out onto the Río Tatín. Prices include two staff members (the caretaker/personal tour guide and the cook) and breakfast. Extra meals can be arranged. The cost is more per person the fewer people there are, ranging from $250 per night for one or two people to $82 per night per person for nine

to 10 people. Tel: USA 866-621-4032, E-mail: info@quintamaconda.com, URL: www.quintamaconda.com. Updated: Jul 11, 2010.

RÍO LÁMPARA

Around seven kilometers (4.35 mi) upstream from Lívingston, in the shadow of Cerro San Gill (1,267 m/4,157 ft), is the Río Lámpara, a southern tributary of the Río Dulce. The lush green scenery and the slow pace of life around the water makes for either a relaxing boat ride as you continue on your journey or a great place to escape, especially if you have just come from buzzing Lívingston. There are a small number of jungle retreats around here (see also Finca Tatín, on the nearby Río Tatín, a northern tributary of the Río Dulce) which provide access to the nature reserves as well as an opportunity to slow down. Updated: Aug 01, 2010.

Getting To and Away

Río Lámpara is upstream from Lívingston, and like its neighbor, only accessible by boat. To get there you will have to hire a boat heading from Río Dulce and Lívingston, or the other way around. No matter the direction, the boat should have no problem dropping you off in Río Lámpara. The jungle lodge El Hotelito Perdido (www.hotelitoperdido.com) in Río Lámpara also offers pick up service from the Livinston municipal dock, usually for around $4. Updated: Aug 25, 2010.

Things to See and Do

El Golfete

Upriver from Lívingston there is a place where very hot sulfurous water flows into the Río Dulce. The public boats going between Río Dulce and Lívingston normally stop here for 10 minutes or so; you can dip your toes in the water where a jetty and café have been built. After passing through the narrow gorge the river opens into El Golfete, a large lake with various points of interest on its shores. On the north side is the Biotopo Chocópn Machacas, a reserve conceived to protect the manatee as well as the wetlands the "sea cow" calls home. Located on the southern bank is the Casa Guatemala charity orphanage (www.casa-guatemala.org) which is linked to Hotel Backpackers in Río Dulce. Updated: Aug 01, 2010.

Lodging

Hotel Perdido

(ROOMS: $5-33) Similar to Finca Tatín, this rustic yet romantic and quiet affordable jungle hideaway, is very near the Manatee reserve making it a great location for moonlit canoeing trips in to the nature park. The communal lounge is relaxed and friendly and where wholesome vegetarian food, including homemade bread, is served. Meals cost $3-9. Dorms ($5.60) and bungalows ($25-35) are available, all powered by solar energy and supplied by collected rain water, in attractive thatched-roofed houses. Activities include kayaking, birdwatching and jungle walks to the waterfalls. Tel: 502-5725-1576, E-mail: contact@hotelitoperdido.com, URL: www.hotelitoperdido.com. Updated: Aug 01, 2010.

RÍO DULCE

Río Dulce refers to the river itself, but also collectively to the twin towns of Fronteras and El Relleno, located on either side of the bridge that crosses the river as it joins Lake Izabal. Both towns have acceptable places to stay and eat, and make for a good base from which to visit the river, lake, Castillo San Felipe and more. Updated: Nov 21, 2006.

When to Go

Río Dulce is hot most of the year but the occasional rain, usually in the afternoon or overnight, helps to freshen things up. You can also escape the heat staying at the hotels on the waterfront. Dry season is November through April and the wet season, from May through October, helps to keep the green vegetation very lush. Hurricanes generally occur between June and November and Río Dulce presents a safe place to escape the storms in the Caribbean. Updated: Aug 30, 2010.

Getting To and Away

There are two bus companies at the Fronteras end of the bridge, Fuentes del Norte on the left and Litegua Pullmans on the right. Buses go to Guatemala City (5-6 hr, every 30 minutes), Puerto Barrios (2 hr, every hour), Poptún in Petén (1.75 hr, every 30 min), and Flores (3.5 hr, every 30 min).

Minibuses also go to El Estor, passing Finca El Paraiso, every hour. You can also get a bus tour to Semuc Champey and Quiriguá ($22), ask at Sundog for info. Public boats leave from the boat station and go to Lívingston ($15.50 one way, $25 round trip). To get to the dock, take the road underneath the bridge down toward the water, passed Bruno's on the right. The trip takes about two hours, passing by the Castillo de San Felipe, hot-springs with a café and toilets, and sometimes a stop

at Ak' Tenamit. Boats leave at 9:30 a.m. and 1:30 p.m. You can also hire private boats and a good place to ask about a private boat is at Bruno's. Updated: Aug 30, 2010.

Getting Around

To get to the hotels around the shore you can take a water-taxi. There are plenty of guys touting for business around the main street or the lancha station but they will usually find you first. Alternatively, if have booked ahead, the hotel may also arrange a boat to pick you up. Taxis station themselves around the end of the bridge near the Litegua office, if you need a ride back over the bridge. The bridge is one kilometer (0.6 miles) long and takes about 15 minutes to walk. Updated: Aug 30, 2010.

Safety

Río Dulce is a busy town and the through-road over the bridge to the north is always chocked with traffic. It is wise to be careful around here, as the trucks steam through, especially at night. There is quite a contrast between the poor working town and the fancy hotels, and the expensive boats in the marina owned by expats or rich city *Guatemaltecos*,. You should be careful not to flash expensive belongings when you're in the main drag. Updated: Aug 30, 2010.

Services

There are a couple of banks with ATMs on the main street in Fronteras, a Banrural and a Banco Industrial. On the same street is the Despensar Familiar supermarket, Monday-Saturday 8 a.m.-8 p.m., closing one hour earlier on a Sunday. There is an Internet café in Bruno's complex, along with a mini market, a swimming pool ($3 for the day) and laundry service ($5 per load). There is also an Internet café next to Río Bravo restaurant. There is a pharmacy where the staff speaks English on the El Relleno side of the bridge, near the Hotel Backpackers. If you need a payphone, there are some on the road by the Litega station. Public bathrooms are by Sundog and by Bruno's under the bridge, both cost $0.25. Updated: Aug 30, 2010.

Things to See and Do

The best thing to do in Río Dulce is make use of the surrounding nature. The jungle around Río Dulce is great for jungle walks and birdwatching. You can also get on the water and hire kayaks from some of the hotels. You can rent jet skis and banana boats from Restaurante Bendición de Dios, by the lancha station.

If you fancy a drink and some entertainment, the Los Pinchos bar on the high street has pool tables and many of the bars have particular happy hours which are a good time to meet other travelers and sailors. The Sundog Café is one of these bars and is also a good place to pick up info on renting bicycles, arranging tours and other local events that may be going on.

Outside of Río Dulce, the Castillo de San Felipe is only 20 minutes from Río Dulce. You could go to Finca El Paraiso and its hot-spring waterfall (*Catarata de Aguas Calientes*) in a day-trip. Ask at your hotel for transport info or look for a microbus on the high street. A taxi to Finca El Paraiso would take about an hour and cost $37. On the shores of Lake Izabal is the Denny's Beach resort, where you can have lunch and a cocktail, swim in the clear lake water, go kayaking or hire jet skis. If you'd like to take a day trip here from Río Dulce ask at your hotel or at Bruno's. Livingston, although a destination in its own right, can also be done in a day. The boat trip goes through the pretty El Golfete, passing the impressive canyon, and stopping at Ak' Tenamit and the hot-water pools. The Hacienda Tijax has a great area for jungle trips and nature hikes. Through the rubber plantation you can follow nature trails and go birdwatching, learn about medicinal trees, go horseback riding, and take monkey and sunset walks.

Kayaking is a fantastic way to explore the Río Dulce and Lake Izabal. It is very peaceful and a great place to spot around 300 species of birds. Nutria Lodge rents out kayaks and boats to explore the river, as does the Hacienda Tijax. Some hotels also run sport-fishing trips on Lake Izabal, where you can catch *robalo*, tilapia and mojarra. Updated: Aug 30, 2010.

Sailing to Belize or Honduras from Río Dulce

Sailing passage to Honduras or Belize, from Río Dulce is $50 per person, per day. This is not easy to do but with a bit of persistence it is possible to secure a place on a yacht bound for either Belize or Honduras' Bay Islands from one of the many marinas in Río Dulce. Most yachties in this area head here for a while before going out to sea, and the best way to catch one is by getting on the boat-wide radio at 7:30 a.m. and making an announcement. Bruno's, as well as other hostels with a radio, will be able to assist. Updated: Nov 21, 2006.

Catarata de Aguas Calientes
(ADMISSION $21.25) This is a unique spot in the jungle where a naturally hot waterfall plunges into a cool swimming hole. With water running at 40°C (104°F) the hot and cold merges in stages to offer you the perfect temperature somewhere in the pool or head behind the waterfall for a steamy experience. In Finca el Paraiso, take bus (45 min) along the north side of the lake, ask to be dropped off there. Updated: Oct 13, 2009.

Boat Trip from Río Dulce to Livingston
This is a great trip that heads from the yachtie heaven of Río Dulce and into El Golfete, past banks full of impressive houses and small flat islands of untouched bird-filled jungle. The most impressive part of the journey, however, is the run through a tall gorge, where the grey rock walls are covered in dense jungle foliage so impressive the site was used to film the original Tarzan movie. The trip ends in the little port town of Livingston (or can be taken the opposite way). Daily boats run 9:30 a.m. and 1:30 p.m. from both ends, but it is possible to catch other launches depending on people traffic, they go when they are full. About $10 one-way. Updated: Nov 21, 2006.

Tours
Otitours, under the bridge opposite going down to the public dock, can arrange local transport and shuttle-buses to Antigua, Guatemala City, Cobán, Copán, Belize, Tikal, as well as day tours to Quiriguá, Finca El Paraíso and jungle tours (Tel: 502-7930-5223). Asociación de Lancheros El Colmaron, the public lancha company, as well as running the collectives up and down the river to Livingston, organize tours and private charters (Tel: 502-7930-5853/5561-9657). Hotel-Marina Vista Río can arrange charters and tours on covered launches and catamarans, Tel: 502-7930-5665, E-mail: info@hotelvistario.com. Updated: Aug 30, 2010.

Lodging
In Río Dulce (an area containing two towns, Fronteras and El Relleno), you can expect hot weather and stunning natural beauty. The towns are located at the mouth of Guatemala's largest lake, Lago de Izabal, which drains along the stunning Río Dulce into the Caribbean Sea. The towns themselves aren't much to see, the real places to go are outside of town and by the water. Río Dulce hotels range from the threadbare, orphanage-run Hotel Backpacker's for about $4 a night, to much nicer options such as Hotel Banana Palms, in nearby San Felipe,

which offers lakefront suites for a little over $100. If you're looking for something in the middle, consider the ecoactivity-rich Hacienda Tijax ($30-50), which offers swinging bridges over mangrove swamps and cheap campgrounds (it's next to a swamp, so take the word "cheap" with a grain of salt). Updated: Jun 29, 2010.

BUDGET

Casa Perico

(ROOMS: $5-13) Hidden among the hanging vines and lush vegetation, Casa Perico is quite a discovery. Accessible only boat, 10 minutes from the dusty town of Río Dulce, Casa Perico is a remote jungle retreat for the weary traveler. Accommodations include dorms, private rooms and even personal cabañas with private washrooms. All rooms come equipped with a much-appreciated mosquito net and are authentically rustic, yet clean. Constructed on stilts, everything hovers above marshy ground, with each separate building connected by a wooden walkway. The main thatched bungalow not only acts as the reception area, but also the restaurant and bar. Along with refreshing beverages, the restaurant offers entertainment in the form of cards, board games and a book exchange. While individual meals are available, the nightly buffet is an excellent value and boasts a wide variety of both local and international cuisine. Everything operates on a trust system with the final bill presented upon checkout. Optional day tours to the town of Lívingston or hot waterfalls of Finca Paraiso can be easily arranged, while personal exploration of Lago de Izabal is made possible through the use of the free kayaks. Tel: 502-7930-5666, URL: www.casa-perico.de.vu. Updated: Mar 18, 2009.

Hotel Backpackers

(ROOMS: $5-48) On the western bank of the river, the quieter El Relleno barrio, Casa Backpackers is a nice place to relax by the river side, and although it has seen better days, it is a lot cheaper and more social than the more up-market river-side hotels. As it says on the tin it is more of a backpackers place with a terrace and bar for socializing, free Internet and book exchange, laundry service, kayak rentals ($2/hr), large dorm rooms for singles or groups of travelers, and opportunities to volunteer at the Casa Guatemala charity, where all profits from the guest house go (URL: www.casa-guatemala.org). Breakfast is also included. There is a range of rooms, such as: beds in dorms only $5 without private bath, $6 with; one single bed with/without bath $10; two single beds and one queen with private bathroom $36. Only the

private rooms come with bed sheets and towels. *Note: 12 percent fee for credit card transactions.* Once in Río Dulce call and they will pick you up. Tel: 502-7930-5480, E-mail: administracion@hotelbackpackers.com, URL: www.hotelbackpackers.com. Updated: Jul 25, 2010.

Hotel y Restaurante Escondido

(ROOMS: $11-15) Apart from being hidden away from the busy main road, the reason to stay at Hotel Escondido is the large pool, great for a dip to cool off just as you've had enough of sweating in the mid-afternoon heat. The restaurant on-site is also a plus. Rooms are basic but clean, have private bathrooms, TVs and hot water, although you won't need it. Better to opt for the second-floor rooms as they're brighter, are away from the parking-lot so are more private and get what little breeze there might be. Rates are $11 per person for a room with a fan, $15 for air conditioning. Dollars are accepted and credit cards carry a 6 percent fee. Barrio La Escuela, Fronteras Tel: 502-7930-5454/5254. Updated: Jul 25, 2010.

Tortugal Marina and Hotel

(ROOMS: $13-80) Tortugal is definitely one of the best places to stay in town, whether mooring your boat or staying in one of the cozy cabins. The all-wooden buildings blend into the surrounding jungle and you can while away hours with a book from the library and a glass of wine, watching satellite TV, playing pool or browsing on WiFi. For singles there are beds in one of the larger houses from $13, or you can hire entire bungalows, some with their own terraces, BBQs and spas. The 'Casita Elegante', designed with romance in mind, is $53 per night and 'La Finca,' which has its own lounge, kitchen and Jacuzzi, has a minimum three-night stay charge at $210, or $700 for the month. Marina rates are from $250 per month. All-inclusive rates are available too. Tel: 502-5306-6432, E-mail: holatortugal@gmail.com, URL: www.tortugal.com. Call for a pick-up or catch a boat from the municipal dock in town. For sailors, contact on VHF 68. Updated: Jul 25, 2010.

Bruno's Hotel and Marina

This pleasant place is more a marina than a backpacker's hotel but it is a great spot to get fantastic facilities at a budget price. A cheap spot in a six-bed dorm gets you access to the large riverside pool and sun loungers, good hot showers and a great bar and restaurant. Owners Steve and Maria are ultra-friendly and also run a travel business so have plenty of tips for the area. Tel: 502-5692-7292, URL: www.mayaparadise.com. Updated: Nov 21, 2006.

MID-RANGE

Hacienda Tijax

(ROOMS: $19-73) This jungle eco-lodge, reachable by boat from Río Dulce or via a fairly well-hidden back road, prides itself on sustainable tourism, with plenty of activities arranged so you may learn about and benefit from the local environment: monkey and sunset walks; birdwatching; kayaking; horseback riding, and there are no TVs, even in the luxury cabins (although they do have air conditioning). There is a small pool surrounded by lush jungle vegetation and a nice bar with views out across the river. The cabins, all well-finished, are available in various combinations: prices for singles are $19 (shared bathroom), $39 (private bath), $67 (air conditioning).There are also bungalows for up to seven people with a private kitchen, living room and hammocks. Tel: 502-7930-5055, E-mail: info@tijax.com, URL: www.tijax.com. Updated: Jul 20, 2010.

Hotel Viñas del Lago

(Rooms: $27-76) About four kilometers (2.5 mi) from Río Dulce, next to Castillo de San Felipe, the Hotel Viñas del Lago is definitely more of a family-oriented holiday resort than a backpacker's hostel: there are 18 rooms all with private bathrooms and hot water, air conditioning, cable TV; for the kids there are two pools and a private zoo. There is even a private jetty out on Lake Izabal, nice gardens for a stroll, plus laundry service, Internet, and parking. Rooms cost from $27 for one person to $75 for five people. San Felipe de Lara. Tel: 502-7930-5053, E-mail: hotelvinasdlago@intelnet.net.gt, URL: www.vinasdelago.com. Updated: Jul 11, 2010.

Restaurants

There is a wide range of eating options in Río Dulce, including street stalls, comedores, and mid-range restaurants where vacationing Guatemalans eat. And then there are the bars the expats frequent for international snacks and beers and their daily happy hours: Bruno's 4-6 p.m.; Hotel Backpackers 3-5 p.m., and Hotel, Restaurante y Marina Vista al Río (both under the bridge on the Relleno/south side) 4-6 p.m. The hotels reached by boat, such as Tijax and Casa Perico, have in-house restaurants too. And, as usual, there is a good fruit and vegetable market off the high street. Updated: Jun 27, 2010.

Sundog Café

(ENTREES: $4-5) The unassuming and very welcoming Sundog Café and Bar, found down a lane on the right just after coming off the big bridge – with the brightly painted Beetle stationed out front, is something of an expat magnet day and night. It's great for a cold beer in the shade, fresh coffee and fantastic sandwiches, all made by Tom, the Swiss owner, barman and chef. There is also plenty of conversation in English, great for gathering travel info, and a free book exchange. Turn right just after coming off the bridge in Fronteras. Tel: 502-5760-7844, E-mail: tom1@gmx.ch. Updated: Jul 06, 2010.

Bruno's Hotel and Marina

(ENTREES: $5) Bruno's hotel and restaurant is also the main marina in town, being right on the waterfront, and is therefore very popular with the sailing crowd. Looking out across the Golfete, it has a pleasant breeze off the water and has a great view of the docked sailing ships. It serves international dishes ($5), bottles of beers and shows US sports games. The Sunday BBQ is worth trying and there are daily specials on the board. It also has a small souvenir store and an Internet café. Access it through the parking lot under the bridge or via a footpath 50 meters (55 yards) to the left down the side of the bridge. Tel: 502-7930-5175. URL: www.mayaparadise.com. Updated: Jun 27, 2010.

Hotel y Restaurante Escondido

(ENTREES: $10-15) Just a five-minute walk from the main road, the Escondido has a large, comfortable, family-orientated restaurant by the pool, which is open for breakfast, lunch and dinner. It has an extensive and varied menu: ceviche, meat and seafood dishes are around $6.20-9.30; tapado soup $12.40 and vegetable soup $2.50; burgers and tacos $2.35-3.50; and desserts such as pie de queso are $1.85. Beers and soft drinks are available. Dollars and credit cards (6 percent fee) are accepted. Barrio La Escuela. Tel: 502-7930-5454/5254. Updated: Jul 06, 2010.

Restaurante Jocelyn

Around the corner from the public lancha station (look for the signs), Restaurante Jocelyn, not to be confused with Cafétería Jocelyn or Comedor Jocelyn on the high street, is a peaceful place by the water to have a seafood meal and take in the view of the spectacular bridge. Breakfast is particularly good and you can watch the local women doing their early morning laundry in the river. It has a large and airy terrace, good for groups as well as families (they have highchairs), and is not typically frequented by the boating crowd. Daily 7 a.m.-11 p.m. Tel: 502-7930-5740. Updated: Jul 06, 2010.

Río Bravo

Next to Sundog, a little farther down the same lane, the Río Bravo serves pizza as well as other Italian pasta favorites and, even better, you can use their WiFi while you eat. It's better to eat here during the day when the big shady terrace on the water is quiet pleasant. Unfortunately the harsh bright lighting used in the evening attracts mosquitos. The good news is they also have delivery and accept dollars. Groups and families are welcome. Daily 7 a.m.-10 p.m. Tel: 502-7930-5167. Updated: Jul 06, 2010.

AROUND RÍO DULCE

PARQUE NACIONAL RÍO DULCE

Río Dulce National Park is a protected wildlife sanctuary spread over 13,000 hectares (32,123 ac) stretching from Lake Izabal to the Caribbean Sea. The park is one of the oldest in the country and is home to dozens of species of birds, manatees, and the acutus crocodile. The Río Dulce cuts through the jungle for 30 kilometers (18.6 mi) before making its way to the sea. Along the length of the river are spectacular views of the dense tropical rainforest as well as hundred meter tall sheer vertical cliffs of La Cueva de la Vaca.

Activities in the park cover a sufficiently broad spectrum as to appeal to everyone. Diving, boating, jet skiing, ecotourism and birdwatching attract visitors year round. Hiking trips, kayaking and bungee jumping from the narrows bridge are all available as well as scuba lessons. One of the more popular (and expensive) activities are sailing cruises to the Belize Cayes. These cruises last from four days to one week and include scuba and snorkeling, sailing lessons and delicious home-cooked meals of fresh seafood.

A popular vacation destination for Guatemalans and foreigners alike, the park has been struggling in recent years to cope with the environmental impact of a large number of tourists. Illegal hunting, logging and construction have been a nagging problem for the park authorities. Higher levels of water pollution can be traced to visiting yachts dumping waste tanks into the river and nearby Caribbean seas.

The park is not all play however. In recent years many non-profits have set up facilities in the area, including Casa Guatemala, an orphanage with an attached school and farm. The orphanage is located on a 17-hectare (42 ac) site and accepts volunteers to perform a variety of tasks including cooking, teaching and special projects such as construction and expansion projects. Volunteers are expected to pay for their room and board and to be able to commit at least three weeks of their time. For more information visit the Hotel Backpackers on the El Relleno side of the narrows bridge in the town of Río Dulce or visit their website at www.casa-guatemala.org.

Most of the accommodations and restaurants in the park can be found on the north side of the narrows bridge near Lake Izabal. There are ecolodges and haciendas scattered the length of the river but most of the services such as travel agency offices, banks and post office will be found on the El Relleno (south side) of the bridge. The Turicentro travel center is home to several bus and tour companies that arrange transport to and from Río Dulce as well excursions into the surrounding areas.

When to Go

Being a tropical region, things will always be hot, wet and sticky on the Río Dulce but owing to a shift in the trade winds, April, May and June tend to be the worst. The air stands still and refreshing offshore breezes that normally provide relief from the heat and humidity are few and far between. Updated: Aug 25, 2010.

Getting To and Away

Unlike most cities and towns in Guatemala there are multiple options for getting to and away from Río Dulce. Serviced by multiple bus routes, waterways and an airport, most visitors will probably end up making their way to Río Dulce via bus.

BY PLANE

The Río Dulce airport is located about 10 km (6.2 mi) outside of town and offers flights to Guatemala City on Fridays and Sundays. Tickets can be booked through Inter which has offices in the Hotel Ensenada on the south side of the river.

BY BUS

Although less comfortable and more time-consuming than air travel, most visitors come and go to Río Dulce by bus. Buses to Guatemala City depart from Fronteras, on the north side of the bridge, several times daily, seven days a week.

Fuentes del Norte in the Turicentro Las Brisas on the south side of the bridge handles service to Poptún and Flores. The 8:30 bus also continues on to the Belizean border. Schedules and prices change often so visit their website to get the latest and most accurate information (URL: www.autobusesfuentedelnorte.com).

Buses are available to the nearby town of El Estor from Fronteras on the north side of the bridge. However there is no set schedule and you are probably better off taking a cheap pick-up truck than sitting around waiting for a bus.

Atitrans also offers an express shuttle from Río Dulce to Guatemala City and Antigua. They are also located in the Turicentro Las Brisas.

BY BOAT

The Cooperativa de Lancheros handles transport on the river and can get you between Lívingston and Río Dulce in around an hour. Boats are nominally scheduled for a 9 a.m. departure but it is not unheard of to delay the launching until the boat is full, and sometimes the entire trip can be canceled if there are not at least ten passengers.

LAKE IZABAL

The majestic and seemingly limitless Lake Izabal is definitely not on most people's itineraries; the majority of tourists only make it as far as the better known Lake Atitlán near Antigua. This is the largest lake in Central America. It is located around 275 kilometers (170 mi) from Guatemala City (5-6 hr by bus).

With no scheduled flights coming out here, if you make the effort you will be rewarded with a more serene Guatemala than you find in most parts, where life has been affected less by expat businesses and where locals see so few tourists that they are curious about your customs.

The northern road around the lake, past El Castillo de San Felipe, leads to El Estor and the only access to the Reserva Boca del Polochic on the west is now more or less paved all the way, providing an alternative and interesting route to the Verapaces, passing the Finca el Paraíso and the hot springs. Around the southern side of the lake is the sleepy town of Mariscos which allows access, at present, to the only development on that shore at Denny's Beach resort.

When to Go

Having a similar environment and climate to Río Dulce, April, May and June tend to be the worst times to visit Lake Izabal.

Getting To and Away

For information on travel to Lake Izabal, please refer to the Getting To and Away section for Río

Dulce National Park (p. 264) as the information for travel to Lake Izabal is the same.

EL CASTILLO DE SAN FELIPE

Jutting out at the upper reaches of the Río Dulce is the historical and strangely diminutive El Castillo de San Felipe. The first defensive tower was built here in 1595 at the entrance to Lake Izabal to protect this strategic location and the only route into the interior of the country on this Caribbean coast. The Spanish King Philip II ordered its construction to protect the provisions stored in villages around the lake. Brazen pirates, many of whom were British like Anthony Shirley and William Parker, would sail up the Río Dulce, through El Golfete and into the lake to raid the bodegas. The fortifications here have been destroyed and rebuilt at least four times over the past five centuries and the castle has been used as a prison (the harsh climate making imprisonment even more tortuous), for defense and now as a tourist attraction.

In 1955, the site was excavated and the castle reconstructed one final time, all the while preserving the different sections built across the eras. It is possible to make out the original tower 'Torre de Bustamante' built in 1604 and the newer sentry towers added nearly a century and a half later in 1736. It is a pleasant place to spend a few hours wandering round the castle, imagining the cannons firing across the mouth of the lake attacking great pirate ships, or relaxing with a picnic in the shade of palm trees. There is also a bathing area marked out in the lake. The site is open every day 8 a.m.–5 p.m., and the $2.50 entry includes a guided tour and info sheet. There are souvenir shops, restrooms and a café inside the complex as well as two comedores at the entrance gate.

Getting To and Away

The road from Río Dulce around the north side of the lake turns left to the castle, where the road ends, and goes right to El Estor. To get to the castle take a minibus, taxi or tuk-tuk from Río Dulce. The journey takes about 20 minutes. Buses leave the castle to go back every 30 minutes or when the bus is full. You can also take a boat from the lancha port in Río Dulce and sail up to the castle for a different view from the river. Updated: Aug 25, 2010.

EL ESTOR

Sitting on the picturesque western shores of Lake Izabal, El Estor is a small, amicable town. Supposedly, its name derives from the English word "store," since back in the day British pirates sailing up the Río Dulce would come across the lake and stop there to buy supplies. The small town's economy used to center around a nickel mine that was active during the 1970s. There has recently been a push by the Guatemalan government to reopen the mine in an effort to export minerals. However, this has been some cause for controversy, since expanding the mine would result in the displacement of several Maya villages, as well as cause the destruction of the area's natural beauty.

Despite the debate over the mine, El Estor mostly gets by on tourism today. It touts itself as being a good destination for ecotourism, serving as a jumping-off point for forays into the nearby El Boquerón canyon and the beautiful Bocas del Polochic Wildlife Refuge. Although the town is still working on developing hotels, restaurants and other tourist amenities, it is a largely tranquil place that is worth a visit. Updated: Sep 20, 2010.

Getting To and Away

Minibuses run to and from El Estor group around 3a Calle. The one hour and 45-minute journey to Río Dulce passes around the lake past El Boquerón and Finca El Paraíso and buses travel hourly. Traveling via El Estor is also an alternative route to Cobán, which is only 160 kilometers (100 mi) away. Ask at the minibus stop on 3a Calle or at your hotel; Oscar Paz at Hotel Vista al Lago or Hotel Calle Real are happy to help with tourist and travel info. Updated: Aug 27, 2010.

Getting Around

El Estor town center is pretty small and you can just wander around the fairly quiet streets. If you need a taxi, they tend to park up along the east side of the plaza. For travel or tours to El Boquerón or Bocas del Polochic ask for boatmen around the plaza. Benjamín Castillo (Tel: 502-7949-7675/502-5818-0850), gives tours on his boat for about Q700/$87 for two people for the day, or visit the office of Defensores de la Naturaleza on 5a Avenida and 2a Calle. URL: www.defensores.org.gt. Updated: Aug 27, 2010.

Safety

El Estor is a safe town. It is very quiet and you can wander the streets freely. As usual, be careful at night, as there is poor street lighting in some areas, and take care with your possessions—El Estor is a relatively poor town, despite the nearby mine, so don't flash expensive cameras or iPods. Updated: Aug 27, 2010.

Services

On the south east corner of the town plaza, 3a Calle and 5a Avenida, there is a Banrural (Monday-Friday 8:30 a.m.-5 p.m., Saturday 9 a.m.-1 p.m.) and a Bam with a Cajero 5B. There is also a Banco Industrial with a Cajero 5B on 3a Calle and 7a Avenida. There is an Internet café on 7a Avenida and 3a Calle that charges $1 an hour and is open Monday-Saturday 8 a.m.-9 p.m. It has Skype and Xbox and the air conditioning is cranked up high. There is a Farmacia Prado on 3a Calle, between 7a and 8a Avenida, which is open early morning until late at night. The post office is on the north-eastern corner of the plaza, on 5a Avenida, and the bright pink municipal office is at the end of 5a Avenida on the waterfront. Updated: Aug 27, 2010.

Things to See and Do

El Boquerón

Although the spectacular cliff faces of El Boquerón tower an impressive 250 meters (820 ft) above the Río Sauce, the canyon is completely hidden from view as you pass by it only 500 meters (1,640 ft) away on the road to El Estor. Indeed, the only way to access the canyon is by boat. In El Estor you will find plenty of boatmen willing to take you, for a small fee, through the ravine and back again, round trip taking about an hour. They will also drop you off and come back for you later if you want to hike further into the canyon, but this is not an easy stroll and you need to be prepared to wrestle with the jungle en route. Updated: Jun 18, 2010.

Bocas Del Polochic

If you really want to be immersed in nature and see a unique part of Guatemala, El Refugio de Vida Silvestre Bocas del Polochic (RVSBP) nature reserve is a good choice. The 208-square-kilometer (130 sq mi) refuge is home to more than 250 species of birds, 39 species of mammals, 138 species of reptiles and 53 different types of fish. It is also home to just over a million inhabitants, mostly settled around the river basins and engaged in agriculture and commerce. About 5,000 indigenous Q'eqchi' also live here in eight communities, benefiting from their fertile surroundings for farming, fishing and firewood.

The park is administered by the Defensores de la Naturaleza, an independent group sanctioned by the government, who collaborate with the communities to find sustainable and alternative ways to live and work in the reserve.

To this end, the area is being developed as an ecotourism center. It is a fantastic place for birdwatching or boating–try a trip in a traditional *cayucos*. In Selempim the Defensores have a base where researchers and tourist can stay and there is the Hostal y Restaurante Chapín Abajo, run by the community of the same name. Alternatively, the Defensores can organize homestays deep in the reserve and will put you in touch with local Q'eqchi', who work as tour guides and craftsmen. It is not an easy place to access. The public lanchas ($10, one hour) make infrequent journeys on odd days and the private hire boats are expensive (up to $150 return). Call the office of the Defensores de la Naturaleza who will know the current boat schedule and can help arrange accommodation and transport (5a Av. and 2a Ca., El Estor. URL: www.defensores.org.gt). If you don't have days to spare hire a local boatmen in El Estor to give you a guided day-tour to the edges of the reserve, usually around $80 for two people. Updated: Jul 20, 2010.

Lodging

If you are used to flash hotels and plush suites then that is not what you're going to get in El Estor. Hostels tend to be a little rough around the edges because the tourist scene has been quiet in this remote part of Guatemala. The accommodation available is decidedly the budget to mid-range level, but there are some nice El Estor hostels with lake views or pretty gardens, so it is worth looking around before you settle. Updated: Jul 13, 2010.

BUDGET

Hospedaje Posada de Don Juan

(ROOMS: $4) If you're on a reduced budget Hotel Don Juan, on the south east corner of the square, can provide you with a basic roof over your head for only $4 a night. The rooms are pretty basic and there are definitely no hidden extras but they do have private bathrooms (squeezed into the corner of the room) and fans, and there is a very green and pleasant courtyard with benches around it. Dollars are accepted. Right next door is the restaurant Café Portal. 5a Av. and 3a Ca. Tel: 502-7949-7296. Updated: Jul 20, 2010.

Finca El Paraíso

(ROOMS: $10-12) The route north around the lake toward El Estor is paved until just before you reach the turn-off south to Finca El Paraíso, 25 kilometers (15.5 miles) from Río Dulce. A winding track leads to the lake front and the relaxed cabaña resort. Have a look at the rooms before you commit to one in particular as they vary: the cabañas on the front with the lake view and, more importantly, the lake breeze cost the same as those further back but they have air conditioning. All have hammocks and a small patio for sitting out and chilling. Up to three people costs $12 each, with a discount offered for more. On the opposite side of the main road is the turn-off north to the hot-spring waterfall; a fascinating geological wonder. The water spilling over the top of the rocks is a scorching temperature, by contrast, before it plunges into the super cold river water. Swim over to the far pool to really take in the full effect of this awesome natural spa and access the bat-filled caves above. In a clearing by the river there is usually someone waiting there to show you through the woods up to the waterfall, and charge you $1.20. Tel: 502-7949-7122. Updated: Jun 12, 2010.

Hotel Vista al Lago !

(ROOMS: $10-18) Run by Oscar Paz, the town's unofficial tourist officer, this lovely wooden hotel is full of old world charm, enhanced further by the claim that it is the actual 'store' raided by marauding pirates, after which the town is named. The rooms are small but all have private bathrooms and the veranda on the second floor is the perfect place to relax while taking in the lake vistas. It is a peaceful place to stay. Rooms cost $10 for a single, $18 for a double and the rooms have fans and TVs. There is also private parking. 6a Ca. (on the lake front). Tel: 502-7949-7205. Updated: Jul 20, 2010.

Cabañas Chaabil

(ROOMS: $16-41) The Chaabil, a short walk past the town square is definitely past its glory days but it is still in a nice setting right on the lake and very quiet. The rooms are in wooden cabins. The cost for a single $16, a double $28, and a triple $41, with private bathrooms, fans and mosquito nets, which you need being so close to the water, is decently priced. The large restaurant serves up tasty Guatemalan dishes. 3a Ca., Tel: 502-7949-7272. Updated: Jul 20, 2010.

MID-RANGE

Hotel Calle Real

(ROOMS: $22-38) This gleaming and well-finished hotel is a good choice if you're looking for a big comfy bed, air conditioning, a fridge in your room as well as a TV, a spacious clean bathroom with 24-hour hot water and delightful garden, around which the rooms are located. Also, there is a small patio area with table and chairs. WiFi is available for free and there is a restaurant on site. Rooms cost $22-25 for a single, $30-38 for a double and dollars are accepted. 3a Ca. Tel: 502-7949-7869, E-mail: callereal@gmail.com. Updated: Jun 19, 2010.

Hotel Ecológico Cabañas del Lago

(ROOMS: $30) About a kilometer (0.6 miles) away from El Estor to the east, this hotel is set on its own grounds on the lake shore and even has a small beach. It's a nice place to stay if you want to get out of town. The well-appointed wooden cabins cost around $30 for a double. The owner, Hugo, can arrange a pick up from the center of town. Tel: 502-7949-7245. Updated: Jul 20, 2010.

Restaurants

There are a good few comedores around town, such as Antojitos El Punto on 8a Avenida and 2a Calle or Antojitos La Negrita on 5a Avenida and 1a Calle, but El Estor is definitely lacking a bunch of decent restaurants to choose from, especially if you stay for more than a few days. Cabañas Chaabil serves up large plates of juicy seafood and Café El Portal is good for breakfast. And if you need some fruit and veggies there is a market on 7a Avenida and 2a Calle, next to the Refresquería Cristi smoothie bar. Updated: Jun 23, 2010.

Café El Portal

Café El Portal is a great place to start the day with breakfast on the small terrace overlooking the town's quiet plaza. A basic 'desayuno típico' will set you back $2.20. Untypically, a drink is not included, but a coffee is just $0.50, along with a fresh juice $0.75) Otherwise, the menu is a little limited but if you want chicken, churrasco or rice and salad for dinner then you're in luck. The café is quite small and it does not have any bathroom facilities. Daily 7 a.m.-9 p.m. 5a Av. and 3a Ca. Tel: 502-7818-0843. Updated: Jun 23, 2010.

Refresquería Cristi

For the best and the cheapest licuado (smoothie) this side of the lake, copy the locals and make sure you find your way to Refresquería Cristi. It is down a quiet street heading toward the lake and with a handful of wooden tables out of the shade plus milkshakes and fruit smoothies served in big ice cream-sundae glasses going for only $0.40. It's the only place to take a break in the mid-afternoon heat. Cakes, candy and chips are also available. 7a Av. between 2a and 3a Ca. Updated: Jun 23, 2010.

MARISCOS

Around Kilometer 218 off the Atlantic highway is the turn-off to the out-of-the-way fishing town of Mariscos. Buses traveling along the CA-9 Carretera al Atlántico can drop you at the junction from where you'll need to catch a ride with a passing minibus. The main reason, perhaps the only reason, to visit Mariscos is to take a boat around the coast of magnificent Lago Izabal to stay at the paradisaical hideaway Denny's Beach. Set on a sandy shore on the south side of the lake against an impressive range of rich green mountains, this blissfully peaceful resort offers a real opportunity to get away from it all.

Go kayaking, indulge in a massage or follow the trails through the woods on horseback and then treat yourself to some nambé home-baked bread with a delicious seafood tapado cooked up by Doña Julia. Rooms range from $25-100. There is Internet available at a charge and dollars and credit cards are accepted. If you call ahead, the Canadian owner Denny can arrange for you to be picked up at the highway junction and will also send a boat to meet you at the jetty in town. Tel: 502-4636-6156, Cel: 502-5171-7477, E-mail: info@dennysbeach.com, URL: www.dennysbeach.com.

On the main street in town there are a few places to eat, the best being the Antojitos Dayli which has an awesome view out over the lake and a nice breeze to cool you down as you eat meat burritos, mojarra fresh fish or a healthy fruit licuado. Comedro Mary and Antojitos Wanda serve cheap breakfasts and lunches and cold beers. There is also the Hotel Leo, which has basic rooms. The Banrural does not have an ATM but will change dollars. If you need to pick up a pair of shorts before you go swimming in the freshwater lake, there are a few stores on the high street. Monday-Friday 8:30 a.m.-5:30 p.m., Saturday 9 a.m.-1 p.m. Updated: Jul 20, 2010.

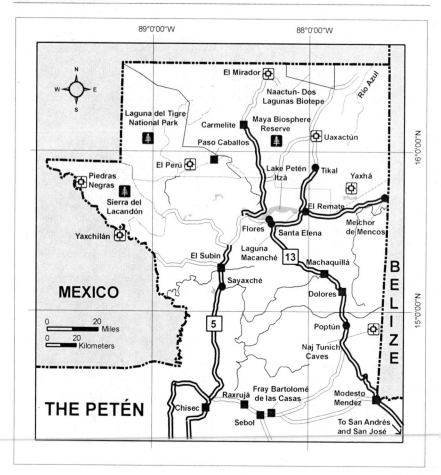

The Petén

The rugged, densely forested northeastern appendage of Guatemala, the Petén, borders both Belize and Mexico. Although the Petén was once home to hundreds of thousands of inhabitants during the reign of the Maya, it is sparsely populated now, and its people live off of basic agriculture, logging and tourism. A vast region, the Petén makes up roughly one-third of Guatemala's total landmass. The Petén is primarily of interest to nature lovers and history buffs. The timeless rainforests are home to thousands of species of mammals, reptiles, birds and insects, and the plant life is abundant to say the least. Some of the more interesting ecosystems are protected, but unfortunately the Petén is in danger of losing much of its biodiversity to logging and development.

The Petén's greatest attraction is, without a doubt, the ruins of the mighty Maya city of Tikal. One of the most important Maya sites, Tikal is a sprawling complex containing hundreds of structures, including some of the most spectacular temples in the Americas. In the remote northern part of the Petén, the site of El Mirador is even more impressive but very difficult to reach. Other important Maya sites in the Petén include Uaxactún, Yaxhá, Seibal and Piedras Negras. Most visitors to the Petén use the picturesque town of Flores as their base of operations. Updated: Oct 02, 2009.

History

Before it became the heartland of Maya Civilization, the Petén was already populated with monumental sites and cities. By the year 750, the Petén had become one of the most densely populated regions of the world at the time. In particular, Tikal was one of the largest urban centers. Experts believe extensive over-farming eventually led to widespread famine of the Maya people, who were also dealing with illnesses from European explorers.

Hermán Cortés led the first expedition through the Petén in 1524, after which the Spanish began to conquer the area. By 1697, the last Maya state was taken over. Today, many Maya sites are preserved throughout the Petén, including Tikal, Uaxactún, Aguateca, Topoxté and Yaxhá, to name just a handful.

The Guatemalan government officially created the Petén department in 1866. In the 1960s, any citizen willing to pay $25 could buy land in the area. An unpaved road that led to Flores brought tourists to the region. The first paved road in the Petén was built in 1982, bringing many new settlers to the region. In an effort to try and protect the tropical lands from further deforestation, the Maya Biosphere Reserve was created in 1990. Updated: Aug 10, 2010.

When to Go

The tourist season in Guatemala runs from December to March, considered the "dry season" throughout the country. The best time to visit the Petén is in December and February, when the weather is dry but the flora is still green. The Petén is hot and humid year round, but April and May are the hottest months. Updated: Aug 10, 2010.

Safety

Traveling is inherently dangerous, so be careful to never let your guard down. In Guatemala, over 70% of the population lives in poverty, so as a traveler you are an easy target for robbery. Remember to never leave your personal items unattended, and do not wear any flashy jewelry or showoff any expensive electronics you may be carrying. If anyone ever tries to rob you, the best thing to do is just give the thief what her or she is looking for. To reduce your risk of becoming a target, never travel alone, especially at night. Updated: Aug 10, 2010.

Things to See and Do

By far, the biggest attraction in the Petén is Tikal National Park, an enormous area of 575 square kilometers (222 sq mi) that contains remnants of one of the Maya civilization's greatest cities. Although your trip would not be complete without a stop in Tikal, there is so much more to explore in

the Petén. On the edge of Tikal is the Maya Biosphere Reserve, the largest protected tropical forest in North America. The colonial city of Flores is also worth at least a one-night stop over and ruin buffs will enjoy the sites of El Mirador and Piedras Negras as well. Updated: Aug 10, 2010.

Highlights

Parque Nacional Tikal–Deep in the lush jungle of northern Guatemala you will find Tikal, one of the largest archeological sites of the pre-Columbian Maya civilization. The dense rainforest is cluttered with thousands of limestone ruins, some as large as 70 meters (230 ft) high. After decades of archeological work, only a fraction of the pyramids, palaces, residences and monuments of Tikal have been unearthed. The site was declared a UNESCO World Heritage Site in 1979.

Flores–Flores, the capital city of the Petén department, is also one of the closest towns to Tikal. Although many travelers just use this island as a resting stop on their way to the ruins, Flores is a destination in itself. The narrow, cobblestone streets of Flores make this colonial town easily walkable, and it takes just 15 minutes to circle the tiny island. Stop by the twin-domed Flores Church, or spend some time people watching in Parque Central.

El Mirador and Piedras Negras–Relatively speaking, these two lesser-known archeological sites are just beginning to be excavated. The pre-Columbian El Mirador was discovered in 1926, but archeological projects did not begin until 1978. As for Piedras Negras, this ruined city is on the north bank of the Usumacinta River. In the 1930s, the Maya hieroglyphic system was first deciphered here by Tatiana Proskouriakoff. The site is extremely remote, so it is suggested you join an organized tour if you plan on visiting. Updated: Aug 10, 2010.

THE PETÉN

Tours

There are many tours of interest to travelers throughout the Petén, particularly if you are a nature lover or enjoy archeology. This area of Guatemala is full of wildlife, including hundreds of bird species—some so rare they are classified as "globally threatened." Here you may even be able to catch a glimpse of the iridescent quetzal, Guatemala's national bird. As for ruins, the entire Petén is dotted with pyramids, temples and other structures. Most famous is Tikal, but there are over a dozen other sites in the Petén waiting to be uncovered. Although you can explore the area on your own, hiring a guide will enhance your experience, as guides are knowledgeable about the wildlife and history of the area. You can arrange for tours in most city centers, or even pre-plan your trip on the Internet before departure. Updated: Aug 10, 2010.

Lodging

The Petén, the northernmost region of Guatemala, is home to many Maya ruins and dense jungles. It is also one of the least inhabited regions of Guatemala, and lodging is hard to come by unless you're looking in the main tourist hubs, Flores and Santa Elena. Most travelers prefer Flores, which has a better selection of hotels and more things to do. El Petén hotels come in an assortment in sizes, prices and accoutrements. For as little as $2 a night, you can find a place to stay, but you get what you pay for. El Petén hostels are harder to find. The only true hostel is the Hostel Los Amigos in Flores, which offers $3.50 rooms and a great atmosphere for backpackers. On the other end of the spectrum lies Hotel del Patio Tikal ($65-80), a higher-end hotel with close proximity to the lake, as well as a courtyard pool, Jacuzzi and international breakfast. Updated: Jun 30, 2010.

POPTÚN

One hundred kilometers (62 mi) south of Flores, Poptún is a small town of 20,000 inhabitants. Nestled 600 meters (1,970 ft) up in the foothills of the Maya mountains, Poptún has a cooler, more appealing climate than the rest of the region, which has made it a popular stop-off point for foreigners and locals alike. The landscape is marked mostly by pine forests.

The first inhabitants were the Maya Mopanes and the Queeckchies from Cahabon, Alta Verapaz. This was a center of government activity during the civil war, though things have long-since returned to normal in the region. The main industries were ranching and the extraction of the resin from the Chicopazote trees to make gum. People dedicate themselves to cattle farming and logging pine, mahogany and cedar trees.

Most people visit Finca Ixobel, the best accommodation choice in the area and an important stop on Guatemala's gringo trail. If you have only one day in Poptún, visit the fascinating caves of Naj Tunich, and then spend the rest of the day relaxing at Finca Ixobel. If you have more time, you can go horseback riding, rafting or explore the other nearby caves. Updated: May 05, 2010.

When to Go

The most pleasant time to visit Poptún is between the months of November and February. Expect some cool nights and mornings, March and April are the hottest and driest months. Rain begins in May and with it come all the mosquitoes. Be sure to bring some repellent if you visit during this time. July to October continues to be muggy and buggy. The town holds a festival in honor of Saint Peter, Martyr of Verona, April 21-29 each year. On the last day, there is a parade which satirizes the daily life in Guatemala and Poptún. Updated: Oct 22, 2009.

Getting To and Away

Most buses and minibuses stop on the main road through the town.

Buses to Flores/Santa Elena ($3.50, 2 hours): Fuentes del Norte goes every hour between 3:30 a.m. and 6:30 a.m., then at 11:30 a.m., 12:30 p.m., 3 p.m., 3:45 p.m., 4:30 p.m., 5:45 p.m. and 8 p.m. Minibuses leave every 30 minutes between 6 a.m. and 6 p.m.

Buses to Fray Bartolome de Las Casas ($6, 6 hr): One bus leaves at 10 a.m. from the market.

Buses to Guatemala City ($7-11, 6-7 hours): Fuentes del Norte leaves at 5:30 a.m., 6:30 a.m., 9 a.m., 9:45 a.m., 10:30 a.m., 11:45 a.m., 2 p.m., 6:30 p.m., 8 p.m., 9:30 p.m., 10:30 p.m., 11:30 p.m. and midnight. Buses to Rio Dulce ($4, 2 hours): Fuentes del Norte leaves at the same hours as the Guatemala City departures listed above. Updated: Oct 22, 2009.

Getting Around

Poptún itself is small and easily walkable. For trips outside the center of town, you can find taxis and tuk-tuks waiting around. Tuk-tuks are always cheaper, but they only do short distances (about 15 minutes, maximum). Of course you wouldn't really want to take a longer tuk-tuk trip on the mountainous roads around Poptún. Updated: Oct 22, 2009.

Safety

Poptún is a small town and has a relatively safe reputation. However, it's still necessary to take some precautions just as you would anywhere else in Guatemala. Don't go out alone late at night, don't accept drinks from strangers, and stick to well-lit, well-populated areas. As always, traveling in a group is safer than traveling alone. Updated: Oct 22, 2009.

Services

MONEY

South of the Flores bus stop, Banco Reformador (5 Calle 7-98) is open Monday-Friday 9 a.m.-5 p.m. and Saturday 9 a.m.-1 p.m. There is a Visa ATM and the bank changes US dollars as well as traveler's checks.

Banrural (5 Calle), one block south of Banco Reformador, is open Monday-Friday 8:30 a.m.-5 p.m. and Saturday 9 a.m.-1 p.m. There is a MasterCard ATM and they change US dollars as well as traveler's checks. Updated: Oct 22, 2009.

KEEPING IN TOUCH

There are no proper cybercafés in Poptún, at least at the time of this writing. If you want to check your E-mail, you will have to go to Finca Ixobel, outside town. There, the hotel charges $1.50 per hour to surf the web. The town's post office is located on 5a. Calle, and it is open Monday-Friday, 9 a.m.-5 p.m., and Saturday, 9 a.m.-1 p.m. Updated: Oct 22, 2009.

MEDICAL

There are two pharmacies on the main street open every day and a clinic with doctors attending Monday to Friday 10 a.m.-6 p.m. and Saturday 8 a.m.-1 p.m. There is also a 24-hour emergency service. Updated: Jul 16, 2010.

Things to See and Do

Activities include treks to remote Maya sites, jungle hikes, caving, tubing or horseback riding. All activities can be organized at Finca Ixobel or Villa de Los Castellanos. Updated: May 05, 2010.

Ixobel Caves

This cave's natural beauty makes it a must-see. Leaving from the Finca Ixobel at 8:30 a.m. and 2 p.m., the tour takes about three hours and costs $4 per person. Wear some good hiking shoes and bring a flashlight. The 45 minute hike goes through the green mountains before arriving at the entrance of the cave. The

crystal pools of water will amaze you as you walk through the formations of stalactites and stalagmites. Don't be afraid to get your feet wet in the icy water. Updated: Jul 06, 2010.

Horseback Riding

Finca Ixobel organizes horseback riding tours leading you through a scenic and refreshing pine forest. Whether you are a beginner or an expert, they have a horse for you. They offer a two-hour trip ($15/person), an all day trek ($30/person including lunch and drink) and an overnight trek ($60/person with a night in a tent). Updated: Jul 06, 2010.

Tubing

(TUBING: $22 per person) Have fun floating down the Machaquila River on inner tubes. The high energy and exciting guided excursion leads you down untamed waters and rapids. This great adventure includes lunch and transportation. You have to know how to swim to participate. Updated: Jul 06, 2010.

Lodging

There are only a handful of hotels in Poptún. Hostels are even harder to come by, but there are a couple low-cost options available in town. You're probably better off at the eco-lodge Finca Ixobel only five kilometers (3.1 mi) south of Poptún, a popular destination among travelers looking to relax in the cozy accommodations of a true jungle lodge. Updated: Jul 19, 2010.

Hotel Izalco

(ROOMS: $6-14) The rooms are small but clean. They all have mosquito nets and TV. Some have private bathrooms. Be sure to get a room with a fan as it's very hot all year round. 4 Ca. 7-11. Tel: 502-7927-7372. Updated: Oct 21, 2009.

Hotel Posada de Los Castellanos

(ROOMS: $7-14) Located in the city center, this hotel offers average rooms with fans and hot-water in the bathrooms. If you're stuck for a place to stay in town, it's your best choice. Corner 4 Ca. and 7 Av. Tel: 502-7927-7222. Updated: Jul 16, 2010.

Finca Ixobel

Finca Ixobel is an ecologically friendly hotel and campground surrounded by mountains, pine forests and jungle. It's a perfect place to relax and enjoy the peacefulness of the surrounding environment. The farm of 162 hectares (400 ac) was bought in 1971 by an American couple. They started with a campground and slowly improved the hotel. Now the finca offers camping, tree houses, private

THE PETÉN

rooms with bathroom and bungalows. The farm has a small organic garden that supplies delicious salads and the chickens provide fresh eggs every day. The restaurant offers a la carte breakfasts and lunches, with prices ranging $1.50-7. Buffet dinner is served at 7 p.m. The hotel offers a wide range of activities from horseback riding ($15 per person for 2 hours), treks in the jungle of 1 to 4 days ($32/person/day), rafting with 5 persons minimum ($25/person) and visit to some caves ($5/person). The hotel also arranges tours to the caves of Naj Tunich for $35/person including transport, entry fee and lunch. On site, there is a natural pond where you can go swimming and relax. Tel: 502-5892-3188, URL: www.fincaixobel.com. Updated: Dec 09, 2009.

Restaurants

There are are a number of comedores and street stalls serving cheap local food in the main street. There is also a popular restaurant in the village, La Fonda Ixobel, that serves baked goods and snacks throughout the day. Updated: Jul 16, 2010.

Street Stalls at the Parque Central

(ENTREES: $1) Food stalls can be found around Parque Central, all dishing up traditional Guatemalan food. You can try the *pupusas* (corn tortillas filled with cheese, beans and/or pork skin), *enchiladas*, *elote* (corn that comes in a variety of sizes and colors) or *rellenos de plátano* (bananas that are sliced, filled with beans, and coated in cream). To drink, try the *arroz con leche* (rice water with milk) or the *atol de elote* (a thick wheat-and-corn-based drink). Updated: Dec 11, 2009.

La Fonda Ixobel

(ENTREES: $4-17) La Fonda Ixobel serves tasty local food and sandwiches all day long. Monday-Saturday 9 a.m.-9 p.m. 4 Ca. Updated: Oct 22, 2009.

AROUND POPTÚN

VILLA DE LOS CASTELLANOS

(ROOMS: $25-40) Villa de Los Castellanos is a beautiful eco-lodge located in the town of Machaquila, seven kilometers (4.35 mi) north of Poptún. The lodge is built on 5 hectares (12.35 ac) of land overlooking the Machaquila River and surrounded by a forest and a medicinal plant garden. If you are interested in heliconia flowers, it's one of the best places to find them in Guatemala. This garden is especially appropriate for anyone who loves tropical flowers as well as for students of anthropology, native medicine or folk healing. The 14 rooms are set in beautiful cabañas made from renewable natural materials found in the region. They all have private bathrooms, mosquito nets and fans. Ecologically focused, the owners have a reforestation program and visitors can participate. So far they have planted 10,000 Spanish Cedars, 800 Jocote Fraile trees, 2,700 Matilishuates, 500 Mahoganies and hundreds of medicinal plants. There is also a good restaurant and the owners organize trips to local caves, ruins, and forest preserves. Aldea Machaquila. Tel: 502-7927-7541, E-mail: ecovilla@ecotourism-adventure.com. Updated: Jul 16, 2010.

NAJ TUNICH CAVES

The caves of Naj Tunich, 35 kilometers (21.75 mi) east of Poptún, are unique for their Maya murals showing religious ceremonies, ball games and erotic scenes, which are not found anywhere else in the Maya world. The name means "paintings on a humid area," and there is evidence of activity from the pre-Classic to the Classic Period (100-900 AD). The caves played an important role in the life of the Maya. They served as a hiding place and later as a sacred place with doors to the afterworld. It was also a place for pilgrimage with people coming from very far away. The caves were closed in 1984 because of vandalism. In 2004, a painter from Guatemala City came to do a reproduction of the murals in a nearby cave, which is open to the public. For now, visitors can only see the entrance of the original caves. There is no public transport to the site but Finca Ixobel can organize tours. Daily 8 a.m.-4:30 p.m. Updated: Dec 03, 2009.

Flores and Santa Elena

Flores is on a small island on Lake Petén Itza, connected to Santa Elena and San Benito by a causeway. The three cities are often referred to collectively as Flores. It was named in honor of Cirilo Flores, one of the first pro-independence leaders in Guatemala. Flores is a good starting point for your trip around Petén. The city itself is beautiful with colonial, red-roofed buildings, narrow cobblestone streets and many restaurants and hotels. The cathedral houses a Black Christ, which are novel across Central America. The town is a quiet and peaceful place and probably the safest place in Petén. You can walk around the whole town in 15 minutes. Santa Elena is modern and requires a little more caution, but the city offers a more authentic Guatemala experience with traffic, litter and street food. Flores has a large selection of hotels for all budgets with view of the lake, and many delicious restaurants. Santa Elena is where the banks, supermarkets and buses are found. The main economy is agriculture (corn, red beans, oranges, chilis and wood) and handicraft (baskets, brooms and leather products). Updated: May 03, 2010

Services

TOURISM

The Inguat tourism office in Flores (Ca. Santa Ana. Tel: 502-7867-5334) is only a block east of Parque Central on Avenida Santa Ana. Open Monday-Friday 9 a.m.-5 p.m. and Saturday 9 a.m.-noon, the friendly staff will give you any information you need about Flores and around. Inguat also has tourism information points at Playa Sur and the airport.There is no post office in Flores. The one in Santa Elena is on 7 Avenida and 2 Calle and is open Monday-Friday 8 a.m.-5 p.m. Updated: Sep 26, 2009.Updated: Sep 26, 2009.

MONEY

There is only one bank in Flores. Banrural, just off the Parque Central, exchanges dollars and traveler's checks. Monday-Friday 9 a.m.-5 p.m., Saturday 9 a.m.-1 p.m. You can also exchange your dollars in many Internet cafés and hotels. There is an ATM next door to Hotel Petén and another one inside the 24-hour shop on Calle 30 de Junio. They both accept Visa and MasterCard. There are many banks in Santa Elena, including Banquetzal in 4 Calle between 4 Avenida and 5 Avenida (Tel: 502-7926-0711), Banrural at the corner of 3 Avenida and 4 Calle and Banco Industrial in 6 Calle. All have an ATM. Updated: Sep 26, 2009.

KEEPING IN TOUCH

There are many Internet cafés in both towns, charging between $1-1.50 an hour. But more and more hotels offer WiFi and computers with Internet connection. MayaNet (Flores), close to the laundry Lavafacil, offers Internet connection for $0.70 per hour between 8

a.m. and 2 p.m. and $1 per hour after that. They offer money exchange and a book exchange. You can make international phone calls for $0.50 a minute. Petén Net (Flores) on Calle Centroamérica offers Internet connection for $1.50 per hour. You can make international phone calls for $0.50 per minute to a landline and $0.70 per minute to a mobile phone. They exchange dollars too. Daily 8 a.m.-10 p.m. Updated: Sep 26, 2009.

MEDICAL

There is no pharmacy or hospital in Flores, but if you go to Santa Elena there are hundreds of them along 4 Calle and 6 Avenida. In case of an emergency, the closest hospital is in San Benito. Tel: 502-7926-1459. Updated: Sep 26, 2009.

LAUNDRY

There are a few laundromats and some hotels have laundry service, so ask at the reception desk. At Laundry Lavafacil (Flores), wash and dry costs $4 a load. They offer Internet connection for $1 per hour so you can surf the Internet while waiting for your clothes. Updated: Sep 26, 2009.

SHOPPING

As a touristy place, Flores has many souvenir shops selling t-shirts, postcards, bags and any other trinkets that you care to take back home. Bargain the prices hard. Most of the shops are in Calle Centroamérica and Calle 30 de Junio. Updated: Sep 26, 2009.

Jade Shop

This store sells jewelry made of Guatemalan jade. If you're looking for a nice present and don't mind paying the price, it's the place to go. The jade comes from the north of Petén. The shop owner also owns Café Yaxhá. Daily 9 a.m.-1 p.m. and 5 p.m.-9 p.m. Ca. 30 de Junio. Tel: 502-4712-4306/5830-2060. Updated: Sep 26, 2009.

Tienda de Artesania

In front of Parque Central, this small art and craft shop is run by an association and sells wooden statues and other souvenirs. Monday-Saturday 9 a.m.-5 p.m. Updated: Sep 26, 2009.

Things to See and Do

Flores is a good starting point for your exploration of Petén, and the jumping-off point for Guatemala's greatest tourist attraction, the ruins of Tikal. There is much more to see and do before you leave Petén.

There are other ruins, if you haven't yet had your fill. Check out El Mirador, which is remote but very impressive. There are also many hikes and good opportunities to see wildlife in the area. There is even more than one way to see Tikal. Most tours go during the daytime, but a true ruins buff will want to book the sunset tour, the sunrise tour or both. In Flores, you can take a tour in a small boat on the lake, rent a canoe at La Villa Del Chef ($4/hour) or go swimming. If you have more time, visit the Zoo or go to visit the Arcas center. Updated: Oct 02, 2009.

Lake Tours

Boats can be hired for any length of time from a half-hour to all day. The rate is $15 for 30 minutes per boat (up to 9 people) or $25 for an hour trip. But prices are negotiable, so bargain hard. They can bring you to the museum on the small island, to the zoo and Arcas or to the Mirador. Ask at your hotel or simply head down to Playa Sur and ask around. Updated: Oct 19, 2009.

Petencito Zoo

Not far down the shore from the village of San Miguel is the Peténcito Zoo. It gives visitors the chance to see a collection of local animals like jaguars, monkeys and macaws. In addition, the visitors can see some of the beautiful regional flora. For people looking for some fun, there are some giant waterslides for splashing in the lake. Open daily from 7 a.m. to 4 p.m., the entrance costs $3. To get there, you need to rent a boat for $20 per group (max 15 people). Daily 7 a.m.-4 p.m. Updated: Oct 19, 2009.

ARCAS Center

(ADMISSION: $2) The Wildlife Rescue and Conservation Association runs an animal rehabilitation center close to San Miguel. They take care of animals rescued from smugglers and illegal pet traders, like jaguars, macaws, monkeys and coatis. You can't visit the animal center but they have an Environmental Education and Interpretation Center for visitors. There is also a one kilometer (0.62 mi) nature trail through the lush rainforest showing medicinal plants, a bird observation platform and an area for animals that cannot be reintroduced to the wild. You can learn about how they get the animals and the rehabilitation process. To get there, take the boat leaving the arch at the entrance of Flores at 8:30 a.m. Monday to Friday, coming back around 3:30 p.m. It costs $7 per person, or you can go by yourself by walking five kilometers (3.1 mi)

east from San Miguel. Daily 9 a.m.-3 p.m. Tel: 502-7926-0946, URL: www.arcas-guatemala.com. Updated: Oct 19, 2009.

Ak'Tun Kan Caves

(ADMISSION: $2.50) If you don't have time to visit the caves in Alta Verapaz or south of Petén, you might want to visit the Ak'Tun Kan Caves, two kilometers (1.2 mi) north of Flores. You'll crawl yourself through the earth's belly in order to observe curious figures sculpted by nature. In the Mayan language, the name means "cave of the serpent" from a legend about a giant snake living in the caves. To get there, walk north out of Santa Elena on 6 Avenida or take a tuk-tuk there for $2. Daily 7 a.m.-5 p.m. There is no light in the caves so bring a flashlight. Giant snake not included. Updated: Sep 26, 2009.

Volunteering

If you want to volunteer with animals or in the protection of the environment around Flores you should contact ARCAS or Volunteer Petén. Updated: Sep 26, 2009.

ARCAS

ARCAS offers volunteer opportunities in its rescue center to anybody who wants to help the conservation of Guatemalan wildlife. Volunteers live in a spacious, two floor wooden building. In addition to the regular daily feeding and caring of the animals, you can help in the construction of cages, trail maintenance, research, giving tours to visitors, participating in educational activities and community projects. The cost is $125/week including lodging and food. E-mail: arcas@intelnet.net.gt, URL: www.arcasguatemala.com. Updated: Sep 26, 2009.

Volunteer Petén

Volunteer Petén in San Andrés offers volunteer opportunities in environment education, reforestation, forest management and medicinal plants. Volunteers are expected to take part in all the program areas. They prefer if volunteers can commit for a minimum of four weeks. Price is $120/week, including lodging in a family, meals, training, activities and resources for the projects. There is a discount from the fourth week on. Tel: 502-5711-0040, E-mail: volunteerPetén@hotmail.com, URL: www.volunteerPetén.com. Updated: Sep 26, 2009.

Tours

Tikal Connection

Inside the Santa Elena Airport, Tikal Connection specializes in ecotourism. They work with local communities to develop responsible tourism and non-timber forest products. They offer jungle tours to different archeological sites and work with eco-lodges around Lake Petén Itza. Airport Santa Elena. Tel: 502-4211-1027, URL: www.tikalcnx.com. Updated: Sep 26, 2009.

Turismo Aventura

Founded in 2003, Turismo Aventura provides the travelers with unique economical services promoting responsible and low-impact tourism. The founders participated in the creation of Green Deal, a certification program for sustainable tourism, in connection with Associacion Alianza Verde. Apart from Tikal, they offer fascinating trips through the jungle to less visited sites. In Flores: Ca. Union (in front of Villa del Chef). In Santa Elena: 6 Av. 4-44. Tel: 502-7926-0398, E-mail: info@toursguatemala.com, URL: www.toursguatemala.com. Updated: Sep 26, 2009.

Zotz Travel Agency

This small travel agency offers typical tours to all the archeological sites and shuttles to Mexico, Cobán and Antigua. They specialize in a four day tour to El Mirador. It costs $250/person for two or three people, $180/person for 4 people or more. Ca. Centroamérica. Tel: 502-5974-4223. Updated: Sep 26, 2009.

Martsam Tour and Travel

This national tour company offers day tours to the different archeological sites such as Tikal, Yaxhá, Aguateca and Ceibal for $65/person with 2 people minimum. The rates include transport, guided tour, entrance fees and lunch. The friendly staff will help you organize your stay in Petén. They also offer a two day trip to the Guacamayas Biological Station for $165 per person and birdwatching trips. Ca. 30 de Junio. Tel: 502-7934-6527, URL: www.martsam.com. Updated: Sep 26, 2009.

The Mayan Adventure

Inside Café Yaxhá, the Mayan Adventure offers tours to different archeological sites. The goal is to give travelers deep insight into the scientific work done at the sites currently under investigation. Travelers usually do not have the opportunity to visit the buildings under excavation or investigation tunnels. They offer day tours to La Banca and Yaxhá ($85/person for two people, $39/person for five including guided tour, transport and family lunch), and Yaxhá and Topoxche ($95/person for 2, $42/person for 5 including guided tour, transport and box lunch). They also organize multi-day trips to Yaxhá and Nakum; El Zolt and Tikal; and El Mirador. Ca. 15 de Septiembre. Tel: 502-5830-2060, URL: www.the-mayan-adventure.com. Updated: Sep 26, 2009.

FLORES

Lodging

Most visitors will want to stay in Flores, as opposed to Santa Elena, as the hotels tend to be better and the town itself is a lot more fun. Santa Elena features hotels at each end of the spectrum: the cheapest of the hostels as well as the fanciest deluxe hotels are in Santa Elena, while Flores offers attractive mid-range options. As the island is small, restaurants and shops are just a few minutes away from the hostels. Flores is hot all year long so make sure the room has a fan or air conditioner. Most hotels have a direct view of the lake and roof terraces to enjoy nice sunsets. Note that many have described the cheapest Santa Elena hostels as potentially dangerous, as they are frequented by coyotes, or criminals who specialize in smuggling illegal immigrants from Guatemala to Mexico. Updated: Jun 29, 2010

BUDGET

Los Amigos

(ROOMS: $3.50-9) Los Amigos Hostel offers an open, traveler-centered environment that allows backpackers used to very basic accommodations a sigh of relief. Rooms start at $3.50, a great deal in a moderately priced city. The dorms feature cupboards where you can lock your bags, comfortable beds, and enough open space to keep the rooms cool despite the heat and humidity common in the Petén region. The common area is filled with multicolored hammocks, couches, tables, and often tons of other travelers, making Los Amigos a great place to kick back. You can enjoy a drink or a cinnamon banana smoothie until around 11 p.m., when the management will kindly ask you to take your fiesta down the street so that others can sleep. The hostel also has a giant selection of documentary films to watch or burn onto a CD, which is wonderful for backpackers who are recovering from one of the many treks in the area. Ca. Central, next door to Pro-Petén. Tel: 502-7867-5075, E-mail: amigoshostel@gmail.com, URL: www.amigoshostel.com. Updated: Jun 18, 2009.

THE PETÉN

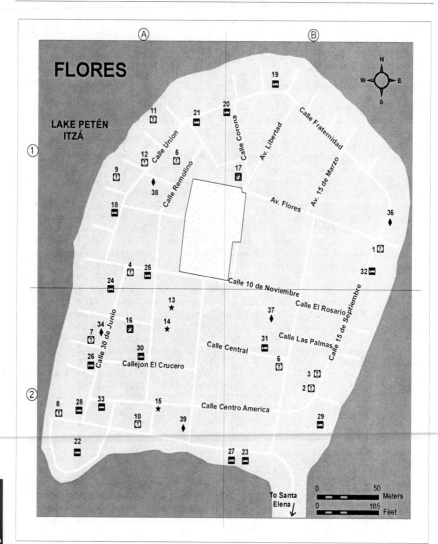

FLORES

LAKE PETÉN
ITZÁ

To Santa
Elena

Hostal Los Amigos

(ROOMS: $3-9) Very popular among budget travelers, Hostal Los Amigos offers cheap lodging in a great atmosphere. You have the choice between sleeping in a hammock, a basic dorm, a luxury dorm with bathroom, or a private room with shared bathroom. The hostel fills quickly and it doesn't take reservations, so make sure to arrive early. The flower garden is a great place to relax, read or chat with other travelers. The restaurant is open between 7 a.m. and 9 p.m. and offers soups, sandwiches and snacks. If you have your laptop, there is free WiFi. If not, they have two computers ($1.50/hr). Ca. Central. Tel: 502-5584-8795, URL: www.amigoshostel. com. Updated: Oct 20, 2009.

Hospedaje Dona Goya

(ROOMS: $4-10) This small hostel will please people traveling on small budgets. The eight-bed dorms with shared bathrooms are spacious and clean. There are also some private rooms with bathrooms available. The roof terrace is a great place to relax in a hammock while enjoying the view of the lake. The restaurant serves breakfast and lunch, and there is

Eating 🍴

1 Café chilero B1
2 Café Yaxha B2
3 Galeria del Zot'z B2
4 La Luna A1
5 Las Brisas A1
6 Las Puertas B2
7 Mayan Sunset Café A2
8 Raices Bar and Grill A2
9 Restaurante Casa Amelia A1
10 Restaurante El Grand Jaguar A2
11 Terrazzo A1
12 Villa del Chef A1

Services ★

13 Lavafacil A2
14 Maya Net A2
15 Peten Net A2

Shopping 🛍

16 Jade shop A2
17 Tienda de Artesanía B1

Sleeping 🛏

18 Casa Amelia A1

19 Casazul B1
20 Dona Goya B1
21 Dona Goya II   A1
22 Grand Hotel de la Isla A2
23 Hotel Casablanca B2
24 Hotel Casona de la Isla A2
25 Hotel Isla de Flores A1
26 Hotel Peten A2
27 Hotel Petenchel B2
28 Hotel Santana A2
29 Hotel Villa del Lago B2
30 La Mesa de los Mayas A2
31 Los Amigos B2
32 Mirador del lago B1
33 Posada de la Jungla A2

Tours ♦

34 Martsam Tour A2
35 Mayan Adventure (See 2)
36 Tikal Connection B1
37 Tourism Office B2
38 Turismo Aventura A1
39 Zotz travel agency A2

a computer available with 15 minutes of free Internet for guests. Ca. Union. Tel: 502-7867-5516. Updated: Oct 20, 2009.

Hotel Mirador del Lago
(ROOMS: $7-9) This is a good value hotel made up of two facing buildings just north of the main street in town. Rooms are simple but clean, and come with fans and some with lake views. All have access to several outdoor communal areas with seats and sun loungers and nice views out over the lake. Popular with travelers, it tends to fill up. Ca. 15 de Septiembre. Tel: 502-926-3211/3276. Updated: Nov 21, 2006.

Mirador del Lago
(ROOMS: $10-15) This friendly, family-run hotel has 29 comfortable rooms with bathrooms, TV, views of the lake and private balconies. From 6:45 a.m. the Mirador offers tasty

breakfasts for a cheap price ($2.50-4). The owner will help you organize your trip. There are computers with Internet connection available for $1 per hour. Ca. 15 de Septiembre. Tel: 502-7867-5409. Updated: Oct 20, 2009.

Hospedaje Dona Goya II
(ROOMS: $13-30) Next door to the Dona Goya, Dona Goya II offers 15 private rooms with bathrooms and TV. Some have an air conditioner, others only a fan. Ask for a room with a view of the lake. Rooms are small and simply decorated but clean. The roof terrace is a plus. Breakfast is served next door. Ca. Union. Tel: 502-7867-5516. Updated: Oct 20, 2009.

Hotel Peténchel
(ROOMS: $15) Cheap and without frills, this eight-room hotel will please travelers on a small budget looking for a private room. The

THE PETÉN

rooms are spacious but lack lake views and have no furniture other than the bed. The hotel's small restaurant has a view of the lake, and offers snacks and hamburgers. Located at the island entrance, it's a good place to begin your stay in Petén. Playa Sur. Tel: 502-7926-3359. Updated: Oct 20, 2009.

Hotel Casablanca

(ROOMS: $15) On the Playa Sur at the entry to Flores, Hotel Casablanca offers simple but spacious rooms and a terrace with a view of the lake. All rooms have bathrooms, some have views of the lake. Playa Sur. Tel: 502-5699-1371. Updated: Oct 20, 2009.

MID-RANGE

Posada de la Jungla

(ROOMS: $19-31) With 20 rooms, this three-level hotel offers comfortable private rooms with TV and bathrooms. Some have an air conditioner, others only a fan. Most of the rooms have a view of the lake and the roof terrace is a good place to catch the breeze. Ca. Centroamérica. Tel: 502-7867-5185. Updated: Oct 20, 2009.

La Mesa de Los Mayas

(ROOMS: $30-45) Decorated with flowers and large corridors, La Mesa de Los Mayas has been around for years. Rooms are small but have ample light. They all have bathrooms, large closets and cable TV. You can choose a room with a fan or with an air conditioner. Each floor has a balcony with a view of Flores, but the best is the roof terrace with its view of the lake. There is a restaurant open every day from 6 a.m. to 11 p.m. that serves typical food at a cheap price. Av. La Reforma. Tel: 502-7867-5268. Updated: Oct 20, 2009.

Hotel Villa del Lago

(ROOMS: $30-40) Don't judge the Hotel Villa Del Lago on its slightly unattractive exterior. The interior is nicely tiled and adorned with flowers and Greek columns, and there are 21 comfortable rooms spread over three levels, each with good furniture, bathrooms, air conditioners, cable TV and WiFi access. There is a computer with free Internet access in the lobby. On each level there is a small terrace with chairs and tables to enjoy the view of the lake. Rates include a continental breakfast. There is also a restaurant. Ca. 15 de Septiembre. Tel: 502-7867-5181, URL: www.hotelvilladellago.com.gt. Updated: Oct 20, 2009.

Casa Amelia

(ROOMS: $30-62) With a waterfront location, this three-level hostel is beautifully decorated in green and white. Every one of the 12 private rooms has a bathroom, TV and air conditioner. Ask for the room on the roof terrace or one of the rooms with an amazing view of the lake. The hostel serves breakfast (buffet $8, a la carte $5) and lunch (buffet $12, box lunch $5). Have a beer on the roof terrace while watching the sunset. Ca. La Union. Tel: 502-7867-5430, URL: reservaciones@hotelcasamelia.com. Updated: Oct 20, 2009.

Casazul

(ROOMS: $38-58) Casazul, meaning Blue House in English, has been painted and decorated in blue. Set in a colonial house, this nine-room hotel will please travelers looking for luxury accommodation at an affordable price. All the rooms have bathrooms, mini-bars, air conditioners and WiFi access. The terrace on the third floor has comfortable chairs where you can sit and relax after a long day. Ca. Fraternidad. Tel: 502-7867-5451, URL: www.hotelesdePetén.com. Updated: Oct 20, 2009.

Hotel Petén

(ROOMS: $40-60) Hotel Petén is a modest brick and stucco building, with 20 nicely decorated rooms, all of which have bathrooms, air conditioners and WiFi access. Ask for a room on the top floor with a private balcony and a view of the lake. The rooms without views don't have much light. There is an indoor courtyard with tropical plants, a swimming pool, Jacuzzi and a lakeside restaurant open from 7 a.m. till 10 p.m. Ca. 30 de Junio. Tel: 502-7867-5203, URL: www.hotelesdePetén.com. Updated: Oct 20, 2009.

Hotel Santana

(ROOMS: $40-60) At the corner of Playa Sur and Calle 30 de Junio, this big blue 35-room hotel can't be missed. Hotel Santana will please travelers looking for a lake view room at an affordable price. Rooms are spacious and the back rooms have a private balcony with a view of the lake. Ask for a room on the third or fourth floor for a better view. All rooms have bathrooms, air conditioners, TV and WiFi access. The outdoor swimming pool has a built-in waterfall and a swim-up bar. There is also a lakefront restaurant offering breakfast, lunch and dinner from 6 a.m. to 10 p.m. Ca. 30 de Junio. Tel: 502-7867-5123, URL: www.santanapeten.com. Updated: Oct 20, 2009.

Hotel La Casona de La Isla

(ROOMS: $45-68) Nicely decorated in blue and yellow with a nautical theme, the tile work on the lobby and stairs is beautifully done. Rooms are large, all with bathrooms, air conditioners, cable TV and WiFi access. Ask for a room with view of the lake. There is an outdoor swimming pool and Jacuzzi where you can cool down after a long day of traveling. The hotel also has an international restaurant. Ca. 30 de Junio. Tel: 502-7867-5200, URL: www.hotelesdePetén.com. Updated: Oct 20, 2009.

HIGH END

Hotel Isla de Flores

(ROOMS: $50-70) One of the most comfortable and expensive hotels in Flores, Hotel Isla de Flores is decorated with white wicker furniture and flowers everywhere. The décor is a mix of modern and colonial elements. Rooms are big and sunny, most have small balconies with views of the lake. Ask for a room on the higher floors with better views. The are a number of bigger rooms for families or groups. All have bathrooms, air conditioners and cable TV. There is also a restaurant where breakfast is served and a helpful tour desk. Av. de la Reforma. Tel: 502-7926-0614, URL: www.hotelisladeflores.com. Updated: Oct 20, 2009.

Grand Hotel de la Isla

(ROOMS: $70-80) Located on the south side of the island, Grand Hotel de Flores will please travelers looking for a large, international-style hotel. Everything here is big. Rooms are nicely presented and most of them have private balconies with a view of the lake. There are two swimming pools, a conference center for 300 people, a modern gym, a restaurant-bar and Internet service. Playa Sur. Tel: 502-7867-5202, URL: www.hoteldelaisla.com. Updated: Oct 20, 2009.

Ni Tun

($120-250) Great little boutique hotel with amazing service and settings. This is comparable to Copolla's all too famous hotel La Lancha but much better in all services. Tel: 502-5201 0759, E-mail: stay@nitun.com, URL: www.nitun.com. Updated: Jun 16, 2009.

Restaurants

Flores has many restaurants for all budgets and tastes: local cuisine, Italian or fast food, take your pick. The local specialties are *tepescuintle* (agouti, a rabbit-sized jungle rodent),

venado (venison), *pavo silvestre* (wild turkey) and *pescado blanco* (white fish). Many restaurants have waterfront terraces, where you can watch the sunset while drinking a beer. Most of the restaurants are along Calle 30 de Junio, Calle Union and Calle 30 de Septiembre. Updated: Sep 28, 2009.

TRADITIONAL GUATEMALAN

Restaurante El Grand Jaguar

(ENTREES: $2-8) Restaurante El Grand Jaguar offers typical Guatemalan dishes with meat, chicken or fish. Prices are cheap and food is good. Open Monday to Saturday 7 a.m.-10 p.m. Ca. Centroamérica. Updated: Sep 26, 2009.

Galeria del Zot'z

(ENTREES: $2-10) Next to Café Yaxhá, Galeria del Zot'z is a colorful restaurant serving pizza, pasta, as well as cheap and delicious seafood. Try the shrimp. Galeria also serves salads, sandwiches and meat dishes, or choose one of its typical economical dishes. Painted in yellow and blue, the walls are decorated with Mayan paintings and pictures. Ca. 15 de Septiembre. Tel: 502-7867-5274, E-mail: restgalezotz@hotmail.com. Updated: Sep 28, 2009.

Café Yaxhá

(ENTREES: $3-10) Opened in 2004 by a German couple passionate about archeology, this restaurant and café is a great place to try tasty traditional Guatemalan dishes. It's cozy and the walls are decorated with pictures, maps and drawings from different Maya sites in Petén. There are also books on Maya culture and archeology that you can read while eating. Dishes include tacos, chicken and traditionally cooked fish filets. Vegetarian meals are also served. Updated: Sep 28, 2009.

Restaurante Las Brisas

(ENTREES: $4-6) Located in front of Il Terrazo, Las Brisas serves breakfast, lunch and dinner from 5 a.m. to 10 p.m. every day. Small and decorated with Maya murals, the restaurant has a selection of traditional dishes as well as sandwiches, hamburgers and fish. Ca. Union Price. Updated: Sep 28, 2009.

Maya Sunset Restaurant

(ENTREES: $6.50) This is a great spot to go for happy hour drinks as the sun goes down beside the small island overlooked by the outside seating area. It is not the cheapest place in town, even at happy hour, but it knows it has the best views for sunsets. Stay for food and you can choose from a wide selection on the menu. Ca. 30 de Junio. Tel: 502-7926-4726, E-mail: quetzal14@hotmail.com. Updated: Nov 21, 2006.

El Tucan

This place has a large dining area with views of the sea and is a popular spot. The food served is simple but pleasant, from barbeque chicken, one of the cheaper options, to the locally caught fish fresh from the lake. Service is a little slow so be prepared to wait. Ca. Centro America, 45. Tel: 502-7926-0536, E-mail: restauranteeltucan@hotmail.com. Updated: Nov 21, 2006.

CAFÉ/BAR

Cool Beans

(ENTREES: $2.50-7.50) Popular among travelers, Cool Beans is more than just a restaurant-bar. There is a large selection of DVDs, board games, and free WiFi access, and the terrace and garden have direct views of the lake. Cool Beans serves sandwiches, chicken, pasta, hamburgers and nachos. Daily 7 a.m.-11 p.m., but know that the kitchen closes at 9:00 p.m. sharp. Ca. 15 Septiembre. Updated: Sep 28, 2009.

MEXICAN

Restaurante Casa Amelia

(ENTREES: $2-6) Between the hotel of the same name and La Villa Del Chef, Restaurant Casa Amelia offers Mexican style cuisine. Tacos, nachos or fajitas, they are all delicious. Or, you can choose between the salads, pastas and hamburgers. They have a lovely lakeside terrace where you can catch the breeze during the day. Ca. Union. Tel: 502-7867-5433, E-mail: restaurantecasaamelia@gmail.com. Updated: Oct 15, 2009.

ITALIAN

Il Terrazzo

(ENTREES: $5-15) Terrazzo serves a large selection of delicious panini, pastas and mixed-fruit smoothies. The Italian restaurant's second floor has a beautiful view of the lake and a refreshing breeze. If you're still hungry, try the homemade tiramisu. Ca. Union. Tel: 502-7867-5479, E-mail: jpzeas@gmail.com.

INTERNATIONAL

Las Puertas

(ENTREES: $3-12) At the corner of Calle Central and Avenida Santa Ana, it getsits name, "the doors," because it has six doors. They have funky décor and serve good food such as steak, prawns and chicken. People who don't want to spend too much money can choose from their extended menu of salads, pastas and sandwiches. The prawns are delicious but expensive. Open 8 a.m.-11 p.m., they have happy hour drinks 6-10 p.m. Ca. Centra and Av. Santa Ana. Tel: 502-7867-5242. Updated: Oct 19, 2009.

La Villa del Chef

(ENTREES: $5-12) Specializing in Arab and Mediterrean food, they also serve a good selection of sandwiches, pastas, chicken and seafood dishes. Don't miss the cheap happy hour drinks all day long on the lakeside terrace. You can rent a canoe there for two or three people for $4/hour. Open 11 a.m.- 11 p.m. every day. Ca. Union. Tel: 502-7926-0296. Updated: Oct 15, 2009.

Restaurant La Luna

(ENTREES: $6-12) In a tropical ambiance with faux ceibal tree and wild wood, this very popular restaurant serves continental food you won't find anywhere else in Guatemala. Try the steak in black pepper cream or the chicken breast in wine sauce. They also serve pastas and vegetarian dishes such as falafel and salads. Daily noon-midnight. Ca. 30 de Junio. Tel: 502-7926-3346. Updated: Oct 19, 2009.

Raices Bar and Grill

(ENTREES: $5-15) With a deck directly on the lake, they serve large portions of grilled steak, chicken and fish that they cook right in front of you. Or just come to watch the sunset and enjoy the happy hour special drinks. Daily 2-10 p.m., Friday-Saturday 2 p.m.-1 a.m. Playa Sur. Tel: 502-5521-1843/502-5117-4963, E-mail: raicesrestaurante@gmail.com. Updated: Oct 19, 2009.

SOUTH AMERICAN STEAKHOUSE

La Hacienda del Rey

(ENTREES: $8-15) At the corner of Playa Sur and Calle 30 de Junio, this two-level open-air restaurant is a South American steak house. They serve tacos in addition to sizable *parrilladas* (South American-style BBQ beef). Go there if you want to eat a big juicy steak, but bear in mind it's good but it's not cheap. With its wooden interior decorated with flags, it has a special atmosphere. Playa Sur. Tel: 502-7926-3647. Updated: Oct 19, 2009

THE PETÉN

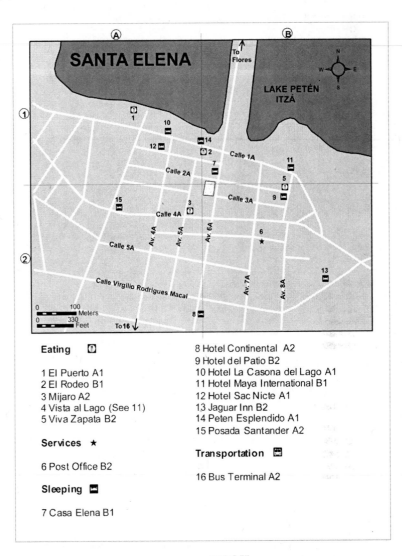

Eating 🍴

1 El Puerto A1
2 El Rodeo B1
3 Mijaro A2
4 Vista al Lago (See 11)
5 Viva Zapata B2

Services ★

6 Post Office B2

Sleeping ▣

7 Casa Elena B1

8 Hotel Continental A2
9 Hotel del Patio B2
10 Hotel La Casona del Lago A1
11 Hotel Maya International B1
12 Hotel Sac Nicte A1
13 Jaguar Inn B2
14 Peten Esplendido A1
15 Posada Santander A2

Transportation 🚌

16 Bus Terminal A2

SANTA ELENA

Lodging

Santa Elena is a scenic town overlooking one of the largest lakes in the country, Lago de Petén Itzá. If you have the choice, choose to stay in Flores over Santa Elena. Santa Elena's hotels are beautiful but expensive. Many are on the lakeshore with views of Flores. There are some cheap options in the city center. Like in Flores, check that the room has a fan or air conditioner as it gets very hot during the day.

BUDGET

Hotel Continental

(ROOMS: $5-12) The 51-room Continental, with its friendly staff, has a range of rooms on three levels. Some have bathrooms, but only with cold water, and all have fans. Rooms are basic but clean. 6 Av., South of Calzada Rodrigo Macal. Tel: 502-7926-0095. Updated: Oct 20, 2009.

Posada Santander

(ROOMS: $7-10) Family run, this small and clean hotel is a good budget option in

Santa Elena. Some rooms have bathrooms, but only with cold water. Another problem is the location: it can get a bit loud during the day. The restaurant next door serves good cheap meals for $2. 4 Ca. Tel: 502-7926-0574. Updated: Oct 20, 2009.

Hotel Sac-Nicte

(ROOMS: $9-11)This small hotel has very clean rooms with bathrooms and fans all for a budget price. Ask for a room upstairs with a balcony where you can have a view of the lake. The hotel has a desk at the airport and free shuttle service. 1 Ca. Tel: 502-7626-0092. Updated: Oct 20, 2009.

MID-RANGE

Jaguar Inn Hotel

(ROOMS: $17-25) Jaguar Inn is one of the best options for travelers on a budget. The rooms are tastefully decorated with Guatemalan art and textiles and are set around a lovely garden courtyard. All rooms have bathrooms, cable TV, WiFi access and fans; but, for $6 more you can have an air conditioner. There is a small open-air pizzeria on site. The Inn is close to the airport but a long walk to Flores so it is better if you have a car. Calzada Rodriguez Macal. Tel: 502-7926-0002, URL: www.jaguartikal.com. Updated: Oct 05, 2009.

Casa Elena

(ROOMS: $30-40) Just a block from the causeway to Flores, Casa Elena will appeal most to travelers looking for a business-style hotel. Rooms are small, but cozy, with private bathrooms and cable TV. Some have a view of the lovely interior courtyard, the plaza or the swimming pool. Kids will love the waterslide. Casa Elena has a restaurant-bar, rooftop terrace and spa service. 6 Av. and 2 Ca. Tel: 502-7926-2239. Updated: Oct 05, 2009.

HIGH END

Hotel del Patio

(ROOMS: $65-80) A short walk from the lake, Hotel del Patio's Neocolonial building has 21 simple, but modern, comfortable rooms with bathrooms and air conditioning. Ask for a room on the second floor where you can admire the courtyard. There is a pool and a small gym. The international restaurant is open every day between 6 a.m. and 10 p.m. Rates include breakfast. 8 Ca. and 2 Av. Tel: 502-7926-1229, URL: www.hoteldelpatio.com.gt. Updated: Oct 05, 2009.

Hotel Maya International

(ROOMS: $70-100) Set on a small hillside just off the lake, the Hotel Maya International is one of the oldest hotels in the area. Its 24 standard rooms and two junior suites are tastefully decorated with tiled floors and have lots of space. Most of the rooms have balconies with an amazing view of the lake, and all have bathrooms, air conditioners, cable TV and WiFi access. There is a swimming pool and a restaurant on the lakeshore with an impressive high-pitched thatch roof. The hotel is close to the airport. 1 Ca. Tel: 502-7926-2083, URL: www.villasdeguatemala.com. Updated: Oct 05, 2009.

Hotel La Casona del Lago

(ROOMS: $70-120) Set in a beautiful blue house on the lakeshore across from Flores, this new luxury hotel has 30 spacious, sunny rooms with excellent views of the lake. All rooms have bathrooms, air-conditioners, WiFi access, cable TVs and are centered around a swimming pool and Jacuzzi. The restaurant overlooks the lake and serves delicious international cuisine. The lobby is decorated with old pictures dating from the 1920s and 1940s along with more modern scenes. 1 Ca. Tel: 502-7952-8700, URL: www.hotelesdePetén.com. Updated: Oct 20, 2009.

Hotel Petén Esplendido

(ROOMS: $90-180) The most modern hotel in the area, Hotel Petén Esplendido is built along the lakeshore and will please travelers looking for an American-type luxury hotel. The rooms are very modern and all have bathrooms, air conditioners, cable TVs and WiFi access. There is a single elevator and four rooms fitted for travelers with disabilities. Ask for a room on the second floor with balconies directly fronting the lake. The waterfront restaurant serves good international food and there is a pool and a Jacuzzi. The Petén offers a free shuttle from the airport for those arriving by plane. 1 Ca. Tel: 502-2360-8140, E-mail: reservaciones@Peténesplendido.com, URL: www.Peténesplendido.com. Updated: Oct 20, 2009.

Restaurants

Although Flores is more popular for its restaurants, Santa Elena has a few good restaurants, including a few inexpensive options. Updated: May 05, 2010.

Restaurante Mijaro

(ENTREES: $3-5) Open daily from 7 a.m. until 10 p.m., this friendly comedor has an extensive menu including fish, meats, burgers and pastas. It has fans inside and has a little thatch-roofed garden area, a perfect place to cool off after a long day of traveling. 4 Ca., across from the Catholic church. Updated: Sep 25, 2009.

Viva Zapata

(ENTREES: $3-8) This Mexican restaurant across the street from Hotel del Patio serves good tacos, burritos and other Mexican specialties in a lively atmosphere. Some nights they have live music. Open every day 10 a.m-10 p.m. 8 Ca. Updated: Sep 28, 2009.

Restaurante El Rodeo

(ENTREES: $5-10) Across the street from the hotel Petén Esplendido, El Rodeo serves delicious chicken, fish, steak and pastas. Ask for the specialty of the house, the *Lomito al Rodeo*, which is a fillet steak with a mushroom sauce. Also try the grilled winkles. The restaurant has a very cowboy atmosphere with big wood wheels and wood furniture. There is a terrace with view of the lake. Daily 10 a.m.-10 p.m., there is WiFi. 1 Ca. and 5 Av. Tel: 502-7924-8045. Updated: Oct 15, 2009.

Restaurante El Puerto

(ENTREES: $5-10) On the lakefront, the restaurant El Puerto is an open-air steak house serving tender steaks along with other meals. Go there to enjoy the views of the lake and Flores while drinking a beer. It's packed with locals during the weekends. Daily 11 a.m.-11 p.m. 1 Ca. 2-15. Updated: Oct 19, 2009.

Vista al Lago

(ENTREES: $5-15) Inside the Hotel Maya International, the Restaurant Vista al Lago offers beautiful views from its covered wooden deck. They serve international as well as local dishes. Don't miss the large buffet and barbecue for Sunday brunch. Daily 7 a.m.-9 p.m. Hotel Maya International, 1 Ca. Updated: Sep 25, 2009.

AROUND FLORES

PARQUE NATURAL IXPANPAJUL

Located just 10 kilometers east (6.2 mi) of Santa Elena on the road to Guatemala City, the Parque Ixpanpajul has an area equivalent to 450 hectares (1,112 ac). It's a private natural reserve classified as subtropical forest. It's a beautiful place to walk, do some birdwatching and experience the jungle in a way you have never experienced. You can camp for $5 with your own tent or rent a tent and mattress for $13. The adventurous will want to try out the hanging sky-way bridges. The Tarzan Canopy Tour ($30/person) of two hours is a circuit of nine platforms and cables installed in beautiful leafy trees. It's accessible to anybody. The spotlightning ($25/person) is a tour by night in 4x4 vehicle to see the animals. Other activities include horseback riding ($15/hr), bicycle rental ($8/hr) and tractor ride ($5/person). The restaurant, open 7 a.m.-9 p.m., serves typical food with prices ranging $2-9.

To get there, take any bus going to Tikal, El Remate or Guatemala City and ask the driver to let you out at the entrance of the park, or take a taxi from your hotel for $25 round trip. Monday-Sunday 6 a.m.-6 p.m. Km 468 de Río Dulce until Flores. Tel: 502-2236-0576/5619-0513, E-mail: servicioalcliente@ixpanpajul.com, Web: www.ixpanpajul.com Updated: Sep 24, 2009.

Skyway

You'll get a bird's-eye view of the park as you walk 40 meters (131 ft) in the air on the twisting skyway paths. During the journey, you will be able to see the different strata of the tropical forest, before arriving at the top of Miramas Hill. You can rest in a hammock as you admire a 360-degree view of the majestic Petén forest. Daily 6 a.m.-6 p.m. URL: www.ixpanpajul.com. Updated: Oct 14, 2009.

TAYASAL

Tayasal is a small archeological site close to the village of San Miguel. It was occupied by the Maya Itzaes around 1194 A.D., Hernan Cortez visited the site in 1525, and the city was finally destroyed in 1697. The site is covered by vegetation so you can't see the pyramids; but, there is a wonderful lookout point called El Mirador constructed on top of a pyramid where you get a good view of Flores and Lake Petén Itzá. There is a small beach ($0.70) nearby where you can go swimming.

To get to San Miguel, take a boat ($0.70) on the north side of Flores close to the Hotel Sabana. Walk up the hill on the main street until you get to the football field. Turn left and follow the sign for the Playa. You will enter the Tayazal archeological site and at the next intersection, take the left uphill road to get to the Grand Plaza. From there follow the signs to the Mirador. The whole trip takes two hours. Bring water and mosquito repellent. Updated: Sep 24, 2009.

LAGO PETÉN ITZÁ

Lake Petén Itzá is the second-largest lake in Guatemala after Lake Izabal. Thirty-two kilometers (20 mi) long and five kilometers (3.1 mi) wide, the lake is vital to the region due to its wood, oil and agricultural resources. Because of the numerous archeological sites close by, around 150,000 tourists pass through this region yearly. The lake is a wildlife paradise with more than a hundred native species such as the red snook fish, crocodiles, jaguars, pumas, white-tailed deer, red brockets and several bird species, including parrots, toucans and macaws. The quiet town of El Remate is on the eastern shore. On the western shore, San Andrés and San José offer a pleasant lakeside atmosphere and an excellent place to learn Spanish. Updated: Sep 24, 2009.

SAN ANDRÉS

San Andrés is a small town of 20,300 inhabitants on the north west side of Lake Petén Itza. The town was founded in 1820 and the name was given in honor of the apostle Saint Andrew. Eighty percent of the population work in agriculture, cultivating mostly rice, black beans and corn. Cattle farming also has an important place in the economy.

Getting To and Away

To reach San Andrés, get a minibus at the market in Santa Elena. Minibuses leave every 30 minutes between 5:30 a.m. and 4 p.m. and cost $1 for the 45-minute drive. Updated: Sep 24, 2009.

Things to See and Do

Nueva Juventud Ecological Park

Volunteer Petén runs an ecological park that travelers can visit for free. When you arrive in San Andrés, call them or go to the library close to the Municipalidad. Open every day from 7 a.m. til 6 p.m., the 60 hectare (148 ac) park has a well-maintained trail. The main purpose of the park is to teach the students of San Andrés about forest management, ecology and the flora and fauna of Guatemala. Tel: 502-5711-0040, URL: www.voluntcerpe-ten.com. Updated: Oct 12, 2009.

Studying Spanish

Eco-Escuela de Español

Most travelers come to San Andrés to learn Spanish or volunteer. Eco-Escuela de Español was created in 1996 in partnership with Conservation International and is run by fifty families. They use a percentage of their income to manage and protect a community reserve. It costs $150/week including the stay with a local family. Students can volunteer in community projects in environment and ecology. Tel: 502-5940-1235, E-mail: ecoescuelaespanol@gmail.com, URL: www.ecoescuelaespanol.org. Updated: Oct 12, 2009.

Volunteer Petén

The Nueva Juventud Spanish School offers Spanish classes for $120/week with volunteer activities such as reforestation projects, environmental education and conservation projects. Travelers can also come solely to volunteer with a minimum one month commitment. Tel: 502-5711-0040, E-mail: volunteerPetén@hotmail.com, URL: www.volunteerPetén.com. Updated: Oct 12, 2009.

Lodging

San Andrés, Guatemala is a remote town to the northwest of Lago de Petén Itzá. It is home to a couple of Spanish schools and a few lodging options, but not much else. You're better off looking for places in nearby Santa Elena. However, there is a really nice eco-lodge just a few kilometers outside of town. Updated: Jul 19, 2010.

Villa Benjamín

(ROOMS: $25-32) Villa Benjamín is the only proper restaurant and hotel in San Andrés. Built with old stones, this beautiful three-level hotel features a panoramic view of the lake and direct access to the water. It will please travelers looking for a romantic getaway from touristy places. The three rooms are tastefully decorated and have an amazing view ($25/person, $32/two people). The restaurant (meals $5-12) has an extensive menu serving fish, chicken, pastas, sandwiches and pizzas. Tel: 502-5926-9917/5521-0677. Updated: Oct 12, 2009.

Ni'tun Ecolodge

(ROOMS: $100-235) Located three kilometers (1.86 mi) east of San Andrés, the rustic Ni'tun Eco lodge ($100-235) is a luxurious option. Set on the lakeshore with comfortable cabins made of stone, sticks and mortar, it's a beautiful place to come and relax. All cabins have bathrooms and the rate includes breakfast. The owners run Monkey Eco Tours, which can take you to any remote place in Petén. Tel: 502-5201-0759, URL: www.nitun.com. Updated: Oct 14, 2009.

SAN JOSÉ

A few kilometers west of San Andrés, San José has one of the best beaches on the lake. The majority of its 2,000 inhabitants are descendants of the Maya from Chichen Itza. The town was founded in a place known as Ixtutz, which means "place populated with corozo trees," and was renamed San José in 1851. The economy is based on agriculture and tourism. San José is a nice place to relax on the beach away from the tourists.

Getting To and Away

Go to San Andrés and take a minibus from the market in Santa Elena. They leave every half-hour between 5:30 a.m.-4 p.m. It costs $1.50 for the one-hour drive. Updated: Sep 24, 2009.

Studying Spanish

Spanish School Bio-Itzá

The community-owned Escuela Bio-Itza is part of an association created to save the Itza culture and the language. They own the Reserve Bio-Itza, a 3,600-hectare (8,896 ac) biological corridor between the southern section of El Zotz and the southwestern part of the Tikal National Park. It's the first ethno-botanical reserve in the country. To study Spanish, it costs $150/week for 20 hours of class and accommodation with a local family in San José. Or you can study in the Bio-Itza reserve for $200/week including accommodation in a cabaña, meals and transportation from San José. The school can organize visits to the reserve for travelers for $15/day. Tel: 502-7928-8056, E-mail: escuelabioitza@hotmail.com. Updated: Sep 24, 2009.

Lodging

Hotel Bahía Taitza

(ROOMS: $45-80) Along the lakeshore you'll find the splendid hotel Bahia Taitza. Its eight beautifully decorated rooms have bathrooms, tile floors and balconies with direct views of the lake. Rates include transportation to and from the airport, Internet and a full breakfast. There is also a restaurant offering delicious meals and cocktails. Order some food and drinks and take in the sunset. Tel: 502-7928-8125, URL: www.taitza.com. Updated: Oct 14, 2009.

EL REMATE

El Remate is a small, laid-back village home to around 370 families on the eastern shore of Lago Petén Itza, located between Flores and Tikal. Travelers looking for a quiet environment surrounded by nature will most probably prefer it to Flores. The sunsets are superb and the color of the lake is turquoise blue in the morning. It's a good place to sample local Guatemalan culture, have a swim in the crystal clear water, sunbathe on a dock, rent a canoe or simply relax. El Remate is known for its wood carving: you can shop in the handicraft shop along the road. The town has many beautiful hotels with direct access to the lake and some very good restaurants. Updated: Jul 16, 2010.

Highlights

If you're staying at El Remate, you should visit the **Biotopo Cerro Cahui** on the north shore of the lake. You can do some horseback riding, a walking tour to the **Laguna Sal Petén** or rent a bicycle, a canoe or a kayak for a few hours. If you're here for a few days, many hotels offer treks and tours to the archeological sites of **Tikal**, **Yaxhá**, **Uaxactún** and **Ceibal**. Updated: Oct 22, 2009.

When to Go

If you're staying at El Remate, you should visit the Biotopo Cerro Cahui on the north shore of the Lake. El Remate is a small roadside settlement on the shores of a huge lake, about 40 kilometres closer to the Mayan temples of Tikal than Flores, the usual Tikal stopover. El Remate is a relaxing alternative. Updated: Feb 04, 2011.

Getting To and Away

Minibuses run from Santa Elena hourly between 5 a.m. and 1 p.m. for $2.50. A Taxi from the airport costs $20.

Getting Around

A minibus leaves El Remate for Tikal at 5:30 a.m., coming back from Tikal at 2 p.m. ($4 round trip). Alternatively, you can catch any regular buses passing through El Remate and going to Tikal. They charge $2.50. Central El Remate is small and walkable but if you're staying along the north road of the Lake you might want to rent a bike. Updated: Oct 22, 2009.

Safety

El Remate is known to be really safe but it's necessary to take the usual precautions.

THE PETÉN

Don't go out too late alone, don't accept drinks from strangers and it's always safer to walk in groups. Updated: Jul 16, 2010.

Services

MONEY

There are no banks, no post offices and no tourism office in El Remate. So you'd better get enough cash before going there. But if you're stuck, you can change your U.S. dollars and traveler's checks at La Casa de Don David at a good rate. Updated: Oct 22, 2009.

KEEPING IN TOUCH

There is an Internet shop just before the junction to go to Biotopo Cahui. They charge $1.50/hr. They are open from 10 a.m. til 5 p.m. but services are variable. Some hotels such as La Casa de Don David and Mon Ami offer free WiFi Internet access for guests. Updated: Oct 22, 2009.

MEDICAL

There are neither pharmacies nor doctors in El Remate. The closest are in Santa Elena and Flores. Updated: Oct 22, 2009.

LAUNDRY

There is no laundry in El Remate but most of the hotels offer laundry facilities to their guests. Ask at the reception. Updated: Jul 16, 2010.

SHOPPING

El Remate is well-known for the very high quality woodcarvings made by indigenous families. The variety is indescribable and can't be found anywhere else in Guatemala. There are numerous woodcarving shops along the road. Some of the largest and most intriguing carvings can be found at La Casa de Don David. Updated: Oct 22, 2009.

Things to See and Do

El Remate is a good starting point for exploring Tikal and other archeological sites such as Ixlu and Yaxhá. Other tours and activities available include the visit of Biotopo Cerro Cahui, birdwatching, horseback riding, kayaking and cycling. Updated: Oct 22, 2009.

Biotopo Cerro Cahui

(ADMISSION: $2.50) Two kilometers (1.2 mi) west of El Remate and along the shore of Lake Petén Itza, Biotopo Cerro Cahui is a rainforest reserve spanning over 600 hectares (1,483 ac). It is one of the most accessible wildlife reserves in Petén. The elevation ranges between 100-360 meters (328-1,180 ft), offering scenic hiking. The reserve is home to nearly 200 species of birds, including toucans, trogons, woodpeckers and parrots. Depending on the season, you might spot numerous spider monkeys, herons, hawks, squat rodents and ocellated turkeys (big birds resembling peacocks). There are two particular trails that are great for hiking. One is the trail of Los Ujuxtes. A 5 kilometers (3.1 mi) long trail that offers spectacular views of the lake. The other trail is Tzu'unte which leads to the Mirador Moreltii, nicknamed the "Crocodile Hill" because the cliffs look like a half-submerged crocodile. Maps and information are available at the entrance kiosk. Open every day 6 a.m.-6 p.m., the entrance fee costs $2.50 and includes the right to camp or sling your hammock under small thatch shelters. There are toilets, showers and a dock where you can swim. Daily 6 a.m.-6 p.m. Updated: Jul 05, 2010.

Ixlu

The turnoff for the road heading to Belize is known as "El Cruce." Just 200 kilometers (124 mi) off the road are the ruins of Ixlu on the shores of Laguna SalPetén. There are small mounds, trails and a few stones but little else to see. During the excavation, they found a Maya altar that you can now see at the central park in Flores. Ixlu is a good place to rest and enjoy some tranquil nature after a long drive. Updated: Jul 16, 2010.

Birdwatching

The best place to go birdwatching is Biotopo Cerro Cahui. It's best to go early in the morning when the birds start flying around. La Casa de Don David offers birdwatching tours with knowledgeable English speaking guides. A three to six hour tour costs between $40 and $75. Updated: Oct 22, 2009.

Horseback Riding

Many hotels can book you a five-hour horseback riding tour to Ixlu and Lagoon SalPetén for $20/person. Palomino Ranch hotel, on the road to the biotope, also offers horseback riding tours for $20/person and riding classes for $5/hour. Updated: Oct 22, 2009.

Kayaking

Renting a kayak or canoe to discover the lake is one of the most popular activities in El Remate. Any hotel can arrange it for you and rates are around $2-4/hour and $10/day. Ask at Casa Mobego and Casa Dona Tonita. Updated: Oct 22, 2009.

THE PETÉN

Mountain Biking

Various places rent bicycles for $2/3.50/4.50 for two/four/24 hours with a $30 deposit. The road that circles Lake Petén Itza is excellent for a mountain bike ride. You can also cycle to Biotopo Cerro Cahui or Ixlu. Updated: Jul 16, 2010.

Lodging

El Remate lies at the eastern tip of Lago Petén Itza and is the closest town to Tikal where you can find a decent hotel. You could pay higher prices for the few options just outside of the park, but since El Remate is just a 30 kilometer (18.64 mi) paved highway drive away, it's a better option. El Remate hotels are varied, but offer threadbare options for backpackers, including campsites, as well as a luxury Westin Hotel for about $125 a night. El Remate hostels are limited, but La Casa de Don David offers beautiful views of the lake and a nice ambiance for about $12 a night. Updated: Jul 16, 2010.

BUDGET

Hotel Sak Luk

(ROOMS: $2-13) A nice creative place with an awesome view over the lake, a the hotel is located 200 meters (656 ft) north of the main beach in El Remate. You can recognize the place by a little colored house in the form of a Maya face right next to the road. The hostel has camping, hammocks and private rooms with or without bathrooms. All rooms have mosquito nets, fans and lake views. There is a restaurant serving delicious Italian meals and vegetarian dishes. You can do your laundry and use the guest kitchen. Tel: 502-5494-5925, E-mail: tikalsakluk@hotmail.com. Updated: Jul 07, 2010.

Gringo Perdido Ecological Inn

(ROOMS: $4-80) Set right on the lakeshore within the boundaries of Biotopo Cerro Cahui, Gringo Perdido is one of the oldest jungle lodges in Guatemala. Splurge for a night in this offbeat paradise. The hotel offers a camping area, simple dorms and private bungalows with private bathrooms. All rooms have mosquito nets and fans. Rates include breakfast and a tasty four-course dinner. Biotopo Cerro Cahui. Tel: 502-2334-2305, URL: www.hotelgringoperdido.com. Updated: Oct 22, 2009.

Casa Mobego

(ROOMS: $5-8) On the road to the biotope, Casa Mobego is a popular place among budget travelers. They offer dorms in attractive two level, open walled thatched houses spread out over a hill. All beds have mosquito nets and bathrooms are shared. The main house is nicely decorated with curious sculptures and paintings. They serve breakfast ($5), snacks and sandwiches. Tel: 502-7909-6999. Updated: Jul 07, 2010.

Hotel Mon Ami

(ROOMS: $7-25) Close to Biotopo Cerro Cahui, Hotel Mon Ami offers a six-bed dorm and private rooms in rustic bungalows set in a jungle environment. All private rooms have bathrooms and fans. Rates include WiFi access. The garden is full of local plants and the hotel has a dock on the lake to go swimming. The friendly French owner is a character and known very well in Petén. He organizes his own trips to Tikal and other archeological sites. The restaurant offers some of the best food in El Remate with a mix of French and local dishes. Tel: 502-7928-8413, E-mail: hotelmonami@hotmail.com, URL: www.hotelmonami.com. Updated: Jul 07, 2010.

Hostal Hermano Pedro

(ROOMS: $9-27) Set in a two-level wood and stone house just off the main road, this charming hostel offers comfortable wooden bedrooms with high ceilings, hot-water bathrooms and fans. Rates include breakfast. The upstairs patio has hammocks and swinging chairs to relax after a long day. There is also a restaurant offering cheap breakfast, lunch and dinner. Tel: 502-2261-4181, E-mail: infotikal@hhpedro.com, URL: www.hhpedro.com. Updated: Jul 07, 2010.

Hotel Sun Breeze

(ROOMS: $10-13) Close to the lake shore and walking distance from several decent restaurants, this pleasant little hotel has clean rooms with mosquito nets and fans. Some have private cold-water bathrooms. The helpful staff can do your laundry or organize guide tours to Yaxhá or Tikal. Tel: 502-7928-8044. Updated: Oct 22, 2009.

Hotel Las Gardenias

(ROOMS: $12-24) On the main road to Tikal, Hotel Las Gardenias offers nine large and comfortable private rooms with bathrooms. Some have air-conditioning, others only fans. Rates include WiFi if you have your computer or a one-hour free session on the hotel's computer. They have a restaurant open 6 a.m.-9 p.m. serving local dishes. The friendly family owners can help you organize your trip and book any tours you might be interested in. They change U.S. dollars, traveler's checks

THE PETÉN

and Euros. Tel: 502-7928-8477, E-mail: ho-
telasgardenias@yahoo.com, URL: www.ho-
telasgardenias.com. Updated: Jul 07, 2010.

MID-RANGE

La Casa de Don David

(ROOMS: $19-26) At the junction with the
road going to Tikal, La Casa de Don David
will please travelers looking for comfort at
an affordable price. They offer fifteen private rooms all with bathrooms. Most have
air conditioning and verandas with a view
of the lake. Rates include a meal a day
(breakfast, lunch or dinner) and WiFi Internet access. There is an open-air octago-
nal hammock hut for resting and reading
after a long day of traveling. The friendly
owner is very knowledgeable about the
area and offers trips to Petén, Yaxhá and
other sites. The restaurant serves international cuisine daily 6 a.m.-9 p.m.. Tel:
502-7928-8469, E-mail: info@lacasad-
edondavid.com, URL: www.lacasadedon-
david.com. Updated: Jul 07, 2010.

Posada del Cerro

(ROOMS: $25-37) At the entrance of Bio-
topo Cerro Cahui, this wonderful little
retreat is right in front of the lake. It will
please travelers looking for luxury and tran-
quility. Wake up to the sound of the hurling
monkeys and enjoy the striking views of the
lake. They offer elegant and comfortable
rooms in stone and wood houses. All rooms
have bathrooms and fans. They also offer
two cozy apartments, with fully-equipped
kitchens, perfect for families or groups.
Rates include WiFi access and laundry.
The restaurant offers delicious traditional
meals all day long. Biotope Cerro Cahui.
Tel: 502-5376-8722, E-mail: mailto@
posadadelcerro.com, URL: www.posad-
adelcerro.com. Updated: Jul 07, 2010.

La Mansion del Pajaro Serpiente

(ROOMS: $40-80) Perched on a hillside
overlooking the lake and connected with
stone paths, the rooms are in modern stone
cabins with thatched roofs. Rooms are large
with great views of the lake and have private
bathrooms. Some have air conditioning,
others only fans. The grounds of the hotel
are beautiful, with a lovely collection of gardens. They have peacocks and giant iguanas. There is a swimming pool to cool off in
after a hot day, and an open-air restaurant
specializing in traditional dishes. Tel: 502-
7928-8498. Updated: Jul 07, 2010.

HIGH END

Maya ZacPetén Jungle Lodge

(ROOMS: $90-180) The hotel/jungle lodge
is located on the Peninsula Salpetén and is a
great place to relax. Its comfortable, if pricey, accommodations are located in private
bungalows, all of which have views of the
lake. This lodge has a restaurant, swimming
pool and hiking trails on its grounds. The
staff can also arrange tours of surrounding
areas like Tikal National Park and Yaxhá
National Park, located only 30 minutes
from the lodge. Peninsula Sal Petén. Tel:
502-7823-5843, E-mail: info@mayazacpe-
tenjunglelodge.com, URL: www.mayazacpe-
tenjunglelodge.com. Updated: May 10, 2010.

Camino Real Tikal

(ROOMS: $120-155) Inside Biotopo Cerro
Cahui, Camino Real Tikal is a 72-luxury room
complex with all the comfort you would expect from an international resort chain. Set
on a hill, the rooms are spacious and feature
contemporary and tasteful decor, as well as
a range of modern amenities. Every room
has a private balcony or porch with beautiful
lake views, bathroom, cable TV, mini bar and
a safety box. Ask for a room on the third floor
for the best views. There are two restaurants
and a lovely outdoor pool area. Down by the
water, there's a dock out into the lake, a sandy
beach area for swimming, and a wood-fired
sauna. The hotel offers a free shuttle to the
park and the airport. Biotopo Cerro Cahui.
Tel: 502-7926-0204, URL: www.camino-
real.com.gt. Updated: Jul 07, 2010.

La Lancha Resort

(ROOMS: $125-210) Farther west along the
lakeshore in the village of Jobompiche is the
latest addition to filmmaker Francis Ford Cop-
pola's hotel dynasty in the Maya world. La Lancha Resort is a deluxe jungle resort overlooking
the beautiful and unspoiled Lake Petén Itza.
The Main Lodge with its soaring thatch roof
and splendid views houses the restaurant, offering delicious local Guatemalan dishes. Enjoy
breakfast surrounded by a myriad of bird life including parrots and toucans. A family of howler
monkeys lives nearby and visits the Lodge every
night stimulating guests with their loud roars.
From the Main Lodge, winding paths lead down
the slopes to the secluded guest houses each
furnished with beautiful Guatemalan furniture
and fabrics. The Rainforest Casitas have a view
of the surrounding forest and partial view of the
lake, while the Lakeview Casitas offer a breathtaking panorama of the lake. A short walk takes

you down to the lake where guests may choose to swim in the cool pristine waters or go fishing with a knowledgeable guide. Lancha is the ideal choice for the perfect combination of relaxation, adventure, nature, culture and comfort. Village of Jobompiche. Tel: 502-7928-8331, URL: www.coppolaresorts.com. Updated: Jul 07, 2010.

Restaurants

There are a number of adequate places to eat in El Remate, from cheap local joints to expensive international restaurants. Most of the hotels have their own restaurants. Most of them can be found along the main road to Tikal and the road to Biotopo Cerro Cahui. Updated: Jul 16, 2010.

Mon Ami

(ENTREES: $2-8) Further along the road to the biotope, Mon Ami serves a mix of tasty French and Guatemalan dishes in a peaceful palm-thatched open air restaurant. Try the *carne al vino* with rice and tomato salad. Before or after your meal, you can refresh yourself in the blue water of the lake from their dock. Daily 8 a.m.-9 p.m. Road to the Biotope. Tel: 502-7928-8413, E-mail: hotelmonami@hotmail.com, URL: www.hotelmonami.com. Updated: Oct 22, 2009.

Restaurante Cahui

(ENTREES: $4-6) This popular restaurant overlooks the lake. People come to eat on their wooden open-air deck while enjoying the views. They have an extensive menu of cheap dishes and a large wine and beer list. Updated: Oct 22, 2009.

Restaurante Las Orquídeas

(ENTREES: $4-12) Next door to Casa de Dona Donita, Las Orquideas is a good Italian restaurant serving pizzas, pastas and sandwiches. The Italian owner/chef cooks delicious desserts you can't find anywhere else in El Remate. Try the homemade tiramisu. Daily Tuesday to Sunday 11 a.m.-10 p.m. Road to the Biotope. Tel: 502-5701-9022, E-mail: asorquideasremate@yahoo.com. Updated: Oct 22, 2009.

LAGUNA MACANCHÉ

The Macanché Lagoon is the smallest lake in the Petén, with a shoreline of only seven kilometers (4.35 mi). Its shore is home to a large, modern community, and, as a consequence of this large and growing settlement, most of the land surrounding the lake has been cleared for housing, farming and cattle ranching. Little of the original tropical forest remains in the basin.

Set on the bank of the lagoon, El Retiro Sanctuary Eco-Lodge ($20-30, Tel.: 502-5751-1876/5704-1300, URL: www.retiro-guatemala.com) is one of the best accommodation options in the area. The lodge is located in a private reserve some 2 kilometers (1.24 mi) north of the village of Macanche. The owners are committed to the preservation of nature and developing sustainable tourism, and they offer comfortable, thatched-roof bungalows with hot-water bathrooms and porches. Visitors can also camp on raised wooden platforms. If you don't have your own tent, you can rent one at the lodge. There is a bar and a dock for swimming in the turquoise lagoon. A serpentarium houses over twenty species of native snakes (including the deadly fer-de-lance) and the venomous beaded lizard, all in secure glass tanks.

On top of the hill, behind the property, lie the stone remains of ancient Maya residential complexes. Even more intriguing are the *chultuns*, holes carved into the ground rock with a narrow entrance on top capped with a circular stone. Their purpose remains unknown, but archeologists guess they were used either for storage or to conduct ceremonial and religious rites.

El Retiro is part of an extensive crocodile sanctuary. Visitors can participate in the crocodile-spotting night tours ($40). The lodge also offers boat tours on the lagoon ($30/person) and guided hikes through the jungle to remote lagoons and *cenotes* (limestone sinkholes).

Getting To and Away

Mananché is located seven kilometers (4.35 mi) east of Ixlu. Any bus heading to the Belize border can drop you at the village of Macanché. To get to the hotel, call ahead to get picked up because there are not many taxis in the village. Updated: Oct 01, 2009.

MELCHOR DE MENCOS

On the Belize-Guatemala border, this small town of 16,500 inhabitants is fairly pleasant as far as border towns go. There is little reason to stay here for the night but if you do do, there are two proper hotels. Right at the border and overlooking the Rio Mopan is the Rio Mopan Lodge ($20-70). Owned by a friendly Swiss-Spanish couple, the lodge is set on lush jungle grounds. They offer large, well-decorated private rooms, all with private bathrooms and balconies overlooking the river. The restaurant, open daily 7 a.m.-9 p.m., serves delicious Mediterranean meals. It's the perfect place to relax after a long trip while enjoying the beauty of Rio Molpan. The owners organize tours to remote archeological sites such as Holmul as well as water rafting, canoeing and tubing (Tel: 502-7926-5196, E-mail: info@tikaltravel.com). The other option is Hotel La Cabana ($40) in Barrio El Centro. They offer comfortable private rooms with hot-water bathrooms, air conditioning and cable TV. There is a swimming pool and a restaurant serving local and international dishes. To eat, there are a few snack and drink stands on the road to the border. The two restaurants at the hotels are the best option.

Getting To and Away

From Flores ($3.50, 2 hours, 100 km/62 mi), minibuses leave the terminal of Santa Elena every hour between 5 a.m. and 6 p.m. To Flores, minibuses leave the border every hour. On the Belize side, taxis run between the border and Benque Viejo del Carmen, where you can catch a bus for Belize City between 11 a.m. and 4 p.m. ($4, 3 hours) Most travelers take a shuttle from Flores directly to Belize City ($20). Updated: Apr 30, 2010.

Crossing into Belize

Crossing the border with Belize is very straightforward. You shouldn't pay any fees at the border for leaving Guatemala or entering Belize. Sometimes travelers have been asked to pay $1.50 to leave or enter Guatemala, but this is illegal. You can try to ask for a receipt, which might work to dissuade potential bribe-seekers. When leaving Belize by land, you'll have to pay $18.75/BZ$37.50. There are money changers at the border with whom you can exchange enough money for immediate needs. The border is always open. Updated: Apr 30, 2010.

TIKAL

Once home to 100,000 Maya, Tikal was one of the most important cities in the Maya empire. It was abandoned when the empire collapsed and was re-discovered relatively recently. Today it is one of the most important Maya sites, with over 4,000 structures, the oldest of which date back to around 800 BC. The most important structures are the imposing Temple of the Giant Jaguar, which stands over 51 meters (170 ft) tall and was once the tomb of a high priest. Across the immense square from this structure is the Temple of Masks, which is an impressive 42 meters (139 ft) tall.

Tikal is also known for its impressive stelae, or intricately carved standing stones. There are over two hundred of them at the site, the oldest of which has been dated to 292 BC. There is a museum at the site, which features ceramics, jade and wood carvings and other relics from the various digs that have taken place over the years at Tikal.

An added boon for the traveler are the natural surroundings. The archeological site at Tikal is part of a large national park, which is home to spider and howler monkeys, parrots, toucans, macaws, and other varied and spectacular wildlife. In fact, it is the only place on earth declared by UNESCO to be both a world culture and nature heritage site. Updated: Oct 02, 2009.

History

TIKAL'S FOUNDING

Around 700 BC, the first settlers arrived in the vicinity of Tikal, drawn by the abundance of flint and water in the area. Tikal was built on a series of low hills surrounded by *bajos* (low swampy areas) and several water holes. Flint was used to make spearheads and knives for hunting and was also a valuable trade resource. The first village was small and the early Mayas built timber-framed houses with thatched roofs and earthen floors. During this formative period, there was little class distinction and the society remained fairly homogeneous.

TIKAL IN THE EARLY CLASSIC PERIOD

During the next five hundred years, the Maya communities gradually expanded, forming social classes and building ceremonial structures. Little archeological remains were found to shed light on this pre-Classic period. By around 200 BC, the first temples at the North Acropolis had been built. Around 100 BC, the Gran Plaza was as impressive as any in the Late Classic era. By then, Tikal was a major ceremonial and commercial hub.

TIKAL IN THE CLASSIC PERIOD

The Classic period saw Tikal reaching its zenith as it grew into a significant and populous religious center. Society was stratified into distinct classes, with castes like priests, nobles, slaves and farmers. Architecture advanced in aesthetic intricacy and sophistication, enhancing the majesty of the ceremonial grounds. This vital era also saw the development of an advanced system of hieroglyphics writing, the Maya calendar, and monumental art. At a time when Europeans insisted that the Earth was flat, the Mayas had built their temples with foundations tangential to the Earth, proving their awareness of the planet's spherical curvature.

In many respects, the Maya had become extremely advanced for their time. Around AD 230, King Yax Moch Xoc founded the ruling dynasty and became the first ruler of the kingdom. Tikal was the first metropolitan area to adopt an Emblem Glyph, a Maya coat-of-arms representation. The ruler exercised control over the people and forced them to worship him as a deity. Human sacrifices and ritualized bloodletting became common and more elaborated. By AD 350, during the ruling of King Great Jaguar Paw, warring and conflict between Tikal and neighboring states had intensified. By forming alliance with Teotihuacán, Tikal emulated the Central Mexican city-state's method of warfare by attacking its enemies with spears from above. This allowed Tikal to conquer its military and political rival, Uaxactún, thereby becoming the dominant kingdom.

TIKAL IN THE LATE CLASSIC PERIOD
The Late Classic era, around 550 AD, saw Tikal's population swell to its height of 100,000 people. Tikal's military was powerful and won many battles with neighboring Maya states. Its only defeat was to Caracol (present-day southwestern Belize) in 562 AD. Adopting Tikal's brutal warfare method, Caracol sacrificed Tikal's ruler, and continued to control Tikal for another century.

Around 700 AD, King Ah-Cacau (Lord Chocolate) reclaimed Tikal from Caracol. Tikal once again thrived as the most influential Maya city-state. It was during Lord Chocolate's reign that most of the surviving temples took shape. His successors completed his ambitious construction projects. The ceremonial buildings then were gloriously painted in rich colors (especially red), and finished with shiny smooth stucco.

Tikal's second shot at revival only lasted two centuries. By 900 AD, Tikal's power had declined. The pressure of overpopulation, and the environmental deterioration resulting from the constant warring, had caused a great strain on Tikal's society. Experts have concluded that such strain led to its gradual downfall.

ABANDONMENT AND DISCOVERY
When Tikal was abandoned, however, the process was not gradual, but quite abrupt. Evidence shows that between 1200 and 1530, the Itzáes, who occupied Tayasal (modern-day Flores), were the only ones aware of Tikal. The Guatemalan government ordered the first expedition to the site in 1848, headed by Modesto Méndez and Ambrosio Tut. Previous discoveries of Tikal dated back to the Spanish colonization period, when missionary friars stumbled upon the ruins. English archeologist Alfred Maudslay made many pioneering discoveries at the site after his arrival in 1881. His studies were continued by other important scientists like Teobert Maler and Alfred Tozzers; the causeways within the national park are named after these men. Tikal National Park was declared a UNESCO World Heritage site in 1979. Updated: Nov 24, 2009

When to Go
The tropical climate of Tikal ensures hot and humid weather all year round. The best time to visit is during the dry season, from December to February, when comfortable temperatures prevail. With a year round average temperature of 26°C (79°F), dehydration is common in such powerful heat. Bring plenty of water, though there are also drink stalls throughout the park. The Tikal National Park is located within the rainforest where it rains for at least part of the day during most of the year. Be sure to bring a raincoat to protect you from the unpredictable downpours. Christmas and New Year's are the peak periods for tourism here, therefore make reservations in advance if you want to visit at that time. Updated: Sep 30, 2009.

Getting To and Away

GETTING TO TIKAL FROM FLORES, SANTA ELENA AND EL REMATE
Tikal is easily accessible from Flores, where most travelers are based. Buses from Flores to Tikal leave hourly, although you should always check with the visitors' center for updated schedules. To get to Tikal from Flores, the fastest and most straightforward way might be on a shuttle bus (1.5 hours) that leaves hourly, picking you up straight from your hotel. The first bus to Tikal leaves at 5 a.m. and subsequent buses run hourly until 10 a.m, while returning buses leave from Tikal to Flores leave from noon to 6 p.m. You can reserve these tickets one hour in advance from any hotel or tour operator.

Tickets cost $7, the same for both one-way and return tickets. When returning in the late afternoon, be prepared for a long wait (especially during low season) as buses may not even arrive without sufficient passengers. Colectivos (buses) to Tikal leave from the main bus terminal in Santa Elena, but the whole journey can take up to 2.5 hours as it stops in each community along the way. Each way costs $2.50.

GETTING TO TIKAL FROM EL REMATE

From El Remate, the Tikal-bound shuttle bus leaves at 5:30 a.m., returning at 2 p.m. and costs $3.75 each way. Alternatively, you can also catch the hourly buses from Flores and pay the same price. Any hotel in El Remate can make reservations for you.

GETTING TO TIKAL BY TAXI AND TOUR

Tour operators also organize guided group tours to Tikal that usually leave at 4:30 a.m. and last for four hours. These tours cost $18.50 including two-way transport and a bilingual guide, but they only bring you to the major ruins. The entrance fee is not included.

A private taxi can take you directly from Flores to Tikal for $20 each way. Inquire at La Posada de Don Juan, or directly at the bus terminal in Santa Elena.

GETTING TO THE REST OF GUATEMALA AND BELIZE FROM TIKAL

To head to other regions in Guatemala, you can easily find public transport services and shuttle buses leaving from Flores and Santa Elena. You can also catch a domestic flight from the airport in Flores to Guatemala City. The frontier with Belize is only 100 kilometers (62 mi) east of Tikal. To get there on public transport, stop at Puente Ixlú and catch a microbus eastwards. Alternatively, a taxi from Tikal to the border costs $50. Updated: Sep 30, 2009.

Safety

Since the introduction of the tourist police and security guards within the temple grounds, crime in Tikal has been relatively low. You should still exercise caution, especially on remote paths, and avoid carrying valuables with you. Incidents of robbery and rape have been reported around the Temple of Inscriptions (Temple VI), so be sure to go in a group or with a guide. Check with the visitors' center beforehand to see if there are any specific areas to avoid. Updated: Sep 30, 2009.

Things to See and Do

Sunrise Tour of Tikal

This tour begins at the ugly hour of 4:30 a.m. and the guide leads you by flashlight (bring your own) past a few interesting spots for information and up to Temple IV, which you climb in the early dawn with the stars still shining above. You then sit there for around two hours while the mists rise and the sun comes up. The guide offers little in the way of stimulation during this wait.

If the sunrise is good, it is worth it, but much of the time it is simply mist rising and it looks like an overcast dawn. You may be better off taking an early day tour. There is a small walk after sunrise detailing information on several areas and it depends significantly on the guide you have as to how much you will get out of it. Updated: Nov 16, 2006.

Sunset Tour of Tikal

The main reason to take this tour is to stay in the park until sunset, so don't expect to be overloaded by information from your guide. Beginning at either the car park or the site of Perdido del Mundo (Lost World), you climb the lofty pyramid for a great view over Tikal's towers and the surrounding jungle.

Since Temple I is closed for climbing, this is the best spot to watch the sun go down to the left of Temple IV. The guide then steers you to Temple II to climb and look at the moonlit Temple I then leads you out by flashlight. This is basically a surcharge for sunset masquerading as a tour, but it is the only way to see it. Updated: Nov 16, 2006.

Gran Plaza

The heart of the ancient Maya civilization lies in this plaza, the focal point of the king's realm. Temple I, also known as the Pyramid of the Giant Jaguar, faces west toward the setting sun, which was believed to be the gateway to the underworld. Built above the tomb of King Ah-Cacau by his son after succeeding his throne in 734 AD, this temple was dedicated to the king himself. His tomb was richly adorned with jade objects, pearl and stingray spines, which were extravagant items for the Mayas. It is prohibited to climb the stairs of the 44 meter (145 ft) temple, as fatal cases of falling have been reported here. You can still climb Temple II though, and the views of the plaza from its roof comb are equally inspiring. Temple II is given the name 'Pyramid of the Masks' due to the monstrous faces that flank the steep stairs. Across the field from Temple I, it faces the rising sun. The 38 meter (125 ft)-high temple was dedicated to the king's wife, known among the Mayas as the Queen of the Sun. Acrópolis del Norte is a complex of pyramids and palaces, under which tunnels and passageways display colossal masks and ceramics that the elites of Tikal used in their daily lives. An area where the upper-class civilians resided, this complex is of great significance, especially since more than 100 structures dating back to 400 BC have been uncovered here. Updated: Oct 27, 2009.

Acrópolis Central
This maze of residential palaces and small temples is found on the south side of Gran Plaza. Believed to be where the royal family and their relatives lived, some chambers still have remnants of low platforms which served as beds. The tiny rooms are believed to be sacred ritual sites with graffiti illustrating this. Out of the 45 buildings in the complex, the Maler Palace was used by one of the pioneering archeologists, Teobert Maler, as his residence between 1895 and 1904. You can still see his signature on the door jambs of the main entrance. Updated: Sep 30, 2009.

Plaza Oeste
North of Temple II is Plaza Oeste where a considerable late-Classic temple is buried under the earth. The entire area is yet to be restored, allowing you to see it through the eyes of the first explorers who had found the ancient city. At the southern corner of the plaza, the crumbling rocks of Temple III can be seen peeking through layers of roots and vegetation. Updated: Sep 30, 2009.

Acrópolis del Sur and Templo V
South of Gran Plaza is Acrópolis del Sur, which is a massive area yet to be restored. This two-hectare (5 ac) mass of stonework is still covered by vines and trees. The palaces atop the masonry date back to the late-Classic period. Beside the acropolis stands the majestic Templo V, one of the tallest pyramids in Tikal standing at 58 meters (190 ft). Built around 700 AD and abandoned in 900 AD, excavations were only started in 1991. A civil war was believed to have taken place in the vicinity as remnants of buildings destroyed by the Mayans were uncovered here. Inside the temple, excavators also found the human remains of an 18-23 year old individual who was believed to have been sacrificed, thereby blessing the construction of this temple. It is also believed to be a royal tomb of the ruler, Kinich Wayan, who had

sponsored its construction. Climb the steep wooden stairway for an unobstructed view of the ancient grounds. Updated: Sep 30, 2009.

Plaza de los Siete Templos
Next to the Acrópolis del Sur is the complex comprised of seven little temples built in a row. Although the temples were assembled during the late Classic period, there are other structures in the complex dating back to the pre-Classic times. On the north end of the complex, archeologists had an intriguing find, a triple ball court. This was where they played the Mesoamerican ballgame, a ritual sport popular among the pre-Columbian people for over 3,000 years. Updated: Oct 27, 2009.

El Mundo Perdido (The Lost World)
This sizable complex consists of 38 structures oriented in a traditional Maya pattern serving as an astronomy observatory. The ancient Maya observed solstices, equinoxes and planetary cycles with clever formations of these structures. The 30-meter (90 ft) high Great Pyramid, assembled around 200 AD in the center of the complex, functioned as an important ceremonial center for Tikal. Unlike the rest of Tikal, El Mundo Perdido contains structures from different time periods. Beneath the surface of the Great Pyramid lie four other pyramids, one of which dates back to 700 BC, making it the oldest structure in Tikal. Updated: Sep 30, 2009.

Templo IV and Complejo N
The largest pyramid at Tikal, Templo IV is the second tallest surviving Maya structure, reaching a height of 65 meters (213 ft). The only taller Maya pyramid is located at the ruins of El Mirador. Famed for the splendid panoramic view from the top of the temple, this is where you come to see the postcard-perfect image of the surrounding ruins peaking through the forest canopy. At sunrise, watch the sun's first golden rays dispel the early-morning mist as the ruins seemingly rise from the woods. Built in 740 AD by King Ah-Cacau's son, Yik'in Chaan K'awil, archeologists believe that his tomb is buried under the pyramid. Also known as the Temple of the Double-headed Serpent, the temple's doorway was ornamented with a wooden lintel painted with an image of the deadly snake. The original lintel was taken by Dr. Gustav Bernoulli of Switzerland in 1885 and can be found in the Völderkunde Museum in Basel. Complex N is a model of the Twin Pyramid formation, a special architectural style developed at Tikal. These

THE PETÉN

complexes were built to commemorate the ending of a katun, a period of 20 years in the Maya calendar. Updated: Sep 30, 2009.

Templo de las Inscripciones (Templo VI)

Only discovered in 1951, this temple is located 1.2 km (0.75 mi) southeast of Gran Plaza. Unlike Copán and several other Maya sites, most Tikal temples bear comparatively few inscriptions, but this temple is an exception. The 55 meter (180 ft)-high pyramid took shape in 766 AD, under the command of Yik'in Chaan K'awil. It was completed by the final ruler of Tikal, King Chi'taam (also known as Yaxkin Caan Chac), who ascended his throne. An impressive display of hieroglyphics can be found at the rear central panel of the 12 meter (40 ft)-high roof comb. The sides and cornice also have writings. Standing before the temple is a stela illustrating Yik'in Chaan K'awil's ascension to his father's throne. Updated: Oct 27, 2009.

Northern Complexes

These complexes are found one kilometer (0.62 ft) away from the Gran Plaza via the isolated Maudslay Causeway. Each are late-Classic twin pyramid complexes that are erected to honor the end of a katun, or 7,200 days on the Maya calendar. These complexes are composed of two identical pyramids on the east and west sides of the plaza. In the north lies a roofless chamber containing a portrait of the ruler, while in the south is a palace with nine doors, associated with the nine levels of the underworld. Complexes P and M are found at the far end of Tikal. A huge carved stela lies nearby. Clearly depicting the capture of a foreign ruler by Tikal's King Yik'in Chaan K'awil, the stela dates back to December 8th 748 AD. Complex Q is found 300 meters (985 ft) south, and is mostly restored, giving a clearer picture of its original exterior. Note that tour groups seldom visit this area, but more wildlife can also be spotted here. Frequent visitors include the keel-billed toucan and collared araçari. Updated: Oct 27, 2009.

Museum Lítico

The bigger of the two museums in Tikal, Museum Lítico, houses the important stelae excavated from within the ancient temples. It displays imposing carved rocks with interpretations of what the illustrations mean. Explanations of the Maya hieroglyphics also give an interesting insight into their literary world. Photographs taken during each step of the discovery by Alfred Mausdlay and Teobert Maler in the 19th century are worth a look. Located inside the visitors' center, you can easily take an hour to explore this museum when the sun is the strongest. No photos are allowed in the museum. Beside the museum, there is a big 3D model of how Tikal would have looked around 800 AD. Monday-Friday 8 a.m.-4:30 p.m., Saturday-Sunday 8 a.m.-4 p.m. Updated: Sep 30, 2009.

Museo Tikal/Museo Cerámico

Situated right behind the park ticket stand, the entrance of Museum Cerámico is flanked by beautiful orchids and thick plants. It has more exhibits of valuable items discovered in the temple's tombs than Museum Lítico. Ceramics, jade, inscribed bones and shells found buried in tombs are exceptionally exquisite and were deemed as highly valuable objects by the Maya. Also found here are precious items buried in the tomb of King Ah-Cacau under Temple I. Photography is not allowed. Monday-Friday 8 a.m.-4:30 p.m., Saturday-Sunday 8 a.m.-4 p.m. Updated: Oct 27, 2009.

Birdwatching

Tikal is an outstanding place to watch birds of prey. Thanks to its protected status, it attracts wildlife in abundance. Its dense tropical vegetation and sultry weather provide an excellent habitat for many of these creatures. There are 300 species of migratory and endemic birds found in Tikal and many can be seen especially in the early morning and at dusk. Stay in the park until 8 p.m. to catch some nocturnal wildlife in action—check with the guards in advance. Grab your binoculars and tread softly through the jungle, even amateurs will be able to spot something. The following areas present excellent birdwatching opportunities:

Temple IV—The ornate hawk-eagle, American kestrel and red-crowned ant-tanager can be admired from the temple's roof comb, usually just before the rain starts.
Temple of the Inscriptions—During the migration season, you can see hundreds of swallow-tailed kite flying over the ruins. Colorful ocellated turkeys are commonly spotted near the ruins as well.
Northern Complexes—The collared araçari and the stunning keel-billed toucan can feed on the fruits of the guarumo palms close to the temples.
Gran Plaza—From the back of Temple II, you can often observe the emerald toucanet and golden-fronted woodpeckers.
El Mundo Perdido—The road to this complex is a habitat of the mealy parrot.
Reservoir near the entrance—Three

species of kingfisher, the blue ground dove, and blue herons can be seen in this area. Updated: Oct 27, 2009.

Lodging

Hotels in Tikal are hard to come by; only three exist in close proximity to the ruins. The closest town to Tikal, El Remate (30 km/19 mi), has a much wider range of options. However, if you're willing to pay for an overpriced room (or plot of land for camping) in order to have convenient access to the ruins, there are a couple of possibilities. The nicest option is the Hotel Tikal Inn, replete with quaint bungalows and a pool. The best value may be the Jungle Lodge, which also offers bungalows and hammocks, but is a bit more cramped. Tikal hostels, unfortunately, do not exist, but the closest thing to it is camping near Tikal. At the Jaguar Inn, you can rent a campsite for about $4 and a tent for another $7, or fork over $23 to stay in a bungalow (just be warned, electricity ends at 9 p.m.). Across from the Jaguar Inn is Camping Tikal, a bare minimum campsite with easy access to Tikal. To rent a plot of land on the mowed lawn (really, that's all it is!) is $3 a night, so if you have gear and we're planning on camping out already it's the best budget option near Tikal. Updated: Jun 30, 2010.

Camping Tikal

(CAMPING: $3) This simply offers a space in a nicely mowed field and is a good option if you have a tent and want to save your money. It is just across the way from the Jaguar Inn but is a much bigger area and is often occupied in part by tour groups. There is an eatery nearby.

Jaguar Inn

(ROOMS: $22.50-40) This country-style lodge might be the cheapest in Tikal, but its prices are not justified by the basic standards. With a quaint tranquil setting among the forest, it is still a comfortable place to get a good night's sleep after exploring the temples. You can also camp for $8.70 per person, with picnic tables and clean bathrooms available in the inn. Duplex bungalows with hammocks on the porch are modern and cozy. Electricity ends at 9 p.m., after which only lights and fans can be used. Internet is available at a hefty price of $5 an hour. It is located just five minutes from the park's entrance. Be sure to reserve in advance during the Christmas season. Updated: Oct 02, 2009.

Hotel Tikal Inn

(ROOMS: $37.50-69) An old-fashioned vintage lodge located beside the Jaguar Inn, this hotel can be a good value for families despite the high prices. There are two double beds in every room, so a family of four can easily split the cost of the room. A large swimming pool sits in the center of the establishment, surrounded by thatch-roofed *cabañas*. The bungalows (*cabañas*) cost $30 more than the rooms. You can also choose to include breakfast and dinner, with an extra charge of $40 per day. For dinner, guests can choose from BBQ steak, fish, chicken and vegetarian food. Electricity stops at 10 p.m. Tikal National Park. Tel: 502-7861-1939, Fax: 502-7861-2445, E-mail: tikalinn@yahoo.com, URL: www.tikalinn.com. Updated: Oct 02, 2009.

Jungle Lodge

(ROOMS: $40-69) The only lodge with standards and facilities that fit the price, Jungle Lodge makes an excellent choice for travelers seeking comfort and proximity to nature and the ruins. This lodge is luxuriously fitted with a gorgeous swimming pool, a restaurant/bar and self-contained bungalows on the spacious hotel grounds. Some rooms are equipped with mosquito nets, creating a dreamy setting. The best part of all: wildlife is abundant at the entrance and throughout the jungle setting of the lodge. Don't forget to look out for colorful keel-billed toucans in the trees! Note that the lodge is closed in the month of September (low season). Contact the hotel before your arrival. Tel: 502-2477-0570, E-mail: reservaciones@junglelodgetikal.com, URL: www.junglelodgetikal.com. Updated: Sep 30, 2009.

Restaurants

Jaguar Inn Restaurant

(ENTREES: $4.50-7.50) This place is a surprisingly reasonable place to dine considering the décor and ambiance. It is much nicer than the more rustic restaurants down the road but matches them for price. If you are looking for a cheap but tasty meal, then a burger and fries will do the trick. If you want a bit more, there is a menu to cater to all tastes. It is associated with the Jaguar Inn hotel. Tel: 502-7926-0002, E-mail: contacto@jaguartikal.com. Updated: Nov 21, 2006.

Comedor Ixim Kúa

(ENTREES: $5-7.50) Across the road from Museo Lítico, this is one of many affordable dining options lining the main road to Flores. From cheap sandwiches ($3-4) to typical main courses ($5-7.5), there is something to fill up your tummy whether you are a meat-eater or salad-lover. Offering great value with huge portions and low prices, you sure can't get a better deal in this tourist-laden area. Interestingly, the tables are made out of tree trunks, while its shady interior provides a relief from the blazing sun. Beer and fruit juices are also a bonus here. Updated: Sep 30, 2009.

Restaurant El Mesón !

As the only restaurant within the temple grounds, El Mesón is just a few minutes' walk from Complex Q, along the turnoff road toward Uaxactún. It has to be the finest dining option in Tikal, with first-class services, exquisite food presentation, and even a professional chef working at the grill. The daily lunch menu costs $10, including a soup, main course, coffee and dessert. Choose from BBQ steak, chicken and fish (from nearby Lake Petén Itza). A perfect way to reward yourself after a full day of trudging through the forests! Next to the Northern Complexes. Updated: Oct 27, 2009.

El Muelle

(ENTREES: $5-10) Along the road to Tikal, El Muelle serves meat dishes, lake fish, pastas, vegetarian dishes and an assortment of desserts. Enjoy the great views of the lake in the pleasant atmosphere and plunge into the turquoise water while waiting for your food. There is a small gift shop selling books and wood carvings. Daily 11 a.m.-9 p.m. Tel: 502-5514-9785. Updated: Oct 22, 2009.

THE MAYA BIOSPHERE RESERVE

The Maya Biosphere Reserve is located in the north of Guatemala, on the border with Mexico and Belize. With an area of 1.5 million hectares (3.7 million ac), it represents 20 percent of the national territory and hosts the largest remaining tropical forest in Mesoamerica. It is part of the UNESCO world biosphere reserve network, and recognized as the most important conservation area in Central America.

The Reserve is separated into three zones: the nucleus zone (protected for investigation, conservation and protection, and with only low-impact ecotourism allowed); a multi-use zone (which allows for the extraction of resources through approved plans); and, the buffer zone (in which economic activities are permitted within a framework of environmental protection). The reserve is relatively flat and the

temperatures range from 26-35°C (79-95°F), with frequent rain. The area has an abundance of species of flora and fauna, including more than 3,000 species of plants, 327 species of reptiles and amphibians, as well as 220 species of fish. In the Reserve, there are 73 known pre-Columbian archeological sites which include the Serria del Lacandon, Tikal, El Mirador, Dos Laguna, Río Azul, El Zotz, Cerro Cahui and San Miguel La Palotada.

The Maya Biosphere Reserve has the potential to spur sustainable development in Petén but only if the economic activities are compatible with both environmental preservation and development. Presently, that is not the case and the reserve is in danger because of deforestation. Deforestation has affected more than 37% of the original forest especially in the Buffer Zone. Illegal logging is the biggest culprit, with local communities exploiting the supply of wood. The government plans for the reserve are not clear but they include community concessions as well as permits for the wood and oils industries. Updated: Oct 01, 2009.

UAXACTÚN

Located 23 kilometers (14.3 mi) north of Tikal, Uaxactún (pronounced wha-shahk-toon) is another Maya ceremonial center and is believed to be the oldest astrological observatory yet discovered in the Maya world. The name means "height stones" as a reference to a stone dating of the 8th baktun in the Maya calendar. It is believed that Uaxactún was built at the same time as Tikal, at the end of the pre-Classic Period. Grand Jaguar, the monarch of Tikal who governed for 62 years between 317 and 379 AD, kept Uaxactún under his power.

The town was abandoned in the 10th Century and was discovered in 1916 by the American archeologist Sylvanus Morley. In the late 70s a road was opened to get to Tikal and in 1982 the site was included in Tikal's protected area. The only access is an unpaved road through the jungle, only approachable by 4WD vehicle. Open daily 6 a.m.-6 p.m., the entrance is free if you have been to Tikal before. If not you have to pay the $2 park entrance.

Uaxactún village lies alongside an abandoned airstrip. Villagers live off the collection of chicle (natural gum used for chewing gum), pimienta (spices) and xate (leaves of palm trees) in the surrounding forest.

There are only two hotels where visitors can spend the night. Campamento El Chiclero

($3-17), on the north side of the airstrip, has ten small, basic rooms, with mosquito-netted ceilings and windows. You also can camp or string a hammock for $3. They have the best restaurant in town with large portions of good, affordable food ($6 for a soup and main course), and a small museum with local artifacts. The friendly owner can arrange trips to more remote sites such as El Zotz, Río Azul, Nakbé, La Muralla and El Miradot (Tel: 502-7926-1095).

Aldana's lodge ($2.50-4), just off the street leading to group A and B, is the cheapest option. You can camp or sleep in a simple thatched-roof cabaña. The owner can arrange trips to more remote sites such as El Zotz, Río Azul, Nakbé, La Muralla and El Mirador. You can eat in one of three comedores in town: comedor Uaxactún, comedor la Bendicion and comedor Imperial. They all serve cheap local food.

Getting To and Away

There is only one bus going to Uaxactún: it usually leaves Santa Elena terminal at 1 p.m. and stops in Tikal around 3 p.m. The schedule can change, and the bus sometimes arrives in Tikal around 5 p.m. and in Uaxactún as late as 6:30 p.m. The return bus to Santa Elena leaves at 6 a.m. If you have a 4WD, you can go on your own. The last chance to fill your tank is at Puente Ixly, south of El Remate. You can also travel with a one day organized tour from Flores or Tikal. It costs around $60 per person for one to four people. Updated: Apr 30, 2010.

Things to See and Do

The Ruins

Uaxactún's importance as a ceremonial and astronomical site is reflected in its ruins. The most impressive set of ruins is called Group E and is a 15 minute walk south of the airstrip. The structures E1, E2 and E3 are aligned north-south and form an astronomical observatory, the first round observatory of the Maya world. From an observation point on a nearby pyramid, Structure E-VII-B, the Maya could watch the sun rising behind these buildings and identify the winter and summer solstices as well as the vernal and autumnal equinoxes. The foundation dates to about 2000 BC. Structure E-VII-B is a truncated pyramid with stairs and four sides that are flanked by huge masks representing jaguars, turtles, eagles, parrots and other animals sacred to them. There is also an impressive stela

on the eastern stairway carved on four sides which is the mark of the observation point.

About 20 minutes to the northwest, the Grupo B and Grupo A ruins are where you'll find the earliest Maya arch and the main pyramid. Early excavations destroyed many of the temples, which are now in the process of being reconstructed. Daily 6 a.m. .-6 p.m. Updated: Apr 30, 2010.

Biotopo El Zotz-San Miguel La Palotada

Completely un-restored and barely excavated, El Zotz is a Maya archeological site, located 30 kilometers (19 mi) west of Tikal. An important Classical Maya city, El Zotz, was never ruled by Tikal despite its proximity. There are inscriptions at the site which point to a connection with El Perú in the north. El Zotz earned its name from the large number of bats living within the site's cliffs. Each night around sunset, tens of thousands of bats exit the caves en masse creating a spectacular sight. The site is part of San Miguel La Palotadad National Park, on the border with the Tikal Park. The ruins are divided into four main groups: the north, the central, the south and El Diablo, which is the highest temple and has views of the Tikal ruins. The monumental architecture includes 49 large structures, including four pyramids, several palaces, a ball court and four chultuns, probably used as water reservoirs. The last mention of this site is in the context of a conquest war against Naranjo in 744 AD. To get to El Zotz, it is best to organize your trip with a tour agency. It can be combined with Tikal or you can visit just El Zotz by making arrangements in Uaxactún. Updated: May 03, 2010.

YAXHÁ

The archeological site Yaxhá is inside the Yaxhá-Nakum-Naranjo National Park. The park is part of the larger Maya Biosphere and covers an area of 37,160 hectares (91, 824 ac), bordered on the west by the Tikal National Park, to the north by the Biological corridor Tikal-Mirador-Río Azul, and to the east and south by the Zone of Multiple uses (operation, use and extraction of resources through approved plans). The site is 11 kilometers (6.8 mi) north of Puente de Ixlú–Melchor de Menchos road and is built on a hill overlooking Lake Yaxhá and Lake Sacnab. The entrance fee is $10 per person and the park is open between 6 a.m. and 6 p.m. You can camp for free but you need to bring your own food. You can also stay at El Campamento Ecologico El Sombrero ($20-40, Tel: 502-7861-1687) on the southern shore. There are good-sized bungalows with mosquito nets facing the lake, and the restaurant serves delicious Guatemalan dishes. Tours by boat can be organized to Topoxté ($20 up to 4 persons, $26 for more people), or by 4x4 to Nakum. Updated: Sep 24, 2009.

Getting To and Away

To get to Yaxhá, go with an organized tour from Flores or El Remate. The other option is to take the colectivo leaving Flores at 7 a.m. and returning around 3 p.m. ($20/person round-trip). Any tour operator in Flores can book it for you. If you want to do it independently, take a bus or minibus going to Melchor de Mencos and get out at the Yaxhá turnoff. If you're lucky you will find a car to take you the last 11 kilometers (87 mi), otherwise you will have to walk. Updated: Sep 24, 2009.

Crossing into Mexico
VIA BETHEL, LA TÉCNICA AND FRONTERA COROZAL

The only route with regular public transportation into Mexico is via Bethel or La Técnica on the Guatemalan side and Frontera Corozal on the Mexican bank of the Río Usumacinta. From Santa Elena, travelers can catch the bus to Bethel ($4, 4 hr). Fuente del Norte departs at 6 a.m. and Pinita at 5 a.m., 8 a.m., noon and 1 p.m. Return buses are at 4 p.m. on Fuente del Norte and 5 a.m., noon and 2 p.m. for Pinita. Travelers can also take the bus to La Tecnica from Santa Elena ($6, 5 hr, 140 km/87 mi). Pinita leaves Santa Elena at 5 a.m. and 1 p.m., returning from La Técnica at 4 a.m. and 11 a.m. Guatemala immigration is in Bethel, so buses to La Técnica will stop there and wait for you to do the formalities. Boats crossing from Bethel charge $7 per person for the 30-minute ride, but they charge only $0.70 per person for the crossing at La Técnica. It's cheaper to go to La Técnica, but it takes longer.

You shouldn't pay any fees at the border for leaving Guatemala and entering Mexico. Sometime travelers have been asked to pay $1.50 to leave or enter Guatemala, but this is illegal. You can try to ask for a receipt; sometimes it works to dissuade the collection of the border bribe. You will have to pay a $20 fee when leaving Mexico by land. If you need to spend the night in Bethel, stay at the community-run Posada Maya ($20), which has simple rooms in thatched-roof bungalows. The

hotel's restaurant serves decent meals. Buses leave from Frontera Corozal to Palenque ($5, 3 hr) at 5 a.m., 10 a.m., noon and 3 p.m. and from Sayaxché to Benemérito via the Río de la Pasión and Benemérito de las Américas.

You can also cross into Mexico by boat down Río de la Pasión to Benemérito de las Américas, but there is no regular passenger service. You will have to rent a private boat for $100 for the four-hour trip. There are five buses from Benemérito to Palenque (9 hr) and the last leaves at 2:30 p.m. There is no immigration office in Benemérito so ask the driver to stop at Boca Lacantún, a few kilometers north, to collect your tourist card. Updated: Oct 01, 2009.

Things to See and Do

The Ruins of Yaxhá

Yaxhá is a unique religious site and the third largest Maya ceremonial archeological site in Petén. The temples were built on the Zenith so the Maya could observe the sun from sunrise until sunset. The site, whose name means Green Water, was stumbled upon by Teobert Maler, a German explorer who devoted his life to the ruins of the Maya civilization, in 1904 during one of his expeditions. The restoration work began in 1989 and over the years archeologists have excavated and restored many of the buildings. The urban complex was inhabited for 16 centuries (600 BC-900 AC) by 20,000 inhabitants and was represented by more than 500 buildings, including temples, pyramids, palaces, platforms for public ceremonies and dances, sanctuaries and houses. Outside the ceremonial center, commoners worked in artisanal workshops, in the fields, or as cleaners or servants. The city was organized in plazas where the administrative, civic and religious activities took place. The main buildings were the Royal Palace, where the governor and his family lived, the Northern Acropolis, the astronomic complex, the two courts to play ball games, the Eastern Acropolis, the Place of the Shade, and the complex of the twin pyramids, all connected by roads. The highest point is Temple 216 in the East Acropolis where there is a beautiful view of the lakes and sunset. This temple was built 30 meters (90 ft) higher than the others just for this purpose. The whole visit should take about two hours. Each site is well documented with explanations on boards. Daily 6 a.m.-6 p.m. Updated: Oct 28, 2009.

Nakum

On the banks of the Holum River, Nakum flourished during the Late Classic (700-900 AD) period because it was on an important trade and communication route. The name means "house of the pot." It was discovered in 1905 by Frenchman Maurice de Perigny. In 1989, the conservation and restoration of the damaged monuments by the Guatemalan authorities began. There are 15 structures. Structure A, with a triadic pod, along with structure C form an astronomical complex. Structure V has vaults and vertical walls. Outside Tikal, the largest corpus of ancient Maya script graffiti in a Classic Maya site can be seen. Seventeen kilometers (10.5 mi) north of Yaxhá and 25 kilometers (15.5 mi) east of Tikal, Nakum is not often visited by travelers. To get there, you can access Yaxhá via a 4x4, but only during the dry season. Updated: Oct 20, 2009.

Topoxté

The ruins are on an island of the same name on Lake Yaxhá. It is a pre-Columbian Maya archeological site and was occupied by local elites from the Middle pre-Classic Period as the capital of the Ko'woj Maya. Topoxté, meaning "seed of the Ramon tree," which was an important component of the ancient Maya diet, was named by Teobert Maler in 1904. The pyramids have archeological similarities with Yaxhá. To get there, take a boat for $20 per group from the eco-lodge in Yaxhá. This site is for people interested in archeology. Updated: Oct 20, 2009.

SAYAXCHÉ

Situated on the southern bank of the Río de la Pasión, this busy town is more of a base from which to visit surrounding attractions rather than a place to see in itself. It is also used by people traveling between the Cobán area and Flores as a place to stop and rest for a night. Sayaxché doesn't have the best reputation when it comes to safety; incidents of robbery have been reported. However, there are half a dozen or so decent Maya sites in the vicinity so if you want to visit those, then a stay in Sayaxché is convenient. There are several hotels in the town, all reasonably priced at around $10-20 a night for a private room. They are not luxury establishments but are generally comfortable and clean. There are also one or two nice dining options in Sayaxché. To get to one such café you have to cross the river but the views, privacy and tasty local food are worth it. Another eatery will prepare packed lunches on request, ideal for those heading out sightseeing for the day. In terms of services, there is a Banrural located just up the street from the popular Hotel Guayacán where you can change US dollars and traveler's checks. Updated: Aug 11, 2010.

Getting To and Away

There are two ways of getting to and from Sayaxché: by water or by land. If you choose to travel along the Río de la Pasión there are plenty of boats that you can take down by the docks. It may be easier to book a trip with an operator. Again, these trips can be found down at the docks and a trip all the way down the river to Benemérito de las Américas in Mexico shouldn't set you back more than $130-180, including stops at Maya ruins and Immigration at Pipiles. By bus from Cobán, the journey usually takes around 5 hours and costs about $7. Buses usually leave from the riverbank or from the Texaco station near the Hotel Guayacán. There are also buses to Sebol, San Antonio Las Cuevas and Raxrujá where you can change to go to Chisec. Updated: Aug 09, 2010.

AROUND SAYAXCHÉ

The easiest way to travel between Sayaxché and its surrounding Maya sites is most certainly by boat along the Río de la Pasión and its tributaries. A combination of taking the local bus to a point and then hiking the rest of the way is also an option and is usually cheaper. However, it generally takes much longer and is a more difficult journey in the end. An organized trip through an operator with a guide is the most popular choice and there are several operators to be found in the town and down by the docks. Some boat owners will offer to take you on round-trip to a specific site and will also act as a guide for a reasonable fee. Usually a round-trip starts from around $45 for the first person and an additional $3-5 for each person thereafter. Updated: Aug 11, 2010.

CEIBAL

Many of the various monuments and ruins at Ceibal would not appear to have been constructed until the 9th century AD. What had previously been quite a small settlement grew rapidly after the arrival of the Putun Maya merchant warrior culture. This new influx of people and influences from the Tabasco area of Mexico meant the region's population increased quickly, peaking at some 10,000 between 830 and 910 AD. The temples and monuments at Ceibal feature beautiful carvings

Photo by: Douglas J. Klostermann

although many people say that the ruins don't quite seem Maya. Waist-length hair, straight noses and unusual dress have led some people to believe that the inhabitants of the area were not always of Maya descent. Besides the small temples covered in jungle foliage there are also 57 stelae at the site. The majority of these carved stelae are located in the Central Plaza or the South Plaza. Structure 79, as it is known, is a large circular platform that may have been used for religious ceremonies or astronomical observation. The ruins are also surrounded by a protected forest full of the majestic Ceibal trees after which the area is named. By far, the best way to get there is along the Río la Pasión. The journey by boat takes about an hour from Sayaxché and often the boatmen can also serve as guide at the site. A round trip for one person shouldn't cost much more than $45 and it's usually $3 per for every extra person. The local bus from Sayaxché can also take you to the ruins but you have to walk the final 8 kilometers (5 mi) and the terrain is not always easy. The boat trip is generally a much more enjoyable experience. Updated: Aug 11, 2010.

LAGUNA PETEXBATÚN

This placid lagoon is home to many fascinating species of animals including freshwater turtles, crocodiles and herons. Beyond the shores of the lake lies a rich rainforest where visitors may encounter howler monkeys and an array of native birds. Laguna Petexbatún is part of the Petexbatún Wildlife Reserve and the nearby ruins are well looked after by conscientious park rangers year round.

Visitors have several locally run accommodation options to choose from, generally involving comfortable thatched cabañas or bungalows. Packages including meals, a night's board, a guided tour and transportation from Sayaxché usually start around $150. You can also opt for packages without transportation and organize your own from Sayaxché. Posada Caribe, Petexbatún Lodge and Chiminos Island Lodge are the more popular choices among visitors. Updated: Aug 11, 2010.

AGUATECA

Aguateca was only discovered in the late 1950s and so is one of the newer more exciting Maya cultural monuments in the area. Located at the southern edge of Laguna Petexbatún, this historic site is divided in two by a dramatic chasm filled with exuberant vegetation. The two main features of Aguateca are the Palace Group and the Main Plaza. There is a concerted effort to conserve the ruins and relics and you will find excellent replicas of original stelae in the Main Plaza beside the remnants of the original ones. Back in the pre-Classic period, along with Dos Pilas, Aguateca was the capital of a powerful dynasty that originated in Tikal. However, judging by the remains of an unfinished temple and the scattered nature of found relics it would appear the settlement was quickly abandoned at the beginning of the 9th century. A causeway connects the two core areas of the ruins and the journey there alone makes for an exciting adventure by canoe and through lush jungle. There is a modest visitor's center and a place selling snacks and refreshments located near the entrance to the site. The rangers will usually let you camp there for free provided you have your own equipment. It is common to give them a small gift of food by way of thanks. As is the case for Dos Pilas and other sites, there are several tour operators with whom you can arrange a guided trip to the ruins. Nearby lodging options such as Chiminos Island and Posada Caribe also offer guided tours. Updated: Aug 11, 2010.

PUNTA DE CHIMONES

About four kilometers (2.5 mi) north of Aguateca is Punta de Chimino. This peninsula served as the last barrier of defense for the local Maya population. It was once home to a man-made fortress with trenches and ramparts to keep back northern invaders. The ruins of such

THE PETÉN

Photo by: Johnathon Nolasco

defenses have all but disappeared and only mounds and barely recognizable remnants can are visible. However, Punto de Chimino is still a beautiful part of the Petén jungle that's well worth a visit. The area is also home to the renowned Chiminos Island Lodge. Thatched bungalows with hot-water bathrooms and lake views give weary travelers a sense of luxury in the jungle. Updated: Aug 11, 2010.

DOS PILAS

While Dos Pilas is only 16 kilometers (10 mi) from Sayaxché, it isn't the easiest of Petén's Maya sites to get to. Unfortunately, the ruins aren't as intact or as impressive as others but their history is a lot more dramatic than some. The intricate carvings are certainly worth a look as are the nearby caves and the partially excavated hieroglyphic staircase that leads to the ruins of the royal palace in the main plaza. Thanks to several aggressive rulers, Dos Pilas clashed with neighboring settlements frequently. By 760 AD, the majority of its inhabitants had fled to nearby Aguateca and those who chose to remain were forced to evacuate when it was overrun during the 9th century. An extensive conservation project has been undertaken and some of the stelae have been replaced with replicas to prevent theft or vandalism. It is recommended that you take a guided tour to Dos Pilas from Sayaxché. Getting there is less than straightforward and the guides have extensive knowledge of the site's history making a visit there all the more interesting. Updated: Aug 11, 2010.

REMOTE MAYA SITES

The Petén forest, situated in north Guatemala, hosts well-preserved and un-restored Maya sites, some discovered as recently as 1998. You will find that some ruins have easier access than

others. Tours to Tikal can be booked easily from everywhere in the country, whereas the visit to some remote sites, such as El Mirador or Piedras Negras, have to be prepared in advance. During your visit, you will also be able to observe the jungle and its exciting wildlife. Only a few sites will let you walk around without a guide.

Don't expect to find luxury tours. In most cases reaching the remote Maya sites involves making your way through the dense jungle and braving mosquitoes! Several agencies organizing those trips exist in Flores, El Remate and San Andrés. In this northern part of Guatemala, there are at least 25 Maya temples, including the largest pre-Columbian constructions in the Americas. Updated: Jul 29, 2010.

EL PERÚ (WAKA') AND AROUND

Part of the Petén forest, Laguna del Tigre is an area where only few archeological searches have been done. El Perú is a site that was recently discovered there. In 2004 the tomb of a queen, dating back to 620 AD was found, and some similar discoveries were made in 2006. El Perú must have been an important commercial and political center due to its ideal location on the Río San Pedro.

The city was founded around 400 AD and was taken over by the Tikal people around 743 AD. Presently, several well-preserved stelae can be observed there. Don't forget to have a look at the *Mirador de los Monos* (Monkey lookout).

On the road to the site, you will probably be able to see some guacamayas or scarlet macaws, especially in their nesting season, from February to June. The Parque Nacional Laguna del Tigre has much to offer. At the scientific station Estación Biológica Las Guacamayas, near the Río San Juan, you will be able to observe scarlet macaws and white tortoises, while being surrounded by a splendid rain forest. It is often possible to take a tour combining the visit of El Perú and the station. Twenty kilometers (12.5 mi) west of El Perú is La Joyanca, a classic-period site with restored structures and several walking trails. Updated: Jul 29, 2010.

EL TINTAL

Situated 21 kilometers (13 mi) south of El Mirador, El Tintal is generally the first stop for trekkers on their way to the large Maya city. El Tintal is more than a camping spot.

With similar constructions to El Mirador, El Tintal's temples have not been restored. However, if you climb up its highest temple you will have a wonderful view of the rainforest and of El Mirador. It is definitely worth taking time to visit El Tintal. Updated: Jul 29, 2010.

PIEDRAS NEGRAS

Located on the banks of the Río Usumacinta, at the border with Mexico, Piedras Negras has some of the best preserved Maya curved monuments. It is here that, in 1930, Russian epigrapher Tatiana Proskouriakoff deciphered many of the Maya glyphs, though her theories were not adopted until the 1960s. Piedras Negras was founded around 300 AD, 40 kilometers (25 miles) downstream a river, in the middle of a dense rainforest, Sierra del Lacandón, now a national park.

The city led a struggle to control Usumacinta's trade routes and created alliances with Tikal for this purpose. It is thought the city housed approximately 10,000 inhabitants at its peak period. The presence of soldiers in the area during the Guatemalan civil war helped to protect the site from looters. This is why Piedras Negras has many fine pieces, some now being displayed in the National Archeological Museum in Guatemala City.

The entrance to the site, made of black cliffs, is what gave its name to the site and is probably the most impressive part of the visit. The depiction of a man making an offering to a woman stands at the beginning of the stairs leading up the riverbank to the ruins 100 meters (328 ft) above. Among the most impressive pieces are several stelae and hieroglyphic panels. Other well-preserved monuments are a sweat bath (Maya sauna) and an Acropolis which contains a large twin-palace complex. In general, the architecture here is a mix of styles, from the Classic to pre-Classic periods. Because of its remoteness, Piedras Negras is visited by a small number of tourists; in fact, only about 200 visitors come to Piedras Negras each year. Nowadays, Piedras Negras is classified among the "100 Most Threatened Landmarks" in the world, mostly because of a Mexican hydroelectric project that could flood Piedras Negras and some smaller sites nearby.

The best way to visit Piedras Negras is by organized tour. Among the agencies offering trips, there are Maya Expeditions (www.mayaexpeditions.com) and Posada Maya in Bethel. If you want to stay overnight, a campsite is located near a sandy beach a few hundred meters downstream from Piedras Negras.

YAXCHILÁN

Yaxchilán, though difficult to access, is one of the most spectacular Maya sites in the region. Built off the shore of Río Usumacinta, surrounded by hills and dense forest, Yaxchilán enjoys a sublime location. The sounds of the fauna (birds, insects and howler monkeys) add to the breathtaking atmosphere of the place. The temples still show well-preserved inscriptions and are decorated with stucco and stone, mainly depicting scenes of ceremonies and conquests. The most beautiful artwork pieces are situated on door lintels and roof combs, so be on the lookout for them!

All along the river's banks, visitors will be able to visit plazas and ball courts in the style of Classic Maya period. The palaces are situated on the lower parts of the former Maya city. Unfortunately many have been removed to be placed in museums all around the world. From the plaza, you can access the most impressive structure of the site by taking a long staircase: Temple 33 features carved lintels under its doorways.

If Yaxchilán has so many richly decorated temples, it's because the city had a special status in the Maya world. From 350-810 AD, the city evolved from a small agricultural village to one of the most important Maya center in the region. Yaxchilán became the capital of the region under the reign of Cráneo-Mahkina (526 AD), and the city expanded its power with Escudo Jaguar I (681 AD). During its wealthier period, in the 7th century AD, Yaxchilán dominated most of the trade on the river, and even formed powerful alliances with neighboring cities such as Tikal and Palenque.

The ruins are open daily from 9 a.m. to 5 p.m. and the entrance fee is $4.50. To stay overnight, you can camp at the INAH site on the banks of the Usumacinta. To get there you have several possibilities. You can take a motorboat for one hour, departing from Echeverria. The price is approximately $67 for up to four people and $92 for more than five people. To get a chance to meet other tourists and to share a boat with them, plan to arrive at Echeverria before 9 a.m. By car from Palenque, it is a 173 kilometer (107 mi) drive via Carretera 307. Stop at Echeverria to take the motorboat. Otherwise, Posada Maya in Bethel organizes trips for $100 round trip.

Photo by: Johnathan Nolasco

EL ZOTZ

El Zotz (meaning "bat" in many Maya languages) got its name from the hundreds of furry animals flying out of nearby caves at dusk in search of insects and fruits. Located in the San Miguel La Palotada Biotope, adjacent to the Tikal National Park, El Zotz remained un-restored: the three major temples are covered with soil and moss. It is still possible to climb up the tallest one (Pirámide del Diablo) and enjoy a panoramic view of Tikal's temples 24 kilometers (15 mi) to the west. It is possible to hike from the tropical forest and wetlands of El Zotz to Tikal, and the other way round. For organized trips, try Tour Operators in Flores and El Remate. They offer trekking, jeep and horse tours to El Zotz, often incorporating Tikal. If you come independently, the hike from Cruce Dos Aguadas is five hours long (30 km/18.6 mi). Camping exists on the site. You will need to bring all your supplies with you and talk with the guards at the Cecon station. Updated: Jul 29, 2010.

RÍO AZUL

Río Azul, part of the Parque Nacional Mirador-Río Azul, is located up north where the Guatemala, Belize and Mexico borders meet. This city reached its peak between 410 and 530 AD, when the new Teotihuacan ruler took power in Tikal. It is estimated that around 5,000 people lived in Río Azul then. Encompassing an area of about 300 hectares (750 ac), the city served as the extension of Tikal in the Petén area. Río Azul was an ideal transition point for *cacao* trade from the Caribbean to Tikal and Mexico. Tikal also used the city as an ally against its rival Calakmul. However, Río Azul was conquered by Calakmul in 530 AD before being regained by Tikal during its resurgence in its late Classic era. The architecture in Río Azul reflects its status as a frequently fought-over vassal city. This pre-Classic Maya site, rediscovered in 1962, is presently famous for its red painted tombs. The burial scenes depicted represent Teotihuacan's culture, proving the city's influence on Río Azul. Among the 350 structures that can be seen at Río Azul, you will find three round altars with carvings representing ritual executions. Unfortunately, the Maya city fell victim to looters in the years following its rediscovery. It's hard to tell what percentage of artifacts were stolen then, but it is said that an archeological team found 150 trenches dug in their absence probably by looters. It is reported that some carved objects such as jade masks, murals and pendants were missing. Thus, only a small part of murals and paintings in the tombs remain intact.

The main attraction of a visit to Río Azul is probably its tallest temple (AIII), reaching 47 meters (154 ft) in height. From its top, visitors have a pretty amazing panoramic view of the jungle. To get to Río Azul, a road exists between the site and Uaxactún (95 km/60 mi), although this road is only open during the dry season. If you do not have a 4x4, you can hike or horseback there, but this is a four- to five-day trip.

From Campamento El Chiclero in Uaxactún, you can arrange a trip to Río Azul. If you wish to stay overnight, the guard's campsite is situated on the other side of the Río Ixcán, six kilometers (3.7 mi) away from the Maya site. Updated: Jul 29, 2010.

EL MIRADOR AND AROUND

El Mirador is a massive Maya city found in the far north of El Petén, just four kilometers (2.49 mi) below the Mexican border. The city is home to some of the most fascinating structures of the Maya empire, including one of the tallest pyramids in all of Maya civilization, La Danta Complex, which towers to 70 meters (230 ft). El Tigre, another pyramid standing at 55 meters (180 ft), is found in El Mirador and has a massive base of 19,600 square meters (210,972 sq ft). Many of the buildings are decorated with stucco masks and designs, which are somewhat eroded but still visible.

The city's stature and population peaked in pre-Classic times, between the 3rd century BC and the 1st century AD. Then, the population waxed and waned for the next 750 years until it was finally abandoned in the 9th century. There is a lot of speculation concerning El Mirador's downfall, and some archeologists have attributed it to changing trade patterns, while others attribute it to natural disasters, warfare or internal strife. The El Mirador site, along with other smaller cities, was "discovered" in 1926, but it wasn't until 1978, when American archeologists launched a major mapmaking project and archaelogical excavation of the area, that El Mirador was put on the map-so to speak. In 2003, another series of American archaelogists and preservationists returned to El Mirador for further studies. There are 26 known sites, but only 14 have been thoroughly studied. Many factors are threatening the preservation of the region, including deforestation and looting. Fortunately, the area is so remote and access to the site is so difficult that the area hasn't been damaged by much tourist activity. Hopefully, with the inclusion of El Mirador and its neighboring cities into a national park, the Guatemalan government can preserve the Maya cities effectively. Updated: Jul 22, 2010.

Getting To and Away

The trek to the El Mirador area is extremely difficult and only manageable by healthy, hearty hikers during the dry season. Otherwise, the trail can turn into shoulder deep mud, making the hike nearly impossible. The trek lasts between three to four days, and covers 70 kilometers (43.5 mi) of dense, mean jungle with no amenities except the contents of your backpack. Expeditions leave from a small settlement called Carmelita, which is already very remote, so don't expect to stock up on supplies there. However, during the dry season the trek is doable, and you will be rewarded by seeing a place that very few others have seen. (During this time, the peak population of El Mirador is said to be over 100,000.)

To get to the El Perú (Waka') site, go to the Parque Nacional Laguna del Tigre, situated 62 kilometers (38.5 mi) northwest of Flores. Take the road heading to the village of Paso Caballos, it is a two-hour ride. From there you will have to take a motorboat up the Río Sacluc for 20 minutes. To go to Río Azul, coming from Uaxactún, you can take the 95 kilometer-long (59 miles) road (five-hours drive) that links both sites. Public transportation does not exist in this remote region. So, unless you have a vehicle, you will have to walk, or horseback (four-days trip) or book a tour, departing from Flores, Uaxactún or El Remate.

Although tours offering trekking, jeep and horse trips exist (leaving from Flores and El Remate), you can take the road to El Zotz by yourself: it is a 30-kilometer (18.6 miles) (5 hr) trek from Cruce Dos Aguadas. Due to its remote location, it is always advised to get a guided visit for Piedras Negras. Once again, you will find tour agencies in Flores, Guatemala City and San Andrés. The easiest way to get to Yaxchilán is to start from Bethel, where you can also find tours Updated: Jul 29, 2010.

NAKBÉ

Nakbé lies about 13 kilometers (8 mi) south of El Mirador and is connected to it (and other smaller cities) by a causeway. The ancient city was founded around 1000 BC, earlier than El Mirador, but its downfall occurred around the same time as its larger counterpart. It is almost equally difficult to get to as El Mirador and was only discovered by aerial photographs in 1930. Excavations didn't begin in earnest until the 1980s. The ancient city is home to fewer impressive structures than El Mirador and is considerably smaller in size. However, Structure I, standing at 48 meters (157 ft), is a sight to behold. Updated: Jul 22, 2010.

NAACHTUNG
DOS LAGUNAS BIOTOPE

The Dos Lagunas Biotope mainly attracts tourists for its amazing wildlife and its well-preserved Maya ruins. If the site looks untouched by time, it is because of its remote location and the absence of roads. The area in which the Biotope is situated forms a connection between El Mirador and Río Azul, inside the National Park. The Dos Lagunas Biotope's abundant wildlife makes it a unique spot for visitors. Many of Guatemala's endangered species can be observed there, including jaguars and other jungle cats such as marguays and ocelots, brocket deer, crocodiles, river turtles, monkeys, tapirs and more. The flora is considered to be the most diverse in the region, with a high concentration of Mahogany trees.

The Biotope also hosts Naachtung, a Late-Classic Maya site. Its architecture shows a strong influence from larger Maya cities: Tikal and Calakmul. It is believed that Naachtung was caught in the war between the two rival cities. Located 25 kilometers (25.5 mi) east of El Mirador and one kilometer (0.62 mi) from the Mexican border, Naachtung displays more than 45 stelae.

The Biotope, managed by Guatemala's University of San Carlos Center for Conservation Studies (CECON), was originally created to protect the endangered white-tailed deer. The center decided not to promote tourism in the reserve, explaining why The Dos Lagunas Biotope remains a secret treasure off the beaten tourist trail. Updated: Jul 29, 2010.

Getting To and Away

As the Dos Lagunas Biotope is situated off the roads in a remote area, visitors can access the reserve only during the dry season and only by 4WD. The access to the biotope is located along the road connecting Uaxactún to Río Azul, about halfway. Visitors can also hike or ride on horseback in about two days from Uaxactún. Those trips can be booked through Campamento El Chiclero. Updated: Jul 29, 2010.

PARQUE NACIONAL
LAGUNA DEL TIGRE

The Laguna del Tigre National Park hosts the largest wetlands in all of Central America and the only remaining scarlet macaws population. Only particular parts of the park are recommended to tourists. Due to population pressure, most parts of the Laguna del Tigre National Park have been lost and the local habitat is almost nonexistent. Also, oil drilling has been going on in the western part of the reserve since before the creation of the park, despite pressure from environmental groups. Because of that, only some parts of the park are worth recommending: the Scarlet Macaw Biological Research station and the site of Waka'-Perú. The Scarlet Macaw Biological Research station is tirelessly working to preserve Petén's most beautiful bird. Its population has dropped during the past years due to habitat loss and wildlife poaching by the international pet trade. Hence the work at the Scarlet Macaw Biological Research station is crucial to preservation.

The Waka'-Perú site is still being excavated by archeologists. The latest discovery dates back to 2006. Several Maya royal tombs have been excavated there and a good number of stelae can still be observed on the site. Waka'-Peru was said to be a commercial and political center thanks to its location near the Río San Pedro, explaining the richness of the site. Explorations in the Laguna del Tigre park are not yet done. While visiting, tourists can wonder what treasures the park is still hiding. To stay overnight, camping is allowed at the site's ranger station, a 25 minutes walk from the river bank. To go to the park, take the dirt road heading northwest, starting in Flores, to the village of Paso Caballos. It is a two-hour drive. From there you will have to take a boat for 20 minutes on the Río Sacluc to access the biological station and Waka'-Peru. Updated: Jul 29, 2010.

LAS GUACAMAYAS BIOLOGICAL RESEARCH STATION

Visitors who want to observe wildlife while following easy trekking trails in the rainforest will find what they are searching for here in Las Guacamayas Biological Research station. The station offers easy access to the Waka'-Peru site. Owned by ProPetén, a group working for the protection of the area, the research station is situated in a dense jungle near the Río San Pedro.

ProPetén is currently trying to educate the local population on the need to conserve the site after angry members from the community burned down the first station in the 1990s. Plenty of trails are around the station. The shortest of them leads you to an observation tower, providing nice views of the river, the wetlands of the Laguna del Tigre National Park and the hills of Sierra del Lacandón. The station even offers activities at night like tours led by the station's staff that take you out on the river to observe crocodiles. Birdwatching tours are also available in the mornings.

The principal activity here is to observe scarlet macaws. Several observation platforms were set up inside the site of Waka'-Peru. The nesting season is during February and March, but you will have a better chance to catch a glimpse of the birds between November and April. A two-day, three-nights package costs $300. This package, departing from Flores, includes accommodation, meals, transportation, birdwatching and a tour of Waka'-Peru. However, you may find cheaper options with travel agencies in Flores. It is recommended to stay at Las Guacamayas overnight since it is situated in a remote location. To go there independently of a package tour, call ProPetén to book a room. The accommodations are pretty basic with shared bathrooms and a common kitchen (although you can arrange your stay to get all meals included). Some dorms can fit up to 20 people. Updated: Jul 29, 2010.

PARQUE NACIONAL SIERRA DEL LACANDÓN

Sierra del Lacandón is located in a mountain chain in the western part of Petén, on the northern bank of the Usumacinta River. The area, elevated at 600 meters (1,970 ft) above sea level, is surprisingly well-preserved. During the Guatemalan civil war, soldiers hid in the mountains, protecting the site from looters and environmental degradation.

The park hosts the largest population of jaguars in all of Central America. Its jungle also shows an amazing diversity. In the forest, several Maya sites can be visited. The most important of them is Piedras Negras, situated on the shore of the Usumacinta River. The site has some of the best carved monuments from the Maya world. Its remoteness makes you feel like a privileged visitor.

Yaxchilán is one of the most important Maya sites in the area, as the city used to dominate trade on the Usumacinta river. Several temples can be observed there. Bethel is a pretty village, often considered as the starting point for tourists who want to visit the Park's ruins or to head toward Mexico. Most of the boats heading to the different Maya sites, going downstream the Usumacinta river, depart from here. A good place to stay is the Posada Maya, offering accommodations in bungalows and a restaurant. It is also here that visitors will be able to book tours for a decent price.

Few of the sites and trekking trails in the jungle can be visited alone. You will find that most of the time visitors have to book tours that include a guide. Several agencies, located in Flores, El Remate and San Andrés offer packages for day-trips to those sites. Some freelance guides can take you to the sites for a cheaper price, but those generally know little about the sites and responsible tourism. Updated: Jul 29, 2010.

))))

Index

INDEX

INDEX

INDEX

I

INDEX

INDEX

INDEX

INDEX

ENVIRONMENTAL TIPS FOR TRAVELERS
By Nicola Robinson, Nicola Mears and Heather Ducharme, Río Muchacho Organic Farm

While traveling in a foreign country, it is important to minimize your impact. Here are some tips and information that you should try and remember. We acknowledge that some of this advice may be more difficult to take on board while traveling than it would be to incorporate into your daily lives at home. However, even if you only put into practice three or four of our suggestions, be it while on the road or while at home, it will certainly contribute to reducing our impact on the planet.

GARBAGE
• Most plastic bottles are not recyclable in Guatemala. Try to use glass bottles (returnable) for sodas etc. Aluminum cans are the next best option as they are at least recyclable. To avoid buying more disposable bottles, carry a water bottle and always check if there is somewhere to fill it up at your hotel/restaurant (most hotels and restaurants have purified water in large 20-litre bottles called *botellones*). These places also sell water in small bottles and so they might be reluctant to begin with as they think they are losing a sale. Of course you will need to pay for the refill also. The concept of reducing garbage is new for Guatemalans, so don't be surprised if you have to explain it, but if more request it, the more common place it will become. If you have to buy bottles, buy the biggest you can and just refill from there, especially if you plan to be in the same place for a while.

• Consider purifying your own water to avoid creating garbage.

• Try to avoid excessive wrapping and plastic bags which are all too readily dished out for each small purchase. If you can, explain to the shop keeper why you want to give the bag back. If you shop in a local market take your own bag or have them place everything in one large plastic bag instead of numerous small ones.

• You can also reduce the amount of garbage you produce as a result of traveling by using a digital camera instead of using film. The process of developing film can produce a lot of waste. Unwanted photos are non recyclable and often end up in the trash.

• Use a reusable container for your soap so that you can use your own instead of the small hotel soaps which come individually wrapped. If you use the hotel soap, use one and take the remainder with you-it will just be thrown out.

• Avoid using excessive cosmetic products e.g. hairspray, mousse, aftershave and perfume, or try to find effective environmentally friendly alternatives such as biodegradable shampoos, crystal deodorants which last longer etc... (most containers for these products are non recyclable). Avoid using disposable products like plastic razors and single use contact lenses.

• Try to use rechargeable batteries or eliminate use of batteries entirely. For instance, use a wind-up or solar flashlight or radio.

• Where available use recycled paper for letters home, trip diaries and toilet paper.

• Buy in bulk if you are traveling in a large group to reduce packaging.

• Please remember to recycle whatever you can in the country you are traveling. However, some products that can not be recycled in the host country can be recycled in your home countries, so please take them home if possible.

INDEX

FOOD AND HEALTH

• Avoid eating foods that you know are from endangered or threatened species (research these before you come to the country). Buy and eat locally grown and locally processed foods wherever possible, rather than food products shipped from long distances, which use more energy and packaging.

• Consider using alternative natural medical products for common travelers' illnesses. This may be healthier for you and keeps you from leaving behind pharmaceuticals in the local water and soil (this is becoming a detectable problem in first world countries, thought to affect aquatic organisms like fish and frogs).

NATURE, FLORA AND FAUNA

• Avoid buying souvenirs of local fauna. Many stores sell cases of bright colored butterflies, spiders and insects; these are caught by the hundreds in the Amzon and the sales people will tell you that they are not caught but that they raise them-it is not true!

• Avoid buying souvenirs that are made with endangered species or species that have to be killed to be made into a craft. Support crafts made from renewable resources.

• Don't collect insects, flora and fauna, without a permit. Leave them for everyone to enjoy.

• When walking, stay on the trails and close gates behind you.

CAMPING AND WATER

• Use toilets where they exist, if not bury human waste in a hole 20 centimeters deep. Human waste should be buried at least 50 meters (164 ft.) from water sources.

• Use biodegradable soaps and detergents.

• Don't wash shampoo and detergent off directly in rivers, but rather as far away as you can (4 m/13 ft) minimum).

• Avoid making fires.

• Use a T-shirt when snorkeling as sunscreen is harmful to marine life.

TRANSPORT

• Use public rather than private transport (e.g. bus instead of rental car) where possible to reduce fossil fuel use. Share rental cars and taxis with others. If possible, walk or use a bicycle. It not only helps the planet, but it keeps you in shape as well!

ELECTRICITY

• Lights, fans, TVs, radios, and computers: if you are not using it, turn it off!

TRAVELING WITH CHILDREN AND BABIES

• Try to teach your child about the local environmental issues. Point out good and bad practices.

• Encourage your child to snack on fruit, which has a biodegradable wrapper!

• If traveling with a baby use cotton diapers. Disposable diapers are becoming a major waste issue in developed countries and are becoming a desirable product in the developing world. Using cotton will set a good example to others and reduce the promotion of disposable diapers.

LOCAL ENVIRONMENTAL ISSUES

• Try to find out what the important environmental issues are in the country. Good environmental practices (e.g. reduce, reuse, recycle!) are often the same in different countries, but the specific issues are often different (e.g. different recycling options, different endangered habitats and species, different laws and policies, etc...)

• Think about where you are eating and staying, and support the more environmentally friendly businesses. If you stay in an ecolodge, talk to the owners/managers, ask how they manage their garbage (including human waste). Do they recycle, do they use grey water systems to be able to reuse their water? Where do their building materials, food, and power come from? Do they practice or contribute to conservation? Do they support the local community? Be constructive, rather than critical, if you don't get a good response. Some people truly think that it can be called an ecolodge if it is built with natural materials.

• Many countries have interesting volunteer opportunities with envronmentally oriented organizations. Perhaps support these efforts by volunteering. Research carefully—some volunteer opportunities are not what they say they are.

The following is a list of helpful environmental websites for further information:

• *www.ecomall.com*
• *www.greenhome.com*
• Fundacaión Natura: *www.fnatura.org*
• Ministry of the Environment of Guatemala: *http://www.marn.gob.gt/*
• Ministry of the Environment and Natural Resources of Guatemala: *en.centralamericadata. com*

INDEX

USEFUL SPANISH PHRASES

CONVERSATIONAL

Hello	Hola
Good morning	Buenos días
Good afternoon	Buenas tardes
Good evening	Buenas noches
Yes	Sí
No	No
Please	Por favor
Thank you	Gracias
It was nothing	De nada
Excuse me	Permiso
See you later	Hasta luego
Bye	Chao
Cool	Buena onda
How are you (formal)	¿Cómo está?
" " " (informal)	¿Qué tal?
I don't understand	No entiendo.
Do you speak English?	¿Habla inglés?
I don't speak Spanish.	No hablo español.
I'm from England	Soy de Inglaterra
the USA	Soy de los Estados Unitos.

FOOD AND DRINK

Breakfast	Desayuno
Lunch	Almuerzo
Dinner	Cena
Check please	La cuenta por favor.
Main Course	Plato Fuerte
Menu	la carta
Spoon	Cuchara
Fork	Tenedor
Knife	Cuchillo
Bread	pan
Fruit	fruta
Vegetables	verduras
Potatoes	papas
Meat	carne
Chicken	pollo
Beer	cerveza
Wine	vino
Juice	jugo
Coffee	café
Tea	té

HEALTH/EMERGENCY

Call a....	¡Llame a...!
Ambulance	una ambulancia
A doctor	un médico
The police	la policía
It's an emergency.	Es una emergencia.
I'm sick	Estoy enfermo/a
I need a doctor	Necesito un médico.
Where's the hospital?	¿Dónde está el hospital?

I'm allergic to...	Soy alérgico/a
Antibiotics	los antibióticos
Nuts	nuez
Penicillin	la penicilina

GETTING AROUND

Where is...?	¿Dónde está...?
The bus station	la estación de bus?
The train station	la estación de tren?
A bank?	¿El banco?
The bathroom?	¿El baño?
Left, right, straight	Izquierda, derecha, recto.
Ticket	Boleto
Where does the bus leave from?	¿De dónde sale el bus?

ACCOMMODATION

Where is a hotel?	¿Donde hay un hotel?
I want a room.	Quiero una habitación.
Single / Double / Marriage	Simple / Doble / Matrimonial
How much does it cost per night?	¿Cuanto cuesta por noche?
Does that include breakfast?	¿Incluye el desayuno?
Does that include taxes?	¿Incluye los impuestos?

VIVA recommends travel insurance. Get it at vivatravelguides.com/insurance/

V!VA TRAVEL GUIDES BRINGS YOU A TEAR-OUT LIST OF USEFUL CONTACTS IN GUATEMALA

Feel free to photocopy this sheet for your use, to give to your dog, or to wallpaper your room.

EMERGENCY NUMBERS

| All Emergencies | 1500 | Police | 110 |
| Fire | 123 | Medical | 120 |

HOSPITALS / DOCTORS / PHARMACIES

Hospital General San Juan de Dios
Av. Elena 9 and 10 C Zona 1
Zacapa, Guatemala
Tel: 502-2-232-3741/3744
Main Public Hospital

Centro Medico de Guatemala
6a Av. 3-47 Zona 10
Guatemala, Cuidad, C.A.
Tel: 502-2-279-4949
Private Hospital

Guatemala Medical Travel, Treatment Referral and Travel Services Agency:
Lori Shea, Guatemala City (Tel: 502-5737-3023), in Miami, FL. (Tel: 305-797-0540)
E-mail: GuatemalaMedicalTravel.com

ENGLISH SPEAKING LAWYERS IN GUATEMALA (CRIMINAL)

Sergio Leonardo Penagos Mijangos
14 Ca. 8-14, Z-1
Edificio Armagua, 4 Nivel, Ofic. 4-6
Guatemala City
Tel: 502-2-220-6183/221-2817
E-mail: licmijangos@hotmail.com/licmijangos@gmail.com

TRAVELER GUIDANCE: V!VA Travel Guides: www.vivatravelguides.com

Guatemalan Tourism Commission (INGUAT)
7 Av. 1-17 Zona 4
Centro Civico, Guatemala City
Tel: 502-2-421-2800
E-mail: info@inguat.gov.gt
www.visitguatemala.com

POST OFFICE (CORREOS)
Main: 7 Av./12 Ca. Zona 1
DHL: 12a Ca. 5-12, Zona 10
www.dhl.com

INTERNET CAFÉS
SERVICIOS ESPAÑA: 20th St. 18-65 Zona 10
MABER CYBER Internet: 8th St. 33-51, colony,
Justo Rufino Barrios, Zona 21

TRANSPORT
Taxis – Blanco y Azul, Tel: 502-2-360-0903; Elegance Cabs, S.A., Tel: 502-2-484-4550

Bus Terminal – main bus terminal is Fuente del Norte bus station in Guatemala City.

Complete the sections below for your convenience:

My tour operator:

My hotel address:

INDEX

Get free E-books when you reserve your hotel or hostel at vivatravelguides.com/hotels/

AIRLINES:

Aeromexico (Mexican)
10a Calle 6-21 "A", Zona 9
Nivel 3
Guatemala City
Tel: 502-2-331-9507
e-mail: discover-guate@guate.net

Air France (French)
Avenida Reforma 9-00, Zona 9
Plaza Panamericana, Planta Baja
Guatemala City
Tel: 502-2-334-0043/5
e-mail: afguate@infovia.com.gt

American Airlines (U.S.)
Avenida Reforma 15-54, Zona 9
Edificio Reforma Obelisco, No. 401-A
Guatemala City
Tel: 502-2-334-7379

Continental Airlines (U.S.)
18 Calle 5-56, Zona 10
Edificio Unicentro, Niveles 3 and 7
Guatemala City
Tel: 502-2-366-9985

Canadian Airlines International (Canadian)
10a. Calle 6-21 "A", Nivel 3, Zona 9.
Guatemala City
Tel: 502-2-331-9507

Delta Airlines (U.S.)
15 Calle 3-20, Zona 10
Edificio Centro Ejecutivo,
Nivel 2, Oficina 201
Guatemala City
Tel: 502-2-337-0642/70/80/88

Korean Air (Korean)
Edificio Plaza Marititma, Nivel 5
6a. Avenida 20-21, Zona 10
Oficina 5-4
Guatemala City
Tel: 502-2-333-5755

Copa Airlines (Panamanian)
1a. Avenida 10-17, Zona 10
Telefono: 502-2-361-1517/87/97
Guatemala City

British Airways
1a. Avenida 10-81, Zona 10
Edificio Inexa, Nivel 6
Guatemala City
Tel: 502-2-332-3402 al 4

Lan (Chile)
Avenida Reforma 9-00, Zona 9
Edificio Plaza Panamericana, No. 8
Guatemala City
Tel: 502-2-331-2070
E-mail: rique@pronet.net.gt

EMBASSIES IN GUATEMALA CITY:

Argentina
2a. Avenida 11-04, Zona 10
Tel: 332-6419/331-4969/96894
Fax: 332-1654
E-mail: embargen@concyt.gob.gt

Belize
Avenida La Reforma 1-50, Zona 9
Edificio El Reformador, 8th Floor, Office 803
Tel: 334-5531/1137
E-mail: embelguat@yahoo.com

Canada
13 Calle 8-44, Zona 10
Edificio Edyma Plaza, 8th Floor
Tel: 333-6102
Fax: 333-6153
URL: www.canadainternational.gc.ca/guatemala/

Costa Rica
Avenida La Reforma 8-60, Zona 9
Edificio Galerías Reforma Torre I, Office 702
Tel: 331-9604/332-1522
Fax: 332-1522
E-mail: embarica@c.net.gt

El Salvador
4a. Avenida 13-60, Zona 10
Tel: 366-6147/2240
Fax: 366-2234
E-mail: emsalva@pronet.net.gt

Honduras
9a. Avenida 16-34, Zona 10
Tel: 368-0842
Fax: 337-3921
E-mail: embhond@intelnet.net.gt

Mexico
15 Calle 3-20, Zona 10
Tel: 333-7254/58
Fax: 333-7615
E-mail: embguatemala@sre.gob.mx

United Kingdom
16 Calle 0-55, Zona 10
Edificio Torre Internacional, 11th Floor
Tel: 2380-7300
E-mail: embhon@infovia.com.gt
URL: http://ukinguatemala.fco.gov.uk/en/

United States
Avenida La Reforma 7-01, Zona 10
Tel: 331-1541/55
Fax: 331-6660
URL: http://guatemala.usembassy.gov/

PACKING LISTS
(* indicates something that might not be available in Guatemala)

GENERAL PACKING LIST:
There are a number of items that every traveler should consider bringing to Guatemala as follows:

- ☐ **Medicines and prescriptions** (Very important. Bringing all relevant medical info and medicines may well save you a lot of grief in Guatemala.)
- ☐ **Photocopies of passport** and other relevant ID documents
- ☐ Paperback novels (sometimes you'll be sitting on buses, in airports, or somewhere else for a long time. Bring some books with you so you're not bored. It is possible to find and/or exchange books in several places in Guatemala, but don't count on much selection)
- ☐ Plug converter (Guatemala uses two-prong flat blade outlets (like in the U.S), two-prong flat blade in a "V" shape, and outlets with two parallel flat pins with a ground pin. Voltage is 120 V/60 Hz).
- ☐ A good camera (see photography section)
- ☐ Water bottle (bottled water is readily available in Guatemala, but you may want your own bottle)
- ☐ Sunglasses
- ☐ Motion sickness medicine
- ☐ Lip balm
- ☐ *Tampons (difficult to find outside the major cities)
- ☐ Sun hat
- ☐ Condoms and other contraceptives
- ☐ *Foot powder
- ☐ Antacid tablets, such as Rolaids
- ☐ Mild painkillers such as aspirin or ibuprofen
- ☐ *GPS device (especially for hikers)
- ☐ Watch with alarm clock
- ☐ Diarrhea medicine (i.e. Imodium)
- ☐ Warm clothes

BACKPACKER PACKING LIST:
- ☐ All of the above, plus:
- ☐ Rain poncho
- ☐ Plastic bags
- ☐ Swiss army knife/leatherman *
- ☐ Toilet paper
- ☐ Antibacterial hand gel *
- ☐ Small padlock

RAINFOREST PACKING LIST:
- ☐ Rubber boots (most jungle lodges have them, call ahead)
- ☐ *Bug spray (with DEET)
- ☐ Flashlight
- ☐ Waterproof bags
- ☐ Rain poncho
- ☐ First aid kit
- ☐ *Compass
- ☐ Whistle
- ☐ Long-sleeved shirt and pants
- ☐ Malaria/yellow fever medicine
- ☐ Original passport
- ☐ Mosquito net (if your destination does not have one; call ahead)
- ☐ Biodegradable soap

INDEX

ADDITIONAL ITEMS TO PACK:

☐ _____
☐ _____
☐ _____
☐ _____
☐ _____

ANTI-PACKING LIST: THINGS NOT TO BRING TO GUATEMALA

- Expensive jewelry. Just leave it home.
- Nice watch or sunglasses. Bring a cheap one you can afford to lose.
- Go through your wallet: what won't you need? Leave your driver's license (unless you're planning on driving), business cards, video-club membership cards, 7-11 coffee club card, social security card and anything else you won't need at home. The only thing in your wallet you will want is a student ID, and if you lose it you will be grateful that you left the rest at home.
- Illegal drugs. You didn't need us to tell you that, did you?
- Stickers and little toys for kids. Some tourists like to hand them out, which means the children pester every foreigner they see.
- Really nice clothes or shoes, unless you're planning on going to a special event or dining out a lot.

INDEX